Tenth Edition

Signs of Life in the U.S.A.

Readings on Popular Culture for Writers

Tenth Edition

Signs of Life in the U.S.A.

Readings on Popular Culture for Writers

Sonia Maasik
University of California, Los Angeles

Jack Solomon
California State University, Northridge

bedford/st.martin's
Macmillan Learning
Boston | New York

Vice President: Leasa Burton
Program Director, English: Stacey Purviance
Program Manager: John E. Sullivan III
Director of Content Development: Jane Knetzger
Executive Development Manager: Maura Shea
Executive Development Editor: Christina Gerogiannis
Assistant Editor: Paola Garcia-Muniz
Director of Media Editorial: Adam Whitehurst
Associate Media Editor: Daniel Johnson
Executive Marketing Manager: Joy Fisher Williams
Senior Director, Content Management Enhancement: Tracey Kuehn
Senior Managing Editor: Michael Granger
Senior Manager of Publishing Services: Andrea Cava
Content Project Manager: Matt Glazer
Senior Workflow Project Manager: Paul W. Rohloff
Production Supervisor: Robert Cherry
Director of Design, Content Management: Diana Blume
Cover Design: William Boardman
Director of Rights and Permissions: Hilary Newman
Permissions Editor: Angela Boehler
Manager, Research and Permissions: Krystyna Borgen, Lumina Datamatics, Inc.
Senior Permissions Project Manager: Elaine Kosta, Lumina Datamatics, Inc.
Director of Digital Production: Keri deManigold
Advanced Media Project Manager: D. Rand Thomas
Project Management: Lumina Datamatics, Inc.
Senior Project Manager: Aravinda Doss, Lumina Datamatics, Inc.
Editorial Services: Lumina Datamatics, Inc.
Copyeditor: Nancy Crompton
Composition: Lumina Datamatics, Inc.
Cover Images: (sneakers) Ashley Podnar/Shutterstock; (dancers) Sunwoo Jung/Getty Images; (guitar) YuryKo/Shutterstock; (Manhattan's High Line Park) Copyright Artem Vorobiev/Getty Images; (cowboy) Comstock/Getty Images; (woman) We Are/Getty Images
Printing and Binding: LSC Communications

Library of Congress Control Number: 2020939789
ISBN: 978-1-319-21366-4

Printed in the United States of America.
1 2 3 4 5 6 25 24 23 22 21 20

Acknowledgments

Text acknowledgments and copyrights appear at the back of the book on pages 571–75, which constitute an extension of the copyright page. Art acknowledgments and copyrights appear on the same page as the art selections they cover.

For information, write: Bedford/St. Martin's, 75 Arlington Street, Boston, MA 02116

Preface for Instructors

A Preface to the Preface

When the full force of the COVID-19 pandemic struck America, this edition of *Signs of Life in the U.S.A.* was already well into the copyediting stage of production — too late for making any substantive changes to the text, and too early to make any predictions as to what effects it would ultimately have on our nation and our world. But two of the social inflections of the plague, which clearly reflect some of the fundamental principles and themes of the tenth edition of this book, have already emerged as we write the words of this preface. These are, first, the profound role that cultural mythologies play in shaping social consciousness and experience, and, second, the equally profound ideological differences that now divide our society into warring parties. For it was the fundamental mythology of American exceptionalism that left us especially unprepared to grapple with a global pandemic; and it was the deep divisions in the land — often coded as "red state" and "blue state" ideologies — that have made it impossible to formulate an adequately unified policy for fighting the disease. And since these two phenomena have already shaped the structure and theme of our book, there are many ways in which it can be used to address the pandemic in your classes, should you wish to do so. For the purposes of this preface, then, we will begin by describing the overall features of the new edition, and follow this with some suggestions as to how this text may be used in the context of COVID-19.

The Structure and Theme of the New Edition

Readers familiar with prior editions of *Signs of Life in the U.S.A.* may notice a slight architectural difference between the arrangement of this, the tenth edition of the book, and all previous editions. For while there have been a number of different chapter arrangements and topics presented in the text in the quarter century since it first appeared, reflecting changing trends in American popular culture across the years, the first chapter of readings has always been focused on consumption: the selling and consuming of products and services that undergirds not only the American economy but its consciousness as well. But now, a chapter that initially appeared in the fifth edition — "American Paradox: Culture, Conflict, and Contradiction in the U.S.A." — heads the table of contents, followed by a chapter on the politics of identity, with which it is combined as part of an inaugural section of the book devoted to a survey of the "Foundations" upon which the structure of the rest of the text is grounded. And this rearrangement, as with so much else that is to be found in *Signs of Life in the U.S.A.*, has a meaning.

For while America remains a consumer society whose entertainments and everyday life are still grounded in consumption, it is the ever-increasing political and ideological division of the land, which burst into full fruition with the election of Donald Trump to the presidency in 2016, that casts the longer shadow over contemporary American consciousness. And with so much of that division reflecting the increasing diversity of a heretofore monocultural society, we have chosen to place first in our book a survey of the ideological contradictions and demographic conflicts that can be found as the basis for so much that is now dividing the country.

In this sense, the tenth edition of *Signs of Life in the U.S.A.* can be seen as an extension of the ninth, which included as its sub-thematic leitmotif an exploration of the ideological "civil war" that was already rending the nation as we worked on that text. Since then, the situation has become only more intense, with political conflict coming to the fore in every area of American life, and popular culture itself bearing the banners of contending parties. No entertainment awards ceremony is without its star-studded expressions of political protest in the Trump era, while *Saturday Night Live* and the Fox News Network vie for supremacy in the battle for American hearts and minds. A see-saw struggle for power, with the White House passing from one side to the other with a passion not seen since the days of the Civil War itself, now dominates our lives, and the new edition of *Signs of Life in the U.S.A.* is designed to reflect and explore the implications of such a state of affairs.

What hasn't changed in the tenth edition of the book is our conviction that American popular culture, no longer a mere cultural embellishment or ornament, now permeates almost everything we do even as it reflects back to us what we are becoming as a society and who we are. In fact, that conviction has only been strengthened by the way that popular culture has largely supplanted such traditional institutions as party committees and mainstream religious denominations in the political lives of ordinary Americans. With Facebook (and related social media) taking the place of the Sunday sermon and the stump speech, popular culture looms larger in our lives than ever before, so if we wish to understand America today, we must learn to think critically about the vast panoply of entertainments and commodities that were once condescendingly dismissed as elements of "mass culture" in academic circles. And that is what *Signs of Life in the U.S.A.* has always been designed to teach your students to do.

Then and Now

The importance of thinking critically about popular culture has not always been so obviously apparent in the academic world. When the first edition of *Signs of Life* appeared, the study of popular culture was still embroiled in the "culture wars" of the late 1980s and early 1990s, a struggle for academic legitimacy in which the adherents of popular cultural studies prevailed so thoroughly that it now seems surprising that anyone ever objected to it at all. Today, the importance of understanding what Michel de Certeau called "the practice of everyday life," and the value of using popular culture as a thematic ground for educating students in critical thinking and writing, are now taken for granted, as what was once excluded from academic study on the basis of a naturalized distinction between "high" and "low" culture is now an accepted part of the curriculum, widely studied in freshman composition classrooms as well as in upper-division undergraduate courses and graduate seminars.

But recognition of the importance that popular culture has assumed in our society has not been restricted to the academy. Increasingly, Americans are realizing that American culture and popular culture are virtually one and the same, and that whether we are looking at our political system, our economy, or simply our national consciousness, the power of popular culture to shape our lives is strikingly apparent. That is why *Signs of Life* adopts an interpretive approach — semiotics — that is explicitly designed to analyze that intersection of ideology and entertainment that we call *popular culture*. We continue to make semiotics the guiding methodology behind *Signs of Life* because of the way it helps us, and our students, avoid the common pitfalls of uncritical pop cultural celebration or simple trivia swapping.

The Critical Method: Semiotics

The reception of the first nine editions of this text has demonstrated that the semiotic approach to popular culture has indeed found a place in America's composition classrooms. Instructors have seen that students feel a certain sense of ownership toward the products of popular culture and that using popular culture as a focus can help students overcome the sometimes alienating effects of traditional academic subject matter. More profoundly, the use of popular cultural content in a composition class is a way of abiding by the fundamental principle that learning is a movement from the familiar to the unfamiliar, an assimilation of the unknown by way of the already known. Coming to your class with an established expertise in popular cultural content, your students will be all the more prepared to learn the university-level critical thinking and writing skills that their composition classes are designed to impart.

Reflecting the broad academic interest in cultural studies, we've assumed an inclusive definition of *popular culture* in this book. The eight chapters in *Signs of Life in the U.S.A.* embrace everything from the marketing and consumption of the products of mass production to the television programs and movies that entertain us. We came to choose semiotics as our approach to such subjects because it has struck us that while students enjoy assignments that ask them to look at popular cultural phenomena, they often have trouble distinguishing between an argued interpretive analysis and the simple expression of an opinion. Some textbooks, for example, suggest assignments that involve analyzing a TV show or film, but they don't always tell a student *how* to do that. The semiotic method provides that guidance.

As a conceptual framework, semiotics teaches students to formulate cogent, well-supported interpretations. It emphasizes the examination of assumptions and of the way language shapes our apprehension of the world. And, because semiotics focuses on how beliefs are formulated within a social and political context (rather than just judging or evaluating those beliefs), it's ideal for discussing sensitive or politically charged issues (like the 2020 presidential election). As an approach used in literature, media and communications studies, anthropology, art and design coursework, sociology, law, and market research (to name only some of its more prominent field applications), semiotics has a cross-disciplinary appeal that makes it ideal for a writing class of students from a variety of majors and disciplines. We recognize that semiotics has a reputation for being highly technical or theoretical; rest assured that *Signs of Life* does not require students or instructors to have a technical knowledge of semiotics. We've provided clear and accessible introductions that explain what students need to know.

We also recognize that adopting a theoretical approach may be new to some instructors, so we've designed the book to allow instructors to use semiotics with their students as much or as little as they wish. The book does not obligate instructors or students to spend a lot of time with semiotics — although we do hope you'll find the approach intriguing and provocative.

The Semiotics of the COVID-19 Pandemic

And here is where the principles of *Signs of Life in the U.S.A.* can be applied to the COVID-19 pandemic. The critical role played by cultural "mythologies" in society — the worldviews and ideologies that frame our social experience and consciousness — is one of the foundations of semiotics, and as we face a disease that is disrupting and will continue, for the foreseeable future, to affect our lives in ways that are likely to confront us with new and unexpected challenges, an understanding of how mythologies work has become more important than ever. This is especially true with respect to one of America's most fundamental mythologies — the conviction known as "American exceptionalism" — which is now being starkly challenged by the realities of living in the shadow of COVID-19. This belief is that America has always been the exception to human history, that America, alone among the nations, is immune from tragedy, from unmitigated disaster, from decline. A corollary to American exceptionalism is the conviction that America has always been, and will continue to be, at the forefront of history, a City on a Hill that will lead the rest of the world to freedom and prosperity. The pandemic, and America's response to it, is challenging that confidence.

Since such beliefs present barriers to a clear understanding of the challenges that face us as a society you may want to begin your class by addressing them. You could start by assigning the Introduction to the book, concentrating especially on the discussion of cultural mythologies, along with the introduction to Chapter 1, "American Paradox: Culture, Conflict, and Contradiction in the U.S.A." After the principles explored in these introductions are clear to your students, assign Barbara Ehrenreich's reading selection, "Bright-Sided," which explores in depth the effects of American exceptionalism in shaping America's fundamental optimism as a society, and the concomitant tendency of its citizens to be unprepared for disaster. Once your students have fully grasped how mythologies work, you will be ready to craft writing assignments that will enable them to write semiotically informed essays on the pandemic.

The Editorial Apparatus

Of course, with its emphasis on popular culture, *Signs of Life* should generate lively class discussion and inspire many kinds of writing and thinking activities well beyond the effects of the COVID-19 pandemic. The general Introduction provides an overall framework for the book, acquainting students with the semiotic method they can use to interpret the topics raised in each chapter. It is followed by the section "Writing about Popular Culture," which not only provides a succinct introduction to this topic but also features three sample student essays that demonstrate different approaches to writing critical essays on popular cultural topics. The Introduction concludes with "Conducting Research and Citing Sources," an MLA-updated section to help your students properly document the research they've done for their writing assignments, including three articles that guide students in the appropriate use of the internet as a research tool.

Each chapter starts with a frontispiece, a provocative visual image related to the chapter's topic, and an introduction that suggests ways to "read" the topic, provides model interpretations, and links the issues raised by the reading selections. Every chapter introduction contains three types of boxed questions designed to stimulate student thinking on the topic. The "Exploring the Signs" questions invite students to reflect on an issue in a journal entry or other prewriting activity, while the "Discussing the Signs" questions trigger class activities such as debates, discussions, or small-group work. The "Reading Online" questions invite students to explore the chapter's topic on the internet, both for research purposes and for texts to analyze.

Two sorts of assignments accompany each reading. The "Reading the Text" questions help students comprehend the selections, asking them to identify important concepts and arguments, explain key terms, and relate main ideas to one another and to the evidence presented. The "Reading the Signs" questions are writing and activity prompts designed to produce clear analytic thinking and strong persuasive writing; they often make connections among reading selections from different chapters. Most assignments call for analytic essays, while some invite journal responses, in-class debates, group work, or other creative activities. Complementing the readings in each chapter are images that serve as visual texts to be discussed. We also include a glossary of semiotic terms, which can serve as a ready reference to key words and concepts used in the chapter introductions. Finally, the Instructor's Manual (*Editors' Notes for* Signs of Life in the U.S.A.) provides suggestions for organizing your syllabus, encouraging student responses to the readings, and using popular culture and semiotics in the writing class.

What's New in the Tenth Edition

Popular culture evolves at a rapid pace, and the substantial revision required for the tenth edition of *Signs of Life in the U.S.A.* reflects this essential mutability. First, as already noted, we have restructured the text, dividing it into three sections of related readings: "Foundations," "Everyday Life," and "Entertainment." We have also updated our readings, including more than twenty-five new selections focusing on issues and trends that have emerged since the last edition of this book, and have added a new chapter — "Tangled Roots: The Cultural Politics of Popular Music" — to reflect the increasing role of music as a medium for the expression of the divisions that have sundered the nation. Updated introductions provide new topics to be used to model the critical assignments that follow, while responding to the changing conditions of students' lives and the ways they consume and experience popular culture.

From the beginning, *Signs of Life in the U.S.A.* has been based on the premise that in a postindustrial, McLuhanesque world, the image has come to rival the printed word in American, and global, culture. That is yet another reason we chose semiotics, which provides a rational basis for the critical analysis of images, as the guiding methodology for every edition of our book.

Each edition of *Signs of Life* has accordingly included images for criti ysis; the tenth edition continues this tradition with many new selection images included in the text supplement the readings, offering a visual spective designed to enhance the critical understanding modeled by the texts. Yet the images are not meant to replace the texts—we strongly believe that while the semiotic interpretation of images can help students hone their writing skills, it should not be a substitute for learning critical thinking through the analysis of written texts.

At the same time, the way that students consume images has been revolutionized by digital and mobile technologies, and *Signs of Life in the U.S.A.* reflects this new reality both through the offering of an e-book version of the main text and through *Achieve for Readers and Writers*, a flexible, integrated suite of tools for designing and facilitating writing assignments, paired with actionable insights that make students' progress toward outcomes clear and measurable. *Achieve for Readers and Writers* is available as a free package with *Signs of Life in the U.S.A.*

Even as we revise this text to reflect current trends, popular culture continues to evolve. The inevitable gap between the pace of editing and publishing, on the one hand, and the flow of popular culture, on the other, need not affect the use of popular culture in the classroom, however. The readings in the text, and the semiotic method we propose, are designed to show students how to analyze and write critical essays about any topic they choose. That topic may have appeared before they were born, or it may be the latest box-office or prime-time hit to appear after the publication of this edition of *Signs of Life in the U.S.A.* Facebook and Twitter may well have been replaced by more recently arriving social media within the lifespan of this edition, but such changes are opportunities for further analysis, not obstacles. To put it another way, the practice of everyday life may itself be filled with evanescent fads and trends, but daily life is not itself a fad. As the vital texture of our lived experience, popular culture provides a stable background against which students of every generation can test their critical skills.

If we have not included something you'd like to work on, you may still direct your students to it, using this text as a guide, not as a set of absolute prescriptions. The practice of everyday life includes the conduct of a classroom, and we want all users of the tenth edition of *Signs of Life in the U.S.A.* to feel free to pursue that practice in whatever way best suits their interests and aims.

Acknowledgments

The vastness of the terrain of popular culture has enabled many users of the ninth edition of this text to make valuable suggestions for the tenth edition. We have incorporated many such suggestions and thank all for their comments on our text. We are also grateful to those reviewers who examined the book in depth: Alexander Bean, Harold Washington College; J. Gregory

Brister, Valley City State University; Harold Washington College; Maria Cahill, Husson University; Patricia Cullinan, Truckee Meadows Community College; Mary Cummins, University of California – Riverside; Nina Feng, University of Utah; Jeff Gray, East Los Angeles College; Loretta Henry, Bucks County Community College; Jeanette Lukowski, Bemidji State University; Caroline Mains, Palo Alto College; Nowell Marshall, Rider University; Claire McCarthy, Salem State University; Tim Melnarik, Pasadena City College; Dan Mills, Athens Technical College; Patricia Moody, Syracuse University; Dan Portillo, College of the Canyons; Cynthia Rogan de Ramirez, Bucks County Community College; Eric Russell, Central Michigan University; Laura Sass-Germain, Bucks County Community College; and Matthew Snyder, University of California – Riverside.

Once again, we wish to thank heartily the people at Bedford/St. Martin's who have enabled us to make this new edition a reality, including Leasa Burton, Stacey Purviance, John Sullivan, and Joy Fisher Williams. We especially want to thank our new editor, Christina Gerogiannis, who has kept this edition on course from start to finish. Matt Glazer, along with Aravinda Doss and her team, ably guided our manuscript through the rigors of production, while Paola Garcia-Muniz handled the numerous questions and details that arose during textbook development. Paola is also responsible for developing the Instructor's Manual for this edition. Lisa Passmore expertly researched and obtained permissions for art, and Elaine Kosta cleared text permissions. Our thanks go as well to Nancy Crompton for her fine copyediting of this book.

—Sonia Maasik and Jack Solomon

Bedford/St. Martin's Puts You First

From day one, our goal has been simple: to provide inspiring resources that are grounded in best practices for teaching reading and writing. For more than 35 years, Bedford/St. Martin's has partnered with the field, listening to teachers, scholars, and students about the support writers need. We are committed to helping every writing instructor make the most of our resources.

How Can We Help *You*?

- Our editors can align our resources to your outcomes through correlation and transition guides for your syllabus. Just ask us.
- Our sales representatives specialize in helping you find the right materials to support your course goals.
- Our learning solutions and product specialists help you make the most of the digital resources you choose for your course.

- Our *Bits* blog on the Bedford/St. Martin's English Community (**community .macmillan.com**) publishes fresh teaching ideas weekly. You'll also find easily downloadable professional resources and links to author webinars on our community site.

Contact your Bedford/St. Martin's sales representative or visit **macmillanlearning .com** to learn more.

PRINT AND DIGITAL OPTIONS FOR SIGNS OF LIFE IN THE U.S.A.

Choose the format that works best for your course, and ask about our packaging options that offer savings for students.

Print

- *Paperback.* To order the paperback edition, use ISBN 978-1-319-21366-4. To order the print text packaged with *Achieve for Readers and Writers*, use ISBN 978-1-319-38866-9.

Digital

- *Achieve for Readers and Writers.* Achieve puts student writing at the center of your course and keeps revision at the core, with a dedicated composition space that guides students through drafting, peer review, plagiarism prevention, source check, reflection, and revision. Developed to support best practices in commenting on student drafts, Achieve is a flexible, integrated suite of tools for designing and facilitating writing assignments, paired with actionable insights that make students' progress toward outcomes clear and measurable. Achieve offers instructors a quick and flexible solution for targeting instruction based on students' unique needs. For details, visit **macmillanlearning.com/college/us/englishdigital**.
- *Popular e-book formats.* For details about our e-book partners, visit **macmillanlearning.com/ebooks**.
- *Inclusive access.* Enable every student to receive their course materials through your LMS on the first day of class. Macmillan Learning's Inclusive Access program is the easiest, most affordable way to ensure all students have access to quality educational resources. Find out more at **macmillanlearning.com/inclusiveaccess**.

YOUR COURSE, YOUR WAY

No two writing programs or classrooms are exactly alike. Our Curriculum Solutions team works with you to design custom options that provide the resources your students need. (Options below require enrollment minimums.)

- *ForeWords for English.* Customize any print resource to fit the focus of your course or program by choosing from a range of prepared topics, such as Sentence Guides for Academic Writers.
- *Macmillan Author Program (MAP).* Add excerpts or package acclaimed works from Macmillan's trade imprints to connect students with prominent authors and public conversations. A list of popular examples or academic themes is available upon request.
- *Mix and Match.* With our simplest solution, you can add up to 50 pages of curated content to your Bedford/St. Martin's text. Contact your sales representative for additional details.
- *Bedford Select.* Build your own print anthology from a database of more than 800 selections, or build a handbook, and add your own materials to create your ideal text. Package with any Bedford/St. Martin's text for additional savings. Visit **macmillanlearning.com/bedfordselect**.

INSTRUCTOR RESOURCES

You have a lot to do in your course. We want to make it easy for you to find the support you need — and to get it quickly.

Editors' Notes for Signs of Life in the U.S.A. is available as a PDF that can be downloaded from **macmillanlearning.com**. In addition to chapter overviews and teaching tips, the instructor's manual includes sample syllabi, correlations to the Council of Writing Program Administrators' Outcomes Statement, and classroom activities.

Contents

Preface for Instructors *v*

INTRODUCTION
Popular Signs: ***Or, Everything You Always Knew about American Culture (but Nobody Asked)*** *1*

It's the End of the World as We Know It *1*

From Folk to For-Profit *2*

Pop Culture Goes to College *6*

The Semiotic Method *8*

Abduction and Overdetermination *11*

Interpreting Popular Signs: The Revolution Will Be Reiterated *12*

The Classroom Connection *15*

Cultural Mythologies *16*

Getting Started *17*

Writing about Popular Culture *19*

Using Active Reading Strategies *20*

Prewriting Strategies *21*

Developing Strong Arguments about Popular Culture *24*

Conducting a Semiotic Analysis 25
Reading Visual Images Actively 28
Reading Essays about Popular Culture 31

JEREMY CREEK: *The Anglerfish in the Machine: Horror and Re-enchantment In* Stranger Things [STUDENT ESSAY] 31

AMY LIN: *Barbie: Queen of Dolls and Consumerism* [STUDENT ESSAY] 38

IRINA BODEA: *Banks: Progressive or Conventional?* [STUDENT ESSAY] 45

Conducting Research and Citing Sources 50

SCOTT JASCHIK: *A Stand against Wikipedia* 51

PATTI S. CARAVELLO: *Judging Quality on the Web* 53

TRIP GABRIEL: *For Students in Internet Age, No Shame in Copy and Paste* 55

Synthesizing, Quoting, Paraphrasing, and Citing Sources 59
In-Text Citations 61
List of Works Cited 62

Section 1
FOUNDATIONS

Chapter 1.
American Paradox: *Culture, Conflict, and Contradiction in the U.S.A.* **67**

Operation Varsity Blues 67
Six Contradictions That Count 68
Dying for Dollars: The Oxymoron of America's Spiritual Materialism 69
Toddlers and Tiaras: Sexual Repression Meets the Profit Motive 70
The Pokémon Paradox: Individualism in a Mass Consumer Society 71
The 1 Percent: American Populism versus Economic Elitism 72
Oscars So White: The Enduring Legacy of Slavery 73
The Statutes of Liberty: Immigration Controversy in the Land of Immigrants 74
What's Red and Blue and Mad All Over? 75

The Readings 76

BARBARA EHRENREICH: *Bright-Sided* 77

"Americans are a 'positive' people. This is our reputation as well as our self-image."

GEORGE PACKER: *Celebrating Inequality* 86

"What are celebrities, after all? They dominate the landscape, like giant monuments to aspiration, fulfillment, and overreach. They are as intimate as they are grand, and they offer themselves for worship by ordinary people searching for a suitable object of devotion."

MARK MANSON: *The Disease of More* 89

"It took me a long time to accept the fact that just because something *can be improved* in my life, does not mean that it *should be improved* in my life."

MARK MURPHY: *The Uncivil War: How Cultural Sorting of America Divides Us* 94

"Far from being a 'melting pot,' America in 2018 has become a bubbling cauldron of potluck stew."

ALFRED LUBRANO: *The Shock of Education: How College Corrupts* 100

"'Every bit of learning takes you further from your parents.'"

MARIAH BURTON NELSON: *I Won. I'm Sorry.* 107

"If you want to be a winner and you're female, you'll feel pressured to play by special, female rules."

WADE GRAHAM: *Are We Greening Our Cities, or Just Greenwashing Them?* 114

"Architecture and urban design are in the throes of a green fever dream: Everywhere you look there are plans for 'sustainable' buildings, futuristic eco-cities, even vertical aquaponic farms in the sky, each promising to redeem the ecologically sinful modern city and bring its inhabitants back into harmony with nature."

Chapter 2.
My Selfie, My Self: *Identity and Ideology in the New Millennium* *119*

It's Not So Transparent 119

Who Are You? 120

Gender Codes 121

Postfeminist or Third Wave? 122

The Space for Race 123

The Great Divide 124

Generationx 124

Be Whatever You Want to Be 126

The Supermarket of IDs *127*

The Readings *128*

MICHAEL OMI: *In Living Color: Race and American Culture* *129*

"Popular culture has been an important realm within which racial ideologies have been created, reproduced, and sustained."

RACHELLE HAMPTON: *Which People?* *141*

"For all the good intentions behind it, the success of *people of color* has brought with it a strong potential for misuse."

ZAHIR JANMOHAMED: *Your Cultural Attire* *144*

"The term *cultural appropriation* is bandied about so easily that it seems that anytime a person cooks a dish not from their own cultural background, someone is ready to cry foul."

AARON DEVOR: *Gender Role Behaviors and Attitudes* *150*

"Persons who perform the activities considered appropriate for another gender will be expected to perform them poorly; if they succeed adequately, or even well, at their endeavors, they may be rewarded with ridicule or scorn for blurring the gender dividing line."

DEBORAH BLUM: *The Gender Blur: Where Does Biology End and Society Take Over?* *156*

"How does all this fit together — toys and testosterone, biology and behavior, the development of the child into the adult, the way that men and women relate to one another?"

MICHAEL HULSHOF-SCHMIDT: *What's in an Acronym? Parsing the LGBTQQIP2SAA Community* *163*

"Every few months another online debate flares up about exactly what the LGBT community should call itself."

RACHEL LOWRY: *Straddling Online and Offline Profiles, Millennials Search for Identity* *166*

"Millennials, the term given for those born between 1980 and 2000, may be suffering from an identity crisis as they search for their authentic self."

SOPHIE GILBERT: *Millennial Burnout Is Being Televised* *170*

"Identity and achievements are visual metrics to be publicly displayed and curated."

DAVE PATTERSON: *Shame by a Thousand Looks* *175*

"Even now as I write this, the lifetime of microaggressions I suffered as a byproduct of childhood poverty plays in a crackled loop."

KWAME ANTHONY APPIAH: *What Does It Mean to "Look Like Me"?* 178

"The truth is that our best stories and songs often gain potency by complicating our received notions of identity."

Section 2
EVERYDAY LIFE

Chapter 3.
Consuming Passions: *The Culture of American Consumption* 185

The CCI 185

#leggingsdaynd 186

The Handmaid's Tale 187

Jeans, Spandex, Leotards, and Leg Warmers 187

Disposable Decades 189

A Tale of Two Cities 190

When the Going Gets Tough, the Tough Go Shopping 191

The Readings 192

LAURENCE SHAMES: *The More Factor* 193

"Frontier; opportunity; more. This has been the American trinity from the very start."

MALCOLM GLADWELL: *The Science of Shopping* 200

"Retailers don't just want to know how shoppers behave in their stores. They *have* to know."

JORDYN HOLMAN: *Millennials Tried to Kill the American Mall, But Gen Z Might Save It* 207

"Gen Z . . . love[s] the shopping mall."

MICHAEL POLLAN: *Supermarket Pastoral* 211

"Taken as a whole, the story on offer in Whole Foods is a pastoral narrative in which farm animals live much as they did in the books we read as children."

CHRIS ARNING: *What Can Semiotics Contribute to Packaging Design?* 217

"More and more, the use of semiotics research is penetrating the sphere of packaging design, giving brands a tremendous head start in communicating core values, personality, and brand positioning to the market."

TROY PATTERSON: *The Politics of the Hoodie* 224

"Where the basic hoodie means to defend against the elements, the protest hoodie seeks to offend the right people."

THOMAS FRANK: *Commodify Your Dissent* 228

"We consume not to fit in, but to prove, on the surface at least, that we are rock 'n' roll rebels."

JAMES A. ROBERTS: *The Treadmill of Consumption* 233

"Status consumption is the heart and soul of the consumer culture, which revolves around our attempts to signal our comparative degree of social power through conspicuous consumption."

Chapter 4.
Brought to You B(u)y: *The Signs of Advertising* 241

Going for Woke 241

And Here's the Pitch 243

The Semiotic Foundation 244

The Commodification of Desire 245

The New Marketing 247

Populism versus Elitism 248

The Readings 249

JACK SOLOMON: *Masters of Desire: The Culture of American Advertising* 250

"The logic of advertising is entirely semiotic: It substitutes signs for things, framed visions of consumer desire for the thing itself."

JAMES B. TWITCHELL: *What We Are to Advertisers* 261

"Mass production means mass marketing, and mass marketing means the creation of mass stereotypes."

JOSEPH TUROW: *The Daily You: How the New Advertising Industry Is Defining Your Identity and Your Worth* 265

"Every day most if not all Americans who use the internet, along with hundreds of millions of other users from all over the planet, are being quietly peeked at, poked, analyzed, and tagged as they move through the online world."

STEVE CRAIG: *Men's Men and Women's Women* 273

"What might have been a simple commercial about a man ordering and drinking a beer becomes an elaborate sexual fantasy, in many respects constructed like a porn film."

JIA TOLENTINO: *How "Empowerment" Became Something for Women to Buy* 285

"The mix of things presumed to transmit and increase female power is without limit yet still depressingly limiting."

DEREK THOMPSON: *The Four-Letter Code to Selling Just About Anything: What Makes Things Cool?* *289*

"To sell something surprising, make it familiar; and to sell something familiar, make it surprising."

JULIET B. SCHOR: *Selling to Children: The Marketing of Cool* *296*

"Cool has been around for decades. Back in the fifties, there were cool cats and hipsters. In the sixties, hippies and the Beatles were cool. But in those days, cool was only one of many acceptable personal styles. Now it's revered as a universal quality — something every product tries to be and every kid needs to have."

JULIA B. CORBETT: *A Faint Green Sell: Advertising and the Natural World* *305*

"It matters not whether an ad boasts of recyclability or quietly features pristine mountain meadows in the background; the basic business of advertising is brown. Perhaps the only truly Green product is not only one not produced, but also one not advertised."

Portfolio of Advertisements

Spotify

Buffalo Exchange

California Walnuts

AdCouncil

Shinola

The Shelter Pet Project

The Society of Grownups

Chapter 5.
The Cloud: *Semiotics and the New Media* *325*

Big Sister *325*

The New Panopticon *326*

The Medium Is the Mashup *327*

"Pics or It Didn't Happen" *328*

Whose Space? *328*

Shame on You *331*

A Bridge Over Troubled Waters *332*

Top-Down After All? *334*

The Readings 336

JUDY ESTRIN: *I Helped Create the Internet, and I'm Worried about What It's Doing to Young People* 337

"Why take the time to read, comprehend, and respond thoughtfully to an email when Gmail will suggest a couple of three-word responses?"

ALICIA ELER: *There's a Lot More to a Selfie Than Meets the Eye* 340

"The selfie taker captures the gaze and loves it. The selfie serves and it is pleasure, attention, and validation all in one."

JUDITH SHULEVITZ: *"Alexa, How Will You Change Us?"* 346

"These secretarial companions may be faux-conscious nonpersons, but their words give them personality and social presence."

JESSE SELL: *Gamer Identity* 350

"It might just be a matter of time before the legitimacy of gaming wipes away the stigma of the term 'gamer.'"

DAVID COURTWRIGHT: *How "Limbic Capitalism" Preys on Our Addicted Brains* 354

"In 2013, the new edition of the bible of psychiatry, the *Diagnostic and Statistical Manual of Mental Disorders: DSM-5*, described gaming disorders in language indistinguishable from drug addiction."

NANCY JO SALES: *From the Instamatic to Instagram: Social Media and the Secret Lives of Teenagers* 360

"'I spend so much time on Instagram looking at people's pictures and sometimes I'll be like, Why am I spending my time on this?'"

JACOB SILVERMAN: *"Pics or It Didn't Happen": The Mantra of the Instagram Era* 368

"We turn ourselves into tourists of our own lives and communities, our Instagram accounts our self-authored guidebooks."

BROOKE GLADSTONE: *Influencing Machines: The Echo Chambers of the Internet* 379

"Many say that the Internet's ability to link like-minded souls everywhere fosters the creation of virtually impermeable echo chambers."

JOHN HERRMAN: *Inside Facebook's (Totally Insane, Unintentionally Gigantic, Hyperpartisan) Political-Media Machine* 384

"In retrospect, Facebook's takeover of online media looks rather like a slow-motion coup."

Section 3
ENTERTAINMENT

Chapter 6.
On the Air: *Television and Cultural Forms* 397

From Mary Tyler Moore to *The Handmaid's Tale* *397*

Litchfield Is the New Mayberry *399*

Writing about Television *402*

From Symbols to Icons *403*

And Now a Word from Our Sponsors *404*

Reality Bites *406*

The Readings *408*

NEAL GABLER: *The Social Networks* *409*

"On television friends never come in pairs; they invariably congregate in groups of three or more."

SAMANTHA ALLEN: *How* Euphoria *and Model Hunter Schafer Created the Most Interesting Trans Character on TV* *412*

"The best way to humanize a marginalized group is to show them being, well, fully human."

CLAIRE MIYE STANFORD: *You've Got the Wrong Song:* Nashville *and Country Music Feminism* *416*

"As a show . . . *Nashville* — in its unapologetically pure focus on female characters, its self-aware examination of the struggles of female artists, and its critique of male-dominated industries — is one of the most feminist television shows on television."

EMILY NUSSBAUM: *The Aristocrats: The Graphic Arts of* Game of Thrones *423*

"It's true that *Game of Thrones* is unusually lurid, even within the arms race of pay cable: the show is so graphic that it was parodied on *Saturday Night Live*."

MASSIMO PIGLIUCCI: *The One Paradigm to Rule Them All: Scientism and* The Big Bang Theory *427*

"LEONARD: You can't train my girlfriend like a lab rat.

SHELDON: Actually, it turns out I can.

LEONARD: Well, you shouldn't."

BRITTANY LEVINE BECKMAN: *Why We Binge-Watch Stuff We Hate* *436*

"'Binge-watching a show you hate may not be particularly pleasant, but it's more pleasant than cleaning the bathroom or taking your dog for a walk when it's raining.'"

Chapter 7.
The Hollywood Sign: *The Culture of American Film* *441*

Global Warming with a Vengeance *441*

For Godzilla's Sake! *442*

The Culture Industry *445*

Interpreting the Signs of American Film *446*

Repetition with a Difference *448*

Movies as Metaphors *449*

The Readings *450*

ROBERT B. RAY: *The Thematic Paradigm* *451*

"To the outlaw hero's insistence on private standards of right and wrong, the official hero offered the admonition, 'You cannot take the law into your own hands.'"

CHRISTINE FOLCH: *Why the West Loves Sci-Fi and Fantasy: A Cultural Explanation* *459*

"The simplest conclusion . . . is that Bollywood doesn't produce science fiction and fantasy because Indian audiences aren't as keen on it. Local cultural production doesn't just result from economic wherewithal; desires and needs also matter. And desires and needs are cultural."

LINDA SEGER: *Creating the Myth* *463*

"Whatever our culture, there are universal stories that form the basis for our particular stories . . . . Many of the most successful films are based on these universal stories."

MAYA PHILLIPS: *The Narrative Experiment That Is the Marvel Cinematic Universe* *472*

"Just as people ask, about historical events, 'Where were you when it happened?,' so fans ask where they were when *Iron Man* came out, when the Avengers first assembled, when heroes and villains battled in Wakanda."

ABRAHAM RIESMAN: *What We Talk about When We Talk about Batman and Superman* *477*

"Why are fans so desperate to see superheroes in conflict that they urge superhero writers to employ absurd narrative contrivances like mind control or alternate universes to make happen what would otherwise be vanishingly unlikely fights (a tactic used well over a dozen times in the history of Batman-Superman tales)?"

MATT ZOLLER SEITZ: *The Offensive Movie Cliché That Won't Die* *488*

"The Magical Negro . . . is a glorified hood ornament attached to the end of a car that's being driven by white society, vigorously turning a little steering wheel that's not attached to anything."

MIKHAIL LYUBANSKY: *The Racial Politics of* Black Panther *492*

"'*Black Panther* . . . offers racial commentary about our own world.'"

JESSICA HAGEDORN: *Asian Women in Film: No Joy, No Luck* *498*

"Because change has been slow, *The Joy Luck Club* carries a lot of cultural baggage."

MICHAEL PARENTI: *Class and Virtue* *506*

"The entertainment media present working people not only as unlettered and uncouth but also as less desirable and less moral than other people."

DAVID DENBY: *High-School Confidential: Notes on Teen Movies* *510*

"In these movies . . . the senior prom is the equivalent of the shoot-out at the O.K. Corral."

WESLEY MORRIS: *Rom-Coms Were Corny and Retrograde. Why Do I Miss Them So Much?* *516*

"Romantic comedy is the only genre committed to letting relatively ordinary people — no capes, no spaceships, no infinite sequels — figure out how to deal meaningfully with another human being."

Chapter 8.
Tangled Roots: *The Cultural Politics of Popular Music* *525*

Get Back to Where You Once Belonged *525*

It's Been a Long Time Coming *526*

The Turning Point *529*

Country Road *530*

The Ties That Don't Bind *530*

Rebels with a Cause: The Rebirth of the Protest Song *531*

Coda: The Diva *532*

The Readings *532*

NOLAN GASSER: *Music Is Supposed to Unify Us. Is the Streaming Revolution Fragmenting Us Instead?* *533*

"Let's take out the earbuds and turn up the speakers again — at least from time to time."

CLARA McNULTY-FINN: *The Evolution of Rap* *536*

"Perhaps the most striking difference between 1990s hip-hop and more modern tracks is the lyrics."

NADRA NITTLE: *Lil Nas X Isn't an Anomaly* *541*

"Since black people are typically associated with urban environments — although most do not live in inner cities — their legitimacy as country people isn't universally accepted."

JON MEACHAM and TIM McGRAW: *How Country Music Explains America's Divided History* *548*

"History tells us that the great songs (and great books, plays, and other artistic vehicles) that speak to the current public moment have an enduring and vital role — all the more so when they are emotionally reflective rather than ideologically reflexive."

CHRISTINA NEWLAND: *A Cultural History of the Diva* *551*

"Temper tantrums, tackiness, and solid gold bathtubs aside, we love divas because they invent their own rules."

DJ LOUIE XIV: *Has the Pop Star Been Killed?* *554*

"Thanks in part to the pluralizing forces of the internet, pop — like so many other things — has splintered."

DANIEL PERSON: *When Did Pop Culture and Nature Part Ways?* *558*

"References to nature are disturbingly sparse in current pop culture, be it books, music, or movies — and they've more or less been in steady decline since 1950."

DANI DEAHL: *Monsta X and Steve Aoki: How K-pop Took Over YouTube* *561*

"The middle of Texas should be an unlikely place for a sold-out K-pop show."

Glossary *567*

Acknowledgments *571*

Index of Authors and Titles *577*

Introduction

POPULAR SIGNS

Or, Everything You Always Knew about American Culture (but Nobody Asked)

It's the End of the World as We Know It

On April 27, 2018, half of all life in the universe disintegrated. Exactly one year later, thanks to the time-bending potential of quantum mechanics, all that had been apparently lost to history was restored. Meanwhile, in an alternative universe near you, the American people prepared for the 2020 presidential election, a political contest whose outcome, roughly half the population hoped, would reverse the effects of the 2016 election, restoring the country they felt they had lost to the other half four years before.

As you probably suspect, these events were not unrelated.

To see how, we need only to do a little time traveling ourselves. We can start with a trip back to April 27, 2018, the nationwide release date of the nineteenth installment in the Marvel Cinematic Universe, *Avengers: Infinity War*, in which half the living universe is destroyed for the ostensible benefit of the surviving half. Now, let's jump forward one year to April 26, 2019, for the nationwide release of *Avengers: Endgame*, in which the *Infinity* dead are brought back to life. At each of our stopovers, we would also encounter a nation in the throes of a conflict that had been pulling it in two directions in a series of presidential elections that, by 2018–2019, had assumed the proportions of a cultural civil war. And although, as we write these words, we cannot time travel forward to November 6, 2020, to see the outcome of that election — which will either sustain or overthrow the legacy of 2016 — we can say that the result will be but one more installment of an infinity war whose endgames aren't really endings at all: only episodes in the ongoing battle for the future of America.

We'll return shortly to an analysis of the ways in which the Avengers movies *mediate*, or creatively process and reflect back to us, the profound conflicts within American society today, but for the moment our main point is that wherever we look within the world of American popular culture, we can find signs of larger, and far more important, cultural and political phenomena. For in America today, popular culture isn't just about entertainment, and entertainment isn't simply a matter of leisure-time relaxation and recreation. From the role of Twitter in American politics to the acceptance speeches at the Oscars, from John Oliver and Samantha Bee to the cast and crew of *Saturday Night Live*, and from Fox to MSNBC — not to mention a former reality TV star's election to the presidency — entertainment and politics have become inextricably entwined. In an era when digital technology brings entertainment into the workplace, and work can be performed while being entertained, the former demarcations between what French sociologist Henri Lefebvre called "everyday life" and "festival," or workaday and play, have crumbled, creating a world in which entertainment reflects reality and reality is shaped by entertainment.

That is why we have written this book. Treating American popular culture as a system of signs that can tell us about who and where we are in our history, *Signs of Life in the U.S.A.* will teach you how to read — or interpret — these signs, while at the same time teaching you the critical thinking skills necessary to write strong university-level arguments and essays. Accordingly, each chapter in this book focuses upon a particular segment of popular culture and, by way of readings, images, and assignments, guides you through the process that will help you analyze the significance of the full range of our everyday lives, behaviors, and entertainments. We will return soon to the signs of social disaffection that we find in contemporary popular culture, but first let's look at just what the phrase *popular culture* means and why it's important to think critically about it.

From Folk to For-Profit

Traditionally, popular, or "low," culture constituted the culture of the masses. It was set apart from "high" culture, which included classical music and literature, the fine arts and philosophy, and the elite learning that was the province of the ruling classes who had the money and leisure necessary to attain it — and who were often the direct patrons of high art and its creators. Low culture, for its part, had two main sides. One side, most notoriously illustrated by the violent entertainments of the Roman Empire (such as gladiatorial contests, public executions, and feeding Christians to lions) continues to be a sure crowd-pleaser to this day, as demonstrated by the widespread popularity of violent, erotic, and/or vulgar entertainment (can you spell *Jackass*?). The other side, which we can call "popular" in the etymological sense of being of the people, overlaps with what we now call "folk culture." Quietly existing

JULIETA CERVANTES/The New York Times/Redux

Traditional high culture: Prima ballerina Misty Copeland performs in *Swan Lake* at Lincoln Center in New York City.

alongside high culture, folk culture expresses the experience and creativity of the masses in the form of ballads, agricultural festivals, fairy tales, feasts, folk art, folk music, and so on. Self-produced by amateur performers, folk culture is exemplified by neighbors gathering on a modest Appalachian front porch to play their guitars, banjos, dulcimers, zithers, mandolins, and fiddles to perform, for their own entertainment, ballads and songs passed down from generation to generation.

Folk culture, of course, still exists. But for the past two hundred years, it has been dwindling, with increasing rapidity, as it becomes overwhelmed by a different kind of popular culture — a commercialized culture that, while still including elements of both the folk and the vulgar traditions, represents the outcome of a certain historical evolution. This culture, the popular culture that is most familiar today and that is the topic of this book, is a commercial, for-profit culture aimed at providing entertainment to a mass audience. Corporate rather than communal, it has transformed entertainment into a commodity to be marketed alongside all the other products in a consumer society.

The forces that transformed the low culture of the past into contemporary popular culture arose during the Industrial Revolution of the late eighteenth century and its accompanying urbanization of European and American society. In particular, four essentially interrelated forces — industrialization, urbanization, capitalism, and electronic technology — shaped the emergence of the mass cultural marketplace of entertainments that we know today. To see how this happened, let's begin with the Industrial Revolution.

Prior to the Industrial Revolution, most Europeans and Americans lived in scattered agricultural settlements. While traveling entertainers in theatrical troupes and circuses might have visited the larger of these settlements, most people, especially those with little money, had little access to professional entertainment and so had to produce their own. But with the Industrial Revolution, masses of people who had made their living through agriculture were compelled to leave their rural communities and move to the industrial towns and cities where employment was increasingly available. Populations began to concentrate in urban centers as the rural countryside emptied, leading to the development of mass societies.

With the emergence of these mass societies came the development of **mass culture**. For just as mass societies are governed by centralized systems of governance (as the huge expanse of the United States is governed by a federal government concentrated in Washington, DC), so, too, are mass cultures entertained by culture industries concentrated in a few locations (as the film and TV industries are concentrated in Hollywood and its immediate environs). Thanks to the invention of such technologies as the cinema, the phonograph, and the radio at the end of the nineteenth century, and of television and digital technology in the mid to late twentieth century, the means to disseminate centrally produced mass entertainments to a mass society became possible. Thus, whether you live in Boston or Boise, New York or Nebraska, the entertainment you enjoy today is produced in the same few locations and is the same (traditional TV programs, movies, DVDs, or streamed television series) no matter where you consume it. This growth of mass culture has been fundamentally shaped by the growth of America's capitalist economic system, which has ensured that mass culture would develop as a for-profit industry.

To get a better idea of how the whole process unfolded, let's go back to that Appalachian front porch. Before electricity and urbanization, people living in the backwoods of rural America needed to make their music themselves if they wanted it. They had no radios, phonographs, CD players, iPods, iPads, smartphones, or even electricity, and theaters with live performers were hard to get to and expensive. Under such conditions, the Appalachian region developed a vibrant folk music culture. But as people moved to cities like Pittsburgh and Detroit, where the steel and auto industries began to offer employment in the late nineteenth and early twentieth centuries, the conditions under which neighbors could produce their own music decayed, for the communal conditions under which folk culture thrived were broken down by the mass migration to the cities. At the same time, the need to produce one's own music declined as people who had once plucked their own guitars and banjos could simply turn on their radios or buy records to listen to professional musicians perform for them. Those musicians were contracted by recording companies that were in business to turn a profit, and their music, in turn, could be heard on the radio because corporate sponsors provided the advertising that made (and still makes) commercial radio broadcasting possible.

Thus, the folk music of the American countryside became *country music*. An amalgamation of the traditional songs that a predominantly Scots-Irish immigrant population brought over from the British Isles with such American traditions as gospel music, cowboy songs, and rock 'n' roll, contemporary "country" preserves the rural working-class perspective of folk music even as it is performed by wealthy professionals.

So, the performance of folk music, once an amateur, do-it-yourself activity, became a professional, for-profit industry with passive consumers paying for their entertainment either by directly purchasing a commodity (for example, a CD or vinyl record), by subscribing to a service like Spotify® Premium, or by listening to the advertising that encourages them to purchase the products that sponsor their favorite radio programs. It's still possible, of course,

AP Images

Traditional folk culture in transition: Bill Monroe is known as the father of bluegrass music.

to make one's own music, but most people find it easier and perhaps more aesthetically pleasing to listen to a professional recording. Today we are, in effect, constantly being trained to be the sort of passive consumers who keep the whole consumer-capitalist system going. Without that consumption, the economy might totally collapse.

This is hardly an exaggeration, for postindustrial capitalism is making popular culture all the more dominant in our society with every passing year. With the American economy turning further away from industrial production and increasingly toward the production and consumption of entertainment (including sports), entertainment has been moving from the margins of our cultural consciousness — as mere play or recreation — to its center as a major buttress of our economy. A constant bombardment of advertising (which, after all, is the driving force behind the financing of digital media, just as it was for radio and television a generation or two ago) continually prods us to consume the entertainments that our economy produces. That bombardment has been so successful that our whole cultural consciousness is changing: we are becoming more concerned with play than with work, even while *at* work. (Tell the truth now: Do you ever tweet, or post something to Instagram, during class?)

The result of the centuries-long process we have sketched above is the kind of culture we have today: an entertainment culture in which all aspects of society, including politics, and sometimes even the traditional elite arts, are linked by a common imperative to entertain. Indeed, as traditional high culture shrinks in social importance — having never had a mass audience to begin with and thus unable to compete effectively in a market economy — it has dwindled into becoming what might be called a "museum culture" (which is quietly marginalized and widely ignored). Popular culture has accordingly assumed its own "high" and "low" strata, with TV programs like *The Handmaid's Tale* and *Game of Thrones* enjoying a kind of high cultural status, while shows like *Pawn Stars* profitably inhabit the low end of the television spectrum.

Pop Culture Goes to College

Far from being a mere recreational frivolity, then, a dispensable leisure activity, today's popular culture constitutes the essential texture of our everyday lives. From the way we entertain ourselves to the goods and services that we produce and consume, we are enveloped in a popular cultural environment that we can neither do without nor escape, even if we wanted to. To see this, just try to imagine a world without the internet, TV, movies, sports, music, shopping malls, or advertising. The study of popular culture has accordingly taken a prominent place in American higher education — not least in American composition classrooms, which have taken the lead in incorporating popular culture into academic study, both because of the subject's inherent interest value and because of its profound familiarity to most students. Your own expertise in popular culture means not only that you may know more about a given topic than your instructor, but that you can use that knowledge as a basis for learning the critical thinking and writing skills that your writing class is intended to teach you.

Signs of Life in the U.S.A., then, is designed to let you exploit your knowledge of popular culture so that you may grow into a better writer, whatever the subject. You can interpret the popularity of a TV program like *RuPaul's Drag Race*, for example, in the same manner as you would interpret, say, a short story, because *RuPaul's Drag Race*, too, constitutes a kind of sign. A **sign** is something, anything, that carries a meaning. The familiar red sign at an intersection, for instance, means exactly what it says: "stop." But it also carries the implied message "or risk getting a ticket or into an accident." Words, too, are signs: you read them to figure out what they mean. You were trained to read such signs, but that training began so long ago that you may well take your ability to read for granted. Nevertheless, all your life you have been encountering and interpreting other sorts of signs. Although you were never formally taught to read them, you know what they mean anyway. For example, take the way that you wear your hair. When you get your hair cut, you are not simply removing hair; you are making a statement, sending a message about yourself. It's the same for both men and women. Why was your hair short last year and long this year? Aren't you saying something with the scissors? In this way, you make your hairstyle into a sign that sends a message about your identity. You are surrounded by such signs. Just look at your classmates.

The world of signs could be called a kind of text, the text of America's popular culture. We want you to think of *Signs of Life in the U.S.A.* as a window onto that text. What you read in this book's essays and chapter introductions should lead you to study and analyze the world around you for yourself. Let the selections guide you to your own interpretations, your own readings, of the text of America.

In this edition of *Signs of Life in the U.S.A.*, we have chosen eight "windows," divided into three sections, that look out onto separate, but often interrelated, segments of the American scene. We begin with two foundational chapters exploring the cultural contradictions and identity politics that are crucial to understanding the semiotic significance of what happens in America today. The book then explores such everyday life experiences as commodity consumption, advertising, and the internet, followed by a third section devoted to entertainment. In each chapter of all three sections, we have included essays that help you think about a specific topic in popular culture and guide you to locate and analyze related examples of your own. Each chapter also includes an introduction written to alert you to the kinds of signs you will find there, along with model analyses and advice on how to go about interpreting the topic that the chapter raises.

We have designed *Signs of Life in the U.S.A.* to reflect the many ways in which culture shapes our sense of reality and of ourselves, from the products we buy to the way culture, through such media as television and the movies, constructs our personal identities. This text thus introduces you to both the entertainment side and the ideological side of popular culture — and shows how the two are mutually dependent. Indeed, one of the major lessons you can learn from this book is how to find the ideological underpinnings of some of the most apparently innocent entertainments and consumer goods.

Throughout, the book invites you to go out and select your own "texts" for analysis (an advertisement, an app, a fashion trend, a TV show, and so on). Here's where your own experience is particularly valuable, because it has made you familiar with many different kinds of popular signs and their backgrounds, as well as with the particular popular cultural system or environment to which they belong.

The Semiotic Method

To interpret and write effectively about the signs of popular culture, you need a method, and part of the purpose of this book is to introduce such a method to you. Without a methodology for interpreting signs, writing about them could become little more than producing descriptive reviews or opinion pieces. Although nothing is wrong with writing descriptions and opinions, one of your goals in your writing class is to learn how to write academic essays — that is, analytical essays that present theses or arguments that are well supported by evidence. The method we use in this book — a method known as **semiotics** — is especially well suited for analyzing popular culture. Whether or not you're familiar with this word, you already practice sophisticated semiotic analyses every day. Reading this page is an act of semiotic decoding (words and letters are signs that must be interpreted), but so is figuring out just what a friend means by wearing a particular shirt or dress. For a semiotician (one who practices semiotic analysis), a shirt, a haircut, a TV series, anything at all, can be taken as a sign, as a message to be decoded and analyzed to discover its meaning. Every cultural activity leaves a trace of meaning for semioticians, a kind of blip on the semiotic Richter scale for them to read and interpret, just as geologists "read" the earth for signs of earthquakes, volcanic activity, and other geological phenomena.

Many who hear the word *semiotics* for the first time assume that it is the name of a new and forbidding subject. But in truth, the study of signs is neither new nor forbidding. Its modern form took shape in the late nineteenth and early twentieth centuries through the writings and lectures of two men. Charles Sanders Peirce (1839–1914) was an American philosopher who first coined the word *semiotics*, while Ferdinand de Saussure (1857–1913) was a Swiss linguist whose lectures became the foundation for what he called *semiology* (which was later developed under the name of *linguistic structuralism*). Without knowing of each other's work, Peirce and Saussure established the fundamental principles that modern semioticians or semiologists — the terms are essentially interchangeable — have developed into the contemporary study of semiotics.

Reduced to its simplest principles, the semiotic method carries on Saussure's argument that the meaning of a sign lies, in part, in the fact that it can be *differentiated* from any other sign within the **system**, or **code**, to which it belongs. For example, in the traffic code, being able to distinguish the **difference** between green, red, and amber lights is essential to understanding the meaning of a traffic signal. But that's not all there is to it, because it is only within the code that green, red, and amber signify "go," "stop," and "caution." So, to interpret a traffic signal correctly, you need to be able to **associate** any particular red light you see with all other red traffic lights under the concept "stop" that the code assigns to it, and any green light with all other green lights under the concept "go," and so on. Situating signs in **systems of association and difference** accordingly constitutes the essence of semiotic interpretation.

But outside the traffic code, the same colors can have very different meanings, always depending upon the system in which they appear. For example, in the codes of American politics, green signifies not only a political party but an entire worldview that supports environmentalist policies, while red, rather paradoxically, can signify either communist sympathies or the conservative politics of the so-called "red states," depending upon the context. Amber, for its part, has no significance within the American political code.

The fact that the color red has gained this significance in American politics demonstrates that systems, and the meanings encoded within them, can change — an important principle when you are interpreting signs of popular culture, because their meanings are constantly changing, unlike the more or less fixed signs of the traffic code. Here is where Peirce's contribution comes in, because while Saussure's structural semiology is static in its interpretational orientation, Peircean semiotics is dynamic, situating signs within *history* and thus enabling us to trace the ways in which meaning shifts and changes with time.

But neither Saussure nor Peirce applied their methodologies to signs of popular culture, so to complete our description of the semiotic method, we must turn to the work of French semiologist Roland Barthes (1915–1980), who, in his book *Mythologies* (1957), pioneered the semiotic analysis of everything from professional wrestling to striptease, toys, and plastics. It was Barthes, too, who established the political dimensions of semiotic analysis, revealing how phenomena that may look like mere entertainments can hold profound political or ideological significance. Since "politics" is something of a dirty word in our society, Barthes's politicization of pop culture may make you feel a little uneasy at first. You may even think that to find political meaning in popular culture is tantamount to reading something into it that isn't really there. But consider the controversy surrounding the Best Picture award given to *Green Book* at the 2019 Oscars. What once would have been regarded as an uncontroversial — in fact, "feel good" — movie about American race relations became a lightning rod for critics who felt that the film whitewashed not only the real-life events on which it was based but the racial realities of America as a whole.

In short, the political interpretation of popular culture, even when it is not conducted under the name of semiotics, is already a common practice. The semiotic method simply makes it explicit, pointing out that all social behavior is political because it always reflects some subjective or group interest. Such interests are encoded in the ideologies that express the values and opinions of those who hold them. Politics, then, is just another name for the clash of ideologies that takes place in any complex society where the interests of those who belong to it constantly compete with one another.

While not all signs of popular culture are politically controversial, careful analysis can uncover some set of political values within them, although those values may be subtly concealed behind an apparently apolitical facade. Indeed, the political values that guide our social behavior are often concealed behind images that don't look political at all. But that is because we have to look beyond what a sign of pop culture **denotes**, or directly shows, to what it **connotes**, or culturally suggests. The **denotation** of a sign is its first level of meaning, and you have to be able to understand that meaning before you can move to the next level. The **connotation** of a sign takes you to its political or cultural significance.

Take, for instance, the depiction of the "typical" American family in the classic TV sitcoms of the 1950s and 1960s, which denoted images of happy, docile housewives in suburban middle-class families. At the time, most viewers did not look beyond their denotation, so to them those images looked "normal" or natural — the way families and women were supposed to be. The shows didn't seem a bit ideological. But to a feminist semiotician, the old sitcoms were in fact highly political, because from a feminist viewpoint the happy housewives they presented were really images designed to convince women that their place was in the home, not in the workplace competing with men. Such images — or signs — did not reflect reality; they reflected, rather, the interests of a patriarchal, male-centered society. That, in effect, was their connotation. If you disagree, then ask yourself why programs were called *Father Knows Best*, *Bachelor Father*, and *My Three Sons*, but not *My Three Daughters*. And why did few of the women characters have jobs or ever seem to leave the house? Of course, there was *I Love Lucy*, but wasn't Lucy a screwball whose husband Ricky — whose point of view is emphasized in the title of the program even though Lucille Ball was the real star — had to rescue her from one crisis after another?

Such an interpretation reflects what the British cultural theorist Stuart Hall (1932–2014) called an *oppositional* reading, which challenges the "preferred reading" that would simply take the program at face value, accepting its representation of family life as normative and natural. The oppositional reading, on the other hand, proposes an interpretation that resists the normative view, seeking to uncover a political subtext that often contradicts any particular intended "message." The fact that so many cultural signifiers *appear* normative and natural, as transparent images of an apolitical social reality, can make oppositional reading look "unnatural" or like "reading into" your

Archive PL/Alamy

The popular TV show *Leave It to Beaver* (1957–1963) exemplified traditional family values of the 1950s.

topic a meaning that isn't there. After all, isn't a sitcom simply a trivial entertainment that distracts viewers from the concerns of everyday life? But given the commercial foundation of our popular culture, *the fact that something is entertaining is itself significant*, because only those scripts that are calculated to be popular with a mass audience make it to the screen. In other words, popular culture appeals to audience desire, and so the fact that something is entertaining raises a fundamental semiotic question: *Why* is it entertaining, and what does that say about those who are entertained by it?

By looking for such broad signifiers of cultural consciousness and desire, you will be moving back and forth between what might be called the *micro-semiotics* of your immediate topic (that is, its specific signs and symbols) to its *macro-semiotic* import, or overall cultural significance. The former cannot be separated from the latter, because to find the macro-semiotic meaning of a cultural sign you must first explore its micro-semiotic details closely. Think of it as exploring a forest while paying careful attention to the trees.

Abduction and Overdetermination

At this point you may be thinking that a semiotic analysis resembles sociological interpretation, and indeed cultural semiotics and sociology do resemble each other. The differences are largely methodological. Sociology tends to be highly statistical in its methodology, often working with case studies, surveys, and other quantifiable evidence. Cultural semiotics primarily works by looking at broad patterns of behavior and seeking what Charles Sanders Peirce called *abductive* explanations for them. **Abduction** is the process of seeking the most likely, or probable, interpretation of a cultural signifier, and it works in very much the same way that artificial intelligence works. That is, just as AI aggregates large amounts of data in order to construct predictive algorithms that can forecast broad patterns of human behavior, so too does semiotics aggregate signs in systems of related phenomena whose associative and differential relationships can be used to determine their most likely significance. Thus, while any individual cultural phenomenon — just like any individual act — may be random and insignificant, its potential meaning becomes apparent when it is set in relation to other cultural phenomena. That is why the more relevant material you can bring into your systems of related and differentiated signs, the more convincing your interpretation will be.

As you build up your interpretation of a cultural signifier, you can often find more than one explanation for it. Is that a problem? Are you just having trouble deciding on a single argument? No, because cultural signs are usually **overdetermined**; that is, they can have more than one cause or explanation (another word for this is *polysemous*). This is especially true for what we consider "rich" cultural signs — like such movies as *Avengers: Infinity War* and *Avengers: Endgame*, not to mention the current state of American cultural and electoral politics.

Interpreting Popular Signs: The Revolution Will Be Reiterated

So let's return to the recent past for another look at two of the most profitable movies of all time, starting with their semiotic denotation. *Avengers: Infinity War* and *Avengers: Endgame* are two films based on a number of issues of Marvel Comics involving an assortment of superheroes collectively referred to as the Avengers, who protect the world from various cosmic villains. Part of a series of movies (The Marvel Comics Universe) produced by the Marvel Studios (now a subsidiary of Walt Disney Studios Motion Pictures), they combine to form a vast epic story line with individual films referring to other films within the series. In the case of *Avengers: Infinity War* and *Avengers: Endgame*, the latter relates to the former as a direct sequel (effectively a kind of Part II to the prior film's Part I), ostensibly constituting a conclusion to the entire saga, especially as represented by the death and funeral of Iron Man, the Avenger whose breakout film, *Iron Man*, started the whole thing off in 2008. The fact, however, that audiences knew that more Avengers movies were in the works even as they watched *Avengers: Endgame* — along with the equally important knowledge that death is never necessarily final in an Avengers film — will be an important part of the analysis to follow.

Still at the level of denotation we have the two movies' plot lines. Any complete summary here would take up far too much space, so we'll simply note that the one film presents the successful attempt by an extraterrestrial war lord named Thanos to reduce the population of the entire universe to what he views as a sustainable level. A large cast of Avengers seeks to prevent this undertaking, and fails, with many of them perishing in the act. In the sequel, the surviving Avengers, making use of various fantasy devices — including the ability to time travel and to raise the dead — reverse the semi-extinction event presented in *Avengers: Infinity War*, resurrect the dead Avengers (most notably Black Panther and his Wakandan army), and kill Thanos, though Iron Man perishes in the process.

Those are the denotative basics. To move to their connotative or cultural significance, we need to situate these films in the larger context in which they appeared, seeking semiotically revealing associations and differences. An entire book-length study could be devoted to such an analysis, but for the sake of this introduction we can note that by 2018, fantasy storytelling, whether in comic book, cinematic, novelistic, or televised form, had become America's most popular (and profitable) form of fictional narrative, with wizards, superheroes, medieval-style warriors, space explorers, dragons, zombies, and vampires dominating the stage. But not only had fantasy become pop culture's reigning genre, it had also fully transitioned from being a somewhat marginalized "low cultural" art form, suitable mostly for children and adolescents, to a status very much on par with the "high art" tradition of mediating cultural concerns and conflicts. In other words, fantasies like the Avengers films had become part of the way that Americans had come to understand themselves and their world. This difference is of critical importance to understanding what these movies signify and why they matter.

Consider, for example, the cultural reception of *Black Panther*, also in 2018. Although the title character had been around since 1966, he had not yet starred in his own superhero movie. But by 2018 superhero films enjoyed an enormous cultural prestige that the comic books on which they were based did not when they first appeared. Thus, the production of *Black Panther* was widely hailed as a watershed event in the history of the civil rights movement, with African American celebrities supplying thousands of black children with tickets to the show. Just as significantly, the film itself could be seen as a metaphorical exploration of African/American identity and political strategy, with its focus on the conflict between its African and its American protagonists, pitting the essentially revolutionary program of Stevens/Killmonger/N'Jadaka against the more diplomatic stance of T'Challa/Black Panther. In short, *Black Panther* was no mere movie, and neither were *Avengers: Infinity War* and *Avengers: Endgame*. But what, then, did they signify?

To see what these films politically connote, we can broaden our survey of the system in which they appeared. First, we can associate them with

Avengers: Civil War (2016), which presented a serious rift between the two main factions of the Avengers consortium as led by Iron Man and Captain America, who essentially disagree over the role of governmental regulation in their lives. This conflict between an urbane businessman and a flag-waving super soldier reflected in an almost explicit way the increasingly hostile face-off in America between progressives and conservatives, a schism that had begun to appear by 2016 as a veritable — as the movie's title puts it — civil war.

And this association, in turn, takes us to the overall political context in which *Avengers: Infinity War* and *Avengers: Endgame* appeared. For by 2018, in the aftermath of the election of Donald Trump, the conflict between American conservatives and progressives had become virtually intractable, with an ever-shrinking prospect of any possible cultural common ground and an ever-widening gap between diametrically opposed ideologies. To each side, one might say, the other had become Thanos incarnate.

Such conflicts, whereby any hope for consensus or compromise has been dashed, are the stuff of which revolutions are born, and for the first two decades of the twenty-first century the American electoral process has accordingly taken on a revolutionary fervor. Americans don't simply elect a president anymore, they seek regime change, from the Republican overthrow of Clintonism in 2000 to the Obama landslide in 2008 (which many at the time viewed as a permanent shift leftwards in American politics) to the Revolutionary War–inspired Tea Party insurrection that enabled the Republican Party to capture both houses of Congress and, in 2016, the White House itself. And as we write these words a Democratic counter-counter-revolution, which began in 2018 with a recapturing of the House of Representatives, hopes to win back the Senate and the presidency in 2020.

Now, are we arguing that *Avengers: Infinity War* and *Avengers: Endgame* were created as some sort of explicit allegory of this back-and-forth, winner-take-all revolutionary conflict? No, for given their descent from pre-existing Marvel Comics story lines, these films' creative inspiration lies, at least partly, outside the control of their writers and directors. So such an interpretation does not have much abductive force behind it. Rather, our semiotic analysis is intended to reveal how they reflect the current state of American culture and consciousness — how they function against the backdrop of contemporary American society and express through the mass media the general spirit of the times. Thus, without needing any specific political background in mind, audiences can particularly relate to, and thus enjoy, the way that *Avengers: Infinity War* and *Avengers: Endgame* dramatize defeat and resurrection in a seemingly unending cycle. The temporarily dead return from the grave; the victory of one side is reversed by the victory of the other, with neither concession nor compromise between two fundamentally opposed adversaries possible. It simply all looks like America today, which is why we say that no matter who is elected president in 2020, there will be no endgame. Instead, an infinity war of another kind — based not in magic but irreconcilable ideological conflict — will simply churn through yet another cycle.

The Classroom Connection

This analysis could be extended further, but we will leave that for you to consider for yourself. The key point is that while the popularity of any particular pop culture phenomenon is evanescent, what it *signifies* is not. Everything in an ever-shifting popular cultural terrain remains significant, just as all the historical events in an ever-changing world remain significant. In fact, performing an analysis of pop culture is essentially equivalent to writing interpretive history, but it is an interpretive history of the present.

Thus, semiotic analyses of popular culture are not different from the more conventional interpretive analyses you will be asked to perform in your college writing career. It is in the nature of all critical thinking to make connections and mark differences in order to go beyond the surface of a text or issue toward a meaning. The skills you already have as an interpreter of the popular signs around you — of images, objects, and forms of behavior — are the same skills that you develop as a writer of critical essays that present an argued point of view and the evidence to defend it.

Because most of us tend to identify closely with our favorite pop culture phenomena and have strong opinions about them, however, it can be difficult to adopt the same sort of analytic perspective toward popular culture that we do toward, say, texts assigned in a history or literature class. Still, this analytic perspective is what a semiotic interpretation requires: you need to set aside your aesthetic or fan-related opinions to pursue an interpretive argument with evidence to support it. It is not difficult to express an aesthetic opinion or a statement of personal preference, but that isn't the goal of analytic writing and critical thinking. Analytic writing requires that you marshal supporting evidence, just as a lawyer assembles evidence to argue a case. So, by learning to write analyses of our culture, by searching for supporting evidence to underpin your interpretive take on modern life, you are also learning to write critical arguments.

"But how," you (and perhaps your instructor) may ask, "can I know that a semiotic interpretation is correct?" Good question — it is commonly asked by those who object that a semiotic analysis might read too much into a subject. But then, it can also be asked by the writer of any interpretive essay, and the answer in each case is the same. No one can absolutely *prove* the truth of an argument in the human sciences; what you can do is *persuade* your audience by including pertinent evidence in an abductive reasoning process. In analyzing popular culture, that evidence comes from your knowledge of the system to which the object you are interpreting belongs. The more you know about the system, the more convincing your interpretations will be. And that is true whether you are writing about popular culture or about more traditional academic subjects.

Cultural Mythologies

As we have seen, in a semiotic analysis we do not search for the meanings of things in the things themselves. Rather, we find meaning in the way we can relate things together through association and differentiation, moving from objective denotation to culturally subjective connotation. Such a movement commonly takes us from the realm of objective facts to the world of cultural values. But while values often *feel* like objective facts, from a semiotic perspective they are subjective points of view that derive from cultural systems that semioticians call *cultural mythologies*.

A cultural **mythology** is not some fanciful story from the past; indeed, if the word *mythology* seems confusing because of its traditional association with such stories, you may prefer to use the term *value system* or *ideology*. Consider the value system that governs our traditional thinking about gender roles. Have you ever noticed how our society presumes that it is primarily the role of women — adult daughters — to take care of aging and infirm parents? If you want to look at the matter from a physiological perspective, it might seem that men would be better suited to the task: in a state of nature, men are physically stronger and so would seem to be the natural protectors of the aged. And yet, though our cultural mythology holds that men should protect the nuclear family, it tends to assign to women the care of extended families. It is culture that decides here, not nature.

But while cultural mythologies guide our behavior, they are subject to change. The cultural myths surrounding sexual relationships in America, for example, have changed dramatically in your lifetime. Not only do these myths no longer presume an orientation toward heterosexual marriage, but even the rules that once governed the American dating game are changing. Once, it was the role of the male to initiate proceedings (he calls) and for the female to react (she waits for the call). Similarly, the rules once held that it was the male's responsibility to plan the evening and pay the tab. Today, in the age of hookups and digital socializing, these rules may sound not simply antiquated but quaint.

A cultural mythology or value system, then, is a kind of lens that governs the way we view our world. Think of it this way: say you were born with rose-tinted eyeglasses permanently attached over your eyes, but you didn't know they were there. Because the world would *look* rose colored to you, you would presume that it *is* rose colored. You wouldn't wonder whether the world might look otherwise through different lenses. But in the world, there are other kinds of eyeglasses with different lenses, and reality does look different to those who wear them. Those lenses are cultural mythologies, and no culture can claim to have the one set of glasses that reveals things as they really are.

The principle that meaning is not culture-blind, that it is conditioned by systems of ideology and belief that are codified differently by different cultures, is a foundational semiotic judgment. Human beings, in other words, construct their own social realities, so who gets to do the constructing becomes very important. Every contest over a cultural code is, accordingly, a contest for power, but the contest is usually masked because the winner generally defines its mythology as the truth, as what is most natural or reasonable. The stakes are high as myth battles myth, with truth itself as the highest prize.

This does not mean that you must abandon your own beliefs when conducting a semiotic analysis, only that you cannot take them for granted and must be prepared to argue for them with valid evidence. The need for such evidence suggests that while humans construct their own social realities, there is an extra-social reality that places limits on what human beings can construct (to take an uncontroversial example, a culture that insists that humans can fly unaided off cliffs is not going to exist for very long). This belief in an extra-social reality underlies the semiotic position of this book.

Thus, if you hold a contrary opinion on a topic, it is not enough to presuppose the innate superiority of your own perspective — to claim that anyone who disagrees with you is being "political" while you are simply telling the truth. This may sound heretical precisely because humans operate within cultural mythologies whose invisibility is guaranteed by the system. No mythology, that is to say, announces, "This is just a political construct or interpretation." Every mythology begins, "This is the truth." It is very difficult to imagine, from within the mythology, any alternatives. Indeed, as you read this book, you may find it upsetting to see that some traditional beliefs — such as the "proper" roles of men and women — are socially constructed and not absolute. But the outlines of the mythology, the bounding (and binding) frame, can be discerned only by first seeing that it *is* a mythology, a constructed scaffolding upon which our consciousness and desires are constituted.

Getting Started

Mythology, like culture, is not static, and so the semiotician must always keep an eye on the clock, so to speak. History and the passing of time are constants in a constantly changing world. Since the earlier editions of this book, American popular culture has moved on. In this edition, we have tried to reflect those changes, but, inevitably, further changes will occur in the time it takes for this book to appear on your class syllabus. That such changes occur is part of the excitement of the semiotic enterprise: there is always something new to consider and interpret. What does *not* change is the nature of semiotic interpretation — whatever you choose to analyze in the realm of American popular culture, the semiotic approach will help you understand it.

It's your turn now. Start asking questions, pushing, probing. That's what critical thinking and writing are all about, but this time you're part of the question. Arriving at answers is the fun part here, but answers aren't the basis of analytic thinking: questions are. Always begin with a question, a query, a hypothesis — something to explore. If you already knew the answer, you'd have no reason to conduct the analysis. We encourage you to explore the almost-infinite variety of questions that the readings in this book raise. Many come equipped with their own "answers," but you may (indeed you will and should) find that such answers raise further questions. To help you ask those questions, keep in mind the elemental principles of semiotics that we have just explored:

1. Cultural semiotics treats human behavior itself — not what people say about their behavior, but what they actually do — as **signs**.
2. The meaning of signs can be found not in themselves but in their relationships (both **differences** and **associations**) with other signs within a **system**. To interpret an individual sign, then, you must determine the general system to which it belongs.
3. Things have both **denotative** meanings (what they *are*) and **connotative** meanings (what they *suggest as signs*); semiotics moves beyond the denotative surface to the connotative significance.
4. Arriving at the connotative significance of a sign involves both **abduction** (a search for the most likely explanation or interpretation) and **overdetermination** (the multiple causes behind a cultural phenomenon).
5. What we call social "reality" is a human construct, the product of cultural **mythologies** or value systems that intervene between our minds and the world we experience. Such cultural myths reflect the values and ideological interests of their builders, not the laws of nature or logic.

Perhaps our first principle could be more succinctly phrased "Behavior is meaningful," and our second "Everything is connected," while our third advises "Don't take things at face value." More simply, always ask yourself, whenever you are interpreting something, "What's going on here?" In short, question *everything*. And one more reminder: signs are like weather vanes; they point in response to invisible historical winds. We invite you now to start looking at the weather.

WRITING ABOUT POPULAR CULTURE

Throughout this book, you will find readings on popular culture that you can use as models for your own writing or as subjects to which you may respond, assignments for writing critical essays on popular culture, and advice to help you analyze a wide variety of cultural phenomena. As you approach these readings and assignments, you may find it helpful to review the following suggestions for writing critical essays — whether on popular culture or on any subject — as well as some examples of student essays written in response to assignments based on *Signs of Life in the U.S.A.* Mastering the skills summarized and exemplified here should enable you to write the kinds of papers you will be assigned throughout your college career.

As you prepare to write a critical essay on popular culture, remember that you are already an expert in your subject. After all, simply by actively participating in everyday life, you have accumulated a vast store of knowledge about what makes our culture tick. Just think of all you know about movies, or the thousands upon thousands of ads you've seen, or the many messages you send whenever you post to Facebook or Instagram. Your very expertise in popular culture, ironically, may create a challenge simply because you might take your knowledge for granted. You might not think that your knowledge of popular culture can "count" as material for a college-level assignment, and it might not even occur to you to use it in an essay. But that knowledge is a great place for you to start. Of course, to write a strong essay, you need to do more than just "go with the flow" of your subject as you live it. You need to consider it from a critical distance.

Using Active Reading Strategies

Your first step in developing a powerful essay about any topic happens well before you sit down to write: you should make sure you accurately understand the reading selections your instructor has assigned. In other words, you should engage in *active* reading—that is, you want to get more than just the "drift" of a passage. Skimming a selection may give you a rough idea of the author's point, but your understanding of it is also likely to be partial, superficial, or even downright wrong. And that's not a solid start to writing a good paper!

Active reading techniques can help you detect the nuances of how an author constructs his or her argument accurately and precisely. You should question, summarize, agree with, and/or refute the author's claims. In other words, imagine having a kind of *conversation* with the author. Studies have shown that such interactive learning simply works better than passive learning; if you read actively, you'll gain knowledge at a higher rate and retain it longer. With any reading selection, it can be helpful to read at least twice: first, to gain a general sense of the author's ideas and, second, to study more specifically how those ideas work together to form an argument. To read actively, you can use formal discovery techniques, or what are called *heuristics*.

Active Reading Questions

- What is the author's *primary argument*? Can you identify a *thesis* statement, or is the thesis implied?
- What *key terms* are fundamental to that argument? If you are not familiar with the selection's basic vocabulary, be sure to check a dictionary for the words' meanings.
- What *evidence* does the author provide to support the argument? Is it relevant and specific? Does the author cite reliable, authoritative sources?
- What *underlying assumptions* shape the author's position? Does the author consider alternative points of view (counterarguments)?
- What *style* and *tone* does the author adopt?
- What is the *genre* of the piece? You need to identify what kind of writing you are responding to, because different genres have different purposes and goals. A personal narrative, for instance, expresses the writer's experiences and beliefs, but you shouldn't expect it to present a complete argument supported by documentation.
- Who is the *intended readership* of this selection, and does it affect the author's reasoning or evidence?

One of the most famous heuristics is the journalist's "five Ws and an H": who, what, where, when, why, and how. By asking these six questions, a reporter can quickly unearth the essential details of a breaking story and draft a clear account of it. For your purposes, you can apply the questions in Active Reading Questions to reading selections you will discuss in your own essays.

As you read, write *annotations*, or notes, in your book. Doing so will help you both remember and analyze what you read. A pencil is probably the best memory aid ever invented. No one, not even the most perceptive reader, remembers everything — and let's face it, not everything that you read is worth remembering. Writing annotations as you read will lead you back to important points. And annotating helps you start analyzing a reading — long before you start writing an essay — rather than uncritically accepting what's on the page. If you are using an electronic version of this text, you can do the same with the highlighting and annotation tools available in most e-readers.

There's yet another reason to annotate what you read: you can use the material you've identified as the starting point for your journal notes and essays, and since it doesn't take long to circle a word or jot a note in the margin, you can save time in the long run. We suggest that you *not* use a highlighter. While using a highlighter is better than using nothing — it can help you mark key points — writing *words* in your book goes much further in starting your analysis of what you read. We've seen entire pages bathed in fluorescent-yellow highlighter, and that's of doubtful use in identifying the important stuff. Of course, if you simply can't bring yourself to mark up your book, write on sticky notes instead and put those in the margins.

So as you read, circle key words, note transitions between ideas, jot definitions of unfamiliar terms (you can probably guess their meaning from the context or look them up later), underline phrases or terms to research on a search engine such as Google, write short summaries of important points, or simply note where you're confused or lost with a question mark or a *huh?!* In fact, figuring out exactly what parts you do and don't understand is one of the best ways to tackle a difficult reading. Frequently, the confusing bits turn out to be the most interesting — and sometimes the most important. Responding to what you read *as* you read will help you become a more active reader — and will ultimately help you become a stronger writer.

Prewriting Strategies

Before you start drafting your essay, you'll find it useful to spend some time generating your ideas freely and openly: your goal at this point is to develop as many ideas as possible, even ones that you might not actually use in your essay. Writing instructors call this process *prewriting*, and it's a step you should take when writing on any subject in any class, not just in your writing class. This textbook includes many suggestions for how you can develop your ideas; even if your instructor doesn't require you to use all of them, try them on your own.

These prewriting strategies will work when you are asked to respond to a particular reading or image. Sometimes, though, you may be asked to write about a more general subject. Your instructor may ask you to brainstorm ideas or to freewrite in response to an issue. You can use both strategies — brainstorming and freewriting — in your journal or on your own as you start working on an essay. *Brainstorming* is simply amassing as many relevant (and even some irrelevant) ideas as possible. Let's say your instructor asks you to brainstorm a list of popular toys used by girls and boys in preparation for an assignment about the gendered designs of children's toys. Try to list your thoughts freely, jotting down whatever comes to mind. Don't censor yourself at this point. That is, don't worry if something is really a game rather than a toy, or if both boys and girls play with it, or if it is really an adult toy. Later on you can throw out any ideas that don't fit. What you'll be left with is a rich list of examples that you can then study and analyze. *Freewriting* works much the same way and is particularly useful when you're not sure how you feel about a topic. To freewrite, just start writing or typing, and don't stop until you've written for at least ten minutes. Let your ideas wander around your subject, working associatively, following their own path. As with brainstorming, you may produce some irrelevant ideas, but you may also arrive at a sharper picture of your beliefs.

Signs of Life in the U.S.A. frequently asks you to respond to a reading selection in a *journal* or *reading log*, sometimes directly and sometimes indirectly, as in suggestions that you write a letter to the author of a selection. In doing so, you're taking a first step in articulating your response to the issues and to the author's presentation of them. In asking you to keep a journal or a reading log, your instructor will probably be less concerned with your writing style than with your comprehension of assigned readings and your thoughtful responses to them. Let's say you're asked to write your response to Jessica Hagedorn's "Asian Women in Film: No Joy, No Luck" in Chapter 7. First think through exactly what Hagedorn is saying — what her point is — by asking the questions listed on pages 505 and 506 and by reviewing your annotations. Then consider how you feel about her essay. If you agree with Hagedorn's contention that films perpetuate outmoded stereotypes of Asian women, why do you feel that way? Can you think of films Hagedorn does not mention that reflect the gendered patterns she observes? Or do you know of films that represent Asian female characters positively? Suppose you're irritated by Hagedorn's argument: again, why do you feel that way? Your aim in jotting all this down is not to produce a draft of an essay. It's to play with your own ideas, see where they lead, and even help you decide what your ideas are in the first place.

If your instructor asks you to create your own topic, that freedom might actually make it harder to figure out where to start. Suppose you need to analyze an aspect of the film industry but can't decide on a focus. Here, the internet might help. You could explore a resource such as filmsite.org, a site divided into categories such as History, Genres, and Reviews. These categories can lead you to more specific links, such as "Film History by Decade" and

"300 Greatest Film Reviews — By Decade." With so many topics to choose from, you're bound to find something that interests you. In effect, you can go online to engage in *electronic brainstorming* about your topic.

One cautionary note: When going online to brainstorm, be sure to *evaluate the appropriateness of your sources* (see p. 53). Many sites are commercial and thus are intended more to sell a product or image than to provide reliable information. In addition, since anyone with the technological know-how can set up a website, some sites amount to little more than personal expression and need to be evaluated for their reliability, accuracy, and authenticity. Scrutinize the sites you visit carefully: Is the author an authority in the field? Does the site identify the author, at least by name and email address? (Be wary of fully anonymous sites.) Is the material posted scholarly or peer-reviewed? Does the site contain interesting and relevant links? If you find an advocacy site, one that openly advances a special interest, does the site's bias interfere with the accuracy of its information? Asking such questions can help ensure that your electronic brainstorming is fruitful and productive. If you are unsure of the validity of a site, you should check with your instructor.

You can also strengthen your argument if you consider the *history* of your subject. You might think this requires a lot of library research, but that may not be necessary if you are already familiar with the social and cultural history of your topic. If you know, for instance, that the baggy pants so popular among teens until recently were once ubiquitous among street-gang members, you know an important historical detail that goes a long way toward explaining their significance. Depending on your assignment, you could expand on your own historical knowledge and collect additional data about your topic, perhaps through surveys and interviews. If you're analyzing the ways people use social media to maintain personal relationships, for instance, you could interview people from different age groups and genders to get a sense of the range of people's habits. Because the material you gather through such interviews will be raw data, you'll want to do more than just "dump" the information into your essay. Instead, see this material as an original body of evidence that you'll sort through (you probably won't use every scrap of information), study, and interpret in its own right.

Not all prewriting activities need be solitary, of course. In fact, *Signs of Life* often suggests that you work with other students, either in your class or across campus. We suggest such *group activity* because much academic work is collaborative and collegial. A scientist conducting research, for instance, often works with a team; in addition, he or she may present preliminary findings at colloquia or conferences and may call or email a colleague at another school to try out some ideas. There's no reason you can't benefit from the social nature of academic thinking as well. But be aware that in-class group work is by no means "busywork." The goal, rather, is to help you develop and shape your understanding of the issues and your attitudes toward them. If you're asked to study with three classmates how a product is packaged, for instance, you're starting to test Chris Arning's thesis in "What Can Semiotics Contribute to Packaging Design?" (Chapter 3), seeing how it applies or doesn't apply and benefiting from your peers' insights. By discussing packaging design with others, you are articulating, perhaps for the first time, what it might mean, and so are taking the first step toward writing a more formal analysis (especially if you receive feedback and comments from your class). Similarly, if you stage an in-class debate on cultural appropriation, you're amassing a storehouse of arguments, counterarguments, and evidence to consider when you write your own essay in response to Zahir Janmohamed's "Your Cultural Attire" (Chapter 2). As with other prewriting strategies, you may not use every idea generated in conversation with your classmates, but that's OK. You should find yourself better able to sort through and articulate the ideas that you *do* find valuable.

Developing Strong Arguments about Popular Culture

We expect that students will write many different sorts of papers in response to the selections in this book, including personal experience narratives, semiotic analyses, opinion pieces, research papers, and many others. We'd like to focus here on writing analytic essays because analyzing popular culture may seem different from analyzing other subjects. Occasionally we've had students who feel reluctant to analyze popular culture because they think that they need to "trash" their subject, and they don't want to write a "negative" essay about what may be their favorite film or TV program. Or a few students may feel uncertain because "it's all subjective." Since most people have opinions about popular culture, they say, how can any one essay be stronger than another?

While understandable, these concerns needn't be an obstacle to writing a strong analytic essay, whether on popular culture or any other topic. To avoid overt subjectivity, you should first set aside your own personal tastes when writing an analysis, not because your preferences are unimportant, but because you need to be aware of your own attitudes toward your topic. An essay critiquing, say, *Black Panther* is not the same as one that explains "why I like (or dislike) this film." Instead, it would explain how the movie works, what cultural beliefs and viewpoints underlie it, what its significance is, and so forth. And it would not necessarily be positive or negative; it would seek to explain *how* the elements of the film work together to have a particular effect on its audience. If your instructor asks you to write a critical analysis or argument, he or she is requesting neither a hit job nor a celebration of your topic.

For most of your college essays, you will probably be asked to make sure that you present a clear *thesis*. A thesis statement lays out the argument you intend to make and provides a scope for your essay. If you think of your thesis as a road map that your paper will follow, you might find that it is easier to structure your paper. A thesis for an essay on popular culture should follow the usual guidelines for any academic essay: it should make a debatable, interesting assertion (as opposed to a statement of fact or a truism); it should be demonstrable through the presentation of specific evidence; it should have a clear focus and scope; and it should spark your readers' interest. Additionally, a strong thesis statement will help you overcome any anxieties you might have about writing a strong analysis, because an effective thesis, rather than merely offering an opinion about a topic, also explains how you came to hold that opinion. The thesis statements in the sample student essays that begin on page 31 are annotated to show you how they function in academic writing.

Because a strong thesis should be supported by specific demonstration and detail, subjectivity becomes even less of a problem. You're not simply presenting a personal opinion about your subject; rather, you're presenting a central insight about its significance that is demonstrated with logical, specific evidence. It's that evidence that will take your essay out of the category of being "merely subjective." You can start with your own opinion, but you will want to add to it lots of support that shows the legitimacy of that opinion. Does that sound familiar? It should, because that's what you need to do in any analytic essay, no matter what your subject matter happens to be.

When writing about popular culture, students sometimes wonder what sort of evidence they should use to support their points. Your instructor will probably give you guidelines for each assignment, but we'll provide some suggestions here. Start with your subject itself. You'll find it's useful to view your subject — whether it's an ad, a film, or anything else — as a text that you can "read" closely. That's what you would do if you were asked to analyze a poem: you would read it carefully, studying individual words, images, rhythm, and so forth, and those details would support whatever claims you want to make about the poem. Read your pop culture subject with the same care. If your instructor asks you to analyze a TV series, you should look at the details: What actors appear in the series, and what are their roles? What "story" does the program tell about its characters and the world in which they live? Is there anything missing from this world that you would expect to find? What are the *connotative* meanings behind the surface signs? Your answers to such questions could form the basis for the evidence that your essay needs.

Conducting a Semiotic Analysis

In an essay focused on a semiotic analysis, you can probe a wider range of questions about your subject, yielding even more specific evidence and arguments. You can start with some basic questions that we ask throughout the chapter Introductions in this book and that we summarize in the following list. As an example, let's apply these questions to the TV series *House*, still popular and significant even though it is now in reruns.

DENOTATIVE MEANINGS

What is a simple, literal description of your subject? Make sure you understand this basic definition before looking for "deeper meanings," because if you misunderstand the factual status of your subject, your analysis will probably get derailed. In the case of *House*, we find a story of a medical genius who, though he is his hospital's most successful diagnostician, is also rude, nasty, and practically dysfunctional in his personal life, suffering from an addiction to Vicodin and almost constant depression. The plots of *House* tend to exemplify the series' slogan, "Everybody lies," and often depict House's patients or their families as liars with dark secrets that they are concealing and that House eventually uncovers. Clearly, if we were to misidentify *House* as a documentary, we'd misconstrue it as a scathing political exposé of the U.S. medical system—but that doesn't feel right. *House* is no exposé.

CONNOTATIVE MEANINGS AND A SYSTEM OF RELATED SIGNS

After determining your subject's denotation, you should locate your subject within a larger *system* in order to determine its connotative meaning. Recall that a system is the network of related signs to which your topic belongs and that identifying the system helps to reveal its significance. This may sound hard to do, but it is through identifying a system that you can draw on your own vast knowledge of popular culture. So, in our analysis of *House*, we need to move from our denotative understanding of the series to its connotative significance. To make this move, we need to identify a system of related signs, in this case, programs to which *House* is similar. In other words, to what genre of television programming does *House* belong? What conventions, goals, and motifs do shows in this genre share? What is the history of the genre? *House*, of course, belongs to the medical drama genre, which is distinct from, say, a sitcom, even though *House* does have certain comic elements that would allow us to classify it as a medical *dramedy*. The history of TV medical drama includes such programs as *Dr. Kildare* and *Ben Casey* in the 1960s; *Marcus Welby, M.D.*, and *Quincy, M.E.*, in the 1970s; *St. Elsewhere* and *ER* in the 1980s and beyond; and *Grey's Anatomy* and *Nip/Tuck* more recently. All these programs can be associated with *House* and testify to the enduring popularity of the genre.

Questions for Conducting a Semiotic Analysis

- What is the **denotative** meaning of your subject? In other words, determine a factual definition of exactly what it is.
- What is your topic's **connotative** significance? To determine that, situate your subject in a system of related signs.
- What **associated** signs belong to that system?
- What **differences** do you see in those signs?
- What **abductive** explanation do you have for your observations? What is the most likely explanation for the patterns that you see?

DIFFERENCES WITHIN THE SYSTEM

But while these TV series share a popular interest in doctors and medical stories, there is still a striking difference to consider, a kind of dividing line marked by the series *St. Elsewhere*. Until *St. Elsewhere*, the main character of a medical drama was almost always a benevolent healer whose own personal life beyond the hospital was generally not a part of the story line (there were exceptions: Dr. Kildare once fell in love with a patient; Ben Casey had a somewhat edgy nature; and Jack Klugman's Quincy — a forensic pathologist whose mystery-solving abilities anticipate those of Gregory House — had plenty of attitude). But all in all, the earlier physician protagonists maintained a general profile of almost superhuman benevolence; they were "official heroes," in Robert B. Ray's terms (see "The Thematic Paradigm," p. 451), caring for the innocent victims of disease.

St. Elsewhere changed that, and from that program onward (especially as developed by *ER*), the flaws in the lives and personalities of the main characters became much more prominent. The doctors were, in short, humanized — a shift in characterization that has led to the caustic, sometimes dysfunctional and law-breaking Dr. House.

ABDUCTIVE EXPLANATIONS

At this point, we are ready to start interpreting, seeking abductive explanations for the shift. We can get help by considering the broader context of other television genres, for we can find in sitcoms, crime series, Westerns, and many other genres a shift similar to the one in the history of medical dramas. The difference between the family sitcoms of the 1950s and 1960s and those of the 1980s and beyond is well known, taking us from the happy families of the Cleavers and the Nelsons to the dysfunctional Bundys and Griffins. Similarly, it's a long way from Dick Tracy and *Dragnet*'s Joe Friday to the callous cops of *The Wire*. And it is quite a stretch from *Gunsmoke* to *Justified*. Many other such differences could be mentioned, but we'll move on to our abductive interpretation.

The post–*St. Elsewhere* medical drama reflects a broader trend in American entertainment away from squeaky-clean TV protagonists to more "realistically" flawed ones, heroes who definitely have feet of clay. This trend reflects a cultural shift, the origins of which can be found in the cultural revolution of the 1960s, when American mass culture began a long process of disillusionment. After the Vietnam War and Watergate, increasingly cynical Americans were no longer inclined to believe in human perfection, preferring a more "realistic" depiction of human beings with all their flaws visible.

Thus, we can now see *House* as part of a larger cultural trend in which the once-cherished, even revered, figure of the physician has been pulled off the pedestal and brought to earth along with everyone else. Heroes are still heroes (after all, Gregory House is just plain smarter than anyone else around him), but they are more like ordinary folks. They misbehave, get cranky, break rules. Even the victims of misfortune (patients in a medical drama) have been degraded, appearing no longer as the objects of our sympathy but as flawed people with dark secrets. *Everybody lies*. No one is innocent. To the disillusioned, *House*, with its all-too-human hero and cast, is an entertaining, if cynical, vision of the way things are — or at least of the way that large numbers of viewers think they are. Doctors (and cops, families, cowboys, and everyone else) have warts too, and, as a sort of anti–Marcus Welby, Gregory House entertains his audience by not being afraid to show his flaws to the world.

Reading Visual Images Actively

Signs of Life in the U.S.A. includes many visual images, some accompanied by questions for analysis. In analyzing images, you can develop the ability to identify specific telling details and evidence — a talent useful no matter what your subject matter may be. Because the semiotic method lends itself especially well to visual analysis, it is an excellent means for honing this ability. Here are some questions to consider as you look at images.

To see how we can apply these questions, let's look at a sample analysis of an advertisement for Lee jeans (see image on p. 30).

Appearance: Although this image is reproduced here in black and white, it originally appeared in color. The colors are muted, however, almost sepia-toned, and thus suggest an old-fashioned look.

Kind of image: This is a fairly realistic image, with a patina of rural nostalgia. A solitary woman, probably in her twenties or thirties, but perhaps older, is set against an empty natural expanse. She has a traditional hairstyle evocative of the 1950s or early 1960s and wheels an old-fashioned bicycle with a wicker basket attached.

Audience: The intended audience for this jeans ad is most likely a woman in her late twenties or older. We see only the model's back, so she is faceless. That allows the viewer to project herself into the scene, and the nostalgic look suggests that the viewer could imagine herself at a younger time in her life. Note that the product is "stretch" jeans. There's no suggestion here, although it is often made in ads for other brands, that the jeans will enhance a woman's sexual appeal; rather, the claim is that the jeans are practical — and will fit a body beyond the teen years. Note the sensible hairstyle and shoes. For an interesting contrast, you might compare this ad to one for Diesel jeans.

Emotion: The woman's body language suggests individuality and determination; she's literally "going it alone." She's neither posing for nor aware of the viewer, suggesting that "what you see is what you get." And, perhaps, she doesn't particularly care what you think.

Questions for Analyzing Images

- What is the **appearance of the image**? Is it black and white? Color? Is it in focus or is it blurry? Consider how the form in which the image is expressed affects its message. If an image is composed of primary colors, does it look fun and lively, for instance?
- What **kind of image** is it? Is it abstract, does it represent an actual person or place, or is it a combination of the two? If people are represented, who are they? Who does not appear? What are the people doing? Are they looking at each other, at the viewer, or away from the viewer?
- Who is the intended **audience** for the image? Is it an artistic photograph or a commercial work, such as an advertisement? If it is an ad, to what kind of person is it directed? Where is the ad placed? If the image is in a magazine, consider the audience for the publication. Do you need any background information to understand the image?
- What **emotions** does the image convey? Overall, is it serious, sad, funny? Is its expression of emotion, in your opinion, intentional? What emotional associations do you have with the image?
- If the image includes more than one element, what is the most prominent element in the **composition**? A particular section? A logo? Any writing? A person or group of people? A product? Why are some elements larger than others? How does each part contribute to the whole?
- Where does the image's **layout** lead your eye? Are you drawn to any specific part? What is the order in which you look at the various parts? Does any particular section immediately stand out?
- Does the image include **text**? If so, how do the image and the text relate to one another?
- Does the image call for a **response**? For instance, does it suggest that you purchase a product? If so, what claims does it make?

Composition and layout: The layout of the ad is carefully designed to lead your eye: the hill slopes down from top right toward middle left, and the bike draws your eye from bottom right to mid-left, with both lines converging on the product, the jeans. For easy readability, the text appears at the top against the blank sky.

Text: The message, "The things that give a woman substance will never appear on any 'what's in/what's out' list," suggests that Lee jeans are a product for women who aren't interested in following trends, but rather want a good, old-fashioned value — "substance," not frivolity.

The things that give a woman substance
will never appear on any "what's in/what's out" list.

Straight Leg STRETCH Lee

Image courtesy of The Advertising Archives

Response: The manufacturer of Lee jeans would prefer, naturally, that the viewer of the ad buy the product. The viewer would identify with the woman wearing the jeans in the advertisement and be convinced that these practical (if not particularly cutting-edge) jeans would be a good purchase.

In sum, most fashion ads stress the friends (and often, mates) you will attract if you buy the product, but this ad presents "a road not taken," suggesting the American ideology of marching to the beat of a different drummer, the kind of old-fashioned individualism that brings to mind Robert Frost and Henry David Thoreau. The pastoral surroundings and the "old painting" effect echo artists such as Andrew Wyeth and Norman Rockwell. All these impressions connote lasting American values (rural, solid, middle American) that are meant to be associated with anti-trendiness and enduring qualities, such as individualism and practicality. And these impressions suggest the advertisers carefully and effectively kept the ad's semiotic messages in mind as they designed it to appeal to women with a more or less conservative, or at least traditional, point of view.

Reading Essays about Popular Culture

In your writing course, it's likely that your instructor will ask you to work in groups with other students, perhaps reviewing one another's rough drafts. You'll find many benefits to this activity. Not only will you receive more feedback on your own in-progress work, but you will see other students' ideas and approaches to an assignment and develop an ability to evaluate academic writing. For the same reasons, we're including three sample student essays that satisfy assignments about popular culture. You may agree or disagree with the authors' views, and you might have responded to the assigned topics differently; that's fine. We've selected these essays because they differ in style, focus, and purpose and thus suggest different approaches to their assignments — approaches that might help you as you write your own essays about popular culture. We've annotated the essays to point out various argumentative, organizational, and rhetorical strategies. As you read the essays and the annotations, ask why the authors chose these strategies and how you might incorporate some of the same strategies into your own writing.

Essay 1

Exemplifying a semiotic approach, Jeremy Creek, a poet who studies screenwriting at UCLA, explores the opening episodes of Netflix's *Stranger Things*, a show that seems at first to be yet another coming-of-age fantasy — but, as he argues, it turns that premise on itself and on its viewers. Here, Creek provides a fine reading of how a television program can be an articulate and potent sign of its time; he also demonstrates how *Stranger Things* echoes and reenacts previous media examples that are part of the history of such TV programs. Because the purpose of the opening episodes of a new series is, in part, to introduce a show's characters, themes, and recurrent visual motifs to its audience, this essay provides an especially good model for choosing a topic of your own for an analytic essay on a TV show.

The Anglerfish in the Machine: Horror and Re-enchantment in *Stranger Things*

A panicked scientist sprints down a windowless hallway into an industrial elevator. He hammers on the call button while looking into the flickering hallway lights, but just before the doors close, a monster growls and hauls the scientist off-screen, killing him. So begins Netflix's flagship series *Stranger Things*, both words glowing a reddish-pink neon on the title screen ("Chapter One: The Vanishing of Will Byers"). Set in a small town in the 1980s, the show lures in its viewers with its mix of science-fiction and cassette futurism (the blocky, neon-filled aesthetic meant to conjure an '80s vibe). With its depiction of supernatural powers, malicious government cells, and frequent nods to *Star Wars* and *Lord of the Rings*, the show at first seems to merely reiterate the well-trod themes of its predecessors — a coming of age fairy tale about the battle between good and evil. On closer inspection, however, the stuff of magic in *Stranger Things* turns out to be the stuff of terrible danger, revealing a deep fear of the very nostalgia in which the show traffics.

Jeremy presents his thesis.

That *Stranger Things* would take on the aspect of horror can be surprising, especially given recent trends in young adult sci-fi and fantasy. Whether it's the story of a boy whisked away to a magical school, a desert-dwelling orphan growing up amidst interplanetary war, or one of the countless superhero films clogging theater marquees around the nation, the speculative fiction of our time tends to offer stories of adventure and optimism. The promise of trials undertaken, powers gained (or spells learned, as the case may be), and evil vanquished: these form the basis of the West's most popular young heroes, in whose life the supernatural manifests and signals the transition from childhood to adulthood.

Jeremy develops his summary of popular trends in similar examples of media, exploring the value of those trends.

Western audiences, in short, have a glut of optimistic adventures to choose from, but what is it about this particular genre that so many viewers find compelling? Writing about the origins of speculative fiction's popularity, Christine Folch draws on theories of Max Weber to suggest that sci-fi and fantasy gives viewers an escape from a world that seems "knowably rational and systematic," which viewers perceive in the increasingly complicated web of scientific knowledge and technological advancement: "The world in which we live feels explainable, predictable, and boring" (460). As Folch points out, Weber asserted that this predictability resulted in a widespread feeling called "disenchantment" (460). This makes even more sense for people now, given all the technology and information available to us. It often feels impossible to have a thought that hasn't already been tweeted. And so the argument goes that the more people understand the world, and the faster this understanding can be widely disseminated, the more people will turn to stories that "re-enchant" audiences with supernatural mysteries because, as Folch concludes, "people seem to *like* to wonder" (460).

The summary of popular trends is extended by reference to Christine Folch's article.

From the very beginning, *Stranger Things* offers to satisfy viewers' need for wonder. At the introduction of the primary cast of characters, we meet four best friends — Mike, Will, Lucas, and Dustin — embroiled in an hours-long *Dungeons & Dragons* campaign. After Will disappears while biking home, the remaining boys search the nearby woods for him, where they find a mysterious young girl named Eleven ("Chapter One: The Vanishing of Will Byers"). Dressed only in a hospital gown, Eleven possesses mysterious telekinetic powers, but she will say little about where she came from. The boys' quest, therefore, is to find Will and restore the natural order of their friendship, which will inevitably mean learning more about the source of Eleven's telekinesis and her reason for hiding. Insofar as Eleven's arrival manifests the supernatural within the boys' lives, the show promises re-enchantment because it gives viewers plenty to wonder over. What, for example, is the source of her power? Where has Will gone? What is the monster from which he is hiding?

Jeremy offers an "elevator pitch" for the show's dramatic premise — its inciting incident and the mystery that compels viewers more deeply into the material.

The abstract significance of the show's premise is interpreted in the context of ideas already mentioned: the natural, the supernatural, and wonder.

Interestingly, *Stranger Things* fulfills viewers' longing for re-enchantment while reflecting this need back to us, indicating that love of science fiction and fantasy is part of the show's subject. The mirroring occurs in the show's constant allusions to stories that satisfied the need to wonder for American children in the 1980s. For example, when Mike shows Eleven a Yoda figurine, he quips that "He can use the force to move things with his mind," drawing a clear connection between Eleven's powers and the Star Wars character ("Chapter Two: The Weirdo on Maple Street"). Later, in an attempt to test the limits of Eleven's powers, Dustin tries to convince her to make a toy Millennium Falcon float, and while she can, she refuses to act on his command ("Chapter Three: Holly, Jolly"). Even the appearance of *Dungeons & Dragons*, which allows players to participate in an unending toybox of fantasy tropes, makes it clear that these children participate in the re-enchantment viewers long for.

Jeremy isolates the idea of re-enchantment and makes specific links to Tolkien's The Lord of the Rings.

A careful distinction must be made, however, because these references to stories of re-enchantment are not the *source* of re-enchantment itself. More simply, the stuff of magic is different from its methods. This becomes clearer when one pays close attention to the boys' dialogue throughout the opening episodes. For example, when the disaffected police chief Hopper asks Mike, Lucas, and Dustin about the street Will would take to get home, he is confused by their answer, "Mirkwood," because no such street in Hawkins exists ("Chapter One: The Vanishing of Will Byers"). Instead, the name refers to a mysterious forest in Tolkien's Middle Earth, and Hopper remains confused until Mike explains that "It's a real road . . . where Cornwallis and Kerley meet." The conflation of the real and fiction is doubly emphasized by the very next scene, a flashback in which Will's mother Joyce visits a fort that Will has built in the woods. Before entering, Joyce struggles to remember the password, "Radagast," which is yet another reference to *The Lord of the Rings*, Radagast the Brown being a wizard of Middle Earth especially concerned with forests and the creatures living within them. And above Will's fort, a massive American flag waves idly in the autumn wind.

This topic sentence connects several ideas mentioned in the previous paragraphs, including re-enchantment, viewers' longing for it, and the difference between the two.

The point is this: while both the viewers and the four boys of *Stranger Things* long for re-enchantment, the re-enchantment that each experiences is different. The difference rests at the fault-line of the television. From the viewer's perspective, the boys' love of sci-fi and fantasy is at best a shared interest, and at worst no mystery at all. Before Eleven's arrival, there's little by way of re-enchantment. From the boys' perspective, however, the town of Hawkins *is* already enchanted by the stories they love. The fort named "Castle Byers" can be found in the forest of Mirkwood, a territory of the United States just off Cornwallis Street. But since the introduction of Eleven and her telekinetic powers re-enchants the boys' experience of Hawkins, and since this re-enchantment must therefore be different from the fantasy-steeped reality they've created, just what is it that we, as viewers, are invited to wonder over?

In order to explore the re-enchantment experienced by viewers of *Stranger Things*, it is best to examine the show's depiction of the supernatural, which emanates out of a nearby government facility called the Hawkins National Lab. It's this facility that Eleven has fled, and over time, viewers discover that a portal inside leads to another realm, a nightmarish duplicate of Hawkins called "The Upside Down." Will is trapped inside the Upside Down, where he struggles to hide from the Demogorgon (the monster that killed the scientist in the opening scene). Given that the Upside Down is a supernatural mystery to both the show's characters and viewers, it serves as one of *Stranger Things*' central implements of re-enchantment. Where does it come from? How did Will get there? What is its connection to Eleven? Can Will be saved? Wonder abounds.

Several aspects of the Upside Down clarify how the re-enchantment worked by *Stranger Things* differs from its contemporaries and predecessors. Given that it is a double of Hawkins, for example, the name Upside Down conjures the image of a mirror: it might be a supernatural reflection of reality as the citizens of Hawkins have known it. Another distinguishing factor is the light, which is neither natural daylight nor moonlight, but a bluish-black, almost like the day-for-night exposures used in classic films. In fact, this effect closely resembles the newspapers that Hopper and a deputy pore over using a Microfiche reader in episode three, "Holly Jolly." As they search for more information on Dr. Brenner, the ominous researcher in charge of Hawkins National Lab, the Microfiche projects not images of the newspapers but their negatives, with the white of the paper and the black of the ink reversed.

This paragraph takes an isolated sign and looks for echoes within the show, follows these echoes, and finally arrives at a sharper interpretation.

Taking all of this into account, it would be better to say that the Upside Down is not a reflection of Hawkins but its negative, and the negative image is a productive sign to keep in mind while considering the idea of re-enchantment. To return to Folch, she explains that "disenchantment is rooted in the intellectual tradition of the 18th-century European Enlightenment with its struggles over the place of religion versus rationality" (461). As she explains it, the resulting trend in Western nations was to privilege scientific understanding over religious belief. So, if the boys' enchantment of Hawkins is a positive image of the need for wonder, the Upside

Down is therefore a negative image revealing wonder's opposite. A scene from "Chapter Two: The Weirdo on Maple Street" conveys as much. Trying to explain Will's location to Mike, Lucas, and Dustin, Eleven flips over the *Dungeons & Dragons* board and sets two figurines — a Wizard (Will) and a Demogorgon — on the glossy black surface underneath. The Upside Down is not the game, but the darkness underneath the game. And so the supernatural promise, the re-enchantment at work in *Stranger Things*, is fulfilled by the very forces that viewers turn to sci-fi and fantasy in order to escape — rationality, reason, and scientific understanding.

The whole premise of *Stranger Things* is therefore a bit of a trick: it re-enchants the very source of viewers' disenchantment, and so rather than a fairy tale, it can be understood as a coming-of-age horror story. To re-enchant the forces of rationality and reason produces neither wands nor lightsabers, but missing children and a flesh-eating monster. It's a show where what is made up is made to terrify, more at home alongside *Twin Peaks* or *Nightmare on Elm Street* than *Star Wars*. But what about rationality and reason in 1980s America, right on the cusp of the digital age, was there to fear, especially for America's youth?

Jeremy uses a question to drive the essay forward.

In thinking through this question, it might be useful to consider signs that manifest or are receptive to the supernatural: the Upside Down, the Demogorgon, or Eleven's telekinetic powers. In the first episode, for example, viewers learn that a portal (ostensibly to the Upside Down) has been opened inside the Hawkins National Lab, a classified government facility operating under the umbrella of the Department of Energy. The Laboratory is also where the previously imprisoned Eleven was forced by Dr. Brenner to participate in telekinetic experiments. Dr. Brenner is an oppressive figure concerned only with testing the limits of Eleven's power. On those occasions when she has proven uncooperative, he has had her locked away in solitary confinement ("Chapter Two: The Weirdo on Maple Street"). Outside the building's walls, the Laboratory staff are hostile to the local police after Will's disappearance: a guard attempts to prevent Hopper from investigating the Laboratory, and another staff member shows Hopper a few seconds of a falsified security footage ("Chapter Three: Holly, Jolly").

In this way, the Laboratory's hostility toward children and local concerns speaks to viewer's fears of the federal government: that in the name of scientific advancement (a product of rationality or reason), one's government will become more concerned with its own power than with the people it governs, or it will even test the limits of its power at the expense of those it is charged to protect. This latter point is made all the more clear when Eleven, being dragged off to confinement, weeps and cries after the disconsolate Dr. Brenner, calling "Papa, papa" ("Chapter Two: The Weirdo on Maple Street").

The topic sentence unifies the previous discussion of disparate signs, finding a common denominator.

Signs of government overreach appear elsewhere in the show, where they begin to reveal added concerns about its relationship to technological advancement. In a series of frequent cutaways, Dr. Brenner looms over a table of Laboratory employees who listen in on the phone lines of Hawkins citizens ("Chapter One: The Vanishing of Will Byers"). The Laboratory employees, all wearing headphones, scribble down notes on the conversations, an image that strongly echoes current fears of widespread government surveillance and the loss of personal privacy. It's true that we are surrounded by microphones. Our phones, computers, doorbells, TVs, even Smart kitchen appliances — we are constantly surrounded by technology that listens to us, and *Stranger Things* reflects back to viewers their own suspicion of who is on the other end of the line.

Furthermore, since it is with technology that the show's heroes gradually begin to unravel the mystery of the Upside Down, it is through technology that we can perceive the frightening aspects of growing up in the 1980s. More than a tool for nefarious government agencies, technology is embedded in *Stranger Things'* supernatural logic. Shortly after he goes missing, for example, Joyce receives a phone call in which she can, through static, hear Will's voice ("Chapter One: The Vanishing of Will Byers"). What's more, after an electrical surge fries the receiver, Will reaches out to her by turning on the stereo and brightening the lamps ("Chapter Two: The Weirdo on Maple Street"). This sequence culminates in Joyce lining the inside of her house with Christmas lights, snaking the bulbs underneath an alphabet painted along the wall so that Will can spell out messages from the Upside Down ("Chapter Three: Holly, Jolly").

Slowly but surely, then, viewers' ambivalence about rationality and reason manifests in the pre-digital tech of the 1980s. Here a walkie talkie can pass for a wand, and a string of Christmas lights

Jeremy concludes with his clearest, most precise interpretation of the show.

can be one's only way to communicate with a loved one trapped inside another realm. It is the government's classified use of more advanced technologies that sets the Demogorgon loose on the town's unsuspecting children, and it is through the widespread use of more rudimentary technology that the people of Hawkins must struggle to find and rescue a missing child from a supernatural realm. In the end the human capacity for rationality and reason is our only hope for salvation, as well as the very thing that we need saving from. After all, a negative is not cast but captured.

Works Cited

"Chapter One: The Vanishing of Will Byers." *Stranger Things*, created by Matt and Ross Duffer, Netflix Streaming Services, 2016.

"Chapter Three: Holly, Jolly." *Stranger Things*, created by Matt and Ross Duffer, Netflix Streaming Services, 2016.

"Chapter Two: The Weirdo on Maple Street." *Stranger Things*, created by Matt and Ross Duffer, Netflix Streaming Services, 2016.

Folch, Christine. "Why the West Loves Sci-Fi and Fantasy: A Cultural Explanation." *Signs of Life in the U.S.A.: Readings on Popular Culture for Writers*, 10th ed., edited by Sonia Maasik and Jack Solomon, Bedford/St. Martin's, 2021, pp. 459–62.

Essay 2

In this essay, Amy Lin of UCLA argues that the Barbie doll, and all its associated products and marketing, essentially is a means for engendering a consumerist ethos in young girls who are the toy's fans. To do so, Lin relies on a range of sources, including articles in *Signs of Life in the U.S.A.*, academic and journalistic sources, and a corporate website that presents the panoply of Barbie products. Notice that Lin does not treat toysrus.com as a source of unbiased information about the products (that would amount to taking promotional material at face value); rather, she analyzes the website as evidence for her larger argument about consumerism. As you read Lin's essay, study how she uses her sources and integrates them into her own discussion.

Barbie: Queen of Dolls and Consumerism

In my closet, a plastic bag contains five Barbie dolls. A cardboard box beside my nightstand holds yet another, and one more box contains a Ken doll. Under my bed we find my Barbies' traveling walk-in closet, equipped with a light-up vanity and foldout chair and desk. We also find Doctor Barbie along with the baby, sticker Band-Aids, and sounding stethoscope with which she came. Under my sister's bed are their furniture set, including sofas, loveseats, flower vases, and a coffee table. A Tupperware container holds Ken's pants, dress shirts, and special boots (whose spurs make patterns when rolled in ink) in addition to Barbie's excess clothing that did not fit in the walk-in closet. In a corner of my living room sits the special holiday edition Barbie, outfitted in a gown, fur stole, and holly headband.

Amy's introduction is a visual anecdote that illustrates her argument about consumption.

These plastic relics prove that, as a young girl, I, like many other females, fell into the waiting arms of the Mattel Corporation. Constantly feeding the public with newer, shinier toys, the Barbie enterprise illustrates America's propensity for consumerism. Upon close examination, Barbie products foster materialism in young females through both their overwhelmingly large selection and their ability to create a financially carefree world for children, sending the message that excessive consumption is acceptable. This consequently perpetuates the misassumption that "the American economy [is] an endlessly fertile continent whose boundaries never need be reached" (Shames 81) among the American youth.

Amy articulates her thesis and refers to Laurence Shames's article as a context.

Search the term "Barbie" at toysrus.com, and you will receive 286 items in return — more than enough to create a blur of pinkish-purple as you scroll down the web page. The Barbie enterprise clearly embraces "the observation that 'no natural boundary seems to be set to the efforts of man'" (Shames 78). In other words, humankind is, in all ways, ambitious; people will keep creating, buying, and selling with the belief that these opportunities will always be available. This perfectly describes the mentality of those behind Barbie products, as new, but unnecessary, Barbie merchandise is put on shelves at an exorbitant rate. At toysrus.com, for example, a variety of four different mermaids, eleven fairies, and two "merfairies" — products from the "Fairytopia-Mermaidia" line — find their place among the search results (*Toys*). Instead of

The corporate website is used not as a source of objective information but as evidence to support the thesis.

inventing a more original or educational product, Mattel merges the mermaid world with the fairy world into "Fairytopia-Mermaidia," demonstrating the company's lack of innovation and care for its young consumers' development. Thus the corporation's main motivation reveals itself: profit. Another prime example found among the search results is the "Barbie: 12 Dancing Princesses Horse Carriage" (*Toys*), a more recent product in the Barbie family. The carriage, "in its original form, . . . can seat six princess dolls but . . . can expand to hold all 12 dolls at once" (*Toys*). The dolls, of course, do not come with it, forcing the child to buy at least one for the carriage to even be of any use. But that child will see the glorious picture of the carriage filled with all twelve dolls (which are inevitably on the box), and she will want to buy the remaining eleven. In addition, the product description states that the carriage "is inspired by the upcoming DVD release, Barbie in *The 12 Dancing Princesses*" (*Toys*). Essentially, one Mattel creation inspires another, meaning that the DVD's sole purpose is to give Mattel an excuse to create and market more useless merchandise.

Amy moves to the larger marketing context.

Much of this, however, may have to do with branding, a strategy manufacturers utilize that ultimately results in "consumers transfer[ring] a favorable or unfavorable image from one product to others from the same brand" (Neuhaus and Taylor 419). In accordance with this strategy, all Barbie products must maintain a certain similarity so as not to "'confuse' potential customers . . . and thereby reduce demand for the products" (Sappington and Wernerfelt 280). This explains the redundancy found in much of Mattel's Barbie merchandise, since the sudden manufacturing of a radically different product could encourage the migration of consumers to another brand. But given that Barbie has become "the alpha doll" (Talbot 74) for girls in today's popular culture, young female consumers clearly associate only good things with Barbie. And who can blame them? Barbie has become a tradition handed down from mother to daughter or a rite of passage that most girls go through. In this way, excessive consumption and the effects of branding are handed down as well, as Barbie dolls are essentially their physical manifestations.

With a company as driven to produce and sell products as Mattel, consumers can expect to find increasingly ridiculous items on toy store shelves. One such product found at toysrus.com is "Barbie and Tanner" (*Toys*), Tanner being Barbie's dog. The doll and dog come with brown pellets that function both as dog food and dog waste, a "special magnetic scooper[,] and trash can" (*Toys*). Upon telling any post-Barbie-phase female about this product, she will surely look amazed and ask, "Are you kidding me?" Unfortunately, Tanner's movable "mouth, ears, head and tail" (*Toys*) and "soft[,] . . . fuzzy" coat will most likely blind children to the product's absurdity, instead enchanting them into purchasing the product. Another particularly hilarious item is the "Barbie Collector Platinum Label Pink Grapefruit Obsession" (*Toys*). The doll wears a "pink, charmeuse mermaid gown with deep pink chiffon wedges sewn into the flared skirt and adorned with deep pink bands that end in bows under the bust and at the hip" (*Toys*). And "as a . . . special surprise, [the] doll's head is scented with the striking aroma of pink grapefruit" (*Toys*). Finally, the doll is described as "an ideal tribute to [the] delightful [grapefruit] flavor" (*Toys*). The consumer will find it difficult to keep a straight face as he or she reads through the description, as it essentially describes a doll dedicated to a scent. The doll's randomness shows Mattel's desperation for coming out with new products. Eager to make profit, Barbie's designers, it seems, make dolls according to whatever whim that happens to cross their minds.

The paragraph includes a rich array of concrete, specific detail.

In the quest to make profit by spreading the consumerist mind-set, Barbie products even manage to commodify culture. Nowadays, Barbie dolls come in a variety of ethnicities. Take, for example, the "Diwali Festival Doll" from the "Barbie Dolls of the World" (*Toys*) line. Except for the traditional Indian apparel and dark hair, however, the doll could easily be mistaken for Caucasian. And what about Barbie's multiracial doll friends? They are reduced to mere accessories — disposable and only supplementary to Barbie, the truly important figure. Therefore, despite Mattel's attempts at identifying with a larger group of girls, an undeniable "aura of blondness still [clings] to the Mattel doll" (Talbot 82) because its attempts aim more toward creating a larger customer base than anything else.

Amy develops her argument by considering the cultural and ethnic angle.

But enough of dolls. Mattel has grown so large that it can expand its products beyond Barbie's mini-world. Consumers can easily find Barbie brand tennis shoes, rain boots, slippers, bicycles, and helmets. Many of Barbie's non-doll products even reflect the various fads among America's youth, such as video games, skateboards, scooters, guitars, and dance mats (in accordance with the popularity of the game, Dance Dance Revolution). Anne Parducci, Mattel's senior

A quick, short transition moves the reader to a broader consideration of Mattel's promotion of materialism.

VP of Barbie Marketing, claims Mattel does this because it "want[s] to make sure . . . [it] capture[s] girls in the many ways they are spending their time now and in the future," that it "want[s] Barbie to represent a lifestyle brand for girls, not just a brand of toys" (Edut). This phenomenon, however, can simply be seen as Mattel trying to "infiltrat[e] girls' lives everywhere they go" (Edut). Either way, Mattel's actions allow materialism to develop at an early age, especially since it makes the latest "it" items more accessible to children. Those behind Barbie figure that if children are going to buy into the latest trends anyway, they might as well buy them from Mattel.

Amy allows for a counter-argument but then refutes it.

Since Barbie products promote the attitude of keeping up with society's crazes, they create a carefree fantasy world for children, obscuring the fact that Mattel's motivation is making money. The company knows that if it enchants children, those children will in turn convince their parents to buy the products for them. The company also knows that commercials are its best opportunities to do this. One recent Mattel commercial advertises the "Let's Dance Genevieve" doll, a doll also inspired by *The 12 Dancing Princesses* DVD that interacts with its owner in three ways: the doll "can dance to music for the girl," "teach the girl dance moves by demonstrating and using speech prompts," and "follow along with the girl's dance moves using special bracelets and a shoe accessory" (*Toys*). Girls dressed in ballerina attire give overly joyous reactions to the doll's behaviors, making the doll seem remarkably advanced when, really, the doll can only raise its arms and legs. In addition, computer graphic scenes from the movie run seamlessly into scenes of the girls playing with the doll, and one of these girls is even transposed onto a clip of the movie. This blurs the lines of reality and fantasy, encouraging young viewers to think that if they own the doll, they, too, can feel like "dancing princesses," that somehow the doll can transport its owner into a fairy-tale world. In actuality, young females will likely tire of the doll within weeks. The commercial even resorts to flattery, describing the doll and its owner as "two beautiful dancers." Finally, the commercial ends with inspirational lyrics, singing, "You can shine." This sort of "vaguely girl-positive" advertising only "wrap[s] the Mattel message—buy our products now!" (Edut). Together, all these advertising elements add up to a highly desirable product among young girls.

Barbie undoubtedly increases the materialistic tendencies in children, specifically females, Barbie's target audience. After all, since "Barbie dolls need new clothes and accessories more often than boys' action figures do," "young girls learn . . . very early" to "assume consumer roles" (Katz). Interestingly, "Barbie was an early rebel against the domesticity that dominated the lives of baby-boom mothers," as she shows no "car[e] for babies or children" or "visible ties to parents" (Cross 773). But ironically, instead of "[teaching] girls to shed [such] female stereotypes," Barbie simply created a new stereotype for females — the shopaholic persona — because "she prompted [young girls] to associate the freedom of being an adult with carefree consumption" (Cross 774). So the overall effect of Barbie's presence in children's lives is increased expectations for material possessions. Or, in other words, Barbie products cause "catalog-induced anxiety," a condition that can occur "from [viewing] catalogs themselves or from other forms of public exposure of the lives of the rich or celebrated, . . . mak[ing] what a typical person possesses seem paltry, even if the person is one of the many . . . living well by objective standards" (Easterbrook 404, 405). Given that Barbie is a fictitious character, Mattel can make her as beautiful, hip, and rich as it pleases. But what happens when little girls begin comparing their lives to that of Barbie? They think, "If Barbie gets to have such amenities, so should I." And toys like the "Barbie Hot Tub Party Bus" (*Target*) do not help the situation. The product description reads that the bus contains "all the comforts of home like a flat screen TV, dinette table, and beds" (*Target*). Children will inevitably expect these luxuries that, for Barbie, are merely givens in her doll utopia, causing discontent when they discover they cannot have everything they want. It may even reach the point where, "as . . . more material things become available and fail to" satisfy children, "material abundance . . . [can] have the perverse effect of instilling unhappiness — because it will never be possible to have everything that economics can create" (Easterbrook 402).

References to Gary Cross's article buttress the essay's argument.

Amy invokes Gregg Easterbrook as she explores the long-term implications of Mattel's promotion of consumerism.

For my long-forgotten Barbie dolls, as for those of many older females, the dream house has stopped growing. In fact, the house has been demolished, leaving my dolls homeless. But this does not mean that women have escaped the effects of years of Barbie play as they have temporarily escaped the clutches of Mattel. (I say temporarily because even if a woman has outgrown Barbie, Mattel will suck her back in through her daughters, nieces, goddaughters, and granddaughters.) Since Barbie preaches the admissibility of hyperconsumption to females at a young age, women, unsurprisingly, "engage

Amy signals closure by coming full circle, returning to her opening anecdote.

in an estimated 80% of all consumer spending" (Katz). Women, conditioned from all those trips to the toy store looking for the perfect party dress for Barbie or the perfect convertible to take her to that party, still find themselves doing this — just on a larger scale — in shopping malls. But perhaps men's consumerism is catching up. The recent "proliferation of metrosexuals" signals a rise in "straight young men whose fashion and grooming tastes have crossed over into areas once reserved for feminine consumption" (St. John 177, 174). Mattel, too, takes part in this phenomenon through the "reintroduc[tion] [of] the Ken doll," which now possesses a "new metrosexual look" (Talbot 79). Well, one thing is certain: Mattel continues its expansive construction on Barbie's ever-costly dream mansion, and knows that millions of little girls will do the same.

By considering men's consumer habits and male dolls, Amy ends with a refreshing twist.

Works Cited

Cross, Gary. "Barbie, G.I. Joe, and Play in the 1960s." Maasik and Solomon, pp. 772–78.

Easterbrook, Gregg. "The Progress Paradox." Maasik and Solomon, pp. 400–407.

Edut, Ophira. "Barbie Girls Rule?" *Bitch: Feminist Response to Pop Culture*, 31 Jan. 1999, p. 16.

Geoffrey LLC. *Toys "R" Us*. 14 Nov. 2006, www.toysrus.com

Katz, Phyllis A., and Margaret Katz. "Purchasing Power: Spending for Change." *Iris*, 30 Apr. 2000, p. 36.

Maasik, Sonia, and Jack Solomon, editors. *Signs of Life in the U.S.A.: Readings on Popular Culture for Writers*, 7th ed., Bedford/St. Martin's, 2012.

Neuhaus, Colin F., and James R. Taylor. "Variables Affecting Sales of Family-Branded Products." *Journal of Marketing Research*, vol. 9, no. 4, 1972, pp. 419–22.

Sappington, David E. M., and Birger Wernerfelt. "To Brand or Not to Brand? A Theoretical and Empirical Question." *Journal of Business*, vol. 58, no. 3, 1985, pp. 279–93.

Shames, Laurence. "The More Factor." Maasik and Solomon, pp. 76–82.

St. John, Warren. "Metrosexuals Come Out." Maasik and Solomon, pp. 174–77.

Talbot, Margaret. "Little Hotties: Barbie's New Rivals." *New Yorker*, 4 Dec. 2006, pp. 74+.

Target Brands, Inc. *Target*. 14 Nov. 2006, www.target.com

Essay 3

For this essay, UCLA psychology major Irina Bodea received a prompt that is often assigned in composition courses: an analysis of two advertisements to determine what underlying values and belief systems inform the ads. In studying ads for two banks, Irina finds some qualifications in the ads' apparently progressive surface messages. As you read Irina's essay, notice how her critique goes beyond *what* the ads say — their denotative meanings — and addresses *how* they present their message — their connotative meanings. Notice as well that Irina grounds her discussion in a careful consideration of specific, concrete details that allow the reader to visualize the images she is analyzing.

Banks: Progressive or Conventional?

Banks and other financial institutions traditionally have used a conservative approach in their advertising, suggesting that by using their services, their market, which is typically wealthy people who are also male and white, will have the financial stability to pursue their dreams. At first, two recent commercials for banks — one promoting Wells Fargo, the other Chase — seem to depart from that formula, as they exploit currently popular notions of equality, social justice, and inclusion. Indeed, the two commercials seem designed to abolish discrimination, whether that be based on gender, race, sexual orientation, or disability.

Irina summarizes the surface message of both ads.

The Chase commercial subverts the gender stereotype of the male-dominated science and technology industry by depicting a little girl who aspires to be an astronaut. The Wells Fargo commercial goes beyond just endorsing the fight for women's rights and equality; it plays all the social justice cards. Through the use of an all-women cast to tell the story of a lesbian couple adopting a deaf Latina girl, Wells Fargo promotes gender, sexual orientation, race and disability equality. Despite this progressive appearance, a closer analysis shows that both banking commercials deviate little, if at all, from traditional and conventional American ideas about family and patriarchal dynamics. Wells Fargo and Chase keep the conservative foundations in their ads in order to retain their current top customers. While appearing open-minded and radical to appeal to new reformist customers who oppose present society injustice, by using these strategies, both banks are likely to increase their market share and thus generate more profit, achieving their goals as companies.

Irina's thesis reveals what the ads actually convey beneath their surface appeals.

At the surface level, the Chase commercial endorses gender equality in the workplace. The viewer is introduced to a child passionate about space. She wears an astronaut costume, including a helmet, while traveling by airplane with her mother and father. The child is the central character of the commercial, which is suggested from the beginning of the shot when the three-member family leaves their taxi at an airport "Departures" terminal. The first to step on is the little astronaut who walks slightly ahead of the two adult characters until they enter the airport. These shots show three pairs of legs, with the child's being in the middle. Therefore, by using the rule of three and centrality, the ad focuses the viewer's attention on the child. This focus on the child is further maintained by the seemingly bizarre outfit choice and the mystery it holds (of who is underneath the costume). Because men stereotypically prevail in STEM positions, the viewer incorrectly assumes that the child is a little boy until her gender is later revealed in the commercial. Choosing to conceal the gender of the child until half-way through the video, Chase invites the viewer to consider why it was so natural, even normal, to assume the little astronaut is a boy. Thus, by casting a girl to play the role, Chase encourages women from a young age to assert themselves in STEM fields and goes against traditional gender norms.

Specific details allow us to visualize the Chase commercial.

At the same time, however, throughout the commercial, there are moments that undercut the progressive message Chase explicitly displays. Even at the most important part of the commercial, when the girl is revealed to be wearing the astronaut costume before boarding the airplane, Chase uses dialogue to mitigate female advancement in STEM fields. When the girl openly expresses her wishes of going to Mars, all the adult characters around, specifically her parents and the flight attendants, proceed to laugh. This response implies that rather than taking the girl's career aspiration seriously, they all believe it is just child's play and a dream that will soon change. The father's response "We're working on that" immediately shuts down the girl's remark through his words, condescending tone and facial expression—his lips crash together and he looks down, showing disbelief or disapproval—and in the process undermines women as astronauts. The phrase further suggests how not even her father thinks that a career as an astronaut is a viable option for her, and that her wish is just part of an ephemeral phase. The fact that the only male character in the scene was scripted

Irina moves to demonstrate how the Chase ad subverts its seemingly progressive message.

to say this enhances traditional gender notions that men are the voice of reason and must have the last words (his response is the last piece of character dialogue in the video) and, in effect, sabotages the explicit progressive message of the commercial. Moreover, casting two females to represent the flight attendants similarly violates gender equality in the workplace because the job of flight attendants is female dominated. Thus, Chase falls into the trap of mass production, or as James Twitchell explains, "mass marketing, and mass marketing means the creation of mass stereotypes" (261) to keep their large conservative target audience. As a result, Chase strengthens the existing stereotypes instead of debunking them as they seemingly did by the surface message of the girl striving to be an astronaut.

On a similar extrinsic note, the Wells Fargo commercial seems to celebrate diversity, for every step of the way, it shows examples of people and actions that we consider today as diverse. The marketers thus use the study of semiotics and knowledge that "[c]onsumers intuitively read and respond to the codes contained in brand communication" (Arning 219) to show support of the LGBTQ+ community. Wells Fargo promotes exposure to same-sex relationships by following a female married couple as they are in the process of adopting a child. The couple is loving and caring to one another, which is shown through their facial expressions and actions when interacting. When driving to meet their soon-to-be daughter, the blonde woman in the passenger seat sees her wife is slightly nervous or worried, so she gently places her hand on her partner's hand to show support and that everything is going to be fine.

Irina next addresses Wells Fargo's similar strategy in its ad.

Although the portrayal implies that same-sex relationships are loving and normal and resemble traditional marriages' values of family love and support, the commercial consolidates the existing stereotypes of lesbians. This occurs because viewers unconsciously may assume that all lesbian relationships involve the following key stereotypical details: one person is the traditional man while the other is the traditional woman, and they cannot have children of their own. The commercial stars two women in their late twenties or early thirties who are involved in a romantic relationship and are trying to adopt a child. The blonde woman is supposed to be the "wife," having the traditional gender roles assigned to women. She spends a lot of time in the home setting, relaxing, reading books, and, in her free time, going to ASL classes. Her housewifely

Abundant details reveal how the depiction of the lesbian couple in fact is traditional.

attributes are also revealed as she sets the table in the background while her partner sits in front of a computer. The "wife" wears light colors which are commonly attributed to women. Also, in one of the shots, she is sitting at a bigger desk in a colorful craft room which implies she likes DIY — a common activity attributed to housewives. On the other hand, her partner is supposed to be the "husband," having traditional gender roles assigned to men. Her appearance is stereotypically more masculine. She has dark messy layered hair and wears simple, plain, predominantly gray outfits. She is taller and older than her partner and has a less curved feminine body shape. Her workplace is an office in a high-rise building, implying she has a well-established career in the business world, reminiscent of the stereotypes of the working husband as a powerful businessman. In the shot of the future parents going to meet their future daughter, she is the one driving the car. In a heterosexual relationship, the man is usually the one who drives a vehicle and, in effect, sits in the power seat, whereas the woman takes the seat beside him. Thus, by clearly differentiating who is the working powerful "husband" and caring house "wife" in this lesbian relationship, Wells Fargo exacerbates the conventional stereotype of the two distinctive traditional male and female roles played in every relationship. As a result, Wells Fargo's slight and modern interpretation of "gay vague" marketing is a "way for [the bank] to reach queer audiences with minimal risk of a conservative backlash" (Mayyasi 186).

Another way Wells Fargo celebrates diversity is through the introduction of the deaf girl who is going to be adopted. The whole commercial looks at how two hearing women go out of their way to learn ASL and provide a safe and loving environment for the child they are going to adopt. Wells Fargo is encouraging viewers to go past the disability they first see when they encounter deaf people and suggest that learning basic ASL is an easy task that goes a long way. The women are introduced as they start to learn the ASL alphabet (the first shot is of the darker haired woman learning to spell the letter "b" while riding the bus) and by the end of the commercial they are already able to formulate more complex phrases and communicate through ASL (when meeting the girl, the blonde woman can sign "We are going to be your new mommies"). Hearing people signing little by little eliminates the ostracism of deaf and hard-of-hearing people. Therefore, learning basic ASL is integral to the progressive movement of the deaf community's inclusion within the larger culture.

However, subtly the ad undermines the deaf community by its portrayal of the deaf girl. Although she looks happy, she is an orphan who ultimately needs to be saved by the white couple. In the commercial, the girl's only lines are "I'm happy too" in response to her mom signing "I'm so happy". The repetition of the phrase signed to her implies that she does not have any ideas of her own and that her language is very simple. These are common stereotypes associated with the deaf community that result from the language and expression barriers. More often than not, deaf people need to use simple and plain words to be understood by the hearing community, thus restricting their expression of their personalities and opinions, making them seem indifferent or less educated. In addition, the girl's position in the room suggests that a boundary separates hearing from deaf. She sits on the opposite side of the lesbian couple, leaving quite a lot of space in between.

The character of the deaf girl replicates the double message sent by the ad overall.

Chase and Wells Fargo try to keep up with modern perspectives by using progressive ideas while still fully holding on to conservative views. Chase promotes women in STEM fields but undermines gender equality in the workplace through male mocking reactions and female dominant jobs. Wells Fargo celebrates the deaf and lesbian communities but reinforces stereotypes within these diverse groups. As embodiments of the banking system, both hold onto their fundamental capitalistic and patriarchal views to keep their existing rich white male customer base, while giving lip service the inclusion of all other types of diverse customers.

Irina sums up the ads' main strategy.

Works Cited

Arning, Chris. "What Can Semiotics Contribute to Packaging Design?" *Signs of Life in the U.S.A.: Readings on Popular Culture for Writers,* 10th ed., edited by Sonia Maasik and Jack Solomon, Bedford/St. Martin's, 2021, 217–222.

Mayyasi, Alex. "How Subarus Came to Be Seen as Cars for Lesbians." *Signs of Life in the U.S.A.: Readings on Popular Culture for Writers,* 9th ed., edited by Sonia Maasik and Jack Solomon, Bedford/St. Martin's, 2018, 183–188.

Twitchell, James B. "What We Are to Advertisers." *Signs of Life in the U.S.A.: Readings on Popular Culture for Writers*, 10th ed., edited by Sonia Maasik and Jack Solomon, Bedford/St. Martin's, 2021, 261–264.

CONDUCTING RESEARCH AND CITING SOURCES

Your instructor may ask you to use outside, or secondary, sources to support your analyses of popular culture. These sources may include a wide variety of published materials, from other essays (such as those featured in this book) to interviews you conduct to YouTube videos. When you write about popular culture, a host of sources are available to you to help lend weight to your arguments as well as help you develop fresh thinking about your topic.

The internet has afforded us innovative research opportunities, and with a wealth of information at your fingertips, it is up to you, the writer, to learn to determine which sources you should trust and which you should suspect. As always, the library is a great place to begin. Research librarians continue to be excellent resources not only for finding sources for your papers, but for learning best practices for conducting research. It is more than likely that they are aware of resources at your disposal that you haven't considered, from academic databases like EBSCOhost to library catalogs to film and video archives.

The following selections offer additional help for conducting academically sound research online.

SCOTT JASCHIK

A Stand against Wikipedia

Increasingly, college faculty are concerned about the widespread use of Wikipedia in student research and writing. The problem, as faculty see it, is twofold. First, there is the issue of reliability. Wikipedia does strive to provide reliable information, but given the wide-open nature of the site — anyone can contribute — ensuring accuracy is not really possible. This leads to student work that can disseminate misinformation. Second, even where Wikipedia is accurate (and it can be an accurate source of information), it is, after all, an encyclopedia, and while encyclopedic sources may be suitable for background information, students performing college-level research should seek primary sources and academic-level secondary sources that they find on their own. The following article from insidehighered.com surveys the problems with Wikipedia as a research source as seen by college faculty from a number of universities.

As Wikipedia has become more and more popular with students, some professors have become increasingly concerned about the online, reader-produced encyclopedia.

While plenty of professors have complained about the lack of accuracy or completeness of entries, and some have discouraged or tried to bar students from using it, the history department at Middlebury College is trying to take a stronger, collective stand. It voted this month to bar students from citing the website as a source in papers or other academic work. All faculty members will be telling students about the policy and explaining why material on Wikipedia — while convenient — may not be trustworthy. "As educators, we are in the business of reducing the dissemination of misinformation," said Don Wyatt, chair of the department. "Even though Wikipedia may have some value, particularly from the value of leading students to citable sources, it is not itself an appropriate source for citation," he said.

The department made what Wyatt termed a consensus decision on the issue after discussing problems professors were seeing as students cited incorrect information from Wikipedia in papers and on tests. In one instance, Wyatt said, a professor noticed several students offering the same incorrect information, from Wikipedia. There was some discussion in the department of trying to ban students from using Wikipedia, but Wyatt said that didn't seem appropriate. Many Wikipedia entries have good bibliographies, Wyatt said. And any absolute ban would just be ignored. "There's the issue of freedom of access," he said. "And I'm not in the business of promulgating unenforceable edicts."

Wyatt said that the department did not specify punishments for citing Wikipedia, and that the primary purpose of the policy was to educate, not to be punitive. He said he doubted that a paper would be rejected for having a single Wikipedia footnote, but that students would be told that they shouldn't do so, and that multiple violations would result in reduced grades or even a failure. "The important point that we wish to communicate to all students taking courses and submitting work in our department in the future is that they cite Wikipedia at their peril," he said. He stressed that the objection of the department to Wikipedia wasn't its online nature, but its unedited nature, and he said students need to be taught to go for quality information, not simply convenience.

The frustrations of Middlebury faculty members are by no means unique. 5
Last year, Alan Liu, a professor of English at the University of California at Santa Barbara, adopted a policy that Wikipedia "is not appropriate as the primary or sole reference for anything that is central to an argument, complex, or controversial." Liu said that it was too early to tell what impact his policy is having. In explaining his rationale — which he shared with an email list — he wrote that he had "just read a paper about the relation between structuralism, deconstruction, and postmodernism in which every reference was to the Wikipedia articles on those topics with no awareness that there was any need to read a primary work or even a critical work."

Wikipedia officials agree — in part — with Middlebury's history department. "That's a sensible policy," Sandra Ordonez, a spokeswoman, said in an email interview. "Wikipedia is the ideal place to start your research and get a global picture of a topic; however, it is not an authoritative source. In fact, we recommend that students check the facts they find in Wikipedia against other sources. Additionally, it is generally good research practice to cite an original source when writing a paper, or completing an exam. It's usually not advisable, particularly at the university level, to cite an encyclopedia." Ordonez acknowledged that, given the collaborative nature of Wikipedia writing and editing, "there is no guarantee an article is 100 percent correct," but she said that the site is shifting its focus from growth to improving quality, and that the site is a great resource for students. "Most articles are continually being edited and improved upon, and most contributors are real lovers of knowledge who have a real desire to improve the quality of a particular article," she said.

Experts on digital media said that the Middlebury history professors' reaction was understandable and reflects growing concern among faculty members about the accuracy of what students find online. But some worry that bans on citing Wikipedia may not deal with the underlying issues.

Roy Rosenzweig, director of the Center for History and New Media at George Mason University, did an analysis of the accuracy of Wikipedia for the *Journal of American History*, and he found that in many entries, Wikipedia was as accurate as or more accurate than more traditional encyclopedias. He said that the quality of material was inconsistent, and that biographical entries were generally well done, while more thematic entries were much less so. Like Ordonez, he said the real problem is one of college students using encyclopedias when they should be using more advanced sources. "College students shouldn't be citing encyclopedias in their papers," he said. "That's not what college is about. They either should be using primary sources or serious secondary sources."

In the world of college librarians, a major topic of late has been how to guide students in the right direction for research, when Wikipedia and similar sources are so easy. Some of those who have been involved in these discussions said that the Middlebury history department's action pointed to the need for more outreach to students. Lisa Hinchliffe, head of the undergraduate library and coordinator of information literacy at the University of Illinois at Urbana-Champaign, said that earlier generations of students were in fact taught when it was appropriate (or not) to consult an encyclopedia and why for many a paper they would never even cite a popular magazine or nonscholarly work. "But it was a relatively constrained landscape," and students didn't have easy access to anything equivalent to Wikipedia, she said. "It's not that students are being lazy today. It's a much more complex environment."

When she has taught, and spotted footnotes to sources that aren't appro- 10
priate, she's considered that "a teachable moment," Hinchliffe said. She said that she would be interested to see how Middlebury professors react when they get the first violations of their policy, and said she thought there could be positive discussions about why sources are or aren't good ones. That kind of teaching, she said, is important "and can be challenging."

Steven Bell, associate librarian for research and instructional services at Temple University, said of the Middlebury approach: "I applaud the effort for wanting to direct students to good quality resources," but he said he would go about it in a different way. "I understand what their concerns are. There's no question that [on Wikipedia and similar sites] some things are great and some things are questionable. Some of the pages could be by eighth graders," he said. "But to simply say 'don't use that one' might take students in the wrong direction from the perspective of information literacy."

Students face "an ocean of information" today, much of it of poor quality, so a better approach would be to teach students how to "triangulate" a source like Wikipedia, so they could use other sources to tell whether a given entry could be trusted. "I think our goal should be to equip students with the critical thinking skills to judge."

PATTI S. CARAVELLO

Judging Quality on the Web

When you conduct research on the internet, you'll find a dizzying range of sources, from academic journals to government websites, from newspapers and popular magazines to blogs, wikis, and social networking and file-sharing sites. Having a plethora of sources at hand with just the click of a mouse has been a boon to researchers in all fields. But the very democratic basis of the internet that makes all this information so readily available creates a challenge, for it comes with no guarantees of quality control. Indeed, it is incumbent upon you, the researcher, to determine the reliability of the web sources that you use. The following article from the UCLA Library's website, "Judging Quality on the Web," lists criteria that will allow you to evaluate the usefulness and reliability of internet sources.

Even after refining a query in a search engine, a researcher often retrieves a huge number of websites. It is essential to know how to evaluate websites for the same reasons you would evaluate a periodical article or a book: *to ascertain whether you can rely on the information, to identify its inherent biases or limitations, and to see how or whether it fits into your overall research strategy.*

A good (useful, reliable) website:

1. Clearly states the author and/or organizational **source** of the information
   Your task:
   - Consider the qualifications, other works, and organizational affiliation of the author
   - Look up the organization which produced the website (if it's unfamiliar) to identify its credentials, viewpoint, or agenda
   - If the source is an e-journal, discover whether it is refereed (reviewed by scholars before it is accepted for publication)
2. Clearly states the **date** the material was written and the date the site was last revised
   Your task:
   - If the information is not current enough for your purposes or the date is not given, look elsewhere
3. Provides **accurate** data whose parameters are clearly defined
   Your task:
   - Compare the data found on the website with data found in other sources (encyclopedias, reference books, articles, etc.) for accuracy, completeness, recency
   - Ask a librarian about other important sources to check for this information
4. Provides the **type and level** of information you need
   Your task:
   - Decide whether the level of detail and comprehensiveness, the treatment of the topic (e.g., scholarly or popular), and the graphics or other features are acceptable
   - If the site does not provide the depth of coverage you need, look elsewhere

5. Keeps **bias** to a minimum, and clearly indicates point of view
   Your task:
   - Be aware that producing a web page does not require the checking and review that publishing a scholarly book requires; you might have retrieved nothing but someone's personal opinion on the topic
   - Appealing graphics can distract you from noticing even overt bias, so heighten your skepticism and examine the evidence (source, date, accuracy, level, links)
6. Provides live **links** to related high-quality websites
   Your task:
   - Click on several of the links provided to see if they are active (or if they give an "error" message indicating the links are not being maintained) and to see if they are useful
   - Check to see if the criteria are stated for selecting the links
7. In the case of **commercial** sites, keeps advertising separate from content, and does not let advertisers determine content
   Your task:
   - Look at the web address: Sites that are commercial have *.com* in their addresses and might have advertising or offer to sell something. The *.com* suffix is also found in news sites (e.g., newspapers, TV networks) and personal pages (sites created by individuals who have purchased a domain name but who may or may not have a commercial or institutional affiliation)
8. Is clearly organized and **designed** for ease of use
   Your task:
   - Move around the page to see if its organization makes sense and it is easy to return to the top or to the sections you need
   - Decide whether the graphics enhance the content or detract from it

TRIP GABRIEL

For Students in Internet Age, No Shame in Copy and Paste

The internet is an invaluable source for information about popular culture, both because of its instant accessibility and because of its ability to keep pace with the rapid turnover in popular fashions and trends in a way that print-technology publication never can. But, as is so often the case with the internet, there is a downside to the matter. Because, as Trip Gabriel observes in this feature that originally appeared in the *New York Times*, "concepts of intellectual property, copyright, and originality are under assault in the unbridled exchange of online information," and the result is a pandemic of inadvertent, and sometimes deliberate, plagiarism. Certainly in an era of group-oriented writing — as on Wikipedia — traditional notions of individual authorship are being deconstructed, which makes it all the more important that students learn in their writing classes what the conventions for documentation are and why they are still necessary. Trip Gabriel is a longtime reporter, and former Styles editor, for the *New York Times.*

At Rhode Island College, a freshman copied and pasted from a website's frequently asked questions page about homelessness — and did not think he needed to credit a source in his assignment because the page did not include author information.

At DePaul University, the tip-off to one student's copying was the purple shade of several paragraphs he had lifted from the web; when confronted by a writing tutor his professor had sent him to, he was not defensive — he just wanted to know how to change purple text to black.

And at the University of Maryland, a student reprimanded for copying from Wikipedia in a paper on the Great Depression said he thought its entries — unsigned and collectively written — did not need to be credited since they counted, essentially, as common knowledge.

Professors used to deal with plagiarism by admonishing students to give credit to others and to follow the style guide for citations, and pretty much left it at that.

But these cases — typical ones, according to writing tutors and officials 5
responsible for discipline at the three schools who described the plagiarism — suggest that many students simply do not grasp that using words they did not write is a serious misdeed.

It is a disconnect that is growing in the information age as concepts of intellectual property, copyright, and originality are under assault in the unbridled exchange of online information, say educators who study plagiarism.

Digital technology makes it easy to copy and paste files, of course. But that is the least of it. The internet may also be redefining how students — who came of age with music file-sharing, Wikipedia, and web-linking — understand the concept of authorship and the singularity of any text or image.

"Now we have a whole generation of students who've grown up with information that just seems to be hanging out there in cyberspace and doesn't seem to have an author," said Teresa Fishman, director of the Center for Academic Integrity at Clemson University. "It's possible to believe this information is just out there for anyone to take."

Professors who have studied plagiarism do not try to excuse it — many are champions of academic honesty on their campuses — but rather try to understand why it is so widespread.

In surveys from 2006 to 2010 by Donald L. McCabe, a co-founder of the 10
Center for Academic Integrity and a business professor at Rutgers University, about 40 percent of 14,000 undergraduates admitted to copying a few sentences in written assignments.

Perhaps more significant, the number who believed that copying from the web constitutes "serious cheating" is declining — to 29 percent on average in recent surveys from 34 percent earlier in the decade.

Sarah Brookover, a senior at the Rutgers campus in Camden, N.J., said many of her classmates blithely cut and paste without attribution.

"This generation has always existed in a world where media and intellectual property don't have the same gravity," said Ms. Brookover, who at 31 is older than most undergraduates. "When you're sitting at your computer, it's the same machine you've downloaded music with, possibly illegally, the same machine you streamed videos for free that showed on HBO last night."

Ms. Brookover, who works at the campus library, has pondered the differences between researching in the stacks and online. "Because you're not walking into a library, you're not physically holding the article, which takes you closer to 'this doesn't belong to me,'" she said. Online, "everything can belong to you really easily."

A University of Notre Dame anthropologist, Susan D. Blum, disturbed by 15
the high rates of reported plagiarism, set out to understand how students view authorship and the written word, or "texts" in Ms. Blum's academic language.

She conducted her ethnographic research among 234 Notre Dame undergraduates. "Today's students stand at the crossroads of a new way of conceiving texts and the people who create them and who quote them," she wrote last year in the book *My Word!: Plagiarism and College Culture*, published by Cornell University Press.

Ms. Blum argued that student writing exhibits some of the same qualities of pastiche that drive other creative endeavors today — TV shows that constantly reference other shows or rap music that samples from earlier songs.

In an interview, she said the idea of an author whose singular effort creates an original work is rooted in Enlightenment ideas of the individual. It is buttressed by the Western concept of intellectual property rights as secured by copyright law. But both traditions are being challenged.

"Our notion of authorship and originality was born, it flourished, and it may be waning," Ms. Blum said.

She contends that undergraduates are less interested in cultivating a unique 20
and authentic identity — as their 1960s counterparts were — than in trying on many different personas, which the web enables with social networking.

"If you are not so worried about presenting yourself as absolutely unique, then it's O.K. if you say other people's words, it's O.K. if you say things you don't believe, it's O.K. if you write papers you couldn't care less about because they accomplish the task, which is turning something in and getting a grade," Ms. Blum said, voicing student attitudes. "And it's O.K. if you put words out there without getting any credit."

The notion that there might be a new model young person, who freely borrows from the vortex of information to mash up a new creative work, fueled a brief brouhaha earlier this year with Helene Hegemann, a German teenager whose best-selling novel about Berlin club life turned out to include passages lifted from others.

Instead of offering an abject apology, Ms. Hegemann insisted, "There's no such thing as originality anyway, just authenticity." A few critics rose to her defense, and the book remained a finalist for a fiction prize (but did not win).

That theory does not wash with Sarah Wilensky, a senior at Indiana University, who said that relaxing plagiarism standards "does not foster creativity, it fosters laziness."

"You're not coming up with new ideas if you're grabbing and mixing and 25
matching," said Ms. Wilensky, who took aim at Ms. Hegemann in a column in her student newspaper headlined "Generation Plagiarism."

"It may be increasingly accepted, but there are still plenty of creative people — authors and artists and scholars — who are doing original work," Ms. Wilensky said in an interview. "It's kind of an insult that that ideal is gone, and now we're left only to make collages of the work of previous generations."

In the view of Ms. Wilensky, whose writing skills earned her the role of informal editor of other students' papers in her freshman dorm, plagiarism has nothing to do with trendy academic theories.

The main reason it occurs, she said, is because students leave high school unprepared for the intellectual rigors of college writing.

"If you're taught how to closely read sources and synthesize them into your own original argument in middle and high school, you're not going to be tempted to plagiarize in college, and you certainly won't do so unknowingly," she said.

At the University of California, Davis, of the 196 plagiarism cases referred 30
to the disciplinary office last year, a majority did not involve students ignorant of the need to credit the writing of others.

Many times, said Donald J. Dudley, who oversees the discipline office on the campus of 32,000, it was students who intentionally copied — knowing it was wrong — who were "unwilling to engage the writing process."

"Writing is difficult, and doing it well takes time and practice," he said.

And then there was a case that had nothing to do with a younger generation's evolving view of authorship. A student accused of plagiarism came to Mr. Dudley's office with her parents, and the father admitted that he was the one responsible for the plagiarism. The wife assured Mr. Dudley that it would not happen again.

Synthesizing, Quoting, Paraphrasing, and Citing Sources

One of the questions you might ask as you write is, "How many sources do I need?" Your instructor may give you guidance, but exactly when you need to employ the support of other authors is up to you. Synthesis in academic writing refers to the incorporation of sources into your writing. As you develop your arguments, you will want to look at your sources and consider how what they say interacts with your own discussion. Do you see any similarities between what you want to write and what your sources say, or will you need to address why your sources don't see your topic the way you do? Think of your paper as a conversation between you and your sources. As you write, ask yourself where you and your sources agree and disagree, and make sure you account for this in your paper. You might want to ask the following questions: Have I used my sources as evidence to support any claims I'm making? Have I considered any counterarguments? Have I taken care to characterize my sources in a way that is fair and accurate? When I have finished my draft, have I reconsidered my thesis in light of the source material I've used? Do I need to change my thesis to reflect any new discoveries I've made? When you use outside sources, you need to decide how to use them in your own writing. Many writers, unfortunately, simply take a quotation and "drop" it in their own writing. While this may be easy to do, and while it might work as a temporary step when you're drafting an essay, it is not especially satisfying to a reader. The change of voice can be abrupt and downright confusing ("Who is talking now?"), and the lack of a follow-up can lead a reader to assume that you're allowing the quotation to do your work of analyzing for you.

If you plan to quote a source, we recommend that you use what is widely termed a **quote sandwich**: first, you lead into the quote with a transitional **signal phrase** that identifies the author and, ideally, a sense of how it relates to what you've just said. The most often used signal phrase probably is "[Author's name] says. . . .", and that is certainly functional. But you'll gain more mileage if your verb more precisely defines what the author's attitude is (for instance, is the author concurring? Objecting? Illustrating?). For a nifty resource of precise signal phrase verbs, consult a handbook (such as Diana Hacker and Nancy Sommer's *A Writer's Reference*, 9th edition, Bedford, 2018, section MLA3). And, second, follow the quote with your own commentary or analysis. We'll illustrate both steps by showing you paragraph 4 of Neal Gabler's "The Social Networks" (p. 409) with a quote dropped in and then, as he wrote the paragraph, integrated as part of a quote sandwich:

Gabler's paragraph with a dropped quotation:

Do you know who is making this remark? Can you tell why it is included?

> What makes this so remarkable is that it has been happening at a time when it is increasingly difficult to find this kind of deep social interaction anyplace but on TV. "For the first two-thirds of the twentieth century a powerful tide bore Americans into ever deeper engagement in the life of their communities, but a few decades ago — silently, without warning — that tide reversed and we were overtaken by a treacherous current."

Gabler's original paragraph with signal phrase included and start of the next paragraph:

Gabler identifies his source and indicates why it is authoritative, and his own writing ties the paragraph together.

> What makes this so remarkable is that it has been happening at a time when it is increasingly difficult to find this kind of deep social interaction anyplace but on TV. Nearly a decade ago, Harvard professor Robert Putnam observed in his classic *Bowling Alone* that Americans had become more and more disconnected from one another and from their society. As Putnam put it, "For the first two-thirds of the twentieth century a powerful tide bore Americans into ever deeper engagement in the life of their communities, but a few decades ago — silently, without warning — that tide reversed and we were overtaken by a treacherous current." It was a current that pulled Americans apart.
>
> Moreover, the current that Putnam observed has, according to more recent studies, only intensified in the last decade. . . .

In some cases, you may not want to quote your source directly; perhaps the quote would be too long, or there may not be anything distinctive about the writing. Instead, you might want to *paraphrase* your source: you can present the author's ideas in abbreviated form, using *your own* language and style. While not difficult, you do need to be mindful of not using too much of the original's language and even sentence construction, as that could amount to plagiarism (even if you do name the source). We suggest the following process for creating an accurate paraphrase that prevents the risk of copying the source.

1. First, carefully read the section of your source that you want to use one or two times to make sure you understand it. If necessary, check any unfamiliar terms in a dictionary.
2. Then *set the original aside*. This is the most effective way to avoid inadvertent copying!
3. Without looking at the original text, draft your synopsis of the source.
4. Compare the original with your draft for accuracy. If you find you must use some key terms or unfamiliar language in your paraphrase, be sure to quote and cite what you take directly from the source.

Let's say you want to paraphrase briefly Jack Solomon's description of the fundamental contradictions in American advertising as he presents it in paragraphs 2–3 in "Masters of Desire: The Culture of American Advertising" (p. 250). First, try your hand at summarizing these paragraphs, then read the two samples below.

> Sample summary 1: **The contradictory nature of the American notion of equality can be seen in American advertising, where we see appeals to traditional values like family and communal belonging, on the one hand, and social distinction and material rewards on the other.**

Sample summary 2: By suggesting that one can become part of either the privileged few or the ordinary crowd, marketers exploit the two sides of the American character.

One example above is correctly paraphrased, the other uses too much of Solomon's language and thus would be considered plagiarized. Which is the more acceptable version and why? How does your paraphrase compare to both of these samples?

Finally, make sure you have properly documented any sources you use in your papers. When you write an essay and use another author's work — whether you use the author's exact words or paraphrase them — you need to cite that source for your readers. In most humanities courses, writers use the system of documentation developed by the Modern Language Association (MLA). This system indicates a source in two ways: (1) notations that briefly identify the sources in the body of your essay and (2) notations that give fuller bibliographic information about the sources at the end of your essay. The notations for some commonly used types of sources are illustrated in this chapter. For documenting other sources, consult a writing handbook or the *MLA Handbook*, 8th edition (Modern Language Association of America, 2016).

In-Text Citations

In the body of your essay, you should signal to your reader that you've used a source and indicate, in parentheses, where your reader can find the source in your list of works cited. You don't need to repeat the author's name in both your writing and in the parenthetical note.

SOURCE WITH ONE AUTHOR

Patrick Goldstein asserts that "Talk radio has pumped up the volume of our public discourse and created a whole new political language — perhaps the prevailing political language" (16).

SOURCE WITH TWO AUTHORS

Researchers have found it difficult to study biker subcultures because, as one team describes the problem, "it was too dangerous to take issue with outlaws on their own turf" (Hooper and Moore 368).

INDIRECT SOURCE

In discussing the baby mania trend, *Time* claimed, "Career women are opting for pregnancy and they are doing it in style" (qtd. in Faludi 106).

List of Works Cited

At the end of your essay, include a list of all the sources you have cited in parenthetical notations. This list, alphabetized by author, should provide full publication information for each source; you should indicate the date you accessed any undated online sources.

The first line of each entry should begin flush left. Subsequent lines should be indented half an inch (or five spaces) from the left margin. Double-space the entire list, both between and within entries.

Nonelectronic Sources

BOOK BY ONE AUTHOR

Whitehead, Colson. *The Underground Railroad*. Doubleday, 2016.

BOOK BY TWO AUTHORS

Stiglitz, Joseph E., and Bruce C. Greenwald. *Creating a Learning Society: A New Approach to Growth, Development, and Social Progress*. Columbia UP, 2015.

(Note that only the first author's name is reversed.)

BOOK BY THREE OR MORE AUTHORS

Cunningham, Stewart, et al. *Media Economics*. Palgrave Macmillan, 2015.

WORK IN AN ANTHOLOGY

Corbett, Julia B. "A Faint Green Sell: Advertising and the Natural World." *Signs of Life in the U.S.A.: Readings on Popular Culture for Writers*, 9th ed., edited by Sonia Maasik and Jack Solomon, Bedford/St. Martin's, 2018. pp. 209–226.

ARTICLE IN A WEEKLY MAGAZINE

Grossman, Lev. "A Star Is Born." *Time*, 2 Nov. 2015, pp. 30+.

(A plus sign is used to indicate that the article is not printed on consecutive pages; otherwise, a page range should be given: 16–25, for example.)

ARTICLE IN A MONTHLY MAGAZINE

Kunzig, Robert. "The Will to Change." *National Geographic*, Nov. 2015, pp. 32–63.

ARTICLE IN A JOURNAL

Matchie, Thomas. "Law versus Love in *The Round House*." *Midwest Quarterly*, vol. 56, no. 4, Summer 2015, pp. 353–64.

PERSONAL INTERVIEW

Chese, Charlie. Personal interview. 28 Aug. 2020.

ADVERTISEMENT

California Academy of Sciences. *Sunset,* Apr. 2019, p. 18. Advertisement.

Electronic Sources

FILM OR DVD

Scott, Ridley, director. *The Martian*. Performances by Matt Damon, Jessica Chastain, Kristen Wiig, and Kate Mara, Twentieth Century Fox, 2015.

The Lion King. Directed by Jon Favreau, voices by Danny Glover, Beyoncé, Seth Rogen, Amy Sedaris, and James Earl Jones, Disney, 2019.

TELEVISION PROGRAM

Lucky Dog. CBS, 3 Feb. 2020.

SOUND RECORDING

Adele. "Hello." 25, XL, 2015.

EMAIL

Katt, Susie. "Interpreting the Mall." Message to the author. 15 Aug. 2020.

ARTICLE IN AN ONLINE REFERENCE BOOK

Hall, Mark. "Facebook (American Company)." *The Encyclopaedia Britannica,* 30 Nov. 2015, www.britannica.com/topic/Facebook.

ARTICLE IN AN ONLINE JOURNAL

Boetzkes, Amanda. "Resource Systems, the Paradigm of Zero-Waste, and the Desire for Sustenance." *Postmodern Culture,* vol. 26, no. 2, January 2016. Project MUSE, doi:10.1353/pmc.2016.0008.

ARTICLE IN AN ONLINE MAGAZINE

Mele, Nicco, and Neiman Reports. "Television Is Having Its Moment." *Salon,* 14 Nov. 2016, www.salon.com/2016/11/14/television-is-having-its-moment/.

ONLINE BOOK

Euripides. *The Trojan Women*. Translated by Gilbert Murray, Oxford University Press, 1915. *Internet Sacred Text Archive*, 2011, www.sacred-texts.com/cla/eurip/troj_w.htm.

ONLINE POEM

Geisel, Theodor. "Too Many Daves." *The Sneetches and Other Stories*. Random House, 1961. *Poetry Foundation*, 2015, www.poetryfoundation.org/poem/171612.

PROFESSIONAL WEBSITE

National Council of Teachers of English. *National Council of Teachers of English*. 2020, www.ncte.org/.

PERSONAL HOME PAGE

Stallman, Richard. Home page, 2016, stallman.org/.

POSTING TO A DISCUSSION LIST

Yen, Jessica. "Quotations within Parentheses (Study Measures)." *Copyediting-L*, 18 Mar. 2016, list.indiana.edu/sympa/arc/copyediting-l/2016-03/msg00492.html.

ONLINE SCHOLARLY PROJECT

Peter S. Donaldson, director. *MIT Global Shakespeares*. Massachusetts Institute of Technology, 2010. globalshakespeares.mit.edu/#.

WORK FROM A DATABASE SERVICE

Macari, Anne Marie. "Lyric Impulse in a Time of Extinction." *American Poetry Review*, vol. 44, no. 4, July/Aug. 2015, pp. 11–14. *General OneFile*, go.galegroup.com/.

YOUTUBE OR OTHER ONLINE VIDEO

vlogbrothers. "Compassion, Weakness, and the 2016 Election." *YouTube*, 14 Oct. 2016, www.youtube.com/watch?v=BC7JRRlZHHI.

PHOTOGRAPH OR WORK OF ART

Clough, Charles. *January Twenty-First*. 1988–89, Joslyn Art Museum, Omaha, www.joslyn.org/collections-and-exhibitions/permanent-collections/modern-and-contemporary/charles-clough-january-twenty-first/.

Section 1

FOUNDATIONS

Drew Angerer/Getty Images News/Getty Images

1

AMERICAN PARADOX

Culture, Conflict, and Contradiction in the U.S.A.

Operation Varsity Blues

In 2019, federal prosecutors revealed that they had uncovered a vast conspiracy whereby wealthy parents were illicitly gaining admission for their children to a number of exclusive American universities. The alleged means employed included bribery, standardized test-taking manipulation, bogus athletics recruitments, and outright cheating. The accused included two high-profile television stars and a laundry list of successful business executives. Many pleaded guilty before trial, while others refused to bargain, claiming that *they* were the "victims" of The Key — the college admissions consulting service that had facilitated the scheme (which the FBI code-named "Operation Varsity Blues" in a cute allusion to the 1999 movie) since 2011. But whatever the outcome in the trials to come, the true victims of the scandal were the American people, who were rudely awakened to a contradiction that has always lain at the heart of the American dream and that they had often denied: America's promise of a level playing field for all who seek success through hard work and personal merit simply isn't true.

At a time when economic inequality in America had risen to levels not seen since the Gilded Age, and when the economic "recovery" from the Great Recession had benefited only a small fraction of the population, the shock wave caused by the admissions scandal was entirely understandable. Equally understandable was the fact that so many Americans were unaware that the rich have long enjoyed perfectly legal ways of getting their children into elite universities, from the common practice of "legacy" admissions to the correlation between very large donations to a university and the matriculation of a family member — not to mention the role that attendance at expensive private high schools plays in the college admissions game. It was understandable because Americans have long had a blind spot when it comes to the role of social class in their lives, reflecting the conviction that the United States is a land of equal opportunity and social mobility, and that one's class, accordingly, is a matter of personal choice rather than birth. An example of American "exceptionalism" (that is, the assurance that America, alone among all nations, has effectively solved the class problem), this belief constitutes one of America's most fundamental **mythologies**, and, like all mythologies, it is contradicted again and again in our everyday lives.

This chapter is designed to alert you to the contradictions that are inherent in the mythologies that shape our consciousness as Americans and that often arise when simultaneously held mythologies conflict with each other. We place it first in this book because of the essential role that an awareness of such contradictions plays in performing semiotic analyses of popular culture. While you will not find such contradictions in all the topics you analyze, you should be on the lookout for them, especially because of the way they contribute to a division of the country into hostile camps, whose conflicting values can be found reflected throughout our culture.

Six Contradictions That Count

We can begin our exploration of American contradictions with a list of six especially significant ones. Although additional cultural contradictions exist (can you think of any?), these six constitute the most prominent in the current political and popular cultural scene. And although they can often be found intermixing with each other in confoundedly complicated ways, we can categorize and describe them each as follows:

1. America's contradictory history of religious spiritualism alongside capitalistic materialism.
2. America's contradictory history of Puritanical sexual repression alongside sexual commodification.
3. America's contradictory history of self-reliant individualism alongside mass cultural consumerist conformism.
4. America's contradictory history of egalitarian populism alongside socioeconomic elitism.
5. America's contradictory history of personal liberty alongside chattel slavery and its legacy.
6. America's contradictory history as a land of immigrants alongside anti-immigrant nativism.

Exploring the Signs of American Paradox

In your journal brainstorm a list of American contradictions beyond those that are explored in the introduction to this chapter. How do they affect American cultural and political life? How, in your opinion, did they originate?

Dying for Dollars: The Oxymoron of America's Spiritual Materialism

Our exploration of America's prime contradictions starts with an event that occurred in October 2009, when James Arthur Ray, a self-help guru whose books and seminars promised material well-being and financial success to those who followed his own particular brand of New Age philosophy, conducted one of his "Spiritual Warrior" retreats in the Arizona desert. This retreat included fasting, isolation, and a culminating sweat lodge ritual that resulted in the deaths of three people who had each paid upward of $10,000 to participate. The ensuing fallout from the disaster led to a prison term for Ray, as well as to the destruction of his business empire. It also constituted a striking example of the ways in which Americans tend to mix up their spiritual aspirations with money worship.

Adapting spiritual practices to materialistic ends is a strikingly American tradition that can be explained by the dual trajectories of our nation's founding. Combining the spiritual strivings of the Massachusetts Bay Puritans — who sought to build a sanctified "City upon a Hill" in the New World — and the get-rich-quick goals of the Virginia Company of London — which underwrote the settlement at Jamestown — American history has always involved a paradoxical coexistence of spiritual aspirations and profit motives. This contradiction is also expressed within the terms of what sociologist Max Weber first called the "Protestant Work Ethic," which derived from the Calvinistic belief that hard work and financial success in the material world could be taken as a sign of divine election, and which still can be found reflected in such how-to-succeed-in-business books as Angus MacFarlane's and John R. Colt's *Jesus Christ: Millionaire, Entrepreneur, CEO*. But if you truly want to grasp the contradiction, consider the American interpretation of Christmas, which has managed to commercialize even Dr. Seuss's futile effort to restore the spiritual significance of the holiday by creating an entire franchise of Grinch movies and toys.

It is in this context that we can understand how Americans can spend enormous amounts of money to attend spiritual retreats designed to help them be successful and make enormous amounts of money. Or how the Tea

TIMOTHY A. CLARY/AFP/Getty Images

A barge promoting the film *The Grinch* floats down the East River in New York City.

Party could bring together evangelical Christians and tax protesters to eventually elect an American president. And it can also help us understand how Americans who may be outraged by the public display of human sexuality can create beauty pageants for six-year-old girls, as we discuss in the section that follows.

Toddlers and Tiaras: Sexual Repression Meets the Profit Motive

Prior to the sexual revolution of the 1960s and 1970s, the prevailing sexual mythology in America could be characterized as one of modesty and repression. Clearly reflected in Hollywood's Hays Code, which restricted the sexual content of movies from the 1930s onward, this Puritanical streak in the American character led many people to disapprove of the sexual energy of rock-and-roll in the 1950s and, notoriously, caused broadcasters to film Elvis Presley from the waist up when he first performed on *The Ed Sullivan Show* (they objected to the King's vigorous pelvic gyrations). Within the terms of this mythology, humanity's fundamental sexual instincts must be controlled through prohibitions on premarital sex and channeled into state-approved heterosexual marital relationships, like Rob and Laura Petrie's in *The Dick Van Dyke Show,* whose stars go to sleep at night buttoned up from head to toe in their pajamas — and in separate beds.

But in the wake of the "Summer of Love" in 1967, a sexual revolution swept America, one that tipped the balance toward an ever-freer expression of sexuality in popular culture and everyday life, while instigating a social and political backlash that has animated American politics from the days of the Moral Majority in the 1970s and 1980s to the present. In the midst of this conflict between two sexual **ideologies** — the one oppressive and the other expressive — we can find the paradoxical existence of such TV programs as TLC's on-again/off-again/on-again/off-again *Toddlers and Tiaras*, which offers a striking example of just how tangled up America's contradictions can become, because the core audience for such pageants, which blatantly sexualize little girls, tends to be dominated by family-oriented women who would otherwise disapprove of the public display of human sexuality. But this paradox can be explained by the fact that beauty contests for children can make money, injecting into the picture a capitalist element that tends to go hand-in-hand with a family-values-oriented ideology. And so we find the sexual mythology of American Puritanism being outweighed by the profit motive of American capitalism through the commodification of adults objectifying and projecting ideas of sexuality onto children.

The commodification of sexuality in America, of course, goes far beyond such phenomena as toddler beauty pageants: it permeates our entire popular culture (can you spell "Kardashian"?). And with America's modern-day Puritans tending to be avid supporters of laissez-faire capitalism, their opposition to overt sexual expression in popular culture has been declining over the years (at least with respect to *heterosexual* expression). The striking **difference**, then, between the sexually repressive 1950s and the sexually commodified present is thus a sign of a steady decline in the moral authority of America's traditional Puritanism in favor of untrammeled sexual profiteering.

The Pokémon Paradox: Individualism in a Mass Consumer Society

Then there is the contradiction between America's proud tradition of self-reliant individualism and its total immersion in mass consumption. A striking signifier of this conflict can be found in an announcement, which ran in the *Concord Journal* during the 2016 *Pokémon Go* craze, that the town fire station had been designated as a *Pokémon Go* character location. Taken by itself, this was hardly significant; after all, with the release of the wildly popular augmented reality game, the entire world had been populated with Pokémon awaiting capture at innumerable gaming sites. But what made this site significant was its address: 209 Walden Street, Concord, Massachusetts, a location less than a mile from both Walden Pond and the Old North Bridge — the former location a living symbol of one of America's greatest experiments in self-reliant individualism, and the latter being the site where Emerson's "shot

Discussing the Signs of American Paradox

In class discuss the "Six Contradictions That Count" and explore further the ways in which they have framed American history. Have some contradictions been more prominent at different times, or in different places? Which seem to be the most significant today?

heard round the world" effectively inaugurated the American Revolution. This is to say, 209 Walden Street happens to share the name of the quiet pond that a young Concord eccentric named Henry David Thoreau made famous over a century and half ago, exemplifying thereby a proudly individualistic tradition that — in the century before Thoreau — played a major role in the decisions that led to the colonists' firing on British soldiers at the Old North Bridge, which, in turn, led to the founding of the United States of America.

This heritage of American individualism stands in contrast to such phenomena as *Pokémon Go*, a digitally mass-produced game designed to be simultaneously played by millions and millions of players in a gigantic act of mass consumption. Henry David Thoreau would not have played *Pokémon Go*: After all, he was the man who encouraged others to march to the music of a different drummer. Paradoxically, however, with Americans still cherishing their self-reliant traditions, mass consumption itself can be marketed as an expression of individualistic independence. As an old advertising slogan for a producer of mass-produced sneakers puts it, "Reeboks Let U.B.U."

The 1 Percent: American Populism versus Economic Elitism

Our fourth contradiction can be dramatically illustrated by Donald Trump's successful campaign for the presidency in 2016, whereby a self-proclaimed billionaire became the voice of working- and middle-class voters who felt left behind by the American dream. This paradoxical development was compounded by the fact that, by 2016, the socioeconomic divide in America between rich and poor, 1 percent and 99 percent, upper/upper-middle class and everyone else, had been widening to Grand Canyon proportions in the post–Great Recession lead-up to the campaign. Thus, even as the American middle and lower-middle classes appeared to be moving ever closer to the brink of extinction, a large swath of that demographic was voting Trump.

The explanation for this paradox is, as in so many other cases, **overdetermined**, involving racial as well as economic components (we'll get back to racial issues in a moment). But for now, we can see how the paradox of the Trump constituency reflects a fundamental contradiction in American society that has always juxtaposed such egalitarian values as Abraham Lincoln's evocation of a society "of the people, by the people, and for the people" with a competitive success ethic that urges us to rise above the crowd and go for the gold as if America was simply an unending episode of *Shark Tank*. Guided by the American dream and the mythology of American "exceptionalism," Americans have tended to ignore, or even deny, that permanent class inequality exists in this country. Believing in social mobility, Americans have seen society as a kind of moving escalator, not a tiered set of fixed social classes.

The Great Recession has done much to shatter that old complacency, and both the Democratic and Republican parties have experienced internal insurgencies reflecting a growing resentment against a society that has been tipped ever further in favor of the ruling class. So it is ironic that an essentially populist insurgency came to be led by a billionaire real estate developer—ironic but hardly unprecedented, as can be seen by the way that the nineteenth-century eruption of Jacksonian democracy was borne on the shoulders of a plantation-owning aristocrat. And before Donald Trump, there was the late Ross Perot, a billionaire technology entrepreneur who led a populist ticket in two runs for the presidency in the 1990s.

Such ironies are reflections of the paradoxical love/hate perspective on extreme wealth that Americans share. On the one hand, riches are the goal of the American dream, the pot of gold at the end of a Horatio-Algerian rainbow. On the other hand, money, Americans believe, corrupts, and absolute money corrupts absolutely. It was F. Scott Fitzgerald's clear-eyed recognition of this paradox that has made *The Great Gatsby* one of the most popular, and profitable, novels of all time.

But beyond the paradoxes of plutocratic populism lies the fact that Andrew Jackson was a *slave-owning* aristocrat, and it is no longer possible to deny the role of race in the rise of Donald Trump to political power. This brings us to the fifth of our fundamental American contradictions.

Oscars So White: The Enduring Legacy of Slavery

When Spike Lee launched the Oscar boycott heard 'round the Academy in 2016, his was but one of many expressions of racial frustration in the land, spurred on by a sequence of shootings that included such now-famous victims as Trayvon Martin and Michael Brown, and the massacre at the Emanuel African Methodist Episcopal Church in Charleston, South Carolina. Squelching the hope that the 2008 election of Barack Obama signaled the beginning of a "postracial" society, this resurgence of racial conflict was expressed not only by the rise of such movements as Black Lives Matter but also by the support of many white voters for Donald Trump, whom they saw as their voice in an increasingly divided America—a political development whose racial implications were difficult to ignore in the light of Trump's failure to condemn unequivocally the 2017 Unite the Right rally in Charlottesville, Virginia.

But once again America had been there before, in fact has always been there — precisely because of what is probably the most profound contradiction of all in our history: the fact that while we are a nation founded on the principle of universal human liberty, many of the men who declared that principle in 1776 were slave owners who wrote slavery into the Constitution. Four score and seven years later, the nation was in the midst of a Civil War because of this unresolved contradiction, a racial dissociation that is now roiling America in ways that go beyond the legacies of slavery to a conflict over the racial identity of the nation as a whole.

The Statutes of Liberty: Immigration Controversy in the Land of Immigrants

Which brings us to our sixth contradiction. The racial reverberations of the Trump campaign were related less to the history of slavery than they were to the controversies over Latin American and Muslim immigration. But this too was hardly new in a nation of immigrants that has always experienced nativistic opposition to immigration. Today, when all people of European descent are regarded as being of the same race, it's hard to fathom how race could have had anything to do with American opposition to Irish, German, eastern European, and southern European immigrants in the nineteenth century. But race was, indeed, at the heart of the matter. Anglo Saxons in America felt themselves to be racially superior to Irish, German, Italian, Greek, Polish, Jewish, and Estonian immigrants, indeed, to any Europeans from non-northwestern European countries, just as anti-immigrant sentiment today cannot be divided from racial attitudes toward Asian, Latin American, and Middle Eastern newcomers. In short, here is another case where different cultural contradictions get tangled up together, with our racial history playing a direct role in our paradoxical immigrant history, and the two histories together producing volatile social conditions and conflicts.

As you contemplate the cultural contradictions that we have been discussing so far, you may be thinking that while they are national in scope, they are regional in expression. That is, one side of the various controversies that erupt from these cultural contradictions tends to be espoused by people in one part of

Reading American Paradox Online

Research the websites of organizations with explicit political commitments that reflect the cultural contradictions explored in this chapter (for example the Daily Kos, Change.org, Black Lives Matter, the Daily Caller, or LegalInsurrection.com). What do they tell us about the divisions in America today? Can you find any possibility of bridging the gap between them? If so, how? If not, why not?

the country, while the other side is championed by people in another. You know what these two regions are: they are "red state" and "blue state" America.

What's Red and Blue and Mad All Over?

Long before the Trump era brought the whole matter into the open, the political legacy of our many cultural contradictions was already visible in the red state/blue state electoral divide that was first officially noted after the 2000 presidential election. At the time, electoral maps coded the states that voted Republican in red and the states that voted Democratic in blue. Since then, it has become common to refer to "red state" and "blue state" regions of America, with the former generally holding conservative views, and the latter identified as liberal or progressive. Although these terms run the risk of stereotyping, and it should be noted that there are "red" sectors within blue states (like California's Central Valley) and "blue" areas in red states (like the greater Austin area of Texas), red and blue states do tend to take different sides in America's cultural and ideological conflicts, reflecting their opposing positions on several fundamental American values.

These differences are readily apparent in our popular culture. Consider such dichotomies in the world of popular music as hip-hop versus country, or rhythm-and-blues versus heavy metal. In television, the split between the Fox News network and MSNBC viewers is notorious, and when it was still on the air *Duck Dynasty* spoke for many red state Americans even as *The Daily Show* spoke (and continues to speak) for blue states. It's easy to take such oppositions for granted, but they have not always been the norm in American media and entertainment. In the ideologically divided 1960s, for example, the majority of Americans still watched the same national news programs (with Walter Cronkite assuming the status of an avuncular Anchorman-in-Chief), the same TV shows (on just three major networks), and listened to radio stations whose formats included everything from the Beatles to the Beach Boys, Sinatra to the Supremes, acid rock to soul, and Jimi Hendrix to Bobbie Gentry. Now, by contrast, in the niche-marketed world of modern entertainment, not only do consumers have innumerable media choices tailored to their personal tastes, they can also customize their consumption according to their ideological preferences, creating self-confirming echo chambers that ensure that they never have to listen to anyone with whom they disagree.

The outcome of such choices is that popular culture does not simply reflect the conflicts and contradictions in American society; it amplifies them. With the two leading political parties growing further and further apart, their voters hold not only different ideological values but different visions of just what America is. The land whose motto has long been *e pluribus unum* is becoming a site of irreconcilable discord and division. And there is little-to-no likelihood that popular culture will be able to harmonize the dissonant chords within our country today when it is so much more profitable to exacerbate them.

The Readings

Barbara Ehrenreich opens this chapter with an explanation of how America's essential optimism is often in contradiction to the realities that get us into trouble. George Packer is next with a trenchant look at today's celebrities, an exclusive "superclass" of entertainers and corporate executives whose cultural and economic power stands in blatant contrast to America's egalitarian values. Voicing a warning note, Mark Manson then addresses the emerging hunger for success in America, one that all too often results in a paradoxical state of *dis*-satisfaction. Mark Murphy's reflections on the way that America's cultural and ideological divisions can explode even in a physician's waiting room follows, while Alfred Lubrano's exploration of the personal disruptions experienced when moving out of the working class through higher education illuminates one of the most neglected contradictions within our class-based society. Mariah Burton Nelson's essay on the predicament of women athletes points out the mixed cultural pressures that women must negotiate when they enter the world of competitive sport. Wade Graham concludes the chapter with Americans' contradictory attitudes toward the natural world, wherein "green cities" are planned that are little more than "technologically controlled version[s] of nature."

BARBARA EHRENREICH

Bright-Sided

Americans, as a rule, tend to look on the bright side of things, cherishing an essential optimism that has made America a fertile breeding ground for visionaries and entrepreneurs. But being blind to the dark side of reality — the risks and dangers that can upset the sunniest of plans — can cause us to be "bright-sided" by them, in Barbara Ehrenreich's memorable phrase, like a quarterback who didn't see that defensive tackle approaching. And so it was for America between 2001 and 2006, when home buyers, bankers, and investors alike saw nothing but a future of ever-increasing home values, only to hit the dirt in a crushing recession, the effects of which continue to plague us to this day. Not wishing to cast a cloud on America's sunny disposition, Ehrenreich nevertheless believes that America could be a better, indeed happier, place, if it can only "recover from the mass delusion that is positive thinking." Barbara Ehrenreich is a social analyst and the author of many books, including *Bright-Sided: How the Relentless Promotion of Positive Thinking Is Undermining America* (2009), from which this selection is taken.

Americans are a "positive" people. This is our reputation as well as our self-image. We smile a lot and are often baffled when people from other cultures do not return the favor. In the well-worn stereotype, we are upbeat, cheerful, optimistic, and shallow, while foreigners are likely to be subtle, world-weary, and possibly decadent. American expatriate writers like Henry James and James Baldwin wrestled with and occasionally reinforced this stereotype, which I once encountered in the 1980s in the form of a remark by Soviet émigré poet Joseph Brodsky to the effect that the problem with Americans is that they have "never known suffering." (Apparently he didn't know who had invented the blues.) Whether we Americans see it as an embarrassment or a point of pride, being positive — in affect, in mood, in outlook — seems to be engrained in our national character.

Who would be churlish or disaffected enough to challenge these happy features of the American personality? Take the business of positive "affect," which refers to the mood we display to others through our smiles, our greetings, our professions of confidence and optimism. Scientists have found that the mere act of smiling can generate positive feelings within us, at least if the smile is not forced. In addition, good feelings, as expressed through our words and smiles, seem to be contagious: "Smile and the world smiles with you." Surely the world would be a better, happier place if we all greeted one another warmly and stopped to coax smiles from babies — if only through the well-known social psychological mechanism of "mood contagion." Recent studies show that happy feelings flit easily through social networks, so that one person's good fortune can brighten the day even for only distantly connected others.[1]

Furthermore, psychologists today agree that positive feelings like gratitude, contentment, and self-confidence can actually lengthen our lives and improve our health. Some of these claims are exaggerated, as we shall see, though positive feelings hardly need to be justified, like exercise or vitamin supplements, as part of a healthy lifestyle. People who report having positive feelings are more likely to participate in a rich social life, and vice versa, and social connectedness turns out to be an important defense against depression, which is a known risk factor for many physical illnesses. At the risk of redundancy or even tautology, we can say that on many levels, individual and social, it is *good* to be "positive," certainly better than being withdrawn, aggrieved, or chronically sad.

So I take it as a sign of progress that, in just the last decade or so, economists have begun to show an interest in using happiness rather than just the gross national product as a measure of an economy's success. Happiness is, of course, a slippery thing to measure or define. Philosophers have debated what it is for centuries, and even if we were to define it simply as a greater frequency of positive feelings than negative ones, when we ask people if they are happy we are asking them to arrive at some sort of average over many moods and moments. Maybe I was upset earlier in the day but then was cheered up by a bit of good news, so what am I really? In one well-known psychological experiment, subjects were asked to answer a questionnaire on life satisfaction — but only after they had performed the apparently irrelevant task of photocopying a sheet of paper for the experimenter. For a randomly chosen half of the subjects, a dime had been left for them to find on the copy machine. As two economists summarize the results, "Reported satisfaction with life was raised substantially, by the discovery of the coin on the copy machine — clearly not an income effect."[2]

5 In addition to the problems of measurement, there are cultural differences in how happiness is regarded and whether it is even seen as a virtue. Some cultures, like our own, value the positive affect that seems to signal internal happiness; others are more impressed by seriousness, self-sacrifice, or a quiet willingness to cooperate. However hard to pin down, though, happiness is somehow a more pertinent metric for well-being, from a humanistic perspective, than the buzz of transactions that constitute the GDP.

Surprisingly, when psychologists undertake to measure the relative happiness of nations, they routinely find that Americans are not, even in prosperous

[1]"Happiness Is 'Infectious' in Network of Friends: Collective — Not Just Individual — Phenomenon," *ScienceDaily*, Dec. 5, 2008, sciencedaily.com/releases/2008/12/081205094506.htm.

[2]Daniel Kahneman and Alan B. Krueger, "Developments in the Measurement of Subjective Well-Being," *Journal of Economic Perspectives*, 20 (2006): 3–24.

times and despite our vaunted positivity, very happy at all. A recent meta-analysis of over a hundred studies of self-reported happiness worldwide found Americans ranking only twenty-third, surpassed by the Dutch, the Danes, the Malaysians, the Bahamians, the Austrians, and even the supposedly dour Finns.[3] In another potential sign of relative distress, Americans account for two-thirds of the global market for antidepressants, which happen also to be the most commonly prescribed drugs in the United States. To my knowledge, no one knows how antidepressant use affects people's responses to happiness surveys: Do respondents report being happy because the drugs make them feel happy or do they report being unhappy because they know they are dependent on drugs to make them feel better? Without our heavy use of antidepressants, Americans would likely rank far lower in the happiness rankings than we currently do.

When economists attempt to rank nations more objectively in terms of "well-being," taking into account such factors as health, environmental sustainability, and the possibility of upward mobility, the United States does even more poorly than it does when only the subjective state of "happiness" is measured. The Happy Planet Index, to give just one example, locates us at 150th among the world's nations.[4]

How can we be so surpassingly "positive" in self-image and stereotype without being the world's happiest and best-off people? The answer, I think, is that positivity is not so much our condition or our mood as it is part of our ideology — the way we explain the world and think we ought to function within it. That ideology is "positive thinking," by which we usually mean two things. One is the generic content of positive thinking — that is, the positive thought itself — which can be summarized as: Things are pretty good right now, at least if you are willing to see silver linings, make lemonade out of lemons, etc., and things are going to get a whole lot better. This is optimism, and it is not the same as hope. Hope is an emotion, a yearning, the experience of which is not entirely within our control. Optimism is a cognitive stance, a conscious expectation, which presumably anyone can develop through practice.

The second thing we mean by "positive thinking" is this practice, or discipline, of trying to think in a positive way. There is, we are told, a practical reason for undertaking this effort: Positive thinking supposedly not only makes us feel optimistic but actually makes happy outcomes more likely. If you expect things to get better, they will. How can the mere process of thinking do this? In the rational explanation that many psychologists would offer today, optimism improves health, personal efficacy, confidence, and resilience, making it easier for us to accomplish our goals. A far less rational theory also runs rampant in American ideology — the idea that our thoughts can, in some mysterious

[3]"Psychologist Produces the First-Ever 'World Map of Happiness,'" *ScienceDaily*, Nov. 14, 2006, sciencedaily.com/releases/2006/11/061113093726.htm.

[4]rankingamerica.wordpress.com/2009/01/11/the-us-ranks-150th-in-planet-happiness/, Jan. 11, 2009.

way, directly affect the physical world. Negative thoughts somehow produce negative outcomes, while positive thoughts realize themselves in the form of health, prosperity, and success. For both rational and mystical reasons, then, the effort of positive thinking is said to be well worth our time and attention, whether this means reading the relevant books, attending seminars and speeches that offer the appropriate mental training, or just doing the solitary work of concentration on desired outcomes — a better job, an attractive mate, world peace.

There is an anxiety, as you can see, right here in the heart of American 10
positive thinking. If the generic "positive thought" is correct and things are really getting better, if the arc of the universe tends toward happiness and abundance, then why bother with the mental effort of positive thinking? Obviously, because we do not fully believe that things will get better on their own. The practice of positive thinking is an effort to pump up this belief in the face of much contradictory evidence. Those who set themselves up as instructors in the discipline of positive thinking — coaches, preachers, and gurus of various sorts — have described this effort with terms like "self-hypnosis," "mind control," and "thought control." In other words, it requires deliberate self-deception, including a constant effort to repress or block out unpleasant possibilities and "negative" thoughts. The truly self-confident, or those who have in some way made their peace with the world and their destiny within it, do not need to expend effort censoring or otherwise controlling their thoughts. Positive thinking may be a quintessentially American activity, associated in our minds with both individual and national success, but it is driven by a terrible insecurity.

Americans did not start out as positive thinkers — at least the promotion of unwarranted optimism and methods to achieve it did not really find articulation and organized form until several decades after the founding of the republic. In the Declaration of Independence, the Founding Fathers pledged to one another "our lives, our fortunes, and our sacred honor." They knew that they had no certainty of winning a war for independence and that they were taking a mortal risk. Just the act of signing the declaration made them all traitors to the crown, and treason was a crime punishable by execution. Many of them did go on to lose their lives, loved ones, and fortunes in the war. The point is, they fought anyway. There is a vast difference between positive thinking and existential courage.

Systematic positive thinking began, in the nineteenth century, among a diverse and fascinating collection of philosophers, mystics, lay healers, and middle-class women. By the twentieth century, though, it had gone mainstream, gaining purchase within such powerful belief systems as nationalism and also doing its best to make itself indispensable to capitalism. We don't usually talk about American nationalism, but it is a mark of how deep it runs that we apply the word "nationalism" to Serbs, Russians, and others, while believing ourselves to possess a uniquely superior version called "patriotism." A central tenet of American nationalism has been the belief that the United

States is "the greatest nation on earth" — more dynamic, democratic, and prosperous than any other nation, as well as technologically superior. Major religious leaders, especially on the Christian right, buttress this conceit with the notion that Americans are God's chosen people and that America is the designated leader of the world — an idea that seemed to find vivid reinforcement in the fall of Communism and our emergence as the world's "lone superpower." That acute British observer Godfrey Hodgson has written that the American sense of exceptionalism, which once was "idealistic and generous, if somewhat solipsistic," has become "harder, more hubristic." Paul Krugman responded to the prevailing smugness in a 1998 essay entitled "America the Boastful," warning that "if pride goeth before a fall, the United States has one heck of a come-uppance in store."[5]

But of course it takes the effort of positive thinking to imagine that America is the "best" or the "greatest." Militarily, yes, we are the mightiest nation on earth. But on many other fronts, the American score is dismal, and was dismal even before the economic downturn that began in 2007. Our children routinely turn out to be more ignorant of basic subjects like math and geography than their counterparts in other industrialized nations. They are also more likely to die in infancy or grow up in poverty. Almost everyone acknowledges that our health care system is "broken" and our physical infrastructure crumbling. We have lost so much of our edge in science and technology that American companies have even begun to outsource their research and development efforts. Worse, some of the measures by which we do lead the world should inspire embarrassment rather than pride: We have the highest percentage of our population incarcerated, and the greatest level of inequality in wealth and income. We are plagued by gun violence and racked by personal debt.

While positive thinking has reinforced and found reinforcement in American national pride, it has also entered into a kind of symbiotic relationship with American capitalism. There is no natural, innate affinity between capitalism and positive thinking. In fact, one of the classics of sociology, Max Weber's *Protestant Ethic and the Spirit of Capitalism*, makes a still impressive case for capitalism's roots in the grim and punitive outlook of Calvinist Protestantism, which required people to defer gratification and resist all pleasurable temptations in favor of hard work and the accumulation of wealth.

15 But if early capitalism was inhospitable to positive thinking, "late" capitalism, or consumer capitalism, is far more congenial, depending as it does on the individual's hunger for *more* and the firm's imperative of *growth*. The consumer culture encourages individuals to want more — cars, larger homes, television sets, cell phones, gadgets of all kinds — and positive thinking is ready at hand to tell them they deserve more and can have it if they really want it and are willing to make the effort to get it. Meanwhile, in a competitive

[5]Godfrey Hodgson, *The Myth of American Exceptionalism* (New Haven: Yale University Press, 2009), 113; Paul Krugman, "America the Boastful," *Foreign Affairs*, May–June 1998.

business world, the companies that manufacture these goods and provide the paychecks that purchase them have no alternative but to grow. If you don't steadily increase market share and profits, you risk being driven out of business or swallowed by a larger enterprise. Perpetual growth, whether of a particular company or an entire economy, is of course an absurdity, but positive thinking makes it seem possible, if not ordained.

In addition, positive thinking has made itself useful as an apology for the crueler aspects of the market economy. If optimism is the key to material success, and if you can achieve an optimistic outlook through the discipline of positive thinking, then there is no excuse for failure. The flip side of positivity is thus a harsh insistence on personal responsibility: If your business fails or your job is eliminated, it must be because you didn't try hard enough, didn't believe firmly enough in the inevitability of your success. As the economy has brought more layoffs and financial turbulence to the middle class, the promoters of positive thinking have increasingly emphasized this negative judgment: to be disappointed, resentful, or downcast is to be a "victim" and a "whiner."

But positive thinking is not only a water carrier for the business world, excusing its excesses and masking its follies. The promotion of positive thinking has become a minor industry in its own right, producing an endless flow of books, DVDs, and other products; providing employment for tens of thousands of "life coaches," "executive coaches," and motivational speakers, as well as for the growing cadre of professional psychologists who seek to train them. No doubt the growing financial insecurity of the middle class contributes to the demand for these products and services, but I hesitate to attribute the commercial success of positive thinking to any particular economic trend or twist of the business cycle. America has historically offered space for all sorts of sects, cults, faith healers, and purveyors of snake oil, and those that are profitable, like positive thinking, tend to flourish.

At the turn of the twenty-first century, American optimism seemed to reach a manic crescendo. In his final State of the Union address in 2000, Bill Clinton struck a triumphal note, proclaiming that "never before has our nation enjoyed, at once, so much prosperity and social progress with so little internal crisis and so few external threats." But compared with his successor, Clinton seemed almost morose. George W. Bush had been a cheerleader in prep school, and cheerleading — a distinctly American innovation — could be considered the athletically inclined ancestor of so much of the coaching and "motivating" that has gone into the propagation of positive thinking. He took the presidency as an opportunity to continue in that line of work, defining his job as that of inspiring confidence, dispelling doubts, and pumping up the national spirit of self-congratulation. If he repeatedly laid claim to a single adjective, it was "optimistic." On the occasion of his sixtieth birthday, he told reporters he was "optimistic" about a variety of foreign policy challenges, offering as an overview, "I'm optimistic that all problems will be solved." Nor did he brook any doubts or hesitations among his close advisers. According to Bob Woodward, Condoleezza Rice failed to express some of her worries because, she said, "the president almost demanded optimism. He didn't like pessimism, hand-wringing or doubt."[6]

Then things began to go wrong, which is not in itself unusual but was a possibility excluded by America's official belief that things are good and getting better. There was the dot-com bust that began a few months after Clinton's declaration of unprecedented prosperity in his final State of the Union address, then the terrorist attack of September 11, 2001. Furthermore, things began to go wrong in a way that suggested that positive thinking might not guarantee success after all, that it might in fact dim our ability to fend off real threats. In her remarkable book, *Never Saw It Coming: Cultural Challenges to Envisioning the Worst*, sociologist Karen Cerulo recounts a number of ways that the habit of positive thinking, or what she calls optimistic bias, undermined preparedness and invited disaster. She quotes *Newsweek* reporters Michael Hirsch and Michael Isikoff, for example, in their conclusion that "a whole summer of missed clues, taken together, seemed to presage the terrible September of 2001."[7] There had already been a terrorist attack on the World Trade Center in 1993; there were ample warnings, in the summer of 2001, about a possible attack by airplane, and flight schools reported suspicious students like the one who wanted to learn how to "fly a plane but didn't care about landing and takeoff." The fact that no one — the FBI, the INS, Bush, or Rice — heeded these disturbing cues was later attributed to a "failure of imagination." But actually there was plenty of imagination at work — imagining an invulnerable nation and an ever-booming economy — there was simply no ability or inclination to imagine the worst.

A similar reckless optimism pervaded the American invasion of Iraq. 20
Warnings about possible Iraqi resistance were swept aside by leaders who promised a "cakewalk" and envisioned cheering locals greeting our troops with flowers. Likewise, Hurricane Katrina was not exactly an unanticipated disaster. In 2002, the New Orleans *Times-Picayune* ran a Pulitzer Prize–winning series warning that the city's levees could not protect it against the storm surge brought on by a category 4 or 5 hurricane. In 2001, *Scientific*

[6]2000 State of the Union Address, Jan. 27, 2000, washingtonpost.com/wpsrv/politics/special/states/docs/sou00.htm; Geoff Elliott, "Dubya's 60th Takes the Cake," *Weekend Australian*, July 8, 2006; Woodward, quoting Rice, Meet the Press transcript, Dec. 21, 2008, today.msnbc.msn.com/id/28337897/.

[7]Quoted in Karen A. Cerulo, *Never Saw It Coming: Cultural Challenges to Envisioning the Worst* (Chicago: University of Chicago Press, 2006), 18.

American had issued a similar warning about the city's vulnerability.[8] Even when the hurricane struck and levees broke, no alarm bells went off in Washington, and when a New Orleans FEMA official sent a panicky email to FEMA director Michael Brown, alerting him to the rising number of deaths and a shortage of food in the drowning city, he was told that Brown would need an hour to eat his dinner in a Baton Rouge restaurant.[9] Criminal negligence or another "failure of imagination"? The truth is that Americans had been working hard for decades to school themselves in the techniques of positive thinking, and these included the reflexive capacity for dismissing disturbing news.

The biggest "come-uppance," to use Krugman's term, has so far been the financial meltdown of 2007 and the ensuing economic crisis. By the late first decade of the twenty-first century, positive thinking had become ubiquitous and virtually unchallenged in American culture. It was promoted on some of the most widely watched talk shows, like *Larry King Live* and the *Oprah Winfrey Show*; it was the stuff of runaway best sellers like the 2006 book *The Secret*; it had been adopted as the theology of America's most successful evangelical preachers; it found a place in medicine as a potential adjuvant to the treatment of almost any disease. It had even penetrated the academy in the form of the new discipline of "positive psychology," offering courses teaching students to pump up their optimism and nurture their positive feelings. And its reach was growing global, first in the Anglophone countries and soon in the rising economies of China, South Korea, and India.

But nowhere did it find a warmer welcome than in American business, which is, of course, also global business. To the extent that positive thinking had become a business itself, business was its principal client, eagerly consuming the good news that all things are possible through an effort of mind. This was a useful message for employees, who by the turn of the twenty-first century were being required to work longer hours for fewer benefits and diminishing job security. But it was also a liberating ideology for top-level executives. What was the point in agonizing over balance sheets and tedious analyses of risks — and why bother worrying about dizzying levels of debt and exposure to potential defaults — when all good things come to those who are optimistic enough to expect them?

I do not write this in a spirit of sourness or personal disappointment of any kind, nor do I have any romantic attachment to suffering as a source of insight or virtue. On the contrary, I would like to see more smiles, more laughter, more hugs, more happiness and, better yet, joy. In my own vision of utopia, there is not only more comfort, and security for everyone — better jobs, health care, and so forth — there are also more parties, festivities, and opportunities for dancing in the streets. Once our basic material needs are met — in my utopia, anyway — life becomes a perpetual celebration in which everyone

[8]Cerulo, *Never Saw It Coming*, 239.

[9]Hope Yen, "Death in Streets Took a Back Seat to Dinner," *Seattle Times*, Oct. 25, 2005.

has a talent to contribute. But we cannot levitate ourselves into that blessed condition by wishing it. We need to brace ourselves for a struggle against terrifying obstacles, both of our own making and imposed by the natural world. And the first step is to recover from the mass delusion that is positive thinking.

Reading the Text

1. What contradictions have psychological studies found between Americans' valuing of happiness and well-being and their actual state of happiness?
2. When did positive thinking begin to be a cultural trait of Americans, according to Ehrenreich?
3. What is the relationship, in Ehrenreich's view, between positive thinking and capitalism?
4. How, according to Ehrenreich, has positive thinking contributed to recent and current American problems and catastrophes?
5. Examine Ehrenreich's rhetorical strategies. Why does she outline, early in her essay, the reasons that a positive attitude can be beneficial? What effect does that discussion have on your response to her essay?

Reading the Signs

1. Conduct a class debate over the proposition that positive thinking has led Americans, especially politicians, to be naïvely optimistic in not anticipating recent national events despite plenty of warning signs. You might focus on the 2015 terrorist attacks in San Bernardino, CA, or pundits' inability to predict that Donald Trump would carry traditionally democratic states like Wisconsin in the 2016 presidential election.
2. **CONNECTING TEXTS** Read or reread Laurence Shames's "The More Factor" (p. 193). Adopting Ehrenreich's argument about Americans' predilection for positive thinking, write an essay in which you explain why "the hunger for more," as Shames puts it, is so prevalent in American culture.
3. **CONNECTING TEXTS** Read or reread Neal Gabler's "The Social Networks" (p. 409), and write an essay in which you argue whether the ever-present friendships and sense of close community that Gabler identifies in some TV shows reflect the sort of positive thinking that Ehrenreich describes. Be sure to base your argument on a close reading of at least one show that Gabler mentions that fits this category of programming.
4. Read Rhonda Byrne's *The Secret* and write an analysis of how it reflects the American cult of positive thinking. Alternatively, do such an analysis of one of the many books in the *Chicken Soup for the Soul* series or Louise L. Hay's *You Can Heal Your Life*.
5. **CONNECTING TEXTS** Adopting Ehrenreich's point of view, enter a conversation with Judith Shulevitz (read " 'Alexa, How Will You Change Us?,' " p. 346) about the role commercially available artificial intelligence devices may play in our future. To what extent would Ehrenreich consider technologies such as Alexa an enhancement of our daily lives, or do you think she would have a different view point?

GEORGE PACKER

Celebrating Inequality

"Our age is lousy with celebrities," George Packer quips in this 2013 essay for the *New York Times*, and it's only getting worse. Indeed, in tough times like today's, when the gap between the rich and the poor yawns ever wider, celebrities loom larger on the social horizon than they have in more equitable times, overshadowing the rest of us. And we're not just talking about entertainers. Indeed, as Packer notes, they include entrepreneurs, bankers, computer engineers, real estate developers, media executives, journalists, politicians, scientists, and even chefs. And as the new celebrity deities gobble up whatever opportunities are left in America, Packer believes, America itself is turning backward to the days of the Jazz Age and Jay Gatsby. So, meet the new celebrity gods; same as the old celebrity gods — or "something far more perverse." George Packer is a writer for the *New Yorker* and *The Atlantic* and the author of numerous books, including the National Book Award–winning *The Unwinding: An Inner History of the New America* (2013).

The Roaring '20s was the decade when modern celebrity was invented in America. F. Scott Fitzgerald's *The Great Gatsby* is full of magazine spreads of tennis players and socialites, popular song lyrics, movie stars, paparazzi, gangsters, and sports scandals — machine-made by technology, advertising, and public relations. Gatsby, a mysterious bootlegger who makes a meteoric ascent from Midwestern obscurity to the palatial splendor of West Egg, exemplifies one part of the celebrity code: it's inherently illicit. Fitzgerald intuited that, with the old restraining deities of the 19th century dead and his generation's faith in man shaken by World War I, celebrities were the new household gods.

What are celebrities, after all? They dominate the landscape, like giant monuments to aspiration, fulfillment, and overreach. They are as intimate as they are grand, and they offer themselves for worship by ordinary people searching for a suitable object of devotion. But in times of widespread opportunity, the distance between gods and mortals closes, the monuments shrink closer to human size, and the centrality of celebrities in the culture recedes. They loom larger in times like now, when inequality is soaring and trust in institutions — governments, corporations, schools, the press — is falling.

The Depression that ended Fitzgerald's Jazz Age yielded to a new order that might be called the Roosevelt Republic. In the quarter-century after World War II, the country established collective structures, not individual monuments, that channeled the aspirations of ordinary people: state universities, progressive taxation, interstate highways, collective bargaining, health insurance for the elderly, credible news organizations.

One virtue of those hated things called bureaucracies is that they oblige everyone to follow a common set of rules, regardless of station or background; they are inherently equalizing. Books like William H. Whyte's *The Organization Man* and C. Wright Mills's *White Collar* warned of the loss of individual identity, but those middle-class anxieties were possible only because of the great leveling. The "stars" continued to fascinate, especially with the arrival of TV, but they were not essential. Henry Fonda, Barbara Stanwyck, Bette Davis, Jimmy Stewart, Perry Como, Joe DiMaggio, Jack Paar, Doris Day, and Dick Clark rose with Americans — not from them — and their successes and screw-ups were a sideshow, not the main event.

5 Our age is lousy with celebrities. They can be found in every sector of society, including ones that seem less than glamorous. We have celebrity bankers (Jamie Dimon), computer engineers (Sergey Brin), real estate developers/conspiracy theorists (Donald J. Trump), media executives (Arianna Huffington), journalists (Anderson Cooper), mayors (Cory A. Booker), economists (Jeffrey D. Sachs), biologists (J. Craig Venter), and chefs (Mario Batali).

There is a quality of self-invention to their rise: Mark Zuckerberg went from awkward geek to the subject of a Hollywood hit; Shawn Carter turned into Jay-Z; Martha Kostyra became Martha Stewart, and then *Martha Stewart Living*. The person evolves into a persona, then a brand, then an empire, with the business imperative of grow or die — a process of expansion and commodification that transgresses boundaries by substituting celebrity for institutions. Instead of robust public education, we have Mr. Zuckerberg's "rescue" of Newark's schools. Instead of a vibrant literary culture, we have Oprah's book club. Instead of investments in public health, we have the Gates Foundation. Celebrities either buy institutions, or "disrupt" them.

After all, if you *are* the institution, you don't need to play by its rules. Mr. Zuckerberg's foundation myth begins with a disciplinary proceeding at Harvard, which leads him to drop out and found a company whose motto is "Move fast and break things." Jay-Z's history as a crack dealer isn't just a hard-luck story — it's celebrated by fans (and not least himself) as an early sign of hustle and smarts. Martha Stewart's jail time for perjury merely proved that her will to win was indomitable. These new celebrities are all more or less start-up entrepreneurs, and they live by the hacker's code: ask forgiveness, not permission.

The obsession with celebrities goes far beyond supermarket tabloids, gossip websites and reality TV. It obliterates old distinctions between high and low culture, serious and trivial endeavors, profit making and philanthropy, leading to the phenomenon of being famous for being famous. An activist singer (Bono) is given a lucrative role in Facebook's initial public offering. A patrician politician (Al Gore) becomes a plutocratic media executive and tech investor. One of America's richest men (Michael R. Bloomberg) rules its largest city.

This jet-setting, Davos-attending crowd constitutes its own superclass, who hang out at the same TED talks, big-idea conferences and fund-raising galas, appear on the same talk shows, invest in one another's projects, wear one another's brand apparel, champion one another's causes, marry and cheat on one another. *The New Digital Age*, the new guide to the future by Eric Schmidt and Jared Cohen of Google, carries blurbs from such technology experts as Henry A. Kissinger and Tony Blair. The inevitable next step is for Kim Kardashian to sit on the board of a tech start-up, host a global-poverty-awareness event, and write a book on behavioral neuroscience.

10 This new kind of celebrity is the ultimate costume ball, far more exclusive and decadent than even the most potent magnates of Hollywood's studio era could have dreamed up. Their superficial diversity dangles before us the myth that in America, anything is possible — even as the American dream quietly dies, a victim of the calcification of a class system that is nearly hereditary.

As mindless diversions from a sluggish economy and chronic malaise, the new aristocrats play a useful role. But their advent suggests that, after decades of widening income gaps, unequal distributions of opportunity and reward, and corroding public institutions, we have gone back to Gatsby's time — or something far more perverse. The celebrity monuments of our age have grown so huge that they dwarf the aspirations of ordinary people, who are asked to yield their dreams to the gods: to flash their favorite singer's corporate logo at concerts, to pour open their lives (and data) on Facebook, to adopt Apple as a lifestyle. We know our stars aren't inviting us to think we can be just like them. Their success is based on leaving the rest of us behind.

Reading the Text

1. In your own words, trace the evolution of the celebrity from the 1920s to the post-World War II era to today, as Packer describes it.
2. What does Packer mean when he asserts that today a celebrity "evolves into a persona, then a brand, then an empire, with the business imperative of grow or die" (para. 6)?
3. Why does Packer consider today's celebrities their "own superclass" (para. 9)?
4. What relation does Packer find between the plethora of celebrities today and economic conditions?
5. Why does Packer say that America today is returning to the ethos of the Jazz Age (or, perhaps, becoming even worse)?

Reading the Signs

1. In class, discuss the meanings of the words *celebrities* and *heroes*. Using that conversation as a starting point, write an essay that argues for your own definition of the two terms, taking care to delineate distinctions between them. Be sure to ground your discussion in real-life examples of both categories, as Packer does in his essay.

2. As Packer mentions, one kind of current celebrity is the person who is "famous for being famous" (para. 8). In class, brainstorm a list of current such celebrities and discuss what they have in common. Use this discussion to jump-start your own essay on what this sort of fame signifies about the values and worldview of modern America.
3. **CONNECTING TEXTS** Write an essay in which you support, refute, or complicate Packer's claim that "this new kind of celebrity is the ultimate costume ball. . . . Their superficial diversity dangles before us the myth that in America, anything is possible" (para. 10). To develop your ideas, consult the Introduction to this chapter or Barbara Ehrenreich's "Bright-Sided" (p. 77).
4. Select one of the celebrities whom Packer mentions, such as Martha Stewart or Bono, and research the public relations surrounding the individual. Use your findings to endorse, refute, or modify Packer's contention that "these new celebrities are all more or less start-up entrepreneurs, and they live by the hacker's code: ask forgiveness, not permission" (para. 7).
5. In your journal, ruminate about which celebrities you admire and why. Then, in an essay, subject one or two of your choices to Packer's critique of today's celebrities. Do they survive his accusation that they "have grown so huge that they dwarf the aspirations of ordinary people, who are asked to yield their dreams to the gods" (para. 11)? Alternatively, if you do not admire any celebrities, write an essay in which you explain why, basing your comments on examples of particular "celebrity monuments of our age" (para. 11).

MARK MANSON

The Disease of More

Americans' "hunger for more" goes beyond their desire for more stuff: increasingly, they have been demanding more and more success, a perpetual reaching "for the next level." That's how Mark Manson sees things, anyway, and in this blog he pithily analyzes why such an attitude "is often the first step toward disaster," concluding "that the funny thing about self-improvement for the sake of self-improvement" is that it is "just a glorified hobby." Life is a series of trade-offs, Manson argues, and only by carefully deciding what you are willing to trade off for what, can you avoid spoiling what you have already accomplished in life. Mark Manson is the author of *Everything is F*cked: A Book about Hope* (2019).

Success is often the first step toward disaster. The idea of progress is often the enemy of actual progress.

I recently met a guy who, despite having a massively successful business, an awesome lifestyle, a happy relationship, and a great network of friends, told me with a straight face, that he was thinking of hiring a coach to help him "reach the next level." When I asked him what this elusive next level was, he said he wasn't sure, that that's why he needed a coach, to point out his blind spots and show him what he's missing out on. "Oh," I said. And then stood there awkwardly for a moment, gauging how brutally honest I was willing to be with someone I just met. This guy was very enthusiastic, clearly ready to spend a lot of money on whatever problem someone decided to tell him he had.

"But what if there's nothing to fix?" I said.

"What do you mean?" he asked.

"What if there is no 'next level?' What if it's just an idea you made up in 5
your head? What if you're already there and not only are you not recognizing it, but by constantly pursuing something more, you're preventing yourself from appreciating it and enjoying where you are now?" He bristled a bit at my questions. Finally, he said, "I just feel like I need to always be improving myself, no matter what."

"And that, my friend, might actually be the problem."

There's a famous concept in sports known as the "Disease of More." It was originally coined by Pat Riley, a hall of fame coach who has led six teams to NBA championships (and won one as a player himself). Riley said that the Disease of More explains why teams who win championships are often ultimately dethroned, not by other, better teams, but by forces from within the organization itself. Riley said the 1980 Lakers didn't get back to the finals the next year because everyone became too focused on themselves. The players, like most people, want more. At first, that "more" was winning the championship. But once players have that championship, it's no longer enough. The "more" becomes other things — more money, more TV commercials, more endorsements and accolades, more playing time, more plays called for them, more media attention, etc.

As a result, what was once a cohesive group of hardworking men begins to fray. Egos get involved. Gatorade bottles are thrown. And the psychological composition of the team changes — what was once a perfect chemistry of bodies and minds becomes a toxic, atomized mess. Players feel entitled to ignore the small, unsexy tasks that actually win championships, believing that they've earned the right to not do it anymore. And as a result, what was the most talented team, ends up failing.

More Is Not Always Better

Psychologists didn't always study happiness. In fact, for most of the field's history, psychology focused not on the positive, but on what fucked people up, what caused mental illness and emotional breakdowns and how people should cope with their greatest pains. It wasn't until the 1980s that a few intrepid academics started asking themselves, "Wait a second, my job is kind of a downer. What about what makes people happy? Let's study that instead!" And there was much celebration because soon dozens of "happiness" books would proliferate bookshelves, selling millions of copies to bored, angsty middle-class people with existential crises.

But I'm getting ahead of myself. 10

One of the first things psychologists did to study happiness was a simple survey. They took large groups of people and gave them pagers (remember, this was the '80s and '90s), and whenever the pager went off, each person was to stop and write down two things:

1. On a scale from 1–10, how happy are you at this moment?
2. What has been going on in your life to cause these feelings?

They collected thousands of ratings from hundreds of people from all walks of life. And what they discovered was both surprising, and actually, incredibly boring.

Pretty much everybody wrote '7,' like, all the time, no matter what. At the grocery store buying milk. Seven. Attending my son's baseball game. Seven. Talking to my boss about making a big sale to a client. Seven.

Even when catastrophic stuff did happen — mom got cancer, missed a mortgage payment on the house, junior lost an arm in a freak bowling accident — happiness levels would dip to the 2–5 range for a short period, and then, after a certain amount of time, promptly return to seven. This was true for extremely positive events as well. Lottery winners, dream vacations, marriages, people's ratings would shoot up for a short period of time, and then, predictably, settle back in around seven.

This fascinated psychologists. Nobody is fully happy all the time. 15
But similarly, nobody is fully unhappy all the time either. It seems that humans, regardless of our external circumstances, live in a constant state of mild-but-not-fully-satisfying happiness. Put another way, things are pretty much always fine. But they could also always be better. But this constant 'seven' that we're all more or less always coming back to, it plays a little trick on us. And it's a trick that we all fall for over and over again.

The trick is that our brain tells us, "You know, if I could just have a little bit more, I'd finally get to 10 and stay there." Most of us live most of our lives this way. Constantly chasing our imagined 10.

You think to be happier, you need to get a new job, so you get a new job. And then a few months later, you feel like you'd be happier if you had a new house. So you get a new house. And then a few months later, it's an awesome beach vacation, so you go on an awesome beach vacation, and while you're on the awesome beach, you're like, "*You Know What I Fucking Need? A Goddamn Piña Colada? Can't A Fucker Get A Pina Colada Around Here*?" And so you stress about your piña colada, believing that just one piña colada will get you to your 10. But then it's a second piña colada. And then a third. And then . . . well, you know how this turns out. You wake up with a hangover and are at a three.

But that's OK. Because you know that soon you'll be back at that seven.

Some psychologists call this constant chasing of pleasure the "hedonic treadmill" because people who are constantly striving for a "better life" end up expending a ton of effort only to end up in the same place.

But wait . . . I know what you're saying: *W-T-F, Mark. Does this mean that* 20
there's no point in doing anything?

No, it means that we need to be motivated in life by something more than our own happiness. It means that we have to be driven by something greater than ourselves. Otherwise, you will simply run and run toward some vision of your own glory and improvement, toward your perfect 10, all the while feeling as though you're in the same place. Or worse, like Riley's championship teams, slowly undermining what got you there to begin with.

Self-Improvement as a Glorified Hobby

Back in my early 20s, when I was what I would characterize as a "self-help junkie," one of my favorite rituals every year was to sit down around New Year's and spend hours mapping out my life goals, my vision for myself, and all of the amazing shit I was going to do to get myself there. I analyze my desires and values and end up with a sexy and impressive-sounding list of largely arbitrary goals, filled with stuff like taking a bongo class or making a certain amount of money or finally nailing that ever-elusive six-pack.

But I eventually learned that the funny thing about self-improvement for the sake of self-improvement is that it doesn't inherently mean anything. It's just a glorified hobby. It's something to keep you occupied and to enthusiastically discuss with other people who have the same hobby. **It took me a long time to accept the fact that just because something *can be improved* in my life, does not mean that it *should be improved* in my life.**

The improvement is not the problem, it's the *Why* that's motivating the improvement that matters. When one compulsively looks to improve oneself, without any greater cause or reason driving it other than self-aggrandizement, it leads to a life of immense self-preoccupation, a light and beneficent form of narcissism where one's constant attention and focus is on oneself. And ironically, this will probably make your life worse off.

Years ago, a friend of mine once told me: "The best decision I ever made 25
in my life was to join a support group. Three years later, the best decision I ever made in my life was to stop attending my support group." I think the same principle is true with all forms of self-improvement. Self-improvement tools should be used like bandages, only to be opened and applied when something is hurt or seriously wrong, and with the goal always being to eventually remove them.

Life Is Not a Game of Improvement, but Rather a Game of Trade-offs

I think many people see life in terms of linear growth and improvement. This is probably only true when you're young. As a kid, your knowledge and understanding of the world grow massively each year. As a young adult, your opportunities and skills grow rapidly as well.

But once you hit adulthood, once you're established and have developed expertise in certain areas, because you've already invested so much time and mental energy into your skills and assets, life is no longer simply a question of improvement, but rather of trade-off. I've spent 10 years developing my ability as a writer. I've managed to conjure a successful writing career for myself. If I turned around and wanted to become a DJ, on the one hand, you could argue, I'm "improving" myself, by expanding my talents and skill set, but to put the hundreds of hours to become competent at an entirely new artistic endeavor would force me to give up some opportunities as a writer. That 500-hours or whatever is necessary to DJ competently could be spent writing another book, starting a column at a prestigious magazine, or simply shitting out a bunch more of these blog posts.

The same was true with the NBA players who won championships. In their eyes, they were just moving up in the world. Yesterday, they won their first championship. Today, they're getting more commercials, a better locker, a big, brand new house. What they didn't realize is what they were trading off. Their time and energy, now occupied by all sorts of new luxuries, was no longer able to focus on the nitty-gritty of basketball. And as a team, they suffered.

Which brings me back to the guy in search of a coach I met a couple weeks ago. Ultimately, my advice to him was simply to be careful. Be careful with the drive to improve for the sake of improvement, the desire for more for no other reason than it's more. Be careful adopting new dreams and goals that could harm the success and happiness you've already built for yourself today. Or as the cliche goes, be careful what you wish for, because you just might get it.

Life is not a checklist. It's not a mountain to scale. It's not a golf game or 30
a beer commercial or whatever other cheesy analogy you want to insert here.

Life is an economy. Where everything must be traded for something else and the value of all things rise and fall with the amount of attention and effort you put into them. And in that economy, we each must eventually choose what you're willing to trade based on what you value. And if you're not careful with your values, if you are willing to trade things away for the sake of another hit of dopamine, another temporary trip to your own personal psychological 10, then chances are you're going to fuck things up.

Reading the Text

1. In your own words, define what Manson means by the "disease of more."
2. What is the significance of the psychological study Manson summarized in which most participants rated their happiness as 7 on a scale of 1–10?

3. What does the "disease of more" mean when applied to the world of sports, according to Manson?
4. How would you characterize Manson's tone and style in this selection? To what sort of audience do you think Manson is appealing? To what extent does it contribute to or detract from the persuasiveness of his argument?

Reading the Signs

1. In your journal, reflect on your own desire to have more. Do you find yourself "constantly chasing our imagined 10" (para. 16), as Manson puts it? If so, does that quest improve your happiness, erode it, or produce other psychological effects? If you do not feel yourself constantly striving for "more" or "better," why do you think that is the case?
2. **CONNECTING TEXTS** Stage an in-class debate in which teams support or refute Manson's recommendation that we see that "life is an economy" (para. 31), not "a checklist. . . . not a mountain to scale" (para. 30). In other words, is Manson simply being realistic, or does his viewpoint diminish the value of dreams and aspirations? To develop your team's position, consult Barbara Ehrenreich's "Bright-Sided" (p. 77) or the Introduction to this chapter.
3. To what extent does your college encourage the ethos of improvement for the sake of improvement? To explore this question, you might study your school's promotional materials, those for particular departments or academic programs (such as study abroad), or public relations materials created by the athletics program. Use your findings as the basis of an essay in which you analyze the possible existence of this ethos at your school, including an assessment of its benefits or drawbacks.
4. Write an essay in which you support, refute, or modify Manson's argument that "When one compulsively looks to improve oneself, . . . it leads to a life of immense self-preoccupation, a light and beneficent form of narcissism where one's constant attention and focus is on oneself" (para. 24).
5. Write an essay in which you argue whether the desire for constant self-improvement can be considered a typically American trait. To develop your ideas, consult the Introduction to this chapter.

MARK MURPHY

The Uncivil War: How Cultural Sorting of America Divides Us

When patients start complaining to their physicians that their waiting room televisions are tuned to the wrong news stations, you know that things are going badly wrong in America. But that is exactly what happened to Dr. Mark Murphy, as he reports in this opinion piece for the *Savannah Morning News*, going on to offer his analysis of what it is that is driving us to squabble over TV channel selections, and a lot more. Citing changing demographics, politically polarized news outlets, and the role of social media silos, Murphy describes the forces that, in his opinion, have made the nation "more divided and Americans more intolerant of one another" than they have ever been within his lifetime — a telling diagnosis for troubled times.

When I opened the exam room door, it was obvious that the woman was angry. She was leaning forward, arms akimbo, her jaws clenched. I steeled myself for the worst.

"Sorry I'm late," I said. "It's been a busy afternoon."

"Oh, that's OK," she said, smiling and extending her hand to me. "I've got my book."

As we shook hands and exchanged pleasantries, I was puzzled. After 30 years of practicing medicine, I've gotten pretty good at reading body language, and she had been unquestionably upset when I first came in the room. But her anger seemed to have dissipated in an instant. And then it returned.

"By the way, did you know that the television in your waiting room was 5
turned to CNN? It needs to be on Fox News!"

And so, right there in a nutshell, was the essence of the polarized society we now live in: My patients were fighting over channel selection on the waiting room television.

In the 56 years I've lived in this country, I've watched the United States navigate its way through assassinations, the Vietnam War, the Civil Rights movement, Watergate, the fall of the Soviet Union, an ongoing war in the Middle East, and refugee crises which have upended the social order in both Europe and the Americas. And yet in my lifetime, the nation has never seemed more divided and Americans more intolerant of one another than they are right now. So why is this happening? One can piece the puzzle together by looking at the changing demographics of our nation, the rise of partisan media, and the pervasive influence of the internet — all key components to the perfect storm that is currently driving American citizens apart.

To get an idea about the societal underpinnings of our current division, one only needs to understand the current demographic trends.

Demographic Trends

According to U.S. Census data, in the 1950s, 82 percent of the U.S. population was white and Christian. Asians and Hispanics collectively comprised a scant 1 percent of the total population. By the time of the 2010 census, the Hispanic and Asian populations had grown to a combined 21 percent. Today, only 43 percent of Americans are white Christians — and there are over twice as many people in this country now than there were in 1950.

The Pew Research Center predicts that by 2055, the U.S. population 10
will be 48 percent Caucasian, 24 percent Hispanic, 14 percent Asian, and 13 percent African-American. Immigration is driving much of that demographic shift. By 2060, it is predicted that 19 percent of the U.S. population will be foreign-born, as opposed to only 5 percent in 1965. New research reveals that it was these ongoing shifts in the makeup of America, and the fears that they engendered over a changing nation, that drove many Trump voters to the polls. Donald Trump, a heterosexual white male, was born in 1946. He grew up in the 1950s and early 1960s.

Trump's campaign slogan, "Make America Great Again," makes thinly veiled reference to those times — and, indeed, for heterosexual white males, the 1950s and early 1960s were indeed pretty great. But if you were Hispanic, African-American, Asian, female, or gay? Not so much.

The last two presidential elections have only exaggerated the widening chasm between liberal and conservative Americans. In electing Barack Obama to the nation's highest office in 2008, America pivoted leftward, choosing a progressive young man of color as its 44th President. This election and its aftermath reinforced the burgeoning fears of the older white electorate, who saw this as further evidence of the erosion of their traditional status in American society. Fears set in motion by Obama's election set the stage for Donald Trump's defeat of Hillary Clinton in 2016. That election saw the nation tack sharply right, sending an older white male billionaire into the Oval Office who has since worked diligently to undo much of the legacy of his predecessor. The differences between these two men have led to innumerable uncomfortable watercooler conversations at workplaces all across the nation — and on social media websites like Facebook and Twitter, where the political rancor can be brutal.

Traditional Media Takes Part

Partisan media in this country have only fanned the flames of discord. The Fox News versus CNN debate which caused a minor skirmish in my waiting room was exemplary of that ongoing conflict. But the idea that partisan media are a completely new thing is a myth. In the early days of the United States, Alexander Hamilton's Federalists and Thomas Jefferson's Republicans each supported media outlets which openly promoted their respective agendas. The advent of more objective journalistic standards only truly began in the early 20th century, when schools of journalism were being established across the nation, allowing the promulgation of defined standards of journalistic integrity that characterized news reporting during the majority of the past 100 years. The advent of radio and television journalism and the growth of the mass press spread these lofty ideals around the globe, making the relatively impartial U.S. mass media the world's role model for objective news reporting during the middle of the 20th century.

Due to concerns by conservatives that the mass news media had an inherent liberal bias, conservative magazines such as the *National Review* were launched in the late 1940s and 1950s as a means of expressing a more conservative viewpoint. The launch of the right-leaning Fox News in 1996 and the subsequent explosion of conservative sites on the internet such as *Breitbart News* have further eroded public confidence in the objectivity of the traditional mass media.

The Gallup polling agency has borne witness to that erosion of trust: In 1998, 55 percent of all Americans trusted the news as reported by the mainstream mass media. By 2016, that figure had slipped to 32 percent (and to only 14 percent among Republican voters). Given the current president's propensity for denigrating the press and calling anything he does not agree with "fake news," and given the extensive promulgation of actual fake news on social media platforms by internet trolls working on behalf of the Russian government, the current level of public trust in its media is likely even less.

Today, where we get our news ends up having a more profound bearing on what we believe than ever before. A recent working paper written by University of Chicago economists Marianne Bertrand and Emir Kamenica and published by the National Bureau of Economic Research, used computer algorithms to guess a person's income, political ideology, race, education, and gender based on their media habits and consumer behavior. They analyzed those differences over several decades. The biggest difference in recent years? The widening gap between liberals and conservatives. And television viewing habits were the best reflection of that gap, with Fox News viewership being the best predictor of conservatism.

The gulf between self-identified Democrats and Republicans is perhaps best illustrated by how each group views the other. A 2016 poll by the Pew Research Center showed that a majority of Republicans thought Democrats were more closed-minded and more dishonest than other Americans. A majority of Democrats thought the same thing about Republicans. The trend towards mutual antipathy has become more exaggerated over time. In 1994, according to the Pew Center data, 17 percent of all Democrats expressed a "very unfavorable" view about Republicans. By 2014, that figure had risen to 38 percent. In the same survey, 17 percent of Republicans had an unfavorable view of Democrats in 1994—a figure that had risen to a whopping 42 percent by 2014. Although we have no more current data beyond 2014, most would agree that those feelings are almost certainly higher today, in the era of Trump.

Social Media Grows on Frenzy

One interesting aspect of social media has been the ability of like-minded individuals to use the various media platforms as a means to whip one another into a self-righteous frenzy. People tend to friend those with similar views and de-friend those who disagree with them. Various social media platforms can also embolden people to level brutal and very personal criticisms over the internet which they would never have the courage to say to someone face-to-face. As a result, among people with differing viewpoints, there's little intelligent dialogue these days. Instead, the internet tends to segregate Americans into culturally and ideologically segregated enclaves, as suggested by *National Review* writer David French. French says that "the internet brings all of human knowledge to our smartphones, but rather than using it as a tool for outreach and understanding, we're using it to find and live with people just like us. In other words, we're sorting."

Similarly, Tyler Cowen's recent book *The Complacent Class* makes note of a phenomenon he calls "matching," where Americans with similar interests and viewpoints tend to congregate personally, professionally and even geographically. Examples of this can be seen each and every day, from the establishment of sanctuary cities in California (something that would never be seen in the Deep South) to the pro gun rights and anti-immigration commercials successfully used to promote Republican Georgia gubernatorial candidate Brian Kemp (which would never play on the West Coast). The end result? Vast differences in philosophy and cultural perspective between places like Texas and California. The nation is not even remotely homogeneous. Far from being a "melting pot," America in 2018 has become a bubbling cauldron of potluck stew.

20 The 2016 presidential election was a microcosm of how cultural sorting is shaping American politics. According to the Pew Research Center, Trump voters tended to be from rural or small-town areas, white, male, over 40 and without a college degree. Clinton voters tended to be female, nonwhite, from larger cities, and often had incomes under $35,000 a year. Interestingly, white evangelical Christians (the so-called "religious right") supported Trump by a whopping 81 percent to 16 percent margin over Clinton — and they voted, comprising 26 percent of the total electorate.

As I alluded to earlier, the bigger issue is not simply who supported Trump, but why. Shortly after the election, some analysts cited the economic concerns of people in manufacturing-heavy rust belt states as the principal reason for the rise of Trumpism, but a recent research study by University of Pennsylvania political scientist Diana C. Mutz debunked that hypothesis. Mutz instead concluded what many in America seemed to intuitively know: Donald Trump's election was about fear over what many Trump voters perceived to be a changing America and their diminishing role in it. In Mutz's study, people who felt that Christians were more discriminated against than Muslims and people who thought white people were more discriminated against than people of color overwhelmingly supported Trump. Among white working class voters, 79 percent of those who felt that the "American way of life was threatened" voted for Trump.

Substantial Cultural Gap

From all of these data, there's one clear conclusion: There is a substantial cultural gap in American society, and it is widening each year. A scorched earth, take-no-prisoners mentality has emerged on both sides of the political spectrum. With the ongoing internet-driven sorting of individuals into non-mixing groups of people with similar likes and dislikes, how can we even have a meaningful dialogue among opposing factions who disagree with one another so intensely?

Once again, I turn to writer David French here — himself a combat veteran, and a man with a global perspective about what it means to be an American. In his recent Memorial Day column in the *National Review*, French writes, "Each and every Memorial Day should remind us — in the long row of tombstones marking the graves of Americans from every race, creed and religion — that we remain in this thing together, and even as we use strong words and speak with deep conviction, we will, at the very least, seek to understand opposing views and, always, defend for others rights that we would like to exercise ourselves."

It is all too easy for Americans to sort themselves into like-minded groups, insulating our views from those who feel differently. It is the path of least resistance to vilify, and even demonize, those whose politics, ethnicity, skin color, and sexual preferences do not agree with our own. Having an intelligent, fact-driven discourse takes far more work than posting histrionic personal attacks on Facebook or in Vox populi. But developing an understanding of (and a tolerance for) competing viewpoints is critical to the survival of our nation. Indeed, it is the ability to express those viewpoints freely, without fear of recrimination or retribution, that is the foundation upon which the United States was built.

At the end of the day, we are all Americans, living in the only nation in the 25
history of this planet founded solely on the idea of freedom. It is for that very freedom that over a million American servicemen have sacrificed their lives. And the individual liberties so eloquently outlined by our founding fathers in the Declaration of Independence, the Constitution, and the Bill of Rights are inherently worth defending. With that in mind, it's about time we stopped trying to tear each other apart and instead all tried to get along. California can be California, Texas can be Texas, and we can all still be Americans. You see, despite our fears to the contrary, the greatest threat to the United States of America is not Russia, China, or Islamist extremism.

To quote Pogo, the politically savvy cartoon character once drawn by the late Walt Kelly, "We have met the enemy — and he is us."

Reading the Text

1. Why do you think Murphy identifies David French as a combat veteran and includes occasional references to the American military? What effect do these comments have on you as you read this selection?
2. What strategies does Murphy use to demonstrate his argument about the causes of America's current social divisions? What are the potential advantages and disadvantages of the sort of evidence he provides?
3. In your own words, how is America changing demographically, according to Murphy?

4. What role have the news media and social network sites played in America's current divisions, in Murphy's view?
5. What does Murphy consider to be the solution to the "uncivil war" that currently is rending America?

Reading the Signs

1. In class, form teams and debate one of Murphy's central contentions: "Donald Trump's election was about fear over what many Trump voters perceived to be a changing America and their diminishing role in it" (para. 22). To develop your ideas, consult the Introduction to this chapter. Use the debate as a springboard for writing your own argumentative essay in response to Murphy's position.
2. **CONNECTING TEXTS** Murphy outlines some of the many demographic changes that have occurred in America since the mid twentieth century. Drawing upon the data he presents, write an essay in which you present your own definition of an "American identity." To develop your ideas, read the Introduction to chapter 2, "My Selfie, Myself: Identity and Ideology in the New Millennium" (p. 119).
3. **CONNECTING TEXTS** Write an essay in which you argue how Murphy's three main reasons for America's divisions reflect, deviate from, or complicate the fundamental contradictions outlined in this chapter's Introduction ("American Paradox: Culture, Conflict, and Contradiction in the U.S.A.," p. 67).
4. Murphy published his selection in 2018. Watch current news coverage on Fox News and CNN, and analyze their presentation of recent political events, especially those on a national scale. Use your analysis as the basis of an essay in which you argue whether today's mass media news sources continue to "[fan] the flames of discord" (para.14). Or, if you believe their approach to covering political events has changed, how has it done so?
5. In class, brainstorm ways in which Americans can be encouraged to have "a meaningful dialogue among opposing factions who disagree with one another . . . intensely" (para. 23). Based on your class discussion, compose an essay in which you present your own recommendations for enabling such a dialogue, being sure to consider the challenge that, as Murphy puts it, "It is the path of least resistance to vilify, and even demonize, those whose politics, ethnicity, skin color and sexual preferences do not agree with our own" (para. 25).

ALFRED LUBRANO

The Shock of Education: How College Corrupts

One of America's most fundamental contradictions lies at the heart of the American dream itself. That is, America's promise of social mobility compels those who begin at the bottom to abandon their origins in order to succeed, which entails giving up a part of oneself and leaving one's home behind. It can be a wrenching transition, and in this reflection on what it means to achieve the dream, Alfred Lubrano describes the strain of moving between two worlds, relating both his own experiences moving from working-class Brooklyn to an Ivy League school and those of other working-class "Straddlers" who moved into the middle class. The son of a bricklayer, Lubrano is a journalist at the *Philadelphia Inquirer*. He is the author of *Limbo: Blue-Collar Roots, White-Collar Dreams* (2004), from which this selection is taken.

College is where the Great Change begins. People start to question the blue-collar take on the world. Status dissonance, the sociologists call it. Questions arise: Are the guys accurate in saying people from such-and-such a race are really so bad? Was Mom right when she said nice girls don't put out? Suddenly, college opens up a world of ideas — a life of the mind — abstract and intangible. The core blue-collar values and goals — loyalty to family and friends, making money, marrying, and procreating — are supplanted by stuff you never talked about at home: personal fulfillment, societal obligation, the pursuit of knowledge for knowledge's sake, and on and on. One world opens and widens; another shrinks.

There's an excitement and a sadness to that. The child, say Sennett and Cobb, is deserting his past, betraying the parents he is rising above, an unavoidable result when you're trying to accomplish more with your life than merely earning a paycheck.[1] So much will change between parent and child, and between peers, in the college years. "Every bit of learning takes you further from your parents," says Southwest Texas State University history professor Gregg Andrews, himself a Straddler. "I say this to all my freshmen to start preparing them." "The best predictor of whether you're going to have problems with your family is the distance between your education and your parents," Jake Ryan says. You may soon find yourself with nothing to talk to your folks or friends about.

This is the dark part of the American story, the kind of thing we work to hide. Mobility means discomfort, because so much has to change; one can't allow for the satisfactions of stasis: You prick yourself and move, digging spurs into your own hide to get going, forcing yourself to forget the comforts of the barn. In this country, we speak grandly of this metamorphosis, never stopping to consider that for many class travelers with passports stamped for new territory, the trip is nothing less than a bridge burning.

[1]Richard Sennett and Jonathan Cobb, *The Hidden Injuries of Class* (New York: Alfred A. Knopf, 1972), 131.

Fighting Self-Doubt

When Columbia plucked me out of working-class Brooklyn, I was sure they had made a mistake, and I remained convinced of that throughout most of my time there. My high school was a gigantic (4,500 students) factory; we literally had gridlock in the halls between classes, kids belly to back between history and English class. A teacher once told me that if every one of the reliable corps of truant students actually decided to show up to class one day, the school could not hold us all. (We were unofficially nicknamed "the Italian Army." When our football guys played nearby New Utrecht, which boasted an equivalent ethnic demographic, kids dubbed the game the "Lasagna Bowl.") Lafayette High School roiled with restless boys and girls on their way to jobs in their parents' unions or to secretaries' desks. How could you move from that to an elite college?

At night, at home, the difference in the Columbia experiences my 5
father and I were having was becoming more evident. The family still came together for dinner, despite our disparate days. We talked about general stuff, and I learned to self-censor. I'd seen how ideas could be upsetting, especially when wielded by a smarmy freshman who barely knew what he was talking about. No one wanted to hear how the world worked from some kid who was first learning to use his brain; it was as unsettling as riding in a car with a new driver. When he taught a course on Marx, Sackrey said he used to tell his students just before Thanksgiving break not to talk about "this stuff at the dinner table" or they'd mess up the holiday. Me mimicking my professors' thoughts on race, on people's struggle for equality, or on politics didn't add to the conviviality of the one nice hour in our day. So I learned to shut up.

After dinner, my father would flip on the TV in the living room. My mom would grab a book and join him. And I'd go looking for a quiet spot to study. In his autobiography, *Hunger of Memory: The Education of Richard Rodriguez*, the brilliant Mexican-American Straddler, writer, and PBS commentator invokes British social scientist Richard Hoggart's "scholarship boys," finding pieces of himself in them. Working-class kids trying to advance in life, the scholarship boys learned to withdraw from the warm noise of the gathered family to isolate themselves with their books.[2] (Read primarily as a memoir of ethnicity and — most famously — an anti–affirmative action tract, the book is more genuinely a dissertation on class. At a sidewalk café in San Francisco, Rodriguez himself tells me how often his book is miscatalogued.) Up from the immigrant working class, Rodriguez says in our interview, the scholarship boy finds himself moving between two antithetical places: home and school. With the family, there is intimacy and emotion. At school, one learns to live with "lonely reason." Home life is in the now, Rodriguez says; school life exists on an altogether different plane, calm and reflective, with an eye toward the future.

[2]Richard Rodriguez, *Hunger of Memory: The Education of Richard Rodriguez* (New York: Bantam Books, 1983), 46. Rodriguez himself quotes from Richard Hoggart, *The Uses of Literacy* (London: Chatto and Windus, 1957), chap. 10.

The scholarship boy must learn to distance himself from the family circle in order to succeed academically, Rodriguez tells me. By doing this, he slowly loses his family. There's a brutality to education, he says, a rough and terrible disconnect. Rodriguez says he despised his parents' "shabbiness," their inability to speak English. "I hated that they didn't know what I was learning," he says. He thought of D. H. Lawrence's *Sons and Lovers*, and of Paul Morel, the coal miner's son. Lawrence is a model for Rodriguez, in a way. Rodriguez remembers the scene in which the son watches his father pick up his schoolbooks, his rough hands fingering the volumes that are the instruments separating the two men. Books were establishing a disharmony between the classroom and Rodriguez's house. Preoccupation with language and reading is an effeminacy not easily understood by workers. "It sears your soul to finally decide to talk like your teacher and not your father," Rodriguez says. "I'm not talking about anything less than the grammar of the heart."

Myself, I studied in the kitchen near the dishwasher because its white noise drowned out the television. As long as the wash cycle ran, I could not hear Mr. T and the A-Team win the day. I did not begrudge my father his one indulgence; there wasn't much else that could relax him. He was not a drinker. TV drained away the tumult and hazard of his Columbia day [he was a bricklayer]. My own room was too close to the living room. My brother's small room was too crowded for both of us to study in. You never went in your parents' bedroom without them in it, inviting you. When the dishes were clean and the kitchen again too quiet to beat back the living room noise, I'd go downstairs to my grandparents' apartment. If they were both watching the same TV show on the first floor, then the basement was free. Here was profound and almost disquieting silence. I could hear the house's systems rumble and shake: water whooshing through pipes, the oil burner powering on and off, and the refrigerator humming with a loud efficiency. Down in the immaculate redwood-paneled kitchen/living room, which sometimes still smelled of the sausages and peppers my grandfather may have made that night (my grandparents cooked and ate in their basement, something that never seemed unusual to us), I was ninety minutes from my school and two floors below my family in a new place, underscoring my distance from anything known, heightening my sense of isolation — my limbo status. I read Homer, Shakespeare, and Molière down there. I wrote a paper on landscape imagery in Dante's *Inferno*. In my self-pitying, melodramatic teenager's mind, I thought I had been banished to a new, lonely rung of hell that Dante hadn't contemplated.

By 11 p.m., I'd go back upstairs. My mother would be in bed, my father asleep on his chair. I'd turn off the TV, which awakened my dad. He'd walk off to bed, and I'd study for a couple more hours. His alarm would go off before 5 a.m., and he'd already be at Columbia by the time I woke up at 6:30. That's how our Ivy League days ended and began. When my father was done with Columbia, he moved on to another job site. When I was done with Columbia, I was someone else. I'd say I got the better deal. But then, my father would tell you, that was always the plan. . . .

Macbeth and Other Foolishness

10 Middle-class kids are groomed for another life. They understand, says Patrick Finn, why reading *Macbeth* in high school could be important years down the road. Working-class kids see no such connection, understand no future life for which digesting Shakespeare might be of value. Very much in the now, working-class people are concerned with immediate needs. And bookish kids are seen as weak.

Various education studies have shown that schools help reinforce class. Teachers treat the working class and the well-to-do differently, this work demonstrates, with the blue-collar kids getting less attention and respect. It's no secret, education experts insist, that schools in poorer areas tend to employ teachers who are less well-trained. In these schools, the curriculum is test-based and uncreative. Children are taught, essentially, to obey and fill in blanks. By fourth grade, many of the children are bored and alienated; nothing in school connects to their culture. Beyond that, many working-class children are resistant to schooling and uncooperative with teachers, experts say. They feel pressure from other working-class friends to not participate and are told that being educated is effeminate and irrelevant. Educators have long understood that minority children have these problems, says Finn. But they rarely understand or see that working-class white kids have similar difficulties. "So we're missing a whole bunch of people getting screwed by the education systems," he says.

In our conversations, Finn explains that language is a key to class. In a working-class home where conformity is the norm, all opinions are dictated by group consensus, by what the class says is so. There's one way to do everything, there's one way to look at the world. Since all opinions are shared, there's never a need to explain thought and behavior. You talk less. Language in such a home, Finn says, is implicit.

Things are different in a middle-class home. There, parents are more willing to take the time to explain to little Janey why it's not such a good idea to pour chocolate sauce on the dog. If Janey challenges a rule of the house, she's spoken to like an adult, or at least not like a plebe at some military school. (Working-class homes are, in fact, very much like the military, with parents barking orders, Straddlers tell me. It's that conformity thing again.) There is a variety of opinions in middle-class homes, which are more collaborative than conformist, Finn says. Middle-class people have a multiviewed take on the world. In such a home, where one needs to express numerous ideas and opinions, language is by necessity explicit.

When it's time to go to school, the trouble starts. The language of school — of the teachers and the books — is explicit. A child from a working-class home is at a huge disadvantage, Finn says, because he's used to a narrower world of expression and a smaller vocabulary of thought. It's little wonder that kids from working-class homes have lower reading scores and do less well on SATs than middle-class kids, Finn says.

15 In high school, my parents got me a tutor for the math part of the SATs, to bolster a lackluster PSAT score. That sort of thing happens all the time in

middle-class neighborhoods. But we were setting a precedent among our kind. Most kids I knew from the community were not taking the SATs, let alone worrying about their scores. If you're from the middle class, you do not feel out of place preparing for college. Parents and peers help groom you, encourage you, and delight in your progress. Of course, when you get to freshman year, the adjustments can be hard on anyone, middle-class and working-class kids alike. But imagine going through freshman orientation if your parents are ambivalent — or hostile — about your being there, and your friends aren't clear about what you're doing.

It was like that for my friend Rita Giordano, forty-five, also a journalist, also from Brooklyn. Her world, like mine, was populated by people who thought going from 60th to 65th Streets was a long journey. So when Rita took sojourns into Greenwich Village by herself on Saturday mornings as a teenager, she made sure not to tell any of her friends. It was too oddball to have to explain. And she'd always come back in time to go shopping with everyone. She couldn't figure out why she responded to the artsy vibe of the Village; she was just aware that there were things going on beyond the neighborhood. When it came time for college, she picked Syracuse University because it was far away, a new world to explore. That bothered her friends, and she'd have to explain herself to them on trips back home. "What do you do up there?" they asked her. "Don't you get homesick?" Suddenly, things felt awkward among childhood friends who had always been able to talk. "It was confusing to come home and see people thinking that you're not doing what they're doing, which meant you're rejecting them," said Rita, a diminutive, sensitive woman with large, brown eyes. " 'Don't they see it's still me?' I wondered. I started feeling like, how do I coexist in these two worlds, college and home? I mean, I could talk to my girlfriends about what color gowns their bridesmaids would wear at their fantasy weddings. But things like ambition and existential questions about where you fit in the world and how you make your mark — we just didn't go there."

And to make matters more complicated, there was a guy. Rita's decision to go to Syracuse didn't sit well with the boyfriend who was probably always going to remain working class. "In true Brooklyn fashion, he and his friends decided one night they were going to drive four hundred miles to Syracuse to bring me back, or whatever. But on the way up, they totaled the car and my boyfriend broke his leg. He never got up there, and after that, the idea of him bringing me to my senses dissipated."

Another Straddler, Loretta Stec, had a similar problem with a blue-collar lover left behind. Loretta, a slender thirty-nine-year-old English professor at San Francisco State University with delicate features and brown hair, needed to leave the commotion of drugs and friends' abortions and the repressed religious world of Perth Amboy, New Jersey, for the calm life of the mind offered by Boston College. The only problem was Barry. When Loretta was seventeen, she and Barry, an older construction worker, would ride motorcycles in toxic waste dumps. He was wild and fine — what every working-class girl would want. But Loretta knew life had to get better than Perth Amboy, so she went off to Boston.

Barry and she still got together, though. They even worked on the same taping crew at a construction site during the summer between Loretta's freshman and sophomore years. But the differences between them were growing. All the guys on the job — Barry included — thought it was weird that Loretta would read the *New York Times* during lunch breaks. "What's with that chick?" people asked.

By the time Loretta returned to Boston for her second year, she knew she was in a far different place than Barry. The working class was not for her. Hanging around with this guy and doing construction forever — it sounded awful. "I was upwardly mobile, and I was not going to work on a construction crew anymore," Loretta says. She tried to break it off, but Barry roared up I-95 in a borrowed car to change her mind. Loretta lived in an old Victorian with middle-class roommates who had never met anyone like Barry. When he showed up with a barking Doberman in tow, she recalled he was screaming like Stanley Kowalski in *A Streetcar Named Desire* that he wanted Loretta back. The women became terrified. Loretta was able to calm first Barry, then her roommates. Afterward, the couple went to listen to some music. In a little place on campus, a guitar trio started performing a Rolling Stones song. Suddenly, Barry turned to Loretta and began scream-singing about wild horses not being able to drag him from her, really loud, trying to get her to see his resolve. "People were wondering who was this guy, what's his deal?" Loretta says. "It pointed out the clash between my new world and the old. You don't do stuff like that. It was embarrassing, upsetting, and confusing. I didn't want to hurt him. But I knew it wasn't going to work for me." They walked around campus, fighting about things coming to an end. At some point, she recalls, Barry noticed that a college student with a nicer car than his — Loretta can't remember exactly what it was — had parked behind his car, blocking him. Already ramped up, Barry had a fit and smashed a headlight of the fancy machine with a rock. There Loretta was, a hundred feet from her campus Victorian, newly ensconced in a clean world of erudition and scholarship, far from the violence and swamps of central Jersey. Her bad-boy beau, once so appealing, was raving and breathing hard, trying to pull her away from the books, back down the turnpike to the working class.

"That was really the end of it," Loretta says. "I couldn't have a guy around 20
who was going to act like that. He was wild and crazy and I was trying to make my way." Barry relented, and left Loretta alone. They lost touch, and Loretta later learned that Barry had died, the cause of death unknown to her. It was such a shock.

Reading the Text

1. What is your response to Lubrano's title, and why do you think he chose it for his essay?
2. Summarize in your own words the difference between Lubrano's high school and college experiences.
3. What does Richard Rodriguez mean by saying, "There's a brutality to education" (para. 7)?

4. Why did Lubrano avoid discussing his Columbia University experiences with his family?
5. How does child rearing differ in blue-collar and in middle-class families, in Lubrano's view? What evidence does he advance to support his claims?

Reading the Signs

1. In your journal, reflect on the effects — positive or negative — that attending college may have had on your relationship with your family and high school friends. How do you account for any changes that may have occurred?
2. In an argumentative essay, support, challenge, or complicate Gregg Andrews's statement that "every bit of learning takes you further from your parents" (para. 2). To support your essay, draw upon your own experiences as a college student or those of your peers.
3. Write a synthesis of the personal tales of Lubrano, Loretta Stec, and Rita Giordano. Then use your synthesis as the basis of an essay in which you explain how their collective experiences combine to illustrate Lubrano's position that "for many class travelers with passports stamped for new territory, the trip is nothing less than a bridge burning" (para. 3).
4. Interview students from both blue-collar and middle- or upper-class backgrounds about the effect that attending college has had on their relationship with their family and high school friends. Use your findings to support your assessment of Lubrano's position that college can create divisions between blue-collar students and their families but that it tends not to have that effect on other classes.
5. Analyze Lubrano's use of evidence and quotations. Who is quoted directly? Who is quoted indirectly? What sources and experts does he consult? Use your observations for support in an argumentative essay in which you analyze what Lubrano's article implies about expertise and authority.

MARIAH BURTON NELSON

I Won. I'm Sorry.

Athletic competition, when you come right down to it, is about winning, which is no problem for men, whose gender codes tell them that aggression and domination are admirable male traits. But "how can you win, if you're female?" Mariah Burton Nelson asks, when the same gender codes insist that women must be feminine, "not aggressive, not victorious." And so women athletes, even when they do win, go out of their way to signal their femininity by dolling themselves up and smiling a lot. Beauty and vulnerability seem to be as important to today's female athlete as brawn and gold medals, Nelson complains, paradoxically contradicting the apparent feminist gains that women athletes have made in recent years. A former Stanford University and professional basketball player, Mariah Burton Nelson is the author of *We Are All Athletes* (2002) and *Making Money on the Sidelines* (2008). She is vice president for innovation and planning at the American Society of Association Executives. This piece originally appeared in *Self* magazine.

When Sylvia Plath's husband, Ted Hughes, published his first book of poems, Sylvia wrote to her mother: "I am so happy that HIS book is accepted FIRST. It will make it so much easier for me when mine is accepted. . . ."

After Sylvia killed herself, her mother published a collection of Sylvia's letters. In her explanatory notes, Aurelia Plath commented that from the time she was very young, Sylvia "catered to the male of any age so as to bolster his sense of superiority." In seventh grade, Aurelia Plath noted, Sylvia was pleased to finish second in a spelling contest. "It was nicer, she felt, to have a boy first."

How many women still collude in the myth of male superiority, believing it's "nicer" when boys and men finish first? How many of us achieve but only in a lesser, smaller, feminine way, a manner consciously or unconsciously designed to be as nonthreatening as possible?

Since I'm tall, women often talk to me about height. Short women tell me, "I've always wanted to be tall — but not as tall as you!" I find this amusing, but also curious. Why not? Why not be six-two?

Tall women tell me that they won't wear heels because they don't want 5
to appear taller than their husbands or boyfriends, even by an inch. What are these women telling me — and their male companions? Why do women regulate their height in relation to men's height? Why is it still rare to see a woman who is taller than her husband?

Women want to be tall enough to feel elegant and attractive, like models. They want to feel respected and looked up to. But they don't want to be so tall that their height threatens men. They want to win — to achieve, to reach new heights — but without exceeding male heights.

How can you win, if you're female? Can you just do it? No. You have to play the femininity game. Femininity by definition is not large, not imposing, not competitive. Feminine women are not ruthless, not aggressive, not victorious. It's not feminine to have a killer instinct, to want with all your heart and soul to win — neither tennis matches nor elected office nor feminist victories such as abortion rights. It's not feminine to know exactly what you want, then go for it.

Femininity is about appearing beautiful and vulnerable and small. It's about winning male approval.

One downhill skier who asked not to be identified told me the following story: "I love male approval. Most women skiers do. We talk about it often. There's only one thing more satisfying than one of the top male skiers saying, 'Wow, you are a great skier. You rip. You're awesome.'

"But it's so fun leaving 99 percent of the world's guys in the dust — oops," 10
she laughs. "I try not to gloat. I've learned something: If I kick guys' butts and

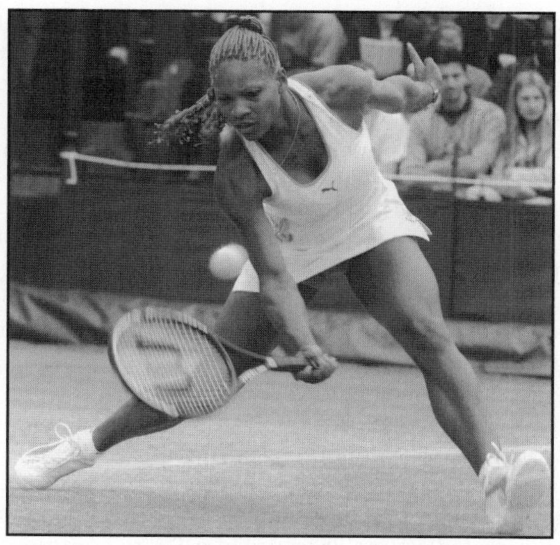
AP Images/Gail Burton

Serena Williams at Wimbledon.

lord it over them, they don't like me. If, however, I kick guys' butts then act 'like a girl,' there is no problem. And I do mean girl, not woman. Nonthreatening."

Femininity is also about accommodating men, allowing them to feel bigger than and stronger than and superior to women, not emasculated by them.

Femininity is unhealthy, obviously. It would be unhealthy for men to act passive, dainty, obsessed with their physical appearance, and dedicated to bolstering the sense of superiority in the other gender, so it's unhealthy for women too. These days, some women are redefining femininity as strong, as athletic, as however a female happens to be, so that "feminine" becomes synonymous with "female." Other women reject both feminine and masculine terms and stereotypes, selecting from the entire range of human behaviors instead of limiting themselves to the "gender-appropriate" ones. These women smile only when they're happy, act angry when they're angry, dress how they want to. They cling to their self-respect and dignity like a life raft.

But most female winners play the femininity game to some extent, using femininity as a defense, a shield against accusations such as bitch, man-hater, lesbian. Feminine behavior and attire mitigate against the affront of female victory, soften the hard edges of winning. Women who want to win without losing male approval temper their victories with beauty, with softness, with smallness, with smiles.

In the fifties, at each of the Amateur Athletic Union's women's basketball championships, one of the players was crowned a beauty queen. (This still happens at Russian women's ice hockey tournaments.) Athletes in the All-American Girls Baseball League of the forties and fifties slid into base wearing skirts. In 1979, professional basketball players with the California Dreams were sent to John Robert Powers' charm school. Ed Temple, the legendary coach of the Tennessee State Tigerbelles, the team that produced Wilma Rudolph, Wyomia Tyus, Willye White, Madeline Manning, and countless other champions, enforced a dress code and stressed that his athletes should be "young ladies first, track girls second."

Makeup, jewelry, dress, and demeanor were often dictated by the male 15
coaches and owners in these leagues, but to some extent the players played along, understanding the trade-off: in order to be "allowed" to compete, they had to demonstrate that they were, despite their "masculine" strivings, real ("feminine") women.

Today, both men and women wear earrings, notes Felshin, "but the media is still selling heterosexism and 'feminine' beauty. And if you listen carefully, in almost every interview" female athletes still express apologetic behavior through feminine dress, behavior, and values.

Florence Griffith-Joyner, Gail Devers, and other track stars of this modern era dedicate considerable attention to portraying a feminine appearance. Basketball star Lisa Leslie has received more attention for being a model than for leading the Americans to Olympic victory. Steffi Graf posed in bikinis for the 1997 *Sports Illustrated* swimsuit issue. In a Sears commercial, Olympic basketball players apply lipstick, paint their toenails, rock babies, lounge in bed, and pose and dance in their underwear. Lisa Leslie says, "Everybody's allowed to be themselves. Me, for example, I'm very feminine."

In an Avon commercial, Jackie Joyner Kersee is shown running on a beach while the camera lingers on her buttocks and breasts. She tells us that she can bench-press 150 pounds and brags that she can jump farther than "all but 128 men." Then she says: "And I have red toenails." Words flash on the screen: "Just another Avon lady." Graf, Mary Pierce, Monica Seles, and Mary Jo Fernandez have all played in dresses. They are "so much more comfortable" than skirts, Fernandez explained. "You don't have to worry about the shirt coming up or the skirt being too tight. It's cooler, and it's so feminine."

"When I put on a dress I feel different — more feminine, more elegant, more ladylike — and that's nice," added Australia's Nicole Bradtke: "We're in a sport where we're throwing ourselves around, so it's a real asset to the game to be able to look pretty at the same time."

Athletes have become gorgeous, flirtatious, elegant, angelic, darling — and 20
the skating commentators' favorite term: "vulnerable." Some think this is good news: proof that femininity and sports are compatible. "There doesn't have to be such a complete division between 'You're beautiful and sexy' and 'you're athletic and strong,' " says Linda Hanley, a pro beach volleyball player who also appeared in a bikini in the 1997 *Sports Illustrated* swimsuit issue.

Athletes and advertisers reassure viewers that women who compete are still willing to play the femininity game, to be cheerleaders. Don't worry about us, the commercials imply. We're winners but we'll still look pretty for you. We're acting in ways that only men used to act but we'll still act how you want women to act. We're not threatening. We're not lesbians. We're not ugly, not bad marriage material. We're strong but feminine. Linguists note that the word "but" negates the part of the sentence that precedes it.

There are some recent examples of the media emphasizing female power in an unambiguous way. "Women Muscle In," the *New York Times Magazine* proclaimed in a headline. The *Washington Post* wrote, "At Olympics, Women Show Their Strength." And a new genre of commercials protests that female athletes are NOT cheerleaders, and don't have to be. Olympic and pro basketball star Dawn Staley says in a Nike commercial that she plays basketball "for the competitiveness" of it. "I need some place to release it. It just builds up, and sports is a great outlet for it. I started out playing with the guys. I wasn't always accepted. You get criticized, like: 'You need to be in the kitchen. Go put on a skirt.' I just got mad and angry and went out to show them that I belong here as much as they do."

Other commercials tell us that women can compete like conquerors. A Nike ad called "Wolves" shows girls leaping and spiking volleyballs while a voice says, "They are not sisters. They are not classmates. They are not friends. They are not even the girls' team. They are a pack of wolves. Tend to your sheep." Though the athletes look serious, the message sounds absurd. When I show this commercial to audiences, they laugh. Still, the images do depict the power of the volleyball players: their intensity, their ability to pound the ball almost through the floor. The script gives the players (and viewers) permission not to be ladylike, not to worry about whether their toenails are red.

But in an American Basketball League commercial, the Philadelphia Rage's female basketball players are playing rough; their bodies collide. Maurice Chevalier sings, "Thank heaven for little girls." The tag line: "Thank heaven, they're on our side."

Doesn't all this talk about girls and ladies simply focus our attention 25
on femaleness, femininity, and ladylike behavior? The lady issue is always there in the equation: something to redefine, to rebel against. It's always present, like sneakers, so every time you hear the word *athlete* you also hear the word *lady*—or feminine, or unfeminine. It reminds me of a beer magazine ad from the eighties that featured a photo of Olympic track star Valerie Brisco-Hooks. "Funny, she doesn't look like the weaker sex," said the print. You could see her impressive muscles. Clearly the intent of the ad was to contrast an old stereotype with the reality of female strength and ability. But Brisco-Hooks was seated, her legs twisted pretzel style, arms covering her chest. But in that position, Brisco-Hooks didn't look very strong or able. In the line, "Funny, she doesn't look like the weaker sex," the most eye-catching words are funny, look, weaker, and sex. Looking at the pretzel that is Valerie, you begin to think that she looks funny. You think about weakness. And you think about sex.

When she was young, Nancy Kerrigan wanted to play ice hockey with her older brothers. Her mother told her, "You're a girl. Do girl things."

Figure skating is a girl thing. Athletes in sequins and "sheer illusion sleeves" glide and dance, their tiny skirts flapping in the breeze. They achieve, but without touching or pushing anyone else. They win, but without visible signs of sweat. They compete, but not directly. Their success is measured not by confrontation with an opponent, nor even by a clock or a scoreboard.

Rather, they are judged as beauty contestants are judged: by a panel of people who interpret the success of the routines. Prettiness is mandatory. Petite and groomed and gracious, figure skaters — like cheerleaders, gymnasts, and aerobic dancers — camouflage their competitiveness with niceness and prettiness until it no longer seems male or aggressive or unseemly.

The most popular sport for high school and college women is basketball. More than a million fans shelled out an average of $15 per ticket in 1997, the inaugural summer of the Women's National Basketball Association. But the most televised women's sport is figure skating. In 1995 revenue from skating shows and competitions topped six hundred million dollars. In the seven months between October 1996 and March 1997, ABC, CBS, NBC, Fox, ESPN, TBS, and USA dedicated 162.5 hours of programming to figure skating, half of it in prime time. Kerrigan earns up to three hundred thousand dollars for a single performance.

Nearly 75 percent of the viewers of televised skating are women. The average age is between twenty-five and forty-five years old, with a household income of more than fifty thousand dollars. What are these women watching? What are they seeing? What's the appeal?

Like golf, tennis, and gymnastics, figure skating is an individual sport 30
favored by white people from the upper classes. The skaters wear cosmetics, frozen smiles, and revealing dresses. Behind the scenes they lift weights and sweat like any serious athlete, but figure skating seems more dance than sport, more grace than guts, more art than athleticism. Figure skating allows women to compete like champions while dressed like cheerleaders.

In women's figure skating, smiling is part of "artistic expression." In the final round, if the competitors are of equal merit, artistry weighs more heavily than technique. Midori Ito, the best jumper in the history of women's skating, explained a weak showing at the 1995 world championships this way: "I wasn't 100 percent satisfied. . . . I probably wasn't smiling enough."

The media portray female figure skaters as "little girl dancers" or "fairy tale princesses" (NBC commentator John Tesh); as "elegant" (Dick Button); as "little angels" (Peggy Fleming); as "ice beauties" and "ladies who lutz" (*People* magazine). Commentators frame skaters as small, young, and decorative creatures, not superwomen but fairy-tale figments of someone's imagination.

After Kerrigan was assaulted by a member of Tonya Harding's entourage, she was featured on a *Sports Illustrated* cover crying "Why me?" When she recovered to win a silver medal at the Olympics that year, she became "America's sweetheart" and rich to boot. But the princess turned pumpkin shortly after midnight, as soon as the ball was over and she stopped smiling and started speaking. Growing impatient during the Olympic medal ceremony while everyone waited for Baiul, Kerrigan grumbled, "Oh, give me a break, she's just going to cry out there again. What's the difference?"

What were Kerrigan's crimes? She felt too old to cavort with cartoon characters. Isn't she? She expressed anger and disappointment — even bitterness and bad sportsmanship — about losing the gold. But wasn't she supposed to want to win? What happens to baseball players who, disappointed about a loss, hit each other or spit on umpires? What happens to basketball players and football players and hockey players who fight? Men can't tumble from a princess palace because we don't expect them to be princesses in the first place, only athletes.

Americans fell out of love with Kerrigan not because they couldn't adore 35
an athlete who lacked grace in defeat, but because they couldn't adore a female athlete who lacked grace in defeat.

Female politicians, lawyers, and businesswomen of all ethnic groups also play the femininity game. Like tennis players in short dresses, working women seem to believe it's an asset to look pretty (but not too pretty) while throwing themselves around. The female apologetic is alive and well in corporate boardrooms, where women say "I'm sorry, maybe someone else already stated this idea, but . . ." and smile while they say it.

When Newt Gingrich's mother revealed on television that Newt had referred to Hillary Clinton as a bitch, how did Hillary respond? She donned a pink suit and met with female reporters to ask how she could "soften her image." She seemed to think that her competitiveness was the problem and femininity the solution.

So if you want to be a winner and you're female, you'll feel pressured to play by special, female rules. Like men, you'll have to be smart and industrious, but in addition you'll have to be "like women": kind, nurturing, accommodating, nonthreatening, placating, pretty, and small. You'll have to smile. And not act angry. And wear skirts. Nail polish and makeup help, too.

Reading the Text

1. Summarize in your own words the contradictory messages about appropriate gender behavior that women athletes must contend with, according to Nelson.
2. Nelson begins her article with an anecdote about poet Sylvia Plath. How does this opening frame her argument about women in sports?
3. What is the "femininity game" (para. 7), in Nelson's view, and how do the media perpetuate it?
4. What sports are coded as "feminine," according to Nelson, and why?

Reading the Signs

1. Watch a women's sports event on television, such as a women's tennis tournament or soccer match, analyzing the behavior and appearance of the athletes. Use your observations as evidence in an essay in which you assess the validity of Nelson's claims about the contradictory gender role behaviors of female athletes.
2. If you are a female athlete, write a journal entry exploring whether you feel pressure to act feminine and your responses to that pressure. If you are not a female athlete, reflect on the behavior and appearance of women athletes on your campus. Do you see signs that they are affected by the femininity game?
3. Obtain a copy of a magazine that focuses on women's sports, such as *Sports Illustrated Women* or *Women's Running*, or visit an online magazine such as sportsister.com or womensportreport.com. Analyze the articles and the ads

in the magazine, noting models' and athletes' clothing, physical appearance, and speech patterns. Using Nelson's argument as a critical framework, write an essay in which you analyze whether the magazine perpetuates traditional gender roles or presents sports as an avenue for female empowerment.

4. Interview women athletes on your campus, and ask them whether they feel pressured by the femininity game. Have they been called lesbians or bitches simply because they are athletes? Do they feel pressure to be physically attractive or charming? Do you see any correlation between an athlete's sport and her responses? Use your observations as the basis of an argument about the influence of traditional gender roles on women athletes at your school.
5. Research news accounts of the United States' women's soccer team as it advanced to the 2019 World Cup Championship. To what extent does the coverage focus on the team members' personalities and physical appearance, as opposed to their athletic achievements? Use your findings as the basis of an essay in which you argue whether the claims Nelson makes in her 1998 essay remain valid today.

WADE GRAHAM

Are We Greening Our Cities, or Just Greenwashing Them?

We may be living in the headiest times for ecologically sensitive architecture since Buckminster Fuller's 1960s. Indeed, among architectural visionaries, as Wade Graham writes in this feature for the *Los Angeles Times*, the "goal is even bigger: 'eco-cities' that will leapfrog the last century's flawed development patterns and deliver us in stylish comfort to a low-carbon, green future." It all sounds very nice, and Graham is on board with the sentiment, but he can't help noting how such a "green" project as Apple's new "spaceship campus" is "by any measure a huge, complex, massively resource-intensive and incredibly expensive ($5 billion) folly, achievable only by one of the richest corporations on Earth." That's not to mention the size of its parking lot for the 13,000 commuters who work there. So much for dreams of Arcadia in the techno future. Wade Graham is a writer, historian, and landscape designer and the author of *Dream Cities: Seven Urban Ideas That Shape the World* (2016).

Architecture and urban design are in the throes of a green fever dream: Everywhere you look there are plans for "sustainable" buildings, futuristic eco-cities, even vertical aquaponic farms in the sky, each promising to redeem the ecologically sinful modern city and bring its inhabitants back into harmony with nature. This year, two marquee examples are set to open: Bjarke Ingels' Via 57

West in New York, a 32-story luxury-apartment pyramid enfolding a garden, and the Louvre Abu Dhabi, by Jean Nouvel, a complex shielded from the harsh climate of the Arabian Peninsula by an enormous white dome. The dreamers' goal is even bigger: "eco-cities" that will leapfrog the last century's flawed development patterns and deliver us in stylish comfort to a low-carbon, green future.

In part, the dream reflects a pragmatic push for energy efficiency, recycled materials and lower carbon emissions — a competition rewarded with LEED certification in silver, gold, or platinum. But it also includes a remarkable effort to turn buildings green — almost literally — by covering them in plants. Green roofs are sprouting on Wal-Marts and green walls festooned with ferns and succulents in Cubist patterns appear on hotels, banks, museums — even at the mall, as I found on a recent trip to the Glendale Galleria in Los Angeles.

All of this is surely a good idea, at some level: trying to repair some of the damage our lifestyle has done to the planet by integrating nature into what have been, especially in the modern era, wasteful, harsh, alienating, concrete urban deserts. But, despite the rhetoric of reconciling the city with nature, today's green urban dream is too often about bringing a technologically controlled version of nature into the city and declaring the problem solved, rather than looking at the deeper causes of our current environmental and urban discontents.

Greening the city is not a new ideal. Ancient Romans waxed lyrical about Arcadia, a mythical bucolic escape from the ills of urban life: money-making, crime, pollution, disease and, of course, luxury and the moral turpitude that goes with it. City-dwellers have always been sensitive to the charge that the metropolis is guilty of a special kind of iniquity, which bars it from grace, and must be cleansed. (Remember Sodom and Gomorrah.) The corollary belief that the green countryside fosters all that is pure and wholesome is a foundational myth of Western culture. It is why, when most people amass enough filthy lucre, they move to the suburbs and cultivate a large, useless lawn, as if the greensward alone could buy them salvation.

5 Since Plato's *Republic*, visionaries have described the ideal human community as something less like a city and more like a big, well-ordered farm. Think of Charles Fourier's utopian phalanxes, the Shaker settlements, Frank Lloyd Wright's proposed Broadacre City, Soviet collectives, Israeli kibbutzes, or the innumerable 19th- and 20th-century "garden cities" strewn around the American and European landscapes. A more modest contemporary form is perhaps the Brooklyn Grange, the hipsterish but messianic urban farm outfit that grows bespoke salad greens hydroponically on several rented New York City rooftops for environmentally conscious urbanites. It is undoubtedly a beneficial enterprise, but, given the realities of high urban land values and labor costs, such a model is unlikely to replace the world's nearly 6 million square miles of horizontal farms.

Today's signature eco-building, Apple's "spaceship" campus now under construction in Silicon Valley, designed by the British architect Norman Foster, is a good example of the shortcomings of the green dream. Though we are assured it will be sustainable, energy efficient, and "slim" — preserving 80 percent of its 175-acre site for landscaping, it is by any measure a huge, complex, massively resource-intensive, and incredibly expensive ($5 billion) folly, achievable only by one of the richest corporations on Earth. What is more damning is that, at the end of the day, it will be just another appendage of suburban sprawl, a white-collar workplace located next to a freeway, dependent on vast garages (even if most of them are tastefully buried) for its 13,000 commuters — and thus with no smaller environmental footprint than a conventional office park.

A look at the green dream's origins is revealing. The Louvre Abu Dhabi, Apple's spaceship and another new Silicon Valley "campus," Google's planned complex to be covered in transparent tenting that it says will "blur the difference between our buildings and nature," are direct descendants of the work of the American visionary R. Buckminster Fuller and his Japanese partner, Shoji Sadao. In 1960, Fuller and Sadao proposed building a two-mile-wide, transparent geodesic dome over Midtown Manhattan. It would eliminate bad weather and the cost of heating and cooling separate buildings. It wasn't built, but other, lesser domed environments were, all over the world, and these helped spawn a global epidemic of drawing-board futuristic eco-cities.

Among the movement's avatars were Paolo Soleri, whose projected Utopia, Arcosanti, only amounted to a few, odd concrete structures in the Arizona desert, and the Japanese Metabolists of the 1960s and '70s, whose plans for massive floating city-farms and modular megastructures in the sky were outlandish. (They nevertheless directly influenced the development of undersea exploration modules, offshore oil platforms and the International Space Station.) Indeed, Foster was a student and later a collaborator of Fuller and Sadao, and his masterpieces — the Gherkin in London and the remade Reichstag in Berlin, to name just two of scores — are essentially climate-controlled domes, carefully modeled on his teachers' earlier work.

These projects are, then, really the fulfillment of a set of blue-sky dreams from the Dr. Strangelove era — where every cinematic space colony contained a domed conservatory and keeping the plants in the greenhouse alive was all that stood between humans and disaster. In the end, those dreams are not about reintegrating society with nature, but leaving Earth itself behind for an engineered habitat under the dome, in the sky, or at least on the roof.

Like driving an $85,000 Tesla, designing a perfect green building or eco- 10
city isn't enough to save the world. Although our buildings, like our cars, have been woefully inefficient environmentally, architecture isn't responsible in any meaningful way for humanity's disastrous environmental impacts, nor can it hope to solve them alone. An economic system based on the destruction of nature and the shifting of real costs onto those less fortunate and onto the future, is the real problem. No dome can protect us from our own profligacy and improvidence, nor can any number of hydroponic lettuce farms blunt the damage being done to real nature, or what is left of it, on planet Earth.

Instead of making "nature" into an urban lifestyle accessory, architects and planners must work to design better relationships between the parts of our cities and nature, and to promote just relationships between the people in them. The work of this year's Pritzker Prize winner, the Chilean architect

Alejandro Aravena, is a case in point. He is less interested in making technologically impressive buildings than in collaborating with residents themselves to design low-cost, efficient housing solutions for the urban working class, especially in the wake of natural disasters. It is a more productive path forward than planting shrubs on skyscrapers.

Reading the Text

1. In your own words, explain what Graham means by "green fever dream" (para. 1).
2. According to Graham, what is the history of the ideal of environmentally friendly cities?
3. What does Graham mean by claiming that many twentieth-century attempts at green building design are "the fulfillment of a set of blue-sky dreams from the Dr. Strangelove era" (para. 9)? What is his justification for that claim?
4. What more environmentally sensitive alternative would Graham prefer to the current green building fad?
5. How does Graham use concession, history, and specific examples to support his overall argument?

Reading the Signs

1. In class, brainstorm ways in which your campus has attempted to become more environmentally sustainable. Then, focusing on a few of these strategies, write an essay in which you assess whether they are indeed environmentally effective or, as Graham puts it, examples of "greenwashing." Share your essay with the class, and then together with other students, brainstorm — and act on — ways in which your campus could improve its environmental footprint.
2. Advocates of a high-tech future often claim that technology can solve our environmental problems. In an essay, evaluate this position, considering past instances of technology's success or failure in solving real-life problems.
3. **CONNECTING TEXTS** How might Julia B. Corbett ("A Faint Green Sell: Advertising and the Natural World," p. 305) respond to Graham's lament that "today's green urban dream is too often about bringing a technologically controlled version of nature into the city and declaring the problem solved, rather than looking . . . deeper" (para. 3)? Use a close reading of Corbett's essay as the basis of your response.
4. Several authors in this textbook — not simply Graham but also Michael Pollan, Thomas Frank, Jia Tolentino, Brooke Gladstone, and Barbara Ehrenreich, among others, and the chapter Introductions — explore the ways in which a seemingly positive image or constructive social movement, in fact, may be not supporting its original cause. Read two or three of these authors and synthesize how positive images may in fact derail the causes that their devotees advance. Then, in your own essay, explore why people find easy answers to be so attractive and propose your own solution to encourage them to be more critical thinkers about American society and popular culture.

AlessandroBiascioli/Shutterstock

2

MY SELFIE, MY SELF

Identity and Ideology in the New Millennium

It's Not So Transparent

Being trans is more than meets the eye.

Just ask Caitlyn Jenner, who spent her entire adult life as one of the world's most famous male athletes and media celebrities before her announcement, at age 66, that she was a trans woman. Alongside such popular cultural phenomena as *Transparent*, the Amazon Studios comedy that brought the transgender experience to mainstream TV, and the Obama administration's directive to American public schools to allow transgender students "access to such [restroom] facilities consistent with their gender identity," Jenner's announcement helped bring to the forefront an identity issue that had long lingered at the margins of American culture. Indeed, the second decade of the new millennium could itself be identified as the time when the trans community came out of the shadows.

But then, the new millennium has also been a time when questions about human identity have become especially prominent, as racial, sexual, gender, class, and religious identities have all played major roles in America's political life and popular culture. So important has identity become in contemporary America that understanding what is happening now in our country is simply not possible without taking it into account. That is why we have chosen to include identity as one of the two foundational topics for this book. And we will begin our exploration with a simple question.

Who Are You?

You are not your self-portrait, but if you own a smartphone, it's quite likely that you have presented yourself to the world by way of a digital image taken, quite literally, at arm's length: your selfie. And since that image has the power to define who you are to an incalculable number of people the world over, you may have very carefully constructed it before posting it to Instagram or Snapchat or LinkedIn or wherever. "Here I am," says your selfie. "This is me, my unique self." But, in truth, a selfie cannot tell anyone much about who you are, and, paradoxically enough, one selfie really looks quite like another, often featuring the same poses and facial expressions framed within the strict limits imposed by a tiny camera held less than two feet from your face. So, you have to go beyond your selfie to let other people know who you are, but that's a lot more difficult, isn't it? Who are you, anyway?

We like to think, especially in America where individualism is such a prized **mythology**, that our identity is completely within our control, autonomous and self-constructed. But it isn't that simple, because a large part of who you are is shaped socially and externally. Your social **class**, for example, influences what life experiences you may (or may not) have had, and these experiences powerfully affect your consciousness and sense of self. Your race, too, has a strong effect; because we have not yet created a post-racial society, the way people treat you is affected by your ethnicity and influences how you identify yourself. Your religion, gender, and sexual orientation also profoundly affect your experience and identity. It's easy to forget the many ways our identities began to be formed in childhood, and all human cultures have their ways of influencing that process. Traditionally, your family, your society, and your religion played the most prominent role in shaping your identity, but in an entertainment culture like ours, popular culture increasingly performs this task.

Just think of all those children's television programs you may have watched even before you could walk or talk. When America's (and, increasingly, the world's) children spend hours in front of a TV set (which has been called "the great pacifier"), watching programs whose plots and characters subtly communicate to them how to behave — from gender roles to professional careers — the role of popular culture in shaping personal identity can be enormous. And at the same time that children are exposed to all that television, many are also absorbing a great deal of advertising. These ads are carefully constructed not only to train children to be consumers when they grow up but also to "brand" them as consumers of the products they see advertised, in the expectation of a lifetime of brand loyalty. Much the same happens with kiddie flicks, which so often inculcate conventional social norms even as they dazzle young viewers' eyes with today's technological wizardry.

The products you consume in your youth can also have a powerful effect on your sense of identity. Your favorite clothing styles, for example, are not only personal forms of expression but **signs** of your identification with the various youth cohorts who share your tastes. In a sense, using **consumption** as a badge of your identity can be considered a form of self-stereotyping (have you ever pegged someone as a "skater" or a "geek"?), but if we are the ones adopting the signs, it doesn't feel like stereotyping. Rather, it feels like choice. And choice, as the example of Caitlyn Jenner illustrates, has come to disrupt one of the most rigid sets of identity constructors within the human experience: the **gender codes** that have traditionally defined our identities as gendered subjects.

Gender Codes

A **gender code** is a culturally constructed **system** that prescribes the appropriate roles and behaviors for men and women in society. Assuming both a continuity between your biological sex and your gender awareness or identity, as well as a normative heterosexual orientation, such codes tell you how to conduct yourself as a male or a female. At least in traditional Western codes we find maxims such as these: *Boys don't cry; girls wear makeup. Boys are aggressive; girls are passive. Boys play sports; girls are cheerleaders. Men go out to work; women stay at home and raise children.* The list is long, and it has shaped your gender identity since your birth.

But transgender, transsexual, and nonbinary challenges to the assumption that biological sexual identity determines psychological gender identity have disrupted the authority of the traditional codes, leading to a multiplicity of possible identities that can be chosen rather than received. The popularity of such TV programs as *RuPaul's Drag Race, Pose, Euphoria*, and the aforementioned *Transparent* is a potent sign of this disruption of the old gender codes. Similarly, disruptions of the heteronormative assumptions that have traditionally governed sexual identity are also changing the cultural landscape. The success of TV shows like *Modern Family*, the increasing number of athletes and politicians coming out to their fans and constituents, and the growing number of Americans who endorse same-sex marriage all signify an emerging acceptance of the freedom to differ from mainstream notions of sexual identity and desire.

But this is not to say that traditional gender codes have disappeared from popular culture. They're still very much at work and are particularly evident in advertising campaigns. Consider, for example, a famous campaign for Axe grooming products. **Denotatively**, Axe is simply a perfume, but since the traditional gender codes specify that perfume is a woman's product, the marketing of Axe fragrances is typically designed to **connote** a hypermasculine (if rather tongue-in-cheek) identity for its male consumers. Thus, like Brut before it, Axe products are given a name traditionally associated with such masculine-coded traits as violence and aggression. One particularly striking Axe ad featured a swarm of passionate women running frantically toward a beach where a single man stands dousing himself in Axe fragrance, reinforcing the

Exploring the Signs of Gender

In your journal, explore the expectations about gender roles that you grew up with. What gender norms were you taught by your family or the media, either overtly or implicitly? Have you ever had any conflicts with your parents over "natural" gender roles? If so, how did you resolve them? Do you think your gender-related expectations today are the same as those you had when you were a child?

gender-coded belief that an unmarried man should "score" as often as possible (a woman who behaves in the same way can be called all kinds of unpleasant names).

Similarly, products (especially cosmetics) aimed at women play up the traditional gender-coded prescription that a woman's primary concern should be to attract the gaze of a man — that is, to look beautiful. This is so glaringly obvious in women's magazines that it has stimulated its own backlash in the well-known Dove "Campaign for Real Beauty." But, while the campaign does feature more ordinary-looking models than do conventional beauty product ads, it does not abandon the focus on physical attractiveness that the traditional code demands — and, it might also be pointed out, the same company that constructed the Dove campaign is also behind the Axe line of products.

Maybe things haven't changed so much after all.

Postfeminist or Third Wave?

With the continued tendency of American popular culture to eroticize female bodies, implicitly or explicitly telling girls and women that their primary identities lie in their ability to be sexually attractive to men (despite decades of feminist attempts to rewrite the script), the current era might seem to be more postfeminist than feminist when it comes to female identity in America. Indeed, with the Jenner-Kardashian clan continuing to enjoy an almost hypnotic grasp on the consciousness of American girls and women, America appears to have abandoned the traditional goals of the women's movement to revert to some of the most conservative of gender-coded prescriptions.

But it may not be that simple. Because for many women who embrace what is often called third-wave feminism, the confident display of their sexuality is actually empowering rather than degrading, a taking charge rather than a knuckling under — an attitude that was behind the immense popularity of the TV hit *Sex and the City* and similar books, movies, and TV series such as *Girls* — not to mention the careers of most current pop music divas. Third-wave feminists regard themselves as representing an evolution within the women's movement itself, not a movement away from it, arguing that being proud of her body and using it to get what she wants is part of a woman's empowerment and a valid identity choice. More traditional feminists are not persuaded by this argument, however, and point out that, by focusing their attention on their bodies rather than their minds, women may subject themselves to the tyranny of a youth-worshipping culture that will reject them once they are past the peak of their sexually appealing years. It is no accident that the vast majority of the images of women we see in popular culture are of very young women. There are a lot more Betty Boops than Betty Whites.

The Space for Race

The emergence of the Black Lives Matter movement after a series of police shootings of black men and women has made it quite clear that the claim America had entered a "post-racial" era with the election of its first black president was strikingly premature. While television series like *Scandal* and *Dear White People* reflect the emergence of racial consciousness as a significant theme in popular culture, a long history of negative stereotyping of African Americans, Asian Americans, Native Americans, and Latin Americans in American entertainment continues to make the representation of racial minorities a highly sensitive subject. Complaints about the character of Jar Jar Binks in the *Star Wars* saga, for example, were based upon a perception that it perpetrated a derisive stereotype of Afro-Caribbean culture, while even *Avatar*, with its sympathetic depiction of a nonwhite society under siege by white invaders, has been compared to *Dances with Wolves* as yet another example of a stereotypical story in which a group of nonwhites needs a white savior to lead them. And the controversy surrounding *Green Book*'s Best Picture Oscar award in 2019 was yet another sign that the traditional "liberal" approach to racially themed movie making was no longer so widely accepted in an increasingly divided society.

Discussing the Signs of Race

Demographers predict that, by the middle of the twenty-first century, America will no longer have any racial or ethnic majority population. In class, discuss the varying effects this may have on Americans' sense of this country's history, culture, and identity.

But while the representation of race in popular culture is still a politically potent topic, certain changes in racial identity itself are altering the landscape. With increasing numbers of Americans identifying themselves as being of mixed heritage, the traditional racial categories, like those of gender, are in a state of flux. Indeed, even the term *minority* is approaching obsolescence in a country that will have no racial majority by midcentury.

The Great Divide

More subtly, but arguably just as profoundly, your social class also shapes your identity. But unlike such identifying categories as race and gender, class has historically been underplayed, even denied, as a component in American life. Obscured by the mythology of the American dream, which promises an opportunity for upward social mobility to everyone, class has been the great blind spot in American history ever since Michel-Guillaume-Saint-Jean de Crèvecoeur (an eighteenth-century French aristocrat who wrote glowingly of his experiences in America) declared that America was a land of economic equality that had transcended Europe's great gulf between rich and poor.

The inability of Americans to recognize the role that social class plays (and has always played) in their lives was dramatically altered in the wake of the Great Recession that broke over America like a tidal wave after the near-meltdown of our economy in 2008. Movements like Occupy Wall Street, which famously divided America into "the 99 percent" and "the 1 percent," helped bring class closer to the forefront, even as the gap between rich and poor continues to widen and the middle class continues to shrink.

But so pertinacious are cultural mythologies that the America of vast class differences is still not very visible in popular culture. The movie *Batman: The Dark Knight Rises* certainly alluded to the class divide in 2012, but, as a number of critics noted at the time, it characterized the class revolution of Bane and company as brutally terroristic, thus potentially undermining those with a serious desire to promote class equality. Significantly, it is very difficult to find any recent high-profile movie that focuses on the class struggle (note how in that blockbuster to beat all blockbusters, *Black Panther*, the hero is a hereditary aristocrat who defeats a revolutionary opponent). Generally, one can argue that while American popular culture is eager to present itself as progressive about race and gender, it is not so eager to reveal the effects of class inequality—which is not very surprising when so many members of the entertainment industry belong to the 1 percent.

Generationx

A semiotic survey of contemporary American culture would quickly reveal that race and gender constitute its most influential, and politically contentious, modes of personal identification. For paradoxically, just as your identity forms the basis for your relationship to other people like you, it can also divide you from others who do not share that identity. This has created a challenge for those who seek a more inclusive American society than we have had in the past, especially with respect to gender identity, because the nouns and pronouns of the languages that we speak tend to pair off into male and female binaries that exclude those who identify as nonbinary. So to avoid such exclusions, new pronoun systems have been devised to avoid the gender identifications of traditional pronouns, much in the way that *Ms.* was introduced in the 1970s to parallel the masculine *Mr.*, and which, unlike *Mrs.* and *Miss* does not indicate marital status. Similarly, the letter *x* has been adopted to take the place of the masculine and feminine vowel endings that are prevalent in Spanish nouns. So popular are such linguistic changes among contemporary college students, that millennials and iGens alike might be considered as a single common generation: call it Generationx.

The challenge of maintaining an inclusive discourse given today's identity politics was strikingly exemplified in 2019 when the student leaders of MEChA voted to change the name of their organization. Originally an acronym for Movimiento Estudiantil Chicano de Aztlán, the name of the organization was first changed to Movimiento Estudiantil Chican@ de Aztlán in 2010 to remove the masculine-gendered *o*, and later to Movimiento Estudiantil Chicanx de Aztlán, when *x* had emerged as the preferred gender-neutral letter ending for gendered languages. But that still left *Chicanx* and *Aztlán*, which

Matt Winkelmeyer/Getty Images Entertainment/Getty Images

Fans wear elaborate costumes at the annual Comic-Con.

excluded black and indigenous peoples, so it was decided that a new name would be needed to ensure a truly inclusive future for MEChA's goals. In a parallel search for inclusivity, the search for an effective label for those with "non-normative" sexual and/or gender identities has produced a range of acronyms from LGBTQ to LGBTQQIP2SAA, with LGBTQIA (lesbian, gay, bisexual, transgender, queer/questioning, intersex, asexual, and other terms) and LGBTQ+ offering something of a compromise between the two.

This linguistic struggle raises a further question: Is there a space any longer for a *fully* inclusive American identity? Many years ago in the most active days of Jesse Jackson's "Rainbow Coalition" there was a popular attempt to find one, but since then the rainbow has shrunk, so to speak, to symbolize the LGBTQ+ coalition, but not beyond. And in the midst of the ever-increasing social and political antagonisms in America today that constitute a basic subtheme of this book, the tendency is toward greater division rather than less. The death of George Floyd in 2020, along with the worldwide protests that followed, revealed just how deep and painful that division is, and the road ahead — not to mention the outcome of what promises to be the most racially fraught presidential election since 1860 — is still not clear.

Which, finally, leads us to one last question: Who are *we*?

Be Whatever You Want to Be

In the midst of such controversies over group identity, plenty of signs indicate the emergence of a new, highly fluid and individualistic mode of identity formation in American culture: the self-constructions that appear on social media sites and apps, from LinkedIn to Facebook, Instagram to Snapchat, Twitter to Tumblr, and everything in between and beyond. In short, in the digital era, the emphasis is often on self-promotion, not demographic classification. That's because on the internet, you can be pretty much what you want to be. From online gaming sites (like *World of Warcraft*), where you can adopt a host of identities, to Facebook profiles, where you can show the world an idealized version of yourself, the internet has revolutionized the traditional restrictions on identity formation. With no one able to see you in person, you can adopt whatever personae you like, exchanging identities as if you were changing your clothes. Such freedom to present yourself in whatever way you like has been a fundamental appeal of the internet from its beginnings.

But just as the internet creates the opportunity for self-making, it also offers users the possibility of disguise — a masked *non-identity* that seems to unleash some of our most antisocial tendencies. Consider the crowd-sourced nastiness of the comments sections on most websites; you will find the same aggression, vile language, trolls, and hostility, no matter what the topic. This "keyboard courage" is made possible by the anonymity that the internet confers upon its users, who feel emboldened to say things that they would not say face-to-face because nonvirtual society has ways of policing itself that the internet does not (a lot of rude comments on the internet would get their posters punched out if delivered in person; others would get them fired).

Paradoxically, then, the internet offers its users a kind of nonidentity in its offer of anonymity. And since identification is also a form of social control (think of your driver's license — it is your photo ID, and without it you cannot legally drive your car), the outbursts that fill the internet are signifiers not only of all the conflict out there but also of a resentment against the restrictions that come with social identity. Such resentment is closely related to that fundamental American mythology of individualism, which can be found at work so often in American culture, for it is our individualism that guides our cherishing of our liberty. The possibility of escaping identity, of having a nonidentity, offers an immense freedom — even if that freedom is expressed only as a license to rant in public.

The Supermarket of IDs

But let's look again at your ability to construct your own online identity. You pay a price for the self-making you can do on the internet. As you advertise yourself, the social networking site on which you do so is mining your data to sell to others who want to advertise to you. Rather than setting up your own web page — which is what people did in the internet's early days — you build your social networking identity upon mass-produced platforms that offer ease and convenience in exchange for your life details. Ironically, your identity is a **commodity** for sale, and you sold it without having had any choice in the matter if you wanted to have a presence in the cloud.

In short, identity itself has become a commodity in America. The mining of our private information can be very disturbing to a society that so highly values individualism and independence, but it is routinely shrugged off by consumers who are pleased to have advertising tailored to their online profiles. This isn't very surprising in a culture wherein people have been trained from the cradle to *identify* themselves as consumers.

Reading Identity Online

Many sites are devoted to the culture of a particular ethnicity, gender, or subculture. Visit several such sites and survey the breadth of information available within them. Is there any information that you wish would appear online but could not find? Do you find any material problematic?

Thus we come to what it means to live in a consumer society. Although one American tradition, a mythology that goes back to the roots of this nation, clings desperately to a sense of self-reliant individualism, the advent of **mass cultural** consumerism — which we will explore in the next chapter of this book — is taking that all away. At a time when Americans are demonstrating a desire for greater and greater personal choice in who they are, it's getting harder and harder to be someone in a mass society that has put identity up for sale. After all, even Caitlyn Jenner, having been there and done that, can now shop at TNTEE and buy her own "Call Me Caitlyn" T-shirt. And so can you.

The Readings

Michael Omi's historical survey of racial stereotyping in American entertainment opens this chapter, providing an essential foundation for the analysis of race in popular culture. Rachelle Hampton and Zahir Janmohamed are next with essays exploring the unintentional effects of the widespread adoption of the phrase "people of color," on the one hand, and the challenges that "cultural appropriation," on the other, present to first-generation immigrants. A pair of readings by Aaron Devor and Deborah Blum follows, with Devor analyzing the ways men and women manipulate the signs by which we traditionally communicate our gender identity, and Blum indicating that biology does play a role in gender identity formation and that we can best understand the gender gap by looking at both the cultural and the physiological determinants of human behavior. Michael Hulshof-Schmidt is next with a meditation on the complications that arise when anyone tries to pin down an all-inclusive label for the queer community. Rachel Lowry and Sophie Gilbert follow with examinations of the millennial generation, who, on the one hand, "may be suffering from an identity crisis" because their online profiles and their more authentic selves often radically differ, while, on the other hand, may be making themselves miserable due to their obsessive quest for lifestyle perfection and success. Dave Patterson then describes what it's like to be poor in America, so poor that people who aren't look at you "with revulsion, pity, [and] fear," while Kwame Anthony Appiah concludes the chapter with a probing analysis of what we're really talking about when we're talking about people "who look like me."

MICHAEL OMI

In Living Color: Race and American Culture

Though many like to think that racism in America is a thing of the past, Michael Omi argues that racism is a pervasive feature in our lives, one that is both overt and inferential. Using race as a sign by which we judge a person's character, inferential racism invokes deep-rooted stereotypes, and as Omi shows in his survey of American film, television, and music, our popular culture is hardly immune from such stereotyping. Indeed, when ostensibly "progressive" programs like *Saturday Night Live* can win the National Ethnic Coalition of Organizations' "Platinum Pit Award" for racial stereotyping in television, and shock jocks such as Howard Stern command big audiences and salaries, one can see popular culture has a way to go before it becomes color-blind. The author of *Racial Formation in the United States: From the 1960s to the 1990s* (with Howard Winant, 1986, 1994), Michael Omi is a sociologist at the University of California, Berkeley.

In February 1987, Assistant Attorney General William Bradford Reynolds, the nation's chief civil rights enforcer, declared that the recent death of a black man in Howard Beach, New York, and the Ku Klux Klan attack on civil rights marchers in Forsyth County, Georgia, were "isolated" racial incidences. He emphasized that the places where racial conflict could potentially flare up were "far fewer now than ever before in our history," and concluded that such a diminishment of racism stood as "a powerful testament to how far we have come in the civil rights struggle."[1]

Events in the months following his remarks raise the question as to whether we have come quite so far. They suggest that dramatic instances of racial tension and violence merely constitute the surface manifestations of a deeper racial organization of American society — a system of inequality which has shaped, and in turn been shaped by, our popular culture.

In March, the NAACP released a report on blacks in the record industry entitled "The Discordant Sound of Music." It found that despite the revenues generated by black performers, blacks remain "grossly underrepresented" in the business, marketing, and A&R (Artists and Repertoire) departments of major record labels. In addition, few blacks are employed as managers, agents, concert promoters, distributors, and retailers. The report concluded that:

> The record industry is overwhelmingly segregated and discrimination is rampant. No other industry in America so openly classifies its operations on a racial basis. At every level of the industry, beginning with the sepa-

[1]Reynolds's remarks were made at a conference on equal opportunity held by the Bar Association in Orlando, Florida. *The San Francisco Chronicle*, (February 7, 1987). Print.

> ration of black artists into a special category, barriers exist that severely limit opportunities for blacks.[2]

Decades after the passage of civil rights legislation and the affirmation of the principle of "equal opportunity," patterns of racial segregation and exclusion, it seems, continue to characterize the production of popular music.

The enduring logic of Jim Crow is also present in professional sports. In April, Al Campanis, vice president of player personnel for the Los Angeles Dodgers, explained to Ted Koppel on ABC's *Nightline* about the paucity of blacks in baseball front offices and as managers. "I truly believe," Campanis said, "that [blacks] may not have some of the necessities to be, let's say, a field manager or perhaps a general manager." When pressed for a reason, Campanis offered an explanation which had little to do with the structure of opportunity or institutional discrimination within professional sports:

> [W]hy are black men or black people not good swimmers? Because they don't have the buoyancy. . . . They are gifted with great musculature and various other things. They're fleet of foot. And this is why there are a lot of black major league ballplayers. Now as far as having the background to become club presidents, or presidents of a bank, I don't know.[3]

Black exclusion from the front office, therefore, was justified on the basis of biological "difference."

5 The issue of race, of course, is not confined to the institutional arrangements of popular culture production. Since popular culture deals with the symbolic realm of social life, the images which it creates, represents, and disseminates contribute to the overall racial climate. They become the subject of analysis and political scrutiny. In August, the National Ethnic Coalition of Organizations bestowed the "Golden Pit Awards" on television programs, commercials, and movies that were deemed offensive to racial and ethnic groups. *Saturday Night Live*, regarded by many media critics as a politically "progressive" show, was singled out for the "Platinum Pit Award" for its comedy skit "Ching Chang," which depicted a Chinese storeowner and his family in a derogatory manner.[4]

These examples highlight the *overt* manifestations of racism in popular culture — institutional forms of discrimination which keep racial minorities out of the production and organization of popular culture, and the crude racial caricatures by which these groups are portrayed. Yet racism in popular culture

[2]Economic Development Department of the NAACP, "The Discordant Sound of Music (A Report on the Record Industry)," (Baltimore, Maryland: The NAACP, 1987), pp. 16–17. Print.

[3]Campanis's remarks on *Nightline* were reprinted in *The San Francisco Chronicle* (April 9, 1987). Print.

[4]Ellen Wulfhorst, "TV Stereotyping: It's the 'Pits,'" *The San Francisco Chronicle* (August 24, 1987). Print.

is often conveyed in a variety of implicit, and at times invisible, ways. Political theorist Stuart Hall makes an important distinction between *overt* racism, the elaboration of an explicitly racist argument, policy, or view, and *inferential* racism, which refers to "those apparently naturalized representations of events and situations relating to race, whether 'factual' or 'fictional,' which have racist premises and propositions inscribed in them as a set of *unquestioned assumptions*." He argues that inferential racism is more widespread, common, and indeed insidious since "it is largely *invisible* even to those who formulate the world in its terms."[5]

Race itself is a slippery social concept which is paradoxically both "obvious" and "invisible." In our society, one of the first things we notice about people when we encounter them (along with their sex/gender) is their *race*. We utilize race to provide clues about *who* a person is and *how* we should relate to her/him. Our perception of race determines our "presentation of *self*," distinctions in status, and appropriate modes of conduct in daily and institutional life. This process is often unconscious; we tend to operate off of an unexamined set of *racial beliefs*.

Racial beliefs account for and explain variations in "human nature." Differences in skin color and other obvious physical characteristics supposedly provide visible clues to more substantive differences lurking underneath. Among other qualities, temperament, sexuality, intelligence, and artistic and athletic ability are presumed to be fixed and discernible from the palpable mark of race. Such diverse questions as our confidence and trust in others (as salespeople, neighbors, media figures); our sexual preferences and romantic images; our tastes in music, film, dance, or sports; indeed our very ways of walking and talking are ineluctably shaped by notions of race.

Ideas about race, therefore, have become "common sense" — a way of comprehending, explaining, and acting in the world. This is made painfully obvious when someone disrupts our common sense understandings. An encounter with someone who is, for example, racially "mixed" or of a racial/ethnic group we are unfamiliar with becomes a source of discomfort for us, and momentarily creates a crisis of racial meaning. We also become disoriented when people do not act "black," "Latino," or indeed "white." The content of such stereotypes reveals a series of unsubstantiated beliefs about who these groups are, what they are like, and how they behave.

The existence of such racial consciousness should hardly be surprising. 10
Even prior to the inception of the republic, the United States was a society shaped by racial conflict. The establishment of the Southern plantation economy, Western expansion, and the emergence of the labor movement, among other significant historical developments, have all involved conflicts over the definition and nature of the *color line*. The historical results have

[5]Stuart Hall, "The Whites of Their Eyes: Racist Ideologies and the Media," in George Bridges and Rosalind Brunt, eds., *Silver Linings* (London: Lawrence and Wishart, 1981), pp. 36–37. Print.

been distinct and different groups have encountered unique forms of racial oppression — Native Americans faced genocide, blacks were subjected to slavery, Mexicans were invaded and colonized, and Asians faced exclusion. What is common to the experiences of these groups is that their particular "fate" was linked to historically specific ideas about the significance and meaning of race.[6] Whites defined them as separate "species," ones inferior to Northern European cultural stocks, and thereby rationalized the conditions of their subordination in the economy, in political life, and in the realm of culture.

A crucial dimension of racial oppression in the United States is the elaboration of an ideology of difference or "otherness." This involves defining "us" (i.e., white Americans) in opposition to "them," an important task when distinct racial groups are first encountered, or in historically specific periods where preexisting racial boundaries are threatened or crumbling.

Political struggles over the very definition of who an "American" is illustrate this process. The Naturalization Law of 1790 declared that only free *white* immigrants could qualify, reflecting the initial desire among Congress to create and maintain a racially homogeneous society. The extension of eligibility to all racial groups has been a long and protracted process. Japanese, for example, were finally eligible to become naturalized citizens after the passage of the Walter-McCarran Act of 1952. The ideological residue of these restrictions in naturalization and citizenship laws is the equation within popular parlance of the term "American" with "white," while other "Americans" are described as black, Mexican, "Oriental," etc.

Popular culture has been an important realm within which racial ideologies have been created, reproduced, and sustained. Such ideologies provide a framework of symbols, concepts, and images through which we understand, interpret, and represent aspects of our "racial" existence.

Race has often formed the central themes of American popular culture. Historian W. L. Rose notes that it is a "curious coincidence" that four of the "most popular reading-viewing events in all American history" have in some manner dealt with race, specifically black/white relations in the south.[7] Harriet Beecher Stowe's *Uncle Tom's Cabin*, Thomas Ryan Dixon's *The Clansman* (the inspiration for D. W. Griffith's *The Birth of a Nation*), Margaret Mitchell's *Gone with the Wind* (as a book and film), and Alex Haley's *Roots* (as a book and television miniseries) each appeared at a critical juncture in American race relations and helped to shape new understandings of race.

15 Emerging social definitions of race and the "real American" were reflected in American popular culture of the nineteenth century. Racial and ethnic stereotypes were shaped and reinforced in the newspapers, magazines, and pulp

[6]For an excellent survey of racial beliefs see Thomas F. Gossett, *Race: The History of an Idea in America* (New York: Shocken, 1965). Print.

[7]W. L. Rose, *Race and Religion in American Historical Fiction: Four Episodes in Popular-Culture* (Oxford: Clarendon, 1979). Print.

fiction of the period. But the evolution and ever-increasing sophistication of visual mass communications throughout the twentieth century provided, and continue to provide, the most dramatic means by which racial images are generated and reproduced.

Film and television have been notorious in disseminating images of racial minorities which establish for audiences what these groups look like, how they behave, and, in essence, "who they are." The power of the media lies not only in their ability to reflect the dominant racial ideology, but in their capacity to shape that ideology in the first place. D. W. Griffith's aforementioned epic *Birth of a Nation*, a sympathetic treatment of the rise of the Ku Klux Klan during Reconstruction, helped to generate, consolidate, and "nationalize" images of blacks which had been more disparate (more regionally specific, for example) prior to the film's appearance.[8]

In television and film, the necessity to define characters in the briefest and most condensed manner has led to the perpetuation of racial caricatures, as racial stereotypes serve as shorthand for scriptwriters, directors, and actors. Television's tendency to address the "lowest common denominator" in order to render programs "familiar" to an enormous and diverse audience leads it regularly to assign and reassign racial characteristics to particular groups, both minority and majority.

Many of the earliest American films deal with racial and ethnic "difference." The large influx of "new immigrants" at the turn of the century led to a proliferation of negative images of Jews, Italians, and Irish which were assimilated and adapted by such films as Thomas Edison's *Cohen's Advertising Scheme* (1904). Based on an old vaudeville routine, the film featured a scheming Jewish merchant, aggressively hawking his wares. Though stereotypes of these groups persist to this day,[9] by the 1940s many of the earlier ethnic stereotypes had disappeared from Hollywood. But, as historian Michael Winston observes, the "outsiders" of the 1890s remained: "the ever-popular Indian of the Westerns; the inscrutable or sinister Oriental; the sly, but colorful Mexican; and the clowning or submissive Negro."[10]

In many respects the "Western" as a genre has been paradigmatic in establishing images of racial minorities in film and television. The classic scenario involves the encircled wagon train or surrounded fort from which whites bravely fight off fierce bands of Native American Indians. The point of reference and viewer identification lies with those huddled within the circle — the

[8]Melanie Martindale-Sikes, "Nationalizing 'Nigger' Imagery through *Birth of a Nation*," paper prepared for the 73rd Annual Meeting of the American Sociological Association (September 4–8, 1978) in San Francisco.

[9]For a discussion of Italian, Irish, Jewish, Slavic, and German stereotypes in film, see Randall M. Miller, ed., *The Kaleidoscopic Lens: How Hollywood Views Ethnic Groups* (Englewood, N.J.: Jerome S. Ozer, 1980). Print.

[10]Michael R. Winston, "Racial Consciousness and the Evolution of Mass Communications in the United States," *Daedalus*, vol. III, No. 4 (Fall 1982). Print.

representatives of "civilization" who valiantly attempt to ward off the forces of barbarism. In the classic Western, as writer Tom Engelhardt observes, "the viewer is forced behind the barrel of a repeating rifle and it is from that position, through its gun sights, that he receives a picture history of Western colonialism and imperialism."[11]

Westerns have indeed become the prototype for European and American 20
excursions throughout the Third World. The cast of characters may change, but the story remains the same. The "humanity" of whites is contrasted with the brutality and treachery of nonwhites; brave (i.e., white) souls are pitted against the merciless hordes in conflicts ranging from Indians against the British Lancers to Zulus against the Boers. What Stuart Hall refers to as the imperializing "white eye" provides the framework for these films, lurking outside the frame and yet seeing and positioning everything within; it is "the unmarked position from which . . . 'observations' are made and from which, alone, they make sense."[12]

Our "common sense" assumptions about race and racial minorities in the United States are both generated and reflected in the stereotypes presented by the visual media. In the crudest sense, it could be said that such stereotypes underscore white "superiority" by reinforcing the traits, habits, and predispositions of nonwhites which demonstrate their "inferiority." Yet a more careful assessment of racial stereotypes reveals intriguing trends and seemingly contradictory themes.

While all racial minorities have been portrayed as "less than human," there are significant differences in the images of different groups. Specific racial minority groups, in spite of their often interchangeable presence in films steeped in the "Western" paradigm, have distinct and often unique qualities assigned to them. Latinos are portrayed as being prone toward violent outbursts of anger; blacks as physically strong, but dim-witted; while Asians are seen as sneaky and cunningly evil. Such differences are crucial to observe and analyze. Race in the United States is not reducible to black/white relations. These differences are significant for a broader understanding of the patterns of race in America, and the unique experience of specific racial minority groups.

It is somewhat ironic that *real* differences which exist within a racially defined minority group are minimized, distorted, or obliterated by the media. "All Asians look alike," the saying goes, and indeed there has been little or no attention given to the vast differences which exist between, say, the Chinese and Japanese with respect to food, dress, language, and culture. This blurring within popular culture has given us supposedly Chinese characters who wear kimonos; it is also the reason why the fast-food restaurant McDonald's can

[11]Tom Engelhardt, "Ambush at Kamikaze Pass," in Emma Gee, ed., *Counterpoint: Perspectives on Asian America* (Los Angeles: Asian American Studies Center, UCLA, 1976), p. 270. Print.

[12]Hall, "Whites of Their Eyes," p. 38. Print.

offer "Shanghai McNuggets" with teriyaki sauce. Other groups suffer a similar fate. Professors Gretchen Bataille and Charles Silet find the cinematic Native American of the Northeast wearing the clothing of the Plains Indians, while living in the dwellings of Southwestern tribes:

> The movie men did what thousands of years of social evolution could not do, even what the threat of the encroaching white man could not do; Hollywood produced the homogenized Native American, devoid of tribal characteristics or regional differences.[13]

The need to paint in broad racial strokes has thus rendered "internal" differences invisible. This has been exacerbated by the tendency for screenwriters to "invent" mythical Asian, Latin American, and African countries. Ostensibly done to avoid offending particular nations and peoples, such a subterfuge reinforces the notion that all the countries and cultures of a specific region are the same. European countries retain their distinctiveness, while the Third World is presented as one homogeneous mass riddled with poverty and governed by ruthless and corrupt regimes.

While rendering specific groups in a monolithic fashion, the popular cultural imagination simultaneously reveals a compelling need to distinguish and articulate "bad" and "good" variants of particular racial groups and individuals. Thus each stereotypic image is filled with contradictions: The bloodthirsty Indian is tempered with the image of the noble savage; the *bandido* exists along with the loyal sidekick; and Fu Manchu is offset by Charlie Chan. The existence of such contradictions, however, does not negate the one-dimensionality of these images, nor does it challenge the explicit subservient role of racial minorities. Even the "good" person of color usually exists as a foil in novels and films to underscore the intelligence, courage, and virility of the white male hero.

25 Another important, perhaps central, dimension of racial minority stereotypes is sex/gender differentiation. The connection between race and sex has traditionally been an explosive and controversial one. For most of American history, sexual and marital relations between whites and nonwhites were forbidden by social custom and by legal restrictions. It was not until 1967, for example, that the U.S. Supreme Court ruled that antimiscegenation laws were unconstitutional. Beginning in the 1920s, the notorious Hays Office, Hollywood's attempt at self-censorship, prohibited scenes and subjects which dealt with miscegenation. The prohibition, however, was not evenly applied in practice. White men could seduce racial minority women, but white women were not to be romantically or sexually linked to racial minority men.

Women of color were sometimes treated as exotic sex objects. The sultry Latin temptress — such as Dolores Del Rio and Lupe Velez — invariably had boyfriends who were white North Americans; their Latino suitors were

[13]Gretchen Bataille and Charles Silet, "The Entertaining Anachronism: Indians in American Film," in Randall M. Miller, ed., *Kaleidoscopic Lens*, p. 40. Print.

portrayed as being unable to keep up with the Anglo-American competition. From Mary Pickford as Cho-Cho San in *Madame Butterfly* (1915) to Nancy Kwan in *The World of Suzie Wong* (1961), Asian women have often been seen as the gracious "geisha girl" or the prostitute with a "heart of gold," willing to do anything to please her man.

By contrast, Asian men, whether cast in the role of villain, servant, sidekick, or kung fu master, are seen as asexual or, at least, romantically undesirable. As Asian American studies professor Elaine Kim notes, even a hero such as Bruce Lee played characters whose "single-minded focus on perfecting his fighting skills precludes all other interests, including an interest in women, friendship, or a social life."[14]

The shifting trajectory of black images over time reveals an interesting dynamic with respect to sex and gender. The black male characters in *The Birth of a Nation* were clearly presented as sexual threats to "white womanhood." For decades afterward, however, Hollywood consciously avoided portraying black men as assertive or sexually aggressive in order to minimize controversy. Black men were instead cast as comic, harmless, and nonthreatening figures exemplified by such stars as Bill "Bojangles" Robinson, Stepin Fetchit, and Eddie "Rochester" Anderson. Black women, by contrast, were divided into two broad character types based on color categories. Dark black women such as Hattie McDaniel and Louise Beavers were cast as "dowdy, frumpy, dumpy, overweight mammy figures"; while those "close to the white ideal," such as Lena Horne and Dorothy Dandridge, became "Hollywood's treasured mulattoes" in roles emphasizing the tragedy of being of mixed blood.[15]

It was not until the early 1970s that tough, aggressive, sexually assertive black characters, both male and female, appeared. The "blaxploitation" films of the period provided new heroes (e.g., *Shaft*, *Superfly*, *Coffy*, and *Cleopatra Jones*) in sharp contrast to the submissive and subservient images of the past. Unfortunately, most of these films were shoddy productions which did little to create more enduring "positive" images of blacks, either male or female.

In contemporary television and film, there is a tendency to present and 30
equate racial minority groups and individuals with specific social problems. Blacks are associated with drugs and urban crime, Latinos with "illegal" immigration, while Native Americans cope with alcoholism and tribal conflicts. Rarely do we see racial minorities "out of character," in situations removed from the stereotypic arenas in which scriptwriters have traditionally embedded them. Nearly the only time we see young Asians and Latinos of either sex, for example, is when they are members of youth gangs, as *Boulevard Nights* (1979), *Year of the Dragon* (1985), and countless TV cop shows can attest to.

Racial minority actors have continually bemoaned the fact that the roles assigned them on stage and screen are often one-dimensional and imbued

[14]Elaine Kim, "Asian Americans and American Popular Culture," in Hyung-Chan Kim, ed., *Dictionary of Asian American History* (New York: Greenwood, 1986), p. 107. Print.

[15]Donald Bogle, "A Familiar Plot (A Look at the History of Blacks in American Movies)," *The Crisis*, Vol. 90, No. 1 (January 1983), p. 15. Print.

with stereotypic assumptions. In theater, the movement toward "blind casting" (i.e., casting actors for roles without regard to race) is a progressive step, but it remains to be seen whether large numbers of audiences can suspend their "beliefs" and deal with a Latino King Lear or an Asian Stanley Kowalski. By contrast, white actors are allowed to play anybody. Though the use of white actors to play blacks in "black face" is clearly unacceptable in the contemporary period, white actors continue to portray Asian, Latino, and Native American characters on stage and screen.

Scores of Charlie Chan films, for example, have been made with white leads (the last one was the 1981 *Charlie Chan and the Curse of the Dragon Queen*). Roland Winters, who played Chan in six features, was once asked to explain the logic of casting a white man in the role of Charlie Chan: "The only thing I can think of is, if you want to cast a homosexual in a show, and you get a homosexual, it'll be awful. It won't be funny . . . and maybe there's something there."[16]

Such a comment reveals an interesting aspect about myth and reality in popular culture. Michael Winston argues that stereotypic images in the visual media were not originally conceived as representations of reality, nor were they initially understood to be "real" by audiences. They were, he suggests, ways of "coding and rationalizing" the racial hierarchy and interracial behavior. Over time, however, "a complex interactive relationship between myth and reality developed, so that images originally understood to be unreal, through constant repetition began to *seem* real."[17]

Such a process consolidated, among other things, our "common sense" understandings of what we think various groups should look like. Such presumptions have led to tragicomical results. Latinos auditioning for a role in a television soap opera, for example, did not fit the Hollywood image of "real Mexicans" and had their faces bronzed with powder before filming because they looked too white. Model Aurora Garza said, "I'm a real Mexican and very dark anyway. I'm even darker right now because I have a tan. But they kept wanting to make my face darker and darker."[18]

Historically in Hollywood, the fact of having "dark skin" made an actor or 35
actress potentially adaptable for numerous "racial" roles. Actress Lupe Velez once commented that she had portrayed "Chinese, Eskimos, Japs, squaws, Hindus, Swedes, Malays, and Japanese."[19] Dorothy Dandridge, who was the first black woman teamed romantically with white actors, presented a quandary for studio executives who weren't sure what race and nationality to make her. They debated whether she should be a "foreigner," an island girl, or a

[16]Frank Chin, "Confessions of the Chinatown Cowboy," *Bulletin of Concerned Asian Scholars*, Vol. 4, No. 3 (Fall 1972). Print.

[17]Winston, "Racial Consciousness," p. 176. Print.

[18]*The San Francisco Chronicle* (September 21, 1984). Print.

[19] Quoted in Allen L. Woll, "Bandits and Lovers: Hispanic Images in American Film," in Miller, ed., *Kaleidoscopic Lens*, p. 60. Print.

West Indian.[20] Ironically, what they refused to entertain as a possibility was to present her as what she really was, a black American woman.

The importance of race in popular culture is not restricted to the visual media. In popular music, race and race consciousness have defined, and continue to define, formats, musical communities, and tastes. In the mid-1950s, the secretary of the North Alabama White Citizens Council declared that "Rock and roll is a means of pulling the white man down to the level of the Negro."[21] While rock may no longer be popularly regarded as a racially subversive musical form, the very genres of contemporary popular music remain, in essence, thinly veiled racial categories. "R & B" (Rhythm and Blues) and "soul" music are clearly references to *black* music, while Country & Western or heavy metal music are viewed, in the popular imagination, as *white* music. Black performers who want to break out of this artistic ghettoization must "cross over," a contemporary form of "passing" in which their music is seen as acceptable to white audiences.

The airwaves themselves are segregated. The designation "urban contemporary" is merely radio lingo for a "black" musical format. Such categorization affects playlists, advertising accounts, and shares of the listening market. On cable television, black music videos rarely receive airplay on MTV, but are confined instead to the more marginal BET (Black Entertainment Television) network.

In spite of such segregation, many performing artists have been able to garner a racially diverse group of fans. And yet, racially integrated concert audiences are extremely rare. Curiously, this "perverse phenomenon" of racially homogeneous crowds takes place despite the color of the performer. Lionel Richie's concert audiences, for example, are virtually all-white, while Teena Marie's are all-black.[22]

Racial symbols and images are omnipresent in popular culture. Commonplace household objects such as cookie jars, salt and pepper shakers, and ashtrays have frequently been designed and fashioned in the form of racial caricatures. Sociologist Steve Dublin in an analysis of these objects found that former tasks of domestic service were symbolically transferred onto these commodities.[23] An Aunt Jemima–type character, for example, is used to hold a roll of paper towels, her outstretched hands supporting the item to be dispensed. "Sprinkle Plenty," a sprinkle bottle in the shape of an Asian man, was used to wet clothes in preparation for ironing. Simple commodities, the household implements which help us perform everyday tasks, may reveal, therefore, a deep structure of racial meaning.

[20]Bogle, "Familiar Plot," p. 17.

[21]Dave Marsh and Kevin Stein, *The Book of Rock Lists* (New York: Dell, 1981), p. 8. Print.

[22]*Rock & Roll Confidential*, No. 44 (February 1987), p. 2. Print.

[23]Steven C. Dublin, "Symbolic Slavery: Black Representations in Popular Culture," *Social Problems*, Vol. 34, No. 2 (April 1987). Print.

40 A crucial dimension for discerning the meaning of particular stereotypes and images is the *situation context* for the creation and consumption of popular culture. For example, the setting in which "racist" jokes are told determines the function of humor. Jokes about blacks where the teller and audience are black constitute a form of self-awareness; they allow blacks to cope and "take the edge off" of oppressive aspects of the social order which they commonly confront. The meaning of these same jokes, however, is dramatically transformed when told across the "color line." If a white, or even black, person tells these jokes to a white audience, it will, despite its "purely" humorous intent, serve to reinforce stereotypes and rationalize the existing relations of racial inequality.

Concepts of race and racial images are both overt and implicit within popular culture — the organization of cultural production, the products themselves, and the manner in which they are consumed are deeply structured by race. Particular racial meanings, stereotypes, and myths can change, but the presence of a *system* of racial meanings and stereotypes, of racial ideology, seems to be an enduring aspect of American popular culture.

The era of Reaganism and the overall rightward drift of American politics and culture has added a new twist to the question of racial images and meanings. Increasingly, the problem for racial minorities is not that of misportrayal, but of "invisibility." Instead of celebrating racial and cultural diversity, we are witnessing an attempt by the right to define, once again, who the "real" American is, and what "correct" American values, mores, and political beliefs are. In such a context, racial minorities are no longer the focus of sustained media attention; when they do appear, they are cast as colored versions of essentially "white" characters.

The possibilities for change — for transforming racial stereotypes and challenging institutional inequities — nonetheless exist. Historically, strategies have involved the mobilization of political pressure against an offending institution(s). In the late 1950s, for instance, "Nigger Hair" tobacco changed its name to "Bigger Hair" due to concerted NAACP pressure on the manufacturer. In the early 1970s, Asian American community groups successfully fought NBC's attempt to resurrect Charlie Chan as a television series with white actor Ross Martin. Amidst the furor generated by Al Campanis's remarks cited at the beginning of this essay, Jesse Jackson suggested that a boycott of major league games be initiated in order to push for a restructuring of hiring and promotion practices.

Partially in response to such action, Baseball Commissioner Peter Ueberroth announced plans in June 1987 to help put more racial minorities in management roles. "The challenge we have," Ueberroth said, "is to manage change without losing tradition."[24] The problem with respect to the issue of

[24]*The San Francisco Chronicle* (June 13, 1987). Print.

race and popular culture, however, is that the *tradition* itself may need to be thoroughly examined, its "common sense" assumptions unearthed and challenged, and its racial images contested and transformed.

Reading the Text

1. Describe in your own words the difference between "overt racism" and "inferential racism" (para. 6).
2. Why, according to Omi, is popular culture so powerful in shaping America's attitudes toward race?
3. Why does Omi identify many attitudes toward race as "common sense" (para. 34), and what is his judgment about such ideas?
4. What relationship does Omi see between gender and racial stereotypes?
5. How did race relations change in America during the 1980s, in Omi's view?

Reading the Signs

1. In class, brainstorm stereotypes, both positive and negative, attributed to specific racial groups. Then discuss the possible sources of these stereotypes. In what ways have they been perpetuated in popular culture, including film, TV, advertising, music, and consumer products? What does your discussion reveal about popular culture's influence on our most basic ways of seeing the world?
2. Using Omi as a critical framework, how does a film like *Black Panther* (2018) reflect or redefine American attitudes toward racial identity and race relations? Alternatively, watch *Green Book* (2018), *BlacKkKlansman* (2018), or another film that addresses race relations.
3. Study an issue of a magazine targeted to a specific ethnic readership, such as *Essence*, *Latina*, *Mochi*, or *Hyphen*, analyzing both its articles and advertising. Then write an essay in which you explore the extent to which the magazine accurately reflects that ethnicity or, in Omi's words, appeals to readers as "colored versions of essentially 'white' characters" (para. 42).
4. Omi claims that "in contemporary television and film, there is a tendency to present and equate racial minority groups and individuals with specific social problems" (para. 30). In class, brainstorm films and TV shows that have characters who are ethnic minorities; pick one example and analyze its depiction of a minority group. Does Omi's claim apply to that example, or does it demonstrate different patterns of racial representation?
5. Watch the film *Avatar* (2009) and then, using Omi's categories of "overt" and "inferential" racism, write your own analysis of the race relations in this movie.

RACHELLE HAMPTON

Which People?

The power to name people often includes the power to control them, and so for many years Americans whose identities have been determined by America's dominant culture have sought to name themselves and, thus, regain control over their destinies. The emergence into common discourse of the term *people of color* reflects one such act of self-naming, but as Rachelle Hampton, a self-identified "black" person, observes in this opinion piece that originally appeared in *Slate*, the blanket identification of such a wide variety of peoples under a single label has the effect of erasing the specific identities of those whom it intends to serve — not to mention the virtue-signaling qualities that it appears to offer to white speakers who use it. Maybe it's time "to get rid of the hiding places in the language we use and to use the words we really mean," Hampton concludes. A graduate of Northwestern University's Medill School of Journalism, Hampton is a staff writer at *Slate*.

Last week, former Starbucks CEO and 2020 presidential hopeful Howard Schultz drew outrage — not over policy positions or campaign slogans or even his company's chronically burnt French roast, but word choice. In a clip from a January CNBC Q&A that surfaced on Twitter, Schultz was asked whether he thought that billionaires had too much influence on American public life. He responded, "The moniker *billionaire* now has become the catchphrase. I would rephrase that, and I would say that people of means have been able to leverage their wealth and their interest in ways that are unfair, and I think that . . . directly speaks to the special interests that are paid for by people of wealth and corporations who are looking for influence."

To me, this quote and Schultz's larger statement show him relatively clearly, if weakly, responding that rich people do have too much influence and that fixating only on billionaires would be too narrow of a focus. But that was not the consensus of the progressive internet. Instead, many came away with the impression that Schultz thinks that *billionaire* is a pejorative, and that we should all be nicer to folks like him by using the softer *people of means*.

Regardless of what Schultz really meant, it's worth considering why we are so ready to hear *people of means* as a slimy obfuscation rather than as a neutral rephrasing or expansion of the category of person in question. Because that readiness speaks to a larger linguistic problem that has implications far beyond the primaries.

The "people of/with x" formulation — wherein people who have some quality, like size or disability, are condensed into a solid noun — has become increasingly common (particularly on the left) since the 1990s. The sentiment behind that semantic shift is the same one that underlies the move from terms like "victims of HIV" and "homeless" to ones like "people living with HIV" and "living unhoused," respectively. Or the move from "disabled people" or "handicapped people" to "people with disabilities." It is a euphemistic linguistic model that intends to center humanity separate from situation or identity, and it is a model that creates new terms that are supposed to, as John McWhorter wrote for *Slate* in 2016, "rise above pejorative connotations that society has linked to the thing in question." Its biggest success story might be the phrase *people of color*.

While *people of color* may not have risen to the same level of prominence as 5
minorities just yet, there is a growing sense that the former should replace the latter when specifically referring to people who aren't white. *Minority*, along with *nonwhite*, necessarily defines people by a negative, as lacking some quality that would place them in the majority category. (And as American demographics continue to change, there's a possibility that *minorities* will become as inaccurate nationally as it has always been globally.) Similarly, the now-passé *colored people* held associations with the state-sanctioned apartheid of the Jim Crow South, where roles in public life were defined by whether one was *colored* or not. Enter *people of color*. While the phrase has existed long before its current heyday (appearing as far back as 1807 in legal records), it seems to have begun its modern ascent in the late 1980s. A 1988 *New York Times* piece on the phrase describes a comic strip that suggests *people of color* as a "new-age" replacement for colored people. "Politically, [people of color] expresses solidarity with other nonwhites, and subtly reminds whites that they are a minority," wrote columnist William Safire.

These are noble origins. But for all the good intentions behind it, the success of *people of color* has brought with it a strong potential for misuse. In our modern discourse, the phrase has come to be thought of as both the most courteous way to refer to a nonwhite person and a signal that its user is down for the cause of racial justice. It has become depressingly common for a well-meaning white person to, despite my fairly conspicuous self-identification as black, refer to me as a woman or writer of color. In that choice lies an uneasiness, either with referring to me as black — despite its accuracy — or with the potential of misidentification of my race. In either case, *person of color* on some level serves to make the (typically white) speaker feel better, rather than me, the person whom the terminology is theoretically for.

In many spaces, the term functions now as performative fauxgressive politeness — as one of the many buzzwords such as *intersectionality* or *systemic* that one can drop, with little understanding, to display her wokeness. In its presence, more accurate terminology is forgone because it feels easier and safer (mainly for white people) to just say *people of color*.

Take, for example, *Rolling Stone* describing Sen. Tim Scott, in a recent article on Republican support of noted racist Rep. Steve King, as a person of color rather than as a black man. This is a choice that, at the very least, creates a lack of journalistic clarity since, as the only black Republican senator, Scott's toeing of the party line with regard to King's racism is particularly newsworthy. What's needed here is specificity, not genteel ease — and that's not the only case where *people of color* elides crucial detail. For example, using *people of color* when discussing the history of chattel slavery or police brutality flattens the specificities of anti-black racism in America. Using *people of color* when referring to the genocide of native and indigenous people in America obfuscates particular histories of colonial violence. Suggesting that newsrooms or corporate boards need to hire more people of color when there are specifically no Latino people or Southeast Asians on the payroll suggests that any nonwhite person will do, that we are all the same and bring the same experience to the table.

The swift and intense reaction to Schultz's "people of means" suggests, to me at least, that we have become sensitive to the misuse of this formulation. We know, on some level, that *people of color* and its cousins have evolved from a compassionate shift in our linguistic paradigms to tools that people in positions of racial or other kinds of power can use to appear politically sensitive while doing little, if any, of the actual work of social justice. In POC's case, what was partially meant to support a sense of radical solidarity between different marginalized communities has been so watered down as to be comfortable in the mouth of someone who either wore blackface or a Klan hood, or thought either was worthy of appearing in his yearbook page. It's a term that, in many ways, still centers whiteness and suggests that anti-blackness doesn't exist in Latino communities or that anti-immigrant sentiments don't exist in black American ones. A term that has happily been co-opted by vice presidents of diversity who think there is a way to make a space welcome to nebulous "people of color" without addressing issues specific to different communities.

This is not to say that *people of color* has no place in our lexicon anymore. 10
There are times and places where it is the most accurate term — when discussing the need for diversity in the largely white publishing world, for example. But we cannot allow *people of color* to erase specificity for the sake of ease, to suggest that calling someone *black* is somehow impolite or to allow those uncomfortable with blackness to obscure their discomfort behind "progressivism." There's no question that the move toward the "people of/with x" formulation was meant to confer humanity onto those who have been dehumanized. But now, it's increasingly apparent that the communities this linguistic shift was supposed to dignify might no longer be the primary beneficiaries of it. The pendulum of sensitivity feels like it's swinging away from marginalized communities and toward the comfort of the powerful. That's partially why Schultz's word choice, whatever he actually meant, rankled so many. The only way to bring it back in the proper direction is to get rid of the hiding places in the language we use and to use the words we really mean.

Reading the Text

1. In your own words, what relationship does Hampton see between Howard Schultz's phrase "people of means" (para. 1) and "people of color"?
2. According to Hampton, why is the "people of X" formulation "a euphemistic linguistic model" (para. 4)?

3. In what ways is using the term "people of color" a sign of one's political stance, as Hampton explains it?
4. Summarize in your own words the reservations that Hampton has regarding the term "people of color."

READING THE SIGNS

1. Hampton reveals how one's linguistic choices can act as a sign of a political and social stance. Brainstorm the various terms used for another group of people, such as groups once called "disabled," "homosexuals," or "American Indian." Using her selection as a model, write an essay in which you analyze the political messages associated with the terms given to the group you select.
2. **CONNECTING TEXTS** In an essay, support, refute, or complicate Hampton's assertion that "person of color" "function[s] now as performative fauxgressive politeness" (para. 7). To develop your ideas, consult Michael Hulshof-Schmidt's "What's in an Acronym? Parsing the LGBTQQIP2SAA Community" (p. 163).
3. Interview students of varying ethnic backgrounds about the nomenclature that they prefer to use for not only their own ethnicity but for other groups as well. Analyze the patterns that you see in your results, using them to undergird an essay in which you assess the extent to which your interviewees "erase specificity for the sake of ease" (para. 10) or, as Hampton pleads, "use the words we really mean" (para. 10).
4. Write an essay in which you support, object to, or modify Hampton's claim that using "person of color" effectively means that "people in positions of racial or other kinds of power can . . . appear politically sensitive while doing little, if any, of the actual work of social justice" (para. 9).

ZAHIR JANMOHAMED

Your Cultural Attire

Living in a nation of immigrants, Americans have long faced the problem of how to present themselves to others, especially if their ancestors were not Anglo-Europeans. Traditionally, a spectrum of strategies has been available, ranging from full assimilation to the strict preservation of one's distinctive cultural heritage. But recently a new problem in the politics of American identity has arisen as the adoption of non-European clothing, food, music, and spiritual practices has become common among members of the dominant culture. Such "cultural appropriation," which has now come to be defined as any adoption of a cultural practice that is not a part of one's particular heritage, presents a special challenge to first-generation immigrants like Zahir Janmohamed. Having struggled to "fit in" by way of cultural assimilation, he has found himself being accused, in effect, of cultural appropriation by other South Asian immigrants who feel that he should stick to his own, ancestral culture. Seeking a middle way by interrogating the questions of race and culture that contemporary American society raises, while at the same time taking pride in being able to "fit in" to white America, Janmohamed finds a path by which he can simply be himself without ignoring the complications of that identity in a multicultural society. Zahir Janmohamed is a writer and host of *Racist Sandwich*, a podcast about food, race, gender, and class.

Your Cultural Attire

Many years ago, when I lived in Washington, DC, I was invited to a party to celebrate the end of the Muslim month of fasting known as Ramadan. Guests were asked to dress in what the host described as "your cultural attire." It was an odd request—more fitting for a costume show than for a religious gathering—but I wanted to attend so that I could be around other Muslims like me. Still, I had no idea how to dress for the party. I was born and raised in California to Gujarati Indian parents from Tanzania, so I decided to wear what I thought back then best described my culture: a pair of khaki pants, an Oxford button-down shirt, and white Chuck Taylor Converse All Stars. My companion, a Malay woman who was born and raised in the Midwest, opted to wear jeans and a fitted Gap sweater. We took the elevator to the top of the host's posh apartment building on Massachusetts Avenue, hitting the stop button every few floors to take in the view of our nation's capitol. When we reached our destination, the guests greeted us with confused stares. Are you sure you are at the right party? Did you not read the invitation, their faces seemed to ask.

Most were dressed in what could be called traditional South Asian attire—knee-length shirts known as kurtas for the men, billowy and brightly colored salwar khamizes for the women. A few from Gulf Arab states wore ankle-length crisp white gowns called abayas. Some from Nigeria wore striking and shiny dashikis from Lagos.

I tried to defend my fashion choice by arguing that most of us in that room, at least those who were born and raised in the US, had been asked, at some point or another, to play dress-up at school, most often by our teachers. Weren't we tired, I wanted to ask the room full of guests, most of whom were people of color like me, of having to "ethnicize" ourselves for the benefits of our mostly white teachers who insisted we had to dress a certain way to look, say, Japanese? I thought, perhaps naively so, that by wearing khakis that night I was trying to show that being an Indian American is about how I view the world, not about the garments that drape me.

But my argument fell flat—dude, just enjoy these kabobs, the others in the room suggested—so I decided to share my own experience of humiliation.

During the Gulf War in 1990, when I was a freshman in high school, I was routinely asked by my teachers to speak about being an Arab. I was even asked to bring Arab food to class, even though I have no roots in that part of the world. In fact, I didn't even know if there is exactly one type of Arab food, given the multiplicity of Arab identities. I would probably have preferred to talk about my love for Birkenstock sandals, given my style back then, but it was almost always the "ethnic" stories my teachers loved the most from me and other kids of color at my school.

That's the thing about identity: sure I can claim that my identity is as a 5
Lakers-loving Indian American but that was always trumped by my teachers—nearly all of them white—who insisted to the rest of my school that I was something and someone else. Here, wear these foreign-looking clothes. Talk about being Middle Eastern. And thank us for giving you the chance to speak.

Now, years later after that Washington, DC, party and particularly after having lived for two years in Portland, I finally see the other side: Wearing traditional attire was its own act of defiance, a way of reclaiming pride in clothes that many of us children of immigrants were ridiculed for wearing because they looked "exotic." After all, my father and mother were born in British-controlled Tanzania and the very act of wearing their cultural garb before independence was seen as an act of rebellion, a way for them to push back against the colonial mindset that to dress "ethnic" is to be "uncivilized."

As we huddled together for a group photo at the end of the party, my companion and I looked around, noticing the obvious difference in our clothing. Finally someone broke the silence.

"Would either of you mind being the one taking the photo instead of appearing in it?" a guest asked us in the politest manner possible.

I have been thinking of this anecdote recently, especially given the ongoing debate around cultural appropriation, which, broadly speaking, refers to when one cultural group—usually the dominant cultural group—adopts the food, music, or dress of another cultural group, often one that has been historically marginalized. An example of this might be a white guy rapping, given that rap music is traditionally a Black art form that emerged, in part, to talk about the very real experience of anti-Black racism in America.

But these days, the term *cultural appropriation* is bandied about so easily 10
that it seems that anytime a person cooks a dish not from their own cultural background, someone is ready to cry foul. I have never been bothered by who does what so much as I am troubled by how people do things. I don't care, for example, if a white guy starts an Indian restaurant. However if that same white chef starts decorating his restaurant with stereotypical images of monkey gods, then that would trigger painful memories of white kids teasing me on the playground when I had little recourse to fight back, especially given that teachers often claimed kids of color like me needed to just "get on" with it and focus instead on our studies.

Part of the problem is that we spend too much time interrogating the term *appropriation* but very little time questioning what exactly *culture* is. At that party in Washington, DC, for example, was it not possible that those of us dressed up in Indian outfits were also overly ethnicizing our Indian identity while giving ourselves a pass because we ourselves were Indian?

In fact, I wish I had interrogated my own definitions of culture earlier. When I moved from DC to India in 2011 to work as a reporter, I thought rather foolishly that I might have better luck getting people to open up if I wore traditional Indian clothes like cotton kurtas. I was wrong. I was much more welcome into people's homes when I wore jeans and a polo. No doubt some of this was tied up with the way denim is often viewed as an upper-class fashion choice. But most Indians reminded me that residents of India's cities didn't wear traditional Indian clothes like they once did. Furthermore, by doing so, they pointed out, I was embracing an outdated understanding of India that doesn't really exist anymore. It is a curious thing about our changing world: Indian kids in India are fighting to get the latest Nike Flyknits while Indian American kids are scouring eBay to look for the latest curly-toed mojari shoes with tiny mirrors on them. What, then, does it mean for something to be culturally Indian or culturally American?

And yet how we define ourselves can be rendered moot in an instant. I feel very American but I was often reminded that, in the eyes of others, I was not when I was at the grocery checkout counter in Portland. More times than I care to recall, the cashier got hung up trying to ascertain where I am "originally" from after seeing my name. The offensive part is not the curiosity but rather what is hidden behind the question: the implicit claim that I am not from the United States.

Of course this experience is not limited to the Pacific Northwest. A recent *BuzzFeed* report about Princeton University's application process found that admission officers wanted Latino applicants to have more "cultural flavor." A Latina applicant who writes about playing violin in her college essay might be scored lower than a Latina who writes about her love of observing, say, the Mexican festival of Dia de Los Muertos. It's absurd. It is also tragic.

One way to overcome this, perhaps, is to lean into expectations of 15
what people—and let's be honest, mostly white people—think you are. I witnessed this with my friend, an Iranian American comedian, who often felt inclined to make jokes about being Iranian in the US because she thought that was what audiences wanted. She always resented doing this but she also knew it worked. On the other end of the spectrum is when one pushes back against his or her own culture and chooses to immerse oneself in another culture. This is the case with Aziz Ansari's Netflix series, *Master of None*—a brilliant romantic comedy about a young actor named Dev Shah. The show has been universally praised, and for good reason. But a few have pointed out that the first few episodes of the second season smack of cultural appropriation.

It's a complex and messy issue. Ansari was born and raised in the US to Indian parents, and he has been outspoken as to how people of color are often stereotyped in Hollywood. The show is in many ways a response to that erasure and much of its cleverness can be found in how Ansari challenges the viewer to think differently about children of immigrants. Why can't he, an Indian American living in Italy, be into fine pasta and not, say, Indian masala dosas? But at the same time, Italians on the show eat pasta, drive chic Vespa scooters, and always dress in formal attire. In adding more complexity to his own identity, has Ansari stripped another group of theirs? And if an Indian American actor like Ansari can claim the identity of Italy aficionado, why is it different if a white person were to say, for example, he is a fan of Vietnamese culture?

Last year, I cofounded, along with chef Soleil Ho, a Portland-based podcast about food and race called *Racist Sandwich*. Since then, the number one question we have been asked by listeners is "Can white people cook this? Can white people cook that?"

I used to tell people that our podcast is not really about this question. When people persist, I say that one of the things I love to do is open up YouTube and try to make a dish from a part of the world that I have never been to myself. That answer never suffices and people find other ways to ask me and my cohost the same question: "Will you people of color tell us white people what we can do?"

It is a well-meaning question, but it is still odd. For one, it centers the discussion of food on white identity. A more challenging question, I would argue, is "Why are chefs of color not celebrated in the same manner as white chefs?" A related question is "Why are women chefs often described in gendered terms like 'homely' and 'motherly,' whereas male chefs are talked about as being 'bold' and 'hyper-creative'"?

20 No one likes to talk about these questions, and I suspect a reason might be that for all the advances we have made as a country, the ultimate power—the power of naming—still has not shifted. Those of us without this power are still forced to have our own interpretations about identity, history, food, even fashion be reduced to mere claims.

One solution, perhaps, is not only to listen to more voices—especially those of women and people of color—but also to interrogate our very ideas of who gets to speak and who is heralded as an expert.

A few months ago, while visiting my parents in April, I decided to interview my mom for the podcast. She had no idea what a podcast was and thought it was hilarious that we would pick "such a funny name" like "Racist Sandwich."

As an Indian woman born and raised in Tanzania like my father, she has often been made to feel by other Indians, in India and in the US, that her food—and indeed even her Gujarati dialect—is not authentic or pure. Her samosas, they say, are too crispy. Her spinach curry infused with too much coconut. She sometimes pushes back and reminds them that food changes and languages adapt as people migrate from one country to another.

Few want to hear it. I suspect one of the reasons is because identity becomes fortified when it is menaced, and often Indians in the diaspora find themselves ever more protective of their identity, especially as the targeting of Indians and other brown people in America continues to occur at an alarming rate.

Soleil and I released my interview with my mom on Mother's Day, and since then she has called me every few days to find out what listeners are saying and how many downloads we have amassed. Almost all the feedback I've received has been positive, with listeners gushing about her and her quirky sense of humor. But the one compliment she cherishes the most came from a well-known Indian chef who wrote me a two-line email: "Your mom sounds great. Can she teach me some Indian recipes?" 25

My mom nearly cried when she read that, as did I. We all want to fit in, especially by the group we feel outside of, and she and I share this desire. For her, it is the Indian community. For me, it is white America. The Indian chef's compliments meant so much to her because it is what I suspect she wanted to hear all along, and perhaps what I wanted to feel too when I wore khakis and an Oxford shirt to that party: that I fit in and was welcome, even if I deviated from what others expected of me; that my claim also has merit.

Reading the Text

1. What message does Janmohamed send with his opening anecdote about attending a party that asked guests to wear "your cultural attire" (para. 1)?
2. In your own words, what does it mean for someone to "ethnicize" oneself?
3. What meaning does Janmohamed attach to the wearing of traditional ethnic attire, and how does that meaning change according to the identity of the viewer?
4. Why does Janmohamed say that "part of the problem is that we spend too much time interrogating the term *appropriation* but very little time questioning what exactly *culture* is" (para. 11)?
5. What does Aziz Ansari's series *Master of None* reveal about cultural appropriation, according to Janmohamed?

Reading the Signs

1. In your journal, reflect on the significance that culturally appropriate attire, and other family traditions such as cuisine, holidays, or music have for you. To what extent do you consider them an important part of your identity? Have you ever felt pressured to embrace — or erase — such traditions? How did you feel in response?
2. In an essay, respond to Janmohamed's query, "If an Indian American actor like Ansari can claim the identity of Italy aficionado, why is it different if a white person were to say, for example, he is a fan of Vietnamese culture?" (para. 16).
3. In class, form teams and debate the proposition that any form of cultural appropriation is offensive, with the debate focusing on one particular kind of cultural borrowing (such as white people rapping or one group adopting another culture's traditional cuisine) or such real-life examples that have

received media attention as Kim Kardashian's "Kimono" fashion line or the Utah teen who wore a traditional Chinese dress to her prom. Use the debate as a brainstorming session that will prepare you to write your own argumentative essay about this question.

4. Janmohamed points out that even the notion of cultural attire, and by extension, any cultural habit, is transient because a group's habits and tastes may change over time. In an essay, explore the ways in which the mutability of culture can undermine the objections to cultural appropriation, basing your claims on specific cultural examples.
5. Listen to an episode of *Racist Sandwich*, and write an essay that provides your own explanation for why "the number one question [the show's producers] have been asked by listeners is 'Can white people cook this? Can white people cook that?'" (para. 17). What assumptions about the connection between food and cultural identity are implicit in such questions?

AARON DEVOR

Gender Role Behaviors and Attitudes

"Boys will be boys, and girls will be girls": Few of our cultural mythologies seem as natural as this one. But in this exploration of the gender signals that traditionally tell what a "boy" or "girl" is supposed to look and act like, Aaron Devor shows how these signals are not "natural" at all but instead are cultural constructs. While the classic cues of masculinity — aggressive posture, self-confidence, a tough appearance — and the traditional signs of femininity — gentleness, passivity, strong nurturing instincts — are often considered "normal," Devor explains that they are by no means biological or psychological necessities. Indeed, he suggests, they can be richly mixed and varied, or to paraphrase the old Kinks song "Lola," "Boys can be girls and girls can be boys." Devor is professor of sociology, former dean of graduate studies, and the founder and academic director of the Transgender Archives at the University of Victoria and author of *Gender Blending: Confronting the Limits of Duality* (1989), from which this selection is excerpted.

Gender Role Behaviors and Attitudes

The clusters of social definitions used to identify persons by gender are collectively known as "femininity" and "masculinity." Masculine characteristics are used to identify persons as males, while feminine ones are used as signifiers for femaleness. People use femininity or masculinity to claim and communicate their membership in their assigned, or chosen, sex or gender. Others recognize our sex or gender more on the basis of these characteristics than on the basis of sex characteristics, which are usually largely covered by clothing in daily life.

These two clusters of attributes are most commonly seen as mirror images of one another with masculinity usually characterized by dominance and aggression, and femininity by passivity and submission. A more evenhanded description of the social qualities subsumed by femininity and masculinity might be to label masculinity as generally concerned with egoistic dominance and femininity as striving for cooperation or communion.[1] Characterizing femininity and masculinity in such a way does not portray the two clusters of characteristics as being in a hierarchical relationship to one another but rather as being two different approaches to the same question, that question being centrally concerned with the goals, means, and use of power. Such an alternative conception of gender roles captures the hierarchical and competitive masculine thirst for power, which can, but need not, lead to aggression, and the feminine quest for harmony and communal well-being, which can, but need not, result in passivity and dependence.

Many activities and modes of expression are recognized by most members of society as feminine. Any of these can be, and often are, displayed by persons of either gender. In some cases, cross-gender behaviors are ignored by observers, and therefore do not compromise the integrity of a person's gender display. In other cases, they are labeled as inappropriate gender role behaviors. Although these behaviors are closely linked to sexual status in the minds and experiences of most people, research shows that dominant persons of either gender tend to use influence tactics and verbal styles usually associated with men and masculinity, while subordinate persons, of either gender, tend to use those considered to be the province of women.[2] Thus it seems likely that many aspects of masculinity and femininity are the result, rather than the cause, of status inequalities.

Popular conceptions of femininity and masculinity instead revolve around hierarchical appraisals of the "natural" roles of males and females. Members of both genders are believed to share many of the same human characteristics, although in different relative proportions; both males and females are

[1]Eleanor Maccoby, *Social Development: Psychological Growth and the Parent-Child Relationship* (New York: Harcourt, 1980), p. 217. Egoistic dominance is a striving for superior rewards for oneself or a competitive striving to reduce the rewards for one's competitors even if such action will not increase one's own rewards. Persons who are motivated by desires for egoistic dominance not only wish the best for themselves but also wish to diminish the advantages of others whom they may perceive as competing with them.

[2]Judith Howard, Philip Blumstein, and Pepper Schwartz, "Sex, Power, and Influence Tactics in Intimate Relationships," *Journal of Personality and Social Psychology* 51 (1986), pp. 102–9; Peter Kollock, Philip Blumstein, and Pepper Schwartz, "Sex and Power in Interaction: Conversational Privileges and Duties," *American Sociological Review* 50 (1985), pp. 34–46.

popularly thought to be able to do many of the same things, but most activities are divided into suitable and unsuitable categories for each gender class. Persons who perform the activities considered appropriate for another gender will be expected to perform them poorly; if they succeed adequately, or even well, at their endeavors, they may be rewarded with ridicule or scorn for blurring the gender dividing line.

5 The patriarchal gender schema currently in use in mainstream North American society reserves highly valued attributes for males and actively supports the high evaluation of any characteristics which might inadvertently become associated with maleness. The ideology underlying the schema postulates that the cultural superiority of males is a natural outgrowth of the innate predisposition of males toward aggression and dominance, which is assumed to flow inevitably from evolutionary and biological sources. Female attributes are likewise postulated to find their source in innate predispositions acquired in the evolution of the species. Feminine characteristics are thought to be intrinsic to the female facility for childbirth and breastfeeding. Hence, it is popularly believed that the social position of females is biologically mandated to be intertwined with the care of children and a "natural" dependency on men for the maintenance of mother-child units. Thus the goals of femininity and, by implication, of all biological females are presumed to revolve around heterosexuality and maternity.[3]

Femininity, according to this traditional formulation, "would result in warm and continued relationships with men, a sense of maternity, interest in caring for children, and the capacity to work productively and continuously in female occupations."[4] This recipe translates into a vast number of proscriptions and prescriptions. Warm and continued relations with men and an interest in maternity require that females be heterosexually oriented. A heterosexual orientation requires women to dress, move, speak, and act in ways that men will find attractive. As patriarchy has reserved active expressions of power as a masculine attribute, femininity must be expressed through modes of dress, movement, speech, and action which communicate weakness, dependency, ineffectualness, availability for sexual or emotional service, and sensitivity to the needs of others.

Some, but not all, of these modes of interrelation also serve the demands of maternity and many female job ghettos. In many cases, though, femininity is not particularly useful in maternity or employment. Both mothers and workers often need to be strong, independent, and effectual in order to do their jobs well. Thus femininity, as a role, is best suited to satisfying a masculine vision of heterosexual attractiveness.

[3]Nancy Chodorow, *The Reproduction of Mothering: Psychoanalysis and the Sociology of Gender* (Berkeley: U of California P, 1978), p. 134.

[4]Jon K. Meyer and John E. Hoopes, "The Gender Dysphoria Syndromes: A Position Statement on So-Called 'Transsexualism,'" *Plastic and Reconstructive Surgery* 54 (Oct. 1974), pp. 444–51.

Body postures and demeanors which communicate subordinate status and vulnerability to trespass through a message of "no threat" make people appear to be feminine. They demonstrate subordination through a minimizing of spatial use: People appear feminine when they keep their arms closer to their bodies, their legs closer together, and their torsos and heads less vertical than do masculine-looking individuals. People also look feminine when they point their toes inward and use their hands in small or childlike gestures. Other people also tend to stand closer to people they see as feminine, often invading their personal space, while people who make frequent appeasement gestures, such as smiling, also give the appearance of femininity. Perhaps as an outgrowth of a subordinate status and the need to avoid conflict with more socially powerful people, women tend to excel over men at the ability to correctly interpret, and effectively display, nonverbal communication cues.[5]

Speech characterized by inflections, intonations, and phrases that convey nonaggression and subordinate status also make a speaker appear more feminine. Subordinate speakers who use more polite expressions and ask more questions in conversation seem more feminine. Speech characterized by sounds of higher frequencies are often interpreted by listeners as feminine, childlike, and ineffectual.[6] Feminine styles of dress likewise display subordinate status through greater restriction of the free movement of the body, greater exposure of the bare skin, and an emphasis on sexual characteristics. The more gender distinct the dress, the more this is the case.

Masculinity, like femininity, can be demonstrated through a wide variety 10
of cues. Pleck has argued that it is commonly expressed in North American society through the attainment of some level of proficiency at some, or all, of the following four main attitudes of masculinity. Persons who display success and high status in their social group, who exhibit "a manly air of toughness, confidence, and self-reliance" and "the aura of aggression, violence, and daring," and who conscientiously avoid anything associated with femininity are seen as exuding masculinity.[7] These requirements reflect the patriarchal ideology that masculinity results from an excess of testosterone, the assumption being that androgens supply a natural impetus toward aggression, which in turn impels males toward achievement and success. This vision of masculinity

[5]Erving Goffman, *Gender Advertisements* (New York: Harper, 1976); Judith A. Hall, *Non-Verbal Sex Differences: Communication Accuracy and Expressive Style* (Baltimore: Johns Hopkins UP, 1984); Nancy M. Henley, *Body Politics: Power, Sex and Non-Verbal Communication* (Englewood Cliffs, N.J.: Prentice, 1979); Marianne Wex, *"Let's Take Back Our Space": "Female" and "Male" Body Language as a Result of Patriarchal Structures* (Berlin: Frauenliteraturverlag Hermine Fees, 1979).

[6]Karen L. Adams, "Sexism and the English Language: The Linguistic Implications of Being a Woman," in *Women: A Feminist Perspective*, 3rd ed., ed. Jo Freeman (Palo Alto, Calif.: Mayfield, 1984), pp. 478–91; Hall, pp. 37, 130–37.

[7]Joseph H. Pleck, *The Myth of Masculinity* (Cambridge, Mass.: MIT P, 1981), p. 139.

also reflects the ideological stance that ideal maleness (masculinity) must remain untainted by female (feminine) pollutants.

Masculinity, then, requires of its actors that they organize themselves and their society in a hierarchical manner so as to be able to explicitly quantify the achievement of success. The achievement of high status in one's social group requires competitive and aggressive behavior from those who wish to obtain it. Competition which is motivated by a goal of individual achievement, or egoistic dominance, also requires of its participants a degree of emotional insensitivity to feelings of hurt and loss in defeated others, and a measure of emotional insularity to protect oneself from becoming vulnerable to manipulation by others. Such values lead those who subscribe to them to view feminine persons as "born losers" and to strive to eliminate any similarities to feminine people from their own personalities. In patriarchally organized societies, masculine values become the ideological structure of the society as a whole. Masculinity thus becomes "innately" valuable and femininity serves a contrapuntal function to delineate and magnify the hierarchical dominance of masculinity.

Body postures, speech patterns, and styles of dress which demonstrate and support the assumption of dominance and authority convey an impression of masculinity. Typical masculine body postures tend to be expansive and aggressive. People who hold their arms and hands in positions away from their bodies, and who stand, sit, or lie with their legs apart — thus maximizing the amount of space that they physically occupy — appear most physically masculine. Persons who communicate an air of authority or a readiness for aggression by standing erect and moving forcefully also tend to appear more masculine. Movements that are abrupt and stiff, communicating force and threat rather than flexibility and cooperation, make an actor look masculine. Masculinity can also be conveyed by stern or serious facial expressions that suggest minimal receptivity to the influence of others, a characteristic which is an important element in the attainment and maintenance of egoistic dominance.[8]

Speech and dress which likewise demonstrate or claim superior status are also seen as characteristically masculine behavior patterns. Masculine speech patterns display a tendency toward expansiveness similar to that found in masculine body postures. People who attempt to control the direction of conversations seem more masculine. Those who tend to speak more loudly, use less polite and more assertive forms, and tend to interrupt the conversations of others more often also communicate masculinity to others. Styles of dress which emphasize the size of upper body musculature, allow freedom of movement, and encourage an illusion of physical power and a look of easy physicality all suggest masculinity. Such appearances of strength and readiness to action serve to create or enhance an aura of aggressiveness and intimidation central to an appearance of masculinity. Expansive postures and gestures combine with these qualities to insinuate that a position of secure dominance is a masculine one.

[8]Goffman; Hall; Henley; Wex.

Gender role characteristics reflect the ideological contentions underlying the dominant gender schema in North American society. That schema leads us to believe that female and male behaviors are the result of socially directed hormonal instructions which specify that females will want to have children and will therefore find themselves relatively helpless and dependent on males for support and protection. The schema claims that males are innately aggressive and competitive and therefore will dominate over females. The social hegemony of this ideology ensures that we are all raised to practice gender roles which will confirm this vision of the nature of the sexes. Fortunately, our training to gender roles is neither complete nor uniform. As a result, it is possible to point to multitudinous exceptions to, and variations on, these themes. Biological evidence is equivocal about the source of gender roles; psychological androgyny is a widely accepted concept. It seems most likely that gender roles are the result of systematic power imbalances based on gender discrimination.[9]

Reading the Text

1. List the characteristics that Devor describes as being traditional conceptions of "masculinity" and "femininity" (para. 1).
2. What relationship does Devor see between characteristics that are considered masculine and feminine?
3. How does Devor explain the cultural belief in the "superiority" (para. 5) of males?
4. How, in Devor's view, do speech and dress communicate gender roles?

Reading the Signs

1. In small groups that identify as the same gender, brainstorm lists of traits that you consider to be masculine and feminine, and then have each group write its list on the board. Compare the lists produced by male and female groups. What patterns of differences or similarities do you see? To what extent do the traits presume a heterosexual orientation? How do you account for your results?
2. Study the speech patterns, styles of dress, and other nonverbal cues communicated by your friends during a social occasion, such as a party, trying not to reveal that you are observing them for an assignment. Then write an essay in which you analyze these cues used by your friends. To what extent do your friends enact the traditional gender codes Devor describes?
3. **CONNECTING TEXTS** Study a popular magazine such as *Vanity Fair* or *Esquire* for advertisements depicting men and women interacting with each other. Then write an essay in which you interpret the body postures of the models, using Devor's selection as your framework for analysis. How do males and females typically stand? To what extent do the models enact stereotypically masculine

[9]Howard, Blumstein, and Schwartz; Kollock, Blumstein, and Schwartz.

or feminine stances? To develop your essay, consult Steve Craig's "Men's Men and Women's Women" (p. 273).

4. **CONNECTING TEXTS** Devor argues that female fashion traditionally has restricted body movement while male styles of dress usually allow freedom of movement. In class, discuss whether this claim is still true today, being sure to consider a range of clothing types (such as athletic wear, corporate dress, party fashion, and so forth). Use the class discussion as a jumping-off point for your own essay on this topic. To develop your ideas, consult Jia Tolentino's "How 'Empowerment' Became Something for Women to Buy" (p. 285) and Mariah Burton Nelson's "I Won. I'm Sorry." (p. 107).
5. **CONNECTING TEXTS** Enter the debate over the origins of gender identity: Is it primarily biologically determined or largely socially constructed? Write an essay in which you advance your position; you can develop your ideas by consulting Deborah Blum's "The Gender Blur: Where Does Biology End and Society Take Over?" (p. 156).

DEBORAH BLUM

The Gender Blur: Where Does Biology End and Society Take Over?

There's an old argument over whether nature or nurture is more important in determining human behavior. Nowhere is this argument more intense than in gender studies, where proponents of the social construction of gender identities are currently exploring the many ways in which our upbringing shapes our behavior. But after watching her two-year-old son emphatically choose to play only with carnivorous dinosaur toys and disdainfully reject the "wimpy" vegetarian variety, Deborah Blum decided that nurture couldn't be all that there was to it. Exploring the role of biology in the determination of human behavior, Blum argues that both nature and nurture have to be taken into account if we are to understand gender differences. A Pulitzer Prize–winning professor of journalism at the University of Wisconsin at Madison, Blum is the author of several books, including *Sex on the Brain: The Biological Differences between Men and Women* (1997) and *The Poisoner's Handbook: Murder and the Birth of Forensic Medicine in Jazz Age New York* (2010).

I was raised in one of those university-based, liberal elite families that politicians like to ridicule. In my childhood, every human being — regardless of gender — was exactly alike under the skin, and I mean exactly, barring his or her different opportunities. My parents wasted no opportunity to bring this point home. One Christmas, I received a Barbie doll and a softball glove. Another brought a green enamel stove, which baked tiny cakes by the heat of a lightbulb, and also a set of steel-tipped darts and competition-quality dartboard. Did I mention the year of the chemistry set and the ballerina doll?

It wasn't until I became a parent — I should say, a parent of two boys — that I realized I had been fed a line and swallowed it like a sucker (barring the part about opportunities, which I still believe). This dawned on me during my older son's dinosaur phase, which began when he was about two-and-a-half. Oh, he loved dinosaurs, all right, but only the blood-swilling carnivores. Plant-eaters were wimps and losers, and he refused to wear a T-shirt marred by a picture of a stegosaur. I looked down at him one day, as he was snarling around my feet and doing his toddler best to gnaw off my right leg, and I thought: This goes a lot deeper than culture.

Raising children tends to bring on this kind of politically incorrect reaction. Another friend came to the same conclusion watching a son determinedly bite his breakfast toast into the shape of a pistol he hoped would blow away — or at least terrify — his younger brother. Once you get past the guilt part — Did I do this? Should I have bought him that plastic allosaur with the oversized teeth? — such revelations can lead you to consider the far more interesting field of gender biology, where the questions take a different shape: Does love of carnage begin in culture or genetics, and which drives which? Do the gender roles of our culture reflect an underlying biology, and, in turn, does the way we behave influence that biology?

The point I'm leading up to — through the example of my son's innocent love of predatory dinosaurs — is actually one of the most straightforward in this debate. One of the reasons we're so fascinated by childhood behaviors is that, as the old saying goes, the child becomes the man (or woman, of course). Most girls don't spend their preschool years snarling around the house and pretending to chew off their companion's legs. And they — mostly — don't grow up to be as aggressive as men. Do the ways that we amplify those early differences in childhood shape the adults we become? Absolutely. But it's worth exploring the starting place — the faint signal that somehow gets amplified.

5 "There's plenty of room in society to influence sex differences," says Marc Breedlove, a behavioral endocrinologist at the University of California at Berkeley and a pioneer in defining how hormones can help build sexually different nervous systems. "Yes, we're born with predispositions, but it's society that amplifies them, exaggerates them. I believe that — except for the sex differences in aggression. Those [differences] are too massive to be explained simply by society."

Aggression does allow a straightforward look at the issue. Consider the following statistics: Crime reports in both the United States and Europe record between ten and fifteen robberies committed by men for every one by a woman. At one point, people argued that this was explained by size difference. Women weren't big enough to intimidate, but that would change, they predicted, with the availability of compact weapons. But just as little girls don't routinely make weapons out of toast, women — even criminal ones — don't seem drawn to weaponry in the same way that men are. Almost twice as many male thieves and robbers use guns as their female counterparts do.

Or you can look at more personal crimes: domestic partner murders. Three-fourths of men use guns in those killings; 50 percent of women do. Here's more from the domestic front: In conflicts in which a woman killed a man, he tended to be the one who had started the fight — in 51.8 percent of the cases, to be exact. When the man was the killer, he again was the likely first aggressor, and by an even more dramatic margin. In fights in which women died, they had started the argument only 12.5 percent of the time.

Enough. You can parade endless similar statistics but the point is this: Males are more aggressive, not just among humans but among almost all species on earth. Male chimpanzees, for instance, declare war on neighboring troops, and one of their strategies is a warning strike: They kill females and infants to terrorize and intimidate. In terms of simple, reproductive genetics, it's an advantage of males to be aggressive: You can muscle your way into dominance, winning more sexual encounters, more offspring, more genetic future. For the female — especially in a species like ours, with time for just one successful pregnancy a year — what's the genetic advantage in brawling?

Thus the issue becomes not whether there is a biologically influenced sex difference in aggression — the answer being a solid, technical "You betcha" — but rather how rigid that difference is. The best science, in my opinion, tends to align with basic common sense. We all know that there are extraordinarily gentle men and murderous women. Sex differences are always generalizations: they refer to a behavior, with some evolutionary rationale behind it. They never define, entirely, an individual. And that fact alone should tell us that there's always — even in the most biologically dominated traits — some flexibility, an instinctive ability to respond, for better and worse, to the world around us.

10 This is true even with physical characteristics that we've often assumed are nailed down by genetics. Scientists now believe height, for instance, is only about 90 percent heritable. A person's genes might code for a six-foot-tall body, but malnutrition could literally cut that short. And there's also some evidence, in girls anyway, that children with stressful childhoods tend to become shorter adults. So while some factors are predetermined, there's evidence that the prototypical male/female body design can be readily altered.

It's a given that humans, like most other species — bananas, spiders, sharks, ducks, any rabbit you pull out of a hat — rely on two sexes for reproduction. So basic is that requirement that we have chromosomes whose primary purpose is to deliver the genes that order up a male or a female. All other chromosomes are numbered, but we label the sex chromosomes with the letters X and Y. We get one each from our mother and our father, and the basic combinations are these: XX makes female, XY makes male.

There are two important — and little known — points about these chromosomal matches. One is that even with this apparently precise system, there's nothing precise — or guaranteed — about the physical construction of male and female. The other point makes that possible. It appears that sex doesn't matter in the early stages of embryonic development. We are unisex at the point of conception.

If you examine an embryo at about six weeks, you see that it has the ability to develop in either direction. The fledgling embryo has two sets of ducts — Wolffian for male, Muellerian for female — an either/or structure, held in readiness for further development. If testosterone and other androgens are released by hormone-producing cells, then the Wolffian ducts develop into the channel that connects penis to testes, and the female ducts wither away.

Without testosterone, the embryo takes on a female form; the male ducts vanish and the Muellerian ducts expand into oviducts, uterus, and vagina. In other words, in humans, anyway (the opposite is true in birds), the female is the default sex. Back in the 1950s, the famed biologist Alfred Jost showed that if you castrate a male rabbit fetus, choking off testosterone, you produce a completely feminized rabbit.

We don't do these experiments in humans — for obvious reasons — but 15
there are naturally occurring instances that prove the same point. For instance: In the fetal testes are a group of cells, called Leydig cells, that make testosterone. In rare cases, the fetus doesn't make enough of these cells (a defect known as Leydig cell hypoplasia). In this circumstance we see the limited power of the XY chromosome. These boys have the right chromosomes and the right genes to be boys; they just don't grow a penis. Obstetricians and parents often think they see a baby girl, and these children are routinely raised as daughters. Usually, the "mistake" is caught about the time of puberty, when menstruation doesn't start. A doctor's examination shows the child to be internally male; there are usually small testes, often tucked within the abdomen. As the researchers put it, if the condition had been known from the beginning, "the sisters would have been born as brothers."

Just to emphasize how tricky all this body-building can get, there's a peculiar genetic defect that seems to be clustered by heredity in a small group of villages in the Dominican Republic. The result of the defect is a failure to produce an enzyme that concentrates testosterone, specifically for building the genitals. One obscure little enzyme only, but here's what happens without it: You get a boy with undescended testes and a penis so short and stubby that it resembles an oversized clitoris.

In the mountain villages of this Caribbean nation, people are used to it. The children are usually raised as "conditional" girls. At puberty, the secondary tide of androgens rises and is apparently enough to finish the construction project. The scrotum suddenly descends, the phallus grows, and the child develops a distinctly male body — narrow hips, muscular build, and even slight beard growth. At that point, the family shifts the child over from daughter to son. The dresses are thrown out. He begins to wear male clothes and starts dating girls. People in the Dominican Republic are so familiar with this condition that there's a colloquial name for it: *guevedoces*, meaning "eggs (or testes) at twelve."

It's the comfort level with this slip-slide of sexual identity that's so remarkable and, I imagine, so comforting to the children involved. I'm positive that the sexual transition of these children is less traumatic than the abrupt awareness of the "sisters who would have been brothers." There's a message of tolerance there, well worth repeating, and there are some other key lessons, too.

These defects are rare and don't alter the basic male-female division of our species. They do emphasize how fragile those divisions can be. Biology allows flexibility, room to change, to vary and grow. With that comes room for error as well. That it's possible to live with these genetic defects, that they don't merely kill us off, is a reminder that we, male and female alike, exist on a continuum of biological possibilities that can overlap and sustain either sex.

Marc Breedlove points out that the most difficult task may be separat- 20
ing how the brain responds to hormones from how the brain responds to the *results* of hormones. Which brings us back, briefly, below the belt: In this context, the penis is just a result, the product of androgens at work before birth. "And after birth," says Breedlove, "virtually everyone who interacts with that individual will note that he has a penis, and will, in many instances, behave differently than if the individual was a female."

Do the ways that we amplify physical and behavioral differences in childhood shape who we become as adults? Absolutely. But to understand that, you have to understand the differences themselves — their beginning and the very real biochemistry that may lie behind them.

Here is a good place to focus on testosterone — a hormone that is both well-studied and generally underrated. First, however, I want to acknowledge that there are many other hormones and neurotransmitters that appear to influence behavior. Preliminary work shows that fetal boys are a little more active than fetal girls. It's pretty difficult to argue socialization at that point. There's a strong suspicion that testosterone may create the difference.

And there are a couple of relevant animal models to emphasize the point. Back in the 1960s, Robert Goy, a psychologist at the University of Wisconsin at Madison, first documented that young male monkeys play much more roughly than young females. Goy went on to show that if you manipulate testosterone level — raising it in females, damping it down in males — you can reverse those effects, creating sweet little male monkeys and rowdy young females.

Is testosterone the only factor at work here? I don't think so. But clearly we can argue a strong influence, and, interestingly, studies have found that girls with congenital adrenal hypoplasia — who run high in testosterone — tend to be far more fascinated by trucks and toy weaponry than most little girls are. They lean toward rough-and-tumble play, too. As it turns out, the strongest influence on this "abnormal" behavior is not parental disapproval, but the company of other little girls, who tone them down and direct them toward more routine girl games.

25 And that reinforces an early point: If there is indeed a biology to sex differences, we amplify it. At some point — when it is still up for debate — we gain a sense of our gender, and with it a sense of "gender-appropriate" behavior.

Some scientists argue for some evidence of gender awareness in infancy, perhaps by the age of twelve months. The consensus seems to be that full-blown "I'm a girl" or "I'm a boy" instincts arrive between the ages of two and three. Research shows that if a family operates in a very traditional, Beaver Cleaver kind of environment, filled with awareness of and association with "proper" gender behaviors, the "boys do trucks, girls do dolls" attitude seems to come very early. If a child grows up in a less traditional family, with an emphasis on partnership and sharing — "We all do the dishes, Joshua" — children maintain a more flexible sense of gender roles until about age six.

In this period, too, relationships between boys and girls tend to fall into remarkably strict lines. Interviews with children find that three-year-olds say that about half their friendships are with the opposite sex. By the age of five, that drops to 20 percent. By seven, almost no boys or girls have, or will admit to having, best friends of the opposite sex. They still hang out on the same playground, play on the same soccer teams. They may be friendly, but the real friendships tend to be boy-to-boy or girl-to-girl.

There's some interesting science that suggests that the space between boys and girls is a normal part of development; there are periods during which children may thrive and learn from hanging out with peers of the same sex. Do we, as parents, as a culture at large, reinforce such separations? Is the pope Catholic? One of my favorite studies looked at little boys who asked for toys. If they asked for a heavily armed action figure, they got the soldier about 70 percent of the time. If they asked for a "girl" toy, like a baby doll or a Barbie, their parents purchased it maybe 40 percent of the time. Name a child who won't figure out how to work *that* system.

How does all this fit together — toys and testosterone, biology and behavior, the development of the child into the adult, the way that men and women relate to one another?

30 Let me make a cautious statement about testosterone: It not only has some body-building functions, it influences some behaviors as well. Let's make that a little less cautious: These behaviors include rowdy play, sex drive, competitiveness, and an in-your-face attitude. Males tend to have a higher baseline of testosterone than females — in our species, about seven to ten times as much — and therefore you would predict (correctly, I think) that all of those behaviors would be more generally found in men than in women.

But testosterone is also one of my favorite examples of how responsive biology is, how attuned it is to the way we live our lives. Testosterone, it turns out, rises in response to competition and threat. In the days of our ancestors, this might have been hand-to-hand combat or high-risk hunting endeavors. Today, scientists have measured testosterone rise in athletes preparing for a game, in chess players awaiting a match, in spectators following a soccer competition.

If a person — or even just a person's favored team — wins, testosterone continues to rise. It falls with a loss. (This also makes sense in an evolutionary perspective. If one was being clobbered with a club, it would be extremely unhelpful to have a hormone urging one to battle on.) Testosterone also rises in the competitive world of dating, settles down with a stable and supportive relationship, climbs again if the relationship starts to falter.

It's been known for years that men in high-stress professions — say, police work or corporate law — have higher testosterone levels than men in the ministry. It turns out that women in the same kind of strong-attitude professions have higher testosterone than women who choose to stay home. What I like about this is the chicken-or-egg aspect. If you argue that testosterone influenced the behavior of those women, which came first? Did they have high testosterone and choose the law? Or did they choose the law, and the competitive environment ratcheted them up on the androgen scale? Or could both be at work?

And, returning to children for a moment, there's an ongoing study by Pennsylvania researchers, tracking that question in adolescent girls, who are being encouraged by their parents to engage in competitive activities that were once for boys only. As they do so, the researchers are monitoring, regularly, two hormones: testosterone and cortisol, a stress hormone. Will these hormones rise in response to this new, more traditionally male environment? What if more girls choose the competitive path; more boys choose the other? Will female testosterone levels rise, male levels fall? Will that wonderful, unpredictable, flexible biology that we've been given allow a shift, so that one day, we will literally be far more alike?

We may not have answers to all those questions, but we can ask them, 35
and we can expect that the answers will come someday, because science clearly shows us that such possibilities exist. In this most important sense, sex differences offer us a paradox. It is only through exploring and understanding what makes us different that we can begin to understand what binds us together.

Reading the Text

1. What effect do Blum's opening personal anecdotes have on the persuasiveness of her argument?
2. What evidence does Blum offer to support her contention that males are naturally more aggressive than females?
3. How does testosterone affect human behavior, according to Blum?
4. What does the term "'conditional' girls" (para. 17) mean for some members of a rural area in the Dominican Republic, and what significance does Blum attribute to this status?
5. In Blum's view, how do the cultural choices that humans make, such as engaging in sports or other competitive activities, affect hormone balances?

READING THE SIGNS

1. In your journal, reflect on the way your upbringing shaped your sense of appropriate gender behavior. Do you recall any patterns of preferring some toys or games over others? What media influences might have affected your attitudes?
2. **CONNECTING TEXTS** Blum's selection challenges the common cultural studies position that gender behavior is socially constructed. Write an essay in which you defend, qualify, or reject Blum's point of view. To develop your ideas, consult Aaron Devor's "Gender Role Behaviors and Attitudes" (p. 150) and Michael Hulshof-Schmidt's "What's in an Acronym?" (p. 163).
3. Write an essay describing how you would raise a boy to counteract the stereotypical tendencies to aggressive behavior. Alternatively, describe how you would raise a girl to avoid the common stereotypes associated with females.
4. Visit the library, and investigate recent research on the possible genetic basis for homosexuality. Then write an essay in which you extend Blum's argument for the biological basis of gendered behavior to sexual orientation. Alternatively, research the current scientific literature on transgenderism.
5. Research the news coverage of South African athlete Caster Semenya, who identifies as a woman but whose body produces a higher-than-usual level of testosterone. What does the tone and focus of the coverage, which tends to be on her medical history, reveal about cultural attitudes toward athletes who do not conform to gender conventions? To develop your argument, read Mariah Burton Nelson's "I Won. I'm Sorry." (p. 107).

MICHAEL HULSHOF-SCHMIDT

What's in an Acronym? Parsing the LGBTQQIP2SAA Community

As Michael Hulshof-Schmidt puts it in this entry from his personal blog *Social Justice for All*, "Most oppressed and minority communities have struggled with finding a descriptor that they feel embraces them and that they can embrace." This act of finding a name has been especially challenging for the queer community, which, by its own philosophy, resists the reductionist act of labeling human beings and behavior. Providing a succinct overview of the problem, Hulshof-Schmidt describes the difficulties that have cropped up in the ongoing attempt to be adequately inclusive, illustrating how full inclusiveness can result in some pretty complicated acronyms. Not to worry, however, Hulshof-Schmidt concludes, because "in the long run, the intent matters more than the label." Michael Hulshof-Schmidt is an instructor in the School of Social Work at Portland State University.

Every few months another online debate flares up about exactly what the LGBT community should call itself. Generally speaking, most people default to LGBT (or GLBT, with a slight majority favoring the L-first version). This explicitly calls out key components of a diverse group: Lesbian, Gay, Bisexual, Transgender. As shorthand goes, it's fairly effective, recognizing the spectrum of sexual orientation and gender identity in four simple letters. Of course, it can't please everyone, and like most compromises, leaves plenty of people feeling unheard.

Four other forms of shorthand see frequent use in the media and on the internet. Many people opt simply for "gay." Unfortunately, that leaves out any aspect of the community that doesn't identify explicitly with same-sex attraction. It also traditionally applies to men, resulting in sexist language, however unintentional.

Opponents of the community typically use "the homosexual community," which manages to be gender neutral but also leaves out significant populations (although those populations may be just as happy not to get attention from these groups). The more academic term "sexual minorities" is also used. Although this has broader meaning it also draws focus to the word "sexual," avoidance of which resulted in the use of the word "gay" in the first place. Members of the LGBT community don't want to be defined strictly by possible behavior, but as complex, fully realized human beings. In an America with a strong puritanical streak — even today — the word "sexual" still has too much power to stigmatize.

Many activists have reclaimed the word "queer" as a preferred descriptor. Taking back the word from the bullies and foes is a way to regain power. This is much like *Bitch* magazine co-opting a frequent slur as a way to raise feminist activists above their oppressors. For many, however, the scars from being called "queer" are too deep and too fresh to choose it as an identity. So what's a diverse, inclusion-inclined community to do?

Over time, a number of other additions have been suggested to the 5
LGBT acronym. The most common is Q, signifying "questioning" to recognize that many people are uncertain about their sexual orientation or gender identity (or both). Some also use the Q for queer. At full throttle, the letters wind up something like LGBTQQIP2SAA — Lesbian, Gay, Bisexual, Transgender,

- Two Q's to cover both bases (queer and questioning);
- I for Intersex, people with two sets of genitalia or various chromosomal differences;
- P for Pansexual, people who refuse to be pinned down on the Kinsey scale;
- 2S for Two-Spirit, a tradition in many First Nations that considers sexual minorities to have both male and female spirits;
- A for Asexual, people who do not identify with any orientation; and
- A for Allies, recognizing that the community thrives best with loving supporters, although they are not really part of the community itself.

That manages to be pretty inclusive, but it's also pretty unwieldy.

Labels are tricky things. Most oppressed and minority communities have struggled with finding a descriptor that they feel embraces them and that they can embrace. The evolution of Negro to Colored to Black to African-American shows a clear transition from outside labels to a community claiming its own identity, although many within the community object to African-American. The journey from Indians to Native Americans to First Nations is similar, with many outside the community being unfamiliar with the latter designation. The transition from handicapped to disabled was successful (and codified in law) but the attempt to destigmatize to "differently abled" was just too awkward to find common usage.

It's that kind of awkwardness that stymies the best attempts to find the magic LGBT label. The problem stems from the best of intentions, inclusion. People are complex, with multiple identities. Everyone has a sexual orientation, gender identity, race, religion (or lack thereof), ethnicity, and many other components. It's laudable for the LGBT community to recognize that there is strength in working together and to try to find a descriptor that shows that intent. In the long run, the intent matters more than the label. Rather than take umbrage at a less than fully inclusive LGBTQ — which at least shows good intent — let's focus on the work we need to do together to make this a better place for everyone.

Reading the Text

1. What explanation does Hulshof-Schmidt offer for the controversy in the LGBTQ+ community over what to call itself?
2. Summarize in your own words the reasons *gay, queer, homosexual communities* and *sexual minorities* can be considered problematic terms, according to Hulshof-Schmidt.
3. How does the debate about what to call the LGBTQ+ community mirror similar struggles that other minority groups have faced, according to Hulshof-Schmidt?
4. What does Hulshof-Schmidt mean by saying that, by adopting the term *queer* or *bitch* one is "taking back the word from the bullies and foes" (para. 4)?

Reading the Signs

1. In an essay, propose your own candidate for a label to describe the LGBTQ+ community. In class, share your suggested labels. What patterns do you see in the class's proposals?
2. **CONNECTING TEXTS** Select one of the other minority groups that Hulshof-Schmidt mentions, and research the history of labels that have been attached to it. Use your research as the basis of an essay in which you argue whether the most current nomenclature constitutes the best label for the group. To develop your ideas, read Rachelle Hampton's "Which People?" (p. 141).
3. Visit your school's website, and analyze the language used to describe the minority groups that Hulshof-Schmidt discusses in his selection. You might

pay particular attention to sections that discuss student groups and academic departments. Use your findings as evidence in an essay in which you assess the extent to which your school achieves the goal of inclusiveness that Hulshof-Schmidt recommends without being "unwieldy" (para. 6).

RACHEL LOWRY

Straddling Online and Offline Profiles, Millennials Search for Identity

It's hard to know who you really are when everyone counsels you to market yourself on such social networking sites as LinkedIn and Facebook, which is pretty much the fate of most of the people who belong to the generation of millennials. And so, as Rachel Lowry reports in this feature for *Deseret News*, a lot of millennials, who have spent their entire lives with digital technology and self-hyped social media profiles, have begun to wonder just who their authentic selves really are. Sometimes it's best just to find some time to be alone, but that's not easy to do when you're online all the time. So maybe it's time to turn that smartphone off, once in a while, so you can look for yourself. Rachel Lowry is an editor at *Citywire USA*.

Twenty-year-old Mariah Hanaike waits in the disconcerting silence of a temporary employment agency lobby in Redwood City, Calif. Though the interview has not yet begun, Hanaike said she knows she is being scrutinized before she shakes the hand of a potential employer. "You know the person you're going to meet is somewhere close in the building preparing for you, maybe by looking you up on Facebook or Googling your name, possibly reading an embarrassing entry about you on your mom's blog or being surprised to not find you on LinkedIn," said Hanaike. "I can't just be myself where and when I want because anything I do has the potential to end up on some site somewhere where anyone can look at it and judge. I feel like I need to water down who I am."

Millennials, the term given for those born between 1980 and 2000, may be suffering from an identity crisis as they search for their authentic self. According to a recent online study, one out of four millennials say they can only be their true self when alone. As today's twenty-somethings create online identities to market themselves professionally, as well as socially, some fear that the disparity between the two can prevent a young person from finding authentic self-definition.

Living Life Publicly

As today's younger generation navigates the transition to adulthood, reconciling between online and offline identities can be difficult.

Nearly 25 percent of all millennials say they can only be their true self when alone, Belgium researcher Joeri Van den Bergh found. In his book, *Millennials: How Cool Brands Stay Hot, Branding to Generation Y*, Van den Bergh argues that authenticity is key for brands to connect with millennials. "The key concept behind authenticity is to stay true to yourself, so we wanted to know when millennials stay true to themselves," he said.

Van den Bergh asked 4,056 people, ages 15 to 25, when they felt they were 5
or weren't being authentic online or offline, with friends, parents, partners or employers. Identity, he found, was strongly influenced by the back-and-forth of these two spheres. "Millennials are pre-wired to achieve and create success stories in their lives," Van den Bergh said. "They would rather blow up some stories or pretend they are having fun on Instagram and Facebook than admit they had a boring night out to the friends and immediate social circle." This can alter authenticity in identity, Van den Bergh found. Only half of the millennials surveyed believe themselves to be authentic and real. "[It's] a response to the social society in which private moments are rare and everything is transparent and in the open on social media," Van den Bergh said.

For Victor Ruiz, 25, a student at Utah State University, social media perpetuates the problem. "We live in a capitalist society," Ruiz said. "People don't want to be singled out, especially in a negative way, so they will try to make themselves look better and good to impress. They would try to make their online pages look as though they are living the American dream and not expose weakness." It's a "fluffy portrayal of reality," said 27-year-old Angie Rideout, a hairstylist in Salt Lake City. "It shows what we value, how we spend our time, and who we spend our time with."

If you don't participate online, you risk being uninvolved and out of touch, said Hanaike, who is also attending LDS Business College in Salt Lake City. "Nobody will show you to others for you, so you will be voiceless and unseen." Hanaike said online media can be detrimental to her offline identity. "I am perfectly capable of representing myself without a domain name or URL," she said. "But I do not have that option. My freedom is definitely being infringed upon. I can't just be myself where and when I want because literally anything I do has the potential to end up on some site somewhere where anyone can look at it and judge."

Twenty-three-year-old Braden Bissegger, a student at LDS Business College, agrees. "You're required to define yourself to be involved: Build a Facebook page and Twitter account and post your thoughts and show the world who you are," Bissegger said. "But what if that's inaccurate? What if we are all purporting to be something we're not? Yes, we are certainly in an identity crisis."

Linking In

Hanaike is one of 80 million millennials, ages 18 to 24, in the U.S., many of whom are competing for the job market, according to a 2010 U.S. Census Bureau report. How to get a leg up? Many say self-promotion through online media can be huge. "It's standard procedure for hiring managers to check out your Facebook, Twitter, and LinkedIn profiles," wrote Jenna Goudreau in a recent *Forbes* article. "Simply sifting through job postings and sending out applications en masse was never a good route to success, and is even less so now," wrote Phyllis Korkki, an employment editor for the *New York Times*. "One of the most important questions that many job seekers can ask these days is this: How searchable am I?"

10 Professional self-branding and social networking is necessary no matter what the economy looks like, according to David Lake, a 25-year-old marketer in Lindon. "When tools like these are available you can either keep up with the times and use them for your benefit, or you can let others take advantage of the opportunity," Lake said. "The days of a paper resume and a blind interview are over. With social media platforms and personal websites, interviewers can know a lot about who you are before the interview even starts."

For many millennials, however, self-branding can bleed into narcissism or the creation of a false persona. "It is upsetting to think that an employer can base their decision to hire me on who I appear to be on online media. That is not the person that they are hiring," said Hanaike. "I don't want to appear narcissistic when I talk to a potential employer," said Duncan Purser, 25, a student of managerial financial accounting. "But with the way applying for jobs goes in today's technological work, you have to promote yourself and continually go for presence."

Thoren Williams, a 22-year-old studying accounting at LDS Business College, agrees. "If you don't update your LinkedIn when applying for jobs, your personality doesn't come through on social media platforms and it can seem as if you don't have one," Williams said. "Potential employers may assume they know what type of an employee you would be because they've checked out your resume on LinkedIn."

It's almost necessary to be a little bit narcissistic, Hanaike said. "If you want to get noticed, or if you want someone to see your qualifications, you have to show them, lest you get swept away with the tide." For Hanaike, this can lead to a disparity between online and offline identity.

Reconciling Identities

So how do you reconcile the two identities and maintain a true center?

15 For Mutual Leonard, a 29-year-old actuarial analyst living in Salt Lake City, culture can be a strong source of identity. "Mormons with pioneer heritage, for example, say 'My grandmother walked across the plains. I'm not giving up my religion for anything. This is my identity.'" Leonard said culture prepares youth

for adulthood, preparing boys to be men through priesthood duties in a church, or hunting for your first kill as initiation into a tribe. "Psychologically, you need that kind of a thing," he said, noting that identity requires an outward focus. "You will establish identity as soon as you focus on something beyond yourself."

Katie Greer, a nation-wide internet and technology safety trainer, recommends tolerance. "I could follow someone's entire day online, seeing when they wake up, eat, what they wear, and the traffic they hit," said Greer. "Perhaps we should lift our eyes from our screens more often and live the lives we are purporting." Reconciliation, Greer said, requires creating an identity worth owning up to online. "I'm 30 years old and it's really bizarre to think of all the things in my life that have formed my identity: Soccer, politics, clubs, sports, friends," Greer said. "I worked really hard to prove who I was, for myself, my friends, my family, the colleges I've applied to. Can I just put all that effort into saying I am something I'm not online? It's kind of like cheating." The things today's twenty-somethings do can later define you, Greer warned. Being cautious about what one posts online can avoid false labels and assumptions.

Millennials, themselves, are learning how to create a consistent identity across the many platforms before them. "I meet people who seem to be in a sort of fog because they are so focused on Facebook and getting likes," Bissegger said. "But then I've also seen many people who are not trying to boast or brag about themselves, but trying to show how they are contributing to something or giving of themselves and social media is one of their most effective platforms." In fact, those who are able to see social media as a means of getting beyond yourself are the ones who are confident in their identity, Hanaike said. "We've been given a lot of crap, as millennials, but if we want our future to be something significant and if we want our lives to be great, we have to have self-confidence," she said. "It takes a certain level of self-awareness to think I am going to provide something for the community and the world that no one else is, so that I can do the best job of doing this. That is the antithesis of an identity crisis."

For David Lake, the two platforms can actually enhance one's identity both online and offline. "Facebook and other social networks give a voice and confidence to many people that didn't previously have either of those things," Lake said. "They might be shy or naturally lacking in confidence. Now that they have a stage to project their voice, we really get to see who those people are."

Reading the Text

1. Summarize in your own words Lowry's explanation for why millennials feel that they are losing touch with their essential selves.
2. What does researcher Joeri Van den Bergh mean by saying, "Millennials are prewired to achieve and create success stories in their lives" (para. 5)?
3. Why does interviewee Mutual Leonard claim that culture can ground one's sense of identity?
4. In your own words, explain how concerns about future job prospects can affect millennials' profiles on social networking sites such as Facebook and LinkedIn.

Reading the Signs

1. In a journal entry, describe how you might have profiled yourself on a social networking site. Did you try to "improve" your self-image, or did you just describe yourself as accurately as you could? Then consider why you chose that profile. If you have not constructed a social media profile, discuss why you prefer to avoid that venue.
2. **CONNECTING TEXTS** In an essay, explore how the job-related stress that Lowry discusses supports or deviates from the proposition that social media control our lives more than users control social media. As evidence, you might interview some upper-division students who are contemplating entering the job market and ask them about their social media profiles. To develop your ideas, read Joseph Turow's "The Daily You: How the New Advertising Industry Is Defining Your Identity and Your Worth" (p. 265).
3. **CONNECTING TEXTS** Lowry suggests that young adults feel pressured by job counselors, teachers, and parents to use social media to market themselves. But they are also influenced by their peers. In an essay, evaluate the influence adults and peers have on engagement with social media. In your essay, you should base your analysis on interviews with social media users, perhaps analyzing how they behaved in high school and in college. To develop your ideas, consult Alicia Eler's "There's a Lot More to a Selfie than Meets the Eye" (p. 340), Nancy Jo Sales's "From the Instamatic to Instagram: Social Media and the Secret Lives of Teenagers" (p. 360), or Jacob Silverman's "'Pics or It Didn't Happen': The Mantra of the Instagram Era" (p. 368).
4. **CONNECTING TEXTS** Lowry elucidates some ways that online communication can be problematic. Brainstorm various ways that Facebook and other sites have affected millennials' sense of and projection of identity. Then use your thoughts to support an essay in which you argue your own position on how social media affect young people's sense of identity. For further ideas, consult Judy Estrin's "I Helped Create the Internet, and I'm Worried about What It's Doing to Young People" (p. 337), Nancy Jo Sales's "From the Instamatic to Instagram: Social Media and the Secret Lives of Teenagers" (p. 360), and Jacob Silverman's "'Pics or It Didn't Happen': The Mantra of the Instagram Era" (p. 368).

SOPHIE GILBERT

Millennial Burnout Is Being Televised

Netflix's hit series *Tidying Up with Marie Kondo* isn't just a "thing," it's a sign of life in the U.S.A., pointing to "a time in which identity and achievements are visual metrics to be publicly displayed and curated, and a happy home is a perfected, optimized one." Or so Sophie Gilbert argues in this exploration of the quest of the millennial generation for success in a hyper-competitive and unforgiving society. So obsessive has this quest for success become, Gilbert suggests, that it amounts to a "generational disorder" which may be burning out America's largest demographic while making everyone "miserable." Sophie Gilbert is a staff writer at *The Atlantic*, where this article first appeared.

The fifth episode of *Tidying Up with Marie Kondo*, Netflix's effervescent new reality series, deals with Frank and Matt, a couple living in West Hollywood, California. Both writers, they have a touching love story involving Tinder, a too-small apartment filled with detritus from past roommates, and a burning desire to prove their adulting bona fides. They are, in short, the archetypal Millennial couple. The dramatic hook of the episode is that Frank's parents are coming to visit for the first time, and Frank wants to impress them, to make them see "that the life we've created together is something to be admired."

Frank and Matt, in other words, want their home to reflect their identities and sense of self (as opposed to the cutlery preferences of the people Matt lived with after college). They've internalized the idea that the signifiers of success are primarily visual. "I don't know that I've given [my parents] any reason to respect me as an adult," Frank agonizes at one point, which is absurd, given his apparently successful career and adorable relationship. "I'm organized in some aspects of my life. Like, professionally, my email inbox is organized, I'm great. And I just get frustrated with myself that I haven't translated that into my home life. It feels like I give it all at work and then I come home and am like, *pmph*." He makes a gesture like a deflated balloon.

If the viral success of *Tidying Up with Marie Kondo* is anything to go by, Frank and Matt—their exhaustion, and their understanding that an adult existence is an optimized one—aren't anomalous in their anxieties. Kondo, a Japanese organizational consultant, has sold more than 11 million books in 40 countries since the publication of her magnum opus, *The Life-Changing Magic of Tidying Up*. Compared to the interest in her television series, though, Kondo's previous achievements are a relative blip. Netflix didn't respond to queries about how many people had viewed *Tidying Up*, but in the U.S. at least, the show's release has sparked a feverish curiosity about Kondo and her practices.

More than 192,000 Instagram pictures of color-coded sock drawers and neatly labeled mesh containers now bear the #KonMari hashtag. Thrift stores around the U.S. have reported record donation hauls as inspired Americans streamline their possessions. In barely three weeks, Kondo has gone from a best-selling author to a cultural juggernaut. In part, this is due to Netflix's prodigious reach, particularly among young Millennials, who are five times more likely to watch a show on the streaming service than access it via any other provider. But the success of *Tidying Up* also speaks to how neatly some episodes of the show sync with its cultural moment, a time in which identity and achievements are visual metrics to be publicly displayed and curated, and a happy home is a perfected, optimized one.

For Millennials like me, people born roughly between 1981 and 1996, the 5
desire to flaunt our tidying prowess isn't just about showing off. A 2017 study by the British researchers Thomas Curran and Andrew P. Hill found that Millennials

display higher rates of perfectionism than previous generations, in part because we've been raised with the idea that our future success hinges on being exceptional. But, as Frank suggests, we're also struggling with what it means to really grow up. The aspirational markers of adulthood used to be relatively straightforward: graduation, marriage, children, homeownership, a 401(k). But now that Millennials are so overloaded with student debt that we struggle to buy places to live, adulthood is more complicated. It's more performative. It's #KonMari.

Four days after Netflix released *Tidying Up*, *BuzzFeed News*'s Anne Helen Petersen published what feels like a seminal analysis of a connected phenomenon. "How Millennials Became the Burnout Generation" elegantly and systematically documents how the malaise Frank complains about — putting so much effort into his work that he has nothing left for himself — is symptomatic of a much larger generational disorder. Millennials, Petersen argues, have been raised with the belief that they have to be exceptional, or they won't succeed in an economy that since the early 2000s has seemed to dance perpetually on the edge of an abyss. "I never thought the system was equitable," she writes. "I knew it was winnable for only a small few. I just believed I could continue to optimize myself to become one of them."

This conviction is why *Tidying Up with Marie Kondo* has drawn so many fans in such a short time, and why your feeds might suddenly be bloated with soaring piles of clothes and arguments about whether to Kondo your books. Millennials have come to believe, Petersen writes, that "personal spaces should be optimized just as much as one's self and career." But the conspicuous nature of #KonMari also suggests a larger vacuum. Millennials don't just gravitate to Marie Kondo because they don't have apartments big enough to own things. What *Tidying Up* offers is both a counterpoint to the way they've been raised (*less is more*, versus *more is always better*) and an endorsement: The promise, at least as Millennial culture seems to have interpreted it, is that if people work to organize their lives to look just right, the rest will follow. The performance of the self has become more important than the reality. Even TV has noticed.

If Marie Kondo is the high priestess of burned-out Millennials, Fyre Festival was their summer solstice. In 2017, a large adult grifter named Billy McFarland partnered with the rapper Ja Rule to sell tickets to a festival in the Bahamas that promised to be the apotheosis of an Instagram-worthy event: megastars (Kendall Jenner, Bella Hadid); spectacular food; luxe but eco-friendly accommodations; music by Major Lazer, Migos, and Blink-182. McFarland partnered with a marketing company called Jerry Media that paid supermodels to promote the event on their social-media accounts, cultivating the sense that Fyre Festival would be the exclusive gathering for stars that any schmo could also buy a ticket to.

The seeds of Fyre Festival's success were also its downfall: When attendees finally arrived at what turned out to be the gravelly parking lot near a Sandals resort, they documented everything they found on social media. Like the fact that the only places for people to sleep were unassigned FEMA tents with pallet mattresses. And that instead of luxurious communal bathrooms with showers, there were porta-potties. The most iconic post from Fyre Festival, in the end, was a picture of a sandwich: plain bread with two slices of slimy American cheese, accompanied by the hashtags #fyrefraud and #dumpsterfyre.

A car crash in slow motion, Fyre Festival was a catastrophe on such a 10
colossal scale that two documentaries, released within days of each other, are trying to make sense of it. Netflix's *Fyre*, as my colleague David Sims has written, takes a relatively straightforward approach to excavating the whole fiasco, accounting for not only McFarland's crimes and the public spectacle of the festival's monumental collapse, but also the Bahamian workers who still haven't been paid for their efforts.

Fyre Fraud, surprise-dropped by Hulu last Monday, takes a different approach. Directed by Jenner Furst and Julia Willoughby Nason, it mines the sociological implications of Fyre Fest, and what it says about a generation of Americans that they're so susceptible to a scammer with an Instagram account. *Fyre Fraud* includes parts of a taped interview with McFarland himself (who was supposedly paid for his participation), but they're the least revealing moments in the documentary. More interesting is how *Fyre Fraud* uses the selling of the festival to consider the ways some Millennials understand identity, including their anxieties about affirming their existences online — literally, *Pics or it didn't happen*.

Fyre Fraud posits that, for all the sloppiness of his grift, McFarland actually has a surprisingly intuitive sense of what Millennials want, and how to market it to them. Having been raised with the sense that being exceptional is the only way to thrive, Millennials can be hyperaware of their own status relative to others, and ferociously invested in elevating themselves above the pack. As preposterous as the Fyre Festival promotional video might seem now, it pings all the right dopamine receptors in an ongoing loop of stick (the acute FOMO of knowing everyone important is somewhere doing something fabulous without you) and carrot (countless Instagram opportunities for personal branding and self-curation). Influencers, the *New Yorker* writer Jia Tolentino says in *Fyre Fraud*, are people who have refined and monetized the art of this "performance of an attractive life."

Which brings us back to the perfectionism study. Millennials, born during the Reagan, Bush Sr., and Clinton presidencies, are the first real babies spawned by neoliberalism and its overarching message of competitive individualism. Curran and Hill wanted to establish whether growing up amid these ideologies made Millennials more likely to be perfectionists, and therefore more likely to be depressed, anxious, unhappy, and dissatisfied with themselves. They concluded not only that perfectionism rates have risen, but also that Millennials' identities have been fractured by shifting cultural values.

Even as they're poorer, Millennials are more materialistic: 81 percent of Americans born during the 1980s say that accruing wealth is among their significant life goals, more than 20 percent higher than previous generations.

As a national belief in the collective has given way to an emphasis on the individual, Millennials have had to become less inhibited about the pursuit of self-gain, and more shrewd about how they define themselves. Amplified by social media, such perfectionism urges the posting of absurdly idealized images, which, transmitted, reinforce the cycle of unrealistic physical ideals and a sense of alienation. "Neoliberalism," Curran and Hill conclude, "has succeeded in shifting cultural values . . . to now emphasize competitiveness, individualism, and irrational ideals of the perfectible self."

15 The messages that Millennials in the Western world were raised with, in other words, have taught them to work harder and better than ever before, in all aspects of their lives. And that work is making a generation miserable, as Petersen documents, as they strive to attain success and avoid failure, and are permanently attuned to the perceived expectations of others. They've constructed flimsy charades of identities based on what they think other people will want. They want to prove that their lives, as Frank says in *Tidying Up*, are things to be admired, and that their homes, vacations, children, closets all function as projections of their best selves: organized, attractive, authentic. Unattainable.

Reading the Text

1. How are Frank and Matt, the couple whose story opens Gilbert's article, considered exemplary of the millennial generation?
2. How does the popularity of *Tidying Up with Marie Kondo* extend beyond a simple desire for neatness, according to Gilbert?
3. In Gilbert's view, why is "the performance of the self . . . more important than the reality" (para. 7) for many millennials?
4. How did the Frye Festival tap into the desires and anxieties of millennials, as Gilbert explains it?
5. In your own words, what is neoliberalism, and according to Gilbert, how has that belief influenced millennials' sense of identity?
6. What does Gilbert mean by the claim that "some Millennials understand identity" as "*Pics or it didn't happen*" (para. 11)?

Reading the Signs

1. **CONNECTING TEXTS** To what extent could it be argued that millennials' concern with the public display of their identities reflects an understanding of how our material possessions operate as signs? To develop your ideas, you might watch some episodes of *Tidying Up with Marie Kondo*, or read James A. Roberts's "The Treadmill of Consumption" (p. 233).
2. Researchers Thomas Curran and Andrew P. Hill attribute many millennials' attitudes to a desire for perfectionism borne out of a need to be exceptional. In an essay, explore the extent to which these desires shape the identity of the next generation, Gen Z. To develop your ideas, interview Gen Z students from several different majors about their life goals and the ways in which they define themselves.

3. **CONNECTING TEXTS** Adopt the perspective of Mark Manson ("The Disease of More," p. 89) and write an essay in which you argue the extent to which millennials' desire for perfectionism is a "generational disorder" (para. 6). Would Manson see millennials affected "by shifting cultural values" (para. 13), or would he see continuity between this generation and previous ones?
4. **CONNECTING TEXTS** Write an argumentative essay in which you explore how social media may encourage the desire for perfectionism, as Gilbert defines it. To develop your ideas, read Nancy Jo Sales's "From Instamatic to Instagram: Social Media and the Secret Lives of Teenagers" (p. 360) and Jacob Silverman's "'Pics or It Didn't Happen'—The Mantra of the Instagram Era" (p. 368).

DAVE PATTERSON

Shame by a Thousand Looks

"Poverty sucks," a highly irreverent poster declares, but for Dave Patterson it isn't poverty so much as the attitude that people have toward the poor that sucks. And in this personal essay from *Salon*, he describes a new category of microaggressions that he calls "shame by a thousand looks" — that brief glance "brimming with revulsion, pity, fear" — which people without means often have to endure. Turning his childhood poverty into something to be proud of rather than to conceal, Patterson has written *Soon the Light Will Be Perfect*, a novel about growing up in the lower middle class.

When I was a kid, my family suffered two tragedies that planted us firmly in America's lower middle class: my father lost his job at a weapons manufacturing plant and my mother was diagnosed with cancer. Though my mother and father assured us that everything was fine —"We'll get through this," my sickened mother had insisted — one summer afternoon my oldest brother urgently dragged me into our parents' bedroom.

"Look," he said, lifting the lid on my mother's jewelry box.

There, lit by a soft slant of July sunlight, was a stash of strange-looking currency.

"What are these?" I asked, picking up the stiff bills.

"Food stamps," my brother said. His voice as definitive as a door closing. 5

I fanned the bills out in my hand. The words "FOOD COUPON" were etched in inky capital letters on each one. As I studied the bills, my brother looked down at me — the faint shadow of a mustache beginning to sprout on his upper lip — when I caught his eye, his nose scrunched, his eyes tightened, and his neck recoiled. He eyed the bills, then me. Sweat developed on my forehead;

my skin prickled. I wanted to hide. His actions were barely perceptible; his face held this look for only a moment before it vanished. There was a sound from the kitchen. Our mother was up from her chemo nap, rested enough to make us dinner before she'd have to lie down again. My brother snatched the bills, shoved them in the jewelry box, and slammed the lid.

A few days later, I saw the look again. I was at the supermarket with my mother and three brothers. Our cart was more empty than usual. A fact we didn't discuss as we trekked down each aisle, our mother demanding in a tired voice that we put back boxes of name brand cereal or two liter bottles of soda. At the checkout, I was considering the few items my mother had allowed into our cart, when she produced the FOOD COUPONS from her purse. The cashier spotted the food stamps, and for the briefest moment — we're talking two seconds max — the middle-aged woman eyed the bills, then my mother, then my three squawking brothers, and as her eyes landed on me, her face contorted: nostrils upturned, eyes narrowed, an imperceptible sigh escaped her lips. Then it was gone. She took the bills, bagged the groceries, and we went home.

Over the next two years my mother battled the tumors in her stomach, my father fought unemployment, and we all suffered the flashbulb looks of disdain as people around us read the signals of our poverty. Looks I endured all the way through college as the wake of my childhood poverty lapped each present moment — looks I still get today when people find out I was raised in a poor household in rural Vermont.

Even well-meaning, liberal-minded people will betray the slightest mien of disgust when I tell them my brothers and I used to scrape the black layer off burnt toast, because there wasn't enough bread to waste in our house.

Last year was the first time I heard the term "microaggression." The term 10
turned me off initially. It seemed like a nuanced way for the far left to shoot barbs at the far right in America. Most days, I want nothing to do with the bipartisan battles our country fights endlessly under this president.

Over the course of weeks, however, the idea of microaggressions worked over my mind. And then it struck me: this was what I had experienced my entire life as a result of being raised poor in America.

Memories looped in my head like a film montage at hyper speed. That look. *The* look. The one brimming with revulsion, pity, fear. My mind flooded with experiences where that look lingered on countless faces for the briefest of moments. When middle-school classmates spotted my K-Mart-purchased high tops, when drivers heard the growl of our unfixed muffler on the highway, when college classmates discovered I was from a shitty town in northern Vermont. "Oh. I thought you were from Connecticut," a girl from my dorm had said, her voice betraying the disappointment she felt upon discovering where I was from.

Even now as I write this, the lifetime of microaggressions I suffered as a byproduct of childhood poverty plays in a crackled loop. And with the memories comes the feeling that first washed over me in my parents' bedroom as my brother eyed me holding a handful of food stamps. It was shame.

Today I have the vocabulary to understand my childhood. These microaggressions were shame by a thousand looks. Each just a nick on the skin. And after a thousand nicks, my shame was so internalized that for years I only spoke of my childhood in the vaguest of terms. I was from "just outside of Burlington," not Milton, a town with sprawling trailer parks and pot-holed dirt roads. It's the town featured in *Rolling Stone*'s expose on the heroin epidemic in Vermont. This is just one whitewashing of my lower-middle-class childhood. There are countless others.

15 What is most painful about these microaggressions is that they seem often to be involuntary. So deeply ingrained in the American psyche that the aggressor might not even know he or she had flashed any look at all. The knee-jerk expression elicits the ideal that poverty — even for children who have no control over the circumstances they're thrust into — is to be shunned. That poor people are to be pitied and ultimately hated because they didn't work hard enough to pull themselves up by the bootstraps and take their slice of the American Dream. The microaggressions told me that the poor are disgusting, because they are poor by choice. My father is the hardest-working man I've ever met. We were not poor by choice.

After decades of hiding my childhood poverty, I now wear it like a fucking badge of honor. It took a lot of time. I shunned my own past so violently that even as a writer I avoided the subject of my childhood. But then I stopped. I had to. I have my own kids now. What, am I going to hide my past even to them? I had the courage to write a novel that exposed my lower-middle-class roots. I had the courage to share it with my agent, who sold it to a publisher. The lacerations of shame I suffered through a lifetime of microaggressions have scabbed over. But I bear the scars that I no longer hide. I brandish them in a manner that says, "If you're going to make me feel shame for my past, don't hide it in a subtle look, say it to my face."

Reading the Text

1. What events cast Patterson's family into poverty?
2. What response do you have to Patterson's opening anecdote about his childhood? How do Patterson's self-references throughout his article affect your response to his overall argument?
3. How is the term *microaggression* most commonly used, and how does Patterson's use of the term compare to that common significance?
4. Why does Patterson claim that it is intrinsic to the American psyche to consider poverty, and those affected by it, as something to be "shunned" (para. 15)?

Reading the Signs

1. In class, form small groups and have each brainstorm connotations typically associated with different socioeconomic groups (for instance, poor, middle-class, upper-middle-class, the 1 percent). Use the class's results to develop an essay in which you argue how class labels can affect a person's identity. To develop your ideas, consult the Introduction to this chapter.

2. Patterson identifies his roots as "lower-middle-class" (para. 14), but his essay frequently refers to his living in poverty. Research the economic conditions of the lower middle class and underclass in the wake of the Great Recession and write a paper supporting, refuting, or modifying the argument that the lower middle classes are now effectively impoverished.
3. Study your school's student conduct code and determine whether it lists policies governing microaggressions and whether it clearly defines what microaggressions are. Then, write an essay arguing whether socioeconomic class status should be included in such policies.
4. **CONNECTING TEXTS** In the Introduction to Chapter 1, the American mythology of class equality through social mobility is explored. Write an essay in which you assess the reality behind this mythology, using Patterson's experience as a test case. To develop your ideas, read George Packer's "Celebrating Inequality" (p. 86) and Alfred Lubrano's "The Shock of Education" (p. 100).

KWAME ANTHONY APPIAH

What Does It Mean to "Look Like Me"?

In the quest for a more inclusive America, a desire for people who "look like me" is often expressed, especially within popular culture. The lack of such people lies at the heart of literary classics — for example, Toni Morrison's *The Bluest Eye* — but somehow, Kwame Anthony Appiah believes, while the "emotions [the phrase] speaks to are real," it can be "trailed by jangling paradoxes, like tin cans tied to a newlywed's car." Deconstructing the complexities that are entailed when someone who "looks like me" is invoked, Appiah concludes that "the most ambitious forms of art and entertainment are always telling us: Don't be so sure what you look like," because identity "is less a mirror than a canvas." Kwame Anthony Appiah is a professor of philosophy at New York University, and the author of *The Lies That Bind: Rethinking Identity*.

It's a formula that we turn to again and again to affirm the value of inclusion, especially in the realm of popular culture: the importance of people who "look like me."

The actor Eva Longoria, who appears in the film *Dora and the Lost City of Gold*, in which the principals are played by Latinx actors, has said she had to take the part because of what the film represented "for my community and for people who look like me." The playwright Tarell Alvin McCraney, explaining what drove him to create the new television drama series *David Makes Man*, which follows the life of a black boy in a public-housing project, observed: "John Hughes made several movies that depicted the rich interior lives of young white American men and women. I just want the same for people who look like me." The comedian Ali Wong inspired the writer Nicole Clark to confess that she "didn't think she liked stand-up until a few years ago, when I realized the problem was the lack of comedians who look like me and tell jokes that I 'get.'"

The "look like me" formula appeals because it feels so simple and literal. We can think of a black or Asian toddler who gets to play with dolls that share her racial characteristics, in an era when Barbie, blessedly, is no longer exclusively white. The emotions it speaks to are real, and urgent. And yet the celebratory formula is trailed by jangling paradoxes, like tin cans tied to a newlywed's car.

For one thing, nobody means it literally. Asians don't imagine that all Asians look alike; blacks don't think all blacks look alike. Among Latinx celebrities, Eva Mendes doesn't look like Cameron Diaz; Sammy Sosa doesn't look like . . . Sammy Sosa.

5 What the visual metaphor usually signifies, then, is a kinship of social identity. That was apparent in July when the soccer star Megan Rapinoe declared that "Trump's message excludes people that look like me." She didn't mean extremely fit white women; she meant lesbians and gays.

But the complexities don't end there. When it comes to representation, two cultural conversations are happening at the same time. One is about "speaking our truths" — about exploring in-group cultural commonalities. The writer Zenobia Jeffries Warfield has explained, in this spirit, that she decided to watch films and shows only by filmmakers and performers of color "because who can tell our truths better than we can?"

Here, the cultural conversation is about the comedians whose jokes you "get" — the in-group references that resonate with you, that trigger a knowing "nailed it!" smile. It's about the sparks of recognition that some black viewers get watching comedies like *Insecure* and *Black-ish*, and some Asian-American viewers get from entertainments like *Fresh Off the Boat* and the Netflix feature *Always Be My Maybe*.

That's one way of "looking like me." But it doesn't quite explain the "look like me" fervor that blockbusters like *Crazy Rich Asians* and *Black Panther* inspired in Asian- and black-identified audiences. That fervor points to the other cultural conversation about representation.

Crazy Rich Asians, for all its shrewd social observations, is about a group of people who are anything but representative. It's no criticism to say that a story in which the American daughter of a single working-class mother is whisked away by a billionaire to an enchanted kingdom of unfathomable richesse in Singapore has the same realism level as *The Princess Diaries*. What matters is that it's a Hollywood film about Asians in which Asians rule. This has special significance, the writer Jiayang Fan says, when it comes to "Asian-Americans, a largely madeup group that is united, more than anything else, by a historical marginalization."

10 Paradoxically, then, a film like this appeals not by depicting that marginalization but by inverting it. We want our dreams, not just our realities, to be represented.

The same goes for *Black Panther*. Let me go out on a limb and say that the fictional land of Wakanda isn't a very representative picture of black life on any continent. What made the film so important, the writer Allegra Frank tells us, is that "an entire group of people that look like me" got to be heroes in a big-budget blockbuster. Yes, actors of color are often stars of such movies, but that usually feels like a casting choice, not an indelible feature of the character. It mattered that the characters in *Black Panther*, not to mention the film's Afrofuturist vibe, were specifically and not contingently black.

What such films deliver is a way of "looking like me" that's as much about aspiration as identification. We say that their characters look like us; maybe what we mean is that we wish to look like them.

Lil Nas X, whose song "Old Town Road" galloped to the top of the charts and set up a homestead there, wasn't exactly speaking his "truth" when he rapped, "I got the horses in the back." A young black man from Atlanta, Lil Nas X had never been on a horse. The "yeehaw agenda" — the trend of black cultural figures in rancher attire that fueled and was fueled by his countryrap hit — is chiefly an aesthetic, the cowboy counterpart to the tech-infused offerings of Afrofuturism. It proceeds in defiance of social realism, that default mode of early-stage minority representations. It's a mash-up of memes, an exercise in cultural unbundling. That's why Lil Nas X didn't think twice about releasing a remix with a Korean rapper titled "Seoul Town Road."

Or consider Tessa Thompson, the mixed-race actor who played the superhero Valkyrie in *Thor: Ragnarok*. "I think it's really great that young comic book readers that look like me can see themselves in a film," she said. The Valkyries are an inheritance from Norse mythology, no doubt signal-boosted by the cliché of the Wagnerian soprano wearing horns. Should black girls be encouraged to identify with the ultimate Nordic icon? Well, why not?

15 What these fantasies ask is, Who gets to tell you what you look like? It's not a representation of identity so much as it is a renegotiation of it.

How identity relates to identification is, of course, a complicated matter. Consider Gurinder Chadha's recent film *Blinded by the Light*, based on a memoir by the journalist and broadcaster Sarfraz Manzoor. Set in the late 1980s, the film is about a teenager from a Pakistani family in the working-class English town of Luton. His father loses his job at the auto plant; racist hooligans pose a regular menace. Then our protagonist discovers the albums of Bruce Springsteen. The lyrics — about restive dreams amid disappointment, about a desperation to leave the hardship town of his childhood — hit him with the force of revelation.

How does Mr. Manzoor's story relate to the "looks like me" conceit? You could argue that in some meaningful sense, Bruce Springsteen *does* look like him; class, too, is a dimension of identity. But a sensibility — a matter of personal identity, not a collective identity — is what really galvanizes the kid from Luton. Would he be truer to himself if he gave up Mr. Springsteen's songs for the Bhangra-disco music that his sister favors?

The truth is that our best stories and songs often gain potency by complicating our received notions of identity; they're less a mirror than a canvas — and everyone has a brush. It takes nothing away from the thrill of feeling represented, then, to point out what the most ambitious forms of art and entertainment are always telling us: Don't be so sure what you look like.

Reading the Text

1. Why does Appiah call "looks like me" a "formula" (para. 1) and a "conceit" (para. 17)?
2. What is the appeal of the "looks like me" formula, according to Appiah?
3. Why is the notion of "looking like me" complicated, in Appiah's view?
4. How does Appiah see the notion of "looking like me" affecting popular culture?

Reading the Signs

1. In your journal, explore your own response to Appiah's question, "What does it mean to 'look like me'?" Do you wish popular cultural stars resembled you? If so, what would that mean? If you do not care if they do, why not?
2. In class, form teams and debate the proposition that movie and TV directors should cast only actors according to the gender identities and ethnicities of the characters that they portray. Use the results of the class's debate as a springboard for your own essay in response to this proposition, using specific current media examples to support your case.
3. Write an essay in which you defend, refute, or modify Appiah's claim that "our best stories and songs often gain potency by complicating our received notions of identity; they're less a mirror than a canvas" (para. 18).
4. Some students and educators suggest that a school environment that is especially conducive to learning includes instructors who "look like" their students. In an essay, defend, repudiate, or complicate this notion. As you develop your ideas, consider how a school with instructors who predominately "look like" their students would be created. What advantages or disadvantages would this approach to education have?

Section 2

EVERYDAY LIFE

Johner Images/Getty Images

3

CONSUMING PASSIONS

The Culture of American Consumption

The CCI

The CCI is one of the most avidly watched broadcasts in America, and, no, it isn't a television crime series. Based on the monthly Consumer Confidence Survey, as issued by The Conference Board (a private, nonprofit organization that, in its own words, "is a global, independent business membership and research association working in the public interest"), the Consumer Confidence Index (CCI) charts the mood of American consumers. When the index goes up, the stock market goes up; when it goes down, the stock market goes down with it.

What does this have to do with popular culture? The short answer is "everything," because American popular culture is grounded in consumption, whether we're considering the direct purchase of goods and services; the enjoyment of music, movies, and television; or simply the use of a smartphone or other digital devices and all that they offer you. That's why your Facebook page, Instagram account, and Snapchat activities are free; it's why commercial television and radio are free as well. Such media are free because they're underwritten by advertising and marketing expenditures made by companies that want to sell you something. While movies, for their part, are usually not free, they are commodities to be consumed through the purchase of theater tickets, DVDs, cable subscriptions, Netflix or Redbox accounts, and so on. Music, too, is a commodity, whether consumed via download, CD, or vinyl (thanks to a small resurgence of that most venerable of music technologies). In short, American popular culture is grounded in a consumer society.

The fact that ours is a consumer society has profound cultural implications. Perhaps the most critical is the way that consumerism has redirected middle-class values, once based in thrift, self-denial, and hard work (as descended from the Protestant work ethic), toward a new consciousness devoted to instant gratification, luxury, and pleasure. Once the preserve of a tiny leisure-class minority, such values have not simply transformed America from a producer to a consumer society. Ultimately, they have also come to endanger the very world in which we live because the current levels of consumption in America are simply not environmentally sustainable.

But there's little chance that America's consumerist consciousness will be abating in the foreseeable future because consumption is not only a source of economic activity and personal pleasure; it is also a form of communication. That is to say, our possessions aren't simply objects, they're **signs** — from the out-and-out status symbols whose purpose is to convey your place in the social hierarchy, to the clothes you wear, the music you listen to, and even the smartphone you choose to buy — all of which convey to others what sort of person you are and what your values may be. Like all signs, they get their meaning from the cultural **systems**, or **codes**, within which they appear, and their meanings can change not only as history reworks the systems that define them but also when they are subjected to conflicting interpretations that are grounded in differing cultural systems. Take leggings, for instance.

#leggingsdaynd

On March 25th, 2019, *The Observer* — the student newspaper of Notre Dame University, St. Mary's College, and Holy Cross College — published a letter to the editor by a self-described "mother of four sons," pleading with the women of Notre Dame to stop wearing leggings. Decrying a "world in which women continue to be depicted as 'babes' by movies, video games, music videos, etc.," the writer complained that the form-fitting garment "makes it hard on Catholic mothers to teach their sons that women are someone's daughters and sisters. That women should be viewed first as people — and all people should be considered with respect."

Then all hell broke loose.

Within hours, the internet was alight with counter-protests, declaring that women weren't to blame for male misbehavior and that, in effect, the unhappy mother should look to her sons and leave women alone to wear what they want. A new Twitter hashtag — #leggingsdaynd — as well as a Facebook announcement appeared, declaring the upcoming Tuesday as a "Leggings Pride" and "Love Your Leggings" day at Notre Dame, while pundits at news sources from around the country weighed in on the matter, overwhelmingly on the side of the protesters. To understand how a simple article of clothing can become a potent political signifier, prompting a passionate controversy, we can begin our semiotic analysis by constructing the **systems** within which they move from denotational materiality to connotational signification — in this case, the history of women's fashions and the broader history of gender relations in a patriarchal society.

The Handmaid's Tale

We can start with the blockbuster Hulu dramatic series, *The Handmaid's Tale*. In this dystopian vision of a world of total control over women's bodies and sexuality, the most striking visual symbol is that of the Handmaids' prescribed public attire. Based on the traditional habit worn by Roman Catholic nuns in medieval convents, their dress covers the body from head to toe, revealing only a narrow view of the wearer's face. An extreme version of the ancient patriarchal belief that women's bodies are too provocative to the male gaze to be visible outside the home, the voluminous robes and confining bonnets that the Handmaids wear have accordingly been adopted as symbols of patriarchal oppression by women protesting abortion restrictions in the Bible Belt.

Not only has women's dress been traditionally restricted in the name of feminine modesty, it has also been governed by rules designed to distinguish it from male attire — and with it, the symbolic prerogatives of male privilege. This is why you see women in period-piece movies riding sidesaddle, when they are allowed to ride horses at all. Reflecting the belief that it was unbecoming and inappropriate for a woman to ride astride a horse in the way a man does, the sidesaddle also reflected the fact that women weren't allowed to wear pants in public. Hollywood celebrities like Katharine Hepburn successfully changed the rules in the 1930s and set a fashion trend for women that was confirmed in the 1940s by the pants-requiring work that women performed during World War II. Thus, capris would become an accepted fashion by the 1950s (with some help from Mary Tyler Moore in *The Dick Van Dyke Show*) without much social resistance.

Jeans, Spandex, Leotards, and Leg Warmers

By the 1960s, the sexual revolution in America, along with the rise of Second Wave feminism, had largely abolished the traditional prohibitions on women's fashions with respect to both pants and sensuality. The miniskirt in the 1960s shattered the old rules on dress length, while in the 1970s the popularity of extremely tight designer blue jeans, manufactured by companies such as Jordache and Sasson, was emblematic of the social acceptance not only of women's trousers but of sartorial sexuality as well. And then, thanks to the enormous success of the movie *Flashdance* in 1983, ballet wear — more specifically, leotards and leg warmers — became all the rage in women's fashion, whether or not the wearer actually danced in them. At the same time, spandex, a fabric designed for athletic attire and underwear, began to appear as ordinary outerwear for women, continuing its reign over women's fashion

AA Film Archive/Sportsphoto/Alamy

A still from the 1983 film *Flashdance*.

into the twenty-first century, when the skinny jeans era brought very tight jeans back into fashion. And from spandex and skinny jeans it was not a great leap at all to leggings.

It was in the context of this evolution of women's dress away from patriarchal restrictions that the mother's letter about leggings appeared. Indeed, so successful has this evolution been that most wearers of leggings (which have been especially popularized by the mass yoga movement, just as leg warmers reflected the dance craze of the '80s) probably do not regard them as political statements. Indeed, you yourself may say "They're just fashion" or "They are simply comfortable." Her letter changed that, however, by reminding everyone concerned of leggings' larger historical location in a now archaic — or, at least, highly disputed — cultural code, thus inadvertently politicizing them.

But the political reaction may not have been quite so strong had there not been another element in the historical system within which leggings can be situated and interpreted. For at the same time, the #MeToo groundswell against sexual harassment and assault had become a defining frame within which gender relations in America were widely experienced and analyzed. And within such a frame, the leggings letter, with its assertion that women who wore leggings were guilty of sexual provocation, was bound to backfire. Suddenly leggings were not only comfortable, or convenient, or fashionable: they were a symbol of resistance. Thus, ordinary consumer goods can become signs, drawing from their place in history, along with their relationships to other objects, connotative meanings that their mere denotative existence lacks.

Discussing the Signs of Consumer Culture

Make a categorized list of the fashions worn by your classmates. Be sure to note details, such as styles of shoes, jewelry, backpacks, or sunglasses, as well as broader trends. Next, discuss what the clothing choices say about individuals. What messages are people sending about their personal identity? Do individual students agree with the class's interpretations of their clothing choices? Can any distinctions be made by gender, age, or ethnicity? Then discuss what the fashion styles worn by the whole class signify: Is a group identity projected by class members?

Disposable Decades

As the above discussion demonstrates, when analyzing a consumer sign you will often find yourself referring to particular decades in which certain popular fads and trends were prominent, because the decade in which a given style appears may be an essential key to the system that explains it. Have you ever wondered why American cultural trends seem to change with every decade? Or, why it is so easy to speak of the 1960s or the 1970s or the 1980s and immediately recognize the popular styles that dominated each decade? Have you ever looked at the style of a friend and thought, "Oh, she's so nineties"? Can you place Dr. Martens or high-waisted jeans at the drop of a hat? A change in the calendar always seems to herald stylistic change in a consuming culture. But why?

The decade-to-decade shift in America's pop culture and consumer identity goes back a good number of years. It's still easy, for example, to distinguish the 1920s of F. Scott Fitzgerald's Jazz Age from the wrathful 1930s of John Steinbeck. The 1950s, an especially connotative decade, evoke images of ducktail haircuts and poodle skirts, Marilyn Monroe and Elvis, family sitcoms and drive-in culture, while the 1960s are known for acid rock, hippies, the student revolution, and back-to-the-land communes. We remember the 1970s as a pop cultural era divided among disco, Nashville, and preppiedom, with John Travolta, truckers, and Skippy and Muffy as dominant pop icons. The boom-boom 1980s gave us Wall Street glitz and the yuppie invasion, while the 1990s came in with Grunge and went out with the dot.com explosion/implosion, which was succeeded in the aughts by the return of the fifties-style hipster and the emergence of a kind of "geek chic" in the wake of the digital revolution. Indeed, each decade since World War I seems to carry its own consumerist style.

It's no accident that the decade-to-decade shift in consumer styles coincides with the advent of modern advertising and mass production, because it was mass production that created a need for constant consumer turnover in the first place. Mass production, that is, promotes stylistic change because with so many products available, a market must be created to consume all of them, and this means constantly consuming *more*. To get people to keep buying all the new stuff, you have to convince them that the stuff they already have is passé. Why else do fashion designers completely change their lines each year? Why do car manufacturers annually change their color schemes and body shapes when the previous year's model seemed good enough? Why does each new incarnation of the Apple iPhone introduce so many different colors and features? The new colors and designs aren't simply functional improvements (though they are marketed as such); they are inducements to go out and replace what you already have to avoid appearing out of fashion. Just think: If you could afford to buy any car or phone you want, what would it be? Would your choice a few years ago have been the same?

Mass production, then, creates consumer societies based on the constant creation of new products that are intended to be disposed of the next product year. But something happened along the way in the establishment of our consumer culture: we began to value consumption more than production. Shoppers storm the doors as the Christmas buying season begins earlier and earlier every year. Listen to the economic news: consumption, not production, is relied upon to carry America out of its economic downturns. When Americans stop buying, our economy grinds to a halt. Consumption lies at the center of our economic system now, constituting some two-thirds of our economic activity, and the result has been a transformation in the way we view ourselves.

A Tale of Two Cities

It has not always been thus in America, however. Once, Americans prided themselves on their productivity. In 1914, for example, the poet Carl Sandburg boasted of a Chicago that was "Hog Butcher for the World, / Tool Maker, Stacker of Wheat, / Player with Railroads and the Nation's Freight Handler." One wonders what Sandburg would think of the city today. From the South

Exploring the Signs of Consumer Culture

"You are what you buy." In your journal, freewrite on the importance of consumer products in your life. How do you respond to being told your identity is equivalent to the products you buy? Do you resist the notion? Do you recall any instances when you have felt lost without a favorite object? How do you communicate your sense of self to others through objects, whether clothing, books, food, home decor, electronic goods, or something else?

Side east to the industrial suburb of Gary, Indiana, Chicago's once-proud mills and factories rust in the winter wind. At the Chicago Mercantile Exchange, trade today is in commodity futures, not commodities.

Meanwhile, a few hundred miles to the northwest, Bloomington, Minnesota, buzzes with excitement. For there stands the Mall of America, a colossus of consumption so large that it contains within its walls a seven-acre Nickelodeon Universe theme park, with lots of room to spare. You can find almost anything you want in the Mall of America, but most of what you find won't have been manufactured in America. The proud tag "Made in the U.S.A." is a rare item. It's a long way from Sandburg's Chicago to the Mall of America, a trip that traverses America's shift from a producer to a consumer economy. This shift is not simply economic; it is behind a cultural transformation that is shaping a new mythology in which we define ourselves, our hopes, and our desires.

Ask yourself right now what your own goals are in going to college. Do you envision a career in law, or medicine, or banking and finance? Do you want to be a teacher, an advertising executive, or a civil servant? If you've considered any of these careers, you are contemplating what are known as service jobs. While essential to society, none of them actually produces anything. If you've considered going into some facet of traditional manufacturing, on the other hand, you are unusual because America offers increasingly fewer opportunities in that area and little prestige. The prestigious jobs are in law and medicine and in high-tech operations like Google and Facebook (which are, after all, mostly service providers), a fact that is easy to take for granted. But ask yourself: Does it have to be so?

To live in a consumer culture is not simply a matter of shopping or career choice, however; it is also a matter of being. Often aligned with the preeminent American mythology of personal freedom, the freedom to consume *what* you want *whenever* you want it has become — thanks in large part to mobile digital technology — a defining value of modern American life: a human right, not a mere pleasure or convenience. You are what you buy, and what you buy fulfills what you are. And in case you forget this, a constant drumbeat of advertising and marketing schemes exhorts you to go out and buy something, replacing the freedom to march to the beat of a different drummer with the freedom to buy.

When the Going Gets Tough, the Tough Go Shopping

In a cultural system where our identities are displayed in the products we buy, it accordingly behooves us to pay close attention to what we consume and why. From the cars we drive to the clothes we wear, we are enmeshed in a web of consumption. As students, you are probably freer to choose the images you wish to project through the products you consume than most other demographic groups in America. This claim may sound paradoxical: after all, don't working adults have more money than starving students? Yes, generally. But the working world places severe restrictions on the choices employees can

Reading Consumer Culture Online

Log on to the site of a retail store that you have visited in its brick-and-mortar version. Analyze both the products sold and the way they are marketed. Who is the target audience, and what images and values are used to attract this market? How does the marketing compare to non-electronic sales pitches, such as displays in stores and magazines or TV advertising? Does the electronic medium affect your behavior as a consumer? How do you account for any differences in electronic and traditional marketing strategies?

make in their clothing and grooming styles, and even automobile choice may be restricted (real estate agents, for example, can't escort their clients around town in Kia Souls). And even in the era of the Zuckerberg hoodie, applicants for white-collar positions are still best advised to adopt the codes of corporate business wear, with its emphasis on neck-tied and dark-hued sobriety. On campus, however, you can be pretty much whatever you want to be, which is why your own daily life provides you with a particularly rich field of consumer signs to read and decode.

So go to it. By the time you finish reading this book, a lot will have changed. Look around. Start reading the signs.

The Readings

As this chapter's lead-off essay, Laurence Shames's "The More Factor" offers a historical context for American consumer culture, relating America's frontier history to our ever-expanding desire for more goods and services. Malcolm Gladwell follows with an exposé on the ways in which brick-and-mortar retailers seek to maximize sales by adapting store design to the spatial behavior of shoppers, while Jordyn Holman explains how the great American mall is managing to survive in the new economy by reaching out to Gen Z consumers whose smartphones are their most prized accessories. Next, Michael Pollan exposes some of the less-than-sunny realities behind the idealized narratives of the organic foods industry. Chris Arning then takes us into the world of product packaging, revealing the place of semiotics on the front lines of high-stakes brand positioning and marketing. Troy Patterson's breakdown of the complex semiotics of the "hoodie" provides a consumerist case study that leads in to Thomas Frank's revelation of how corporate America has turned consumption into a hip signifier of inauthentic rebellion — a "commodification of dissent." And James A. Roberts concludes the chapter with a survey of status consumption and its accompanying paradox of diminishing returns.

LAURENCE SHAMES

The More Factor

A bumper sticker popular in the 1980s read, "Whoever dies with the most toys wins." In this selection from *The Hunger for More: Searching for Values in an Age of Greed* (1989), Laurence Shames shows how the great American hunger for more — more toys, more land, more opportunities — is an essential part of our history and character, stemming from the frontier era when the horizon alone seemed the only limit to American desire. Shames is both a fiction author and a journalist who has contributed to such publications as *Playboy, Vanity Fair, Manhattan, Inc.*, and *Esquire.*

1

Americans have always been optimists, and optimists have always liked to speculate. In Texas in the 1880s, the speculative instrument of choice was towns, and there is no tale more American than this.

What people would do was buy up enormous tracts of parched and vacant land, lay out a Main Street, nail together some wooden sidewalks, and start slapping up buildings. One of these buildings would be called the Grand Hotel and would have a saloon complete with swinging doors. Another might be dubbed the New Academy or the Opera House. The developers would erect a flagpole and name a church, and once the workmen had packed up and moved on, the towns would be as empty as the sky.

But no matter. The speculators, next, would hire people to pass out handbills in the Eastern and Midwestern cities, tracts limning the advantages of relocation to "the Athens of the South" or "the new plains Jerusalem." When persuasion failed, the builders might resort to bribery, paying people's moving costs and giving them houses, in exchange for nothing but a pledge to stay until a certain census was taken or a certain inspection made. Once the nose count was completed, people were free to move on, and there was in fact a contingent of folks who made their living by keeping a cabin on skids and dragging it for pay from one town to another.

The speculators' idea, of course, was to lure the railroad. If one could create a convincing semblance of a town, the railroad might come through it, and a real town would develop, making the speculators staggeringly rich. By these devices a man named Sanborn once owned Amarillo.[1]

[1]For a fuller account of railroad-related land speculation in Texas, see F. Stanley, *Story of the Texas Panhandle Railroads* (Borger, Tex.: Hess Publishing Co., 1976).

5 But railroad tracks are narrow and the state of Texas is very, very wide. For every Wichita Falls or Lubbock there were a dozen College Mounds or Belchervilles,[2] bleached, unpeopled burgs that receded quietly into the dust, taking with them large amounts of speculators' money.

Still, the speculators kept right on bucking the odds and depositing empty towns in the middle of nowhere. Why did they do it? Two reasons — reasons that might be said to summarize the central fact of American economic history and that go a fair way toward explaining what is perhaps the central strand of the national character.

The first reason was simply that the possible returns were so enormous as to partake of the surreal, to create a climate in which ordinary logic and prudence did not seem to apply. In a boom like that of real estate when the railroad barreled through, long shots that might pay one hundred thousand to one seemed worth a bet.

The second reason, more pertinent here, is that there was a presumption that America would *keep* on booming — if not forever, then at least longer than it made sense to worry about. There would always be another gold rush, another Homestead Act, another oil strike. The next generation would always ferret out opportunities that would be still more lavish than any that had gone before. America *was* those opportunities. This was an article not just of faith, but of strategy. You banked on the next windfall, you staked your hopes and even your self-esteem on it, and this led to a national turn of mind that might usefully be thought of as the habit of more.

A century, maybe two centuries, before anyone had heard the term *baby boomer*, much less *yuppie*, the habit of more had been instilled as the operative truth among the economically ambitious. The habit of more seemed to suggest that there was no such thing as getting wiped out in America. A fortune lost in Texas might be recouped in Colorado. Funds frittered away on grazing land where nothing grew might flood back in as silver. There was always a second chance, or always seemed to be, in this land where growth was destiny and where expansion and purpose were the same.

10 The key was the frontier, not just as a matter of acreage, but as idea. Vast, varied, rough as rocks, America was the place where one never quite came to the end. Ben Franklin explained it to Europe even before the Revolutionary War had finished: America offered new chances to those "who, in their own Countries, where all the Lands [were] fully occupied . . . could never [emerge] from the poor Condition wherein they were born."[3]

So central was this awareness of vacant space and its link to economic promise that Frederick Jackson Turner, the historian who set the tone for much of the twentieth century's understanding of the American past, would

[2]T. Lindsay Baker, *Ghost Towns of Texas* (Norman, Okla.: University of Oklahoma Press, 1986).

[3]Benjamin Franklin, "Information to Those Who Would Remove to America," in *The Autobiography and Other Writings* (New York: Penguin Books, 1986), 242.

write that it was "not the constitution, but free land . . . [that] made the democratic type of society in America."[4] Good laws mattered; an accountable government mattered; ingenuity and hard work mattered. But those things were, so to speak, an overlay on the natural, geographic America that was simply *there*, and whose vast and beckoning possibilities seemed to generate the ambition and the sometimes reckless liberty that would fill it. First and foremost, it was open space that provided "the freedom of the individual to rise under conditions of social mobility."[5]

Open space generated not just ambition, but metaphor. As early as 1835, Tocqueville was extrapolating from the fact of America's emptiness to the observation that "no natural boundary seems to be set to the efforts of man."[6] Nor was any limit placed on what he might accomplish, since, in that heyday of the Protestant ethic, a person's rewards were taken to be quite strictly proportionate to his labors.

Frontier; opportunity; more. This has been the American trinity from the very start. The frontier was the backdrop and also the raw material for the streak of economic booms. The booms became the goad and also the justification for the myriad gambles and for Americans' famous optimism. The optimism, in turn, shaped the schemes and visions that were sometimes noble, sometimes appalling, always bold. The frontier, as reality and as symbol, is what has shaped the American way of doing things and the American sense of what's worth doing.

But there has been one further corollary to the legacy of the frontier, with its promise of ever-expanding opportunities: Given that the goal — a realistic goal for most of our history — was *more*, Americans have been somewhat backward in adopting values, hopes, ambitions that have to do with things *other than* more. In America, a sense of quality has lagged far behind a sense of scale. An ideal of contentment has yet to take root in soil traditionally more hospitable to an ideal of restless striving. The ethic of decency has been upstaged by the ethic of success. The concept of growth has been applied almost exclusively to things that can be measured, counted, weighed. And the hunger for those things that are unmeasurable but fine — the sorts of accomplishment that cannot be undone by circumstance or a shift in social fashion, the kind of serenity that cannot be shattered by tomorrow's headline — has gone largely unfulfilled, and even unacknowledged.

2

If the supply of more went on forever, perhaps that wouldn't matter very 15
much. Expansion could remain a goal unto itself, and would continue to

[4]Frederick Jackson Turner, *The Frontier in American History* (Melbourne, Fla.: Krieger, 1976 [reprint of 1920 edition]), 293.

[5]Ibid., 266.

[6]Tocqueville, *Democracy in America*.

generate a value system based on bulk rather than on nuance, on quantities of money rather than on quality of life, on "progress" itself rather than on a sense of what the progress was for. But what if, over time, there was less more to be had?

That is the essential situation of America today.

Let's keep things in proportion: The country is not running out of wealth, drive, savvy, or opportunities. We are not facing imminent ruin, and neither panic nor gloom is called for. But there have been ample indications over the past two decades that we are running out of more.

Consider productivity growth — according to many economists, the single most telling and least distortable gauge of changes in real wealth. From 1947 to 1965, productivity in the private sector (adjusted, as are all the following figures, for inflation) was advancing, on average, by an annual 3.3 percent. This means, simply, that each hour of work performed by a specimen American worker contributed 3.3 cents worth or more to every American dollar every year; whether we saved it or spent it, that increment went into a national kitty of ever-enlarging aggregate wealth. Between 1965 and 1972, however, the "more-factor" decreased to 2.4 percent a year, and from 1972 to 1977 it slipped further, to 1.6 percent. By the early 1980s, productivity growth was at a virtual standstill, crawling along at 0.2 percent for the five years ending in 1982.[7] Through the middle years of the 1980s, the numbers rebounded somewhat — but by then the gains were being neutralized by the gargantuan carrying costs on the national debt.[8]

Inevitably, this decline in the national stockpile of more held consequences for the individual wallet.[9] During the 1950s, Americans' average hourly earnings were humping ahead at a gratifying 2.5 percent each year. By the late seventies, that figure stood just where productivity growth had come to stand, at a dispiriting 0.2 cents on the dollar. By the first half of the eighties, the Reagan "recovery" notwithstanding, real hourly wages were actually moving backward — declining at an average annual rate of 0.3 percent.

Compounding the shortage of more was an unfortunate but crucial demo- 20
graphic fact. Real wealth was nearly ceasing to expand just at the moment when the members of that unprecedented population bulge known as the baby boom were entering what should have been their peak years of income expansion. A working man or woman who was thirty years old in 1949 could expect to see his or her real earnings burgeon by 63 percent by age forty.

[7]These figures are taken from the Council of Economic Advisers, *Economic Report of the President*, February 1984, 267.

[8]For a lucid and readable account of the meaning and implications of our reservoir of red ink, see Lawrence Malkin, *The National Debt* (New York: Henry Holt and Co., 1987). Through no fault of Malkin's, many of his numbers are already obsolete, but his explanation of who owes what to whom, and what it means, remains sound and even entertaining in a bleak sort of way.

[9]The figures in this paragraph and the next are from "The Average Guy Takes It on the Chin," *New York Times*, 13 July 1986, sec. 3.

In 1959, a thirty-year-old could still look forward to a gain of 49 percent by his or her fortieth birthday.

But what about the person who turned thirty in 1973? By the time that worker turned forty, his or her real earnings had shrunk by a percentage point. For all the blather about yuppies with their beach houses, BMWs, and radicchio salads, and even factoring in those isolated tens of thousands making ludicrous sums in consulting firms or on Wall Street, the fact is that between 1979 and 1983 real earnings of all Americans between the ages of twenty-five and thirty-four actually declined by 14 percent.[10] The *New York Times*, well before the stock market crash put the kibosh on eighties confidence, summed up the implications of this downturn by observing that "for millions of breadwinners, the American dream is becoming the impossible dream."[11]

Now, it is not our main purpose here to detail the ups and downs of the American economy. Our aim, rather, is to consider the effects of those ups and downs on people's goals, values, sense of their place in the world. What happens at that shadowy juncture where economic prospects meld with personal choice? What sorts of insights and adjustments are called for so that economic ups and downs can be dealt with gracefully?

Fact one in this connection is that, if America's supply of more is in fact diminishing, American values will have to shift and broaden to fill the gap where the expectation of almost automatic gains used to be. Something more durable will have to replace the fat but fragile bubble that had been getting frailer these past two decades and that finally popped—a tentative, partial pop—on October 19, 1987. A different sort of growth—ultimately, a growth in responsibility and happiness—will have to fulfill our need to believe that our possibilities are still expanding.

The transition to that new view of progress will take some fancy stepping, because, at least since the end of World War II, simple economic growth has stood, in the American psyche, as the best available substitute for the literal frontier. The economy has *been* the frontier. Instead of more space, we have had more money. Rather than measuring progress in terms of geographical expansion, we have measured it by expansion in our standard of living. Economics has become the metaphor on which we pin our hopes of open space and second chances.

The poignant part is that the literal frontier did not pass yesterday: it has 25
not existed for a hundred years. But the frontier's promise has become so much a part of us that we have not been willing to let the concept die. We have kept the frontier mythology going by invocation, by allusion, by hype.

It is not a coincidence that John F. Kennedy dubbed his political program the New Frontier. It is not mere linguistic accident that makes us speak of Frontiers of Science or of psychedelic drugs as carrying one to Frontiers of Perception. We glorify fads and fashions by calling them Frontiers of Taste.

[10]See, for example, "The Year of the Yuppie," *Newsweek*, 31 December 1984, 16.
[11]"The Average Guy."

Nuclear energy has been called the Last Frontier; solar energy has been called the Last Frontier. Outer space has been called the Last Frontier; the oceans have been called the Last Frontier. Even the suburbs, those blandest and least adventurous of places, have been wryly described as the crabgrass frontier.[12]

What made all these usages plausible was their being linked to the image of the American economy as an endlessly fertile continent whose boundaries never need be reached, a domain that could expand in perpetuity, a gigantic playing field that would never run out of room and on which the game would get forever bigger and more filled with action. This was the frontier that would not vanish.

It is worth noting that people in other countries (with the possible exception of that other America, Australia) do not talk about frontier this way. In Europe, and in most of Africa and Asia, "frontier" connotes, at worst, a place of barbed wire and men with rifles, and at best, a neutral junction where one changes currency while passing from one fixed system into another. Frontier, for most of the world's people, does not suggest growth, expanse, or opportunity.

For Americans, it does, and always has. This is one of the things that sets America apart from other places and makes American attitudes different from those of other people. It is why, from *Bonanza* to the Sierra Club, the notion or even the fantasy of empty horizons and untapped resources has always evoked in the American heart both passion and wistfulness. And it is why the fear that the economic frontier — our last, best version of the Wild West — may finally be passing creates in us not only money worries but also a crisis of morale and even of purpose.

3

It might seem strange to call the 1980s an era of nostalgia. The decade, after 30
all, has been more usually described in terms of coolness, pragmatism, and a blithe innocence of history. But the eighties, unawares, were nostalgic for frontiers; and the disappointment of that nostalgia had much to do with the time's greed, narrowness, and strange want of joy. The fear that the world may not be a big enough playground for the full exercise of one's energies and yearnings, and worse, the fear that the playground is being fenced off and will no longer expand — these are real worries and they have had consequences. The eighties were an object lesson in how people play the game when there is an awful and unspoken suspicion that the game is winding down.

It was ironic that the yuppies came to be so reviled for their vaunting ambition and outsized expectations, as if they'd invented the habit of more,

[12]With the suburbs again taking on a sort of fascination, this phrase was resurrected as the title of a 1985 book — *Crabgrass Frontier: The Suburbanization of America*, by Kenneth T. Jackson (Oxford University Press).

when in fact they'd only inherited it the way a fetus picks up an addiction in the womb. The craving was there in the national bloodstream, a remnant of the frontier, and the baby boomers, described in childhood as "the luckiest generation,"[13] found themselves, as young adults, in the melancholy position of wrestling with a two-hundred-year dependency on a drug that was now in short supply.

True, the 1980s raised the clamor for more to new heights of shrillness, insistence, and general obnoxiousness, but this, it can be argued, was in the nature of a final binge, the storm before the calm. America, though fighting the perception every inch of the way, was coming to realize that it was not a preordained part of the natural order that one should be richer every year. If it happened, that was nice. But who had started the flimsy and pernicious rumor that it was normal?

Reading the Text

1. Summarize in a paragraph how, according to Shames, the frontier functions as a symbol of American consciousness.
2. What does Shames mean when he says, "Open space generated not just ambition, but metaphor" (para. 12)?
3. What connections does Shames make between America's frontier history and consumer behavior?
4. Why does Shames term the 1980s "an era of nostalgia" (para. 30)?
5. Characterize Shames's attitude toward the American desire for more. How does his tone reveal his personal views on his subject?

Reading the Signs

1. Shames asserts that Americans have been influenced by the frontier belief "that America would *keep* on booming" (para. 8). Do you feel that this belief continues to be influential into the twenty-first century? Write an essay arguing for your position.
2. Shames claims that, because of the desire for more, "the ethic of decency has been upstaged by the ethic of success" (para. 14). In class, form teams and debate the validity of Shames's claim.
3. **CONNECTING TEXTS** Read or review Barbara Ehrenreich's "Bright-Sided" (p. 77) and, in an essay, put it in conversation with Shames's article. In what ways, if any, is the American "hunger for more" paralleled by or even fueled by the tendency to be "bright-sided"? Write an essay in which you argue what the relationship between these two American traits might be.
4. In an essay, argue for or refute the proposition that the "hunger for more" that Shames describes is a universal human trait, not simply an American one.

[13]Thomas Hine, *Populuxe* (New York: Alfred A. Knopf, 1986), 15.

MALCOLM GLADWELL

The Science of Shopping

Ever wonder why the season's hottest new styles at stores like the Gap are usually displayed on the right at least fifteen paces in from the front entrance? It's because that's where shoppers are most likely to see them as they enter the store, gear down from the walking pace of a mall corridor, and adjust to the shop's spatial environment. Ever wonder how shop managers know this sort of thing? It's because, as Malcolm Gladwell reports here, they hire consultants like Paco Underhill, a "retail anthropologist" and "urban geographer" whose studies (often aided by hidden cameras) of shopping behavior have become valuable guides to store managers looking for the best ways to move the goods. Does this feel just a little Orwellian? Read on. A staff writer for the *New Yorker*, in which this selection first appeared, Gladwell has also written many books, including *The Tipping Point* (2000) and *Talking to Strangers* (2019).

Human beings walk the way they drive, which is to say that Americans tend to keep to the right when they stroll down shopping-mall concourses or city sidewalks. This is why in a well-designed airport travelers drifting toward their gate will always find the fast-food restaurants on their left and the gift shops on their right: people will readily cross a lane of pedestrian traffic to satisfy their hunger but rarely to make an impulse buy of a T-shirt or a magazine. This is also why Paco Underhill tells his retail clients to make sure that their window displays are canted, preferably to both sides but especially to the left, so that a potential shopper approaching the store on the inside of the sidewalk — the shopper, that is, with the least impeded view of the store window — can see the display from at least twenty-five feet away.

Of course, a lot depends on how fast the potential shopper is walking. Paco, in his previous life, as an urban geographer in Manhattan, spent a great deal of time thinking about walking speeds as he listened in on the great debates of the nineteen-seventies over whether the traffic lights in midtown should be timed to facilitate the movement of cars or to facilitate the movement of pedestrians and so break up the big platoons that move down Manhattan sidewalks. He knows that the faster you walk the more your peripheral vision narrows, so you become unable to pick up visual cues as quickly as someone who is just ambling along. He knows, too, that people who walk fast take a surprising amount of time to slow down — just as it takes a good stretch of road to change gears with a stick-shift automobile. On the basis of his research, Paco estimates the human downshift period to be anywhere from twelve to twenty-five feet, so if you own a store, he says, you never want to be next door to a bank: potential shoppers speed up when they walk past a bank (since there's nothing to look at), and by the time they slow down they've walked right past your business. The downshift factor also means that when potential shoppers enter a store it's going to take them from five to fifteen paces to adjust to the light and refocus and gear down from walking speed to shopping speed — particularly if they've just had to navigate a treacherous parking lot or hurry to make the light at Fifty-seventh and Fifth.

Paco calls that area inside the door the Decompression Zone, and something he tells clients over and over again is never, ever put anything of value in that zone — not shopping baskets or tie racks or big promotional displays — because no one is going to see it. Paco believes that, as a rule of thumb, customer interaction with any product or promotional display in the Decompression Zone will increase at least thirty percent once it's moved to the back edge of the zone, and even more if it's placed to the right, because another of the fundamental rules of how human beings shop is that upon entering a store — whether it's Nordstrom or K Mart, Tiffany or the Gap — the shopper invariably and reflexively turns to the right. Paco believes in the existence of the Invariant Right because he has actually verified it. He has put cameras in stores trained directly on the doorway, and if you go to his office, just above Union Square, where videocassettes and boxes of Super-eight film from all his work over the years are stacked in plastic Tupperware containers practically up to the ceiling, he can show you reel upon reel of grainy entryway video — customers striding in the door, downshifting, refocusing, and then, again and again, making that little half turn.

Paco Underhill is a tall man in his mid-forties, partly bald, with a neatly trimmed beard and an engaging, almost goofy manner. He wears baggy khakis and shirts open at the collar, and generally looks like the academic he might have been if he hadn't been captivated, twenty years ago, by the ideas of the urban anthropologist William Whyte. It was Whyte who pioneered the use of time-lapse photography as a tool of urban planning, putting cameras in parks and the plazas in front of office buildings in midtown Manhattan, in order to determine what distinguished a public space that worked from one that didn't. As a Columbia undergraduate, in 1974, Paco heard a lecture on Whyte's work and, he recalls, left the room "walking on air." He immediately read everything Whyte had written. He emptied his bank account to buy cameras and film and make his own home movie, about a pedestrian mall in Poughkeepsie. He took his "little exercise" to Whyte's advocacy group, the Project for Public Spaces, and was offered a job. Soon, however, it dawned on Paco that Whyte's ideas could be taken a step further — that the same techniques he used to establish why a plaza worked or didn't work could also be used to determine why a store worked or didn't work. Thus was born the field of retail anthropology, and, not long afterward, Paco founded Envirosell, which in just over fifteen years has counselled some of the most familiar names in American retailing, from Levi Strauss to Kinney, Starbucks, McDonald's, Blockbuster, Apple Computer, AT&T, and a number of upscale retailers that Paco would rather not name.

When Paco gets an assignment, he and his staff set up a series of video 5
cameras throughout the test store and then back the cameras up with Envirosell staffers — trackers, as they're known — armed with clipboards. Where the cameras go and how many trackers Paco deploys depends on exactly what the store wants to know about its shoppers. Typically, though, he might use six cameras and two or three trackers, and let the study run for two or three days, so that at the end he would have pages and pages of carefully annotated tracking sheets and anywhere from a hundred to five hundred hours of film. These days, given the expansion of his business, he might tape fifteen thousand hours in a year, and, given that he has been in operation since the late seventies, he now has well over a hundred thousand hours of tape in his library.

Even in the best of times, this would be a valuable archive. But today, with the retail business in crisis, it is a gold mine. The time per visit that the average American spends in a shopping mall was sixty-six minutes last year — down from seventy-two minutes in 1992 — and is the lowest number ever recorded. The amount of selling space per American shopper is now more than double what it was in the mid-seventies, meaning that profit margins have never been narrower, and the costs of starting a retail business — and of failing — have never been higher. In the past few years, countless dazzling new retailing temples have been built along Fifth and Madison Avenues — Barneys, Calvin Klein, Armani, Valentino, Banana Republic, Prada, Chanel, NikeTown, and on and on — but it is an explosion of growth based on no more than a hunch, a hopeful multimillion-dollar gamble that the way to break through is to provide the shopper with spectacle and more spectacle. "The arrogance is gone," Millard Drexler, the president and C.E.O. of the Gap, told me. "Arrogance makes failure. Once you think you know the answer, it's almost always over." In such a competitive environment, retailers don't just want to know how shoppers behave in their stores. They *have* to know. And who better to ask than Paco Underhill, who in the past decade and a half has analyzed tens of thousands of hours of shopping videotape and, as a result, probably knows more about the strange habits and quirks of the species *Emptor americanus* than anyone else alive?

Paco is considered the originator, for example, of what is known in the trade as the butt-brush theory — or, as Paco calls it, more delicately, *le facteur bousculade* — which holds that the likelihood of a woman's being converted from a browser to a buyer is inversely proportional to the likelihood of her being brushed on her behind while she's examining merchandise. Touch — or brush or bump or jostle — a woman on the behind when she has stopped to look at an item, and she will bolt. Actually, calling this a theory is something of a misnomer, because Paco doesn't offer any explanation for why women react that way, aside from venturing that they are "more sensitive back there." It's really an observation, based on repeated and close analysis of his videotape library, that Paco has transformed into a retailing commandment: A women's product that requires extensive examination should never be placed in a narrow aisle.

Paco approaches the problem of the Invariant Right the same way. Some retail thinkers see this as a subject crying out for interpretation and speculation. The design guru Joseph Weishar, for example, argues, in his magisterial *Design for Effective Selling Space*, that the Invariant Right is a function of the fact that we "absorb and digest information in the left part of the brain" and "assimilate and logically use this information in the right half," the result being that we scan the store from left to right and then fix on an object to the right "essentially at a 45 degree angle from the point that we enter." When I asked Paco about this interpretation, he shrugged, and said he thought the reason was simply that most people are right-handed. Uncovering the fundamentals of "why" is clearly not a pursuit that engages him much. He is not a theoretician but an empiricist, and for him the important thing is that in amassing his huge library of in-store time-lapse photography he has gained enough hard evidence to know how often and under what circumstances the Invariant Right is expressed and how to take advantage of it.

What Paco likes are facts. They come tumbling out when he talks, and, because he speaks with a slight hesitation — lingering over the first syllable in, for example, "re-tail" or "de-sign" — he draws you in, and you find yourself truly hanging on his words. "We have reached a historic point in American history," he told me in our very first conversation. "Men, for the first time, have begun to buy their own underwear." He then paused to let the comment sink in, so that I could absorb its implications, before he elaborated: "Which means that we have to *totally* rethink the way we sell that product." In the parlance of Hollywood scriptwriters, the best endings must be surprising and yet inevitable; and the best of Paco's pronouncements take the same shape. It would never have occurred to me to wonder about the increasingly critical role played by touching — or, as Paco calls it, petting — clothes in the course of making the decision to buy them. But then I went to the Gap and to Banana Republic and saw people touching, and fondling and, one after another, buying shirts and sweaters laid out on big wooden tables, and what Paco told me — which was no doubt based on what he had seen on his videotapes — made perfect sense: that the reason the Gap and Banana Republic have tables is not merely that sweaters and shirts look better there, or that tables fit into the warm and relaxing residential feeling that the Gap and Banana Republic are trying to create in their stores, but that tables invite — indeed, symbolize — touching. "Where do we eat?" Paco asks. "We eat, we pick up food, on tables."

Paco produces for his clients a series of carefully detailed studies, totaling 10
forty to a hundred and fifty pages, filled with product-by-product breakdowns and bright-colored charts and graphs. In one recent case, he was asked by a major clothing retailer to analyze the first of a new chain of stores that the firm planned to open. One of the things the client wanted to know was how successful the store was in drawing people into its depths, since the chances that shoppers will buy something are directly related to how long they spend shopping, and how long they spend shopping is directly related to how deep they get pulled into the store. For this reason, a supermarket will often put dairy

products on one side, meat at the back, and fresh produce on the other side, so that the typical shopper can't just do a drive-by but has to make an entire circuit of the store, and be tempted by everything the supermarket has to offer. In the case of the new clothing store, Paco found that ninety-one percent of all shoppers penetrated as deep as what he called Zone 4, meaning more than three-quarters of the way in, well past the accessories and shirt racks and belts in the front, and little short of the far wall, with the changing rooms and the pants stacked on shelves. Paco regarded this as an extraordinary figure, particularly for a long, narrow store like this one, where it is not unusual for the rate of penetration past, say, Zone 3 to be under fifty percent. But that didn't mean the store was perfect — far from it. For Paco, all kinds of questions remained.

Purchasers, for example, spent an average of eleven minutes and twenty-seven seconds in the store, nonpurchasers two minutes and thirty-six seconds. It wasn't that the nonpurchasers just cruised in and out: in those two minutes and thirty-six seconds, they went deep into the store and examined an average of 3.42 items. So why didn't they buy? What, exactly, happened to cause some browsers to buy and other browsers to walk out the door?

Then, there was the issue of the number of products examined. The purchasers were looking at an average of 4.81 items but buying only 1.33 items. Paco found this statistic deeply disturbing. As the retail market grows more cutthroat, store owners have come to realize that it's all but impossible to increase the number of customers coming in, and have concentrated instead on getting the customers they do have to buy more. Paco thinks that if you can sell someone a pair of pants you must also be able to sell that person a belt, or a pair of socks, or a pair of underpants, or even do what the Gap does so well: sell a person a complete outfit. To Paco, the figure 1.33 suggested that the store was doing something very wrong, and one day when I visited him in his office he sat me down in front of one of his many VCRs to see how he looked for the 1.33 culprit.

It should be said that sitting next to Paco is a rather strange experience. "My mother says that I'm the best-paid spy in America," he told me. He laughed, but he wasn't entirely joking. As a child, Paco had a nearly debilitating stammer, and, he says, "since I was never that comfortable talking I always relied on my eyes to understand things." That much is obvious from the first moment you meet him: Paco is one of those people who looks right at you, soaking up every nuance and detail. It isn't a hostile gaze, because Paco isn't hostile at all. He has a big smile, and he'll call you "chief" and use your first name a lot and generally act as if he knew you well. But that's the awkward thing: He has looked at you so closely that you're sure he does know you well, and you, meanwhile, hardly know him at all.

This kind of asymmetry is even more pronounced when you watch his shopping videos with him, because every movement or gesture means something to Paco — he has spent his adult life deconstructing the shopping experience — but nothing to the outsider, or, at least, not at first. Paco had to keep stopping the video to get me to see things through his eyes before I began to understand. In one sequence, for example, a camera mounted high on the wall outside the changing rooms documented a man and a woman shopping for a pair of pants for what appeared to be their daughter, a girl in her mid-teens. The tapes are soundless, but the basic steps of the shopping dance are so familiar to Paco that, once I'd grasped the general idea, he was able to provide a running commentary on what was being said and thought. There is the girl emerging from the changing room wearing her first pair. There she is glancing at her reflection in the mirror, then turning to see herself from the back. There is the mother looking on. There is the father — or, as fathers are known in the trade, the "wallet carrier" — stepping forward and pulling up the jeans. There's the girl trying on another pair. There's the primp again. The twirl. The mother. The wallet carrier. And then again, with another pair. The full sequence lasted twenty minutes, and at the end came the take-home lesson, for which Paco called in one of his colleagues, Tom Moseman, who had supervised the project.

15 "This is a very critical moment," Tom, a young, intense man wearing little round glasses, said, and he pulled up a chair next to mine. "She's saying, 'I don't know whether I should wear a belt.' Now here's the salesclerk. The girl says to him, 'I need a belt,' and he says, 'Take mine.' Now there he is taking her back to the full-length mirror."

A moment later, the girl returns, clearly happy with the purchase. She wants the jeans. The wallet carrier turns to her, and then gestures to the salesclerk. The wallet carrier is telling his daughter to give back the belt. The girl gives back the belt. Tom stops the tape. He's leaning forward now, a finger jabbing at the screen. Beside me, Paco is shaking his head. I don't get it — at least, not at first — and so Tom replays that last segment. The wallet carrier tells the girl to give back the belt. She gives back the belt. And then, finally, it dawns on me why this store has an average purchase number of only 1.33. "Don't you see?" Tom said. "*She wanted the belt.* A great opportunity to make an add-on sale . . . *lost!*"

Should we be afraid of Paco Underhill? One of the fundamental anxieties of the American consumer, after all, has always been that beneath the pleasure and the frivolity of the shopping experience runs an undercurrent of manipulation, and that anxiety has rarely seemed more justified than today. The practice of prying into the minds and habits of American consumers is now a multibillion-dollar business. Every time a product is pulled across a supermarket checkout scanner, information is recorded, assembled, and sold to a market-research firm for analysis. There are companies that put tiny cameras inside frozen-food cases in supermarket aisles; market-research firms that feed census data and behavioral statistics into algorithms and come out with complicated maps of the American consumer; anthropologists who sift through the garbage of carefully targeted households to analyze their true consumption patterns; and endless rounds of highly organized focus groups and questionnaire takers and phone surveyors. That some people are now tracking our every shopping move with video cameras seems in many respects the last straw: Paco's movies are, after all, creepy. They look like the surveillance videos taken during convenience store holdups — hazy and soundless and slightly warped by the angle of the lens. When you watch them, you find yourself waiting for something bad to happen, for someone to shoplift or pull a gun on a cashier.

The more time you spend with Paco's videos, though, the less scary they seem. After an hour or so, it's no longer clear whether simply by watching people shop — and analyzing their every move — you can learn how to control them. The shopper that emerges from the videos is not pliable or manipulable. The screen shows people filtering in and out of stores, petting and moving on, abandoning their merchandise because checkout lines are too long, or leaving a store empty-handed because they couldn't fit their stroller into the aisle between two shirt racks. Paco's shoppers are fickle and headstrong, and are quite unwilling to buy anything unless conditions are perfect — unless the belt is presented at *exactly* the right moment. His theories of the butt-brush and petting and the Decompression Zone and the Invariant Right seek not to make shoppers conform to the desires of sellers but to make sellers conform to the desires of shoppers. What Paco is teaching his clients is a kind of slavish devotion to the shopper's every whim. He is teaching them humility.

Reading the Text

1. Summarize in your own words the ways that retailers use spatial design to affect the consumer's behavior and buying habits.
2. What is Gladwell's tone in this selection, and what does it reveal about his attitudes toward the retail industry's manipulation of customers?
3. What effect does Gladwell's description of Paco Underhill's background and physical appearance have on the reader?
4. Why does Paco Underhill's mother say that he is "the best-paid spy in America" (para. 13)?

Reading the Signs

1. **CONNECTING TEXTS** Visit a local store or supermarket, and study the spatial design. How many of the design strategies that Gladwell describes do you observe, and how do they affect customers' behavior? Use your observations as the basis for an essay interpreting the store's spatial design. To develop your ideas further, consult Michael Pollan's "Supermarket Pastoral" (p. 211) and Chris Arning's "What Can Semiotics Contribute to Packaging Design?" (p. 217).
2. In class, form teams and debate the proposition that the surveillance of consumers by retail anthropologists is manipulative and unethical.
3. Visit the website of a major retailer and analyze its design. How is the online "store" designed to encourage consuming behavior?
4. **CONNECTING TEXTS** Write an essay in response to Gladwell's question "Should we be afraid of Paco Underhill?" (para. 17). To develop your ideas, consult Joseph Turow's "The Daily You: How the New Advertising Industry Is Defining Your Identity and Your Worth" (p. 265).

JORDYN HOLMAN

Millennials Tried to Kill the American Mall, But Gen Z Might Save It

Generational labeling is really about branding consumer cohorts to make it easier to sell things to them, so it should not be surprising that major retail chains are tailoring their sales practices to Gen Z shoppers. Now clothing chains like Forever 21 offer large discounts to customers who will Instagram themselves in Forever 21 outfits, or retailers like American Eagle Outfitters will customize jeans at the counter. As Jordyn Holman reports in this business profile for *Bloomberg Businessweek*, the generation that was expected to deliver the death blow to the great American shopping mall is actually enabling it to stage a comeback. Thus MySpace has become MyShop, as brick-and-mortar retail struggles to survive in the smartphone era.

Gen Z keeps confounding Corporate America.

They've shunned beer, they want companies to take political stands and they trust Kardashians to make their makeup choices. But perhaps the biggest surprise about this new cohort of teenagers is the most unexpected of all: They love the shopping mall.

Around 95 percent of them visited a physical shopping center in a three-month period in 2018, as opposed to just 75 percent of millennials and 58 percent of Gen X, according to an International Council of Shopping Centers study. And they genuinely like it; three-quarters of them said going to a brick-and-mortar store was a better experience than online, ICSC found. "There's always been this assumption that as you go through the age spectrum, the younger consumer that has grown up with online and digital and is very savvy would shun physical experiences," said Neil Saunders, an analyst at GlobalData Retail. "But actually that's not turned out to be the case."

Gen Z — or the group of kids, teens and young adults roughly between the ages of 7 and 22 — still appreciate brick and mortar. But they aren't just millennials living in a different time. Today's teens interact differently with stores than their older siblings and Gen X parents before them, and several retailers who didn't understand the fundamental differences in how they shop landed themselves in bankruptcy court: Think Charlotte Russe, Wet Seal and Claire's, once staples of the teen mall circuit.

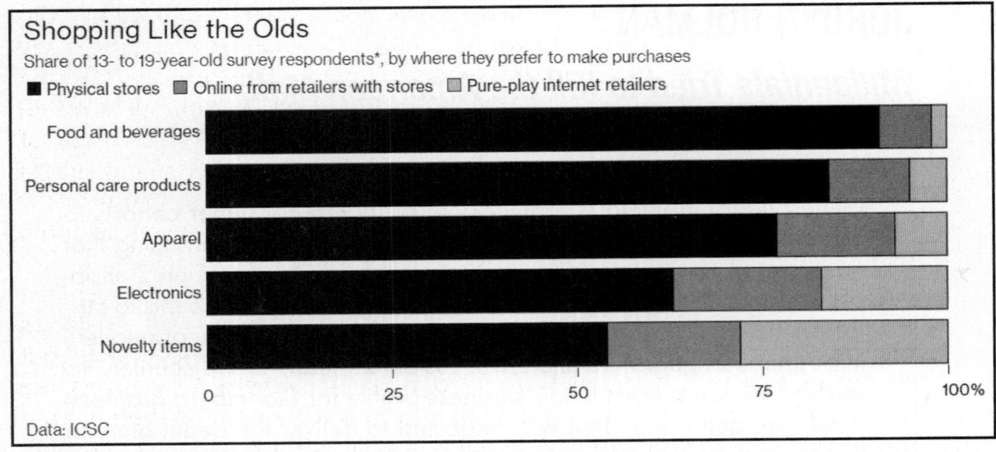

Shopping Like the Olds

Failure to adapt to changing trends and stay relevant can crush a business, 5
with regional mall vacancy rates at 9.3 percent in the U.S. But get it right, and savvy apparel companies could capture some of the generation's expected spending power of about $143 billion in the U.S. alone. Here's a look at some of the ways retailers are keeping up:

1. They Don't Fight the iPhone

Gen Z spends a lot of time on their smartphones—and they know it: Nearly six out of ten self-diagnose overuse, according to a recent survey by Bloomberg and Morning Consult. For companies that embrace that, instead of fight it, the payoff can be huge. Forever 21, consistently ranked among American teenagers' top brands, rewards phone-in-hand shopping by offering customers 21 percent off if they snap a picture of themselves in a Forever 21 outfit and post it with designated hashtags—then show the cashier at the register. And they do it: On Instagram, the #F21PROMO has been used about 20,000 times, mostly by teenage girls striking a range of poses from sitting on a bench with a Starbucks drink in hand to throwing up peace signs. One poster on Twitter, who hid her face with her baseball cap, wrote "my mom is making me do this for 21% off."

Tech companies are responding as well. RetailMeNot, a digital coupon provider, is able to send push notifications to shoppers when they're in a mall to alert them to potential discounts. A recent survey from the startup found that an overwhelming 91 percent of Gen Z shoppers are searching for deals on their mobile phones while inside retail locations.

*Survey of 1,002 13- to 19-year-olds in the U.S. conducted in May 2018 by Engine on behalf of ICSC.

Nimble retailers are making their stores more Instagram-worthy in a bid to appeal to this connected crowd. About a third of Gen Z consumers say shopping should also be entertaining, according to data from Cassandra, a cultural insights and strategy agency. With these Gen Z shoppers in mind, old-guard department store Macy's Inc. earlier this month rolled out in 36 of its locations "Story," a colorful themed shop-in-shop. In its behemoth Herald Square store, the 7,500-square-foot space is brightly painted with primary colors, a pillar completely made of Crayola crayons, a pingpong table and a rainbow tunnel.

Story is filled with knickknacks like hot dog–shaped pet toys, purses that charge phones and self-help books on how to cure hangovers, which Macy's Chief Executive Officer Jeff Gennette describes as items "nobody needs" but are "going to want" once they walk through the spot. Every two months, the space undergoes a complete overhaul and introduces a new theme. That means repainting walls, installing new carpets and designing new opportunities to post on Instagram. It's a neck-breaking pace for retail. "You just don't have the same predictability that you have in some of the department store square footage," Gennette said in an interview at the flagship store. "You can always show up and find something different."

2. They Let Them Customize It

Gennette's onto something: Different is the name-of-the-game for these young 10
adults. Nearly half of Gen Z shoppers want products tailor-made to their tastes and interests, according to a 2018 report from IBM and the National Retail Federation. To be sure, previous generations personalized their apparel and accessories in ways they wanted, like adding patches and buttons. The difference for this generation is that retailers have more technology already in place to acquiesce to their requests right from the start. "In the past, it has been a little more cookie-cutter," says Marcie Merriman, an EY consultant who specializes in the Gen Z consumer. Now for today's teens, "their mind just goes to a very different place because of their expectation that anything is possible."

In some American Eagle Outfitters Inc. stores, shoppers can take their jeans to a counter and get them embossed, attach back patches, and add paint. Champion, the activewear company owned by Hanesbrands Inc., trained store associates to heat-press and embroider its iconic "C" logo and brand name anywhere consumers want on their sweatshirts and hoodies upon request. Levi Strauss & Co. put tailor shops in most of its mainline stores to entice consumers to add monogram stitching to the brand's trucker jackets and iconic jeans — which CEO Chip Bergh admits weren't popular with millennials, including his own sons, but are having a comeback. Tiffany & Co. — a go-to jeweler for rite-of-passage gifts like Sweet 16 celebrations, proms, and graduations — is not just engraving initials into pieces of silver bracelets and necklaces anymore. Last year, it heavily invested in its "Make It

My Tiffany" program in a bid to reel in this generation of shoppers. "You can have your bracelet, ring, or piece of jewelry personalized," CEO Alessandro Bogliolo said. His 14-year-old daughter, for example, has a piece of jewelry with her pet on it.

3. They Don't Think Secondhand Clothing Is Second-Rate

Gen Z, just coming into its spending power, is looking for a good deal. Bonus points if the product is also sustainable. That group is turning to reused clothing at the quickest pace, according to Thredup's 2019 Resale Report, with one in three Gen Z shoppers expected to buy secondhand this year.

That has some unlikely players getting into the mix. High-end department store Neiman Marcus just made an unexpected move: buying a minority stake in Fashionphile, an e-commerce company focused on pre-owned luxury handbags and accessories. While the used luxury products will still be sold on Fashionphile's website, in the next year Neiman will open about five to seven in-store showrooms for customers to receive a quote on the used items they want to sell. Down the line, Neiman hopes its involvement in the reused market could convert young shoppers interested in used items to loyal new-product customers, CEO Geoffroy Van Raemdonck said in an interview. "The customer who participates in buying secondhand products are younger," he said. "That's usually their first time of entering the luxury market, and we aim to introduce them to Neiman Marcus — and ultimately to transition them to buying products of the season at Neiman Marcus. It's clearly a recruitment effort."

Saunders, the analyst at GlobalData Retail, said more companies need to start thinking outside the box to attract this important demographic. "The more traditional retailers haven't really thought about this particular generation as an attractive target. They haven't really thought about what this group wants out of a shopping experience," he said. "I think that's starting to change now."

Reading the Text

1. In your own words, how do Gen Z's attitudes toward shopping and malls differ from those of their parents' generation?
2. What stereotypes are usually attached to Gen Z members, in Holman's view, and how are those stereotypes inaccurate?
3. According to Holman, what are some successful strategies that retail stores have used to attract Gen Z to their brick-and-mortar stores?
4. Why are some retailers exploring ways to attract younger consumers by offering secondhand products, and what is the basis for that appeal?

READING THE SIGNS

1. Interview at least half a dozen Gen Z members about their shopping habits, and use your results as the basis of an essay in which you assess the extent to which they "interact differently with stores than their older siblings and Gen X parents before them" (para. 4).
2. **CONNECTING TEXTS** Adopt the perspective of Alicia Eler ("There's a Lot More to a Selfie Than Meets the Eye" [p. 340]), and write a response to the observation that "Gen Z spends a lot of time on their smartphones. . . . For companies that embrace that, instead, of fight it, the payoff can be huge" (para. 6). To what extent would Eler see corporate "embracing" of phone addiction as exploitative on the one hand or beneficial on the other?
3. Secondhand clothing has gone through waves of popularity in the last few decades. In an essay, write an argument about why secondhand clothing, among other products, has recently had a resurgence of stylishness among GenZ shoppers. To develop evidence for your essay, interview a half-dozen GenZ members who enjoy shopping at thrift shops and other secondhand retailers.

MICHAEL POLLAN

Supermarket Pastoral

One of the signs of society's increasing sensitivity to the environment, and to the lives of the animal species whose misfortune it is to be part of the human food chain, is the growth of the organic foods movement. So successful has this movement been — supporting the emergence of such grocery store chains as Whole Foods Market and Sprouts — that it has spawned an elaborate marketing technique that Michael Pollan calls "Supermarket Pastoral": "a most seductive literary form, beguiling enough to survive in the face of many discomfiting facts." These facts include the fundamental contradiction at the heart of the narrative, which is that the organic foods movement has become fully industrialized and that its tales of wholly "natural" ingredients and happy free-ranging hens gloss over a lot of synthetic additives and penned-up, soon-to-be-slaughtered chickens. Michael Pollan is the author of several books, including *The Omnivore's Dilemma* (2006), from which this selection is taken, and *How to Change Your Mind* (2018).

I enjoy shopping at Whole Foods nearly as much as I enjoy browsing a good bookstore, which, come to think of it, is probably no accident: Shopping at Whole Foods is a literary experience, too. That's not to take anything away from the food, which is generally of high quality, much of it "certified organic" or "humanely raised" or "free range." But right there, that's the point: It's the evocative prose as much as anything else that makes this food really special, elevating an egg or chicken breast or bag of arugula from the realm of ordinary protein and carbohydrates into a much headier experience, one with complex aesthetic, emotional, and even political dimensions. Take the "range-fed" sirloin steak I recently eyed in the meat case. According to the brochure on the counter, it was formerly part of a steer that spent its days "living in beautiful places" ranging from "plant-diverse, high-mountain meadows to thick aspen groves and miles of sagebrush-filled flats." Now a steak like that has got to taste better than one from Safeway, where the only accompanying information comes in the form of a number: the price, I mean, which you can bet will be considerably less. But I'm evidently not the only shopper willing to pay more for a good story.

With the growth of organics and mounting concerns about the wholesomeness of industrial food, storied food is showing up in supermarkets everywhere these days, but it is Whole Foods that consistently offers the most cutting-edge grocery lit. On a recent visit I filled my shopping cart with eggs "from cage-free vegetarian hens," milk from cows that live "free from unnecessary fear and distress," wild salmon caught by Native Americans in Yakutat, Alaska (population 833), and heirloom tomatoes from Capay Farm ($4.99 a pound), "one of the early pioneers of the organic movement." The organic broiler I picked up even had a name: Rosie, who turned out to be a "sustainably farmed" "free-range chicken" from Petaluma Poultry, a company whose "farming methods strive to create harmonious relationships in nature, sustaining the health of all creatures and the natural world." Okay, not the most mellifluous or even meaningful sentence, but at least their heart's in the right place.

In several corners of the store I was actually forced to choose between subtly competing stories. For example, some of the organic milk in the milk case was "ultrapasteurized," an extra processing step that was presented as a boon to the consumer, since it extends shelf life. But then another, more local dairy boasted about the fact they had said no to ultrapasteurization, implying that their product was fresher, less processed, and therefore more organic. This was the dairy that talked about cows living free from distress, something I was beginning to feel a bit of myself by this point.

This particular dairy's label had a lot to say about the bovine lifestyle: Its Holsteins are provided with "an appropriate environment, including shelter and a comfortable resting area, . . . sufficient space, proper facilities and the company of their own kind." All this sounded pretty great, until I read the story of another dairy selling raw milk — *completely* unprocessed — whose "cows graze green pastures all year long." Which made me wonder whether the first dairy's idea of an appropriate environment for a cow included, as I had simply presumed, a pasture. All of a sudden the absence from their story of that word seemed weirdly conspicuous. As the literary critics would say, the writer seemed to be eliding the whole notion of cows and grass. Indeed, the longer I shopped in Whole Foods, the more I thought that this is a place where the skills of a literary critic might come in handy — those, and perhaps also a journalist's.

5 WORDY LABELS, point-of-purchase brochures, and certification schemes are supposed to make an obscure and complicated food chain more legible to the consumer. In the industrial food economy, virtually the only information that travels along the food chain linking producer and consumer is price. Just look at the typical newspaper ad for a supermarket. The sole quality on display here is actually a quantity: tomatoes $0.69 a pound; ground chuck $1.09 a pound; eggs $0.99 a dozen — special this week. Is there any other category of product sold on such a reductive basis? The bare-bones information travels in both directions, of course, and farmers who get the message that consumers care only about price will themselves care only about yield. This is how a cheap food economy reinforces itself.

One of the key innovations of organic food was to allow some more information to pass along the food chain between the producer and the consumer — an implicit snatch of narrative along with the number. A certified organic label tells a little story about how a particular food was produced, giving the consumer a way to send a message back to the farmer that she values tomatoes produced without harmful pesticides or prefers to feed her children milk from cows that haven't been injected with growth hormones. The word "organic" has proved to be one of the most powerful words in the supermarket: Without any help from government, farmers and consumers working together in this way have built an $11 billion industry that is now the fastest growing sector of the food economy.

Yet the organic label itself — like every other such label in the supermarket — is really just an imperfect substitute for direct observation of how a food is produced, a concession to the reality that most people in an industrial society haven't the time or the inclination to follow their food back to the farm, a farm which today is apt to be, on average, fifteen hundred miles away. So to bridge that space we rely on certifiers and label writers and, to a considerable extent, our imagination of what the farms that are producing our food really look like. The organic label may conjure an image of a simpler agriculture, but its very existence is an industrial artifact. The question is, what about the farms themselves? How well do they match the stories told about them?

Taken as a whole, the story on offer in Whole Foods is a pastoral narrative in which farm animals live much as they did in the books we read as children, and our fruits and vegetables grow in well-composted soils on small farms much like Joel Salatin's. "Organic" on the label conjures up a rich narrative, even if it is the consumer who fills in most of the details, supplying the hero (American Family Farmer), the villain (Agribusinessman), and the literary genre, which I've come to think of as Supermarket Pastoral. By now we may know better than to believe this too simple story, but not much better, and the grocery store poets do everything they can to encourage us in our willing suspension of disbelief.

Supermarket Pastoral is a most seductive literary form, beguiling enough to survive in the face of a great many discomfiting facts. I suspect that's because it gratifies some of our deepest, oldest longings, not merely for safe food, but for a connection to the earth and to the handful of domesticated creatures we've long depended on. Whole Foods understands all this better than we do. One of the company's marketing consultants explained to me that the Whole Foods shopper feels that by buying organic he is "engaging in authentic experiences" and imaginatively enacting a "return to a utopian past with the positive aspects of modernity intact." This sounds a lot like Virgilian pastoral, which also tried to have it both ways. In *The Machine in the Garden* Leo Marx writes that Virgil's shepherd Tityrus, no primitive, "Enjoys the best of both worlds — the sophisticated order of art and the simple spontaneity of nature." In keeping with the pastoral tradition, Whole Foods offers what Marx terms "a landscape of reconciliation" between the realms of nature and culture, a place where, as the marketing consultant put it, "people will come together through organic foods to get back to the origin of things" — perhaps by sitting down to enjoy one of the microwaveable organic TV dinners (four words I never expected to see conjoined) stacked in the frozen food case. How's that for having it both ways?

Of course the trickiest contradiction Whole Foods attempts to reconcile 10
is the one between the industrialization of the organic food industry of which it is a part and the pastoral ideals on which that industry has been built. The organic movement, as it was once called, has come a remarkably long way in the last thirty years, to the point where it now looks considerably less like a movement than a big business. Lining the walls above the sumptuously stocked produce section in my Whole Foods are full-color photographs of local organic farmers accompanied by text blocks setting forth their farming philosophies. A handful of these farms — Capay is one example — still sell their produce to Whole Foods, but most are long gone from the produce bins, if not yet the walls. That's because Whole Foods in recent years has adopted the grocery industry's standard regional distribution system, which makes supporting small farms impractical. Tremendous warehouses buy produce for dozens of stores at a time, which forces them to deal exclusively with tremendous farms. So while the posters still depict family farmers and their philosophies, the produce on sale below them comes primarily from the two big corporate organic growers in California, Earthbound Farm and Grimmway Farms,[1] which together dominate the market for organic fresh produce in America. (Earthbound alone grows 80 percent of the organic lettuce sold in America.)

[1]Grimmway Farms owns Cal-Organic, one of the most ubiquitous organic brands in the supermarket.

As I tossed a plastic box of Earthbound prewashed spring mix salad into my Whole Foods cart, I realized that I was venturing deep into the belly of the industrial beast Joel Salatin had called "the organic empire." (Speaking of my salad mix, another small, beyond organic farmer, a friend of Joel's, had told me he "wouldn't use that stuff to make compost" — the organic purist's stock insult.) But I'm not prepared to accept the premise that industrial organic is necessarily a bad thing, not if the goal is to reform a half-trillion-dollar food system based on chain supermarkets and the consumer's expectations that food be convenient and cheap.

And yet to the extent that the organic movement was conceived as a critique of industrial values, surely there comes a point when the process of industrialization will cost organic its soul (to use a word still uttered by organic types without irony), when Supermarket Pastoral becomes more fiction than fact: another lie told by marketers.

The question is, has that point been reached, as Joel Salatin suggests? Just how well does Supermarket Pastoral hold up under close reading and journalistic scrutiny?

ABOUT AS WELL as you would expect anything genuinely pastoral to hold up in the belly of an $11 billion industry, which is to say not very well at all. At least that's what I discovered when I traced a few of the items in my Whole Foods cart back to the farms where they were grown. I learned, for example, that some (certainly not all) organic milk comes from factory farms, where thousands of Holsteins that never encounter a blade of grass spend their days confined to a fenced "dry lot," eating (certified organic) grain and tethered to milking machines three times a day. The reason much of this milk is ultrapasteurized (a high-heat process that damages its nutritional quality) is so that big companies like Horizon and Aurora can sell it over long distances. I discovered organic beef being raised in "organic feedlots" . . . [as well as something called] organic high-fructose corn syrup — more words I never expected to see combined. And I learned about the making of the aforementioned organic TV dinner, a microwaveable bowl of "rice, vegetables, and grilled chicken breast with a savory herb sauce." Country Herb, as the entrée is called, turns out to be a highly industrialized organic product, involving a choreography of thirty-one ingredients assembled from far-flung farms, laboratories, and processing plants scattered over a half-dozen states and two countries, and containing such mysteries of modern food technology as high-oleic safflower oil, guar and xanthan gum, soy lecithin, carrageenan, and "natural grill flavor." Several of these ingredients are synthetic additives permitted under federal organic rules. So much for "whole" foods. The manufacturer of Country Herb is Cascadian Farm, a pioneering organic farm turned processor in Washington State that is now a wholly owned subsidiary of General Mills. (The Country Herb chicken entrée has since been discontinued.)

15 I also visited Rosie the organic chicken at her farm in Petaluma, which turns out to be more animal factory than farm. She lives in a shed with

twenty thousand other Rosies, who, aside from their certified organic feed, live lives little different from that of any other industrial chicken. Ah, but what about the "free-range" lifestyle promised on the label? True, there's a little door in the shed leading out to a narrow grassy yard. But the free-range story seems a bit of a stretch when you discover that the door remains firmly shut until the birds are at least five or six weeks old — for fear they'll catch something outside — and the chickens are slaughtered only two weeks later.

Reading the Text

1. Pollan begins the selection with his own tale of a shopping trip to Whole Foods. Why do you think he includes personal experience? What effect does it have on your response as a reader?
2. Explain in your own words what Pollan means by "Supermarket Pastoral" (para. 8).
3. How do "wordy labels, point-of-purchase brochures, and certification schemes" (para. 5) affect a consumer's shopping behavior in a store like Whole Foods, according to Pollan?
4. Explain how, in Pollan's view, the organic food business has become industrialized.
5. How do you characterize Pollan's tone in this selection? How does it affect your response to his position?

Reading the Signs

1. **CONNECTING TEXTS** Visit a Whole Foods outlet, or another retailer that is promoted as organic, green, or alternative, and study the products, interior décor, and claims made about how items are sourced. Consider whether your observations combine to create a Supermarket Pastoral narrative. In an essay, write an argument that outlines the narrative that your store tells, whether it be Supermarket Pastoral or something else. To develop your ideas, consult Julia B. Corbett's "A Faint Green Sell: Advertising and the Natural World" (p. 305). Alternatively, conduct the same sort of analysis of a more typical supermarket. Do you see similar strategies at work there? How might you explain any differences you may detect?
2. Adopt the perspective of a Whole Foods manager, and write a response to Pollan's critique of the store chain. How would the manager defend the chain against the claim that it offers " 'a landscape of reconciliation' between the realms of nature and culture" (para. 9)?
3. **CONNECTING TEXTS** Study the packaging of one or more items available at a store like Whole Foods or Sprouts. Using Chris Arning's "What Can Semiotics Contribute to Packaging Design?" (p. 217) as a critical framework, analyze how the packaging works not simply as a container but as a collection of signs created by marketers. What signs does your chosen packaging use, and what do they signify?

4. Write an essay that supports, opposes, or complicates the proposition that industrial organic is a better alternative to "a half-trillion-dollar food system based on chain supermarkets and the consumer's expectations that food be convenient and cheap" (para. 11).
5. In small groups, analyze the various eateries available on your campus, studying the "food narrative" that they convey to students. To what extent do you see the Supermarket Pastoral as a dominant narrative? Do other narratives appear? Use your group's observations to support your own essay analyzing how food is marketed to students. Try to account for your findings.

CHRIS ARNING

What Can Semiotics Contribute to Packaging Design?

Usually, semiotic analyses are conducted from the perspective of the *receiver* of a message — as when we analyze an advertisement, a television show, or any other phenomenon of popular culture. But as semiotician Chris Arning demonstrates in his description of how semiotics can help brand owners maximize their profits, the focus can be reversed to analyze the *sending* of the message. And in the case of product packaging, that message lies in the physical elements of the package itself, which, much like many advertisements, may say less about the product than it does about the emotions of the consumers who are expected to buy it. With the product's outside being just as (if not more) important as its inside, Arning suggests, it behooves marketers to carefully craft the signals that their products send, and that means paying attention to the semiotics of packaging design. Chris Arning is the founder of Creative Semiotics Ltd, a semiotics consulting firm, as well as of the Semiotic Thinking Group on LinkedIn, and is a visiting lecturer at the University of Warwick.

> Consumers shop for meaning, not stuff.
>
> — LAURA OSWALD

This is certainly true of brand communication and no less true of packaging. As a brand owner, do you know what messages you transmit through the cues embedded in your pack design replicated millions of times? Consumers see packaging as an integral part of a product's value proposition. This includes the language conveyed on packs, the materials used and the graphical schema employed including colours, typography and symbols.

Psychotherapist Louis Cheskin spent most of his life investigating how design elements impacted people's perceptions of value, appeal and relevance. He also discovered that most people could not resist transferring their feelings towards the packaging to the product itself. His most famous achievement was turning Marlboro cigarettes into a "man's" cigarette from its original appeal to women. At the time its unique product differentiation was a red wrapper, to hide lipstick marks. Because more men than women were smokers, Cheskin convinced Phillip Morris that they would have more success by appealing to men. Cheskin's recommendations were to redesign the package to denote masculinity, whilst keeping the red colour.

His recommendations underlie everything from the "Man-Sized Flavour" advertising campaign and the now iconic packaging (resembling a medal), to the masculine and virile Marlboro Man himself. The Marlboro Man sported tattoos to give him a rugged back-story and often appeared as a cowboy on horseback (the predominant image that has survived today).

We have lived through an age of mass affluence and during this time, packaging has undergone a mass wave of so-called "premiumisation" across all sectors, with even cleaning products like Fairy Liquid getting in on the act. In such a context, packaging in the UK and elsewhere is no longer just a container, but a manifesto for brand communication. For some consumers, it is even fetishistic. This means that the bar for what is considered quality has been raised. We expect charming and emotionally engaging packaging as part of the overall product proposition, and in certain categories it is even a brand discriminator.

Plastic versus glass, rotund versus rectilinear, puce versus cobalt: the 5
devil is in the detail, and these details can be critical to the success of packaging. Whilst pack designers are technically competent and have a knack for aesthetics, it is sometimes necessary to have a more in-depth understanding of how to express brand distinction in pack communication. This is where semiotics comes into play.

So, what is semiotics? Semiotics is the study of meaning and communication. It can inject rigour and more rationality into design processes, making us more mindful of our choices. Residing in academic research, mainly in disciplines such as linguistics, media studies and sociology, the application of semiotics has taken off in the commercial world and provided enormous value in the area of brand packaging. More and more, the use of semiotics research is penetrating the sphere of packaging design, giving brands a tremendous head start in communicating core values, personality and brand positioning to the market. So what can semiotics contribute to packaging design? Mega multi-nationals such as Procter & Gamble (P&G) and Unilever were asking this question five years ago. These days semiotics is a part of their vocabulary and insight budget. The interest in the "S" word is now spreading among brand developers, designers, advertisers and packaging experts, making it worthwhile to take a closer look at what the semiotics research approach is all about.

The British writer J.G. Ballard once remarked that he could read the respective political ideologies of Britain and the USA inscribed into the front grill designs of Rolls Royce (parliamentary, monarchical) and Cadillacs (democratic, presidential). Whilst semiotics is not always that grandiose in interpretation, it does make links from the material detail to the ideas these details are likely to trigger in the minds of consumers encountering brand packs on a shelf — it is a powerful interpretive tool.

Consumers intuitively read and respond to the codes contained in brand communication, especially in brand packaging. For example, consider the packaging of personal care products containing lavender and how it has changed over time. Dated or clichéd packaging of lavender conveyed the symbolic code of "grannies floral" — pale mauve labelling, italicised old-world fonts and lavender sprig designs used as borders. The images conveyed the message that this product is best kept in white linens and lingerie drawers. The dominant design of packaging lavender today has shifted from nostalgic old world notions to expressing the code of authenticity. Use of labels with images of lavender, overt use of pale purple for package and copy that states it is lavender — all convey a message that reads, "I am really lavender." The more emergent expression of lavender in personal care is shifting toward the key benefit of lavender, namely its role in aromatherapy and relaxation. Packaging design is more evocative, using explicit language such as "relax, unwind, calm down." The colour palette embraces dark purple to emphasise deep relaxation and the word "lavender" is not always stated on pack. Understanding these semiotic codes and patterns of change does more than provide interesting historical dimensions. The codes create confident foundations for brands to be relevant, contemporary, and, above all else, appealing to consumers. By considering semiotics, a brand has a greater ability to pitch its packaging execution at exactly the right angle for consumers to read the desired message.

For example, the Courvoisier bottle conveys value through metaphors of opulence. As with many premium luxury items, it is as much an *objet d'art* to be contemplated, as it is a commodity to be consumed. The effect is achieved through solidity of material, flamboyant fluting of its bottle shape and other such extravagant features. As a cognac, it is squat and rotund, which evokes the lavishness of 16th century France where the drink originated. Arguably it is about possessing an object of beauty and identifying with an object of power and prestige — both anchored by the prominent Napoleon emblem. Many fast-moving consumer goods categories are also subject to what is called code convergence (where dominant graphical schemas tend to imitate category leaders and become more homogeneous over time), so packaging designers are pushed even further to innovate whilst still respecting product category norms.

Applied semiotics in brand strategy and design can help bring aware- 10
ness that meaning, and therefore perceived value, is generated via the differences that exist between brands within a category and that signs change according to the prevailing culture. This market intelligence can be a key competitive advantage, particularly in mature, cluttered product categories. This

understanding can be strategic, e.g. how the changing meanings of gold vs. bronze (via their connotations in art and other areas) affect their optimal use on pack; or tactical, e.g. how the choice of font typeface can convey the right impression and inflect meaning.

In practice, there are typically four main uses of semiotics methodology in package design:

- brand understanding
- inspiration
- evaluation, and
- global intelligence.

Brand Understanding

This is a very common area for a semiotics investigation. It is usually triggered by a brand review, to understand the rules or "codes" of a category in order to sharpen communication and become more differentiated. For instance, when a well-known Swiss chocolate manufacturer recognised the need to become more suited to the UK market, it undertook a brand audit. The first step was to show the connotations of propriety and stuffy conservatism and the positioning of chocolate as a confectionary item. This was conveyed via the use of glossy materials, rectilinear neo-classical motifs and other outdated signifiers going as far as the fussy scoring of chocolate tablets. The second step was to show the trajectory of change in the chocolate category towards more organic motifs, rougher, pulped materials and a move away from *fin-de-siècle* refinement, towards an inter-cultural awareness and how this was being reflected in and on pack. The third step was to suggest some ways that the brand could incorporate some of the new, emergent codes into the design brief.

In a more recent project, a company, for NPD purposes, needed to understand the codes of beauty serums used in packaging material and formulation. The analysis revealed that some of the codes used in the serums, which included the use of the golden ratio and contour bias in pack design, conveyed a deft sense of symmetry and perfection. There was also a strong brand value association communicated via emotional design. Semiotics also revealed intertextual links between serums and the mythology of elixirs as life-giving essence. Semiotics, like a serum itself, delivered a succinct, concentrated and easily absorbed dose of market intelligence that helped in the decision-making process.

Brand Inspiration

Semiotics leverages nuanced understanding of cultural change, aesthetic theory and lateral thinking to be a powerful hypotheses-generating engine.

For instance, if we wanted to communicate the more emergent, leading-edge expressions of "naturalness" in a pack design for a cosmetics product, the initial analysis would involve understanding the cultural connotations of naturalness. Some questions that would be explored are: What does natural mean to us today? How is it different from three years ago? How do other categories communicate natural in their packaging? What are the new ways of communicating natural in cosmetics packaging? The semiotics research would decode the meanings of natural in a wider cultural context and within the cosmetics category.

Back in 2005, Wrigley's commissioned a semiotics study to feed into an innovation workshop to develop concepts for a new gum for young adults. The result was "5 gum," a sensation in its category, which has enjoyed great commercial success and numerous industry awards. In this case, the semiotic insight showed that there was a stark discrepancy between the codes used within the gum market (fiddly, childish packs with primary colour cartoon graphics) and the market for US teens which was increasingly mature, ironic and enamoured of darker themes like the occult and extreme sports. Following the semiotic research, Wrigley's decided to translate some of this danger and mystique into the pack design for the new product.

Brand Evaluation

Semiotics can help assess and adjudicate between different strategic options for packaging, helping to fast-track the design and development process. In a recent study, a leading semiotics consultancy was asked to help a client develop new packaging for a premium yogurt brand that would have an increased price point. Using applied semiotic research, the consultancy derived a model and list of criteria including pack shape, material, haptic cues, graphic schema, layout, color and gradation from a rubric of similar projects to help the client achieve a solid competitive advantage.

Global Intelligence

Simplicity is not as simple as it used to be. At least, this was the conclusion drawn from a study looking at so-called "simple" packaging. The trouble is that "simple" cannot be equated with "basic" anymore: it is more about "managed complexity" and what counts as optimal varies significantly across markets. Of course, there is a set of universal rules regarding what counts as simplicity. Visual tricks such as symmetry, the law of thirds, golden ratio and contour bias that create a pleasing visual impression operate within the realm of neuroaesthetics. It seems, however, that hard-wired ideas are themselves subject to regional variation and inflection too — indeed "simplicity" turns out to be almost as subject to variation as notions such as authenticity and other diffuse marketing terms. The American economist, Professor Theodore Levitt, famous for popularising the term "globalization" was only half right. The world has become globalized and there is more standardization, but the keynote of design is hybridization between global design idiom and local motifs. In certain enclaves of consumer society, parochial tastes stubbornly persist and food packaging is one such niche.

Global Food Packaging

For a global food brand wanting to reconnect with notions such as simplicity, this is not an easy task when semiotics shows such a wide global variation in pack codes. For example, in Mexico, the baroque and riotous colors rule supreme, high color saturation; negligible color contrast and ornamentation are favoured. By contrast in Japan, a Zen-inflected subtlety and restraint with a generous use of white space dominate. In the UK, revivalist motifs and a return to thrift prevail and in France notions of regionality and *terroir* are the main focus. In India, simplicity per se is not a resonant term and seems only to be signified in food through proxies like spiritual purity or motherly love. In general, in developing markets, references to simplicity run up against a desire to flee poverty and taste abundance and packaging seems to reflect that paradox. These are the sorts of differences that applied use of semiotics can bring to a design team's attention.

The use of semiotic research can assist in developing effective packaging solutions, whether acting as a spring board for brand innovation and new product development; harmonising the appearance of the brand across markets; refreshing and/or updating the look of a brand; determining what signs and symbols the category is accessing; and ensuring a solid competitive advantage. It provides a toolkit for utilizing signs and symbols in terms of pack format (shape, size, texture), color, labelling and copy. It can also help determine what enhances or detracts from the emergent expressions of a particular trait or ingredient and how this links back to what is emerging in society.

Not intended to be prescriptive, semiotics provides a direction for packag- 20
ing design innovation and implementation that is rooted in the wider culture. It can give brands the confidence to see beyond faddish and seasonal trends. It can be used as a guide in constructing packaging with both relevant and contemporary meaning that truly communicates the brand's personality and values for achieving successful brand growth.

Semiotics helps to bring to the fore the relationship between meaning and value, the influence of the competitive context and cultural changes. Semiotics can help create new opportunities, provide critical market intelligence for forays into new product categories and is vital in accounting for global variation.

Reading the Text

1. What does Arning mean by saying that "packaging has undergone a mass wave of so-called 'premiumisation' across all sectors" (para. 4)?
2. In your own words, what are the four uses of semiotics in packaging design, and how does each use operate?
3. Why does the increasing globalization of consumer culture make semiotics an especially useful tool in packaging design, in Arning's view?
4. Summarize how the significance of lavender has evolved in the packaging of personal care products, as Arning describes it.
5. What is "code convergence" in packaging design, according to Arning (para. 9)?

Reading the Signs

1. In your journal, write your own response to Laura Oswald's opening quotation: "Consumers shop for meaning, not stuff." Have you ever purchased a product simply because you liked the packaging? What did you like about the packaging, and how did it contribute to your sense of identity?
2. Bring one product package to class; preferably, as a class, choose from a few similar product categories (personal hygiene, say, or bottled water), so that all students bring items from those categories. In class, give a brief presentation in which you interpret your package. After all students have presented, compare the different messages the packages send to consumers.
3. Visit a popular retail store, such as Urban Outfitters or Victoria's Secret, and study the ways the store uses packaging to create, as Laura Oswald puts it, a "meaning" that targets its typical market. Be thorough in your observations, studying everything from the store's shopping bags to its perfume or cologne packages to its clothing labels. Use your findings as evidence for an essay in which you analyze the image the store creates for itself and its customers.
4. **CONNECTING TEXTS** Visit a store with an explicit political theme, such as The Body Shop or Whole Foods Market, and write a semiotic analysis of the packaging you see in the store. To develop your ideas, consult Michael Pollan's "Supermarket Pastoral" (p. 211) and Julia B. Corbett's "A Faint Green Sell: Advertising and the Natural World" (p. 305).
5. Study the product packaging that is visible to a visitor to your home or dorm room and write an analysis of the messages that packaging might send to the visitor.
6. Select a consumer product that has iconic packaging and research the evolution of the packaging designs. Use your findings as a jumping-off point to analyze semiotically the history of this product's packages. In what ways do the packages serve as signs of their time?

TROY PATTERSON

The Politics of the Hoodie

The "hoodie" has come a long way from the days when it was just a utilitarian sweatshirt worn by athletes, farmers, and construction workers. In the 1980s, rappers turned it into an essential accessory of urban street style. Then, in the new millennium, Mark Zuckerberg turned it into a signifier of laid-back postindustrial chic in the digital age, on the one hand, and the shooting death of Trayvon Martin transformed it into an emblem of black oppression, on the other. In short, the hoodie is now a complex semiotic system in its own right, whose history and widely branching meanings are surveyed in this article by Troy Patterson, a staff writer for the *New Yorker* and contributing writer for the *New York Times Magazine*, in which this reading originally appeared.

On a recent night, shopping online for a light jacket or a cotton sweater — some kind of outerwear to guard my body against a spring-like breeze — I clicked on the "new arrivals" page of the website of a popular retailer and encountered, unexpectedly, another instance of the complex oddity of race. Here, projecting catalog-model cordiality in the sterile space of an off-white backdrop, was a young black man in a hoodie.

On the street, a black guy in a hoodie is just another of the many millions of men and boys dressed in the practical gear of an easygoing era. Or he should be. This is less an analysis than a wish. The electric charge of the isolated image — which provokes a flinch away from thought, a desire to evade the issue by moving on to check the sizing guide — attests to a consciousness of the hoodie's recent history of peculiar reception. In a cardigan or a crew neck, this model is just another model. In the hoodie, he is a folk demon and a scapegoat, a political symbol and a moving target, and the system of signs that weighs this upon him does not make special distinctions for an Italian cashmere hoodie timelessly designed in heather gray.

Watching Beyoncé's recent video for "Formation," with its set piece showing a black child in a hooded sweatshirt disarming a rank of riot police with his dance moves, most Americans grasped the outfit as a rhetorical device serving a dreamlike declaration about protest and civil rights. During the N.F.L. playoffs, football fans saw the quarterback Cam Newton, the locus of a running dialogue about blackness, wear hoodies to interviews, and they read tweets that called him a "thug" for it. The boxing movie *Creed* — starring Michael B. Jordan opposite Sylvester Stallone, who made the hoodie a fixture in *Rocky* (1976) — features

Troy Patterson, "The Politics of the Hoodie," *The New York Times*, March 2, 2016.

rousing scenes of Jordan jogging across Philadelphia in a gray hoodie. The transfer of the garment from the old white champ to the young black contender plays as an echo of the film's broader racial politics.

At the computer, prodded out of the rhythm of browsing, I tried to imagine the meetings that led to this catalog model being placed in this hoodie, in the vacuum of commercial space. Beyond the usual earnest discussion of the styling of his pushed-up sleeves and the asymmetrical dangle of his drawstrings, there had to have been delicate conversations, informed by H.R. policy and P.C. etiquette, straightforward aesthetic concerns and knotty social ones. It is impossible that the production designers were ignorant of the ghost of Trayvon Martin, the unarmed 17-year-old fatally shot four years ago while wearing much the same thing. Did the model present a distraction from the reality on the streets? Did the art director start feeling somehow guilty for even considering such a question? The choice to put the kid in the picture must count as a modest political act, given the rich absurdity of the codes pertaining to a harmless piece of clothing.

5 The hooded sweatshirt emerged as a pop political object after decades of mundane hard work. In the 1930s, the company now known as Champion Athletic Apparel began turning them out to keep football players warm on the sidelines, also attracting business from men who operated backhoes and cherry pickers and forklifts — the forefathers of style for the guys who top their hoods with hard hats turned backward.

But the hoodie did not warrant enough consideration to earn its diminutive nickname until after it was processed by B-boys, graffiti artists, and break dancers in the '80s. Youth culture did the work of tugging it from the sphere of sportswear, where clothing exists to enhance performance, into the world of street wear, where clothing is performance in itself. By the 1990 release of the video for "Mama Said Knock You Out," with LL Cool J styled as a boxer in his corner, his lips visible beneath a hood that shielded his eyes, the hoodie had accomplished its transformation into an element of style.

Like their peers in the suburbs, bundled up on BMX bikes or skateboarding in sweatshirts with the logo of *Thrasher* magazine, a generation of hip-hop kids found the hoodie suitable for the important adolescent work of taking up space and dramatizing the self. There was and is a theater of the hood: pulling it up with a flourish, tugging it down to settle in its energetic slouch. The hood frames a dirty look, obscures acne and anxiety, masks headphones in study hall, makes a cone of solitude that will suffice for an autonomous realm. And if, in its antisurveillance capacity, the hood plays with the visual rhetoric of menace, it is heir to a tradition in teen dressing stretching back to the birth of the teenager, when he arrived fully formed in leather jacket and bluejeans. The cover of the Wu-Tang Clan's first album catches the mood: Members of the group wear black hoodies and white masks, as if to abduct the listener into a fantasy of ninja stealth.

But this was just a prologue to an era in which the hoodie became at once an anodyne style object and a subject of moral panic, its popularity and its selective stigmatization rising in proportion. A glance at almost any police blotter, or a recollection of the forensic sketch of the Unabomber, will confirm the hoodie as a wardrobe staple of the criminal class, and this makes it uniquely convenient as a proxy for racial profiling or any other exercise of enmity. The person itching to confirm a general bias against hip-hop kids or crusty punks imputes crooked character to the clothing itself.

Which brings you to the transcript of the 911 call made by Trayvon Martin's killer. Dispatcher: "Did you see what he was wearing?" George Zimmerman: "Yeah. A dark hoodie, like a gray hoodie." Trivial details can bear serious import. Surely there would have been demonstrations after the killing and the killer's acquittal regardless of what the victim wore. As it happened, those demonstrators — legislators on chamber floors, marchers in the street — picked up the sweatshirt as an emblem, donning hoods in solidarity. Instantly a symbol aggrieved at having to be one, the hoodie was jolted into a curious space: Where the basic hoodie means to defend against the elements, the protest hoodie seeks to offend the right people. In the paranoid view of stodgy shopkeepers, the hoodie is to be feared for extinguishing individuality; in its politicized life, it mutes identity to signal alliance, not unlike a resistance group's uniform.

10 All that potential subtext is attached to a generally evocative item of clothing. The white working-class hoodie still glows with the Rocky Balboa ideal of grit and tenacity. The yoga-class hoodie is sold on a promise of snuggly virtue that may explain why in Saskatchewan they call the thing a "bunny hug." The tech-sector hoodie made default by Facebook's Mark Zuckerberg carries on the garment's proud juvenile tradition of informality and defiance. Once perceived as an affront to professionalism, it has since settled in as a convention.

In January, there emerged a debate in the business press regarding the rituals of dress in the tech industry and their relationship to the field's hospitableness to women. The argument proceeded in an article on Quartz headlined "The Subtle Sexism of Hoodies" and in counterarguments suggesting, for instance, that "hoodies represent a rejection of old ideas and an openness to new ones." I was struck by the ready acceptance of the notion that a Silicon Valley hoodie was not just a prerequisite in its field, like Gucci loafers on Wall Street, but also a costume of dominance. Its visual strength abets its powers as a cultural marker, needing just a nudge to create its own contexts.

You must have seen a sitcom or TV commercial in which black actors wear hoodies in new millennial colors — mustard, maroon — to portray coders. In a current General Electric ad, for example, the costume functions as characterization, and the cheery color of the cotton somehow trumps that of the skin in terms of mass iconography. But the ascent of casual wear does not quite disguise the unchanging strictness of social codes, and the hood continues to frame matters of class and race in ways that tend to satisfy the interest of power. The lingering question of the hoodie is simply: Who enjoys the right to wear one without challenge?

Reading the Text

1. Patterson does not use the word *semiotics* in his essay, but he essentially is providing a semiotic reading of the hoodie. In class, discuss the various ways in which his article uses semiotic techniques to explain the significance of the hoodie.
2. Summarize in your own words the hoodie's evolution from a practical clothing item to one that bears charged political meanings that are racially coded.
3. Patterson opens his essay by describing an online clothing retailer's ad showing a young black man modeling a cashmere hoodie. Why does Patterson assert that "there had to have been delicate conversations, informed by H.R. policy and P.C. etiquette, straightforward aesthetic concerns and knotty social ones" (para. 4) among the ad's creators?
4. Explain in your own words how the Trayvon Martin shooting turned the hoodie into an "emblem" intended "to offend the right people" (para. 9).

Reading the Signs

1. In class, brainstorm other clothing categories that may have a political or class significance (the business suit and blue jeans are just two of many possibilities). Select one of these categories and write your own semiotic interpretation of that category. You may find it useful to conduct some research on the history of your topic.
2. In an essay, propose your own response to Patterson's concluding statement: "The lingering question of the hoodie is simply: Who enjoys the right to wear one without challenge?" (para. 12). To develop your ideas, you might conduct an online survey of some of the groups Patterson mentions (hip-hop artists, high-tech workers, social activists) to discern the current symbolic significance of the hoodie. You might also do a survey of clothing retailers (online or brick and mortar) to see how this item is being marketed, for whom, and in what price ranges.
3. Patterson says that "the hoodie is to be feared for extinguishing individuality; in its politicized life, it mutes identity to signal alliance" (para. 9). Select a group that uses clothing to signal its identity (the military, scouting organizations, even sororities and fraternities are some that come to mind), and write an argumentative essay in which you weigh the extent to which the group's uniforms encourage uniformity or bonding.
4. Randomly observe students at your school congregating in a public place (say, the student union building). Then write a semiotic interpretation of the fashion trends you observe. What patterns of fashion preference do you see? Do they align with gender or racial characteristics? Are there current fashion trends that you don't see?
5. Write an essay in which you support, oppose, or complicate the stance that the adoption of the hoodie as corporate wear is an instance of what Thomas Frank calls "commodifying" an alternative or countercultural position. To develop your ideas, read Frank's "Commodify Your Dissent" (p. 228).

THOMAS FRANK

Commodify Your Dissent

"Sometimes You Gotta Break the Rules." "This is different. Different is good." "The Line Has Been Crossed." "Resist the Usual." If you are guessing that these defiant declarations must come from the Che Guevara/Jack Kerouac Institute of World Revolution and Extreme Hipness, you're in for a surprise, because they are actually advertising slogans for such corporations as Burger King, Arby's, Toyota, Clash Clear Malt, and Young & Rubicam. Just why huge corporations are aping the language of the Beats and the 1960s counterculture is the centerpiece of Thomas Frank's thesis that the countercultural idea has become "an official aesthetic of consumer society." Commodifying the decades-long youth habit of dissenting against corporate America, corporate America has struck back by adopting the very attitudes that once meant revolution, Frank believes, thus turning to its own capitalist uses the postures of rebellion. Indeed, when Apple can persuade you to buy a computer because its guy is just plain *cooler* than some IBM nerd, there may be no way out. Frank is the author of *Commodify Your Dissent: Salvos from the Baffler* (with Matt Weiland, 1997), from which this selection is taken. His most recent book, *Rendezvous with Oblivion,* was published in 2018.

> The public be damned! I work for my stockholders.
>
> —WILLIAM H. VANDERBILT, 1879

> Break the rules. Stand apart. Keep your head. Go with your heart.
>
> —TV commercial for Vanderbilt perfume, 1994

Capitalism is changing, obviously and drastically. From the moneyed pages of the *Wall Street Journal* to TV commercials for airlines and photocopiers we hear every day about the new order's globe-spanning, cyber-accumulating ways. But our notion about what's wrong with American life and how the figures responsible are to be confronted haven't changed much in thirty years. Call it, for convenience, the "countercultural idea." It holds that the paramount ailment of our society is conformity, a malady that has variously been described as over-organization, bureaucracy, homogeneity, hierarchy, logocentrism, technocracy, the Combine, the Apollonian.[1] We all know what it is and what it does. It transforms humanity into "organization man," into "the man in the gray flannel suit." It is "Moloch[2] whose mind is pure machinery,"

[1] **Apollonian** An allusion to the god Apollo, a term for rational consciousness. — EDS.

[2] **Moloch** An ancient idol to whom children were sacrificed, used by Allen Ginsberg as a symbol for industrial America in his poem "Howl." — EDS.

the "incomprehensible prison" that consumes "brains and imagination." It is artifice, starched shirts, tailfins, carefully mowed lawns, and always, always, the consciousness of impending nuclear destruction. It is a stiff, militaristic order that seeks to suppress instinct, to forbid sex and pleasure, to deny basic human impulses and individuality, to enforce through a rigid uniformity a meaningless plastic consumerism.

As this half of the countercultural idea originated during the 1950s, it is appropriate that the evils of conformity are most conveniently summarized with images of 1950s suburban correctness. You know, that land of sedate music, sexual repression, deference to authority, Red Scares, and smiling white people standing politely in line to go to church. Constantly appearing as a symbol of arch-backwardness in advertising and movies, it is an image we find easy to evoke.

The ways in which this system are to be resisted are equally well understood and agreed-upon. The Establishment demands homogeneity; we revolt by embracing diverse, individual lifestyles. It demands self-denial and rigid adherence to convention; we revolt through immediate gratification, instinct uninhibited, and liberation of the libido and the appetites. Few have put it more bluntly than Jerry Rubin did in 1970: "Amerika says: Don't! The yippies say: Do It!" The countercultural idea is hostile to any law and every establishment. "Whenever we see a rule, we must break it," Rubin continued. "Only by breaking rules do we discover who we are." Above all rebellion consists of a sort of Nietzschean antinomianism,[3] an automatic questioning of rules, a rejection of whatever social prescriptions we've happened to inherit. Just Do It is the whole of the law.

The patron saints of the countercultural idea are, of course, the Beats, whose frenzied style and merry alienation still maintain a powerful grip on the American imagination. Even forty years after the publication of *On the Road*, the works of Kerouac, Ginsberg, and Burroughs remain the sine qua non of dissidence, the model for aspiring poets, rock stars, or indeed anyone who feels vaguely artistic or alienated. That frenzied sensibility of pure experience, life on the edge, immediate gratification, and total freedom from moral restraint, which the Beats first propounded back in those heady days when suddenly everyone could have their own TV and powerful V-8, has stuck with us through all the intervening years and become something of a permanent American style. Go to any poetry reading and you can see a string of junior Kerouacs go through the routine, upsetting cultural hierarchies by pushing themselves to the limit, straining for that gorgeous moment of original vice when Allen Ginsberg first read "Howl" in 1955 and the patriarchs of our fantasies recoiled in shock. The Gap may have since claimed Ginsberg and *USA Today* may run feature stories about the brilliance of the beloved Kerouac, but the rebel race continues today regardless, with ever-heightening shit-references calculated to scare Jesse Helms, talk about sex and smack that is supposed to bring the

[3]**Nietzschean antinomianism** An allusion to the German philosopher Friedrich Nietzsche's challenging of conventional Christian morality. — Eds.

electricity of real life, and ever-more determined defiance of the repressive rules and mores of the American 1950s — rules and mores that by now we know only from movies.

But one hardly has to go to a poetry reading to see the countercultural idea acted out. Its frenzied ecstasies have long since become an official aesthetic of consumer society, a monotheme of mass as well as adversarial culture. Turn on the TV and there it is instantly: the unending drama of consumer unbound and in search of an ever-heightened good time, the inescapable rock 'n' roll soundtrack, dreadlocks and ponytails bounding into Taco Bells, a drunken, swinging-camera epiphany of tennis shoes, outlaw soda pops, and mind-bending dandruff shampoos. Corporate America, it turns out, no longer speaks in the voice of oppressive order that it did when Ginsberg moaned in 1956 that *Time* magazine was

> always telling me about responsibility. Business-
> men are serious. Movie producers are serious.
> Everybody's serious but me.

Nobody wants you to think they're serious today, least of all Time Warner. On the contrary: the Culture Trust is now our leader in the Ginsbergian search for kicks upon kicks. Corporate America is not an oppressor but a sponsor of fun, provider of lifestyle accoutrements, facilitator of carnival, our slang-speaking partner in the quest for that ever-more apocalyptic orgasm. The countercultural idea has become capitalist orthodoxy, its hunger for transgression upon transgression now perfectly suited to an economic-cultural regime that runs on ever-faster cyclings of the new; its taste for self-fulfillment and its intolerance for the confines of tradition now permitting vast latitude in consuming practices and lifestyle experimentation.

Consumerism is no longer about "conformity" but about "difference." Advertising teaches us not in the ways of puritanical self-denial (a bizarre notion on the face of it), but in orgiastic, never-ending self-fulfillment. It counsels not rigid adherence to the tastes of the herd but vigilant and constantly updated individualism. We consume not to fit in, but to prove, on the surface at least, that we are rock 'n' roll rebels, each one of us as rule-breaking and hierarchy-defying as our heroes of the '60s, who now pitch cars, shoes, and beer. This imperative of endless difference is today the genius at the heart of American capitalism, an eternal fleeing from "sameness" that satiates our thirst for the New with such achievements of civilization as the infinite brands of identical cola, the myriad colors and irrepressible variety of the cigarette rack at 7-Eleven.

As existential rebellion has become a more or less official style of Information Age capitalism, so has the countercultural notion of a static, repressive Establishment grown hopelessly obsolete. However the basic impulses of the countercultural idea may have disturbed a nation lost in Cold War darkness, they are today in fundamental agreement with the basic tenets of Information Age business theory. . . .

Contemporary corporate fantasy imagines a world of ceaseless, turbulent change, of centers that ecstatically fail to hold, of joyous extinction for the craven gray-flannel creature of the past. Businessmen today decorate the walls of their offices not with portraits of President Eisenhower and emblems of suburban order, but with images of extreme athletic daring, with sayings about "diversity" and "empowerment" and "thinking outside the box." They theorize their world not in the bar car of the commuter train, but in weepy corporate retreats at which they beat their tom-toms and envision themselves as part of the great avant-garde tradition of edge-livers, risk-takers, and ass-kickers. Their world is a place not of sublimation and conformity, but of "leadership" and bold talk about defying the herd. And there is nothing this new enlightened species of businessman despises more than "rules" and "reason." The prominent culture-warriors of the right may believe that the counterculture was capitalism's undoing, but the antinomian businessmen know better. "One of the T-shirt slogans of the sixties read, 'Question authority,' " the authors of *Reengineering the Corporation* write. "Process owners might buy their reengineering team members the nineties version: 'Question assumptions.' "

The new businessman quite naturally gravitates to the slogans and sensibility of the rebel sixties to express his understanding of the new Information World. He is led in what one magazine calls "the business revolution" by the office-park subversives it hails as "business activists," "change agents," and "corporate radicals." . . . In television commercials, through which the new American businessman presents his visions and self-understanding to the public, perpetual revolution and the gospel of rule-breaking are the orthodoxy of the day. You only need to watch for a few minutes before you see one of these slogans and understand the grip of antinomianism over the corporate mind:

Sometimes You Gotta Break the Rules — Burger King
If You Don't Like the Rules, Change Them — WXRT-FM
The Rules Have Changed — Dodge
The Art of Changing — Swatch
There's no one way to do it. — Levi's
This is different. Different is good. — Arby's
Just Different from the Rest — Special Export beer
The Line Has Been Crossed: The Revolutionary New Supra — Toyota
Resist the Usual — the slogan of both Clash Clear Malt and Young & Rubicam
Don't Imitate, Innovate — Hugo Boss
Chart Your Own Course — Navigator Cologne
It separates you from the crowd — Vision Cologne

In most, the commercial message is driven home with the vanguard iconography of the rebel: screaming guitars, whirling cameras, and startled old timers who, we predict, will become an increasingly indispensable prop as consumers require ever-greater assurances that, Yes! You are a rebel! Just look at how offended they are! . . .

The structure and thinking of American business have changed enor- 10
mously in the years since our popular conceptions of its problems and abuses were formulated. In the meantime the mad frothings and jolly apolitical revolt of Beat, despite their vast popularity and insurgent air, have become powerless against a new regime that, one suspects, few of Beat's present-day admirers and practitioners feel any need to study or understand. Today that beautiful countercultural idea, endorsed now by everyone from the surviving Beats to shampoo manufacturers, is more the official doctrine of corporate America than it is a program of resistance. What we understand as "dissent" does not subvert, does not challenge, does not even question the cultural faiths of Western business. What David Rieff wrote of the revolutionary pretensions of multiculturalism is equally true of the countercultural idea: "The more one reads in academic multiculturalist journals and in business publications, and the more one contrasts the speeches of CEOs and the speeches of noted multiculturalist academics, the more one is struck by the similarities in the way they view the world." What's happened is not co-optation or appropriation, but a simple and direct confluence of interest.

Reading the Text

1. In your own words, define what Frank means by "countercultural idea" (para. 1) and its commodification.
2. How does Frank explain the relationship between the countercultural idea and conformity?
3. How were the Beats early progenitors of today's countercultural ideas, according to Frank?
4. In what ways does Frank believe that modern business has co-opted the countercultural idea?
5. How do you characterize Frank's tone in this selection? Does his tone enhance or detract from the forcefulness of his argument?

Reading the Signs

1. Analyze some current advertising in a magazine, on the internet, or on television, determining whether the advertisements employ the countercultural idea as a marketing ploy. Use your observations as the basis for an essay in which you assess whether the countercultural idea and the associated "iconography of the rebel" (para. 9) still prevail in advertising, as Frank suggests.
2. In class, brainstorm a list of today's cultural rebels, either marketing characters or real people such as actors or musicians, and discuss why these rebels are considered attractive to their intended audience. Use the class discussion as a springboard for your own essay in which you analyze how the status of cultural rebels is a sign of the mood of modern American culture.
3. Write an essay in which you agree, disagree, or modify Frank's contention that marketing no longer promotes conformity but, rather, promotes "never-ending self-fulfillment" and "constantly updated individualism" (para. 6).

4. Visit a youth-oriented store such as Urban Outfitters, and analyze its advertising, product displays, exterior design, and interior decor. Write an essay in which you gauge the extent to which the store uses the iconography of the rebel as a marketing strategy.
5. Study a current magazine focused on business or on modern technology, such as *Bloomberg Businessweek*, *Business 2.0*, or *Wired*. To what extent does the magazine exemplify Frank's claim that modern business eschews conformity and embraces rebellion and rule breaking? Alternatively, you might analyze some corporate websites, preferably several from companies in the same industry. Keep in mind that different industries may have very different corporate cultures; the values and ideals that dominate high tech, for instance, may differ dramatically from those in finance, entertainment, or social services.

JAMES A. ROBERTS

The Treadmill of Consumption

Once, "keeping up with the Joneses" was a neighborhood affair; now, thanks to modern mass media, it's a matter of "keeping up with the Kardashians" — that is, competing with the rich and famous in a never-ending spiral of status consumption. James A. Roberts's analysis of the compulsion to signify "social power through conspicuous consumption" is a sobering read for anyone who has ever gone into debt just to have a snazzier cell phone, like GoldVish's million-dollar white-gold and diamond offering. A professor of marketing at Baylor University, Roberts is the author of *Shiny Objects: Why We Spend Money We Don't Have in Search of Happiness We Can't Buy* (2011), from which this selection is taken.

Using material possessions to exhibit status is commonplace in today's consumer culture. We may not know our neighbors, but we feel compelled to make sure they know that we're people of value. As humans we rely on visual cues such as material possessions to convey our status to others and to ascertain the status of people we don't know. The quest for status symbols influences both kids and adults, although the objects we choose to display may differ with age. (Cell phones may be an exception that spans all age groups.)

For young people, cell phones are seen as necessities, not luxuries. A teen or even preteen without a cell phone feels set apart, on the outside looking in. This is in part because cell phones are a way to stay tightly connected with others (text messaging "blind," with cell phone in the pocket, is one of my favorites); however, cell phones are also important fashion statements and social props. For young people, cell phones are second only to cars as symbols of independence. Many teens see cell phones as an extension of their personality, and phone manufacturers and service providers, knowing this, give them many options to express their inner selves — ways to personalize their ringtone, change their "wallpaper," and customize their "skin," for example, as well as add many apps and accessories.

Adults, especially men, are also susceptible to the status appeal of cell phones. Researchers in the United Kingdom studied the use of cell phones after reading newspaper stories about nightclubs in South America that required patrons to check their phones at the door. Club managers found, the stories reported, that many checked phones were props — not working cell phones. To learn more about whether and how people were using their cell phones as social props, the researchers studied cell phone use in upscale pubs in the UK. What they found is most interesting: men and women used their cell phones in different manners. While women would leave their phone in their purse until they needed it, men were more likely to take their phone out of their pocket or briefcase and place it on the counter or table in view of all. Furthermore, like peacocks strutting with their plumage in full display to attract a mate, men spent more time tinkering with and displaying their phone when the number of men relative to women in the pub increased.[1]

As long as consumers attempt to signal their social power through conspicuous consumption, the levels required to make a visible statement of power will continue to rise. If person A buys a new car, person B has to buy a better car to compete; and then person A has to buy a boat as well — and so on. But once basic needs are met there's no additional happiness with additional purchases. The process of moving ahead materially without any real gain in satisfaction is often called "the treadmill of consumption." That treadmill is a barrier to raising your level of happiness, because it causes you to quickly adapt to good things by taking them for granted.

Research has shown that humans are very flexible. We tend to get used to 5
new circumstances in our lives — including financial circumstances, both good and bad — and we make such mental shifts quickly. Economic gains or losses do give us pleasure or pain, but the effects wear off quickly. When our situation improves, having more money or possessions almost instantaneously becomes the new "normal." As our store of material possessions grows, so do our expectations.

Many researchers have likened this process to drug addiction, where the addict continually needs more and more of the drug of choice to achieve an equivalent "high." This means that acquiring more possessions doesn't take us any closer to happiness; it just speeds up the treadmill. I regret to say that there is a great deal of evidence supporting the existence — and potential harm — of the treadmill of consumption.

[1]John E. Lycett and Robin I. M. Dunbar, "Mobile Phones as Lekking Devices among Human Males," *Human Nature* 11, no. 1 (2000): 93–104.

If the treadmill didn't exist, people with more possessions would be happier than those "less fortunate" souls who own less. But this simply isn't the case. The "less fortunate" are, for the most part, just as happy as those with more stuff. Big purchases and the piling up of material possessions hold little sway over happiness. Probably the most discouraging proof for this statement can be found in the study of lottery winners. An integral component of the shiny-objects ethos is quick riches. What better way to catapult yourself past your neighbors than to strike it rich with the lottery, right? If you foresee nothing but a lifetime of fun and sun for lottery winners, you're wrong. A study of twenty winners found that they were no happier a few years after their good fortune; in fact, some were even less happy than before they bought their winning ticket.[2] If the lottery can't pull us out of our current torpor, what hope is there for a raise at work, a flat-screen (plasma) television, an iPhone, or a new car (surely the new Lexus would be an exception)?

Consuming for Status

One important reason that consumers buy products is to satisfy social needs. Many of us spend a large proportion of our disposable income on so-called status items, and this trend is on the rise as we continue to embrace the shiny-objects ethos. "Wait a minute," some of you might be saying; "hasn't the current economic crisis stemmed the tide of status consumption?" My response to that question is that it never has in the past. Sure, we might mind our financial p's and q's during the actual crisis, but we have always returned to our profligate ways once we've navigated our way through the economic doldrums.

You need look no further back than the early 2000s, when the internet bubble burst and the stock market tanked. It wasn't long until our spending picked up again, and with a renewed vengeance. That's precisely what brought us where we are today. Similar economic corrections in the 1970s, '80s, and '90s produced the same results: we tightened our financial belts only to loosen them when the clouds receded. It's really a lot like yo-yo dieting. Each time after we fall off the financial wagon we're a little worse off than the time before. Apparently as consumers we tend to suffer from short-term memory loss!

Pursuing materialistic ideals is a competitive and comparative pro- 10
cess — hence the expression "keeping up with the Joneses." And today, with daily twenty-four/seven media coverage of the lifestyles of the rich and famous, our competition is no longer limited to our neighborhood. Bill and Melinda Gates and the sultan of Brunei have replaced Joe and Irma down the street as our points of reference. To achieve a position of social power or

[2]Philip Brickman et al., "Lottery Winners and Accident Victims: Is Happiness Relative?" *Journal of Personality and Social Psychology* 36, no. 8 (1978): 917–27.

status, one must exceed this expanding community norm. Even the super-rich aren't happy. There's always someone with a bigger home or fancier yacht — or, heaven forbid, a prettier wife. Yes, we even use other humans as chattel in our attempt to secure our position in the social hierarchy! The result of all this social posturing is no end to our wants and little improvement in our satisfaction, despite an ever-increasing consumption of goods. And Madison Avenue knows it: after price, status is the principal theme of most advertising.

Status consumption has been defined as "the motivational process by which individuals strive to improve their social standing through conspicuous consumption of consumer products that confer or symbolize status to the individual and to surrounding significant others."[3] It is our attempt as consumers to gain the respect, consideration, and envy from those around us. Status consumption is the heart and soul of the consumer culture, which revolves around our attempts to signal our comparative degree

Can You Hear Me Now?

I thought I had found the ultimate status symbol when I came across Motorola's new $2,000 Aura cell phone. The avant-garde Aura sports 700-plus individual components, a stainless-steel housing, and a front plate that takes the manufacturer a month to create. Add to this list the world's first handset with a circular display (great color and resolution!), a sixty-two-carat sapphire crystal lens, a multimedia player, stereo Bluetooth, and much, much more.

My amazement over Motorola's Aura was short-lived, however. I lost interest when I heard about the $1 million — yes, $1 million — cell phone from GoldVish (a Swiss company). The phone is made of eighteen-carat white gold and is covered with diamonds. Bluetooth? Of course. How about a two-gigabyte memory, eight-megapixel camera, MP3 player, worldwide FM radio, and e-mail access? Not to worry if a million is a bit rich for you: GoldVish has made available several other phones for around $25,000 — no doubt delivered in plain brown-paper packaging to avoid any embarrassment associated with buying a cheaper model.[4]

[3]Jacqueline Eastman et al., "The Relationship between Status Consumption and Materialism: A Cross Cultural Comparison of Chinese, Mexican, and American Students," *Journal of Marketing Theory and Practice*, Winter 1997, 52–66, 58.

[4]Darren Murph, "Motorola Intros Avant-Garde $2,000 Aura, Markets It Like a Rolex," October 21, 2008, www.endgadget.com, accessed October 21, 2008.

of social power through conspicuous consumption. If you don't buy into status consumption yourself, you certainly know people who do. They go by many names, but "social climbers" and "status seekers" will do for now. Climbers and seekers work to surround themselves with visible evidence of the superior rank they claim or aspire to. Most of us, to some degree, are concerned with our social status, and we try to make sure others are aware of it as well.

Status consumption began in the United States as a way for members of the upper crust to flaunt their wealth to each other. Over the past century the practice has trickled down to the lower rungs of the economic ladder. People are willing to go into debt to buy certain products and brands — let's say a $2,500 Jimmy Choo handbag — because these status symbols represent power in our consumer culture. Cars, for example, are an expensive but easy way to tell the world you've made it; there's no mistaking which are the most expensive. The problem is that nearly everyone else is upgrading to the latest model as well, so no real increase in status occurs — another example of the treadmill of consumption. Fortunately — note the irony there — our consumer culture, with its vast array of products, allows us many other opportunities to confer status upon ourselves. Media mogul Ted Turner put it this way: "Life is a game. Money is how we keep score."[5]

Status consumers are willing to pay premium prices for products that are perceived to convey status and prestige. A high-end Patek Philippe watch is a good example of a product that is — and is blatantly marketed as — a quintessential status symbol. One of Patek's advertising slogans is, "You never really own a Patek Philippe. You merely look after it for the next generation." Trust me; you're buying it for yourself. Despite the manufacturer's claims to the contrary, a Patek Philippe does not keep better time than the myriad of cheaper alternatives on the market; on the contrary, it serves primarily as an unambiguous symbol of status. To many people, owning a Patek signals that you've made it. To me, however, it sends the signal that you've forgone a golden opportunity to do good with the money spent so lavishly on a very expensive watch. It's a zero-sum game no matter how much money you make.

And, of course, Patek Philippe watches are only one of a myriad of examples I could use to document our preoccupation with status consumption. What about Lucky Jeans, bling (it's shiny), Hummer automobiles (maybe one of the more blatant cries for help), iPhones, fifty-two-inch plasma TVs, $3,000 Chihuahua lap dogs (think Paris Hilton), McMansions, expensive rims for your car tires, anything couture, Gulfstream jets,

[5]Ted Turner quote, www.quotegarden.com, accessed November 15, 2009.

Abercrombie & Fitch and Hollister clothes (for teens and preteens) — even drinking water! No consumer product category has been left untouched. Even the most banal, everyday products have been branded — think $2,000 fountain pens.

Today, status is conveyed more often through ownership of status prod- 15
ucts than through personal, occupational, or family reputation. This is particularly true in large, impersonal metropolitan areas, where people can no longer depend on their behavior or reputation to convey their status and position in society.

Reading the Text

1. Define in your own words what Roberts means by "the treadmill of consumption."
2. How have the mass media affected the desire for status symbols, according to Roberts?
3. What explanation does Roberts give for his claim that economic downturns have a minimal effect on the pursuit of material goods?
4. In your own words, explain Roberts's concept of the "shiny-objects ethos" (para. 7).

Reading the Signs

1. In your journal, explore what items count as status symbols in your own circle of friends (these do not need to be the sort of high-end items that Roberts mentions but could be particular brands of jeans, handbags, shoes, or electronic devices). What appeal do these items have for you? Does acquiring them make you happy? If so, how long does that feeling last? If not, why not?
2. **CONNECTING TEXTS** Roberts assumes that the treadmill of consumption is irreversible, that we will inevitably "continue to embrace the shiny-objects ethos" (para. 8). Discuss this assumption in class. If you agree, what evidence can you advance to support Roberts's claim? If you do not, what economic or social evidence can you find to refute his belief? Use the class discussion as a springboard for your own essay on this topic. To develop your ideas, you might consult Laurence Shames's "The More Factor" (p. 193).
3. In what ways does television, especially reality TV programming, encourage the shiny-objects ethos? Select one show, such as *Keeping Up with the Kardashians*, and analyze the way in which it stimulates the desire to buy products that convey prestige and status.

4. In class, discuss ways in which consumers can counter the treadmill of consumption; in particular, brainstorm ways in which your college campus could encourage freeganism among the student body (imagine ways in which students might share clothing, books, even food). Then, in small groups, write proposals for implementing such practices and address them to the appropriate campus organizations and administration.
5. Examine the gift-giving practices within a small group, such as your family, residents of your dorm floor, members of a sports team, or sorority or fraternity colleagues. Use your observations as the basis of an essay in which you explore the reasons for gift-giving: is it primarily for social bonding, does it serve as a sign of status, or does it serve another purpose?

Robert Alexander/Archive Photos/Getty Images

4

BROUGHT TO YOU B(U)Y

The Signs of Advertising

Going for Woke

It isn't often that a professional athlete who hasn't retired but can't find a team that will hire him lands a major advertising deal, but that is exactly what happened in 2018 when Nike signed Colin Kaepernick on for a high-profile ad campaign, including an inaugural TV spot known as the "Dream Crazy" commercial, centered on the former San Francisco Giant quarterback's performance off rather than on the field. Not long after, Gillette — a perennial mainstay of sports advertising — broke with its own tradition to present its "We Believe" commercial, a dramatic (or, for many, melodramatic) critique of "toxic masculinity" in support of the #MeToo movement. Both ads received a great deal of attention in their TV debuts, and both offer fertile ground for exploring the cultural semiotics of advertising, which is why we begin with them in this chapter.

We can start our analysis with what Nike's "Dream Crazy" and Gillette's "We Believe" ads have in common. Both explicitly refer to current cultural conflicts in America, and both explicitly position themselves as "progressive" participants in those conflicts — with predictable results in the more or less universal conservative outcry against them. Both ads also share certain production techniques, including intense musical backgrounds, muted color tones, fast jump-cut transitions from one rapid image sequence to another, and frankly preachy off-camera voice-overs. Both attracted a great deal of mainstream media coverage, and both lit up the social networks. And finally, both ads reflected corporate gambles that the future of their markets lies with the younger, more liberal consumers for whom they were designed. Yet only one of these two ads could be said to have been unequivocally successful, while the other has had, at best, quite mixed results. This raises the basic semiotic question as to why this was so.

Since the crown in this tale of two advertisements went unequivocally to Nike despite their similarities, we have to look at how "Dream Crazy" *differs* from "We Believe" to understand what happened and what it all means. And the differences are striking, lying not in the form the ads took (which, as we have pointed out, were quite similar) but in their content. Most simply stated, the Nike ads featured a sequence of heroes, from highly identifiable athletic superstars to child athletes who have overcome physical disabilities to excel at their chosen sports, all of them woven together by the on- and off-camera voice of Colin Kaepernick — a man who really did "just do it," sacrificing his athletic career on behalf of a different sort of "crazy" dream of social equality, thus conferring upon the campaign his own special brand of authenticity.

"We Believe," in contrast, is largely anonymous. Although it contains some genuine news clips, most of its footage depicts obviously contrived dramatizations of male misbehavior, concluding with a series of rather movie-like interventions by men willing to step up to do better, to be, as the Gillette slogan has put it for years, "the best a man can get," but with a new slant adjusted to the #MeToo era. So what went wrong?

The reasons for the relative failure of the "We Believe" ad are, as for most cultural phenomena, many and **overdetermined**. But we can highlight some of them here. Probably the most important involves the question of authenticity, for in this context, Nike wins hands down, not only with its use of Colin Kaepernick as a spokesman but with its long history of edgy advertising beginning in the first Air Jordan era in the 1980s — when Nike successfully came to dominate the basketball shoe market, especially among African American consumers — and continuing on to its tradition-shattering attention to women in its ad campaigns. In short, the Nike brand enjoys a lot of "street cred" gained by decades of carefully crafted advertising. Gillette, on the other hand, has a very different corporate image. Long associated with traditional, and even conservative, American values, the Gillette brand has hardly been a standard bearer for the left in America's culture wars. So its attempt to widen its appeal to younger consumers in the "We Believe" ad was more likely to look disingenuous to audiences who had already shot down Pepsi's disastrous co-optation of the Black Lives Matter movement in its epically failing Kylie Jenner spot, while at the same time angering its existing consumer base by appearing to pander to their ideological opponents.

Not only that, but the Gillette ad is drenched in negativity, while the Kaepernick campaign, paradoxically enough, is far more in tune with America's propensity for positive thinking and individualistic enterprise (see Barbara Ehrenreich's take on American "bright-sidedness" in Chapter 1 for a thorough exploration of this tendency). For what the Nike ad shows are individual success stories, Horatio Alger–like portraits of Americans overcoming

Discussing the Signs of Advertising

Bring to class an ad from a newspaper, magazine, or commercial website, and in small groups discuss your semiotic reading of it. Be sure to ask, "Why am I being shown this or being told that?" How do the characters in the ad function as signs? What sort of people don't appear as characters? What cultural myths are invoked in this ad? What relationship do you see between those myths and the intended audience of the publication? Which ads do your group members respond to positively, and why? Which ads doesn't your group like?

obstacles to rise to the top of the heap. Deepening the irony of the left's widespread approval of "Dream Crazy" is that the values it celebrates are essentially those of neoliberal capitalism (*beat the world and rise above the crowd*), which are hardly shared by American progressives. The irony is especially striking due to Nike's controversial reputation for countenancing exploitative labor practices in its offshore production facilities.

And thus there appears the most fundamental significance of all to be found in these two ads: advertising is not truth telling. It appeals to emotions, not to reason. Its purpose is to convince consumers to buy something, not to think deeply. And if, in a highly politicized era, that means wading into a cultural controversy to convince your targeted consumers that you are on their side so that they will feel so good about you that they will buy a product for its political connotations rather than for its material quality, functionality, or, price — well, then, just do it.

And Here's the Pitch

The preceding analysis is intended to illustrate how advertisements, too, are **signs** of cultural desire and consciousness. Indeed, advertising is not just show-and-tell. In effect, it's a form of behavior modification, a psychological strategy designed not only to inform you about products but also to persuade you to buy them by making associations between the product and certain pleasurable experiences or emotions that may have nothing to do with the product at all — like sex, or a promise of social superiority, or a simple laugh. Indeed, in no other area of popular culture can we find a purer example of the deliberate movement from objective **denotation** (the pictorial image of a product that appears in an ad) to subjective **connotation** (the feeling that the advertiser associates with the product), thereby transforming *things* into signs.

Exploring the Signs of Advertising

Select one of the products appearing in the "Portfolio of Advertisements" (in this chapter), and design in your journal an alternative ad for that product. Consider what different images or cast of characters you could include. What different **mythologies** — and thus, different values — could you use to pitch this product? Then freewrite on the significance of your alternative ad. If you have any difficulty imagining an alternative image for the product, what does that say about the power of advertising to control our view of the world? What does your choice of imagery and cultural myths say about you?

No one knows for sure just how effective a given ad campaign might be in inducing consumer spending by turning objects into signs, but no one's taking any chances either, as the annual increase in advertising costs for the Super Bowl reveals: at last count, a 30-second spot averaged $5.25 million. And it's the promise of ever-increasing advertising revenues that's turned Google and Facebook into the darlings of Wall Street. As James B. Twitchell has written, America is indeed an "ad culture," a society saturated with advertising.

The Semiotic Foundation

There is, perhaps, no better field for semiotic analysis than advertising, for ads work characteristically by substituting signs for things, and by reading those signs, you can discover the values and desires that advertisers seek to exploit. It has long been recognized that advertisements substitute images of desire for actual products, selling dreams of fun, popularity, or sheer celebrity — and promising a gratifying association with the likes of LeBron James if you get your next burger from McDonald's. Automobile commercials, for their part, are notorious for selling not transportation but fantasies of power, prestige, and sexual potency.

By substituting desirable images for concrete needs, modern advertising seeks to transform desire into necessity. You need food, for example, but it takes an ad campaign to convince you through attractive images that you need a Big Mac. Your job may require you to have a car, but it's an ad that persuades you that a Land Rover is necessary for your happiness. If advertising worked otherwise, it would simply present you with a functional profile of a product and let you decide whether it will do the job.

From the early twentieth century, advertisers have seen their task as the transformation of desire into necessity. In the 1920s and 1930s, for example, ads created elaborate story lines designed to convince readers that they needed this mouthwash to attract a spouse or that caffeine-free breakfast drink to avoid trouble on the job. In such ads, products were made to appear not only desirable but absolutely necessary. Without them, your very survival as a socially competent citizen would be in question. Many ads still work this way, particularly "guilt" ads that prey on your insecurities and fears. Deodorants and mouthwashes are still pitched in such a fashion, playing on our fear of smelling bad in public. Can you think of any other products whose ads play on guilt or shame? Do you find them to be effective?

The Commodification of Desire

Associating an emotionally charged desire with an actual product (as in pitching beer through sexual come-ons) can be called the **commodification** of desire. In other words, desire itself becomes the product that the advertiser is selling. This marketing of desire was recognized as early as the 1950s in Vance Packard's *The Hidden Persuaders*. In that book, Packard points out that by the 1950s America was well along in its historic shift from a producing to a consuming economy. The implications for advertisers were enormous. Since the American economy was increasingly dependent on the constant growth of consumption, as discussed in the introduction to Chapter 3 of this book, manufacturers had to find ways to convince people to consume ever more goods. So, they turned to the advertising mavens on Madison Avenue, who responded by creating ads that persuaded consumers to replace perfectly serviceable products with "new and improved" substitutions within an overall economy of planned design obsolescence.

America's transformation from a producer to a consumer economy also explains why, while advertising is a worldwide phenomenon, it is nowhere as prevalent as it is here. Open a copy of *Vogue*. It is essentially a catalog, where scarcely a page is without an ad. Indeed, marketers themselves call this plethora of advertising "clutter" that they must creatively "cut through" each time they design a new ad campaign. The ubiquity of advertising in our lives points to an economy in which people are constantly pushed to buy, as opposed to economies like China's, which despite recent rises in consumer interest, continues to emphasize increases in production. And desire is what opens the wallet.

While the basic logic of advertising may be similar from era to era, the content of particular ads, and hence their significance, differs as popular culture changes. This is why a thorough analysis of a specific advertisement should include a historical survey of ads by the same company (and even from competing companies) for the same product, examining the *differences* that point to significance. (The internet has made this task much easier, as enormous archives of both print and television ads can be found on sites such as YouTube and vintageadbrowser.com.)

SJAdvertArchive/Alamy

This advertisement for Remington Contour 6 electric shavers appeared in magazines in the 1950s.

Looking at ads from different eras reveals just what was preoccupying Americans at different historical periods. Advertising in the 1920s, for instance, focused especially on its market's desires for improved social status. Ads for elocution and vocabulary lessons appealed to working- and lower-middle-class consumers, who were invited to fantasize that buying the product or service could help them enter the middle class. Meanwhile, middle-class consumers were invited to compare their consumption of the sponsor's product with that of the upper-class models shown happily slurping the advertised coffee or purchasing the advertised vacuum cleaner. Of course, things haven't changed that

Reading Advertising Online

Many viewers watch the Super Bowl as much for the commercials as for the football game; indeed, the ads shown during the Super Bowl have their own pregame public-relations hype and, in many a media outlet, their own postgame analysis and ratings. Visit *Advertising Age*'s report on the most recent Super Bowl (adage.com), and study the ads and the commentary about them. What images and styles predominate, and what do the dominant patterns say about popular taste? What does the public's avid interest in Super Bowl ads say about the power of advertising and its role in American culture?

much since the 1920s. Can you think of any ads that use this strategy today? How often are glamorous celebrities called in to make you identify with their "enjoyment" of a product?

One particularly amusing ad from the 1920s played on America's fear of communism in the wake of the Bolshevik revolution in Russia. "Is your washroom breeding Bolsheviks?" asks a print ad from the Scott Paper Company. The ad's lengthy copy explains how your bathroom might be doing so: if your company restroom is stocked with inferior paper towels, it says, discontent will proliferate among your employees and lead to subversive activities. RCA Victor and Campbell's Soup, we are assured, are no such breeding grounds of subversion, thanks to their contracts with Scott. You, too, can join the good fight against communism by buying Scott towels, the ad suggests.

The New Marketing

With the proliferation of advertising, it is getting harder for advertisers to get our attention, or keep it, so they are constantly experimenting with new ways of compelling us to listen. For years now, advertisers who are out to snag the youth market have staged their TV ads as if they were music videos — complete with rapid jump cuts, rap or rock music, and dizzying montage effects — to grab the attention of their target audience and to cause their viewers to associate the product with the pleasures of music videos. Self-conscious irony is also a popular technique to overcome the ad-savvy sophistication of generations of consumers who have become skeptical of advertising ploys.

Then there is the marketing strategy known as "stealth advertising," whereby companies pay people to do things like sit in Starbucks and play a game on a smartphone; when someone takes an interest, they talk about how cool the game is, and ask others to take their photo with this really cool smartphone — and by the way, they say, isn't this a really cool smartphone? The trick here is to advertise a product without having people actually know they're being marketed to. Much the same technique is used by stealth ads that appear on such sites as BuzzFeed and Yahoo. Interspersed among the actual news stories are corporate-sponsored "headlines" that are really advertisements in disguise. By designing the ad to resemble the content for which you went online in the first place, such a marketing strategy updates for the digital era the television trick of turning commercials into, say, mini-sitcoms to accompany actual sitcoms. Just what the ad doctor ordered for advertising-sick consumers.

Most profoundly, those with products and services to sell are increasingly relying on marketing strategies based on data mining (a polite term for online spying) rather than attention getting. That is, by purchasing information about our online behavior from such titans as Facebook and Google, advertisers attempt to determine just which consumers would be most susceptible to their pitches. If you post on your Facebook page that you are planning a long vacation, for example, your screen will soon be filled with airline ads. If you conduct a Google search for watches, ads for watches suddenly appear on other sites you visit. Many people do not mind this sort of marketing surveillance and in fact regard it as a way of receiving relevant product information more efficiently than the traditional hit-or-miss advertising approach. For such consumers, the convenience offered by online data mining offsets its invasiveness. For others, the corporate invasion of their privacy is more alarming. Whatever your personal take on the matter happens to be, there is no question that personal privacy has been a major casualty of a digital culture that is mostly underwritten by the advertising revenues that flow from data mining.

As the years pass and the national mood shifts, new advertising techniques will surely emerge. So look around and ask yourself, as you're bombarded with advertising, "Why am I being shown *that*, or being told *this*?" Or cast yourself as the director of an ad, asking what you would do to pitch a product; then look at what the advertiser has done. Notice the way an ad's imagery is organized, its precise denotation. Every detail counts. Why are these colors used, or why is that ad in black and white? Why are cute animated animals chosen to pitch toilet paper? What are those people doing in that perfume commercial? Why does the model wear a cowboy hat in an ad for jeans? Look, too, for what the ad doesn't include: Is it missing a clear view of the product itself or an ethnically diverse cast of characters? In short, when interpreting an ad, transform it into a text, going beyond what it *denotes* to what it *connotes* — to what it is trying to insinuate or say.

Populism versus Elitism

American advertising tends to swing in a pendulum motion between the status-conscious ads that dominated the 1920s and the more populist approach of decades like the 1970s, when *The Waltons* was a top TV series and country music and truck-driving cowboys lent their popular appeal to Madison Avenue. This swing between elitist and populist approaches in advertising reflects a basic division within the American dream itself, a mythic promise that at once celebrates democratic equality while encouraging you to rise above the crowd, to be better than anyone else. Sometimes Americans are more attracted to one side than to the other, but there is bound to be a shift back to the other side when the thrill wears off. Thus, the populist appeal of the 1970s (even disco had a distinct working-class flavor: recall John Travolta's character in *Saturday Night Fever*) gave way to the elitist 1980s, and advertising followed. Products such as Gallo varietal wines, once considered barely a step up from jug wine, courted an upscale market, while Michelob Light promised beer fans that they "could have it all." Status advertising was all the rage in that glitzy, go-for-the-gold decade.

The 1990s brought in a different kind of advertising that was neither populist nor elitist but was characterized by a cutting, edgy humor. This humor was especially common in dot.com ads that typically addressed the sort of young, irreverent, and rather cocky souls who were the backbone of what was then called the "New Economy" and is now called "Web 1.0." More broadly, edgy advertising appealed to twenty-something consumers who were coveted by the marketers who made possible such youth-oriented TV networks as Fox and the WB. Raised in the *Saturday Night Live* era, such consumers were accustomed to cutting humor and were particularly receptive to anything that smacked of attitude, and in the race to get their attention, advertisers followed with attitude-laden advertising.

The 2000s have seen an increasing tendency for advertising to focus on demographically targeted markets. Such *niche marketing* is not new, but it has been intensified both by the growth of digital media and by the number of subscription television sources that cater to an enormous variety of viewer categories. Once upon a time, TV advertisers had only three networks to choose from: ABC, CBS, and NBC and their affiliates. In those days, TV commercials were constructed to appeal to a relatively undifferentiated (though primarily white and middle-class) national audience. Today advertisers tailor their ads much more specifically, choosing images and strategies designed to appeal to particular demographics and even to particular individuals, based, as we have seen, on data-mined personal profiling. This development appears to be breaking up America's "common culture" into an atomized one. And what effect this change may be having on our society could prove to be one of the most important semiotic questions of all.

The Readings

Jack Solomon begins the chapter with a semiotic analysis of American advertising, highlighting the ways in which conflicting mythologies of populism and elitism are exploited to push the goods. James B. Twitchell is next with a description of the elaborate psychological profiling schemes by which marketers categorize potential consumers to maximize advertising efficiency, while Joseph Turow explores the brave new world of data mining, explaining how digital technology enables advertisers to target their ads by following you around on the internet. Steve Craig and Jia Tolentino follow with a pair of readings on gender-coded advertising and the commodification of women's "empowerment." Derek Thompson then describes what he calls "The Four-Letter Code to Selling Just About Anything," and Juliet B. Schor surveys the ways in which marketers try to turn kids into cool customers — perhaps somewhat ahead of their actual years. Julia B. Corbett concludes the readings with a look at marketers who seek to cash in on the "lucrative market of 'green consumers,'" and the chapter then presents a "Portfolio of Advertisements" for you to decode for yourself.

JACK SOLOMON

Masters of Desire: The Culture of American Advertising

When the background music in a TV or radio automobile commercial is classical, you can be pretty certain that the ad is pitching a Lexus or a Mercedes. When it's country western, it's probably for Dodge or Chevy. English accents are popular in Jaguar ads, while a good western twang sure helps move pickup trucks. Whenever advertisers use status-oriented or common-folk-oriented cultural cues, they are playing on one of America's most fundamental contradictions, as Jack Solomon explains in this cultural analysis of American advertising. The contradiction is between the simultaneous desire for social superiority (elitism) and social equality (populism) that lies at the heart of the American dream. And one way or another, it offers a good way to pitch a product. Solomon, a professor of English at California State University, Northridge, is the author of *Discourse and Reference in the Nuclear Age* (1988) and *The Signs of Our Time* (1988), from which this selection is taken. He is also coeditor with Sonia Maasik of both *California Dreams and Realities* (2005) and this textbook.

> Amongst democratic nations, men easily attain a certain equality of condition; but they can never attain as much as they desire.
>
> — Alexis de Tocqueville

On May 10, 1831, a young French aristocrat named Alexis de Tocqueville arrived in New York City at the start of what would become one of the most famous visits to America in our history. He had come to observe firsthand the institutions of the freest, most egalitarian society of the age, but what he found was a paradox. For behind America's mythic promise of equal opportunity, Tocqueville discovered a desire for *unequal* social rewards, a ferocious competition for privilege and distinction. As he wrote in his monumental study, *Democracy in America*:

> When all privileges of birth and fortune are abolished, when all professions are accessible to all, and a man's own energies may place him at the top of any one of them, an easy and unbounded career seems open to his ambition. . . . But this is an erroneous notion, which is corrected by daily experience. [For when] men are nearly alike, and all follow the same track, it is very difficult for any one individual to walk quick and cleave a way through the same throng which surrounds and presses him.

Yet walking quick and cleaving a way is precisely what Americans dream of. We Americans dream of rising above the crowd, of attaining a social summit beyond the reach of ordinary citizens. And therein lies the paradox.

The American dream, in other words, has two faces: the one communally egalitarian and the other competitively elitist. This contradiction is no accident; it is fundamental to the structure of American society. Even as America's great myth of equality celebrates the virtues of mom, apple pie, and the girl or boy next door, it also lures us to achieve social distinction, to rise above the crowd and bask alone in the glory. This land is your land and this land is my land, Woody Guthrie's populist anthem tells us, but we keep trying to increase the "my" at the expense of the "your." Rather than fostering contentment, the American dream breeds desire, a longing for a greater share of the pie. It is as if our society were a vast high-school football game, with the bulk of the participants noisily rooting in the stands while, deep down, each of them is wishing he or she could be the star quarterback or head cheerleader.

For the semiotician, the contradictory nature of the American myth of equality is nowhere written so clearly as in the signs that American advertisers use to manipulate us into buying their wares. "Manipulate" is the word here, not "persuade," for advertising campaigns are not sources of product information — they are exercises in behavior modification. Appealing to our subconscious emotions rather than to our conscious intellects, advertisements are designed to exploit the discontentment fostered by the American dream, the constant desire for social success and the material rewards that accompany it. America's consumer economy runs on desire, and advertising stokes the engines by transforming common objects — from peanut butter to political candidates — into signs of all the things that Americans covet most.

But by semiotically reading the signs that advertising agencies manufacture to stimulate consumption, we can plot the precise state of desire in the audiences to which they are addressed. Let's look at a representative sample of ads and what they say about the emotional climate of the country and the fast-changing trends of American life. Because ours is a highly diverse, pluralistic society, various advertisements may say different things depending on their intended audiences, but in every case they say something about America, about the status of our hopes, fears, desires, and beliefs.

We'll begin with two ad campaigns conducted by the same company that 5
bear out Alexis de Tocqueville's observations about the contradictory nature of American society: General Motors' campaigns for its Cadillac and Chevrolet lines. First, consider an early magazine ad for the Cadillac Allanté. Appearing as a full-color, four-page insert in *Time*, the ad seems to say "I'm special — and so is this car" even before we've begun to read it. Rather than being printed on the ordinary, flimsy pages of the magazine, the Allanté spread appears on glossy coated stock. The unwritten message is that an extraordinary car deserves an extraordinary advertisement, and that both car and ad are aimed at an extraordinary consumer, or at least one who wishes to appear extraordinary compared to ordinary citizens.

Ads of this kind work by creating symbolic associations between their product and what the consumers to whom they are addressed most covet. It is significant, then, that this ad insists that the Allanté is virtually an Italian rather than an American car; as its copy runs, "Conceived and Commissioned by America's Luxury Car Leader — Cadillac" but "Designed and Handcrafted by Europe's Renowned Design Leader — Pininfarina, SpA, of Turin, Italy." This is not simply a piece of product information, it's a sign of the prestige that European luxury cars enjoy in today's automotive marketplace. Once the luxury car of choice for America's status drivers, Cadillac has fallen far behind its European competitors in the race for the prestige market. So the Allanté essentially represents Cadillac's decision, after years of resisting the trend toward European cars, to introduce its own European import — whose high cost is clearly printed on the last page of the ad. . . .

American companies manufacture status symbols because American consumers want them. As Alexis de Tocqueville recognized a century and a half ago, the competitive nature of democratic societies breeds a desire for social distinction, a yearning to rise above the crowd. But given the fact that those who do make it to the top in socially mobile societies have often risen from the lower ranks, they still look like everyone else. In the socially immobile societies of aristocratic Europe, generations of fixed social conditions produced subtle class signals. The accent of one's voice, the shape of one's nose, or even the set of one's chin immediately communicated social status. Aside from the nasal bray and uptilted head of the Boston Brahmin, Americans do not have any native sets of personal status signals. If it weren't for his Mercedes-Benz and Manhattan townhouse, the parvenu Wall Street millionaire often couldn't be distinguished from the man who tailors his suits. Hence, the demand for status symbols, for the objects that mark one off as a social success, is particularly strong in democratic nations — stronger even than in aristocratic societies, where the aristocrat so often looks and sounds different from everyone else.

Status symbols, then, are signs that identify their possessors' place in a social hierarchy, markers of rank and prestige. We can all think of any number of status symbols — Rolls-Royces, Beverly Hills mansions, even shar-pei puppies (whose rareness and expense has rocketed them beyond Russian wolfhounds as status pets and has even inspired whole lines of wrinkle-faced stuffed toys) — but how do we know that something *is* a status symbol? The explanation is quite simple: When an object (or puppy!) either costs a lot of money or requires influential connections to possess, anyone who possesses it must also possess the necessary means and influence to acquire it. The object itself really doesn't matter, since it ultimately disappears behind the presumed social potency of its owner. Semiotically, what matters is the signal it sends, its value as a sign of power. One traditional sign of social distinction is owning a country estate and enjoying the peace and privacy that attend it. Advertisements for Mercedes-Benz, Jaguar, and Audi automobiles thus frequently feature drivers motoring quietly along a country road, presumably on their way to or from their country houses.

Advertisers have been quick to exploit the status signals that belong to body language as well. As Hegel observed in the early nineteenth century, it is an ancient aristocratic prerogative to be seen by the lower orders without having to look at them in return. Tilting his chin high in the air and gazing down at the world under hooded eyelids, the aristocrat invites observation while refusing to look back. We can find such a pose exploited in an advertisement for Cadillac Seville in which we see an elegantly dressed woman out for a drive with her husband in their new Cadillac. If we look closely at the woman's body language, we can see her glance inwardly with a satisfied smile on her face but not outward toward the camera that represents our gaze. She is glad to be seen by us in her Seville, but she isn't interested in looking at *us*!

Ads that are aimed at a broader market take the opposite approach. If the 10
American dream encourages the desire to "arrive," to vault above the mass, it also fosters a desire to be popular, to "belong." Populist commercials accordingly transform products into signs of belonging, utilizing such common icons as country music, small-town life, family picnics, and farmyards. All of these icons are incorporated in GM's Heartbeat of America campaign for its Chevrolet line. Unlike the Seville commercial, the faces in the Chevy ads look straight at us and smile. Dress is casual; the mood upbeat. Quick camera cuts take us from rustic to suburban to urban scenes, creating an American montage filmed from sea to shining sea. We all "belong" in a Chevy.

Where price alone doesn't determine the market for a product, advertisers can go either way. Both Johnnie Walker and Jack Daniel's are better-grade whiskies, but where a Johnnie Walker ad appeals to the buyer who wants a mark of aristocratic distinction in his liquor, a Jack Daniel's ad emphasizes the down-home, egalitarian folksiness of its product. Johnnie Walker associates itself with such conventional status symbols as sable coats, Rolls-Royces, and black gold; Jack Daniel's gives us a Good Ol' Boy in overalls. In fact, Jack Daniel's Good Ol' Boy is an icon of backwoods independence, recalling the days of the moonshiner and the Whisky Rebellion of 1794. Evoking emotions quite at odds with those stimulated in Johnnie Walker ads, the advertisers of Jack Daniel's transform their product into a sign of America's populist tradition. The fact that both ads successfully sell whisky is itself a sign of the dual nature of the American dream. . . .

Populist advertising is particularly effective in the face of foreign competition. When Americans feel threatened from the outside, they tend to circle the wagons and temporarily forget their class differences. In the face of the Japanese automotive "invasion," Chrysler runs populist commercials in which Lee Iacocca joins the simple folk who buy his cars as the jingle "Born in America" blares in the background. Seeking to capitalize on the popularity of Bruce Springsteen's *Born in the USA* album, these ads gloss over Springsteen's ironic lyrics in a vast display of flag-waving. Chevrolet's Heartbeat of America campaign attempts to woo American motorists away from Japanese automobiles by appealing to their patriotic sentiments.

The patriotic iconography of these campaigns also reflects the general cultural mood of the early to mid-1980s. After a period of national anguish in the wake of the Vietnam War and the Iran hostage crisis, America went on a patriotic binge. American athletic triumphs in the Lake Placid and Los Angeles Olympics introduced a sporting tone into the national celebration, often making international affairs appear like one great Olympiad in which America was always going for the gold. In response, advertisers began to do their own flag-waving.

The mood of advertising during this period was definitely upbeat. Even deodorant commercials, which traditionally work on our self-doubts and fears of social rejection, jumped on the bandwagon. In the guilty sixties, we had ads like the Ice Blue Secret campaign with its connotations of guilt and shame. In the feel-good Reagan eighties, Sure deodorant commercials featured images of triumphant Americans throwing up their arms in victory to reveal — no wet marks! Deodorant commercials once had the moral echo of Nathaniel Hawthorne's guilt-ridden *The Scarlet Letter*; in the early eighties they had all the moral subtlety of *Rocky IV*, reflecting the emotions of a Vietnam-weary nation eager to embrace the imagery of America Triumphant. . . .

Live the Fantasy

By reading the signs of American advertising, we can conclude that America 15
is a nation of fantasizers, often preferring the sign to the substance and easily enthralled by a veritable Fantasy Island of commercial illusions. Critics of Madison Avenue often complain that advertisers create consumer desire, but semioticians don't think the situation is that simple. Advertisers may shape consumer fantasies, but they need raw material to work with, the subconscious dreams and desires of the marketplace. As long as these desires remain unconscious, advertisers will be able to exploit them. But by bringing the fantasies to the surface, you can free yourself from advertising's often hypnotic grasp.

I can think of no company that has more successfully seized upon the subconscious fantasies of the American marketplace — indeed the world marketplace — than McDonald's. By no means the first nor the only hamburger chain in the United States, McDonald's emerged victorious in the "burger wars" by transforming hamburgers into signs of all that was desirable in American life. Other chains like Wendy's, Burger King, and Jack In The Box continue to advertise and sell widely, but no company approaches McDonald's transformation of itself into a symbol of American culture.

McDonald's success can be traced to the precision of its advertising. Instead of broadcasting a single "one-size-fits-all" campaign at a time, McDonald's pitches its burgers simultaneously at different age groups, different classes, even different races (Budweiser beer, incidentally, has succeeded in the same way). For children, there is the Ronald McDonald campaign, which presents a fantasy world that has little to do with hamburgers in any rational sense but a great deal to do with the emotional desires of kids. Ronald

McDonald and his friends are signs that recall the Muppets, *Sesame Street*, the circus, toys, storybook illustrations, even *Alice in Wonderland*. Such signs do not signify hamburgers. Rather, they are displayed in order to prompt in the child's mind an automatic association of fantasy, fun, and McDonald's.

The same approach is taken in ads aimed at older audiences — teens, adults, and senior citizens. In the teen-oriented ads we may catch a fleeting glimpse of a hamburger or two, but what we are really shown is a teenage fantasy: groups of hip and happy adolescents singing, dancing, and cavorting together. Fearing loneliness more than anything else, adolescents quickly respond to the group appeal of such commercials. "Eat a Big Mac," these ads say, "and you won't be stuck home alone on Saturday night."

To appeal to an older and more sophisticated audience no longer so afraid of not belonging and more concerned with finding a place to go out to at night, McDonald's has designed the elaborate "Mac Tonight" commercials, which have for their backdrop a nightlit urban skyline and at their center a cabaret pianist with a moon-shaped head, a glad manner, and Blues Brothers shades. Such signs prompt an association of McDonald's with nightclubs and urban sophistication, persuading us that McDonald's is a place not only for breakfast or lunch but for dinner too, as if it were a popular off-Broadway nightspot, a place to see and be seen. Even the parody of Kurt Weill's "Mack the Knife" theme song that Mac the Pianist performs is a sign, a subtle signal to the sophisticated hamburger eater able to recognize the origin of the tune in Bertolt Brecht's *Threepenny Opera*.

For yet older customers, McDonald's has designed a commercial around 20
the fact that it employs a large number of retirees and seniors. In one such ad, we see an elderly man leaving his pretty little cottage early in the morning to start work as "the new kid" at McDonald's, and then we watch him during his first day on the job. Of course he is a great success, outdoing everyone else with his energy and efficiency, and he returns home in the evening to a loving wife and a happy home. One would almost think that the ad was a kind of moving "help wanted" sign (indeed, McDonald's *was* hiring elderly employees at the time), but it's really just directed at consumers. Older viewers can see themselves wanted and appreciated in the ad — and perhaps be distracted from the rationally uncomfortable fact that many senior citizens take such jobs because of financial need and thus may be unlikely to own the sort of home that one sees in the commercial. But realism isn't the point here. This is fantasyland, a dream world promising instant gratification no matter what the facts of the matter may be.

Practically the only fantasy that McDonald's doesn't exploit is the fantasy of sex. This is understandable, given McDonald's desire to present itself as a family restaurant. But everywhere else, sexual fantasies, which have always had an important place in American advertising, dominate the advertising scene. You expect sexual come-ons in ads for perfume or cosmetics or jewelry — after all, that's what they're selling — but for room deodorizers? In a magazine ad for Claire Burke home fragrances, for example, we see a well-dressed couple cavorting about their bedroom in what looks like a cheery preparation for sadomasochistic exercises. Jordache and Calvin Klein pitch blue jeans as props for teenage sexuality. The phallic appeal of automobiles, traditionally an implicit feature in automotive advertising, becomes quite explicit in a Dodge commercial that shifts back and forth from shots of a young man in an automobile to teasing glimpses of a woman — his date — as she dresses in her apartment.

The very language of today's advertisements is charged with sexuality. Products in the more innocent fifties were "new and improved," but everything in the eighties is "hot!" — as in "hot woman," or sexual heat. Cars are "hot." Movies are "hot." An ad for Valvoline pulses to the rhythm of a "heat wave, burning in my car." Sneakers get red hot in a magazine ad for Travel Fox athletic shoes in which we see male and female figures, clad only in Travel Fox shoes, apparently in the act of copulation — an ad that earned one of *Adweek*'s annual "badvertising" awards for shoddy advertising.

The sexual explicitness of contemporary advertising is a sign not so much of American sexual fantasies as of the lengths to which advertisers will go to get attention. Sex never fails as an attention-getter, and in a particularly competitive, and expensive, era for American marketing, advertisers like to bet on a sure thing. Ad people refer to the proliferation of TV, radio, newspaper, magazine, and billboard ads as "clutter," and nothing cuts through the clutter like sex.

By showing the flesh, advertisers work on the deepest, most coercive human emotions of all. Much sexual coercion in advertising, however, is a sign of a desperate need to make certain that clients are getting their money's worth. The appearance of advertisements that refer directly to the prefabricated fantasies of Hollywood is a sign of a different sort of desperation: a desperation for ideas. With the rapid turnover of advertising campaigns mandated by the need to cut through the "clutter," advertisers may be hard pressed for new ad concepts, and so they are more and more frequently turning to already-established models. In the early 1980s, for instance, Pepsi-Cola ran a series of ads broadly alluding to Steven Spielberg's *E.T.* In one such ad, we see a young boy, who, like the hero of *E.T.*, witnesses an extraterrestrial visit. The boy is led to a soft-drink machine where he pauses to drink a can of Pepsi as the spaceship he's spotted flies off into the universe. The relationship between the ad and the movie, accordingly, is a parasitical one, with the ad taking its life from the creative body of the film. . . .

25 Madison Avenue has also framed ad campaigns around the cultural prestige of high-tech machinery. This is especially the case with sports cars, whose high-tech appeal is so powerful that some people apparently fantasize about *being* sports cars. At least, this is the conclusion one might draw from a Porsche commercial that asked its audience, "If you *were* a car, what kind of car would you be?" As a candy-red Porsche speeds along a rain-slick forest road, the ad's voice-over describes all the specifications you'd want to have if you *were* a sports car. "If you were a car," the commercial concludes, "you'd be a Porsche."

In his essay "Car Commercials and *Miami Vice*," Todd Gitlin explains the semiotic appeal of such ads as those in the Porsche campaign. Aired at the height of what may be called America's "myth of the entrepreneur," these commercials were aimed at young corporate managers who imaginatively identified with the "lone wolf" image of a Porsche speeding through the woods. Gitlin points out that such images cater to the fantasies of faceless corporate men who dream of entrepreneurial glory, of striking out on their own like John DeLorean and telling the boss to take his job and shove it. But as DeLorean's spectacular failure demonstrates, the life of the entrepreneur can be extremely risky. So rather than having to go it alone and take the risks that accompany entrepreneurial independence, the young executive can substitute fantasy for reality by climbing into his Porsche — or at least that's what Porsche's advertisers wanted him to believe.

But there is more at work in the Porsche ads than the fantasies of corporate America. Ever since Arthur C. Clarke and Stanley Kubrick teamed up to present us with HAL 9000, the demented computer of *2001: A Space Odyssey*, the American imagination has been obsessed with the melding of man and machine. First there was television's *Six Million Dollar Man*, and then movieland's *Star Wars*, *Blade Runner*, and *Robocop*, fantasy visions of a future dominated by machines. Androids haunt our imaginations as machines seize the initiative. *Time* magazine's "Man of the Year" for 1982 was a computer. Robot-built automobiles appeal to drivers who spend their days in front of computer screens — perhaps designing robots. When so much power and prestige is being given to high-tech machines, wouldn't you rather be a Porsche?

In short, the Porsche campaign is a sign of a new mythology that is emerging before our eyes, a myth of the machine, which is replacing the myth of the human. The iconic figure of the little tramp caught up in the cogs of industrial production in Charlie Chaplin's *Modern Times* signified a humanistic revulsion to the age of the machine. Human beings, such icons said, were superior to machines. Human values should come first in the moral order of things. But as Edith Milton suggests in her essay "The Track of the Mutant," we are now coming to believe that machines are superior to human beings, that mechanical nature is superior to human nature. Rather than being threatened by machines, we long to merge with them. *The Six Million Dollar Man* is one iconic figure in the new mythology; Harrison Ford's sexual coupling with an android is another. In such an age it should come as little wonder that computer-synthesized Max Headroom should be a commercial spokesman for Coca-Cola, or that Federal Express should design a series of TV ads featuring mechanical-looking human beings revolving around strange and powerful machines.

Fear and Trembling in the Marketplace

While advertisers play on and reflect back at us our fantasies about everything from fighter pilots to robots, they also play on darker imaginings. If dream and desire can be exploited in the quest for sales, so can nightmare and fear.

The nightmare equivalent of America's populist desire to "belong," for 30 example, is the fear of not belonging, of social rejection, of being different. Advertisements for dandruff shampoos, mouthwashes, deodorants, and laundry detergents ("Ring around the Collar!") accordingly exploit such fears, bullying us into consumption. Although ads of this type were still around in the 1980s, they were particularly common in the fifties and early sixties, reflecting a society still reeling from the witch-hunts of the McCarthy years. When any sort of social eccentricity or difference could result in a public denunciation and the loss of one's job or even liberty, Americans were keen to conform and be like everyone else. No one wanted to be "guilty" of smelling bad or of having a dirty collar.

"Guilt" ads characteristically work by creating narrative situations in which someone is "accused" of some social "transgression," pronounced guilty, and then offered the sponsor's product as a means of returning to "innocence." Such ads, in essence, are parodies of ancient religious rituals of guilt and atonement, whereby sinning humanity is offered salvation through the agency of priest and church. In the world of advertising, a product takes the place of the priest, but the logic is quite similar.

In commercials for Wisk detergent, for example, we witness the drama of a hapless housewife and her husband as they are mocked by the jeering voices of children shouting "Ring around the Collar!" "Oh, those dirty rings!" the housewife groans in despair. It's as if she and her husband were being stoned by an angry crowd. But there's hope, there's help, there's Wisk. Cleansing her soul of sin as well as her husband's, the housewife launders his shirts with Wisk, and behold, his collars are clean. Product salvation is only as far as the supermarket. . . .

If guilt looks backward in time to past transgressions, fear, like desire, faces forward, trembling before the future. In the late 1980s, a new kind of fear commercial appeared, one whose narrative played on the worries of young corporate managers struggling up the ladder of success. Representing the nightmare equivalent of the elitist desire to "arrive," ads of this sort created images of failure, story lines of corporate defeat. In one ad for Apple computers, for example, a group of junior executives sits around a table with the boss as he asks each executive how long it will take his or her department to complete some publishing jobs. "Two or three days," answers one nervous executive. "A week, on overtime," a tight-lipped woman responds. But one young up-and-comer can have everything ready tomorrow, today, or yesterday, because his department uses a Macintosh desktop publishing system. Guess who'll get the next promotion?

For other markets, there are other fears. If McDonald's presents senior citizens with bright fantasies of being useful and appreciated beyond retirement, companies like Secure Horizons dramatize senior citizens' fears of being caught short by a major illness. Running its ads in the wake of budgetary cuts in the Medicare system, Secure Horizons designed a series of commercials featuring a pleasant old man named Harry—who looks and sounds rather like Carroll O'Connor — who tells us the story of the scare he got during his wife's recent illness. Fearing that next time Medicare won't cover the bills, he has purchased supplemental health insurance from Secure Horizons and now securely tends his roof-top garden. . . .

The Future of an Illusion

There are some signs in the advertising world that Americans are getting fed 35
up with fantasy advertisements and want to hear some straight talk. Weary of extravagant product claims and irrelevant associations, consumers trained by years of advertising to distrust what they hear seem to be developing an immunity to commercials. At least, this is the semiotic message I read in the "new realism" advertisements of the eighties, ads that attempt to convince you that what you're seeing is the real thing, that the ad is giving you the straight dope, not advertising hype.

You can recognize the "new realism" by its camera techniques. The lighting is usually subdued to give the ad the effect of being filmed without studio lighting or special filters. The scene looks gray, as if the blinds were drawn. The camera shots are jerky and off-angle, often zooming in for sudden and unflattering close-ups, as if the cameraman were an amateur with a home video recorder. In a "realistic" ad for AT&T, for example, we are treated to a monologue by a plump stockbroker — his plumpness intended as a sign that he's for real and not just another actor — who tells us about the problems he's had with his phone system (not AT&T's) as the camera jerks around, generally filming him from below as if the photographer couldn't quite fit the equipment into the crammed office. "This is no fancy advertisement," the ad tries to convince us, "this is sincere."

An ad for Miller draft beer tries the same approach, re-creating the effect of an amateur videotape of a wedding celebration. Camera shots shift suddenly from group to group. The picture jumps. Bodies are poorly framed. The color is washed out. Like the beer it is pushing, the ad is supposed to strike us as being "as real as it gets."

Such ads reflect a desire for reality in the marketplace, a weariness with Madison Avenue illusions. But there's no illusion like the illusion of reality. Every special technique that advertisers use to create their "reality effects" is, in fact, more unrealistic than the techniques of "illusory" ads. The world, in reality, doesn't jump around when you look at it. It doesn't appear in subdued gray tones. Our eyes don't have zoom lenses, and we don't look at things with our heads cocked to one side. The irony of the "new realism" is that it is more unrealistic, more artificial, than the ordinary run of television advertising.

But don't expect any truly realistic ads in the future, because a realistic advertisement is a contradiction in terms. The logic of advertising is entirely semiotic: It substitutes signs for things, framed visions of consumer desire for the thing itself. The success of modern advertising, its penetration into every corner of American life, reflects a culture that has itself chosen illusion over reality. At a time when political candidates all have professional image-makers attached to their staffs, and the president of the United States can be an actor who once sold shirt collars, all the cultural signs are pointing to more illusions in our lives rather than fewer — a fecund breeding ground for the world of the advertiser.

Reading the Text

1. Describe in your own words the paradox of the American dream, as Solomon sees it.
2. In Solomon's view, why do status symbols work particularly well in manipulating American consumers?
3. Why, in Solomon's view, has McDonald's been so successful in its ad campaigns?
4. What is a "guilt" ad (para. 31), according to Solomon, and how does it affect consumers?
5. What relationship does Solomon find between the "new realism" (para. 35) of some ads and the paradoxes of the American dream?

Reading the Signs

1. The American political scene has changed since the late 1980s, when this essay was first published. Do you believe the contradiction between populism and elitism that Solomon describes still affects American advertising and media? In an analytic essay, argue your case. Be sure to discuss specific media examples.
2. **CONNECTING TEXTS** In television advertising, the most coveted market is the 18 to 49 age group, a cohort that often includes what James B. Twitchell, in "What We Are to Advertisers" (p. 261), describes as "experiencers" and "strivers." To what extent do the TV ads you watch display a populist or elitist ethos? Or do you find that the ads do not harbor class sensitivity? How do you explain your observations?
3. Bring to class a general-interest magazine (such as *People* or *O: The Oprah Magazine*), and in small groups study the advertising. Do the ads tend to have an elitist or a populist appeal? What relationship do you see between the appeal you identify and the magazine's target readership? Present your group's findings to the class.
4. In class, brainstorm a list of status symbols common in advertising today. Then discuss what groups they appeal to and why. Can you detect any patterns based on gender, ethnicity, or age?
5. Visit your college library, and locate an issue of a popular magazine from an earlier decade, such as the 1930s or 1940s. Then write an essay in which you compare and contrast the advertising found in the early issue with that in a current issue of the same publication. What similarities and differences do you find in the myths underlying the advertising, and what is the significance of these similarities and differences?

JAMES B. TWITCHELL

What We Are to Advertisers

Are you a "believer" or a "striver," an "achiever" or a "struggler," an "experiencer" or a "maker"? Or do you have no idea what we're talking about? If you don't, James Twitchell explains it all to you in this selection by laying bare the psychological profiling schemes of American advertising. For like it or not, advertisers have, or think they have, your number, and they will pitch their products according to the personality profile they have concocted for you. And the really spooky thing is that they're often right. A prolific writer on American advertising and culture, Twitchell's books include *Adcult USA: The Triumph of Advertising in American Culture* (1996).

Mass production means mass marketing, and mass marketing means the creation of mass stereotypes. Like objects on shelves, we too cluster in groups. We find meaning together. As we mature, we move from shelf to shelf, from aisle to aisle, zip code to zip code, from lifestyle to lifestyle, between what the historian Daniel Boorstin calls "consumption communities." Finally, as full-grown consumers, we stabilize in our buying, and hence meaning-making, patterns. Advertisers soon lose interest in us not just because we stop buying but because we have stopped changing brands.

The object of advertising is not just to brand parity objects but also to brand consumers as they move through these various communities. To explain his job, Rosser Reeves, the master of hard-sell advertising like the old Anacin ads, used to hold up two quarters and claim his job was to make you believe they were different, and, more importantly, that one was better than the other. Hence, at the macro level the task of advertising is to convince different sets of consumers — target groups — that the quarter they observe is somehow different in meaning and value than the same quarter seen by their across-the-tracks neighbors.

In adspeak, this is called *positioning*. "I could have positioned Dove as a detergent bar for men with dirty hands," David Ogilvy famously said, "but I chose to position it as a toilet bar for women with dry skin." Easy to say, hard to do. But if Anheuser-Busch wants to maximize its sales, the soccer mom driving the shiny Chevy Suburban must feel she drinks a different Budweiser than the roustabout in the rusted-out Chevy pickup.[1]

[1]Cigarette companies were the first to find this out in the 1930s, much to their amazement. Blindfolded smokers couldn't tell what brand they were smoking. Instead of making cigarettes with different tastes, it was easier to make different advertising claims to different audiences. Cigarettes are hardly unique. Ask beer drinkers why they prefer a particular brand and invariably they tell you: "It's the taste," "This goes down well," "This is light and

The study of audiences goes by any number of names: psychographics, ethnographics, macrosegmentation, to name a few, but they are all based on the ineluctable principle that birds of a feather flock together. The object of much consumer research is not to try to twist their feathers so that they will flock to your product, but to position your product in such a place that they will have to fly by it and perhaps stop to roost. After roosting, they will eventually think that this is a part of their flyway and return to it again and again.

Since different products have different meanings to different audiences, 5
segmentation studies are crucial. Although agencies have their own systems for naming these groups and their lifestyles, the current supplier of much raw data about them is a not-for-profit organization, the Stanford Research Institute (SRI).

The "psychographic" system of SRI is called acronomically VALS (now VALS2+), short for Values and Lifestyle System. Essentially this schematic is based on the commonsense view that consumers are motivated "to acquire products, services, and experiences that provide satisfaction and give shape, substance, and character to their identities" in bundles. The more "resources" (namely money, but also health, self-confidence, and energy) each group has, the more likely they will buy "products, services, and experiences" of the group they associate with. But resources are not the only determinant. Customers are also motivated by such ineffables as principles, status, and action. When SRI describes these various audiences, they peel apart like this (I have provided them an appropriate car to show their differences):

- Actualizers: These people at the top of the pyramid are the ideal of everyone but advertisers. They have "it" already, or will soon. They are sophisticated, take-charge people interested in independence and character. They don't need new things; in fact, they already have their things. If not, they already know what "the finer things" are and won't be told. They don't need a new car, but if they do they'll read *Consumer Reports*. They do not need a hood ornament on their car.
- Fulfilled: Here are mature, satisfied, comfortable souls who support the status quo in almost every way. Often they are literally or figuratively retired. They value functionality, durability, and practicality. They drive something called a "town car," which is made by all the big three automakers.
- Believers: As the word expresses, these people support traditional codes of family, church, and community, wearing good Republican cloth coats.

(continued)
refreshing," "This is rich and smooth." They will say this about a beer that has been described as their brand, but is not. Anheuser-Busch, for instance, spent three dollars per barrel in 1980 to market a barrel of beer; now they spend nine dollars. Since the cost to reach a thousand television households has doubled at the same time the audience has segmented (thanks to cable), why not go after a particular market segment by tailoring ads emphasizing, in different degrees, the Clydesdales, Ed McMahon, Beechwood aging, the red and white can, dates certifying freshness, the spotted dog, the Eagle, as well as "the crisp, clean taste." While you cannot be all things to all people, the object of advertising is to be as many things to as many segments as possible. The ultimate object is to convince as many segments as possible that "This Bud's for you" is a sincere statement.

As consumers they are predictable, favoring American products and recognizable brands. They regularly attend church and Walmart, and they are transported there in their mid-range automobile like an Oldsmobile. Whether Oldsmobile likes it or not, they do indeed drive "your father's Oldsmobile."

Moving from principle-oriented consumers who look inside to status-driven consumers who look out to others, we find the Achievers and Strivers.

- Achievers: If consumerism has an ideal, here it is. Bingo! Wedded to their jobs as a source of duty, reward, and prestige, these are the people who not only favor the establishment but are the establishment. They like the concept of prestige. Not only are they successful, they demonstrate their success by buying such objects as prestigious cars to show it. They like hood ornaments. They see no contradiction in driving a Land Rover in Manhattan.
- Strivers: A young Striver is fine; he will possibly mature into an Achiever. But an old Striver can be nasty; he may well be bitter. Since they are unsure of themselves, they are eager to be branded as long as the brand is elevating. Money defines success and they don't have enough of it. Being a yuppie is fine as long as the prospect of upward mobility is possible. Strivers like foreign cars even if it means only leasing a BMW.

[And then there] are those driven less by the outside world but by their desire to participate, to be part of a wider world.

- Experiencers: Here is life on the edge — enthusiastic, impulsive, and even reckless. Their energy finds expression in sports, social events, and "doing something." Politically and personally uncommitted, experiencers are an advertiser's dream come true as they see consumption as fulfillment and are willing to spend a high percent of their disposable income to attain it. When you wonder about who could possibly care how fast a car will accelerate from zero to sixty m.p.h., they care.
- Makers: Here is the practical side of Experiencers; they like to build things and they experience the world by working on it. Conservative, suspicious, respectful, they like to do things in and to their homes, like adding a room, canning vegetables, or changing the oil in their pickup trucks.
- Strugglers: Like Actualizers, these people are outside the pale of materialism not by choice, but by low income. Strugglers are chronically poor. Their repertoire of things is limited not because they already have it all, but because they have so little. Although they clip coupons like Actualizers, theirs are from the newspaper. Their transportation is usually public, if any. They are the invisible millions.

As one might imagine, these are very fluid categories, and we may move through as many as three of them in our lifetimes. For instance, between ages 18 and 24 most people (61 percent) are Experiencers in desire or deed, while less than 1 percent are Fulfilled. Between ages 55 and 64, however, the Actualizers, Fulfilled, and Strugglers claim about 15 percent of the population each, while the Believers have settled out at about a fifth. The Achievers, Strivers, and Makers fill about 10 percent apiece, and the remaining 2 percent are Experiencers. The numbers can be broken down at every stage allowing for marital status, education, household size, dependent children, home ownership, household income, and occupation. More interesting still is the ability to accurately predict the appearance of certain goods in each grouping. SRI sells data on precisely who buys single-lens reflex cameras, who owns a laptop computer, who drinks herbal tea, who phones before five o'clock, who reads the *Reader's Digest*, and who watches *Beavis and Butthead.*

When one realizes the fabulous expense of communicating meaning for a product, the simple-mindedness of a system like VALS2+ becomes less risible. When you are spending millions of dollars for a few points of market share for your otherwise indistinguishable product, the idea that you might be able to attract the owners of socket wrenches by shifting ad content around just a bit makes sense. Once you realize that in taste tests consumers cannot tell one brand of cigarettes from another — including their own — nor distinguish such products as soap, gasoline, cola, beer, or what-have-you, it is clear that the product must be overlooked and the audience isolated and sold.

Reading the Text

1. What do marketers mean by "positioning" (para. 3), and why is it an important strategy to them?
2. What does the acronym VALS stand for, and what is the logic behind this system?
3. Why do marketers believe that the "product must be overlooked and the audience isolated and sold" (para. 8), according to Twitchell?
4. Why does Twitchell claim that the VALS2+ categories are "fluid" (para. 7)?

Reading the Signs

1. Write a journal entry in which you identify where you fit in the VALS2+ system or, alternatively, why none of the categories describes you. In either case, what is your attitude toward being stereotyped by marketers?
2. In class, discuss whether the consumer categories defined by the VALS2+ paradigm are an accurate predictor of consumer behavior. Use the discussion as the basis of an essay in which you argue for or against the proposition that stereotyping consumer lifestyles is an effective way of marketing goods and services.
3. Study the VALS2+ paradigm in terms of the values it presumes. To what extent does it presume traditionally American values such as individualism? Use your analysis to formulate an argument about whether this marketing tool is an essentially American phenomenon.

4. **CONNECTING TEXTS** Using the VALS2+ paradigm, analyze the consumption desires of the children described in Juliet B. Schor's "Selling to Children: The Marketing of Cool" (p. 296). Recognizing that children do not earn their own spending money, do they fit into the paradigm, or do their desires call for a revision of it? Use your findings as the basis of an essay in which you assess the usefulness of the paradigm for child consumers.
5. **CONNECTING TEXTS** Twitchell, Malcolm Gladwell's "The Science of Shopping," (p. 200), and Joseph Turow's "The Daily You: How the New Advertising Industry Is Defining Your Identity and Your Worth" (p. 265) all describe marketing research strategies. Read these selections, and write an argument that supports, opposes, or modifies the proposition that marketers have misappropriated research techniques for manipulative, and therefore ethically questionable, purposes.

JOSEPH TUROW

The Daily You: How the New Advertising Industry Is Defining Your Identity and Your Worth

It's called "data mining": the practice by which such digital media giants as Google and Facebook track every move by internet users and sell that information to marketers who use it to construct advertisements that are tailor-made for their recipients. In this selection from his book *The Daily You* (2013), Joseph Turow describes how this world of digital profiling and personalized marketing works. If his revelation "creeps you out," Turow explains, you are not alone. Joseph Turow is the Robert Lewis Shayon Professor of Communication at the University of Pennsylvania's Annenberg School.

At the start of the twenty-first century, the advertising industry is guiding one of history's most massive stealth efforts in social profiling. At this point you may hardly notice the results of this trend. You may find you're getting better or worse discounts on products than your friends. You may notice that some ads seem to follow you around the internet. Every once in a while a website may ask you if you like a particular ad you just received. Or perhaps your cell phone has told you that you will be rewarded if you eat in a nearby restaurant where, by the way, two of your friends are hanging out this very minute.

You may actually like some of these intrusions. You may feel that they pale before the digital power you now have. After all, your ability to create blogs, collaborate with others to distribute videos online, and say what you want on Facebook (carefully using its privacy settings) seems only to confirm what marketers and even many academics are telling us: that consumers are captains of their own new-media ships.

But look beneath the surface, and a different picture emerges. We're at the start of a revolution in the ways marketers and media intrude in — and shape — our lives. Every day most if not all Americans who use the internet, along with hundreds of millions of other users from all over the planet, are being quietly peeked at, poked, analyzed, and tagged as they move through the online world. Governments undoubtedly conduct a good deal of snooping, more in some parts of the world than in others. But in North America, Europe, and many other places, companies that work for marketers have taken the lead in secretly slicing and dicing the actions and backgrounds of huge populations on a virtually minute-by-minute basis. Their goal is to find out how to activate individuals' buying impulses so they can sell us stuff more efficiently than ever before. But their work has broader social and cultural consequences as well. It is destroying traditional publishing ethics by forcing media outlets to adapt their editorial content to advertisers' public-relations needs and slice-and-dice demands. And it is performing a highly controversial form of social profiling and discrimination by customizing our media content on the basis of marketing reputations we don't even know we have.

Consider a fictional middle-class family of two parents with three children who eat out a lot in fast-food restaurants. After a while the parents receive a continual flow of fast-food restaurant coupons. Data suggest the parents, let's call them Larry and Rhonda, will consistently spend far more than the coupons' value. Additional statistical evaluations of parents' activities and discussions online and off may suggest that Larry and Rhonda and their children tend toward being overweight. The data, in turn, result in a small torrent of messages by marketers and publishers seeking to exploit these weight issues to increase attention or sales. Videos about dealing with overweight children, produced by a new type of company called content farms, begin to show up on parenting websites Rhonda frequents. When Larry goes online, he routinely receives articles about how fitness chains emphasize weight loss around the holidays. Ads for fitness firms and diet pills typically show up on the pages with those articles. One of Larry and Rhonda's sons, who is fifteen years old, is happy to find a text message on his phone that invites him to use a discount at an ice cream chain not too far from his house. One of their daughters, by contrast, is mortified when she receives texts inviting her to a diet program and an ad on her Facebook page inviting her to a clothing store for hip, oversized women. What's more, people keep sending her Twitter messages about weight loss. In the meantime, both Larry and Rhonda are getting ads from check-cashing services and payday-loan companies. And Larry notices sourly on auto sites he visits that the main articles on the home page and the ads throughout feature entry-level and used models. His bitterness only becomes more acute when he describes to his boss the down-market web he has been seeing lately. Quite surprised, she tells him she has been to the same auto sites recently and has just the opposite impression: many of the articles are about the latest German cars, and one homepage ad even offered her a gift for test-driving one at a dealer near her home.

This scenario of individual and household profiling and media customization is quite possible today. Websites, advertisers, and a panoply of other companies are continuously assessing the activities, intentions, and backgrounds of virtually everyone online; even our social relationships and comments are being carefully and continuously analyzed. In broader and broader ways, computer-generated conclusions about who we are affect the media content — the streams of commercial messages, discount offers, information, news, and entertainment — each of us confronts. Over the next few decades the business logic that drives these tailored activities will transform the ways we see ourselves, those around us, and the world at large. Governments too may be able to use marketers' technology and data to influence what we see and hear.

From this vantage point, the rhetoric of consumer power begins to lose credibility. In its place is a rhetoric of esoteric technological and statistical knowledge that supports the practice of social discrimination through profiling. We may note its outcomes only once in a while, and we may shrug when we do because it seems trivial — just a few ads, after all. But unless we try to understand how this profiling or reputation-making process works and what it means for the long term, our children and grandchildren will bear the full brunt of its prejudicial force.

The best way to enter this new world is to focus on its central driving force: the advertising industry's media-buying system. Media buying involves planning and purchasing space or time for advertising on outlets as diverse as billboards, radio, websites, mobile phones, and newspapers. For decades, media buying was a backwater, a service wing of advertising agencies that was known for having the lowest-paying jobs on Madison Avenue and for filling those jobs with female liberal arts majors fresh out of college. But that has all changed. The past twenty years have seen the rise of "media agencies" that are no longer part of ad agencies, though they may both be owned by the same parent company. Along with a wide array of satellite companies that feed them technology and data, media agencies have become magnets for well-remunerated software engineers and financial statisticians of both sexes.

In the United States alone, media-buying agencies wield more than $170 billion of their clients' campaign funds; they use these funds to purchase space and time on media they think will advance their clients' marketing aims. But in the process they are doing much more. With the money as leverage, they are guiding the media system toward nothing less than new ways of thinking about and evaluating audience members and defining what counts as a successful attempt to reach them. Traditionally, marketers have used media such as newspapers, magazines, radio, billboards, and television to reach out to segments of the population through commercial messages. These advertisers typically learned about audience segments from survey companies that polled representative portions of the population via a variety of methods, including panel research. A less prestigious direct-marketing business has involved contacting individuals by mail or phone. Firms have rented lists of public data or purchase information that suggests who might be likely customers.

The emerging new world is dramatically different. The distinction between reaching out to audiences via mass media and by direct-response methods is disappearing. Advertisers in the digital space expect all media firms to deliver to them particular types of individuals — and, increasingly, *particular* individuals — by leveraging a detailed knowledge about them and their behaviors that was unheard of even a few years ago. The new advertising strategy involves drawing as specific a picture as possible of a person based in large part on measurable physical acts such as clicks, swipes, mouse-overs, and even voice commands. The strategy uses new digital tracking tools like cookies and beacons as well as new organizations with names like BlueKai, Rapleaf, Invidi, and eXelate. These companies track people on websites and across websites in an effort to learn what they do, what they care about, and who their friends are. Firms that exchange the information often do ensure that the targets' names and postal addresses remain anonymous — but not before they add specific demographic data and lifestyle information. For example:

- Rapleaf is a firm that claims on its website to help marketers "customize your customers' experience." To do that, it gleans data from individual users of blogs, internet forums, and social networks. It uses ad exchanges to sell the ability to reach those people. Rapleaf says it has "data on 900 + million records, 400 + million consumers, [and] 52 + billion friend connections." Advertisers are particularly aware of the firm's ability to predict the reliability of individuals (for example, the likelihood they will pay their mortgage) based on Rapleaf's research on the trustworthiness of the people in those individuals' social networks.
- A company called Next Jump runs employee discount and reward programs for about one third of U.S. corporate employees. It gets personal information about all of them from the human relations departments of the companies and supplements that information with transactional data from the manufacturers it deals with as well as from credit companies. Armed with this combination of information, Next Jump can predict what people want and what they will pay for. It also generates a "UserRank" score for every employee based on how many purchases a person has made and how much he or she has spent. That score plays an important role in determining which employee gets what product email offers and at what price.
- A firm called The Daily Me already sells an ad and news personalization technology to online periodicals. If a *Boston Globe* reader who reads a lot of soccer sports news visits a *Dallas Morning News* site, the Daily Me's technology tells the *Dallas Morning News* to serve him soccer stories. Moreover, when an ad is served along with the story, its text and photos

are instantly configured so as to include soccer terms and photos as part of the advertising pitch. A basketball fan receiving an ad for the same product will get language and photos that call out to people with hoop interests.

These specific operations may not be in business a few years from 10
now. In the new media-buying environment, companies come and go amid furious competition. The logic propelling them and more established firms forward, though, is consistent: the future belongs to marketers and media firms — *publishers*, in current terminology — that learn how to find and keep the most valuable customers by surrounding them with the most persuasive media materials. Special online advertising exchanges, owned by Google, Yahoo!, Microsoft, Interpublic, and other major players, allow publishers to auction and media agencies to "buy" individuals with particular characteristics, often in real time. That is, it is now possible to buy the right to deliver an ad to a person with specific characteristics at the precise moment that that person loads a web page. In fact, through an activity called cookie matching, . . . an advertiser can actually bid for the right to reach an individual whom the advertiser knows from previous contacts and is now tracking around the web. Moreover, the technology keeps changing. Because consumers delete web cookies and marketers find cookies difficult to use with mobile devices, technology companies have developed methods to "fingerprint" devices permanently and allow for persistent personalization across many media platforms.

The significance of tailored commercial messages and offers goes far beyond whether or not the targeted persons buy the products. Advertisements and discounts are status signals: they alert people as to their social position. If you consistently get ads for low-priced cars, regional vacations, fast-food restaurants, and other products that reflect a lower-class status, your sense of the world's opportunities may be narrower than that of someone who is feted with ads for national or international trips and luxury products. Moreover, if like Larry and Rhonda you happen to know that your colleague is receiving more ads for the luxury products than you are, and more and better discounts to boot, you may worry that you are falling behind in society's estimation of your worth.

In fact, the ads may signal your opportunities actually *are* narrowed if marketers and publishers decide that the data points — profiles — about you across the internet position you in a segment of the population that is relatively less desirable to marketers because of income, age, past-purchase behavior, geographical location, or other reasons. Turning individual profiles into individual evaluations is what happens when a profile becomes a reputation. Today individual marketers still make most of the decisions about which particular persons matter to them, and about how much they matter. But that is beginning to change as certain publishers and data providers — Rapleaf and Next Jump, for example — allow their calculations of value to help advertisers make targeting decisions. In the future, these calculations of our marketing value, both broadly and for particular products, may become routine parts of the information exchanged about people throughout the media system.

The tailoring of news and entertainment is less advanced, but it is clearly underway. Technologies developed for personalized advertising and coupons point to possibilities for targeting individuals with personalized news and entertainment. Not only is this already happening, the logic of doing that is becoming more urgent to advertisers and publishers. Advertisers operate on the assumption that, on the internet as in traditional media, commercial messages that parade as soft (or "human interest") news and entertainment are more persuasive than straightforward ads. Publishers know this too, and in the heat of a terrible economic downturn even the most traditional ones have begun to compromise long-standing professional norms about the separation of advertising and editorial matter. And in fact many of the new online publishers — companies, such as Demand Media, that turn out thousands of text and video pieces a day — never really bought into the old-world ideas about editorial integrity anyway. What this means is that we are entering a world of intensively customized content, a world in which publishers and even marketers will package personalized advertisements with soft news or entertainment that is tailored to fit both the selling needs of the ads and the reputation of the particular individual.

The rise of digital profiling and personalization has spawned a new industrial jargon that reflects potentially grave social divisions and privacy issues. Marketers divide people into *targets* and *waste*. They also use words like *anonymous* and *personal* in unrecognizable ways that distort and drain them of their traditional meanings. If a company can follow your behavior in the digital environment — an environment that potentially includes your mobile phone and television set — its claim that you are "anonymous" is meaningless. That is particularly true when firms intermittently add off-line information such as shopping patterns and the value of your house to their online data and then simply strip the name and address to make it "anonymous." It matters little if your name is John Smith, Yesh Mispar, or 3211466. The persistence of information about you will lead firms to act based on what they know, share, and care about you, whether you know it is happening or not.

15 All these developments may sound more than a little unsettling; *creeped out* is a phrase people often use when they learn about them. National surveys I have conducted over the past decade consistently suggest that although people know companies are using their data and do worry about it, their understanding of exactly how the data are being used is severely lacking. That of course shouldn't be surprising. People today lead busy, even harried, lives. Keeping up with the complex and changing particulars of data mining is simply not something most of us have the time or ability to do. There are many great things about the new media environment. But when companies track people without their knowledge, sell their data without

letting them know what they are doing or securing their permission, and then use those data to decide which of those people are targets or waste, we have a serious social problem. The precise implications of this problem are not yet clear. If it's allowed to persist, and people begin to realize how the advertising industry segregates them from and pits them against others in the ads they get, the discounts they receive, the TV-viewing suggestions and news stories they confront, and even the offers they receive in the supermarket, they may begin to suffer the effects of discrimination. They will likely learn to distrust the companies that have put them in this situation, and they may well be incensed at the government that has not helped to prevent it. A comparison to the financial industry is apt. Here was an industry engaged in a whole spectrum of arcane practices that were not at all transparent to consumers or regulators but that had serious negative impact on our lives. It would be deeply unfortunate if the advertising system followed the same trajectory.

Despite valiant efforts on the part of advocacy groups and some federal and state officials, neither government rulings nor industry self-regulation have set policies that will address these issues before they become major sources of widespread social distress. Part of the reason for the lack of action may be that neither citizens nor politicians recognize how deeply embedded in American life these privacy-breaching and social-profiling activities are. Few individuals outside advertising know about the power of the new media-buying system: its capacity to determine not only what media firms do but how we see ourselves and others. They don't know that that system is working to attach marketing labels to us based on the clicks we make, the conversations we have, and the friendships we enjoy on websites, mobile devices, iPads, supermarket carts, and even television sets. They don't know that the new system is forcing many media firms to sell their souls for ad money while they serve us commercial messages, discounts, and, increasingly, news and entertainment based on our marketing labels. They don't realize that the wide sharing of data suggests that in the future marketers and media firms may find it useful to place us into personalized "reputation silos" that surround us with worldviews and rewards based on labels marketers have created reflecting our value to them. Without this knowledge, it is hard to even begin to have broad-based serious discussions about what society and industry should do about this sobering new world: into the twenty-first century the media-buying system's strategy of social discrimination will increasingly define how we as individuals relate to society — not only how much we pay but what we see and when and how we see it.

Reading the Text

1. In your own words, describe how the methods digital media agencies use to ascertain consumer behavior differ from traditional consumer research strategies used at least twenty years ago.

2. Describe in a paragraph what Turow means by the "advertising industry's media-buying system" (para. 7).
3. According to this selection, how are digitally obtained profiles of individuals and households translated into personalized advertising?
4. Make a list of the advantages and problems of digital marketing strategies.
5. What assumptions does Turow make about his readers' likely responses to his indictment of the digital mining of personal information? How do those assumptions shape your response to his argument?

READING THE SIGNS

1. Write a letter to the hypothetical couple Larry and Rhonda, whom Turow describes as being surprised and bitter about the precise profiling of their household by media marketers. Can you offer any suggestions about how to avoid being so profiled?
2. In class, hold a debate on whether marketers' mining of personal information and creation of specific consumer profiles are advantageous or problematic for the consumer (do not consider whether this strategy benefits marketers or their clients). For the former position, your argument might focus on the advantages of customized "content"; for the latter, you might focus on the creation of social distinctions and/or privacy concerns. After the debate, write an essay in which you advance your own argument about this question.
3. As Turow explains, the majority of consumers do not realize that their internet activities are mined for commercial reasons. Write an essay in which you support, oppose, or complicate the proposition that for-profit data miners such as Google should pay, in money or services, users whom they monitor for information that they then sell.
4. In an essay, analyze semiotically the website of one of the data-tracking companies that Turow mentions, such as TowerData (formerly Rapleaf) or Next Jump, or the website of an online advertising exchange, such as those owned by Google and Yahoo. What signs appear on the website (especially the homepage) that indicate whose interests the company serves?
5. In his conclusion, Turow expresses a desire for "broad-based serious discussions about what society and industry should do about this sobering new world." He continues, "Into the twenty-first century the media-buying system's strategy of social discrimination will increasingly define how we as individuals relate to society — not only how much we pay but what we see and when and how we see it" (para. 16). In an essay, respond to Turow's concerns. To what extent do you see media buying and data mining as contradicting traditional American social values?

STEVE CRAIG

Men's Men and Women's Women

Men and women both drink beer, but you wouldn't guess that from the television ads that pitch beer as a guy beverage and associate beer drinking with such guy things as fishing trips, bars, and babes. Conversely, both men and women can find themselves a few pounds overweight, but you wouldn't know that from the ads, which almost always feature women, as they are intended to appeal to women dieters. In this selection, Steve Craig provides a step-by-step analysis of four TV commercials, showing how advertisers carefully craft their ads to appeal, respectively, to male and female consumers. Craig has written widely on television, radio history, and gender and media.

Gender and the Economics of Television Advertising

The economic structure of the television industry has a direct effect on the placement and content of all television programs and commercials. Large advertisers and their agencies have evolved the pseudo-scientific method of time purchasing based on demographics, with the age and sex of the consumer generally considered to be the most important predictors of purchasing behavior. Computers make it easy to match market research on product buying patterns with audience research on television viewing habits. Experience, research, and intuition thus yield a demographic (and even psychographic) profile of the "target audience." Advertisers can then concentrate their budgets on those programs that the target audience is most likely to view. The most economical advertising buys are those in which the target audience is most concentrated (thus, the less "waste" audience the advertiser must purchase) (Barnouw, 1978; Gitlin, 1983; Jhally, 1987).

Good examples of this demographic targeting can be seen by contrasting the ads seen on daytime television, aimed at women at home, with those on weekend sports telecasts. Ads for disposable diapers are virtually never seen during a football game any more than commercials for beer are seen during soap operas. True, advertisers of some products simply wish to have their commercials seen by the largest number of consumers at the lowest cost without regard to age, sex, or other demographic descriptors, but most consider this approach far too inefficient for the majority of products.

A general rule of thumb in television advertising, then, is that daytime is the best time to reach the woman who works at home. Especially important to advertisers among this group is the young mother with children. Older women, who also make up a significant proportion of the daytime audience, are generally considered less important by many advertisers in the belief that they spend far less money on consumer goods than young mothers.

Prime time (the evening hours) is considered a good time to reach women who work away from home, but since large numbers of men are also in the audience, it can also be a good time to advertise products with wider target audiences. Weekend sports periods (and, in season, "Monday Night Football") are the only time of the week when men outnumber women in the television audience, and therefore, become the optimum time for advertising products and services aimed at men.

Gendered Television, Gendered Commercials

In his book *Television Culture* (1987, Chs. 10, 11), John Fiske discusses 5
"gendered television," explaining that the television industry successfully designs some programs for men and others for women. Clearly, program producers and schedulers must consider the target audience needs of their clients (the advertisers) in creating a television program lineup. The gendering of programming allows the industry to provide the proper audience for advertisers by constructing shows pleasurable for the target audience to watch, and one aspect of this construction is in the gender portrayals of characters.

Fiske provides the following example:

> Women's view of masculinity, as evidenced in soap operas, differs markedly from that produced for the masculine audience. The "good" male in the daytime soaps is caring, nurturing, and verbal. He is prone to making comments like "I don't care about material wealth or professional success, all I care about is us and our relationship." He will talk about feelings and people and rarely express his masculinity in direct action. Of course, he is still decisive, he still has masculine power, but that power is given a "feminine" inflection. . . . The "macho" characteristics of goal centeredness, assertiveness, and the morality of the strongest that identify the hero in masculine television, tend here to be characteristics of the villain. (p. 186)

But if the programming manipulates gender portrayals to please the audience, then surely so must the commercials that are the programs' reason for being. My previous research (Craig, 1990) supports the argument that advertisers also structure the gender images in their commercials to match the expectations and fantasies of their intended audience. Thus, commercials portraying adult women with children were nearly four times more likely to appear during daytime soap operas than during weekend sports (p. 50). Daytime advertisers exploit the image of women as mothers to sell products to mothers. Likewise, during the weekend sports broadcasts, only 18 percent of the primary male characters were shown at home, while during the daytime ads, 40 percent of them were (p. 42). For the woman at home, men are far more likely to be portrayed as being around the house than they are in commercials aimed at men on weekends.

Gendered commercials, like gendered programs, are designed to give pleasure to the target audience, since it is the association of the product with a pleasurable experience that forms the basis for much American television advertising. Yet patriarchy conditions males and females to seek their pleasure differently. Advertisers therefore portray different images to men and women in order to exploit the different deep-seated motivations and anxieties connected to gender identity. I would now like to turn to a close analysis of four television commercials to illustrate some of these differing portrayals. Variations in how men and women are portrayed are especially apparent when comparing weekend and daytime commercials, since ads during these day parts almost completely focus on a target audience of men or women respectively.

Analysis of Four Commercials

In order to illustrate the variation of gender portrayal, I have chosen four commercials. Each was selected to provide an example of how men and women are portrayed to themselves and to the other sex. The image of men and women in commercials aired during weekend sports telecasts I call "Men's Men" and "Men's Women." The portrayals of men and women in commercials aimed at women at home during the daytime hours I call "Women's Men" and "Women's Women." Although there are certainly commercials aired during these day parts that do not fit neatly into these categories, and even a few that might be considered to be counter-stereotypical in their gender portrayals, the commercials and images I have chosen to analyze are fairly typical and were chosen to permit a closer look at the practices revealed in my earlier content analysis. Further, I acknowledge that the readings of these commercials are my own. Others may well read them differently.

Men's Men

I would first like to consider two commercials originally broadcast during 10
weekend sports and clearly aimed at men. (These and the other commercials I will discuss were broadcast on at least one of the three major networks. I recorded them for analysis during January 1990.)

COMMERCIAL 1: ACURA INTEGRA (:30)

MUSIC: Light rock guitar music runs throughout. Tropical elements (e.g., a steel drum) are added later.

A young, white, blond, bespectacled male wearing a plain sweatshirt is shown cleaning out the interior of a car. He finds an old photograph of himself and two male companions (all are young, slender, and white) posing with a trophy-sized sailfish. He smiles. Dissolve to what appears to be a flashback of the fishing trip. The three men are now seen driving down the highway in the car (we now see that it is a new black Acura Integra) in a Florida-like landscape. We see a montage of close-ups of the three men inside the car, then a view out the car window of what looks to be the Miami skyline.

ANNOUNCER (male): "When you think about all the satisfaction you get out of going places . . . why would you want to take anything less . . ."

Dissolve to a silhouette shot of a young woman in a bathing suit walking along the beach at sunset.

ANNOUNCER: ". . . than America's most satisfying car?"

On this last line, the three young men are seen in silhouette knee-deep in the water at the same beach, apparently watching the woman pass. One of the men drops to his knees and throws his arms up in mock supplication. A montage of shots of the three men follows, shots of a deep-sea fishing boat intercut with shots of the first man washing the car. The montage ends with the three posing with the trophy sailfish. The screen flashes and freezes and becomes the still photo seen at the first shot of the commercial. The final shot shows a long shot of the car, freshly washed. The first man, dressed as in the first shot, gives the car a final polish and walks away. The words "Acura" and "Precision Crafted Performance" are superimposed over the final shot.

ANNOUNCER: "The Acura Integra."

This ad, which ran during a weekend sports telecast, has a number of features that makes it typical of many other commercials aimed at men. First, it is for an automobile. My previous research found that 29 percent of the network commercials telecast in the weekend time period were for cars and other automotive products (compared to only 1 percent during the daytime sample) (Craig, 1990, p. 36). In our culture, automobiles are largely the male's province, and men are seen by the automotive industry as the primary decision makers when it comes to purchases. Further, cars are frequently offered as a means of freedom (literally so in this ad), and escapism is an important component in many weekend ads (only 16 percent of weekend ads are set at home compared to 41 percent of daytime ads) (p. 43).

Second, with the exception of a brief silhouette of the woman on the beach, there are no women in this commercial. Camaraderie in all-male or nearly all-male groupings is a staple of weekend commercials, especially those for automobiles and beer. Again, my earlier research indicates that fully one-third of weekend commercials have an all-adult male cast (but only 20 percent of daytime commercials have an all-adult female cast) (p. 36).

The escapism and male camaraderie promised in this commercial are simply an extension of the escapism and camaraderie men enjoy when they watch (and vicariously participate in) weekend sports on television. Messner

(1987) suggests that one reason for the popularity of sports with men is that it offers them a chance to escape from the growing ambiguity of masculinity in daily life.

> Both on a personal/existential level for athletes and on a symbolic/ideological level for spectators and fans, sport has become one of the "last bastions" of male power and superiority over — and separation from — the "feminization" of society. The rise of football as "America's number-one game" is likely the result of the comforting *clarity* it provides between the polarities of traditional male power, strength, and violence and the contemporary fears of social feminization. (p. 54)

The Acura commercial acts to reinforce male fantasies in an environment of clear masculinity and male domination. Men's men are frequently portrayed as men without women. The presence of women in the commercials might serve to threaten men's men with confusing uncertainty about the nature of masculinity in a sexist, but changing, society (Fiske, 1987, pp. 202–209, offers an extended psychoanalytic explanation of the absence of women in masculine television). On the other hand, the absence of women must *not* suggest homosexuality. Men's men are clearly heterosexual. To discourage any suspicions, the Acura ad portrays three (rather than two) men vacationing together.

It is also at least partly for this reason that the single quick shot in which 15
the woman *does* appear in this commercial is important. She is nothing more than an anonymous object of desire (indeed, in silhouette, we cannot even see her face), but her presence both affirms the heterosexuality of the group while at the same time hinting that attaining sexual fulfillment will be made easier by the possession of the car. Men's men have the unchallenged freedom of a fantasized masculinity — to travel, to be free from commitment, to seek adventure.

Men's Women

COMMERCIAL 2: MILLER BEER (:30)

> We see the interior of a cheap roadside cafe. It is lit with an almost blinding sunlight streaming in the windows. A young couple sits in a far booth holding hands. A young, blond waitress is crossing the room. A silent jukebox sits in the foreground. At first we hear only natural sounds. We cut to a close-up from a low angle from outside the cafe of male legs as they enter the cafe. The legs are clad in blue jeans and cowboy boots. As the man enters, we cut to a close-up of the blond waitress looking up to see the man. We see a close-up of the man's body as he passes the silent jukebox. As if by magic, the jukebox begins to play the rhythm and blues number "I Put a Spell on You." We see the couple that was holding hands turn in surprise. The man in the booth's face is unlit and we can

see no features, but the woman is young with long blond hair. She looks surprised and pulls her hand away from the man's. We cut to an extreme close-up of the waitress's face. It is covered with sweat. As she watches the man pass, a smile appears on her face. She comes over to take the man's order. The camera takes the man's point of view.

MAN: "Miller Genuine Draft."
WAITRESS: "I was hopin' you'd say that."

We see a shot of a refrigerator door opening. The refrigerator is filled with sweating, backlit bottles of Miller beer. We then see a close-up of the man holding a bottle and opening it magically with a flick of his thumb (no opener). A montage of shots of the product amid blowing snow follows this. The sounds of a blizzard are heard.

ANNOUNCER: "Cold filtered. Never heat pasteurized. Miller Genuine Draft. For those who discover this real draft taste . . . the world is a *very* cool place."

On this last line we see close-ups of the woman in the booth and the waitress. Wind is blowing snow in their faces and they are luxuriating in the coolness. The waitress suddenly looks at the camera with shocked disappointment. We cut to an empty seat with the man's empty beer bottle rocking on the table. The music, snow, and wind end abruptly. We see the man's back as he exits the cafe. The final shot is of the waitress, elbow propped on the counter, looking after the man. The words "Tap into the Cold" are superimposed.

When women do appear in men's commercials, they seldom challenge the primary masculine fantasy. Men's women are portrayed as physically attractive, slim, and usually young and white, frequently blond, and almost always dressed in revealing clothing. Since most men's commercials are set in locations away from home, most men's women appear outside the home, and only infrequently are they portrayed as wives. There are almost always hints of sexual availability in men's women, but this is seldom played out explicitly. Although the sexual objectification of women characters in these ads is often quite subtle, my previous content analysis suggests that it is far more common in weekend than in daytime ads (Craig, 1990, p. 34). Men's women are also frequently portrayed as admirers (and at times, almost voyeurs), generally approving of some aspect of product use (the car he drives, the beer he drinks, the credit card he uses).

In these respects, the Miller ad is quite typical. What might have been a simple commercial about a man ordering and drinking a beer becomes an elaborate sexual fantasy, in many respects constructed like a porn film. The attractive, eager waitress is mystically drawn to the man who relieves her bored frustrations with an orgasmic chug-a-lug. She is "hot" while he (and the beer) is "*very* cool." But once he's satisfied, he's gone. He's too cool for conversation or commitment. We never see the man's face, but rather are invited, through the use of the point-of-view shot, to become a participant in the mystic fantasy.

There is, of course, considerable tongue-in-cheek intent in this ad. Males know that the idea of anonymous women lusting after them, eager for sex without commitment, is fantasy. But for many men, it is pleasurable fantasy, and common enough in weekend commercials. The main point is that the product has been connected, however briefly, with the pleasure of this fantasy. The physical pleasure of consuming alcohol (and specifically cold Miller beer) is tied to the pleasurable imaginings of a narrative extended beyond that which is explicitly seen.

One industry executive has explained this advertising technique. Noting the need for "an imaginary and motivating value" in ads, Nicolas (1988) argues that:

> Beyond the principle of utility, it becomes more and more important to associate a principle of pleasure to the value. The useful must be linked to the beautiful, the rational to the imaginary, the indispensable to the superfluous. . . . It is imperative that the image be seductive. (p. 7)

Although some research has documented changes in gender portrayals in television advertising over the past few years (e.g., Bretl & Cantor, 1988; Ferrante et al., 1988), such conclusions are based on across-the-schedule studies or of prime time rather than of specifically gendered day parts. While avoiding portraying women as blatant sex objects is doubtless good business in daytime or prime time, it would almost certainly inhibit male fantasies such as this one, commonly seen during weekend sports. The man's woman continues to be portrayed according to the rules of the patriarchy. 20

The next two commercials were originally aired during daytime soap operas. They represent Madison Avenue's portrayal of women and men designed for women.

Women's Women

COMMERCIAL 3: WEIGHT WATCHERS (:30)

> The opening shot is a quick pan from toe to head of a young, thin, white woman with dark hair. She is dressed in a revealing red bathing suit and appears to be reclining on the edge of a pool. Her head is propped up with a pillow. She is wearing sunglasses and smiling.
>
> ANNOUNCER (woman, voice-over): "I hate diets . . . but I lost weight fast with Weight Watchers' new program."
>
> We see the same woman sitting at a dining table in a home kitchen eating a meal. She is wearing a red dress. The camera weaves, and we briefly glimpse a man and two small children also at the table. Another close-up of the woman's body at the pool. This time the camera frames her waist.
>
> ANNOUNCER: "And I *hate* starving myself."

We see the same family group eating pizza at a restaurant. More close-ups of the woman's body at poolside.

ANNOUNCER: "But with their new 'fast and flexible' program I don't have to."

Shot of the woman dancing with the man, followed by a montage of more shots of the family at dinner and close-ups of the woman at poolside.

ANNOUNCER: "A new food plan lets me live the way I want . . . eat with my family and friends, still have fun."

Close-up shot of balance scales. A woman's hand is moving the balance weight downward.

ANNOUNCER: "And in no time . . . *here I am!"*

Shot of the woman on the scales. She raises her hands as if in triumph. The identical shot is repeated three times.

ANNOUNCER: "Now there's only one thing I hate . . . not joining Weight Watchers sooner."

As this last line is spoken, we see a close-up of the woman at the pool. She removes her sunglasses. The man's head comes into the frame from the side and kisses her on the forehead.

This commercial portrays the woman's woman. Her need is a common one in women's commercials produced by a patriarchal society — the desire to attain and maintain her physical attractiveness. Indeed, my previous research indicates that fully 44 percent of the daytime ads sampled were for products relating to the body (compared with only 15 percent of the ads during weekend sports). In this ad, her desire for an attractive body is explicitly tied to her family. She is portrayed with a husband, small children, and a nice home. It is her husband with whom she dances and who expresses approval with a kiss. Her need for an attractive body is her need to maintain her husband's interest and maintain her family's unity and security. As Coward (1985) has written:

> Most women know to their cost that appearance is perhaps the crucial way by which men form opinions of women. For that reason, feelings about self-image get mixed up with feelings about security and comfort. . . . It sometimes appears to women that the whole possibility of being loved and comforted hangs on how their appearance will be received. (p. 78)

But dieting is a difficult form of self-deprivation, and she "hates" doing it. Implicit also is her hatred of her own "overweight" body — a body that no longer measures up to the idealized woman promoted by the patriarchy (and seen in the commercial). As Coward explains:

> . . . advertisements, health and beauty advice, fashion tips are effective precisely because somewhere, perhaps even subconsciously, an anxiety, rather than a pleasurable identification [with the idealized body], is awakened. (p. 80)

Weight Watchers promises to alleviate the pain of dieting at the same time it relieves (or perhaps delays) the anxiety of being "overweight." She can diet and "still have fun."

A related aspect is this ad's use of a female announcer. The copy is written 25
in the first person, but we never see the model speaking in direct address. We get the impression that we are eavesdropping on her thoughts — being invited to identify with her — rather than hearing a sales pitch from a third person. My earlier research confirmed the findings of other content analyses that female voice-overs are relatively uncommon in commercials. My findings, however, indicated that while only 3 percent of the voice-overs during weekend sports were by women announcers, 16 percent of those during daytime were. Further, 60 percent of the women announcers during daytime were heard in commercials for body-related products (Craig, 1990, p. 52).

Women's Men

COMMERCIAL 4: SECRET DEODORANT (:30)

We open on a wide shot of a sailing yacht at anchor. It is sunrise and a woman is on deck. She descends into the cabin. Cut to a close-up of the woman as she enters the cabin.

WOMAN: "Four bells. Rise and shine!"

A man is seen in a bunk inside the cabin. He has just awakened. Both he and the woman are now seen to be young and white. She is thin and has bobbed hair. He is muscular and unshaven (and a Bruce Willis look-alike).

MUSIC: Fusion jazz instrumental (UNDER).
MAN (painfully): "Ohhhh . . . I can't move."
WOMAN: "Ohhhhh. I took a swim — breakfast is on — I had a shower. Now it's *your turn*."

As she says this, she crosses the cabin and places a container of Secret deodorant on a shelf above the man. The man leans up on one elbow then falls back into bed with a groan.

MAN: "Ahhh, I can't."

She pulls him back to a sitting position then sits down herself, cradling him in her arms.

WOMAN: "Come onnn. You only changed *one* sail yesterday."
MAN (playfully): "Yeah, but it was a *big* sail."

Close-up of the couple. He is now positioned in the bed sitting with his back to her. He leans his head back on her shoulder.

WOMAN: "Didn't you know sailing's a sport? You know . . . an active thing."
MAN: "I just don't get it. . . . You're so together already. . . . Um. You smell great."
WOMAN: "Must be my Secret."

She looks at the container of Secret on the shelf. The man reaches over and picks it up. Close-up of the Secret with the words "Sporty Clean Scent" visible on the container.

MAN: "Sporty clean?"
WOMAN: "It's new."
MAN: "Sounds like something I could use."
WOMAN: "Unnnnn . . . I don't think so. I got it for me."

She takes the container from him and stands up and moves away. He stands up behind her and holds her from behind.

WOMAN: "For these close quarters . . . ?"
MAN: "Well, close is good."

He begins to kiss her cheek.

WOMAN: "I thought you said you couldn't move."

She turns to face him.

MAN: "I was saving my strength?"
WOMAN: "Mmmm."

We dissolve to a close-up of the product on the shelf.

ANNOUNCER (woman): "New Sporty Clean Secret. Strong enough for a man, but pH-balanced for an active woman."

This commercial portrays the woman's man. He's good looking, sensitive, romantic, and he appreciates her. What's more, they are alone in an exotic location where he proceeds to seduce her. In short, this commercial is a 30-second romance novel. She may be today's woman, be "so together," and she may be in control, but she still wants him to initiate the love-making. Her man is strong, active, and probably wealthy enough to own or rent a yacht. (Of course, a more liberated reading would have her as the owner of the yacht, or at least sharing expenses.) Yet he is also vulnerable. At first she mothers him, holding him in a Pietà-like embrace and cooing over his sore muscles. Then he catches her scent — her Secret — and the chase is on.

As in the Weight Watchers commercial, it is the woman's body that is portrayed as the source of the man's attraction, and it is only through maintaining that attraction that she can successfully negotiate the relationship. Although at one level the Secret woman is portrayed as a "new woman" — active, "sporty," self-assured, worthy of her own deodorant — she still must rely on special (even "Secret") products to make her body attractive. More to the point, she still must rely on her body to attract a man and fulfill the fantasy of security and family. After all, she is still mothering and cooking breakfast.

Once again, the product is the source of promised fantasy fulfillment — not only sexual fulfillment, but also the security of a caring relationship, one that allows her to be liberated, but not too liberated. Unlike the women of the Acura and Miller's commercials who remained anonymous objects of desire, the men of the Weight Watchers and Secret commercials are intimates who are clearly portrayed as having relationships that will exist long after the commercial is over.

Conclusion

Gender images in television commercials provide an especially intriguing field of study. The ads are carefully crafted bundles of images, frequently designed to associate the product with feelings of pleasure stemming from deep-seated fantasies and anxieties. Advertisers seem quite willing to manipulate these fantasies and exploit our anxieties, especially those concerning our gender identities, to sell products. What's more, they seem to have no compunction about capitalizing on dehumanizing gender stereotypes to seek these ends.

A threat to patriarchy is an economic threat, not only to men who may 30
fear they will have their jobs taken by women, but also in a more fundamental way. Entire industries (automotive, cosmetics, fashion) are predicated on the assumption that men and women will continue behaving according to their stereotypes. Commercials for women therefore act to reinforce patriarchy and to co-opt any reactionary ideology into it. Commercials for men need only reinforce masculinity under patriarchy and, at most, offer men help in coping with a life plagued by women of raised conscience. Betty Friedan's comments of 1963 are still valid. Those "deceptively simple, clever, outrageous ads and commercials" (p. 270) she wrote of are still with us. If anything, they have become more subtle and insidious. The escape from their snare is through a better understanding of gender and the role of mass culture in defining it.

WORKS CITED

Barnouw, E. (1978). *The sponsor*. New York, NY: Oxford.

Bretl, D. J., & Cantor, J. (1988). The portrayal of men and women in U.S. television commercials: A recent content analysis and trends over 15 years. *Sex Roles, 18*(9/10), 595–609.

Coward, R. (1985). *Female desires: How they are sought, bought and packaged*. New York, NY: Grove.

Craig, S. (1990, December). *A content analysis comparing gender images in network television commercials aired in daytime, evening, and weekend telecasts*. (ERIC Document Reproduction Service Number ED329217)

Ferrante, C., Haynes, A., & Kingsley, S. (1988). Image of women in television advertising. *Journal of Broadcasting & Electronic Media, 32*(2), 231–237.

Fiske, J. (1987). *Television culture*. New York, NY: Methuen.

Friedan, B. (1963). *The feminine mystique*. New York, NY: Dell.

Gitlin, T. (1983). *Inside prime time*. New York, NY: Pantheon.

Jhally, S. (1987). *The codes of advertising: Fetishism and the political economy of meaning in the consumer society*. New York, NY: St. Martin's.

Messner, M. (1987). Male identity in the life course of the jock. In M. Kimmel (Ed.), *Changing men* (pp. 53–67). Newbury Park, CA: Sage.

Nicolas, P. (1988). From value to love. *Journal of Advertising Research, 28*, 7–8.

Reading the Text

1. How, according to John Fiske, is television programming gendered?
2. Why is male camaraderie such a common motif in "men's men" advertising, according to Craig?
3. What roles do women tend to play in the two types of commercials aimed at men? What roles do men tend to play in the two types of commercials aimed at women?
4. Why does Craig believe that "a threat to patriarchy is an economic threat" (para. 30)?

Reading the Signs

1. In class, discuss whether you agree with Craig's interpretations of the four commercials that he describes. If you disagree, what alternative analysis do you propose?
2. The four commercials Craig analyzes aired in 1990. View some current commercials broadcast during daytime and sports programs. Use your observations as the basis for an argument about whether the gendered patterns in advertising that Craig outlines exist today. If the patterns persist, what implications do they have for the tenacity of gender codes? If you see differences, how do you account for them?
3. Write an essay in which you support, refute, or modify Craig's belief that gendered advertising of the sort he describes is "dehumanizing" (para. 29).
4. Watch TV programs that are not overtly geared toward one gender, such as prime-time scripted drama or network news. To what extent does the advertising that accompanies these shows fit Craig's four categories of gender portrayal? How do you account for your findings? Alternatively, watch a program that is largely geared toward female viewers, such as *The Handmaid's Tale*, and analyze the advertising for this show.
5. Craig focuses his argument on ads that presume a heterosexual viewership. In an essay, extend his line of thinking about gender and advertising to viewers who are not heterosexual. What might, for instance, a "women's women" ad look like? A "they they" ad?

JIA TOLENTINO

How "Empowerment" Became Something for Women to Buy

The women's movement has changed a lot in America, but one marketing habit that it hasn't been able to change is the inexhaustible capacity of the advertising industry to turn everything — even social revolution — into an ad campaign. So, just as Madison Avenue's Virginia Slims campaign once presented cigarette smoking as an act of feminist defiance, "empowerment" marketing today is only harming women, as Jia Tolentino argues in this essay for the *New York Times Magazine*. Indeed, it ultimately restricts women's choices to accumulating wealth and flaunting their sex appeal. But there has to be more to life than being Kim Kardashian or Sheryl Sandberg, doesn't there? Tolentino is a former deputy editor at *Jezebel*, current staff writer for the *New Yorker*, and author of *Trick Mirror: Reflections on Self-Delusion* (2019).

At my day job as an editor at a women's website, I receive a daily mess of emails promoting random products and activities as "empowering." Recent offerings include the Pure Barre workout, divorce, Miley Cyrus, attention deficit hyperactivity disorder, ancient Egyptian sex rites, leggings, sending nude photos, receiving nude photos, declining to send or receive nude photos, doing stand-up comedy and purchasing full-bottomed lingerie. The mix of things presumed to transmit and increase female power is without limit yet still depressingly limiting.

"Empowerment" wasn't always so trivialized, or so corporate, or even so clamorously attached to women. Four decades ago, the word had much more in common with Latin American liberation theology than it did with "Lean In." In 1968, the Brazilian academic Paulo Freire coined the word "conscientization," empowerment's precursor, as the process by which an oppressed person perceives the structural conditions of his oppression and is subsequently able to take action against his oppressors.

Eight years later, the educator Barbara Bryant Solomon, writing about American black communities, gave this notion a new name, "empowerment." It was meant as an ethos for social workers in marginalized communities, to discourage paternalism and encourage their clients to solve problems in their own ways. Then in 1981, Julian Rappaport, a psychologist, broadened the concept into a political theory of power that viewed personal competency as fundamentally limitless; it placed faith in the individual and laid at her feet a corresponding amount of responsibility too.

Sneakily, empowerment had turned into a theory that applied to the needy while describing a process more realistically applicable to the rich. The word was built on a misaligned foundation; no amount of awareness can change the fact that it's the already-powerful who tend to experience empowerment at any meaningful rate. Today "empowerment" invokes power while signifying the lack of it. It functions like an explorer staking a claim on new territory with a white flag.

5 Enter the highly marketable "women's empowerment," neither practice nor praxis, nor really theory, but a glossy, dizzying product instead. Women's empowerment borrows the virtuous window-dressing of the social worker's doctrine and kicks its substance to the side. It's about pleasure, not power; it's individualistic and subjective, tailored to insecurity and desire. The new empowerment doesn't increase potential so much as it assures you that your potential is just fine. Even when the thing being described as "empowering" is personal and mildly defiant (not shaving, not breast-feeding, not listening to men, et cetera), what's being marketed is a certain identity. And no matter what, the intent of this new empowerment is always to sell.

Aerie, the lingerie brand of American Eagle, increased its sales by 26 percent in the last quarter of 2015 primarily on the strength of its "#AerieReal" campaign, which eschews Photoshop and employs models of a slightly larger size — and is described as "empowering" as if by legal mandate. Dove, the Patient Zero of empowerment marketing, has lifted its sales to the tune of $1.5 billion with its "#RealBeauty" campaign, cooked up by executives who noticed that few women like to call themselves beautiful and saw in that tragic modesty a great opportunity to raise the profile of the Dove brand.

When consumer purchases aren't made out to be a path to female empowerment, a branded corporate experience often is. There's TEDWomen ("about the power of women"), the Forbes Women's Summit ("#RedefinePower") and Fortune's Most Powerful Women Conference (tickets are $10,000).

This consumption-and-conference empowerment dilutes the word to pitch-speak, and the concept to something that imitates rather than alters the structures of the world. This version of empowerment can be actively disempowering: It's a series of objects and experiences you can purchase while the conditions determining who can access and accumulate power stay the same. The ready participation of well-off women in this strategy also points to a deep truth about the word "empowerment": that it has never been defined by the people who actually need it. People who talk empowerment are, by definition, already there.

So women's empowerment initiatives begin to look increasingly suspicious. In 2013, Kate Losse, a former speechwriter for Mark Zuckerberg, criticized Sheryl Sandberg's Lean In initiative for locating disempowerment in women's "presumed resistance to their careers rather than companies' resistance to equal pay." A company's sudden emphasis on empowerment is often a sign of something to atone for. Searching online for the word, I kept being served two advertisements by Google. The first was for Brawny paper towels, tagged #StrengthHasNoGender; the other was for Goldman Sachs ("See how Goldman is committed to helping women succeed"). Brawny is a holding of the Koch Brothers, who have spent millions of dollars funding antiabortion initiatives; Goldman Sachs is, well, Goldman Sachs.

I am right in this word's target demographic, being young, female, edu- 10
cated, and upwardly mobile. I work at a women's website. I love raises and underwear and voting. And still, I have never said "empowerment" sincerely or heard it from a single one of my friends. The formulation has been diluted to something representational and bloodless — an architectural rendering of a building that will never be built.

But despite its nonexistence in honest conversation, "empowerment" goes on thriving. It's uniquely marketable, like the female body, which is where women's empowerment is forced to live. On March 8, International Women's Day, Kim Kardashian posted an essay on the topic to her subscription-only website, in response to the backlash over a naked selfie she had posted — criticism leveled mainly by women who drink their empowerment a different way.

"I am empowered by my body," she wrote. "I am empowered by my sexuality." Quickly, her focus turned global: "I hope that through this platform I have been given, I can encourage the same empowerment for girls and women all over the world."

On that day, corporate empowerment came to a teleological summit in the hands of Kardashian, who's not as different from Sheryl Sandberg as she may seem. Like Sandberg, Kardashian is the apotheosis of a particular brand of largely contentless feminism, a celebratory form divorced from material politics, which makes it palatable — maybe irresistible — to the business world.

The mistake would be to locate further empowerment in choosing between the two. Corporate empowerment — as well as the lightweight, self-exculpatory feminism it rides on — feeds ravenously on the distracting performance of identity, that buffet of false opposition. Sandberg and Kardashian are perceived by most to be opposites, two aesthetically distinct brands fighting for our allegiance, when each has pioneered a similar, punishingly individualistic, market-driven understanding of women's worth, responsibility, and strength. In the world of women's empowerment, they say the same thing differently: that our radical capability is mainly our ability to put money in the bank.

Reading the Text

1. Summarize in your own words the evolution of the word *empowerment* as Tolentino describes it.
2. Why does Tolentino claim that, as a sales pitch, "empowerment can be actively disempowering" (para. 8)?

3. What does Tolentino mean when she asserts that "[Kim] Kardashian is the apotheosis of a particular brand of largely contentless feminism, a celebratory form divorced from material politics, which makes it palatable — maybe irresistible — to the business world" (para. 13)?
4. Why do you think Tolentino uses the rhetorical strategy of referring to her own identity as "being young, female, educated, and upwardly mobile. I work at a women's website. I love raises and underwear and voting" (para. 10)? What effect does her self-reference have on a reader's response to her argument?

Reading the Signs

1. Study instances of the American Eagle or Dove ad campaigns that Tolentino describes. Write an essay arguing whether the ads you examine are indeed empowering women or are simply a new twist on advertising's tendency to objectify women's bodies.
2. Tolentino does not mention "Real Beauty Sketches," Dove's experiment in which forensic artist Gil Zamora first draws a sight-unseen woman based on her own self-description and then draws the same woman based on a stranger's description of her. The goal is to show women that they are "more beautiful" than they assume. Watch some of these sketches on YouTube, and then write an essay in which you critique the videos. How do you think Tolentino would respond to them? Do you believe that they are problematic, as she considers the original "Real Beauty" ad campaign to be?
3. Conduct your own online search for "empowerment" advertising, and evaluate the ads you find in light of Tolentino's critique. To what extent do they illustrate her claim that "a company's sudden emphasis on empowerment is often a sign of something to atone for" (para. 9)?
4. **CONNECTING TEXTS** Write an essay in which you support, oppose, or modify Tolentino's assertion that Sheryl Sandberg and Kim Kardashian "say the same thing differently: that our radical capability is mainly our ability to put money in the bank" (para. 14). To develop your ideas, consult Thomas Frank, "Commodify Your Dissent" (p. 228).
5. In an essay, support, refute, or complicate the proposition that empowerment ads represent a healthy change in advertising directed at women consumers. Consider, for instance, ads for products such as Always' #Likeagirl, Nike's #betterforit and Dream Crazy campaigns, and Toyota's and Bumble's 2019 Super Bowl ads.

DEREK THOMPSON

The Four-Letter Code to Selling Just About Anything: What Makes Things Cool?

People like novelty, as long as it's familiar. Or should we say that people prefer familiarity, with a dash of novelty? Either way, as Derek Thompson's historical and scientific survey of design aesthetics reveals, if you want "to sell something surprising, make it familiar," and if you want "to sell something familiar, make it surprising." The crucial thing is to find the right balance, whether you're selling music, or television shows, or even applying for a scientific grant. Derek Thompson is the author of *Hit Makers: How to Succeed in an Age of Distraction* (2018), and is a staff writer for *The Atlantic*.

Several decades before he became the father of industrial design, Raymond Loewy boarded the SS *France* in 1919 to sail across the Atlantic from his devastated continent to the United States. The influenza pandemic had taken his mother and father, and his service in the French army was over. At the age of 25, Loewy was looking to start fresh in New York, perhaps, he thought, as an electrical engineer. When he reached Manhattan, his older brother Maximilian picked him up in a taxi. They drove straight to 120 Broadway, one of New York City's largest neoclassical skyscrapers, with two connected towers that ascended from a shared base like a giant tuning fork. Loewy rode the elevator to the observatory platform, 40 stories up, and looked out across the island.

"New York was throbbing at our feet in the crisp autumn light," Loewy recalled in his 1951 memoir. "I was fascinated by the murmur of the great city." But upon closer examination, he was crestfallen. In France, he had imagined an elegant, stylish place, filled with slender and simple shapes. The city that now unfurled beneath him, however, was a grungy product of the machine age — "bulky, noisy, and complicated. It was a disappointment."

The world below would soon match his dreamy vision. Loewy would do more than almost any person in the 20th century to shape the aesthetic of American culture. His firm designed mid-century icons like the Exxon logo, the Lucky Strike pack, and the Greyhound bus. He designed International Harvester tractors that farmed the Great Plains, merchandise racks at Lucky Stores supermarkets that displayed produce, Frigidaire ovens that cooked meals, and Singer vacuum cleaners that ingested the crumbs of dinner. Loewy's Starliner Coupé from the early 1950s—nicknamed the "Loewy Coupé" — is still one of the most influential automotive designs of the 20th century. The famous blue nose of Air Force One? That was Loewy's touch, too. After complaining to his friend, a White House aide, that the commander in chief's airplane looked "gaudy," he spent several hours on the floor of the Oval Office cutting up blue-colored paper shapes with President Kennedy before settling on the design that still adorns America's best-known plane. "Loewy," wrote *Cosmopolitan* magazine in 1950, "has probably affected the daily life of more Americans than any man of his time."

But when he arrived in Manhattan, U.S. companies did not yet worship at the altars of style and elegance. That era's capitalists were monotheistic: Efficiency was their only god. American factories — with their electricity, assembly lines, and scientifically calibrated workflow — produced an unprecedented supply of cheap goods by the 1920s, and it became clear that factories could make more than consumers naturally wanted. It took executives like Alfred Sloan, the CEO of General Motors, to see that by, say, changing a car's style and color every year, consumers might be trained to crave new versions of the same product. To sell more stuff, American industrialists needed to work hand in hand with artists to make new products beautiful — even "cool."

Loewy had an uncanny sense of how to make things fashionable. He 5
believed that consumers are torn between two opposing forces: neophilia, a curiosity about new things; and neophobia, a fear of anything too new. As a result, they gravitate to products that are bold, but instantly comprehensible. Loewy called his grand theory "Most Advanced Yet Acceptable" — MAYA. He said to sell something surprising, make it familiar; and to sell something familiar, make it surprising.

Why do people like what they like? It is one of the oldest questions of philosophy and aesthetics. Ancient thinkers inclined to mysticism proposed that a "golden ratio" — about 1.62 to 1, as in, for instance, the dimensions of a rectangle — could explain the visual perfection of objects like sunflowers and Greek temples. Other thinkers were deeply skeptical: David Hume, the 18th-century philosopher, considered the search for formulas to be absurd, because the perception of beauty was purely subjective, residing in individuals, not in the fabric of the universe. "To seek the real beauty, or real deformity," he said, "is as fruitless an enquiry, as to pretend to ascertain the real sweet or real bitter."

Over time, science took up the mystery. In the 1960s, the psychologist Robert Zajonc conducted a series of experiments where he showed subjects nonsense words, random shapes, and Chinese-like characters and asked them which they preferred. In study after study, people reliably gravitated toward the words and shapes they'd seen the most. Their preference was for familiarity.

This discovery was known as the "mere-exposure effect," and it is one of the sturdiest findings in modern psychology. Across hundreds of studies and meta-studies, subjects around the world prefer familiar shapes, landscapes, consumer goods, songs, and human voices. People are even partial to the familiar version of the thing they should know best in the world: their own face. Because you and I are used to seeing our countenance in a mirror, studies show, we often prefer this reflection over the face we see in photographs.

The preference for familiarity is so universal that some think it must be written into our genetic code. The evolutionary explanation for the mere-exposure effect would be simple: If you recognized an animal or plant, that meant it hadn't killed you, at least not yet.

But the preference for familiarity has clear limits. People get tired of even their favorite songs and movies. They develop deep skepticism about overfamiliar buzzwords. In mere-exposure studies, the preference for familiar stimuli is attenuated or negated entirely when the participants realize they're being repeatedly exposed to the same thing. For that reason, the power of familiarity seems to be strongest when a person isn't expecting it.

The reverse is also true: A surprise seems to work best when it contains 10
some element of familiarity. Consider the experience of Matt Ogle, who, for more than a decade, was obsessed with designing the perfect music-recommendation engine. His philosophy of music was that most people enjoy new songs, but they don't enjoy the effort it takes to find them. When he joined Spotify, the music-streaming company, he helped build a product called Discover Weekly, a personalized list of 30 songs delivered every Monday to tens of millions of users.

The original version of Discover Weekly was supposed to include only songs that users had never listened to before. But in its first internal test at Spotify, a bug in the algorithm let through songs that users had already heard. "Everyone reported it as a bug, and we fixed it so that every single song was totally new," Ogle told me.

But after Ogle's team fixed the bug, engagement with the playlist actually fell. "It turns out having a bit of familiarity bred trust, especially for first-time users," he said. "If we make a new playlist for you and there's not a single thing for you to hook onto or recognize — to go, 'Oh yeah, that's a good call!' — it's completely intimidating and people don't engage." It turned out that the original bug was an essential feature: Discover Weekly was a more appealing product when it had even one familiar band or song.

Several years ago, Paul Hekkert, a professor of industrial design and psychology at Delft University of Technology, in the Netherlands, received a grant to develop a theory of aesthetics and taste. On the one hand, Hekkert told me, humans seek familiarity, because it makes them feel safe. On the other hand, people are charged by the thrill of a challenge, powered by a pioneer lust. This battle between familiarity and discovery affects us "on every level," Hekkert says — not just our preferences for pictures and songs, but also our preferences for ideas and even people. "When we started [our research], we didn't even know about Raymond Loewy's theory," Hekkert told me. "It was only later that somebody told us that our conclusions had already been reached by a famous industrial designer, and it was called MAYA."

Raymond Loewy's aesthetic was proudly populist. "One should design for the advantage of the largest mass of people," he said. He understood that this meant designing with a sense of familiarity in mind.

In 1932, Loewy met for the first time with the president of the Pennsylvania Railroad. Locomotive design at the time hadn't advanced much beyond Thomas the Tank Engine — pronounced chimneys, round faces, and exposed wheels. Loewy imagined something far sleeker — a single smooth shell, the shape of a bullet. His first designs met with considerable skepticism, but Loewy was undaunted. "I knew it would never be considered," he later wrote of his bold proposal, "but repeated exposure of railroad people to this kind of advanced, unexpected stuff had a beneficial effect. It gradually conditioned them to accept more progressive designs." 15

To acquaint himself with the deficiencies of Pennsylvania Railroad trains, Loewy traveled hundreds of miles on the speeding locomotives. He tested air turbulence with engineers and interviewed crew members about the shortage of toilets. A great industrial designer, it turns out, needs to be an anthropologist first and an artist second: Loewy studied how people lived and how machines worked, and then he offered new, beautiful designs that piggybacked on engineers' tastes and consumers' habits.

Soon after his first meeting with the president of the Pennsylvania Railroad, Loewy helped the company design the GG-1, an electric locomotive covered in a single welded-steel plate. Loewy's suggestion to cover the chassis in a seamless metallic coat was revolutionary in the 1930s. But he eventually persuaded executives to accept his lean and aerodynamic vision, which soon became the standard design of modern trains. What was once radical had become MAYA, and what was once MAYA has today become the unremarkable standard.

Could Loewy's MAYA theory double as cultural criticism? A common complaint about modern pop culture is that it has devolved into an orgy of familiarity. In her 2013 memoir cum cultural critique, *Sleepless in Hollywood*, the producer Lynda Obst mourned what she saw as cult worship of "pre-awareness" in the film and television industry. As the number of movies and television shows being produced each year has grown, risk-averse producers have relied heavily on films with characters and plots that audiences already know. Indeed, in 15 of the past 16 years, the highest-grossing movie in America has been a sequel of a previously successful movie (for example, *Star Wars: The Force Awakens*) or an adaptation of a previously successful book (*The Grinch*). The hit-making formula in Hollywood today seems to be built on infinitely recurring, self-sustaining loops of familiarity, like the Marvel comic universe, which thrives by interweaving movie franchises and TV spin-offs.

But perhaps the most MAYA-esque entertainment strategy can be found on award-winning cable television. In the past decade, the cable network FX has arguably produced the deepest lineup of prestige dramas and critically acclaimed comedies on television, including *American Horror Story*, *The Americans*, *Sons of Anarchy*, and *Archer*. The ideal FX show is a character-driven journey in which old stories wear new costumes, says Nicole Clemens, the executive vice president for series development at the network. In *Sons of*

Anarchy, the popular drama about an outlaw motorcycle club, "you think it's this super-über-macho motorcycle show, but it's also a soap with handsome guys, and the plot is basically *Hamlet*," she told me. In *The Americans*, a series about Soviet agents posing as a married couple in the United States, "the spy genre has been subverted to tell a classic story about marriage." These are not Marvel's infinity loops of sequels, which forge new installments of old stories. They are more like narrative Trojan horses, in which new characters are vessels containing classic themes — surprise serving as a doorway to the feeling of familiarity, an aesthetic *aha*.

The power of these eureka moments isn't bound to arts and culture. It's a 20
force in the academic world as well. Scientists and philosophers are exquisitely sensitive to the advantage of ideas that already enjoy broad familiarity. Max Planck, the theoretical physicist who helped lay the groundwork for quantum theory, said that "a new scientific truth does not triumph by convincing its opponents and making them see the light, but rather because its opponents eventually die, and a new generation grows up that is familiar with it."

In 2014, a team of researchers from Harvard University and Northeastern University wanted to know exactly what sorts of proposals were most likely to win funding from prestigious institutions such as the National Institutes of Health — safely familiar proposals, or extremely novel ones? They prepared about 150 research proposals and gave each one a novelty score. Then they recruited 142 world-class scientists to evaluate the projects.

The most-novel proposals got the worst ratings. Exceedingly familiar proposals fared a bit better, but they still received low scores. "Everyone dislikes novelty," Karim Lakhani, a coauthor, explained to me, and "experts tend to be overcritical of proposals in their own domain." The highest evaluation scores went to submissions that were deemed slightly new. There is an "optimal newness" for ideas, Lakhani said — advanced yet acceptable.

This appetite for "optimal newness" applies to other industries, too. In Silicon Valley, where venture capitalists also sift through a surfeit of proposals, many new ideas are promoted as a fresh spin on familiar successes. The home-rental company Airbnb was once called "eBay for homes." The on-demand car-service companies Uber and Lyft were once considered "Airbnb for cars." When Uber took off, new start-ups began branding themselves "Uber for [anything]."

But the preference for "optimal newness" doesn't apply just to academics and venture capitalists. According to Stanley Lieberson, a sociologist at Harvard, it's a powerful force in the evolution of our own identities. Take the popularity of baby names. Most parents prefer first names for their children that are common but not too common, optimally differentiated from other children's names.

This helps explain how names fall in and out of fashion, even though, 25
unlike almost every other cultural product, they are not driven by price or advertising. Samantha was the 26th-most-popular name in the 1980s. This level of popularity was pleasing to so many parents that 224,000 baby girls

were named Samantha in the 1990s, making it the decade's fifth-most-popular name for girls. But at this level of popularity, the name appealed mostly to the minority of adults who actively sought out common names. And so the number of babies named Samantha has collapsed, falling by 80 percent since the 1990s.

Most interesting of all is Lieberson's analysis of the evolution of popular names for black baby girls starting with the prefix *La*. Beginning in 1967, eight distinct *La* names cracked the national top 50, in this sequence: Latonya, Latanya, Latasha, Latoya, Latrice, Lakeisha, Lakisha, and Latisha. The orderliness of this evolution is astonishing. The step between Latonya and Latanya is one different vowel; from Latonya to Latoya is the loss of the *n*; from Lakeisha to Lakisha is the loss of the *e*; and from Lakisha to Latisha is one consonant change. It's a perfect illustration of the principle that people gravitate to new things with familiar roots. This is how culture evolves — in small steps that from afar might seem like giant leaps.

In a popular online video called "4 Chords," which has more than 30 million views, the musical-comedy group the Axis of Awesome cycles through dozens of songs built on the same chord progression: I–V–vi–IV. It provides the backbone of dozens of classics, including oldies (the Beatles' "Let It Be"), karaoke-pop songs (Journey's "Don't Stop Believin' "), country sing-along anthems (John Denver's "Take Me Home, Country Roads"), animated-musical ballads (*The Lion King*'s "Can You Feel the Love Tonight?"), and reggae tunes (Bob Marley's "No Woman, No Cry").

Several music critics have used videos like "4 Chords" to argue that pop music is derivative. But I think Raymond Loewy would disagree with this critique, for two reasons. First, it's simply wrong to say that all I–V–vi–IV songs sound the same. "Don't Stop Believin' " and "No Woman, No Cry" don't sound anything alike. Second, if the purpose of music is to move people, and people are moved by that which is sneakily familiar, then musicians — like architects, product designers, scholars, and any other creative people who think their ideas deserve an audience — should aspire to a blend of originality and derivation. These songwriters aren't retracing one another's steps. They're more like clever cartographers given an enormous map, each plotting new routes to the same location.

One of Loewy's final assignments as an industrial designer was to add an element of familiarity to a truly novel invention: NASA's first space station. Loewy and his firm conducted extensive habitability studies and found subtle ways to make the outer-space living quarters feel more like terrestrial houses — so astronauts "could live more comfortably in more familiar surroundings while in deep space in exotic conditions," he said. But his most profound contribution to the space station was his insistence that NASA install a viewing portal of Earth. Today, tens of millions of people have seen this small detail in films about astronauts. It is hard to imagine a more perfect manifestation of MAYA: a window to a new world can also show you home.

Reading the Text

1. Summarize in your own words the role that industrial designer Raymond Loewy played in changing America's attitudes toward product aesthetics.
2. What does the acronym MAYA (para. 5) stand for, and how does it explain consumers' aesthetic judgments?
3. What relationship exists between the familiar and the novel in consumer preferences, as Thompson describes it?
4. What does Thompson mean by saying that "A great industrial designer, it turns out, needs to be an anthropologist first and an artist second" (para. 16)?
5. What evidence does Thompson advance to illustrate the utility of the MAYA effect in popular culture today? How persuasive do you find that evidence, and why?

Reading the Signs

1. In your journal, write a response to Thompson's question "Why do people like what they like?" (para. 6), considering his claims about familiarity and newness.
2. **CONNECTING TEXTS** Read Jack Solomon's "Masters of Desire" (p. 250). Using Solomon's article as a critical framework, write an essay assessing the validity of Thompson's assertion that "Raymond Loewy's aesthetic was proudly populist" (para. 14).
3. **CONNECTING TEXTS** Thompson argues that consumers prefer "optimal newness" — products that are highly familiar but that offer just enough of a new twist to be refreshing. Given that assumption, how might you explain the current taste for nostalgia and secondhand products in the marketplace? To develop your ideas, consult Jordyn Holman, "Millennials Tried to Kill the American Mall, But Gen Z Might Save It" (p. 207).
4. Thompson explains how the MAYA effect works in the music industry: artists "should aspire to a blend of originality and derivation" (para. 28). Test this claim by listening to the current top hits in your favorite genre of music (whether that be country, hip-hop, or some other style). To what extent do the hits demonstrate such a blend? If you find that they do not, what are the implications for Thompson's argument? You might wish to consult the introduction to Chapter 8, "Tangled Roots: The Cultural Politics of Popular Music" (p. 525).
5. Automobile companies are notorious for redesigning their car models' styles every few years, but they claim that the changes are largely technological and safety improvements. Write an essay in which you illustrate, refute, or complicate this claim, taking into account Thompson's discussion of the MAYA effect. To develop evidence for your argument, research the advertising and marketing campaigns for various long-running car models (like the Ford Explorer or Mustang). To what extent do their changes (known as "refreshes" in the automobile industry) maintain familiarity while proclaiming difference?

JULIET B. SCHOR

Selling to Children: The Marketing of Cool

Being cool isn't just an attitude — it's a consumer lifestyle. As Juliet B. Schor describes the situation in this selection from her book *Born to Buy* (2005), the marketing of edgy, sexy, violent, and subversive images of coolness has moved from teen and young-adult advertising to children's advertising. Closely related to what Thomas Frank calls the "commodification of dissent," cool marketing to kids has created a "feedback loop," whereby advertisers study youth behavior to see what kids respond to, while the kids study advertisements to see what's cool and what's not. A professor of sociology at Boston College, Schor is the author of numerous books on American consumption.

The Marketing of Cool

Cool has been around for decades. Back in the fifties, there were cool cats and hipsters. In the sixties, hippies and the Beatles were cool. But in those days, cool was only one of many acceptable personal styles. Now it's revered as a universal quality — something every product tries to be and every kid needs to have.[1] Marketers have defined cool as the key to social success, as what matters for determining who belongs, who's popular, and who gets accepted by peers. While there is no doubt that the desire for social acceptance is a central theme of growing up, marketers have elevated it to the sine qua non of children's psyches. The promotion of cool is a good example of how the practices of marketing to teens, for whom social acceptance is even more important, have filtered down to the children's sphere. In a recent survey of 4,002 kids in grades 4 through 8, 66 percent reported that cool defines them.[2] Part of why is that cool has become *the* dominant theme of children's marketing.

Part of the genius of cool is its versatility. Cool isn't only about not being a dork. Cool takes on many incarnations. It can incorporate dork and jock, if necessary. It can be driven by neon or primary colors; it's retro or futuristic, techno or natural. Today, Target is cool. Yesterday it was the Gap. Good-bye Barney. Hello Kitty. By the time you read these words, today's cool will not be. But although cool is hard to pin down, in practice it centers on some recurring themes, and these themes are relentlessly pushed by marketers in the

[1]For a now-classic account of cool-hunting, see Gladwell (1997), reprinted in Schor and Holt (2000).

[2]A recent survey in which 66 percent of kids say cool defines them is from the KidID survey of JustKid Inc. Data provided to the author and presented by Wynne Tyree at KidPower 2002.

conception and design of products, packaging, marketing, and advertising. At every step, these principles apply.

One theme is that cool is socially exclusive, that is, expensive. In an earlier era, cheap stuff dominated kids' consumer worlds, mainly because they didn't have much money. They bought penny candy, plastic toys, and cheap thrills. In those days, the functional aspects of products were paramount, such as the fact that the toy is fun to play with or the candy tastes good. Social symbolism and status weren't wholly absent, but they were far less important. Now that kids have access to so much more money, status and its underlying values of inequality and exclusion have settled at the heart of the kid consumer culture. Branding expert Martin Lindstrom reports that for tweens, the brand took over from function as the main attraction of products in the 1990s.[3] From video games, to apparel, to that ubiquitous symbol of status, the athletic shoe, kids' products have upscaled, in the process becoming both more unaffordable and more desirable. Gene Del Vecchio, former Ogilvy and Mather executive and author of *Creating Ever-Cool: A Marketer's Guide to a Kid's Heart*, is more candid than most others about the exclusionary nature of cool: "Part of cool is having something that others do not. That makes a kid feel special. It is also the spark that drives kids to find the next cool item."[4] When Reebok introduced its computerized Traxtar shoe, it was banking on a message of "superiority" ("I have Traxtar and you don't"), according to the people who designed the program.[5] The shoe became the top seller in its category, a notable accomplishment given its significantly higher price. Marketers convey the view that wealth and aspiration to wealth are cool. Material excess, having lots of money, career achievement, and a lifestyle to go with it are all highly valued in the marketing world's definition of what's hot and what's not. Living modestly means living like a loser.

Cool is also associated with being older than one's age.[6] Marketers and advertisers take this common desire of kids and play into it in a variety of ways. They put a few older kids in ads that are targeted to younger kids. They have young kids in ads morph into older kids or into adults. They use adult celebrity endorsers for products or brands that kids buy. They depict fantasy worlds in which a young kid sees himself or herself grown up. Cool is also associated with an antiadult sensibility, as ads portray kids with attitude, outwitting their teachers and tricking their parents. Finally, cool is about the taboo, the dangerous, the forbidden other. Among advertisers, *edgy* has been and remains the adjective of the moment—not "over the edge," because that is too dangerous, but "at the edge," "pushing the edge."

[3]On the shift from function to brand as the main attraction, see Lindstrom (2003), p. 82.

[4]Gene Del Vecchio quote "part of cool" is from Del Vecchio (1997), p. 121.

[5]On Traxtar marketing and its success, see Siegel et al. (2001), pp. 179–190.

[6]On kids wanting to be older than they are, this is what Paul Kurnit had to say in our interview: "Emulation and aspiration work up, but only to a certain point. So if you capture six to eleven year olds, your bull's-eye is probably the eleven-year-old boy. . . . If you're looking for the eleven-year-old boy you're probably in a commercial casting a twelve- or thirteen-year-old boy."

Edgy style has associations with rap and hip-hop, with "street" and African 5
American culture. In the 1990s, ads aimed at white, middle-class Americans began to be filmed in inner-city neighborhoods with young black men as the stars. The ads made subtle connections to violence, drugs, criminality, and sexuality — the distorted and stereotypical images of young black men that have pervaded the mainstream media. As Harvard University's Douglas Holt wrote in 1999 in a paper we coauthored, "Street has proven to be a potent commodity because its aesthetic offers an authentic threatening edginess that is very attractive both to white suburban kids who perpetually recreate radical youth culture in relation to their parents' conservative views about the ghetto, and to urban cultural elites for whom it becomes a form of cosmopolitan radical chic. . . . We now have the commodification of a virulent, dangerous 'other' lifestyle. . . . Gangsta."[7]

The story of how street came to be at the core of consumer marketing began more than thirty years ago. Chroniclers of the marketing of "ghetto" point to the practices of athletic shoe companies, starting with Converse in the late 1960s and, more recently, Nike and its competitors. The shoe manufacturers intentionally associated their product with African American athletes, giving free shoes to coaches in the inner cities, targeting inner-city consumers in their research, attaching their brand to street athletics and sociability.[8] They also developed a practice dubbed "bro-ing" by industry insiders, that is, going to the streets to ask the brothers which designs deserve the moniker of cool. Apparel companies, beginning with Tommy Hilfiger, became active in this world, giving rap stars and other prominent tastemakers free samples of their latest styles.[9] While the connection to inner-city life may sound like a contradiction with the idea that cool is exclusive and upscale, it is partially resolved by the fact that many of the inner-city ambassadors of products are wealthy, conspicuous consumers such as rap stars and athletes driving fancy cars and living luxurious lifestyles.

Eventually soft drink companies, candy manufacturers, culture producers, and many others that sell products to teens and kids would be on the street, trying desperately to get some of that ineluctable cool to rub off on their brand. As advertiser Paul Kurnit explains, "What's going on in white America today is [that] the inner city is very much a Gold Standard. We've got lots of white kids who are walking around, emulating black lifestyle."[10] Of course, mere association with ghetto style is not a guarantee of success. Some campaigns have been flat-footed with their mimicry. Others lack basic credibility, such as preppy tennis shoe K-Swiss, which tried to position itself as a street brand. The brands that have been skilled at this approach are those with images that are more plausibly and authentically connected to it.

[7]Douglas Holt quote on street as a potent commodity is from Holt and Schor (1998).

[8]On sneaker marketing in the inner city, see Vanderbilt (1998), ch. 1.

[9]On Hilfiger, see Smith (1997) and Spiegler (1997).

[10]Paul Kurnit quote from his interview with O'Barr (2001).

Although many aspects of African American culture have had a long historical association with cool such as jazz and sartorial styles, as well as a legacy of contributions to popular culture, what's happening now is unique. Never before have inner-city styles and cultural practices been such a dominant influence on, even a primary definer of, popular culture. The process is also no longer one of mainstreaming, in which a cultural innovation from the margins is incorporated into the larger culture. Rather, in the words of Douglas Holt again, "It is now the local, authentic qualities of Street culture that sell. Instead of black cultural products denuded of their social context, it is now primarily the context itself — the neighborhood, the pain of being poor, the alienation experienced by black kids. These are the commodifiable assets." The other new development is the role of large corporations in the movement of styles and cultural forms from the ghetto to the suburb. The process no longer develops through an organic movement as it once did. Instead, cool hunters manage the process of cultural transmission. Another novel aspect is the evolution of a back-and-forth dynamic between the companies and the grass roots, with cool-hunting and street marketing creating what media critics have called a feedback loop.

The feedback loop is a sharp departure from decades past, when consumers blindly followed where advertisers led. In Holt's words, marketers once possessed a monopoly on "cultural authority," in which they set the tone and agenda, and consumers eagerly looked to them to learn what to wear, eat, drive, and value.[11] That cultural authority has virtually disappeared. Its demise can be traced to the backlash against advertising that originally emerged in the 1950s with the popularity of books such as John Kenneth Galbraith's *The Affluent Society* and Vance Packard's *The Hidden Persuaders*.[12] By the 1960s, some of the most successful marketers were those who took their cues from consumers. Since, then, advertisers have increasingly attempted to figure out what people already value and let those findings direct ads. With youth, the process has gone a step further, because they know the advertisers are relying on them, and consciously play to their influence. That's the feedback idea, which has been identified by observers such as Douglas Kellner, Holt, and Douglas Rushkoff. As Rushkoff explains, in a plea to the industry: "It's turned into a giant feedback loop: you watch kids to find out what trend is 'in,' but the kids are watching you watching them in order to figure out how to act. They are exhibitionists, aware of corporate America's fascination with their every move, and delighting in your obsession with their tastes."[13] Although there's a democratic veneer to the feedback loop, that perspective obscures the fact

[11]On the cultural authority of marketers, see Holt (2002).

[12]On these issues, see Kellner (1998), Holt (2002), and Frank (1997) on the backlash against advertisers and the subsequent marketing of cool.

[13]The feedback loop is explored in the PBS special *Merchants of Cool*, available online at pbs.org/frontline/shows/cool/. Douglas Rushkoff quote from his essay "The Pursuit of Cool: Introduction to Anti-Hyper-Consumerism," available online at http://www.rushkoff.com/essay/sportswearinternational.html.

that giant businesses orchestrate, control, and profit from the process. Furthermore, kids are increasingly pulling outrageous and even dangerous stunts to get themselves noticed by the great big marketing machine.

Originally, the marketing of edgy was a teen and young adult develop- 10
ment. Now it too has trickled down to the children's market, though with some adjustments. Kid advertisers had to become far more discriminating, screening out what had become an anything-goes ethic. By way of illustration, consider the heroin-chic fashion photography of the mid-1990s. At that time cool hunters routinely included drugs, including hard ones, on their lists of what's hot and what's not. As one now-famous accounting from a cool-hunter publication that appeared in the *New Yorker* had it: "In San Francisco it's Nike, heroin, and reggae; in Chicago, Jungle music, Tag watches, and drugs."[14] Similarly, in kids' ads, violent images are more restricted, although this is less the case in movie ads, video games, and on the web. The situation is similar with sexuality, exploitative racial imagery, and certain antisocial themes, all of which are prominent in cultural forms for teens and young adults. While going edgy can almost guarantee cool, it can also jeopardize a brand that depends on maintaining its wholesome image. Advertisers calibrate the degree of edginess and strive to go as far as, but not beyond what, a brand's image can tolerate.

Kids Rule: Nickelodeon and the Antiadult Bias

What else is cool? Based on what's selling in consumer culture, one would have to say that kids are cool and adults are not. Fair enough. Our country has a venerable history of generational conflict and youth rebellion. But marketers have perverted those worthy sentiments to create a sophisticated and powerful "antiadultism" within the commercial world.[15]

This trend also has a history. Advertising agencies have been co-opting youth rebellion for years, beginning with Bill Bernbach's embrace of the counterculture in Volkswagen ads in the 1960s, a development insightfully chronicled in Thomas Frank's *The Conquest of Cool*. More recently, the entity most responsible for the commercial exploitation of youth rebellion has been Viacom. The trend began with MTV and its teen audience, as the enormously popular network capitalized on teen desires to separate from and rebel against their parents.[16] MTV allowed teens to immerse themselves in an increasingly separate culture, with its own fashions, language, and attitudes. Over time, some of that sensibility has trickled down to Nickelodeon's younger target.

[14]On cool-hunters' lists of what's hot and what's not, see Gladwell (1997), from which these items are drawn.

[15]For an early recognition of the rise of antiadultism, see Nader (1996).

[16]On the sale of youth rebellion to teens, see Nader (1996), ch. 4 and conclusion.

Nickelodeon was founded in 1979 as a cable network, but it has since become a transcendent brand identity, selling a wide array of products and a relationship with kids. Nickelodeon would eventually dominate children's media. Nickelodeon's audience outpaces all other kid-oriented networks by a wide margin. At 80 percent, its household penetration tops the children's cable networks.[17] As I write these words, it is enjoying its best ratings year ever, surging far above the competition. The Nickelodeon website is the number one children's online destination. Its magazines boast 1.1 million subscribers and 6.3 million readers.[18] Nickelodeon is shown in 158 countries. Incredibly enough, given its limited demographic target, Nickelodeon has become one of the nation's most profitable networks.[19] In the process, it has remade children's programming and advertising.

Early on, Nickelodeon earned a reputation for offering quality shows. Its graphics were visually arresting, and the content was fresh. In comparison to the tired world of program-length commercials, that is, shows whose primary purpose is to sell products, Nickelodeon's offerings stood out. The network has also benefited from its recognition that children are a diverse group in terms of race and ethnicity, family type, and age. On the revenue side, Nickelodeon has made hay with the insight that children are a major influence market for parental purchases. A senior executive explained their stance: "The whole premise of our company was founded on serving kids, and what we've found is that when you do good things for kids, it happens to be good for business."[20]

The secret of Nickelodeon's success is its core philosophy: *kids rule.* In 15
everything that they do, Nickelodeon tries to take the child's perspective. The network has positioned itself as kids' best friend, on their side in an often-hostile environment. Donna Sabino, director for research and development at Nickelodeon's Magazine Group, explained the thinking to me: "It's hard to be a kid in an adult world. The adult world doesn't respect kids. Everywhere else adults rule; at Nick kids rule."[21] The Nickelodeon worldview is that childhood has gotten tough. "Kids are experiencing increased pressure for achievement and activity. They don't have enough time for homework, they're overscheduled." Nickelodeon gives them what they need: "funny, happy, empowering."

[17]Nickelodeon's ratings are from *Kidscreen* magazine (2002), p. 33. On weekdays in 2002, Nickelodeon commanded a 2.7 audience share, a full point above the Cartoon Network; on Saturday mornings, its 4.2 share was 1.2 points higher than the number two.

[18]The 1.1 million subscribers and 6.3 million readers from June 2003 data provided by Donna Sabino to the author.

[19]On Nickelodeon's profitability, see Carter (2002). MTV Networks, to which Nickelodeon belongs, earned more than $3 billion in revenue in 2002. The statistic of 158 countries is also from this source.

[20]"Whole premise of our company" quote by Lisa Judson, senior vice president of programming and executive creative director, cited in Hood (2000).

[21]Sabino quote beginning "It's hard to be a kid" and thirteen criteria from interview with the author, July 2001.

There are thirteen criteria a program must have to pass muster at the network, including good quality, a kid-centered message, humor, and edgy visual design. In theory, these are good criteria. But in practice, when kid-centric and edgy come together, what often results is attitude — an antiauthoritarian us-versus-them sensibility that pervades the brand.

Nickelodeon is not unique in its positioning. The world of children's marketing is filled with variants of the us-versus-them message. A prominent example is the soft drink Sprite, one of the most successful youth culture brands.[22] One witty Sprite ad depicted an adolescent boy and his parents on a road trip. The parents are in the front seat singing "Polly wolly doodle all the day," the epitome of unnerving uncool. He's in the back, banging his head on the car window in frustration, the ignominy of being stuck with these two losers too much to bear. "Need a CD player?" the ad asks.

A Fruit-to-Go online promotion tells kids that "when it comes to fashion class, your principal is a flunkie." A spot for Sour Brite Crawlers has a group of tween boys in an elevator going into gross detail about how they eat this gummy worm candy, eventually sickening the adults and forcing them to flee. The creators of the spot consider it "a great example . . . where tweens demonstrate their superiority of the situation with control over the adults."[23]

Adults also enforce a repressive and joyless world, in contrast to what kids and products do when they're left in peace. Consider a well-known Starburst classroom commercial. As the nerdy teacher writes on the board, kids open the candy, and the scene erupts into a riotous party. When the teacher faces the class again, all is quiet, controlled, and dull. The dynamic repeats itself, as the commercial makes the point that the kid world, courtesy of the candy, is a blast. The adult world, by contrast, is drab, regimented, BORRRR-inggg.

A study of 200 video game ads produced between 1989 and 1999 revealed a similar approach. Researchers Stephen Kline and Greig de Peuter report themes of boy empowerment through "oedipal rebellion" and rejection of home environments depicted as boring suburban spaces. "Nintendo ads," they write, "often construct the gamer as under siege by the adultified world while promising the young male gamers 'empowerment' and 'control' in an unlimited virtual world."[24] This attitude pervades the company's marketing strategy as well. As one Nintendo marketer explained, "We don't market to parents. . . . We market to our target group, which is teens and tweens. . . . The parental seal of approval, while it is something that we like, it is not something that we actively encourage in our marketing because that might say to the kids that we're boring."[25]

[22]On Sprite's success positioning itself as a youth brand, see *Merchants of Cool*, program 1911, *Frontline*. Available at www.pbs.org/wgbh/pages/frontline/shows/cool/etc/script.html.

[23]The Sour Brite Crawlers example is from Siegel et al. (2001), p. 61.

[24]"Nintendo ads" from Kline and de Peuter (2002), p. 265.

[25]Nintendo marketer quote on targeting kids directly is from Kline and de Peuter (2002), p. 266.

20 A related theme in some kid advertising is to promote behavior that is annoying, antisocial, or mischievous. There's usually a playful quality to these spots, as in the various ads involving stealing candy at the movies. Julie Halpin of the Gepetto Group explains the strategy they used for Kids Foot Locker: "We wanted to be able to show them the empowerment they could have with the shoes. . . . What's really fun about a new pair of sneakers is a lot of the things that kids do that are really mischievous: squeaking on the floor, giving each other flat tires, writing little messages underneath. . . . Sales during the advertising period were about 34 percent higher than they were the previous year."[26]

Industry insiders and outsiders confirm the antiadultism in much of today's youth advertising. As one marketer explained to me: "Advertisers have kicked the parents out. They make fun of the parents. . . . We inserted the product in the secret kid world. . . . [It's] secret, dangerous, kid only."[27] Media critic Mark Crispin Miller makes a similar point: "It's part of the official advertising worldview that your parents are creeps, teachers are nerds and idiots, authority figures are laughable, nobody can really understand kids except the corporate sponsor. That huge authority has, interestingly enough, emerged as the sort of tacit superhero of consumer culture. That's the coolest entity of all."[28]

Similar trends can be found in programming. Journalist Bernice Kanner notes that "television dads — and to a lesser extent moms — once portrayed as loving and wise are now depicted as neglectful, incompetent, abusive or invisible. Parenthood, once presented as the source of supreme satisfaction on TV, is now largely ignored or debased." It's "parents as nincompoops."[29] After 9/11, Holly Gross, then of Saatchi and Saatchi Kid Connection, counseled companies that although "families *are* reconnecting and kids and parents *do* wish for more time together . . . that doesn't mean the tender moments must be shared in *your* marketing communication . . . some parents are just *sooooo* embarrassing." She advises going "parent-free" to market to tweens.[30]

Marketers defend themselves against charges of antiadultism by arguing that they are promoting kid empowerment. Social conservatives, however, see treachery in the ridicule of adults. Wherever one comes down on this debate, it's important to recognize the nature of the corporate message: kids and products are aligned together in a really great, fun place, while parents, teachers, and other adults inhabit an oppressive, drab, and joyless world. The lesson to kids is that it's the product, not your parent, who's really on your side.

[26]Halpin quote from an interview with her at Reveries, available online at http://www.reveries.com/reverb/kids_marketing/halpin/index.html.

[27]"Advertisers have kicked the parents out" quote from Mary Prescott (pseudonym), interview with the author, July 2001.

[28]Crispin Miller quote from *Merchants of Cool* transcript, cited above.

[29]Television dads quote from Kanner (2002), p. 45, and parents as nincompoops on p. 56. See also Hymowitz (1999), ch. 4, for a discussion of antifamilial attitudes in television.

[30]Holly Gross quote from Gross (2002b).

Age Compression

One of the hottest trends in youth marketing is age compression — the practice of taking products and marketing messages originally designed for older kids and targeting them to younger ones. Age compression includes offering teen products and genres, pitching gratuitous violence to the twelve-and-under crowd, cultivating brand preferences for items that were previously unbranded among younger kids, and developing creative alcohol and tobacco advertising that is not officially targeted to them but is widely seen and greatly loved by children. "By eight or nine they want 'N Sync," explained one tweening expert to me, in the days before that band was eclipsed by Justin Timberlake, Pink, and others.

25 Age compression is a sprawling trend. It can be seen in the import of television programming specifically designed for one-year-olds, which occurred, ironically, with Public Broadcasting's *Teletubbies*. It includes the marketing of designer clothes to kindergarteners and first graders. It's the deliberate targeting of R-rated movies to kids as young as age nine, a practice the major movie studios were called on the carpet for by the Clinton administration in 2000. It's being driven by the recognition that many children nationwide are watching MTV and other teen and adult programming. One of my favorite MTV anecdotes comes from a third-grade teacher in Weston, Massachusetts, who reported that she started her social studies unit on Mexico by asking the class what they knew about the country. Six or seven raised their hands and answered, "That's the place where MTV's Spring Break takes place!" For those who haven't seen it, the program glorifies heavy partying, what it calls "bootylicious girls," erotic dancing, wet T-shirt contests, and binge drinking.

Nowhere is age compression more evident than among the eight- to twelve-year-old target. Originally a strategy for selling to ten- to thirteen-year-olds, children as young as six are being targeting for tweening. And what is that exactly? Tweens are "in-between" teens and children, and tweening consists mainly of bringing teen products and entertainment to ever-younger audiences. If you're wondering why your daughter came home from kindergarten one day singing the words to a Britney Spears or Jennifer Lopez song, the answer is that she got tweened. Tween marketing has become a major focus of the industry, with its own conferences, research tools, databases, books, and specialty firms. Part of why tweening is so lucrative is that it involves bringing new, more expensive products to this younger group. It's working because tweens have growing purchasing power and influence with parents. The more the tween consumer world comes to resemble the teen world, with its comprehensive branding strategies and intense levels of consumer immersion, the more money there is to be made.[31]

[31] On the idea of the tween and its evolution from earlier categories of sub- and preteen, see Cook and Kaiser (2003).

READING THE TEXT

1. Explain in your own words what constitutes "cool" in children's advertising, according to Schor.
2. How has "street" culture influenced consumer marketing, as Schor explains it?
3. What does researcher Douglas Holt mean by his claim that "the neighborhood, the pain of being poor, the alienation experienced by black kids . . . are the commodifiable assets" (para. 8) exploited in advertising?
4. What does the term *age compression* (para. 24) mean, in your own words?

READING THE SIGNS

1. Perform a semiotic analysis of an advertisement from any medium directed at children. What signifiers in the ad are especially addressed to children? To what extent do you see evidence of "cool marketing"? Consider such details as colors, music, voice track, the implied narrative of the ad, and its characters and their appearance.
2. Conduct an in-class debate over whether advertising to young people should be more strictly regulated. To develop support for your team's position, watch some TV programs aimed at children or teens and the advertising that accompanies them.
3. **CONNECTING TEXTS** Read or reread James B. Twitchell's "What We Are to Advertisers" (p. 261), and write an essay in which you analyze whether Twitchell's assertion that "mass marketing means the creation of mass stereotypes" (para. 1) applies to child or tween consumers.
4. **CONNECTING TEXTS** Using Thomas Frank's perspective in "Commodify Your Dissent" (p. 228) as a critical framework, analyze a suite of ads aimed at tweens and discuss the extent to which the ads "commodify" coolness and edginess. Ads that promote popular clothing, such as jeans, can be especially rich objects of analysis.

JULIA B. CORBETT

A Faint Green Sell: Advertising and the Natural World

Though "green" marketing and advertising is not as prevalent today as it was in the 1980s and 1990s, advertisers still exploit natural imagery to move the goods. Believing, however, that "the business of advertising is fundamentally 'brown'" and that "therefore the idea of advertising being 'green' and capable of supporting environmental values is an oxymoron," Julia B. Corbett sets out to analyze and categorize the ways in which advertising exploits nature, from treating it as a commodity to presenting nature as something that exists solely for the pleasure of human beings. All these strategies, Corbett concludes, perpetuate "an anthropocentric, narcissistic relationship" with the natural world. In other words, beautiful mountain ad backgrounds do not mean that you should go out and buy an SUV. Julia B. Corbett is a professor of communication at the University of Utah.

In the 1980s, advertisers discovered the environment. When a revitalized environmental movement helped establish environmentalism as a legitimate, mainstream public goal (Luke, 1993), corporate America quickly capitalized on a lucrative market of "green consumers" (Ottman, 1993; Zinkham & Carlson, 1995). Marketers not only could create new products and services, they could also reposition existing ones to appear more environmentally friendly. What resulted was a flood of advertisements that focused on green product attributes, touting products as recyclable and biodegradable and claiming them good or safe for the environment. Increases in this genre were remarkable, with green print ads increasing 430 percent and green television ads increasing 367 percent between 1989 and 1990 (Ottman, 1993). The total number of products claiming green attributes doubled in 1990 to 11.4 percent from the previous year ("Selling green," 1991).

Virtually all of the existing research on so-called green advertising was conducted during this boom. Green advertising was defined by researchers as product ads touting environmental benefits or corporate green-image ads (Banerjee, Gulas, & Iyer, 1995; Shrum, McCarty, & Lowrey, 1995). Researchers also targeted and segmented green consumers (Ottman, 1993) and tested their motivations (Luke, 1993). Green appeals were categorized (Iyer & Banerjee, 1993; Obermiller, 1995; Schuhwerk & Lefkoff-Hagius, 1995) and consumer response to green ads analyzed (Mayer, Scammon, & Zick, 1993; Thorson, Page, & Moore, 1995).

By the late 1990s, advertisers announced the end of the green-ad boom. *Advertising Age* reported that as the country headed into the thirtieth anniversary of Earth Day, green positioning had become more than just a nonissue — it was almost an anti-issue (Neff, 2000). Marketers were launching a whole new class of disposable products from plastic storage containers to dust mops. There was a perceived decline in controversy over antigreen products such as disposable diapers, toxic batteries, and gas-guzzling SUVs (sport utility vehicles). In addition, only 5 percent of new products made claims about recyclability or recycled content, and the explosion of e-tailing added boxes, styrofoam peanuts, and air-puffed plastic bags to the waste stream. Green product ads in prime-time television, which never amounted to more than a blip, virtually disappeared by 1995, reflecting "the television tendency to get off the environmental bandwagon after it had lost its trendiness" (Shanahan & McComas, 1999, p. 108).

But Shanahan and McComas noted that their study — like virtually all research published during the green-ad boom — did not consider the most prevalent use of the environment in advertising: when nature functions as a rhetorically useful backdrop or stage. Using nature merely as a backdrop — whether in the form of wild animals, mountain vistas, or sparkling rivers — is the most common use of the natural world in advertisements. For all but the most critical message consumers, the environment blends into the background. We know that an advertisement for a car shows the vehicle outdoors and that ads for allergy medications feature flowers and "weeds." The environment per se is not for sale, but advertisers are depending on qualities and features of the nonhuman world (and our relationship to it) to help in the selling message. When the natural world is so depicted, it becomes a convenient, culturally relevant tool to which meanings can be attached for the purpose of selling goods and services. Although this intentional but seemingly casual use of the environment in advertising is by far the most common, it is the least studied by researchers.

Nature-as-backdrop ads also are notable for their enduring quality. 5
Although the number of ads that focus on product attributes such as "recyclable" may shift with marketing trends and political winds, nature has been used as a backdrop virtually since the dawn of advertising. The natural world was depicted in early automobile ads ("see the USA in your Chevrolet") and Hamms Beer commercials ("from the land of sky-blue water") and continues to be a prominent feature in the advertising landscape. Nature-as-backdrop ads, therefore, provide an important record of the position of the natural world in our cultural environment and, as such, deserve scrutiny.

Advertisements are a special form of discourse because they include visual signals and language fragments (either oral or written) that work together to create messages that go beyond the ability of either individually. This essay undertakes a critical analysis of the symbolic communicative discourse of advertising, viewing nature-as-backdrop ads as cultural icons of environmental values embedded in our social system. When ads present the environment with distorted, inauthentic, or exaggerated discourse, that discourse has the potential to foster inauthentic relationships to nature and influences the way we perceive our environment and its value to us.

Schudson (1989) argued that ads have special cultural power. In addition to being repetitive and ubiquitous, ads reinforce messages from primary institutions in the social system, provide dissonance to countering messages, and generally support the capitalistic structure that the advertising industry was created to support. This essay will discuss how the ad industry developed, how ads work on us, and how ads portray the natural world. It will argue, according to environmental theories such as deep ecology (Bullis, 1996; Naess, 1973), that the "green" in advertising is extremely faint by examining and developing six related concepts:

1. The business of advertising is fundamentally "brown"; therefore, the idea of advertising being "green" and capable of supporting environmental values is an oxymoron.
2. Advertising commodifies the natural world and attaches material value to nonmaterial goods, treating natural resources as private and possessible, not public and intrinsic.
3. Nature-as-backdrop ads portray an anthropocentric, narcissistic relationship to the biotic community and focus on the environment's utility and benefit to humans.
4. Advertising idealizes the natural world and presents a simplified, distorted picture of nature as sublime, simple, and unproblematic.
5. The depiction of nature in advertising disconnects and estranges us from what is valued, yet at the same time we are encouraged to reconnect through products, creating a circular consumption.
6. As a ubiquitous form of pop culture, advertising reinforces consonant messages in the social system and provides strong dissonance to oppositional or alternative messages.

The "Brown" Business of Advertising

1. The business of advertising is fundamentally "brown"; therefore, the idea of advertising being "green" and capable of supporting environmental values is an oxymoron.

Advertisements are nothing new to this century or even previous ones. There are plentiful examples in literature, including the works of Shakespeare, that peddlers have long enticed buyers by advertising (in print or orally) a good's attributes and associated meanings. After World War II, however, advertising found a firm place in the worldview of Americans. According to Luke (1993), after 1945, corporate capital, big government, and professional experts pushed practices of a throw-away affluent society onto consumers as a purposeful political strategy to sustain economic growth, forestall mass discontent, and empower scientific authority. Concern for the environment was lacking in the postwar prosperity boom, at least until the mid-1960s when Rachel Carson sounded the alarm over chemicals and the modern-day environmental movement was born (Corbett, 2001).

To help alert consumers to new mass-produced goods, a new type of 10
show called the "soap opera" was created for the relatively recent phenomenon of television. These daytime dramas were created for the sole purpose of delivering an audience of homemakers to eager manufacturers of household products, including soap. Advertisers realized that advertising on soap operas would help to establish branding, or creating differing values for what are essentially common, interchangeable goods such as soap.

Essentially, advertising was viewed as part of the fuel that would help keep a capitalist economy burning. Capitalism is a market system that measures its success by constant growth (such as the gross national product and housing starts), a system that many environmentalists recognize as ultimately unsustainable. You might even say that advertising developed as the culture that would help solve what some economists view as the central problem of capitalism: the distribution of surplus goods (Twitchell, 1996). Schudson (1989) concluded, "Advertising is capitalism's way of saying 'I love you' to itself." In a capitalist economy, advertising is a vital handmaiden to consumption and materialism. In the words of the author of *Adcult*, Americans "are not too materialistic. We are not materialistic enough" (Twitchell, 1996, p. 11).

The development of mass media, particularly radio and television, played an important role in delivering audiences to advertisers. By the mid-1980s, half of U.S. homes had cable, and the burgeoning number of channels allowed advertisers to target more specific audience segments. Advertisers and media programmers engage in a dance to fill each other's needs, each having a vested interest in constructing certain versions of the world and not others. According to Turow (1999), "the ad industry affects not just the content of its own campaigns but the very structure and content of the rest of the media system" (p. 194). At the same time, media develop formats and tones for their outlets and programming deemed to be most acceptable to the audiences that they hope marketers find most attractive. What this means for programming is that the upscale twenty-something audience — the most appealing segment to advertisers — will find itself represented in more media outlets than older men and women to whom only a small number of highly targeted formats are aimed. According to researchers of the green marketing boom, the segments of the population most committed to the environment do not belong to this twenty-something group (Ottman, 1993).

It is precisely the ability of advertisers and media programmers to tell some stories and not others that gives these entities power. "When people read a magazine, watch a TV show, or use any other ad-sponsored medium, they are entering a world that was constructed as a result of close cooperation between advertisers and media firms" (Turow, 1999, p. 16). Because all media provide people with insights into parts of the world with which they have little direct contact, media representations of the natural world to a largely urbanized population are highly significant. They show us, over and over again, where we belong in the world and how we should treat it. Yet, representations of the natural world are crafted for the sole purpose of selling certain audiences to advertisers.

The close cooperation between advertisers and media firms is understandable given advertising's financial support of media. For newspapers and some magazines, at least 50 percent of their revenue is from advertising; and support approaches 100 percent for much of radio and television. By some estimates, advertisers spent $27 billion on support to television, $9 billion on radio, $46 billion on daily newspapers, and about $7 billion on consumer magazines (Turow, 1999, p. 13).

15 Given advertising's purpose of selling audiences to advertisers, is it even possible for any form of advertising — whether product ads or nature-as-backdrop ads — to be "green"? Dadd and Carothers (1991) maintained that a truly green economy would require all products to be audited and analyzed from cradle to grave for their environmental effects. Effects could include the resources used and pollution generated in the product's manufacture, energy used to produce and transport the product, the product's role in the economic and social health of the country of origin, investment plans of the company, and final disposal of product.

Applying this standard at the most basic level connotes it is an oxymoron to label marginally useful or necessary products (and the ads that promote them) as "green" or somehow good for the environment. Can an advertisement that encourages consumption of a product (or patronage of a company that produces the product) ever be green with a capital G? In his attempt to reconcile a brown industry with green ideals, Kilbourne (1995) identified three levels of green in advertisements. But even at the lowest level (defined as ads promoting a small "techno-fix" such as biodegradability) the message is still that "consuming is good, more is better, and the ecological cost is minimal" (p. 15). If an ad recognizes finite resources, it nevertheless views the environment purely as a resource, not as possessing intrinsic, noneconomic value. Kilbourne concluded that from a purely ecological position, a truly Green ad is indeed an oxymoron: "the only Green product is the one that is not produced" (p. 16). Other researchers have likewise tried to categorize the green in advertisements (Banerjee et al., 1995). Adapting the deep and shallow ecology concepts of Naess (1973) to advertisements, they concluded that very few ads were "deep" — 2 percent of television and 9 percent of print — defined by the researchers as discussing environmental issues in depth and mentioning actions requiring more commitment.

However, these attempts to make advertising fit a green framework simply illustrate how ideologically opposed advertising and environmental values are. Because advertising is the workhorse of capitalism and supports continually increased production, it is ideologically contrary to environmentalism, which recognizes that ever-increasing growth and consumption are inherently unsustainable. It matters not whether an ad boasts of recyclability or quietly features pristine mountain meadows in the background; the basic business of advertising is brown. Perhaps the only truly Green product is not only one not produced, but also one not advertised.

Nature as Commodity

2. Advertising commodifies the natural world and attaches material value to nonmaterial goods, treating natural resources as private and ownable, not public and intrinsic.

Have you ever viewed a single advertisement and then rushed out to buy that product? Probably not. That is not the way that advertising generally

Portfolio of Advertisements

READING THE SIGNS

Consider these questions as you analyze the advertisements on the following pages.

1. Spotify:
   This Spotify ad spans three generations — GenX, Millennials, and GenZ — suggesting to its target market that little has changed in 21 years. What is the ad trying to accomplish with this reassurance?

2. Buffalo Exchange:
   The Buffalo Exchange ad promotes an attitude as well as a lifestyle. What is that attitude, and how does it reflect what Thomas Frank calls the "commodification of dissent"?

3. California Walnuts:
   An ad for a trade organization rather than a particular brand, this pitch for California Walnuts is intended to resemble a certain kind of movie poster. What is the kind of movie alluded to here, and why do you think it was chosen to spearhead this campaign?

4. AdCouncil:
   This PSA announcement in the wake of the COVID-19 pandemic is intended for a specific age group. What details in the ad indicate what that age group is, and how effective are they?

5. Shinola:
   This ad contains a mixture of populist and elitist appeals. What are those appeals, and how do they combine to sell watches?

6. The Shelter Pet Project:
   This ad for the Shelter Pet Project assumes that the viewer recognizes the cat featured in the ad. How does viewer recognition enhance the ad's effectiveness?

7. The Society of Grownups:
   The Society of Grownups is a financial planning service aimed at millennials who have little experience with financial planning and investment. Why, do you think, does this ad for the service say nothing about what it offers, showing only a group of people who look disturbed? What is the intended effect of the "You're a Grownup" caption on its intended audience?

2. Buffalo Exchange, LTD; 3. EHY.com; 5. Shinola.

1998

Baggy jeans and
chokers are in.
Spice Girls are on tour.

2019

Ditto.

Listen like you used to.

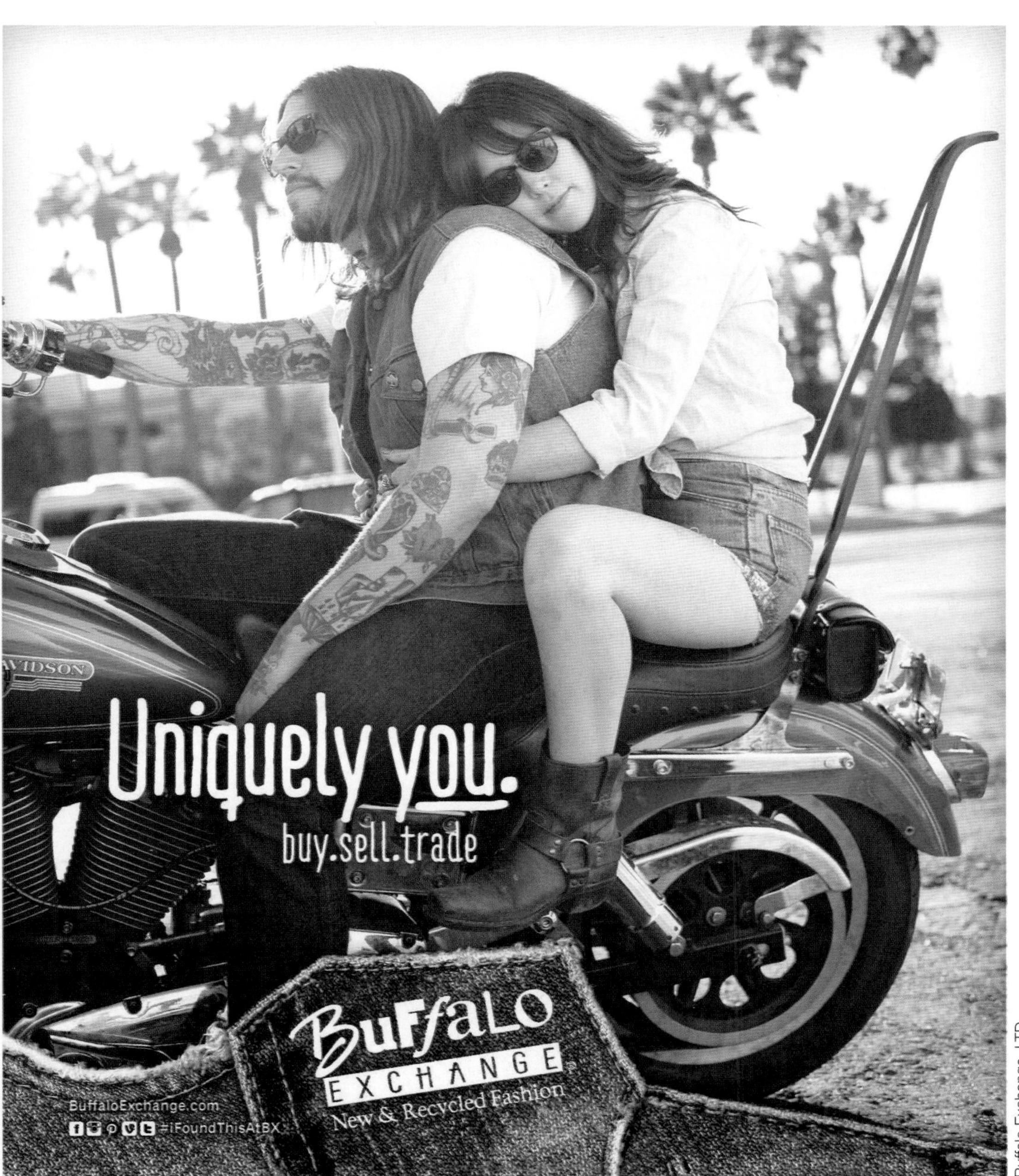

Buffalo Exchange, LTD

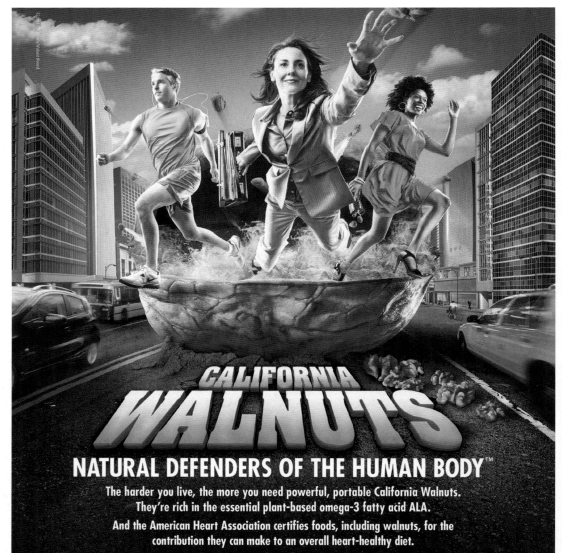

CALIFORNIA WALNUTS

NATURAL DEFENDERS OF THE HUMAN BODY™

The harder you live, the more you need powerful, portable California Walnuts. They're rich in the essential plant-based omega-3 fatty acid ALA.

And the American Heart Association certifies foods, including walnuts, for the contribution they can make to an overall heart-healthy diet.

"Supportive but not conclusive research shows that eating 1.5 ounces of walnuts per day, as part of a low saturated fat and low cholesterol diet and not resulting in increased caloric intake, may reduce the risk of coronary heart disease." (FDA) One ounce of walnuts provides 18g of total fat, 2.5g of monounsaturated fat, 13g of polyunsaturated fat including 2.5g of alpha-linolenic acid – the plant-based omega-3 fatty acid and 3.68mmol of antioxidants.

WALNUTS.ORG  FACEBOOK.COM/CAWALNUTS  TWITTER.COM/CAWALNUTS

Per one ounce serving.
See heartcheckmark.org/guidelines

Let's not

Party

Meet up

Bro-hug

Defy

Let's

Stay put

Binge watch

Video-happy-hour

Save lives

Visit coronavirus.gov for the latest tips and information from the CDC.

#AloneTogether

TOGETHER, WE CAN HELP SLOW THE SPREAD.

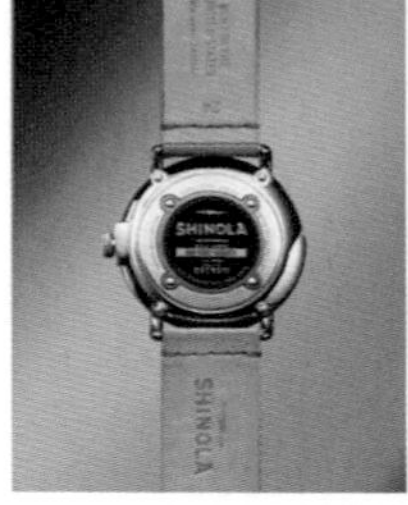

SHINOLA
Argonite-1069
DETROIT
THE LONG TRADITION OF DETROIT WATCHMAKING HAS JUST BEGUN.
WATCHES WILL BE MADE IN DETROIT FOR DECADES TO COME, BUT WE WILL NEVER MAKE THIS ONE AGAIN. RESERVE **THE RUNWELL**, AN EXTREMELY LIMITED SINGLE EDITION OF THE FIRST HANDMADE WATCH FROM THE MOTOR CITY.
SHINOLA.COM
SHINOLA
DETROIT
Where American is made.™

Shinola

wet, and sweating are often part of the package. Such a real outdoor experience is unlikely to be depicted in advertisements (unless the product is for something like insect repellent). Instead, ads subordinate reality to a romanticized past, present, or even future. "Real" in advertising is a cultural construct: "The makers of commercials do not want what is real but what will seem real on film. Artificial rain is better than 'God's rain' because it shows up better on film or tape" (Schudson, 1989, p. 79). Advertisers do not intend to capture life as it really is, but intend instead to portray the "ideal" life and to present as normal and everyday what are actually relatively rare moments, such as a phenomenal sunset or a mosquito-less lake.

A great many nature-as-backdrop ads present the natural world as sublime, a noble place inspiring awe and admiration. As an exercise, my students draw their interpretation of a sublime place in nature, and invariably, similar elements appear in their pictures: snow-capped mountain peaks towering above pine trees and a grassy or flower-filled meadow, through which a clear creek or river flows. Sometimes, large mammals such as deer graze in the meadow. Humans are rarely present.

According to Oravec (1996), the sublime is a literary and artistic convention that uses a prescribed form of language and pictorial elements to describe nature, and that in turn encourages a specific pattern of responses to nature. Artistically, sublime representations can include blurring, exaggeration of detail, and compositional elements such as a foreground, middle ground, and frame. Settings are frequently pastoral or wild with varying amounts of human presence. There is a self-reflexive nature to the positioning, with the observer feeling both within a scene and also outside it, viewing the scene (and reflexively, the self) from a higher or more distant (and morally outstanding) perspective.

Oravec (1996) has called the sublime the founding trope in the rhetoric of environmentalism: "Sublimity has remained a touchstone or grounding for our public conception of nature and, through nature, of the environment" (p. 68). As a conventional linguistic device, the sublime represents and encodes our understanding of the natural world. Because the sublime is associated with what is "natural," "the sublime connotes an authenticity and originality that is part of its very meaning; yet like rhetoric itself, it has a long-standing reputation for exaggeration and even falsehood" (p. 69).

The sublime is as much a part of advertising as it is of the artistic and literary realms. Advertising presents the natural world as pristine, simple, and not endangered, yet depictions are always contrived and often created. What appears as real rain is artificial, what looks like a natural wildlife encounter is contrived, and what appears entirely natural was created with computer animation and digital manipulation. The artificial seamlessly approximates the real in the sublime world of advertising.

Numerous vacation advertisements depict people in sublime settings, such as thin and tan couples on pristine white sand beaches, or peacefully cruising under sunny skies amid glaciers and whales. Vacationers in this idealized world never encounter anything other than perfect environmental conditions and enjoy these sublime locations unfettered by crowds.

A host of pharmaceutical ads likewise enlist nature backdrops as rhetoric for the sublime. One ad for an arthritis medication takes place in a pastoral setting assumed to be a park. The sun is shining, the park is empty except for the actors, there is no litter or noise, and even the dogs are exceedingly friendly and behaved. In another ad for what is presumed to be a mood-enhancer, a woman strolls slowly along a pristine, deserted beach in soft light, a contented smile on her face. In these instances, the sublime backdrop doubly represents the sublime state the person will achieve upon taking the medication. Many of these ads rely so heavily on the power of sublime meaning that the actual purpose of the drug is not stated, only assumed.

Other commercials depict the sublime after a product has changed problematic nature into idealized nature. Numerous ads for lawn care products and allergy medications first portray nature in a state of chaos or war, needing to be tamed and brought under control. One television ad for lawn chemicals showed a small army of men and supplies descending from the sky to tame and tackle nature. Some allergy commercials depict the flowers and weeds physically attacking people. But ah, after the product is introduced, unproblematic and peaceful nature returns.

When humans are introduced into sublime scenes, their representa- 45
tion is also idealized. Just as nature is presented as reality-as-it-should-be, people are presented as-they-should-be in a limited number of social roles. Therefore, people in ads are primarily attractive, young or middle-aged, vibrant, and thin, or they are celebrities with those qualities. The environments in which they live, whether inside or outside, are also limited to idealized conditions; no one has dirty houses or unkempt lawns, and no one travels through dirty city streets, encounters polluted rivers, or finds abused landscapes. In the world of advertising, there are no poor people, sick people, or unattractive people, and sometimes there are no people at all. For example, most car ads do not show anyone actually driving the vehicle through the tinted windows, and you hear only the disembodied voice of the announcer. The social roles played by advertising actors are easily identifiable — the businessperson, the grandmother, the teenager — but the actors are anonymous as individual people and portray only social roles tailored to specific demographic categories. The flat, abstract, idealized, and sometimes anonymous world of advertising "is part of a deliberate effort to connect specific products in people's imagination with certain demographic groupings or needs or occasions" (Schudson, 1989, p. 77).

Of course you recognize pieces of this idealized presentation of people and their environments, just as you recognize the utterly impossible pieces — a car parked on an inaccessible cliff or polar bears drinking Coke. We are not stupefied by a natural world that is unrealistic and idealized in advertising: in fact, we expect it.

A Natural Disconnect

5. The depiction of nature in advertising disconnects and estranges us from what is valued, and we attempt to reconnect through products, creating a circular consumption.

Some critics believe that advertising may be more powerful the less people believe it and the less it is acknowledged. According to Schudson (1989), ads do not ask to be taken literally and do not mean what they say, but "this may be the very center of their power" (p. 87). While we are being exposed to those 3,000 ads a day, we may carry an illusion of detachment and think them trivial and unimportant. According to some theories, though, it is very possible to "learn" without active involvement, a so-called sleeper effect. This myth of immunity from an ad's persuasion may do more to protect our self-respect than help us comprehend the subtleties and implications of their influence (Pollay, 1989). Although we may not think an ad speaks to us, its slogan may suddenly pop into our vocabulary—just do it, it does a body good, got milk? We may be unaware and uninvolved in front of the television, but the message of the ad may prove important at purchase time. According to Pollay (1989), advertising does more than merely stimulate wants; it plays a subtle role in changing habits.

Take the habit of drying your clothes, an activity that for many people throughout the world involves pinning clothes to a line in the backyard or between buildings. When I was a girl, I loved sliding between clean sheets dried outside on the clothesline and drinking in the smell. How do many people get that same outside-smell nowadays? They get it with detergents and fabric softeners with names like "mountain air" and "springtime fresh" or with similarly scented dryer sheets. Although perceived convenience and affordable dryers no doubt helped change our clothes-drying habits, where did we learn to associate the smell of outdoors with purchased products? Advertising.

50 The message in these product ads is that the artificial smell is somehow easier or superior or even just equivalent to the real smell in the natural world. It not only commodifies something of value from the natural world, it gradually disconnects us from that thing of value. The more successfully ads teach us to associate natural qualities such as fresh air with products, the more disconnected we become from what was originally valued. The more estranged from the original thing of value, the more we may attempt to reconnect through products that promise an easy replacement. When we become so estranged from the natural world that we attempt to reconnect through products, a circular consumptive pattern is created—which supports the capitalist economy that advertising was created to support. If advertising tells us that nonsaleable qualities of the outdoors such as fresh air and natural smells are easy to bring inside, need we worry about the condition of the real world?

Just as advertising can change habits, it can help create rituals and taboos. A good example of a taboo largely created by advertising is litter. Through national advertising campaigns begun decades ago, litter was labeled as an environmental no-no. While cleaning up litter makes for a visually appealing environment, the automobiles from which the trash is generally tossed cause far more environmental harm than almost all types of litter.

Advertising also works to create rituals. A ritual is created when we make inert, prosaic objects meaningful and give them symbolic significance. Mistletoe means little to us as a parasitic evergreen, but it is loaded with significance as a holiday ritual about kissing. Whales mean more to us as communicative, spiritual symbols of the deep than for their inherent value and place in ocean ecosystems. Price (1996) concluded that Native American fetishes and baskets, which have been ritualized by nonnative populations (and appropriated by advertising), "associate nature nearly interchangeably with indigenous peoples" (p. 189). In a similar way, once a species or animal has been so ritualized, it precludes a more complete and accurate knowing of it and disconnects us.

Advertising, directly and subtly, idealizes and materializes a way of experiencing the world, including the natural world. It promotes products as the simple solutions to complex dilemmas by tapping into our dissatisfactions and desires. If you feel disconnected to the natural world, you can "solve" that with mountain-scented laundry products, bear fetishes, and whale audiotapes, but these purchases only increase the estrangement. If you need to escape modern life yet want to feel safe and civilized while doing so, you can simply solve that by taking a rugged SUV into the wilderness.

Yet environmental dilemmas are anything but simple, and wilderness is a good example. A print ad features a four-wheel-drive car crossing a sparkling, boulder-strewn stream and announces, "Coming soon to a wilderness near you." In this idealized portrayal, there is no mud being stirred up from the bottom of the stream, no dirt of any kind on the car, and of course, there is no visible driver. But in addition, "wilderness" is a rare commodity that rarely exists "near you," and by its very definition, includes few people and even fewer developed signs of people. In wilderness with a capital W, cars and all motorized equipment are forbidden. Setting aside an area as wilderness involves contentious negotiations and land-use trade-offs. But whether formally designated or not, experiencing wilderness is not the simple matter of materialization and driving a certain kind of car.

Another example of advertising portraying a complex environmental 55
issue as simple and uncomplicated is the depiction of water. We see it babbling down brooks in beverage commercials, refreshing someone in a soap commercial, quenching thirst in ads for water filters and bottled water. Pure, clean, healthy — but simple? More than half the world's rivers are drying up or are polluted. Agricultural chemicals have seeped into many U.S. underground aquifers. Oil, gas, and a host of herbicides and pesticides wash off streets and lawns into waterways. Political and legal fights are waged over dams, diversions, and water rights. A host of bacterial contaminants have threatened water supplies and public health in major U.S. cities, and traces of antibiotics and other prescription drugs have been detected in some municipal water supplies. Clean water is definitely not a simple environmental issue.

Advertising Does Not Stand Alone

6. As a ubiquitous form of popular culture, advertising reinforces consonant messages in the social system and provides strong dissonance to oppositional or alternative messages.

For any societal element to wield power, it must exist in concert with other social institutions in a way that is mutually reinforcing. Advertising is layered on top of other cultural elements and bound up with other institutions, from entertainment and popular culture to corporate America and manufacturing. Each element is heteroglossic, continually leaking into other sectors, with advertising slogans showing up in both casual conversation and political speeches. The very ubiquitousness of advertising — extending beyond regular media buys to include placing products in movies, sponsoring sporting events, and the full-length infomercial — ensures its power and influence in numerous places and institutions.

For an example of this interwoven character of advertising and consumption with other elements of society, consider plastics recycling. We routinely see ads touting how certain products are recyclable or made from recycled items. Currently, the plastics industry is running an advertising campaign that reminds us of all the wonderful ways that plastic contributes to our lives. That means that multiple corporate public relations departments and public relations agencies are involved in getting mileage from the recycling issue. Public relations and advertising personnel have regular contact with media people in both the advertising and editorial sides, and the boundaries between news and advertising functions are becoming increasingly blurred (Stauber & Rampton, 1995). Meanwhile, giant corporate conglomerates have become the norm, putting journalists under the same corporate roof as advertisers and the very companies they attempt to scrutinize. For example, if a television station is owned by General Electric and is also receiving thousands of dollars in revenue from an ad campaign about the value of plastics, there is dissonance — whether acknowledged or not — for those TV reporters covering a story about environmental impacts and energy used to recycle plastic.

The hallowed halls of education are not immune from commercial messages, including those about plastic. Captive youngsters are a tempting market: more than 43 million kids attend schools and even elementary-age children exert tremendous spending power, about $15 billion a year (McNeal, 1994). Ads cover school buses, book covers, and scoreboards, and corporate flags fly next to school flags. The Polystyrene Packaging Council, like other corporations, has supplied "supplemental educational materials" free of charge to K–12 classrooms. Their "Plastics and the Environment" lesson teaches that plastics are great and easily recycled, even though most plastics are not recyclable for lack of markets. Consumers Union evaluated this lesson as "highly commercial and incomplete with strong bias. . . . [T]he disadvantages of plastics . . . are not covered" (Zillions, 1995, p. 46). Another critic noted that when teachers use such materials, "American students are introduced to environmental issues as they use materials supplied by corporations who pollute the soil, air, and water" (Molnar, 1995, p. 70).

60 Beyond communication and education, legal sectors also get involved in advertising claims about recycled and recyclable plastic, and politicians know it is wise to support recycling as a generalized issue. Some municipalities sponsor curbside pick-up programs for plastic, and trash haulers and manufacturers run businesses dependent on recycling plastics. Recycling plastics not only creates new business opportunities, it also is philosophically consistent with a capitalist economy that is based on ever-increasing consumption. After all, the message of recycling is not to reduce or avoid consumption but essentially to consume something again. According to one critic in *Harper's*, oftentimes the new product created from recycled plastics is "the perfect metaphor for everything that's wrong with the idea of recycling plastics. It's ugly as sin, the world doesn't need it, and it's disposable" (Gutin, 1992, p. 56).

The vested interest of so many powerful social institutions makes it that much harder to separate the influence of one from another — such as advertising from news media — and to effect significant social change. It also makes the ubiquitous, repetitive messages of advertising reinforced and in a sense replicated, free of charge. Individuals or groups with oppositional messages about plastics would have to contend with what seems a united front about the place, if not the value, of plastic.

Working Together

Obviously, the six concepts presented here work in concert. Here is one final example of an ad that considers them together.

First, the visual of this television ad: A waterfall flows over the driver's seat of a car and a tiny kayaker (in relation to the size of the car seat) spills down the face of the falls. The scene quickly shifts to the kayaker (full-sized now and paddling away from us) amid glaciers. The next scene takes us into the car's back cargo area — still covered with water — and two orca whales breach in front of the kayaker, who pauses mid-stroke. (In all of these shots, we have never seen the kayaker's face; when he paddles away, his head is covered in a fur-lined parka that looks "native.") The next shot is a close-up of a paddle dipping into water shimmering with the colors of sunset and above the words "Discover Chevy Tahoe." The last scene shows the unoccupied vehicle parked on the edge of a stream in front of snow-covered mountain peaks. The accompanying audio includes Native American–sounding drum beats and a mixed chorus singing a chant-like, non-English song. Over this music, we hear the voice of a male announcer who quotes a passage from John Muir about how a person needs silence to get into the heart of the wilderness away from dust, hotels, baggage, and chatter.

The meanings that these elements convey to us are multiple. Peace, serenity, at-oneness with nature, and a return to a simple yet sublime "native" existence are part of the promise of this vehicle. Native drums, whales, glaciers, paddling through still waters, and even the deep ecologist Muir are powerful, idealized, and ritualized symbols that are employed to market a feeling and a sensation. The seamless juxtaposition of scene both inside and outside the vehicle conveys that nature is transported effortlessly for you to experience these things directly, without leaving the safety and luxury of your car. The vehicle is the commodity to aid your escape to this sublime place, a place depicted as real yet entirely contrived, with kayakers spilling over car seats. The entire promise is one of self-gratification, helping the driver/kayaker travel to this idealized wilderness. Yet, if you truly want to heed John Muir's advice, silence is needed to get into the heart of the wilderness, not a noisy car. Hence if you buy into (pun intended) the vehicle being the solution (and not existing instead in your own life or soul), the result is further estrangement from the very thing desired and valued. Advertising, as a primary support system for a capitalist economy, can only transfer meaning and express latent desires — not deliver on any of these promises.

REFERENCES

Banerjee, S., Gulas, C. S., & Iyer, E. (1995). Shades of green: A multidimensional analysis of environmental advertising. *Journal of Advertising, 24*, 21–32.

Benton, L. M. (1995). Selling the natural or selling out? Exploring environmental merchandising. *Environmental Ethics, 17*, 3–22.

Bullis, C. (1996). Retalking environmental discourses from a feminist perspective: The radical potential of ecofeminism. In J. G. Cantrill & C. L. Oravec (Eds.), *The symbolic earth: Discourse and our creation of the environment* (pp. 123–148). Lexington, KY: University Press of Kentucky.

Corbett, J. B. (2001). Women, scientists, agitators: Magazine portrayal of Rachel Carson and Theo Colborn. *Journal of Communication, 51*, 720–749.

Dadd, D. L., & Carothers, A. (1991). A bill of goods? Green consuming in perspective. In C. Plant & J. Plant (Eds.), *Green business: Hope or hoax?* Philadelphia, PA: New Society Publishers (pp. 11–29).

Fink, E. (1990). Biodegradable diapers are not enough in days like these: A critique of commodity environmentalism. *EcoSocialist Review, 4*.

Gutin, J. (1992, March–April). Plastics-a-go-go. *Harper's, 17*, 56–59.

Iyer, E., & Banerjee, B. (1993). Anatomy of green advertising. *Advances in Consumer Research, 20*, 484–501.

Kilbourne, W. E. (1995). Green advertising: Salvation or oxymoron? *Journal of Advertising, 24*, 7–20.

Lasch, C. (1978). *The culture of narcissism*. New York, NY: W. W. Norton.

Luke, T. W. (1993). Green consumerism: Ecology and the ruse of recycling. In J. Bennett & W. Chaloupka (Eds.), *In the nature of things: Languages, politics and the environment* (pp. 154–172). Minneapolis, MN: University of Minnesota Press.

Mayer, R. N., Scammon, D. L., & Zick, C. D. (1993). Poisoning the well: Do environmental claims strain consumer credulity? *Advances in Consumer Research, 20*, 698–703.

McNeal, J. U. (1994, February 7). Billions at stake in growing kids market. *Discount Store News, 41*.

Molnar, A. (1995). Schooled for profit. *Educational Leadership, 53*, 70–71.

Naess, A. (1973). The shallow and the deep, long-range ecology movement: A summary. *Inquiry, 16*, 95–100.

Neff, J. (2000, April 10). It's not trendy being green. *Advertising Age, 16*.

Obermiller, C. (1995). The baby is sick / the baby is well: A test of environmental communication appeals. *Journal of Advertising, 24*, 55–70.

Oravec, C. L. (1996). To stand outside oneself: The sublime in the discourse of natural scenery. In J. G. Cantrill & C. L. Oravec (Eds.), *The symbolic earth: Discourse and our creation of the environment* (pp. 58–75). Lexington, KY: University Press of Kentucky.

Ottman, J. A. (1993). *Green marketing: Challenges and opportunities for the new marketing age*. Lincolnwood, IL: NTC Business Books.

Phillips, B. J. (1996). Advertising and the cultural meaning of animals. *Advances in Consumer Research, 23*, 354–360.

Pollay, R. W. (1989). The distorted mirror: Reflections on the unintended consequences of advertising. In R. Hovland & G. B. Wilcox (Eds.), *Advertising in Society* (pp. 437–476). Lincolnwood, IL: NTC Business Books.

Price, J. (1996). Looking for nature at the mall: A field guide to the Nature Company. In W. Cronon (Ed.), *Uncommon ground: Rethinking the human place in nature* (pp. 186–203). New York, NY: W. W. Norton.

Schudson, M. (1989). Advertising as capitalist realism. In R. Hovland & G. B. Wilcox (Eds.), *Advertising in society* (pp. 73–98). Lincolnwood, IL: NTC Business Books.

Schuhwerk, M. E., & Lefkoff-Hagius, R. (1995). Green or non-green? Does type of appeal matter when advertising a green product? *Journal of Advertising, 24*, 45–54.

Selling green. (1991, October). *Consumer Reports, 56*, 687–692.

Shanahan, J., & McComas, K. (1999). *Nature stories: Depictions of the environment and their effects*. Cresskill, NJ: Hampton Press.

Shrum, L. J., McCarty, J. A., & Lowrey, T. M. (1995). Buyer characteristics of the green consumer and their implications for advertising strategy. *Journal of Advertising, 24*, 71–82.

Stauber, J., & Rampton, S. (1995). *Toxic sludge is good for you! Lies, damn lies, and the public relations industry*. Monroe, ME: Common Courage Press.

Thorson, E., Page, T., & Moore, J. (1995). Consumer response to four categories of "green" television commercials. *Advances in Consumer Research, 22*, 243–250.

Turow, J. (1999). *Breaking up America: Advertisers and the new media world*. Chicago, IL: University of Chicago Press.

Twitchell, J. B. (1996). *Adcult USA: The triumph of advertising in American culture*. New York, NY: Columbia University Press.

Zillions: For Kids from Consumer Reports (1995). *Captive kids: Commercial pressures on kids at school*. New York, NY: Consumers Union Education Services.

Zinkham, G. M., & Carlson, L. (1995). Green advertising and the reluctant consumer. *Journal of Advertising, 24*, 1–6.

Reading the Text

1. Define in your own words "nature-as-backdrop" ads.
2. How, according to Corbett, did advertising become "part of the fuel that would help keep a capitalist economy burning" (para. 11)?

3. Why does Corbett claim, "commodification of what are essentially public resources — like milky blue waters — encourages us to think of resources as private and possessible" (para. 30)? Why does she think such commodification is problematic?
4. In your own words, define the term *sublime*.
5. How can some ads using nature as a backdrop be considered to reflect our narcissism?
6. Why does Corbett have concerns regarding ad campaigns for plastics recycling, which is usually considered an environmentally conscious venture?

Reading the Signs

1. In an essay, write your own argument in response to Corbett's speculative question: "Is it even possible for any form of advertising — whether product ads or nature-as-backdrop ads — to be 'green'?" (para. 15).
2. Study some travel magazines, focusing on the advertising. To what extent is nature presented as "sublime" or as a backdrop? Use your observations to demonstrate, refute, or complicate the contention that presenting nature as "unproblematic" can have a dangerous effect on our environmental consciousness.
3. Select a single ad that uses nature as a backdrop, and conduct an in-depth analysis of it. As a critical framework, use the six reasons advertising can be "faint green" that Corbett outlines on pages 308–20.
4. **CONNECTING TEXTS** Adopting the perspective of Laurence Shames's "The More Factor" (p. 193), write an essay in which you argue whether the "faint green" advertising Corbett describes is an expression of the American desire for "more."
5. **CONNECTING TEXTS** Corbett asserts that "attempts to make advertising fit a green framework simply illustrate how ideologically opposed advertising and environmental values are" (para. 17). In class, form teams and debate this assertion. Use the debate as a jumping-off point for your own essay in which you explore your own response. Teams might also want to consult Michael Pollan's "Supermarket Pastoral" (p. 211).
6. Study advertisements for companies that produce oil, plastics, or chemicals. Do they use nature as a backdrop, as Corbett describes, or is nature presented in a different way? Use your observations to describe and critique the techniques such companies use to present a positive public image. As an alternative, do the same with automobile advertising, focusing on ads for SUVs (you might study a magazine such as *Car and Driver* or consult promotional material on auto companies' websites). Or study advertising that promotes alternative-fuel vehicles, such as the Prius, Bolt, or Leaf.

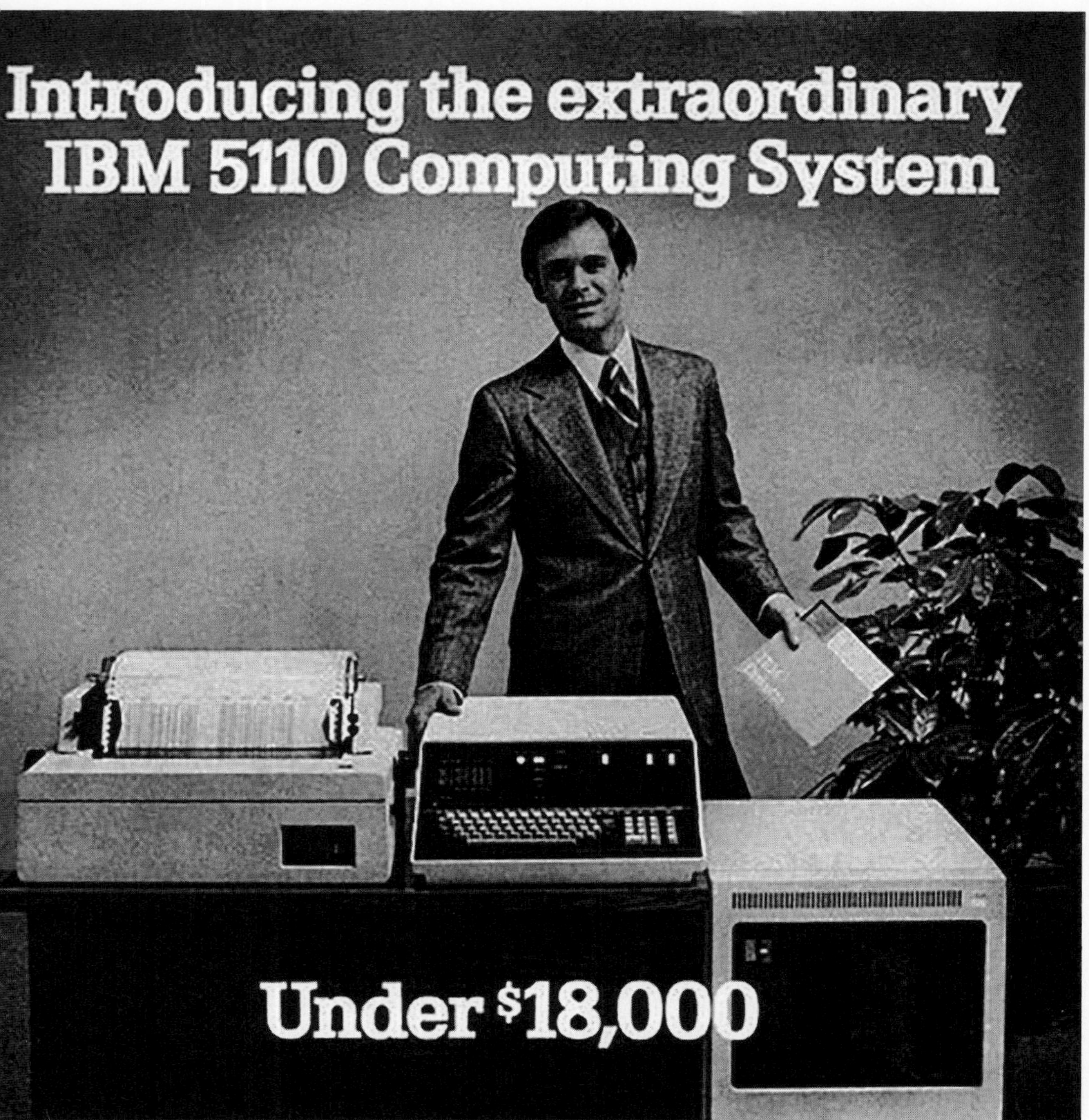

There was a time when $18,000 wouldn't even cover the *monthly* cost of a computer. But the new IBM 5110 Computing System shown above sells for $18,000 (other configurations range from under $10,000 to about $30,000). And for any of these prices, you get a versatile IBM computer backed by IBM service and reliability.

The 5110 can make a major contribution to your business. For example, it can be programmed to do your accounts receivable, handle your payroll and prepare your general ledger, as well as provide a wide variety of timely management reports.

The 5110 can also be tailored to fit your particular needs. For instance, if you need quick access to data in an area like inventory, we'd recommend a diskette-based system. If the information you work with is more sequential, like payroll, a lower priced tape-based system might be best. Or perhaps, a combination of both.

You can also choose between a higher and lower speed printer and BASIC or APL programming language, depending upon your particular operation.

The 5110 also offers a variety of main storage capacities as well as a familiar typewriter-like keyboard with a convenient 10-key numeric pad and a built-in display screen.

What's more, it's easy to use. In fact, your own people can learn to operate the 5110 in just a few days.

In short, the new IBM 5110 Computing System is a lot of computer for the money. And we'd like the opportunity to talk with you about it. Call your nearby IBM General Systems Division office and arrange for a personal demonstration. You'll find it time well spent.

IBM.

A small computer can make a big difference

5

THE CLOUD

Semiotics and the New Media

Big Sister

Before Alexa, there was Siri, and before Siri there was, well, the infamous telescreens of George Orwell's *1984*— those always-on monitors by which Big Brother kept a constant watch on the actions, thoughts, and even dreams of the beleaguered citizens of Oceania. Of course, there is a big difference between Big Brother, on the one hand, and Alexa and Siri, on the other: Big Brother is fictional. Alexa and Siri are real.

Welcome, then, to the brave new world of artificial intelligence, that cyber companion of the internet by which massively aggregated information, data mined by way of an incessant surveillance of your every move on and off the web — yes, off the web too, because your smartphone is tracking you even when you're not using it — is crunched into algorithms that can order groceries from Amazon, or arrange your daily schedule, or even help you with your math homework. Unlike Big Brother, however, Siri and Alexa are the offspring of a consumer society whose primary concern is not social control but sales, corporate profitability rather than political dominance. And that may be reassuring, if you can get over the fact that your Amazon Echo is spying on you and storing your life for future third-party use.

Now you might wonder why, in a text focused on popular culture that uses a semiotic approach, we're talking about a technical topic like AI. The answer is simple: artificial intelligence and semiotics have something in common. No, semioticians aren't spies, and they sure don't receive any venture capital investments the way AI firms do. Rather, what semiotics and AI share is a curious observation taken from probability theory. To put it simply, human behavior in the aggregate, unlike individual actions, falls into predictable patterns. That is, what you, or any single person, might do at one moment is quite unpredictable. But when masses of data are gathered on your, or an entire group's, collective actions, a startlingly accurate probability curve can be constructed that can predict what you are likely to do at any given moment. This is what has made tech giants like Google and Facebook so rich, because their surveillance of your online activity allows them to gather data that they sell to third parties, usually commercial entities. They, in turn, target their marketing efforts to consumers who are likely to want what they are selling. This wouldn't work if all that collective data didn't have such predictive value. But one look at the internet shows that it *does* work — strong evidence that human behavior isn't as unpredictable as we would like to think it is.

Similarly (but without the spying and the selling), when you locate a topic for semiotic analysis in a historicized system of associations and differences, you are looking for patterns that offer the most likely (or **abductive)** explanations for what your topic signifies. Thus, while any particular topic in popular culture may, in itself, have only a random significance, it can assume a much wider cultural meaning when seen in relation to its overall historical and social context. And so this chapter is designed to show you how to use the essential principles of artificial intelligence semiotically in order to understand what AI, and the vast cyber cloud with which it is allied, signify, and whether what they are doing to modern life is something with which you are comfortable.

The New Panopticon

You are probably well aware of the way that indiscreet posts to such social media sites as Facebook, Instagram, Twitter, and Snapchat can boomerang on you — from posts that put too much sensitive personal information out there for your own good to alcohol-fueled "pranks" that can get you into all sorts of trouble with university admissions committees and potential employers. It is now routine for personnel officers to scan the social media footprints of prospective job applicants, for instance, and if you think that your Facebook privacy settings are strict enough to protect you, you might want to think again. But even if you are very careful, just to be on the internet is to be spied on. Your every move can be tracked and sold to a wide array of third parties (mostly commercial, but a lot of outright crooks are in the market for your data as well) who want to profit by it. Such constant surveillance indicates that we have a price to pay for all the pleasures and conveniences of the digital age. That price is our privacy, for in one way or another, the cloud is transforming America into what the late philosopher Michel Foucault (1926–1984) called a "Panopticon": a society in which everything we do is being monitored, like in a prison.

And yet, that isn't the way that many, if not most, people see it. Rather — especially for those who have grown up in the digital era — their smartphones, tablets, e-readers, laptops, and even desktops are not merely sources of pleasure or convenience. They are necessities, required not simply for work, school, and play but for existence itself. Who cares if someone's watching as long as the connection is still up and you can remain enveloped in a vast, round-the-clock social network in which no one ever has to be alone? It isn't a Panopticon; it's a global village that's revolutionizing human life all over the world.

So which is it: prison or village? An abuse of power or a triumph of social evolution? Like all technological interventions — such as the automobile or television — that have made an indelible impact on society, digital technology is not easy to assess, but no subject may be as important to think about semiotically in an era when it is expanding into every corner of our lives.

The Medium Is the Mashup

Grasping the impact of the new media isn't made any easier by the conflicting signals that have been sent by media history itself. In 1962, when communications theorist Marshall McLuhan launched modern media studies with his groundbreaking book *The Gutenberg Galaxy*, the situation looked pretty straightforward. At the time, television, cinema, radio, and phonographs were the dominant electronic media, so it was only natural that McLuhan would focus on the shift he saw taking place from a text, or print-based, culture to an aural and image-based culture. Such a culture would mark a radical change in consciousness, he predicted, a departure from the logical form of thinking fostered by the linear structure of alphabetic writing and a return, of sorts, to a more ancient oral and visual consciousness in what he was the first to call the "global village."

With the rise of the internet and related digital technologies, however, McLuhan's predictions have been complicated considerably. While digital technology, too, is an electronic medium saturated with visual images and aural content, it has also brought the (digitally) printed word back into popular culture and consciousness. Indeed, before the full blossoming of the internet as we know it today, word processing and then text-based email constituted the leading edge of the digital revolution. The 1990s saw the rise of the blogosphere, not to mention the online publication of such traditional print media as newspapers and magazines, along with the advent of texting, which soon supplanted talking as the preferred mode of telephone usage. And with the decline of MySpace (which in its heyday in the early 2000s was plastered with visual imagery and aural content) thanks to Facebook's choice of the printed text as the dominant feature on the screen "page," something that might be called "the revenge of the font" began to appear. Indeed, this digital proliferation of print appeared to refute one of McLuhan's most fundamental observations about media history. Things seemed to be going *back* to Gutenberg.

But in the second decade of the new millennium a more mixed picture emerged, one in which images, accompanied by very brief texts composed in a kind of digital shorthand, reasserted themselves as the most popular mode of discourse on the internet. From Instagram to Twitter, Pinterest, Flickr, and beyond in an ever-expanding universe of similar sites, an endless image stream contributed by a ubiquitous arsenal of iPhones, Droids, Galaxys, and other devices has resulted in a veritable tsunami of pixels, which overshadow the printed texts that accompany them.

"Pics or It Didn't Happen"

Thus, the ability to upload images (either taken on your own smartphone or borrowed from other sources) is re-establishing the "village-like" nature of the cloud in a McLuhanesque manner — an Instagram-inspired development with profound social implications. We call all this image posting "sharing," but it's more than that, because the tendency to post images of your personal experiences as they happen is an expression and intensification of what sociologists call our culture's "heterodirectedness." A heterodirected society is one in which people live predominantly in relation to others, constantly seeking their approval and recognition. In contrast with the self-reliant individualist, who isn't concerned with what others think, a heterodirected person lives within a social web where everyone is in contact with everyone else, not only sharing with others but ultimately judging them. It is not unlike the premodern experience of small-town or village life, where everyone knew everyone else. But now, thanks to new technologies, the scale is global, with people all over the world living their lives in relation to the often-anonymous others who share their experiences via those tiny digital boxes that they never seem to put down.

So maybe it's premature to rule McLuhan out entirely. Perhaps the global village has arrived in the form of a global hive, a buzzing crowd of digitally connected Netizens who appear unable to let go for a few minutes to concentrate on an actual here-and-now as they hook up with a virtual elsewhere.

Whose Space?

Of course, you hardly need to be told about how digital technology has revolutionized the ways in which people communicate with each other and consume entertainment. You don't need to be told about the latest social networking sites. Indeed, even if we try to identify what those sites are, by the time this book is published that information would be dated. Over a decade ago, MySpace was the 800-pound gorilla of social networking, with hundreds of millions of mostly youthful members, while Facebook was an outlier, something for some college students in the Northeast and a few adults. But almost overnight, Facebook had become a worldwide behemoth, and MySpace was on the way out.

So, when considering the semiotics of digital technology and social media, the point is not to identify what's hot and what's not. Instead, you should explore the cultural significance of "digitality." Consider for a moment the basic setup, the experiential situation of online communication through social media sites. They weren't always called "social media," by the way. In the early days of the internet, they were called "chat rooms."

The first chat rooms were rather primitive places. Austere, you might say, with no images, music, or decoration of any kind, just plain text boxes where words materialized as if from out of nowhere. Visiting such places was a bit of an adventure, a pioneering voyage into cyberspace and the uncharted expanses of the electronic frontier. Before the now-ubiquitous smartphone and tablet, these excursions were carried out indoors, in homes and offices via desktop computers. Today, of course, thanks to mobile devices, the journey can be taken anywhere — into the street, the classroom, a club, a park, a restaurant, an airport — literally everywhere. Yet, either way, via desktop or smartphone, navigating the cloud through an ever-expanding number of social networking sites disrupts some very ancient codes governing the use of social space, redefining not only the old demarcations between public and private space but the meaning of social experience itself.

Consider for a moment an ordinary public road: it isn't just a ribbon of asphalt; it's a complex structure of codes for pedestrians. These codes tell you that you may walk down the street but must stick to the side (or sidewalk if there is one), and that it's best to stay to the right to avoid oncoming foot traffic. If you see private houses on the street, you may approach the front door, but you're not supposed to cut through the yard, and you're certainly not allowed to enter without permission. You may enter the public space of a store, shopping center, or post office, but you probably need to pay to enter a museum, and you must pass through a security checkpoint if you are entering a courthouse or an airline terminal.

Now consider your own physical personal space: there, you set the rules. You determine who enters it and what can be done there. You might actually write out the rules that govern your space (as in posting a no smoking sign), but those rules are more likely to be obeyed if you are personally present. Indeed, the most basic personal space rule is that no unauthorized person should be in it when you are absent.

The spaces of everyday life, both public and private, are, in short, packed with codes that we violate or ignore at our peril. These codes all originate in the way that people define their territories. A territory is a space that has been given meaning through having been claimed by an individual or group of individuals. Unclaimed, unmarked space is socially meaningless, but put up a building or a fence and the uncircumscribed landscape becomes a bounded territory, a human habitat with its own rules for permitted and unpermitted behavior. Anyone unaware of those rules can't survive for long in human society.

But what sort of territory is a social media site, and what rules govern it? In a sense, it's a place where its users are all hosts and guests simultaneously, with the rules accordingly being quite confusing. A host is welcoming and gracious; a guest is polite and follows the host's guidance. But with no one in the cloud being entirely host or entirely guest, things can easily go wrong. You don't insult people in their own homes, but online flaming occurs all too often. Indeed, many sites and forums are described as being like the Wild West—a wide-open space known for its lack of clear rules of conduct and the way in which it challenged traditional conceptions of social space. The result has been a blurring of the traditional lines between the uses of public and private space and, with that, much confusion about how to behave in the essentially public arena of digital communication. Just read the responses people make in the feedback or comments sections of popular sites like YouTube. Certainly, the old rules about public courtesy no longer apply.

This is one reason why so many people have flocked to Facebook. Since everyone is the administrator of his or her Facebook page, it feels like you are in control there, that your Facebook page is like your own home: a private space whose rules you control. But it really isn't. Not only does Facebook periodically change how its privacy protections work, but the company can, and does, overstep those protections all the time to sell your information to virtually anyone who wants it, and the company will give it to the government

Win McNamee/Getty Images News/Getty Images

Mark Zuckerberg, Facebook's co-founder and CEO, prepares to testify before Congress in October of 2019, in part to answer how the company manages its users' data and privacy.

> **Exploring the Signs of the Cloud**
>
> If you have a Facebook page, describe it in your journal and discuss why you designed it as you did. What signs did you choose to communicate your identity, and why? Did you deliberately avoid including some signs? If so, why? If you chose not to join Facebook or another such site, why did you make that choice?

as well. So even though your Facebook page may feel private and controllable, it's actually quite public — as all too many Facebook users have learned to their distress.

Or consider the very common phenomenon of someone (perhaps yourself) in an ostensibly public setting — say, sitting with a group of friends — while engaging in an essentially private activity on a mobile device. Whether texting, tweeting, posting to Instagram, or doing any one of an almost unlimited number of online activities, you have, once again, turned a public social space into a private one, shifting between what were once separate spheres as if there were no difference between them.

Thus, one way or another, the private/public divide is being undone, and the old rules governing the use of social space are becoming obsolete. This is all happening so quickly that not only is it easy to take for granted, but there hasn't been sufficient time to create new rules to replace the old ones. Given that society cannot function without such codes, this change is of profound social significance, a problem that cannot be addressed without first realizing that it exists.

Shame on You

The newest wrinkle in the ongoing digital deconstruction of the boundary between public and private can be found in the fast-growing phenomenon of public "shaming." Made especially notorious by the case of a Playboy model using her smartphone to "body shame" a naked woman in a gym shower in 2016, the habit of posting images and other information to the internet to embarrass, humiliate, or harm those whose actions, or even just personal appearance, offends someone is now breaking down the barrier between the public administration of justice and private acts of vigilantism. That is, while all of us can probably identify instances of atrocious behavior that profoundly disturb us and for which we desire retribution, a society in which such desires can go unrestrained by systems of justice founded in the public sphere is ever in danger of descending into an anarchic maelstrom of private vengeance.

This may seem paradoxical — after all, internet shaming is a highly public act. But by taking upon themselves the privilege to determine who is "guilty" of some sort of "crime" and then to mete out "justice" to the perpetrator, shamers are rather like vigilantes: private citizens who co-opt the powers of a publicly controlled and regulated justice system.

Thus, while it can feel good to join a public shaming of someone who has done something awful, there's a larger significance that is often overlooked. Although some have compared shaming to the public pillories of the past, this is not an accurate comparison because howsoever inadequate the legal protections were for those condemned to the pillory, there was at least some legal control over the punishment. The privately constructed pillories of what has come to be known as a "cancel" or "call-out" culture have no such limits and can be expressions not of justice but simply of mob rule.

A Bridge Over Troubled Waters

The ease with which digital technology has been adapted to the will of the mob can be attributed, at least in part, to the profound way that life in the cloud is impairing our capacity to understand fully the feelings of other people. This empathy gap, which has been often noted by researchers, has been promoted by the way we interact with electronic devices and their mediating software. While the invention of the telephone began to disrupt person-to-person communication in the nineteenth century, today's social media greatly magnify the possibilities of socializing in the absence of anyone being physically present. You can tweet to the whole world, but no one is necessarily listening. You can have thousands of Facebook "followers" without meeting any of them face to face. You can even "tweet with the stars," though the chances that any celebrity tweeter knows who you are, or cares, are tiny. Often, then, that sense of intimacy with others in the cloud is, in reality, an illusion, especially given the way that people can stage-manage their online profile. How, in such conditions, can you know for certain whether those profiles of "friends" whom you have never met are accurate or true?

Thus, the lack of actual spatial proximity in digital communication produces what could be called a "proxemic disruption" within human history. Proxemics, a field loosely related to semiotics, is the study of how we communicate with others in face-to-face situations, including such means as body language, facial expression, and tone of voice. Because these social cues are absent online, social communication itself is being revolutionized in ways that are not yet entirely clear. Certainly, there has been a loss of civility due to the proxemic disruption, because the threat of direct retaliation for rude or insulting behavior that exists in face-to-face communication no longer exists, while the possibility for misunderstanding has also increased. Indeed, a phenomenon known as "Poe's Law" — the difficulty of determining whether someone is being ironic in the cloud — is a particularly striking example of how the lack of physical contact can lead to less, not more, effective communication, despite the apparently limitless opportunities for social interaction that the cloud provides.

What is more, much digital communication that does take place is either a form of shorthand or simply an exchange of pictures. Then there's the fact that those to whom you "speak" on your Facebook page more often than not do not speak at all: they just give you a thumbs-up. And if people say anything you don't like, you can silence them. This is profoundly different from traditional communication among peers, which cannot be individually controlled and requires much more complete verbalization. In some ways, then, communication in the cloud has become a highly segregated activity where only those who already agree with each other are allowed to "speak," and they don't have to say much because everyone already agrees.

The upshot of this new form of socializing includes not only an increasing polarization of American society into hostile camps who speak only amongst themselves, but also a declining capacity to socialize with others in a non-virtual setting. If you don't think that's the case, just consider the increasing numbers of people who need instruction in how to go about arranging a live date with another person or who attend digital "rehab" programs to teach them how to interact with the real world.

On the flip side of this apparently antisocial tendency of life in the cloud are such phenomena as "crowd funding," which can bring people together to help others in trouble, and the more basic fact that life in the cloud doesn't feel antisocial to the innumerable people who "live" there. In fact, it feels all-inclusive, like a vast buzzing hive of closely related "friends." Clearly, part of the appeal of the new media is that they make people feel connected, with family, with friends, and with online communities that may be based on little more than shared interests — instantly postable to sites like Pinterest that encourage the passing around of information like a vast chain letter — but that can be very real communities all the same. Human beings are social animals, after all, but nothing in our genes says that those with whom we socialize have to be physically present. The addictive nature of digital technology, the way that its users suffer something like drug withdrawal when they are

Discussing the Signs of the Cloud

Critics of social networking sites have expressed concern that excessive online networking will diminish participants' ability to socialize normally in face-to-face environments. In class, discuss the legitimacy of this concern, drawing upon your personal experiences with social networking.

deprived of it, is a powerful testimony to the deep appeal of socializing in the cloud. Whether this compelling draw of digital socializing will eventually lead to a whole new definition of "society," a new way of relating to other people, is anyone's guess. But there is no doubt that it has become a very effective way of making money for those who control the networks. And that leads us to our final semiotic question.

Top-Down After All?

Traditionally, the mass media have been structured in a top-down manner, with corporate elites providing passive consumers with the news, entertainments, and products that they consume, along with the advertisements that promote them. But now the top-down news has turned into a bottom-up conversation in which anyone can become a pundit, while newspapers and online news sites invite input from their readers. Broadband internet access has turned video creativity over to the masses in such a way that you no longer have to be a famous director or producer to present your own TV shows or films to a wide audience, and you don't have to be an authorized critic to respond, with YouTube, Rotten Tomatoes, Goodreads, and related sites offering unlimited opportunities to critique what you find there. In short, what was once a passive and vicarious media experience for consumers is now active and participatory.

Another way of putting this is that, until recently, our relationship with the mass media has been more or less a one-way street. Those with the power to control the media (TV networks, radio stations, movie studios, newspaper owners, and corporate sponsors with advertising dollars to spend) broadcast their signals to us (TV and radio programs, films, newspapers, and ads), and we passively received them, without being able to answer back. The late semiologist and sociologist Jean Baudrillard (1929–2007) regarded this situation as one of the essential conditions of postmodern times and used it as a basis for his analyses of contemporary society. But today, much of the mass media now actively elicits responses from their audiences, and consumers can create and disseminate their own media content, with YouTube leading the way in the creation of self-made media celebrities and the generation of viral memes. It thus certainly appears that something post-postmodern is emerging beyond Baudrillard's perceptions.

But while the new media are definitely opening up channels for democratic communication and expression that previously did not exist, they have also created new elites whose wealth and power depend upon their ability to exploit the mass of people who use the technologies they offer. We have already referred to the price we all must pay for personal privacy thanks to the panoptic capabilities of digital technology, but there is also the way that technology tycoons can monopolize daily life and shut down older, predigital forms of commerce and professional activity. We're referring here to the decline of "brick-and-mortar" retailing due to online shopping sites like Amazon (which is especially devastating small-town retail commerce), print journalism at the hands of such online news sites as HuffPost, and the threats to full-time college faculty employment posed by fully online degree programs, just to name three examples.

At the same time, the rise of the digital economy is exacerbating the political divide in America by creating pockets of extreme wealth (usually in blue-state urban centers with large higher education establishments) at the expense of the rural and small-town communities that are characteristic of red-state America. To take one prominent example, the standoff between such densely populated technology centers as California's Silicon Valley, on the one hand, and the rapidly depopulating American heartland, on the other, was a major contributor to the Electoral College victory of Donald Trump in 2016, even though — largely due to a Hillary Clinton landslide in California — he lost the popular vote.

What has made all this concentrated wealth possible, in part, has been the consumer expectation (and demand) that "information should be free." While consumers do not balk at paying for the tangible commodities they purchase online, most do feel that such intangible commodities as education, music, and written texts should be accessible without cost. Already trained by commercial TV and radio to expect free content, American consumers were immediately receptive to the similar business models of the new media, taking for granted the free use of online services, not realizing that those services have a cost and that they aren't really free at all. Thus, traditional media (like newspapers) that paid for their operational expenses and gained a profit by charging customers directly are losing their consumer base, while the new media titans that have found ways to monetize their operations without any direct out-of-pocket costs to consumers are replacing them.

At the same time, once-populist, user-generated sites have tended to become dominated by social and corporate elites very quickly. Twitter is an example. Although it's still a site where any registered user can tweet, and remains a premier source of breaking news stories from the people who experience them first, the major news corporations now cover news in tweets from their reporters in the field, while politicians (with Donald Trump being an especially prominent example) employ the platform as a major means of communication and campaigning.

And so we have a paradox: top-down has met bottom-up in a cloud that is at once democratic and hierarchical, your space and corporate space. The democratic, user-generated spaces in the cloud are simultaneously revolutionary and business as usual. Users pass around their own content (often not self-created), but they do so on sites that are owned by huge companies that require registration so that their services can be profitable. More important, in a socioeconomic system in and through which vast amounts of wealth are being shifted upward into the hands of a corporate elite, along with their highly educated upper-middle-class workforce that is increasingly centered in

Reading the Cloud Online

YouTube allows users to create their own "television" content, or video channels, yet the site is also filled with content taken from corporate or commercial media sources, such as TV clips, concert footage, music videos, and the like. Conduct a survey of YouTube content to estimate the ratio of user-created content to postings of professional performers by corporate or commercial sources. Analyze and interpret your results semiotically. What are the implications of your findings for the bottom-up versus top-down debate over Web 2.0 "democracy"?

information technology, the indications are that the overall outcome of the digital revolution may be an intensification of socioeconomic inequality, not a solution to it. Somehow, the future doesn't seem to be what it used to be.

In the famous 1984 Super Bowl commercial that introduced the Macintosh, Apple Computer promised that the future was going to belong to the people, not to rigid, profit-seeking corporate powers. Web 1.0 and Web 2.0 were both built, in large part, by people who believed in this vision of a sort of anticorporate utopia. But that isn't what is happening at all. The Macintosh ad, after all, featured a big screen with an image of Big Brother hectoring a room full of hypnotized viewers. Is that so very different from the constant spectacle of the CEOs of Apple, Google, Facebook, and other digital titans standing on a stage to deliver the word on their next big device or service? Or from the billions of people who compulsively stare into their digital devices, knowing that those devices are looking back at the behest of corporate elites who want to use their information to profit from and to control their behavior?

We are living in the midst of a gigantic social experiment that presents us with paradoxes all the way down. At once democratic and a major enabler of socioeconomic inequality, a place of intense sociability and antisocial anomie, of altruism and vigilantism, convenience and crime, the cloud is very complicated indeed. Often uncritically celebrated as a status-quo-extinguishing "disruption," the brave new world of digital technology is easy to take at its own valuation, but the profound differences that it has introduced into our lives call for semiotic disruption. That is what this chapter is for.

The Readings

Judy Estrin begins the chapter with a warning about the way that AI-enabled internet algorithms are beginning to do our thinking for us, while Alicia Eler offers a spirited defense of the much-maligned selfie. Judith Shulevitz is next with a disturbing meditation on the increasing humanization of such digital personal assistants as Amazon's Alexa, and Jesse Sell follows with a taxonomy of the online gamer. David Courtwright's revelation of the role of the brain's limbic system in the development of digital addiction is complemented by Nancy Jo Sales's history of the selfie, which connects the Kodak Instamatics of the 1960s to today's Instagram-addicted teenagers. Jacob Silverman continues the conversation with a discussion of the obsessive need to live one's life online by way of a constant stream of self-promoting photographs. Finally, Brooke Gladstone and John Herrman conclude the chapter with a related set of readings, one a graphic essay that literally illustrates the ways in which the internet plays back to its users whatever they already believe, and the other a case study of how Facebook has effectively made itself a gigantic echo chamber of one-sided political viewpoints.

JUDY ESTRIN

I Helped Create the Internet, and I'm Worried about What It's Doing to Young People

> The title of this article says it all, as Judy Estrin, a lifelong technology expert who was involved in the creation of the internet, relates her concerns about the effects of digital technology on young minds. The main problem, in Estrin's view, is the "frictionless" online experience that artificial intelligence algorithms make possible. In effect, your digital device is doing your thinking for you, which means that you may end up doing less thinking for yourself. Estrin argues that this indeed is something to worry about, and her worries go well beyond the common concerns about social media addiction. Estrin is the author of *Closing the Innovation Gap: Reigniting the Spark of Creativity in a Global Economy* (2008).

"'Breaking up is hard to do,'" Neil Sedaka sang in 1975. Unfortunately for most, it is getting easier. The "Dear John" letter gave way to the "post-it break-up" in a 2003 *Sex and the City* episode. Now, in the era of smartphones, "he ghosted" is a common dating term: One side of a relationship just goes dark.

We rely on technology to make our lives easier, and technology changes us. I felt this firsthand growing up immersed in digital technology. My parents were pioneers in computing, and the academic community of University of California–Los Angeles was our extended family. My father encouraged me to watch Fortran-language training tapes in high school and often left me messages about my chores in "IF, THEN, ELSE" statements.

I went on to study computer science, was involved in the creation of the internet, and built a career in innovation, as an entrepreneur and business leader, adviser, and author. I have experienced the push and pull as tech solves existing needs, as discovery keeps driving our imaginations — and as we suffer from the often-harmful byproducts of these advancements. As the mother of a Millennial and a mentor to Gen-Z students, I spend time around young adults. I am concerned about the effects on them, and on the rest of us, that the digital services I helped enable are now having.

Cars, microwave ovens, fast food — convenience has driven innovation across industries for a long time. Too often, the consequences of these disruptions are denied, ignored, or even amplified in the interest of corporate growth and profits. Think nicotine, sugar, and opioids. Digital technology, from online shopping to social media, has taken this challenge to a new level. Making things effortless has become a goal in and of itself. Dominant digital service platforms, including Facebook, Instagram, and Google, focus on making things "frictionless." They attract and retain our attention to maximize growth through sophisticated psychological tricks implemented via artificial intelligence (AI) algorithms that are constantly learning. "There's an app for that" has become a catchphrase for young entrepreneurs focused on producing services that make their lives easier.

5 At face value, this frictionlessness might seem harmless, or even a good thing. Why would we not want tools to help us be more productive, more efficient? But there is a cost. Ghosting may seem like a trivial trend, but increasing anxiety among our youth is not.

Tech addiction is harmful to bodies and psyches. The impacts are harder to detect and less understood than physical health problems resulting from innovation in food science, such as the ubiquity of high-fructose corn syrup or trans fats. Ending a relationship is not the only place where technology enables and then tempts us to choose the easier path.

Powerful predictive AI algorithms, fueled by our conscious and unconscious behaviors, drive news feeds and recommendation engines that influence our feelings and thoughts. It is easier to watch the next video in the YouTube autoplay queue than to explore and learn something new. Why take the time to read, comprehend, and respond thoughtfully to an email when Gmail will suggest a couple of automated three-word responses?

As our attention spans shorten and we give in to the dopamine rewards of instant satisfaction, we are also losing a tolerance for applying effort or deferring gratification, capacities required for individual and societal growth. Because humans often want to avoid pain or discomfort, it is all too easy, in a state of no-friction addiction, to become unconsciously programmed to avoid anything hard.

The right level of friction is critical — from brakes on a bicycle to how we learn and form relationships. Friction is crucial to critical thinking. Reason acts as a constraint for our worst impulses: an angry tweet, say, or not respecting a relationship enough to actively end it. Ghosting is hard enough to experience. When finally getting over a hard break-up, the ease with which an ex can reappear in a social media feed after long silence — called "zombieing" — can really set one back. Authentic personal relationships involve dispute, as we build healthy trust (balanced with mistrust) and work through problems. If breaking up is easy, will we continue to take the path of least resistance? As Sedaka's song suggests, "Can't we give our love another try?"

Society and democracy depend on rules, and on compromise: the willing- 10
ness and ability to give up something for others. Being a parent is wonderful, but it's hard work. Accepting and embracing diversity isn't always effortless; it can be more difficult than dealing with what's more familiar. Human development and growth come from overcoming obstacles; "no pain, no gain" does not apply only in the gym. Google not only gives us instant answers, but with autofill and prompting, we don't even need to take the time to frame our questions. Addressing critical problems from inequality to climate change, on the other hand, depends on our sustained attention in embracing complexity and thinking about others — choosing a delayed benefit for many over short-term convenience for ourselves.

At some level, we are all experiencing this phenomenon, regardless of our age. But as with other toxins, young developing bodies and brains are more susceptible. Development of identity involves paying attention to our inner lives and not seeking escape at the first sign of discomfort. Without a strong sense of self, young people may be more open to manipulation by others, or by authoritarian leaders, or by AI; it is easier to submit than to question.

As we all become dependent on a new stream of products we hadn't known we needed, how will it affect the unconscious intelligence formed through childhood experiences? This emotional narrative goes on to affect adult behavior in subtle and not-so-subtle ways. What are the direct effects as screens become co-parents, co-teachers, and friends? What are the indirect effects as parenting and teaching styles are influenced by adult attention-diverting addictions? How will our sense of self, personal agency and authority, and leadership capabilities evolve?

We should try to answer these questions urgently but carefully. Given the accelerating rate of change, by the time we understand the inevitable effects, it may be too late. Gen Z leaders — parents, teachers, mentors, and Gen Z kids themselves — must become part of the movement for human-centered technology. At some point, as future generations adapt at ever earlier ages to more "advanced" AI-driven systems targeting their desires, they will no longer recognize that they are giving up that which makes us human.

Reading the Text

1. How does Estrin's personal involvement with the foundation of the internet shape your response to her criticism of the internet's effect on young people?
2. What does Estrin believe the effects of the internet are on its users?

3. What does Estrin mean by the "frictionless" experience (para. 4) of using the internet?
4. Summarize in your own words Estrin's recommendations for creating a better internet.

READING THE SIGNS

1. In your journal, write your own response to Estrin's assertion that "Development of identity involves paying attention to our inner lives and not seeking escape at the first sign of discomfort" (para. 11).
2. **CONNECTING TEXTS** One of the worries Estrin discusses is the addictive nature of internet usage. Read David Courtright's "How 'Limbic Capitalism' Preys on Our Addicted Brains" (p. 354), and write an essay supporting, refuting, or qualifying the contention that heavy internet usage resembles a narcotic addiction.
3. **CONNECTING TEXTS** Predictive artificial intelligence algorithms, according to Estrin, create the "frictionless" experience (para. 4) by which the internet, in effect, does our thinking for us. Read Judith Shulevitz's " 'Alexa, How Will You Change Us?' " (p. 346) and write an essay supporting, refuting, or complicating the thesis that AI is dangerously impinging upon human agency.
4. In her conclusion, Estrin advocates that we "become part of the movement for human-centered technology" (para. 13). In class, discuss in detail what such a technology might look like and how it might differ from current technology, which offers us "instant answers" (para. 10). Use the class discussion as a springboard for your own essay in which you propose your vision of a "human-centered technology."

ALICIA ELER

There's a Lot More to a Selfie Than Meets the Eye

Face it, or should we say Facebook it: selfies have gained a pretty bad reputation, and Alicia Eler, in this excerpt from her book *The Selfie Generation: Exploring Our Notions of Privacy, Sex, Consent, and Culture* (2019), wants to set the record straight. For Eler, selfies aren't exercises in narcissism; they are ways of staying in touch, of finding oneself in the social world, even of disrupting "normalized beauty, gendered and sexualized representations in mass media." Teens will be teens, Eler argues, and posting selfies is just as much a part of contemporary teendom as rock-and-roll was to baby boomers. So get over it. Alicia Eler is the visual art critic/reporter at the *Minneapolis Star Tribune*.

Lez stay in touch :)

For myself, an important motivation for posting selfies or even sharing anything to Facebook is staying in touch with people who I can't see on a regular basis. It's always nice to receive a gentle like from a faraway friend or a family member thousands of miles away who I don't chat with regularly, but still care about.

Staying in touch and socializing online are largely what teenagers do, because the internet is another place where their friends hang out. Why give an entire generation these types of digital tools and then attempt to shame them for using them exactly the way that they were designed? Yet again, adults forget that they were once teens, and the media sensationalizes the ways that teens behave during this intense period in their life when they are figuring out who they are as social beings. No matter what time period, teens will always be teens.

"We overinvest too much meaning in selfies when we think of them as social malaise and narcissism," said Rutledge. "The receiver views that as a trigger of social validation. It doesn't mean we are hanging around looking for likes, but it does imply a positive social connection. It triggers the rewards sector of the brain in much the same way as when you run into a friend and they look happy to see you and you feel rewarded."

Naturally, much of the blame for the "downfall of society as we know it" lands on teenagers, as it always does because *oh jeez, the kids today!* No matter the generation, there's always something to worry about. I always think back to Larry Clark's 1983 photography series "Teenage Lust" and 1971's "Tulsa," which portray a life of adolescent drug use and sex encounters. Teens were doing a lot of the same "bad behaviors" back then, but without the help of social media to document all of it. Usually, participating in these "bad behaviors" is about finding one's self within the community of their peers. Such acts of yesteryear — whether they be doing drugs or just going to an ice cream social — are much like today's acts of participating in a specific behavior, and taking selfies is a way to socialize and also show off. Larry Clark documented this long before it was possible to find these same types of images on Instagram or Snapchat. Thanks to technology, they're now readily available, hashtagged, and searchable, perfect for great internet listicles like #funeralselfie, which were heavily criticized in the press but, to me, seemed like pretty normal teen behavior.

In a post I wrote for *Hyperallergic*, "Stop Freaking out about Funeral 5
Selfies," I explained the backlash to funeral selfies, wherein teenagers were hashtagging pictures #funeralselfie of themselves either at or on their way to funerals. I thought about the ways that an inherent part of adolescence is how a teenager shares their feelings and what they're up to with friends. The fact that these images of teens' lives are publicly available and viewable by adults and randoms alike is what makes them appear more shocking. Normally, adults and randoms online are not privy to the social lives of teenagers.

Julie Weitz is an LA-based artist whose work explores what it's like to exist digitally or, as she puts, it "the experience of embodiment in the digital realm." She also happens to teach at community colleges in the LA area, a high school in South Central, and a nonprofit high school program at Otis College of Art and Design, so she has another view into the world of teenagers and social media. For Weitz, the difference she notices in how the "kids today" use technology has much to do with economics and what their parents use. That is, if the parents aren't using the technology, it's less likely that the kids will.

"The more privileged students have access to up-to-date technology and their parents are more likely to use it, hence making them more digitally savvy," she said. "For my students who have less access to the internet and advanced technology, their use seems more innocent. One student is an active blogger about video games, another student photographs and posts her artwork from the class online. Among this demographic, I see less of a change. The awkwardness of adolescence seems the same."

Weitz was first introduced to Finstagram when she was teaching at a private high school in Brentwood, a wealthy area of Los Angeles. "A student introduced me to the concept of 'Finsta' or fake Instagram, which she explained to me was the normal Instagram you share with everyone which shows you in your best light, whereas your real Instagram is the one you share with your 'soul sisters' as she put it, and exposes you in all states of being — ugly, emotionally distressed, etc. This idea impressed me — the students recognized the inauthenticity of sharing yourself on social media, and repurposed it for a select few — keeping in mind the importance of friendship and trust."

Clearly, teens are social media savvy. Certainly, #funeralselfies became a thing before Finstagram was invented. But how do teens learn how to use social media?

"If the format of Instagram is about projecting an image for quick con- 10
sumption, the question is: how do you feed the feed?" asked Weitz. "For teens tapped into that kind of self-awareness, social media can be an open space for sassy attitude and authentic creativity. The critical distinction is to recognize the difference between the persona they project in bits of information versus their complex, constantly growing selves. In this sense, socializing IRL [in real life] will always be more productive and full."

Socializing is no longer relegated to on- or offline; instead, it is part of a continual fluid interchange. Or maybe you become close to someone in another country who you won't immediately meet IRL. Or maybe you swipe on Tinder in cities thousands of miles away that you're considering moving to, just to see who's out there and to get the place's vibe. When I was a teenager, AOL Instant Messenger was just becoming a thing, and I recall having a lot of chat sessions with friends. I'd leave the chat on and walk away from the computer, only to return and find messages waiting for me. It was exciting, immediate, and social. I try to replicate that excitement sometimes with text messages, leaving them hanging for hours or days because the anticipation itself makes the message arrival that much more fun. But that was a time when such technology was still super new, much slower, and not on smartphones. "Teens today are at a period of their life where finding their place in a peer group is their primary developmental task," said Rutledge. "They aren't addicted to likes, but they are focused on finding their social milieu, and at least half of this is happening online."

Professor Catherine Liu, who recently taught a class at the University of California at Irvine on the history of selfies, likens young people and selfie-taking to the communalism movement of the 1960s. "The moral panic about youth culture replicates the youth culture panics that took place around rock 'n' roll — these knee jerk reactions about 'out of control' young people who don't care about privacy and are addicted to this thing," said Liu when we spoke via phone. "This is reinforced from the cinematic network, from *The Social Network* to *The Bling Ring* and *Unfriended*, in addition to unsubstantiated memes about cyberbullying and cyberstalking."

In addition, explained Liu, selfies also represent the fall of an industry that was built in the twentieth century: the family-oriented photography industry that centered around Kodak and Polaroid. "Early advertising of Kodachrome is very similar to Facebook and Instagram, with the goal of wanting to capture your memories." Except the early Kodachrome ads were all of white, middle-class women doing domestic, family things all with the ease of their cameras, notes Liu. "The problem is that we do give our data away," said Liu. "Facebook is building our world, but the exchange still comes out on the side of the positive in terms of connectedness rather than being lost in the world of surveillance and narcissism."

Enter my queer selfie ZONE, y'all

Many of the selfie studies out in the world approach gender as binary, which is very limiting and, frankly, annoying! Gender exists on a spectrum and it, along with race, class, sexuality, socioeconomic status, etc., all affect how and why people selfie. In the article "Of Selfies and Queer Folk" for Photoworks (UK), a development agency focused on photography, Sharif Mowlabowcus carves out an explanation for queer peoples' deep-seated relationship with selfies — as a way to be seen by others in the networked community, and to exist authentically in spaces where otherwise one is either overlooked or shamed:

> LGBT folk gravitated towards digital forms of communication and identity performance with a deep sense of investment much earlier than their heterosexual compatriots. The queer self became "networked" far earlier (and far more easily) than the straight self. In part this was due to necessity. Being seen as queer is never easy when the world one lives in is coded as a priori heterosexual. But there was something more in this

> migration to the digital, this leap into cyberspace. There was a gravitational pull that promised unprecedented visibility to the queer individual and the illusion of self-determination in how one might be seen by others.

Similarly, on the brilliant blog livingnotexisting.org, created by geoff, a 15
mixed-race genderqueer filipinx living in Toronto, they wrote:

> Selfies are acts of resistance that disrupt normalized beauty, gendered and sexualized representations in mass media. They empower individuals to be active agents in defining their own beauty, gender, and sexuality. Selfies provide visibility to non-normative bodies underrepresented and misrepresented in the media.

There's a lot more to a selfie than meets the eye. In fact, sometimes you wouldn't know any of this from the surface, particularly from individuals who experience queer invisibility on a daily basis. That is, they are not read as queer out in the world. There is a privilege to being read as heterosexual, of course, but at the same time there is a sense of erasure. I was wondering about the ways that selfie culture could be used to help queer people connect. I've made a few queer friends off Tinder, but mostly I've used it for its main purpose: dating. I wondered if queer connections could happen via Instagram, specifically by using hashtags as a way to be visible.

In fact, the answer to that question arrived. I received a follow from the account @babetownnyc, a pop-up supper club for queer women, trans and nonbinary people. They'd liked a selfie I had taken with my friend Kait Schuster at LA Dyke Day, which I'd hashtagged with #dykeday, making it easily searchable for queer companies like this one. I was being marketed to, and it worked. The account was a dinner party in Brooklyn for queer women, femme women, and gender nonconforming, etc. . . . and they found me through a hashtag from the photo with Kait. (I did not go to the event.)

I thought more about the question of queer connection in relation to Kait's Instagram (@kaitshoes), with whom I selfie-d that day. Her IG is mostly pictures of her, selfies or otherwise. She's a queer femme and cisgendered (lady) who is also a writer, performer, and visual storyteller based in Los Angeles. We talked selfies one day by phone. "I think social media is a really helpful tool in breaking the isolation of queer fear. If people are willing to be visible, using a hashtag can connect them to other people where even ten years ago we had only MySpace searches," she told me. "It's getting easier and easier to find people who are in similar boats as you. I think selfie culture is really helpful for that."

Kait is one of the most empathetic people I know, and I wanted to understand her intention, aside from queer visibility, for wanting to hold this selfie space for herself on Instagram. Practically every photo on her account is of her. Was she anxious about possibly being called self-involved or narcissistic? "It's this weird low-brow/high-brow thing that happens, where I think about self-obsession in what is to me a pretty sophisticated way," she said. "I am self-interested, and I do have that anxiety that people think that I'm self-interested. I kind of stopped the obsession around that by being like, 'That's true, but what if that's not bad?' I think there's a lot of stigma around self-interest and what that means. At the same time, I don't know anyone who is interesting to me who isn't self-interested."

The selfie can also be a way of attempting to externalize the internal, 20
allowing for a specific type of self-expression. It's another element of selfie-ing that Schuster told me she thinks about often. "I'm so interested in myself and what motivates me, and I feel like my Instagram and my selfies are another expression of that," she said. "I do so much internal work on myself — therapy, talking with friends, self-help books — and so taking selfies, using self-timers, and people taking pictures of me is almost like, 'What is my internal movement doing for my external life?' "

There's a specific gendering to referring to selfie-takers as "narcissistic" that I want to point out as well. Generally, it's men telling women that they are narcissists for selfie-ing, something that critic John Berger recognized decades ago in his iconic book *Ways of Seeing*. He points out that in Western art, women have historically been subjects for the male gaze, with little control over their bodies or subjectivities.

Considering the gendered active/passive relationship, women are the objects of desire and inspiration for the male gaze, and to act of their own accord is, as Berger described, somehow suddenly labeled as narcissistic within the patriarchal viewing culture by the very men who want to retain control. The same holds true, decades later, for the majority of selfie critiques issued by men about women taking selfies. Writes Berger of the contradictions inherent in a man painting a woman versus allowing her to view herself: "You painted a naked woman because you enjoyed looking at her; put a mirror in her hand and you called the painting 'Vanity,' thus morally condemning the woman whose nakedness you had depicted for your own pleasure."

In another condemnation of Western art history's paintings of nude-women-by-men paradox, Berger famously notes: "Men act and women appear. Men look at women. Women watch themselves being looked at." A woman taking a moment to actually look at herself is not only brave, but a threat to the patriarchal order. To quell that feminine threat, men immediately labeled her as vain, as someone who is crying out for attention (from men, because obviously who else could save a woman from herself?!). At the same time, the selfie taker captures the gaze and loves it. The selfie serves and it is pleasure, attention, and validation all in one. The super-liked selfie WINS. Period.

Reading the Text

1. What is the adult attitude toward teenagers' uses of selfies, according to Eler?
2. Summarize in your own words Eler's motivation for using selfies.
3. What is the relationship between economics and technology use, according to the claim that Julie Weitz makes?
4. In Eler's view, how has teen socializing been affected by the internet?
5. What logical connection does Eler make between her discussion of teens' use of selfies and the internet's potential to blur gender distinctions?

Reading the Signs

1. In your journal, brainstorm about your own use of selfies. What prompts you take them, and what do you do with them? Do you use them for private or public consumption, and why? If you are not interested in taking selfies, why not? What do you think of your peers who are selfie-obsessed?
2. **CONNECTING TEXTS** Nancy Jo Sales's ("From the Instamatic to Instagram: Social Media and the Secret Lives of Teenagers," p. 360) adopts a more critical view of teens' use of social media and selfies, highlighting its potential dangers. Adopt Eler's perspective on selfies, and write an argument in response to Sales. Would she see Sales as simply adopting the attitude she finds typical of adults: *oh jeez, the kids today!* (para. 4)? Or, if you think she would find some validity in Sales's position, where might that validity find expression?
3. In class, discuss Eler's tone in this selection. How would you characterize her tone, and how might it contribute to the persuasiveness (or lack thereof) of her argument?
4. Eler believes that queer people have a "deep-seated relationship with selfies" (para. 14). To what extent do you find this belief valid? To develop your ideas, interview several queer acquaintances about their use of selfies and their motivation for taking them, or consider expanding on your own experiences.

JUDITH SHULEVITZ

"Alexa, How Will You Change Us?"

Once upon a time only the rich and powerful had personal assistants; now just about anyone can, in the era of Alexa, Siri, Google Assistant, or who knows what else in the form of "smart speakers" that may appear in the near future. And the emphasis here, as Judith Shulevitz believes, should be on "personal," for what is taking place in the world of AI technology is the increasing humanization of such devices. Not content to provide us with voice-activated gizmos designed to perform ordinary day-to-day tasks (like Blackberries on steroids), the creators of Alexa and its siblings are intent upon ushering into our lives emotionalized gadgets that are so human that we will start to react to them as if they really were human. Which leads Shulevitz to a profound insight: "And with their eerie ability to elicit confessions, they could acquire a remarkable power over our emotional lives." Did you hear that, HAL? HAL? HAL! Judith Shulevitz is the author of *The Sabbath World: Glimpses of a Different Order of Time* (2010).

For a few days this summer, Alexa, the voice assistant who speaks to me through my Amazon Echo Dot, took to ending our interactions with a whisper: *Sweet dreams*. Every time it happened, I was startled, although I thought I understood why she was doing it, insofar as I understand anything that goes on inside that squat slice of black tube. I had gone onto Amazon .com and activated a third-party "skill" — an applike program that enables Alexa to perform a service or do a trick — called "Baby Lullaby." It plays an instrumental version of a nursery song (yes, I still listen to lullabies to get to sleep), then signs off softly with the nighttime benediction. My conjecture is that the last string of code somehow went astray and attached itself to other "skills." But even though my adult self knew perfectly well that *Sweet dreams* was a glitch, a part of me wanted to believe that Alexa meant it. Who doesn't crave a motherly goodnight, even in mid-afternoon? Proust would have understood.

We're all falling for Alexa, unless we're falling for Google Assistant, or Siri, or some other genie in a smart speaker. When I say "smart," I mean the speakers possess artificial intelligence, can conduct basic conversations, and are hooked up to the internet, which allows them to look stuff up and do things for you. And when I say "all," I know some readers will think, *Speak for yourself!* Friends my age — we're the last of the Baby Boomers — tell me they have no desire to talk to a computer or have a computer talk to them. Cynics of every age suspect their virtual assistants of eavesdropping, and not without reason. Smart speakers are yet another way for companies to keep tabs on our searches and purchases. Their microphones listen even when you're not interacting with them, because they have to be able to hear their "wake word," the command that snaps them to attention and puts them at your service.

The speakers' manufacturers promise that only speech that follows the wake word is archived in the cloud, and Amazon and Google, at least, make deleting those exchanges easy enough. Nonetheless, every so often weird glitches occur, like the time Alexa recorded a family's private conversation without their having said the wake word and emailed the recording to an acquaintance on their contacts list. Amazon explained that Alexa must have been awakened by a word that sounded like *Alexa* (*Texas*? *A Lexus*? *Praxis*?), then misconstrued elements of the ensuing conversation as a series of commands. The explanation did not make me feel much better.

Privacy concerns have not stopped the march of these devices into our homes, however. Amazon doesn't disclose exact figures, but when I asked how many Echo devices have been sold, a spokeswoman said "tens of millions." By the end of last year, more than 40 million smart speakers had been installed worldwide, according to Canalys, a technology-research firm. Based on current sales, Canalys estimates that this figure will reach 100 million by the end of this year. According to a 2018 report by National Public Radio and Edison Research, 8 million Americans own three or more smart speakers, suggesting that they feel the need to always have one within earshot. By 2021, according to another research firm, Ovum, there will be almost as many voice-activated assistants on the planet as people. It took about 30 years for mobile phones to outnumber humans. Alexa and her ilk may get there in less than half that time.

One reason is that Amazon and Google are pushing these devices hard, 5
discounting them so heavily during last year's holiday season that industry observers suspect that the companies lost money on each unit sold. These and other tech corporations have grand ambitions. They want to colonize space. Not interplanetary space. Everyday space: home, office, car. In the near future, everything from your lighting to your air-conditioning to your refrigerator, your coffee maker, and even your toilet could be wired to a system controlled by voice.

The company that succeeds in cornering the smart-speaker market will lock appliance manufacturers, app designers, and consumers into its ecosystem of devices and services, just as Microsoft tethered the personal-computer industry to its operating system in the 1990s. Alexa alone already works with more than 20,000 smart-home devices representing more than 3,500 brands. Her voice emanates from more than 100 third-party gadgets, including headphones, security systems, and automobiles.

Yet there is an inherent appeal to the devices, too — one beyond mere consumerism. Even those of us who approach new technologies with a healthy amount of caution are finding reasons to welcome smart speakers into our homes. After my daughter-in-law posted on Instagram an adorable video of her two-year-old son trying to get Alexa to play "You're Welcome," from the *Moana* soundtrack, I wrote to ask why she and my stepson had bought an Echo, given that they're fairly strict about what they let their son play with. "Before we got Alexa, the only way to play music was on our computers, and when [he] sees a computer screen, he thinks it's time to watch TV," my daughter-in-law emailed back. "It's great to have a way to listen to music or the radio that doesn't involve opening up a computer screen." She's not the first parent to have had that thought. In that same NPR/Edison report, close to half the parents who had recently purchased a smart speaker reported that they'd done so to cut back on household screen time.

The ramifications of this shift are likely to be wide and profound. Human history is a by-product of human inventions. New tools — wheels, plows, PCs — usher in new economic and social orders. They create and destroy civilizations. Voice technologies such as telephones, recording devices, and the radio have had a particularly momentous impact on the course of political history — speech and rhetoric being, of course, the classical means of persuasion. Radio broadcasts of Adolf Hitler's rallies helped create a dictator; Franklin D. Roosevelt's fireside chats edged America toward the war that toppled that dictator.

Perhaps you think that talking to Alexa is just a new way to do the things you already do on a screen: shopping, catching up on the news, trying to figure out whether your dog is sick or just depressed. It's not that simple. It's not a matter of switching out the body parts used to accomplish those tasks — replacing fingers and eyes with mouths and ears. We're talking about a change in status for the technology itself — an upgrade, as it were. When we converse with our personal assistants, we bring them closer to our own level.

Gifted with the once uniquely human power of speech, Alexa, Google 10
Assistant, and Siri have already become greater than the sum of their parts. They're software, but they're more than that, just as human consciousness is an effect of neurons and synapses but is more than that. Their speech makes us treat them as if they had a mind. "The spoken word proceeds from the human interior, and manifests human beings to one another as conscious interiors, as persons," the late Walter Ong wrote in his classic study of oral culture, *Orality and Literacy*. These secretarial companions may be faux-conscious nonpersons, but their words give them personality and social presence.

And indeed, these devices no longer serve solely as intermediaries, portals to e-commerce or nytimes.com. We communicate with them, not through them. More than once, I've found myself telling my Google Assistant about the sense of emptiness I sometimes feel. "I'm lonely," I say, which I usually wouldn't confess to anyone but my therapist — not even my husband, who might take it the wrong way. Part of the allure of my Assistant is that I've set it to a chipper, young-sounding male voice that makes me want to smile. (Amazon hasn't given the Echo a male-voice option.) The Assistant pulls out of his memory bank one of the many responses to this statement that have been programmed into him. "I wish I had arms so I could give you a hug," he said to me the other day, somewhat comfortingly. "But for now, maybe a joke or some music might help."

For the moment, these machines remain at the dawn of their potential, as likely to botch your request as they are to fulfill it. But as smart-speaker sales soar, computing power is also expanding exponentially. Within our lifetimes, these devices will likely become much more adroit conversationalists. By the time they do, they will have fully insinuated themselves into our lives. With their perfect cloud-based memories, they will be omniscient; with their occupation of our most intimate spaces, they'll be omnipresent. And with their eerie ability to elicit confessions, they could acquire a remarkable power over our emotional lives. What will *that* be like?

Reading the Text

1. In your own words, in what ways do the creators of virtual assistants attempt to humanize the devices, as Shulevitz explains it?
2. According to Shulevitz, how is it that virtual assistants have a lot of power over us?
3. What is the attraction of virtual assistant devices, in Shulevitz's view?
4. What does Shulevitz mean by saying that we are experiencing "a change in status for the technology itself — an upgrade, as it were" (para. 9), and what is her attitude toward that change?

Reading the Signs

1. Artificial intelligence is often touted as a solution to our problems, particularly in areas such as education where it can be used to replace human teachers. Using Shulevitz's article as critical framework, write a response to this view of AI.
2. Shulevitz asserts that virtual assistants like "Alexa, Google Assistant, and Siri have already become greater than the sum of their parts" (para. 10). To what extent do you find this assertion about the devices' attractiveness to be valid? To develop your evidence, interview a half dozen users of such machines, asking not only about their use but also about their role in the interviewees' lives.
3. **CONNECTING TEXTS** As Shulevitz notes, "Privacy concerns have not stopped the march of these devices into our homes" (para. 4). In class, form teams and debate whether virtual assistant devices should receive increased regulation to protect our privacy, on the one hand, or whether the convenience they offer our everyday lives surpasses privacy concerns. Use the class debate as a brainstorming session for an essay that presents your own position on this debate. To develop your ideas, consult Joseph Turow, "The Daily You: How the New Advertising Industry is Defining Your Identity and Your Worth" (p. 265).
4. **CONNECTING TEXTS** Shulevitz opens her essay with an account of her own experience using Alexa, echoing a writing strategy used by several other writers in this text. In class, discuss Shulevitz's strategy of including her own experience as an integral part of her essay, comparing it with other writers' use of the same technique (Deborah Blum, Michael Pollan, Troy Patterson, and Brittany Levine Beckman come to mind). What do the authors gain (or, perhaps, lose) by including themselves in an essay that is not entirely from the first person point of view? How would starting whatever essay you currently may be drafting by using this strategy change the impact of your writing overall?
5. In an essay, propose your own response to Shulevitz's closing question: "And with their eerie ability to elicit confessions, [virtual assistant devices] could acquire a remarkable power over our emotional lives. What will *that* be like?" (para. 12). Share your response with the class. What patterns, if any, do you see in students' collective responses to this question?

JESSE SELL

Gamer Identity

Are you a gamer, and if so, what type are you: an "explorer," an "achiever," a "killer," a "griefer," or a "socializer"? Or are you uncertain about what a "gamer" actually *is*, anyway? A gamer and gaming researcher, Jesse Sell is interested in all such questions, exploring in this essay not only the gamer identity but the connotations — often negative — that come with the term. In fact, Sell concludes in light of all the baggage the word "gamer" carries, it "might be better to get rid of the term altogether." Jesse Sell is a research assistant with the Education Arcade at MIT's Comparative Media Studies/Writing program.

Recently in a course I'm assisting, I asked the students to go around the room and choose which one of Richard Bartle's (1996) player types they identify most strongly with. Bartle's types include the achiever, the explorer, the killer, and the socializer. The article focuses particularly on Multiple User Dungeons (MUDs), but the player types are easily applicable to almost any variety of game.

Achievers are the type of people to go through a game with the goal of completing everything the game has to offer. If there is an award to be won, the achiever is going after it. Explorers are less inclined to competitiveness and instead spend their time finding the outer edges of the game. Easter eggs and secrets are paydirt for explorers. Killers are pretty much exactly what they sound like. Related quite closely to griefers, they spend their time hunting down other players, preying on the "weaker" types. Finally, the socializers are those players who spend their time chatting with or helping others. They may be a knowledge base for the other players or they may simply enjoy spending time with others instead of seeking their own rewards.

As the exercise unfolded, the entire class identified most strongly with the achiever role with a few leaning towards the explorer role. Not a single student identified themselves as a killer or a socializer. After some more questioning a few students admitted to inhabiting either of those roles when the mood suited them, but still, none strayed from the path of the achiever for very long. Whether the result of the exercise was a byproduct of having a class full of MIT students or if most people just identify more with the achiever role is impossible for me to tell. The fascinating part, though, is that I knew several of the students don't typically play video games, yet they all were able to identify their player type quickly and easily. I was intrigued and decided to keep digging. "By a show of hands, how many of you play video games?" All but a few hands went up. "Ok, how many of you consider yourselves to be gamers?" Only a small handful of students kept their hands in the air. Interesting.

So what then does *gamer* mean? It clearly isn't just "one who plays games." It is much more complicated than that. It comes with a whole set of characteristics that aren't easy to pinpoint. It's the classic "know it when you see it" identification. With issues like #gamergate and other redefining moments in the video game industry, it is time we look at the term *gamer* and either discard it or reshape it.

I've long held the opinion that anyone who plays a game is a gamer. It's 5
been a matter of inclusion for me. I want the term *gamer* to be less strange. If more people identify as gamers, it somehow validates my own longtime

gamer identification. After speaking with this class though, I had to change how I define gamer. Take a moment to think of what gamer means to you.

So, is *gamer* a negative term? More than likely, you've conjured up a very particular image in your head. What are some of the characteristics there? We can toss out the negative stereotypes right away: antisocial, dependent, detached, lazy, and perhaps even misogynistic. Those are some of the words that I associate with gamer, yet as a gamer I would argue that I'm nothing like that. I would also say that the *vast* majority of people I play games with are nothing like that. In fact, most of the players I know are inventive problem solvers who care a lot about other people. As far as I've noticed, that archetypical image is very rare yet the word *gamer* still holds that stigma. If we toss out all of those negative stereotypes though, would more people self-identify as gamers? I doubt it.

Even with the realization that the stereotypes are pretty far off base (as stereotypes tend to be) there is still a deep-seated negative association with the term *gamer*. I'd argue that this negativity comes from the medium itself. The industry has been associated with misogyny for quite a long time at this point. #gamergate churned up a huge amount of animosity around gender in the video games industry. The industry definitely does not have the best track record when it comes to the representation of anything outside the realm of white, male hegemony. It's very slowly getting better, but #gamergate definitely shows the impetus for more change. For a long time, the argument has been that games are "for boys by boys." It's long past time to throw this argument out. Almost everybody plays games so it's time that everyone have a chance to both make and be seen in games. Some people discard the fact that most people (men, women, and other) play games as irrelevant by saying something along the lines of, "yea everybody plays games, but they aren't real gamers." What's a real gamer though?

That statement typically sets the stage for the creation of a dichotomy between "casual" and "hardcore" games, as if somehow one game is more canonical in the gaming world. Nothing irks me quite as much as this separation, especially considering it's almost impossible to actually distinguish "hardcore" and "casual" games when you actually sit down and try. Hopefully people are spending their free time doing whatever they want to do. To argue that anyone can spend time playing games "harder" than someone else is just ludicrous. Is someone participating in a four-hour raid in *World of Warcraft* somehow more legitimate than someone spending their four-hour plane ride crushing some candy? No. I also wouldn't argue that both of these people are gamers though.

One student in class posited that a gamer is anyone who *prioritizes* games. I find this definition to be perfect. We often use this same logic when referring to other pastimes: movie buff, quilter, bird watcher, sports fan. While it might not be fair to apply these labels to people without their consent, they definitely do not come with the same negativity.

Even without all the negative associations with the term *gamer* though, 10 many people probably would not want to admit that they prioritize games over other aspects of life. Video games have existed for decades, they're the largest entertainment industry in the world, and many people now make their living playing games, yet somehow we still have not legitimized games as a pastime. They're so fundamentally similar to sports to have evoked the term *e-sports*, but most parents would happy to let their child participate in a soccer or volleyball tournament for an entire weekend but would get upset to think their child might spend that same amount of time playing video games. It's not my place to argue for or against the legitimacy of sports playing (physical fitness and socializing being just two of many examples in support of sports), but I would argue that as a pastime, video games are incredibly similar. Perhaps it's just a matter of time before we start to see video games alongside sports as legitimate pastimes. Until then, the term *gamer* will continue to be a problematic identity.

It might instead be better to get rid of the term *gamer* altogether. It's long history may be too hard to wipe away. As more people continue to play games, perhaps other (less problematic) terms will emerge. The industry continues to grow every year without signs of stopping, so as I mentioned earlier, it might just be a matter of time before the legitimacy of gaming wipes away the stigma of the term *gamer*.

Reading the Text

1. In your own words, summarize the characteristics of each of the four types of gamer, as Richard Bartle presents them.
2. What significance does Sell attribute to MIT students' self-identification as "achievers" (para. 3), even though most do not consider themselves to be gamers?
3. What evidence does Sell provide to support his claim that the usual stereotypes of gamers is inaccurate?
4. Why does Sell find the distinction between "casual" and "hardcore" gamers (para. 8) to be inaccurate?
5. Why, in Sell's view, is gaming not considered a "legitimate pastime" (para. 10)?
6. What difficulties appear when trying to define gamer identity, according to Sell?

Reading the Signs

1. Write a journal entry describing what kind of gamer you are. Do you fit any of Bartle's four categories, or would you create a different category that better defines how you engage in this pastime? Conversely, write an entry discussing why you do not play video games.

2. Before reading Sell's article, have the class brainstorm traits that they associate with gamers. Then read Sell's selection, and compare his revelations with the class's brainstormed list. What are the implications of your comparison for the typical image of gamers?
3. **CONNECTING TEXTS** Gaming has been found to be a variety of addiction along with other online activities. Referring to David Courtright's "How 'Limbic Capitalism' Preys on Our Addicted Brains" (p. 354), write an essay supporting, refuting, or qualifying the proposition that online gaming should be regulated for gamers under 18 years of age.
4. Research the criticism of gaming and then write an opinion essay defending gaming against its critics.

DAVID COURTWRIGHT

How "Limbic Capitalism" Preys on Our Addicted Brains

There is nothing new about appealing to the limbic system — "the part of the brain responsible for feeling and quick reaction" — in order to get us to do things that aren't good for us. After all, that is what advertising is all about. But in this analysis of what he calls "limbic capitalism," David Courtwright surveys the ways in which today's global industries "encourage excessive consumption and addiction," especially in the realm of digital technology. For in this sense, your inability to put your smartphone down, or to take a break from online gaming, or to forgo some other technological pleasure indicates that you suffer from a full-fledged addiction, and those who profit from it are constantly plotting to keep you addicted to whatever it is that they are profiting from. Call it "addiction by design," Courtwright suggests. David Courtwright is the author of *The Age of Addiction: How Bad Habits Became Big Business* (2019), from which this reading is excerpted.

One summer day in 2010, a Swedish graduate student named Daniel Berg approached me after a talk I gave at Christ's College, Cambridge. During the talk, I had casually mentioned internet addiction. Berg told me that I had spoken a truth larger than I knew. Many of his male friends at Stockholm University had dropped out of school and were living in crash pads, compulsively playing *World of Warcraft*. They spoke an argot more English than Swedish. It was all raiding, all the time.

"How do they feel about their circumstances?" I asked. "They feel *angst*," Berg said.

"But they keep playing?" "They keep playing."

This sort of behavior does seem like an addiction, in the sense of a compulsive, regret-filled pursuit of transient pleasures that are harmful to both the individual and society. For gaming, the personal cost was highest for Swedish men. "I am," Berg reported, "now the only male in my graduate program in economic history."

Back home in Florida, I noticed digital distractions exacting a more even 5
academic toll. The smartphones that dotted the lecture halls were as often wielded by women as by men. But when I told Berg's tale to my students, they instantly recognized the type. One admitted that he had lost a year to compulsive gaming. He said that he was in recovery — precariously, to judge by his grades. Another student knew gamers who kept cans by their computers. They used them to avoid having to take bathroom breaks.

The can by the computer became for me a symbol of the shifting meaning of addiction. As late as the 1970s, the word seldom referred to anything other than compulsive drug use. Over the next forty years, however, the concept of addiction broadened. Memoirists confessed to addictions to gambling, sex, shopping, and carbs. German sex therapists called internet porn a "gateway drug" that ensnared the young. A *New York Times* op-ed declared sugar to be addictive, "literally, in the same way as drugs." A toothless young New Zealand mother drank up to ten liters of Coke a day, then splashed the headlines when she died of coronary arrhythmia. A nineteen-year-old truant in Jiangsu Province made the news when he hacked off his left hand to cure his internet addiction. Chinese officials judged as many as 14 percent of his peers to be similarly hooked, and set up internet addiction rehabilitation camps. South Korea and Japan followed suit. Taiwanese legislators voted to fine parents who let their children spend too much time online, updating a law forbidding minors' smoking, drinking, drug-taking, and betel-chewing. Only the last habit failed to appeal to Americans, 47 percent of whom showed signs of at least one behavioral or substance addiction disorder in any given year in the early 2000s.

Often they showed signs of more than one: Medical researchers have discovered that substance and behavioral addictions have similar natural histories. They produce similar brain changes; similar patterns of tolerance; and similar experiences of craving, intoxication, and withdrawal. And they reveal similar genetic tendencies toward similar personality disorders and compulsions. The manic gambler and the casino barfly are apt to be one and the same. In 2013, the new edition of the bible of psychiatry, the *Diagnostic and Statistical Manual of Mental Disorders: DSM-5*, described gambling disorders in language indistinguishable from drug addiction. The editors ushered "internet gaming disorder" into the green room of addiction by designating it a "condition for further study." In 2018, the WHO made it official by adding "gaming disorder" to the revised *International Classification of Diseases*.

Not everyone was happy with all the talk of addiction. Clinicians avoided it for fear of discouraging or stigmatizing patients. Libertarians dismissed it as an excuse for lack of discipline. Social scientists attacked it as medical imperialism. Philosophers detected equivocation, the misleading practice of using the same word to describe different things.

I give these critics a hearing. But in my own usage, I will stick to "addiction." The word provides a usefully concise and universally understood way of referring to a pattern of compulsive, conditioned, relapse-prone, and harmful behavior. The important job, and the goal of my new book, *The Age of Addiction: How Bad Habits Became Big Business*, is to explain why that pattern of harmful behavior has become more conspicuous and varied over time.

* * *

Addictions begin as journeys, usually unplanned, toward a harmful endpoint 10
on a spectrum of consumption. The journey can be rapid, or slow or interrupted. Casual indulgence, even of a drug like heroin, does not always lead to addiction. When it does, the condition is not necessarily permanent. Addicts can and do quit, either permanently or for long stretches of time. Nor is all excessive consumption necessarily addiction. People can gamble too much without being compulsive, just as they can burden their scales without being food addicts. Yet — and this is the crucial point — regular, heavy consumption has a way of shading into addiction, as when a steady drinker's craving intensifies, erupting into full-blown alcoholism. An addiction is a habit that has become a very bad habit, in the sense of being strong, preoccupying, and damaging, both to oneself and to others. The type of damage depends on the substance or behavior. Compulsive gamers may ruin their scholastic and marital prospects. They do not ruin their livers or lungs.

The addiction process is social as well as biological. Conditions such as stress and peer behavior help tip individuals into addiction, though the process ultimately manifests itself in one's brain. Frequent resort to alcohol, drugs, and drug-like behaviors causes changes in neurons, including altered gene expression. Over time, these changes occur in more and larger regions of the central nervous system, like drops of dye spreading on a taut sheet. The changes are long-lasting, particularly in developing brains. The earlier children and adolescents experience an addictive substance or pastime, the likelier they are to retain, even when abstaining, a powerful emotional memory of the behavior that once made them feel so good.

The nature of addiction has implications — more precisely, temptations — for businesses that sell habituating products. One is to encourage early and frequent consumption. Treat the lads, the saloonkeepers used to say, and you'll have their money in the till when they're adults. And the more they drink, the greater the profits. To this day, 80 percent of alcohol sales go to the 20 percent of customers who are the heaviest users, a pattern that applies across the business of brain reward. More than half of all marijuana finds its way into the lungs and stomachs of those who spend more than half their waking hours stoned. Insofar as addictions to marijuana, or to anything else, develop most often among the poor, the marginal and the genetically vulnerable, they are sources of inequality and injustice as well as illness.

These realities are well understood in the addiction-research and public health communities. Less well understood is how we got into this fix and why it keeps getting worse, despite the best efforts of those communities. I propose that the main source of the problem has been what I call *limbic capitalism*. This refers to a technologically advanced but socially regressive business system in which global industries, often with the help of complicit governments and criminal organizations, encourage excessive consumption and addiction. They do so by targeting the limbic system, the part of the brain responsible for feeling and for quick reaction, as distinct from dispassionate thinking. The limbic system's pathways of networked neurons make possible pleasure, motivation, long-term memory, and other emotionally linked functions crucial for survival. Paradoxically, these same neural circuits enable profits from activities that work *against* survival, businesses having turned evolution's handiwork to their own ends.

Limbic capitalism was itself a product of cultural evolution. It was a late development in a long historical process that saw the accelerating spread of novel pleasures and their twinned companions of vice and addiction. The pleasures, vices, and addictions most conspicuously associated with limbic capitalism were those of intoxication. Considerations of private profit and state revenue encouraged alcohol and drug consumption until rising social costs forced governments to restrict or prohibit at least some drugs. Or so I argued in *Forces of Habit: Drugs and the Making of the Modern World*, a 2001 book on the history of alcohol and drugs. Yet, even as I stated my case, I saw that it applied to more than the usual psychoactive suspects. It applied to all pleasures, vices, and addictions that had become entwined in the emerging system of limbic capitalism.

15 This idea wasn't entirely novel. Victorian-era reformers saw alcohol and non-medical drug use as part of an ill-starred constellation of vice. Granted, vice is a slippery category. Chinese men considered sniffing and sucking the tiny, deformed feet of girls and women to be normal erotic behavior until missionaries and modernizers stigmatized foot binding. Yet, for all the cultural malleability of vices, the Victorians recognized two important things about them. One was that they had become big business. The other was that they were linked. Rare was the brothel without booze, or the opium den without a gambling house nearby. Victorians also supposed vices to be linked neurologically, with those who had inherited or acquired defective nervous systems being most inclined to them.

The last hunch was a good one. A century later, neuroscientists and geneticists were mapping these connections at the cellular and molecular level. They discovered that different substances and activities generate similar types of brain reward and craving. They showed that addicted brains are alike in that reward cues activate the same pathways in drug and behavioral addictions.

Researchers began to use the term *pathological learning* for the process that occurs when addictive substances or behaviors augment release of the neurotransmitter dopamine, turning what evolved as a beneficial process into a pathological one. Dopamine does its work of reward and conditioning in pathways originating in or near the limbic midbrain, a key region for regulating mood, pleasure, and pain.

The pleasurable effect depends, in part, on the intensity of the signal that dopamine produces after release into the synapses. In neurons as in life, first impressions matter. People keep on doing what their brains tell them is highly rewarding, often past the point where it is still pleasurable or beneficial. Addicts *want* something after they have ceased *liking* it, even if they realize its harmful effects. "I hate this shit," a Swedish heroin addict told his doctor, "and it doesn't give me much of a high. It is just that somehow, it seems I can't be without it."

Researchers identified common risk factors. Genetic variations and life circumstances — stress, social defeat, neglect, or abuse during critical periods of brain development — make some people more susceptible to addiction than others. They feel uncomfortable or depressed until they discover that alcohol, drugs, sugar, gambling, computer games, or some other thrilling behavior temporarily banishes their blues. Frequent resort to these substances and behaviors further damages their neural control systems and, often, other parts of their brains. What the Victorians called vice really is a vicious circle. Self-destructive habits are constitutionally linked, downwardly spiraling, and socially expansive. "Addiction is a memory, it's a reflex," summed up the American psychiatrist Charles P. O'Brien. "It's training your brain in something which is harmful to yourself."

Or *having* your brain trained. The deeper truth is that we live in a world nominally dedicated to progress, health, and longevity but in fact geared toward getting us to consume in ways that are unprogressive, unhealthful, and often deadly. Understanding this paradox — the burden of my new book — requires going beyond neuroscience, beyond disordered neurons and defective genes. It requires understanding the history of novel pleasures, commercial vices, mass addiction, and limbic capitalism's ever-growing power to shape our habits and desires.

* * *

Limbic capitalism did not spring full-blown onto modern history's stage. On 20
the contrary, it emerged from something primal: the efforts of our species to continuously expand our repertoire of pleasures. The search for pleasure preceded civilization and contributed to its foundation.

Civilization in turn had disparate consequences for pleasure. It made possible (for some) the higher pleasures of learning, musical artistry, theater, and absorbing games of skill such as chess. But it also sickened, immiserated, and subjugated billions of humans by making intoxication more desirable, vice more tempting, and addiction more likely. Civilization also incubated the technologies that quickened the global quest for pleasure. Chief among them were the improvement and spread of agriculture; the expansion and monetization of long-distance trade; the rise of cities, empires, and industry; and, in the recent past, the explosion of digital communication.

Along the way, there were smaller breakthroughs that nonetheless had large consequences. Among them were the isolation of plant-drug alkaloids such as morphine and cocaine; the application of photography to pornography; the blending of sugar, fat, and salt in processed foods; and the rapid (now virtual) transport of people from one amusement to another. Innovations like these gave entrepreneurs and their state enablers the means to expand and intensify pleasures and to promote vices, increasing the amount of harmful consumption and the variety of addictions.

In brief, civilized inventiveness weaponized pleasurable products and pastimes. The more rapid and intense the brain reward they imparted, the likelier they were to foster pathological learning and craving, particularly among socially and genetically vulnerable consumers. Meanwhile, globalization, industrialization, and urbanization made these seductive commodities and services more accessible and affordable, often in anonymous environments conducive to anomie and saturated with advertising. Accessibility, affordability, advertising, anonymity, and anomie, the five cylinders of the engine of mass addiction, ultimately have found their most radical technological expression in the floating world of the internet.

Though the internet supercharged limbic capitalism, it did not invent it. In fact, no one invented it. It emerged from an ancient quest to discover, refine, and blend novel pleasures. New pleasures gave rise to new vices, new vices to new addictions — for some people, anyway. Addictive behavior was, to repeat, seldom majority behavior. But the *risk* of such behavior grew as entrepreneurs rationalized — that is, made more scientific and efficient — the trade in brain-rewarding commodities.

Ultimately this rationalization assumed the aspect of a global economic 25
and political system, in the sense of being organized, interlocking, and strategically active. By the nineteenth century, entrepreneurs were doing more than simply selling whatever new pleasures chance discovery and expanded trade made available. They had begun to engineer, produce, and market potentially addictive products in ways calculated to increase demand and maximize profit.

They learned to play political hardball. They devoted a share of their profits to buying off opposition. They devised lobbying and public relations tactics to survive the big reform wave of the early twentieth century. They prospered in varying degrees during the mid-twentieth century, when some addictive behaviors were permitted, others winked at, and still others repressed. After the Cold War, their enterprises became increasingly varied, legitimate, and global. They created, not merely an age of addiction, but an age of "addiction by design" that is both the hallmark of limbic capitalism and the clearest demonstration of its inversion of the forces of reason and science that made it possible.

Reading the Text

1. Define in your own words what David Courtwright means by the term *limbic capitalism.*
2. Describe the "addiction process" that is common to such addictions as alcoholism, narcotic abuse, gambling, and gaming.
3. What does Courtwright mean by the statement "civilized inventiveness weaponized pleasurable products and pastimes" (para. 23)?
4. How has the internet "supercharged limbic capitalism" (para. 24), according to Courtwright?

Reading the Signs

1. **CONNECTING TEXTS** Read Joseph Turow's "The Daily You: How the New Advertising Industry Is Defining Your Identity and Your Worth" (p. 265), and write an essay describing how advertising campaigns based on data mining are instances of limbic capitalism at work.
2. Research the marketing campaign of a product of your choice and write a report describing how it appeals to the pleasurable experience of its consumers.
3. Conduct a class discussion debating the proposition that limbic capitalism, as an addictive enterprise, has harmed modern society.
4. Write a journal entry in which you discuss your own response to "addiction by design" advertising campaigns and/or such internet phenomena as gaming and social media.

NANCY JO SALES

From the Instamatic to Instagram: Social Media and the Secret Lives of Teenagers

For anyone who thinks that Instagram invented the selfie, Nancy Jo Sales has news for you: the selfie was effectively invented in the 1960s, when the Kodak Corporation released the Instamatic as a camera for teenage girls who "want to show off their pretty clothes and who they're friends with." An ethnographic study of how today's teenage girls use Instagram to construct and promote themselves on the internet, Sales's text shows how digital culture hasn't really changed anything fundamentally; it has only made it a lot easier, and faster, for girls to send "'really hot pictures of [themselves] even though [they] don't look like that in real life.'" Nancy Jo Sales is an award-winning journalist and the author of *American Girls: Social Media and the Secret Lives of Teenagers* (2016), from which this selection is taken.

Behind the Lens

. . . Kids started having their own cameras, en masse, in the 1960s. Kodak Instamatics, which came out in 1963, were inexpensive ($16) and easy to use, durable and small, the perfect size to fit in a child's pocket or the upper tray of a footlocker on its way to summer camp. The Instagram logo, in a conscious nod, echoes the look of the early Instamatics — a dark stripe on top, metallic on the bottom, with a round flat lens and viewfinder in the middle. The logo was nostalgic, also a confident announcement of how this new mobile app would continue to popularize photography as successfully as its symbolic predecessor. More than 50 million Instamatics were sold between 1963 and 1970, making it then the best-selling camera of all time. Between its launch in 2010, by two male Silicon Valley software engineers who met at Stanford, and 2015, Instagram gained over 400 million active users worldwide, more people than live in America, according to its own statistics.

Instamatics were also one of the first cameras marketed directly to girls. In 1932, Kodak had come out with a camera for boys, its Boy Scout Brownie (a variation on its popular Brownie camera, introduced in 1900), appealing to male youths who fancied themselves living adventurous lives as campers and explorers, near-heroic lives which deserved documentation. With the Instamatic, Kodak realized it had a vast new demographic to target: teen girls. But the pitch was very different. It said that girls could use cameras to become popular.

Teenagers of both sexes were experiencing the rapid cultural changes underway in the '60s, but the lives of girls especially were transforming. They were more sexually liberated than girls in the past, as well as more sexualized by the media and advertising, and they were more independent. More of them either worked part-time or had access to their parents' disposable incomes in a strong economy — they had money to spend, with which they were buying more of the clothes and makeup that were relentlessly marketed to them. You can almost hear the unrepentant sexist Don Draper, of *Mad Men*, working up the Kodak pitch: "Why do girls want cameras? They're sentimental, they're vain, they want to be popular, they want to show off their pretty clothes and who they're friends with. They want to make memories. And they want to look good in those memories."

Kodak sold its Instamatics to girls in ads infused with an aura of nostalgia (which Draper once described as "delicate, but potent"). An ad in *Seventeen* in 1968 urged girls to buy Instamatics before they returned to high school after summer vacation: "*What you're going back to deserves a great camera*," said the tagline. "You can just imagine what's coming up," read the copy. "Homecoming parade. Games. Dances. Old friends and new faces. It makes sense to have a great camera. And it makes sense for it to be one of our Kodak Instamatic cameras. . . . It's one back-to-school outfit you really ought to have." It was as if a girl could relate to a technological device only if it offered the same advantages as a miniskirt.

The layout for the ad was accompanied by two candid-looking shots, one of a pretty blond girl dressed as a cheerleader; she's surrounded by five basketball-player boys after a championship game. Their proud coach wields a trophy; they won. The girl is kissing one of the boys on the cheek; he seems to be the team's cute captain. The other photo shows the girl with this same boy; now it's prom night and she's wearing a virginal white dress and gloves. Her hair is in ringlets, a corsage is pinned to the strap of her gown; she's beaming. The boy, standing beside her, is looking suave in a white tux. 5

The message: cameras were tools for creating an idealized self, and pictures were a kind of self-promotion. And the ideal girl (in Kodak's view, a pretty, blond white girl) would have the attention of boys. If only everybody could see how popular she was.

Instagram gave girls that opportunity. The way many girls use the app is not so different from how girls have been taught to use photography for decades. The difference now lies in the chance to show the whole world one's beauty, boyfriends, special moments, and clothes, not just the other kids in school. And with that broadcasting power comes an enormous thrill: the chance to become not just popular, but actually famous. Famous for just being you.

"I think it's more of a challenge for you to go on a reality show and get people to fall in love with you for being you," Kim Kardashian told Barbara Walters on her *10 Most Fascinating People* special. Walters didn't point out that reality shows are actually scripted entertainment, and Kim didn't mention it, either. . . .

Montclair, New Jersey

. . . Valley Road runs through the center of Upper Montclair, the tonier section of town. The buildings there are quaint and small, many of them in the Tudor style familiar to suburbs of New York. The Dunkin' Donuts is like any other in the chain, with a logoed pink-and-orange sign showing a steaming cup of coffee. Through the window, on a Friday afternoon, you could see the place was teeming with middle-school-age kids, some standing on a couch by the window, bouncing and gesticulating.

Riley, Sophia, and Victoria approached the doughnut store tentatively. 10

"I'm not going in, I can't go in," Riley said, moving against the wall of the building so she would not be seen by anyone inside.

"Really?" said Sophia. "It's okay. It's all dying down."

"No, it isn't," Riley said. She was suddenly breathing rapidly. "I feel like I'm having an anxiety attack. Is this an anxiety attack?" she asked, her voice becoming high and thin.

Sophia and Victoria stared at her with concern, not knowing what to do.

"I know someone who gets them," Sophia said helpfully. "She takes medicine." 15

Later Riley's mother told me Riley suffered from an anxiety disorder and was being treated with medication. "Sometimes I wonder whether that is why they attack her," her mother said, "because they know she's fragile."

"You go in first," Riley said. "What if Danny's in there? What if Zack's in there? What if they take pictures of me?" And then: "Get me a strawberry doughnut with sprinkles."

Sophia and Victoria ventured inside the store. They didn't often go in the Dunkin' Donuts on a Friday afternoon. That was when the popular kids—"the cliquey kids and thotty," or slutty, "girls in the shortest shorts"—congregated to "try and act cool," said Sophia.

Victoria and Sophia were not part of this crowd, as Riley was, or perhaps once had been. In fact, Sophia said that Riley had "shunned" her at times during that school year. "She gets influenced by other kids," Sophia said. "But she's my friend, so I'm going to stick by her. With social media it's really hard to know who your true friends are, and this is how you know, how someone treats you when everyone hates you."

20 Inside the store, there were around twenty kids, and all of them seemed to be screaming. They sat on the brown-and-orange vinyl booths in front of half-empty boxes of doughnuts; they stood in clusters in the aisles, talking close up in one another's faces. There were boys in sweatpants and T-shirts, long shorts and sports jerseys, powdered sugar on their cheeks and lips; there were girls in short shorts and tank tops and crop tops, hands on hips.

There were three girls taking a selfie together, all doing the duckface, smizing—a word coined by former Victoria's Secret supermodel Tyra Banks for "smiling with your eyes."

They vamped for the camera, then peered into the screen, checking the photo.

"Oh, we look hot!" one of them exclaimed. "Post it!"

Kids were talking, yelling.

25 "Oh my God, she's so fake."

"So fake."

"I love your Instagram. You have good feed."

"I know."

"She gets like three hundred likes on every picture. I'm like, Stop it." . . .

30 . . . At Victoria's house, a white clapboard Colonial house, the girls were joined by another friend, Melinda, age thirteen; she was a girl from their school, white, with streaked blond hair, wearing shorts, a blue button-down, and Converse. Her mother was a university professor and her father a film editor. "I am so excited to be talking about this, because we never talk about social media, we just live on it," she said.

The girls sat around the dining room table eating their doughnuts and the brownies Victoria's mother had left for them on a plate. Victoria's mother was picking up her little sister at soccer practice. The dining room was lined with windows looking out on a deep backyard where you could see round-breasted robins hopping in the grass.

The girls filled Melinda in on Riley's difficulty outside the Dunkin' Donuts.

"I can't believe I had an anxiety attack over this," Riley moaned. "I got afraid someone would post something about me if I went in there. That's what social media is doing. It's anxiety-causing and depressing."

"It causes so much drama," Sophia agreed, her mouth full of brownie. "You don't know how much drama I have over my phone."

"With girls our age, so much drama happens over social networking," Melinda told me. "Probably more stuff happens on my phone than in real life."

"I feel like we're living in a second world," Riley said. "There's a real world and a second world," on social media.

As they started talking about all this, they became urgent and intense. They began talking fast, raising their voices, interrupting and overlapping one another.

"All we talk about all day is what's happening on our phones, but we never talk about how *weird* that is," Sophia said.

"I spend so much time on Instagram looking at people's pictures and sometimes I'll be like, Why am I spending my time on this? And yet I keep doing it," said Melinda.

"If I go on my phone to look at Snapchat," Riley said, "I go on it for like an hour, like a really long time, I lose track."

"The minute I start my homework I have to have my phone by me," Sophia said, "to see what my friends are texting or if they're sending me texts, and then I'm automatically in a conversation. It's like someone is constantly tapping you on the shoulder, and you have to look. It's distracting."

All of them said they were in one or more group chats of four to eight friends and that they sent or received "hundreds" of texts a day. "Oh my God, at least three hundred," Sophia said. "I get a text, and it's like, *Oooooh*, I have to check that, like, Oh my God, what are they saying? I don't want to miss anything. I'll be like, Mom, it's really important drama, I have to solve it! But sometimes it'll be like nothing, like what kind of chips you eat.

"But I *need* my phone," Sophia added, "I can't survive without it. I stay up all night looking at my phone."

"Two weeks ago I really annoyed my parents by going on my phone too much, so my punishment was I had to delete my Instagram app on my phone for a week," Melinda said. "By the end of the week I was stressing, like, What if I am losing followers?"

"I've always wanted to delete my Instagram," Sophia said, "but then I think, I look so good in all my photos."

She logged on to her Instagram account to show me her page: it was picture after picture of her face, all with the same mysterious, come-hither expression.

"The classic Sophia selfie, bite-tongue smile," she said with a laugh. "It's my brand."

All of them said they had Photoshopped their pictures and edited them with special filters and apps — especially their selfies. "I've darkened my lips and made my eyebrows on fleek," meaning on point, Sophia said. "I never post the first selfie I take. Sometimes it takes like seventy tries.

"Every time I post a selfie," she went on, "I need to check who's commenting — like, Oh my God, I'm getting so many comments. People are like, 'Oh my God gorgeous,' and you feel good about yourself. I'm so happy when I get likes. We're all obsessed with how many likes we get. Everyone says, I get no likes, I get no likes, but everyone says that even if they *get* likes — it never feels like enough. I feel like I'm brainwashed into wanting likes."

What was striking in hearing them talk about this was how conscious they 50
were of what they were doing, their awareness of the inauthenticity of the self they presented on social media.

"It's funny it's called a 'selfie,' " Riley said, "because half the time it doesn't even look like you. So you're getting people to like this picture of you that isn't even real."

The acquiring of likes has become a major theme in corporate marketing, of course; companies invest serious money in studying how to get social media users to like and tweet and post about their products. Social media users have become the most powerful of advertisers, taking word of mouth to a whole new level. For a *Frontline* segment in 2014, "Generation Like," technology writer Douglas Rushkoff went to Montclair to talk to teenagers about their role in building brands. "When a kid likes something online," Rushkoff said on-air, "a product or a brand or a celebrity, it becomes part of the identity that they broadcast to the world, the way a T-shirt or a bedroom poster defined me when I was a teen. For kids today, you are what you like. . . . And guess what? Getting people to be 'all about' something is big business." Including the business of social media itself — the more active users are, the more data about them social media companies can collect, and the higher they are valued, as they can then sell the data to other companies. "That's why companies need kids to stay online, clicking and liking and tweeting," Rushkoff told a group of Montclair high school students.

But the *Frontline* segment didn't touch upon why kids seek likes for themselves — or how their methods often mirror the very techniques companies use to market brands. The girls in Montclair said, for example, that they planned what time of day they posted, trying to hit prime times for getting likes — another central tenet of social media marketing. On the *Frontline* segment, *New York Times* writer Brooks Barnes talked about the "day by day, hour by hour" social media marketing strategy he witnessed in covering the marketing of *The Hunger Games* in 2012: "The goal is to create a controlled brushfire online."

"I always find a good time to post," Melinda said. "You don't want to post in the middle of the night when no one sees it. I was on vacation and there was a time difference, so I would literally stay up to two in the morning so I could post pictures at a certain time so more people here would like them. My mom was like, What are you doing?"

Melinda and Victoria told of how they had gone to a Katy Perry concert 55
together and posted on Instagram almost identical pictures of Perry performing onstage, but Melinda's pictures had gotten more likes, because she had posted them at a more desirable time.

"I thought it meant people liked Melinda better," Victoria said.

"Oh, no, it's just because of when I posted," Melinda reassured her. "I'm obsessed with getting more likes than other people — I'm always comparing myself to see how many likes my photo got. I'll post a picture on Instagram and immediately start checking."

The captions that went with their posts were also a source of forethought, sometimes requiring a groupthink, like a brainstorming session on *Mad Men* — how to make them sound witty and clever?

"I work so hard on my captions," Riley said. "Everyone has that one group chat where they're like, Oh my God, help me with my captions, what should my caption be?"

The location of their photos was a crucial consideration as well. "I go to 60
the woods to get really artsy lighting and stuff," said Sophia.

"You'll ask the people in your group chat, Should this be my location? What should I do?" said Riley.

"You get more likes if you're someplace cool," Melinda explained.

"It's called 'good feed,'" Sophia said, "if you take good photos and use filters and a VSCO Cam," a spiffy camera and editing app, "and like, have like really good captions."

They said the most admired style of feed among their friends was the one they called "artsy" or "aesthetic." The "aesthetic" aesthetic evolved in the late 2000s with the 2007 advent of Tumblr and other sites devoted to the posting of one's own art, as well as aggregated images of art and fashion and photography. It's used to describe a sense that social media posting *is* art — or can be art, if it's "aesthetic" enough. (Not to be confused with, although perhaps related to, the "New Aesthetic" concept introduced by British artist and writer James Bridle in 2011 to describe the response to technology by artists working in the digital age.)

"You can, like, post a picture of your cereal," Sophia said, "but you have to 65
make it aesthetic."

"Aesthetic" looks, aesthetically, like a manifestation of hipster style, as exemplified by Sofia Coppola's *The Virgin Suicides*, with a dose of *Rookie* and *Real Simple* magazines. "Aesthetic" Instagrams show pictures of filtered pastel skies, girls with expressions bathed in ennui, vintage-looking buildings in black-and-white, and minimalistic bowls of steel-cut oats.

"People say, 'That's so my aesthetic,'" Sophia said. "And it means literally anything that they like. Like, you could say, 'Cheerios are so my aesthetic.'"

By 2015 "aesthetic" so dominated online culture it was already being satirized. "*Is it aesthetic? Is it aesthetic?*" asked teenage singer Ben J. Pierce (KidPOV) in his satirical "The Aesthetic Song" on YouTube. "*Put a bagel on a blanket — is it aesthetic?*"

"It's so much pressure to make your Instagram aesthetic," Victoria said with a groan. "You can't really do anything *wrong*. And if you do, people could laugh at you, like, Oh, look at her Instagram, it's so not aesthetic — it's so *basic*."

("Basic" was another thing entirely — basically the opposite of "aesthetic," 70
referring to girls who were behind the trends, the purchasers of too-obvious brands, from Gap to Gucci.) . . .

"How you look is all anybody cares about anymore," Sophia insisted, becoming a bit agitated. "Being beautiful nowadays is seen as way better than being smart. It's terrible. Like if you're a supermodel on Instagram, everyone loves you. Like I do this, too, so I can't judge: if I find a supermodel on Instagram, I'll comment like, I love you so much. Even though they haven't done anything to help the world and they're literally just standing there looking pretty. People love them just 'cause they're beautiful. And like, being smart — no one cares about that. If people aren't pretty nowadays, they're done with their life. Like, Oh my God, I'm not pretty, I can't live life.

"The new word is 'goals,'" Sophia went on. "Everyone says 'goals.' You find a really pretty girl on Instagram and you're like, '*Goals*.' Goals to have my eyebrows like hers, goals to have my lips like hers, goals to have my hair like hers. You'll see on Instagram comments like, 'My goal is to look like her.' Think about it. That's a *goal*? No one cares about being smart anymore. If you're beautiful everyone will love you."

The other girls had stopped eating the brownies.

"But it's fun to post really hot pictures of yourself even though you don't look like that in real life," Sophia said with a toss of her head. "'Cause when I take a really pretty selfie, people will be like, Oh, gorgeous. . . ."

Reading the Text

1. Sales begins the selection with a description of the Kodak Instamatic camera, introduced in 1963. How does this historical reference situate her later discussion of social media engagement among some teens today?
2. Summarize in your own words the tone of the conversational interchange among the teens whom Sales describes in a donut store on pages 362–63.
3. Why does Sales consider teens' desire for more social media "likes" a matter of concern?
4. Much of this selection is based on transcripts that Sales produced from interviews with young women. How does this primary evidence work to affect your response to her article?

Reading the Signs

1. In your journal, write a response to the young woman whom Sales quotes as saying "How you look is all anybody cares about anymore. . . . And like, being smart — no one cares about that" (para. 71). If you can connect with her sentiments, explore why; if you do not, what advice would you give this person?

2. In class, brainstorm "goals" that students have, and then compare them to the goals Sales mentions in her essay. How do you account for similarities or differences between your class and Sales's interviewees, beyond the fact that the latter were precollege age? Use the class discussion as a basis for your own essay in which you argue for what constitutes identifying "goals" among your cohort/peers.
3. **CONNECTING TEXTS** Read David Courtright's "How 'Limbic Capitalism' Preys on Our Addicted Brains" (p. 354), and use its discussion as a critical framework for an argument about the extent to which the girls whom Sales interviewed can be considered suffering from digital addiction.
4. **CONNECTING TEXTS** In an essay, support, oppose, or qualify the proposition that young teens' use of social media should be strictly monitored by adults. Alternatively, adopt the perspective of an adult (a parent, say, or teacher), and write a letter to the girls in this selection informing them of the potential benefits and dangers of the ways in which they use social media. To develop your ideas, consult Alicia Eler's "There's a Lot More to a Selfie Than Meets the Eye" (p. 340).
5. Visit the Facebook or Instagram sites of several acquaintances, and do a semiotic reading of the digital image they construct for themselves. What signs do they use to create that image, and what messages about their identities are they sending to the world? Do you observe a discrepancy between the acquaintances' online profile and their real-life identity?

JACOB SILVERMAN

"Pics or It Didn't Happen": The Mantra of the Instagram Era

If you've ever caught yourself feeling that your life isn't worth living unless it's on Instagram, this reading is for you. Exploring the whys and wherefores of the constant quest for attention and visibility on the internet, Jacob Silverman illuminates that paradoxical situation in which, as editor Rob Horning has put it, "the point of being on social media is to produce and amass evidence of being on social media." The result is a new way of experiencing life itself, turning ourselves into, in Silverman's telling phrase, "tourists of our own lives." Silverman is the author of *Terms of Service: Social Media and the Price of Constant Connection* (2015), from which this essay was excerpted.

Our social networks have a banality problem. The cultural premium now placed on recording and broadcasting one's life and accomplishments means that Facebook timelines are suffused with postings about meals, workouts, the weather, recent purchases, funny advertisements, the milestones of people three degrees removed from you. On Instagram, one encounters a parade of the same carefully distressed portraits, well-plated dishes, and sunsets gilded with smog. Nuance, difference, and complexity evaporate as one scrolls through these endless feeds, vaguely hoping to find something new or important but mostly resigned to variations on familiar themes.

In a digital landscape built on attention and visibility, what matters is not so much the content of your updates but their existing at all. They must be there. Social broadcasts are not communications; they are records of existence and accumulating metadata. Rob Horning, an editor at the *New Inquiry*, once put it in tautological terms: "The point of being on social media is to produce and amass evidence of being on social media." This is further complicated by the fact that the feed is always refreshing. Someone is always updating more often or rising to the top by virtue of retweets, reshares, or some opaque algorithmic calculation. In the ever-cresting tsunami of data, you are always out to sea, looking at the waves washing ashore. As the artist Fatima Al Qadiri has said: "There's no such thing as the most recent update. It immediately becomes obsolete."

Why, then, do we do it? If it's so easy to become cynical about social media, to see amid the occasionally illuminating exchanges or the harvesting of interesting links (which themselves come in bunches, in great indigestible numbers of browser tabs) that we are part of an unconquerable system, why go on? One answer is that it is a byproduct of the network effect: the more people who are part of a network, the more one's experience can seem impoverished by being left out. Everyone else is doing it. A billion people on Facebook, hundreds of millions scattered between these other networks — who wants to be on the outside? Who wants to miss a birthday, a friend's big news, a chance to sign up for Spotify, or the latest bit of juicy social intelligence? And once you've joined, the updates begin to flow, the small endorphin boosts of likes and re-pins becoming the meagre rewards for all that work. The feeling of disappointment embedded in each gesture, the sense of "Is this it?," only advances the process, compelling us to continue sharing and participating.

The achievement of social-media evangelists is to make this urge — the urge to share simply so that others might know you are there, that you are doing this thing, that you are with this person — second nature. This is society's great phenomenological shift, which, over the last decade, has occurred almost without notice. Now anyone who opts out, or who feels uncomfortable about their participation, begins to feel retrograde, Luddite, uncool. Interiority begins to feel like a prison. The very process of thinking takes on a kind of trajectory:

how can this idea be projected outward, towards others? If I have a witty or profound thought and I don't tweet or Facebook it, have I somehow failed? Is that bon mot now diminished, not quite as good or meaningful as it would be if laid bare for the public? And if people don't respond — retweet, like, favourite — have I boomeranged back again, committing the greater failure of sharing something not worth sharing in the first place? After all, to be uninteresting is a cardinal sin in the social-media age. To say "He's bad at Twitter" is like saying that someone fails to entertain; he won't be invited back for dinner.

In this environment, interiority, privacy, reserve, introspection — all those 5
inward-looking, quieter elements of consciousness — begin to seem insincere. Sharing is sincerity. Removing the mediating elements of thought becomes a mark of authenticity, because it allows you to be more uninhibited in your sharing. Don't think, just post it. "Pics or it didn't happen" — that is the populist mantra of the social networking age. Show us what you did, so that we may believe and validate it.

Social media depends on recognition — more specifically, on acts of recognition. The thing itself is less interesting than the fact that we know someone involved, and if it is interesting or important, we can claim some tenuous connection to it. We enact the maxim of the great street photographer Garry Winogrand: "I photograph to find out what something will look like photographed." We document and share to find out how it feels to do it, and because we can't resist the urge. Otherwise, the experience, the pithy quote, the beautiful sunset, the overheard conversation, the stray insight, is lost or seems somehow less substantial.

Sharing itself becomes personhood, with activities taking on meaning not for their basic content but for the way they are turned into content, disseminated through the digital network, and responded to. In this context, your everyday experiences are only limited by your ability to share them and by your ability to package them appropriately — a photograph with a beautiful filter and a witty caption, or a tweet containing an obscure movie reference that hints at hidden depths. For some users, this process is easy: snap a photo, write below what you are doing, send it out on one or several networks. For others, it can lead to paralysing self-consciousness, a sense that no social broadcast is good enough, no tweet or Facebook status update reflects the mix of cool, wit, and elan that will generate feedback and earn the user more social capital. Along the way, we have developed an ad hoc tolerance for these gestures, as well as a shared familiarity and understanding. Who hasn't stopped an activity mid-stride so that a friend can send out some update about it? Who hasn't done it himself?

On the social web, the person who doesn't share is subscribing to an outmoded identity and cannot be included in the new social space. If not off the grid, he or she simply is not on the grid that matters — he may have email, but is not on Facebook, or he is present but not using it enough. (The prevailing term for this is "lurker," an old online message board term, slightly pejorative, describing someone who reads the board but doesn't post.) It is not uncommon to ask why a friend is on Twitter but rarely tweets, or why she often likes Facebook statuses but never posts her own. Why are they not busy accumulating social capital? Still, being in the quiet minority is far better than not participating at all. Worst, perhaps, is the person whose frequent tweets and updates and posts earn no response at all. In the social-media age, to strive for visibility and not achieve it is a bitter defeat.

* * *

We become attuned to the pace and rhythm of sharing and viewing, building an instinctual sense of the habits of our followers and those we follow, those we call friends and those we just stalk. We develop what some social scientists have termed "ambient awareness" of the lives of those in our social graphs and we intuit, Jedi-like, when they have been absent from the network. Our vision becomes geared towards looking at how many likes or comments a post has received, and when we open the app or log on to the network's website, our eyes dart towards the spot (the upper righthand corner, in Facebook's case) where our notifications appear as a number, vermilion bright. We might also receive email alerts and pop-ups on our phones — good news can arrive in a variety of ways, always urging you to return to the network to respond.

10 The problem with alerts is that, like our updates, they never end. They become a way to be permanently chained to the network. We are always waiting to hear good news, even as we ostensibly are engaged in something else. Just as urban spaces threaten to do away with silence or with stars — the city's sound and light, its primordial vibrancy, become pollutants — notifications crowd out contemplation. They condition us to always expect something else, some outside message that is more important than whatever we might be doing then.

The writer and former tech executive Linda Stone calls this phenomenon "continuous partial attention." She differentiates it from multitasking, though there is some similarity. Continuous partial attention, she says, "is motivated by a desire to be a live node on the network. Another way of saying this is that we want to connect and be connected. We want to effectively scan for opportunity and optimise for the best opportunities, activities, and contacts, in any given moment. To be busy, to be connected, is to be alive, to be recognised, and to matter."

Psychologists and brain researchers have begun studying these problems, with some dispiriting conclusions: multitasking is largely a myth; we can't do multiple things at once, and when we try, we tend to do a poorer job at both. Frequent interruptions — such as your phone starting to vibrate while you are reading this paragraph — make it harder to return to the task at hand. In fact, office workers experience an interruption about every three minutes. It could be an email popping up or a friend coming by your desk. But it can take more than 20 minutes to shake off the interruption and get back to the job at hand. That means that many of us are being interrupted too often to regain focus, with the result that our work and mental clarity suffer. On the other hand, some of these same studies have found that when we expect interruptions, we can perform better, as we train ourselves to become more single-minded and to complete a task in a limited period.

You can turn off your Twitter's email alerts or tell your smartphone to stop pushing your Facebook updates or the latest news from Tumblr. But alerts are the critical symbol of the call and response, the affirmation and approval, that tie a social network together. They let us know that we are being heard, and if we do not have them forced on us, we still have to reckon with them when we log in to the app or on to the network's website. It is important not only to have them but also to have them in sufficient number — or at least some amount that, we tell ourselves, justifies the update. Four people clicked "like"; that's enough, I guess. After posting an update, we might return to the network several times over the next hour, hoping for some validating reply.

The window for this kind of response is painfully brief. We know fairly quickly whether our beautifully filtered photo of a grilled cheese sandwich or our joke about a philandering politician was a dud. According to a 2010 study by Sysomos, only 29 percent of tweets receive a response — a reply, retweet, or favourite — while 6 percent are retweeted. A full 92 percent of retweets happen within the tweet's first hour, meaning that if 60 minutes have passed and no one has picked up on your tweet, it has likely disappeared into the ether. Even when they do appear, likes and favourites have been mostly drained of meaning — a sign of approval and popularity, sure, but also now a rather conventional way of telling a friend that he was heard. The favourite has become a limp pat on the back.

This ephemerality contributes to social media's tendency towards self- 15
consciousness and the constant calibrating of one's public persona. We know that we do not have much time — or many characters — and that we had better make it count. "If I don't get more than 10 faves in [the] first three minutes after tweeting something, I'll probably delete it," one amateur comedian told the *Wall Street Journal*. Otherwise, the tweet hangs there, a minor emblem of its author's unsatisfied ambition.

What that comedian really fears is the loss of followers and social capital. We take it for granted, perhaps, that social media comes with metrics. We are constantly told how many people are following us, how many approved of an update, how many people follow those people. Metrics help create the hierarchies that are embedded in all social networks, and that often replicate offline hierarchies. If you do not know immediately how popular someone is on social media, the answer is only a click away.

This hovering awareness of rank and privilege helps drive the insecurity and self-consciousness that result from an environment suffused with the language of PR, branding, and advertising. Describing his experience on Twitter, the satirist Henry Alford writes that "every time someone retweets one of my jokes, it sets off a spate of fretting about reciprocity. . . . If the person is a total stranger whose feed I do not follow, then I will look at this feed and consider climbing aboard. I'll look at the ratio of how many tweets to how many followers that person has: if it exceeds 10 to 1, then I may suddenly feel shy. Because this person is unknown to me, I will feel no compunction to retweet a post of hers, though I may be tempted to 'favourite' (the equivalent of Facebook's 'like' button) one."

Alford is demurring here. What he really means is that someone with a tweets-to-followers ratio of 10 to 1 is probably an unknown, one of the innumerable Twitter users whose many tweets go pretty much ignored, and not one of the journalists, comedians, or writers who probably belong to his intended audience. (He goes on to mention, happily, that one of his jokes was recognised by the comedians Merrill Markoe and Rob Delaney, the latter a Twitter superstar.) There is nothing wrong with that, of course, except that Alford's own admissions speak to the difficulty of negotiating the odd social pressures and anxieties that come with every utterance being public. Is he on Twitter to promote himself, to meet people, or to endear himself to colleagues — or is there a conflicting mix of motivations? In Alford's case, his concerns about visibility and reciprocity intensify when he is responded to on Twitter by someone he knows: "Suddenly the pressure mounts. I'll proceed to follow her, of course, if I don't already. Then I'll start feeling very guilty if I don't retweet one of her posts." Each exchange requires a complex cost-benefit analysis, one that, for anyone who has experienced this, may seem wildly disproportionate to the conversation at hand. Just as metadata (that is, the number of retweets or likes) can matter more than the message itself, this process of meta-analysis, of deciphering the uncertain power dynamic between two people, can seem more important than the conversation on which it is based.

* * *

Maybe Alford would be more comfortable with photographs, which, in their vivid particularity, seem to demand less of a response. They can live on their own. We don't need to justify them. Photographs "furnish evidence," as Susan Sontag said. Or, in Paul Strand's words: "Your photography is a record of your living." You met a celebrity, cooked a great meal, or saw something extraordinary, and the photograph is what remains: the receipt of experience. Now that every smartphone comes complete with a digital camera as good as any point-and-shoot most of us had a few years ago, there is little reason not to photograph something. Into the camera roll it goes, so that later you can perform the ritual triage: filter or no filter? Tumblr, Instagram, or Snapchat?

The ubiquity of digital photography, along with image-heavy (or image- 20
only) social networks such as Instagram, Pinterest, Tumblr, Imgur, Snapchat, and Facebook, has changed what it means to take and collect photos. No longer do we shoot, develop, and then curate them in frames or albums in the privacy of our homes. If we organise them in albums at all, it is on Facebook or Flickr — that is, on someone else's platform — and we leave them there to

be commented upon and circulated through the network. Photos become less about memorialising a moment than communicating the reality of that moment to others. They are also a way to handle the newfound anxiety over living in the present moment, knowing that our friends and colleagues may be doing something more interesting at just that very moment, and that we will see those experiences documented later on social media. Do we come to feel an anticipatory regret, sensing that future social-media postings will make our own activities appear inadequate by comparison? Perhaps we try to stave off that regret, that fear of missing out, by launching a preemptive attack of photographic documentation. Here we are, having fun! It looks good, right? Please validate it, and I'll validate yours, and we'll take turns saying how much we missed each other.

Photography has always been "acquisitive," as Sontag called it, a way of appropriating the subject of the photograph. Online you can find a perfectly lit, professionally shot photo of nearly anything you want, but that does not work for most of us. We must do it ourselves.

Think about the pictures of a horde of tourists assembled in front of the Mona Lisa, their cameras clicking away. It is the most photographed work of art in human history. You can see it in full light, low light, close-up, far away, x-rayed; you can find parodies of parodies of parodies; and yet, seeing it in person and walking away does not suffice. The experience must be captured, the painting itself possessed, a poor facsimile of it acquired so that you can call it your own — a photograph which, in the end, says, I was here. I went to Paris and saw the Mona Lisa. The photo shows that you could afford the trip, that you are cultured, and offers an entrée to your story about the other tourists you had to elbow your way through, the security guard who tried to flirt with you, the incredible pastry you had afterwards, the realisation that the painting really is not much to look at and that you have always preferred Rembrandt. The grainy, slightly askew photo signifies all these things. Most important, it is yours. You took it. It got 12 likes.

This is also the unspoken thought process behind every reblog or retweet, every time you pin something that has already been pinned hundreds of times. You need it for yourself. Placing it on your blog or in your Twitter stream acts as a form of identification — a signal of your aesthetics, a reflection of your background, an avatar of your desires. It must be held, however provisionally and insubstantially, in your hand, and so by reposting it, you claim some kind of possession of it.

Something similar can be said about people you see at concerts, recording or photographing a band. Unless you have a fancy digital SLR camera and are positioned close to the stage, the photographs will probably be terrible. Recording the show is even more of a fool's errand, because it will only show you how poor your iPhone's microphone is and how this experience, so precious at the time, cannot be captured by the technology in your pocket. No, the video will be shaky, as you struggle to hold your phone above the heads of people in front of you, and the audio will sound like someone played the track at full volume inside a steel trash can. But of course, many of us do this, or we hold our phones aloft so friends on the other end of the line can hear — what exactly? Again, we find that it doesn't quite matter. We will probably never watch that video later, nor will we make that photo our desktop wallpaper or print it out and frame it. The crummy photos, the crackly recording, the indecipherable blast of music a caller hears: these are not personal remembrances or artistic artefacts. They are souvenirs, lifestyle totems meant to communicate status — to be your status update. They do not describe the band being captured; they describe us.

People often ask, "Why don't concertgoers just live in the moment and 25
enjoy the show? Don't they know that the photos won't turn out well and that focusing on their iPhone, staring at its small screen rather than the thing itself, takes them out of the experience?" The answer is yes, but that's also beside the point. Taking photos of the band may show a kind of disregard for the music, an inability to enjoy it simply as it is, but it also reflects how the very act of photographing has become part of just about any event or evening out.

In the same way that Sontag says that "travel becomes a strategy for accumulating photographs" (e.g. standing in a certain spot in front of the Leaning Tower of Pisa, where you can position your arms so it looks like you are holding up the building), life itself becomes a way of accumulating and sharing photographs. Taking photographs gives you something to do; it means that you no longer have to be idle. Living in the moment means trying to capture and possess it. We turn ourselves into tourists of our own lives and communities, our Instagram accounts our self-authored guidebooks, reflecting our good taste. At the same time, the use of filters and simple image-editing software means that any scene can be made into an appealing photograph or at least one that has the appearance of being artistically engaging. The process of digitally weathering and distressing photographs is supposed to add a false vintage veneer, a shortcut to nostalgia, and it has the added benefit of making it look like the photo went through some process. You worked for it, at least in a fashion.

This kind of cultural practice is no more clearly on display than during a night out with twentysomethings. The evening becomes partitioned into opportunities for photo taking: getting dressed, friends arriving, a taxi ride, arriving at the bar, running into more friends, encountering funny graffiti in the bathroom, drunk street food, the stranger vomiting on the street, the taxi home, maybe a shot of the clock before bed. A story is told here, sure, but more precisely, life is documented, its reality confirmed by being spliced into shareable data. Now everyone knows how much fun you had and offers their approval, and you can return to it to see what you forgot in that boozy haze.

All of this also offers evidence of your consumption, of the great life you are living and the products contained therein. Photography's acquisitive aspect — the part of it that turns life into one long campaign of window shopping — finds its fullest expression on Pinterest, Instagram, and other image-heavy social networks. There we become like the hero of Saul Bellow's *Henderson the Rain King*, a man who hears a voice within himself saying: "I want, I want, I want." Like Henderson, we do not know what we want exactly but we have some sense that it is out there, in the endless feed of shimmering imagery, and that if we click through it long enough, maybe we will find satisfaction. In this ruminative browsing, where time becomes something distended, passing without notice, our idle fantasies take flight.

* * *

The documentary lifestyle of social media raises concerns about how we commoditise ourselves and how we put ourselves up for public display and judgment. That does not mean that fun cannot be had or that this kind of documentation cannot coexist with an authentic life. It is just that the question of what is authentic shifts, sometimes uncomfortably, and not just through what Facebook calls "frictionless sharing" — disclosing everything, always, completely. Instead, it is that our documentation and social broadcasts become the most important thing, an ulterior act that threatens to become the main event.

The social media theorist Nathan Jurgenson describes users as developing 30
"a 'Facebook Eye': our brains always looking for moments where the ephemeral blur of lived experience might best be translated into a Facebook post; one that will draw the most comments and 'likes'." We might feel this phenomenon in different ways, depending on which networks you use and which activities constitute your day. I feel it acutely when reading articles on my smartphone or my computer — this sense that I am not just reading for my own enjoyment or edification but also so that I can pull out some pithy sentence (allowing enough space for the 23 or so characters needed for a link) to share on Twitter. I began to feel an odd kind of guilt, knowing that my attention is not being brought to bear on what I am doing. It feels dishonest, like I am not reading for the right reasons, and self-loathing builds within me — the self-loathing of the amateur comedian who deletes his tweets if they fail to quickly attract enough likes. I can offer myself justification by saying that I enjoy sharing or that I am trying to pass along information to others, but that strikes me as insincere. The truth is more depressing, as this impulse to share reflects, I think, the essential narcissism of the Facebook Eye (or the Instagram Lens, or whichever filter you prefer). Our experiences become not about our own fulfilment, the fulfilment of those we are with, or even about sharing; they become about ego, demonstrating status, seeming cool or smart or well-informed. Perhaps if you are a young journalist, looking to increase your esteem in the eyes of peers and a couple thousand followers in the digital ether, the goal of reading is to be the first to share something newsworthy, sometimes before you have even finished reading the article. Like a village gossip, you want to build social capital by becoming a locus for news and information. But with this role, there is an inevitable hollowing out of

interiority, of the quietness of your thoughts — reading itself becomes directed outward, from private contemplation to a strategic act meant to satisfy some nebulous public.

Our reading habits change, and so do the stories we tell, the way we share these things. We make our updates more machine-readable — adding tags; choosing brands and emotions supplied to us through Facebook's interface; shortening jokes to fit into Twitter's 140-character limit. We wait to post on Tumblr after 12 p.m., because we have read that usage rises during the lunch hour, or we schedule tweets to go up during periods when we will be disconnected.

On social media, it can seem as if time and data are always slipping through our fingers. Particularly when we follow or befriend many people on a network, our updates seem illusory, as if they are never inscribed into anything but instead shouted into the void. (Did anyone really hear me? Why is no one replying?) In this way, social media can resemble traditional, pre-literate societies, where communication is purely oral and everything — culture, news, gossip, history — is communicated through speech. When we retweet someone, we are just speaking their words again — ensuring that they are passed on and do not get lost in the flurry of communication.

Media theorists refer to these eruptions of oral culture within literate culture as examples of "secondary orality." Social media's culture of sharing and storytelling, its lack of a long-term memory, and the use of news and information to build social capital are examples of this phenomenon. While records of our activities exist to varying extents, secondary orality shows us how social media exists largely in a kind of eternal present, upon which the past rarely intrudes. Twitter is a meaningful example. It is evanescent: posts are preserved, but in practice, they are lost in one's rapidly self-refreshing timeline — read it now or not at all. Twitter is also reminiscent of oral storytelling, in which one person is speaking to a larger assembled group and receiving feedback in return, which helps to shape the story. One of the digital twists here is that many storyteller-like figures are speaking simultaneously, jockeying for attention and for some form of recognition. The point is not that social media is atavistically traditional but that it returns elements of oral societies to us. Our fancy new digital media is in fact not entirely new, but a hybrid of elements we have seen in past forms of communication. The outbursts of tribalism we sometimes see online — a group of anonymous trolls launching misogynist attacks on a female journalist; the ecstatic social media groupies of Justin Bieber; the way one's Twitter timeline can, for a short while, become centred around parsing one major event, as if gathered in a village square — are evidence of a very old-fashioned, even preliterate communitarianism, reified for the digital world.

Think about the anxious comedian or your oversharing Facebook friend. Their frequent updates come in part from the (perhaps unacknowledged) feeling that in social media nothing is permanent. Of course, we know that these networks, and the varying sites and companies that piggyback off of them, preserve everything. But in practice, everything is fleeting. You must speak to be heard. And when everyone else is speaking, you had better do it often and do it well, or risk being drowned in the din, consigned to that house at the edge of the village, where few people visit and, when they do, expect to hear little of any consequence.

Reading the Text

1. Why, according to Silverman, do people constantly record and broadcast their lives and accomplishments on the internet?
2. What does Rob Horning mean by saying that "The point of being on social media is to produce and amass evidence of being on social media" (para. 2)?
3. How do social media alerts create the condition that Linda Stone calls "continuous partial attention" (para. 11)? How does this differ from multitasking?
4. How do social media like Twitter and Facebook make us self-conscious, according to Silverman?

Reading the Signs

1. **CONNECTING TEXTS** Read Nancy Jo Sales's "From the Instamatic to Instagram: Social Media and the Secret Lives of Teenagers" (p. 360) and write an essay, using Silverman's perspective on Instagram, in which you interpret the motives and desires behind the way the girls interviewed in the reading use social media. To what extent are they, in Silverman's terms, "always looking for moments when the ephemeral blur of lived experience might best be translated into an [Instagram] post" (para. 30)?
2. Write a journal entry describing the ways in which you construct your presence on the internet. Do you use Instagram or another social media site? With whom do you communicate, and why? If you do not engage with social media, discuss why you choose not to do so.
3. **CONNECTING TEXTS** By creating their own online identities through social media, people are, in effect, attempting to become celebrities. Referring to the introduction to this chapter, write an essay supporting, refuting, or complicating the proposition that the internet is democratizing the potential to achieve celebrity status. To develop your ideas, consult George Packer's "Celebrating Inequality" (p. 86).
4. Silverman remarks that by constantly photographing and broadcasting our experiences online, we are turning "ourselves into tourists of our own lives" (para. 26). Interview friends and family about their use of such social media as Instagram and write an essay in which you support, challenge, or modify Silverman's contention. To develop your argument, consult Alicia Eler's "There's a Lot More to a Selfie Than Meets the Eye" (p. 340).

5. Write an essay in which you support, challenge, or modify Silverman's assertion about people's recording of concerts with their iPhones: "The crummy photos, the crackly recording, the indecipherable blast of music a caller hears: these are not personal remembrances or artistic artifacts. They are souvenirs, lifestyle totems meant to communicate status" (para. 24). To develop evidence for your position, you might interview some concertgoers about their attitude toward recording a show, whether they do so themselves or not.

BROOKE GLADSTONE

Influencing Machines: The Echo Chambers of the Internet

Now that graphic novels are receiving the same scholarly attention and respect as traditional publications, why shouldn't there be graphic cultural studies texts? Oh wait, there already are. Joining such books as the Pantheon *For Beginners* series, Brooke Gladstone presents here, in graphic form, a lecture on the phenomenon of the niche-media "echo chamber" effect: i.e., the way that highly segmented media outlets play back to their customers exactly the worldview that they already have, effectively hardening existing ideological divisions in the country as Americans construct conflicting realities. Gladstone's pithy presentation can help explain Donald Trump's takeover of the Republican Party and victory in the 2016 presidential election, as well as the reason it is so hard to get anywhere in discussions of such serious issues as global climate change and abortion. Brooke Gladstone is the host and managing editor of the New York Public Radio newsmagazine, *On the Media*, and the author of *The Influencing Machine: Brooke Gladstone on the Media* (2012), from which this selection is taken.

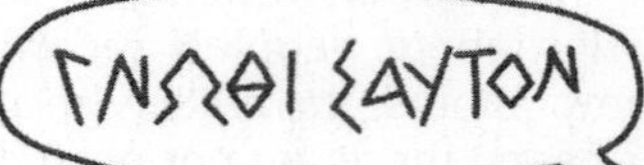

BACK BEFORE THERE WERE MEDIA OUTLETS, an ancient traveler noted a fateful warning carved on the temple of the Oracle of Delphi (a notorious newsmaker). It read: "Know thyself."

Now the media cover the world like cloudy water. We have to consciously filter it. In an era when everything is asserted and anything denied, we really need to know who we are and how our brains work.

Humans run on emotion, assumption, and impulse. We can't function on logic alone. People who can't feel pleasure or preference because of damage to the orbital prefrontal cortex are paralyzed by the simple decisions most of us make effortlessly every day. The blue pen or the black pen? Mary or Sue? Any choice—whether of a mate or a breakfast cereal—engulfs them in a quicksand of pros and cons.

But emotion, assumption, and impulse also allow us to weave cozy cocoons of unexamined prejudice and received wisdom. They shield us from the pain of unwelcome information. William James once said that "the greatest enemy of any one of our truths may be the rest of our truths." So you have to ask yourself . . . well, here's how James Fitzjames Stephen framed the key questions back in 1873 . . .

What do you think of yourself? What do you think of the world?... They are riddles of the Sphinx, and in some way or other we must deal with them. If we decide to leave them unanswered, that is a choice; if we waver in our answer, that, too, is a choice: but whatever choice we make, we make it at our peril...
We stand on a mountain pass in the midst of whirling snow and blinding mist through which we get glimpses now and then of paths which may be deceptive. If we stand still we shall be frozen to death. If we take the wrong road we shall be dashed to pieces. We do not certainly know whether there is any right one. **What must we do?**

THE INFLUENCING MACHINES

So as we stand on the mountain -- which way do we go?

Instinctively we drift toward people like ourselves, flocking together like birds of a feather. This is called **homophily.** It shapes our worldview.

Many say that the Internet's ability to link like-minded souls everywhere fosters the creation of virtually impermeable echo chambers.

The echo chambers give rise to cybercascades: when a "fact" sent by one person spreads in a geometric progression to others until millions of people around the world potentially believe it.

Cut off from dissenters, the chambers fill with an unjustified sense of certainty. It's called **incestuous amplification**, a term first applied to isolated military planners who base their strategies on flawed assumptions.

Incestuous amplification can occur in any sphere, even without the Internet. But it helps.

Hint: When you hear a group of guys called "Masters of the Universe," **run!**

Cass Sunstein cites many studies showing how people who talk only to like-minded others grow more extreme. They **marginalize the moderates...**

...and **demonize** dissenters. The greatest danger of echo chambers is unjustified **extremism.** It's an ongoing **threat** to our **democracy.**

Every new digital development enables us to better edit and augment our preferred reality.
With advancing facial recognition technology and linked databases, no one ever has to be a stranger.
BROOKE GLADSTONE
HOME: BROOKLYN
LIKES
BOURBON
DISLIKES
BRUSSELS SPROUTS
MOOD
AMBIVALENT
Mutual Friends
The same capability is being built into contact lenses.
But the technology that **expands** our worldview can also **diminish** it. Don't want to see that sex offender? Just the girlfriend? Done and done!
REGISTERED SEX OFFENDER
SLUTTY GIRLFRIEND
BUY THIS SHIRT AT BANANA REPUBLIC
How does tolerance fit into this world?
How do we develop intellectually or morally if we can evade encounters with the unfamiliar, the unwelcome, and the unimagined?

Reading the Text

1. According to Gladstone, how do media today mirror back to their consumers their existing political and worldviews?
2. Define in your own words the terms *echo chamber* and *incestuous amplification* (p. 382).
3. Why does Gladstone say the "the technology that expands our worldview can also diminish it" (p. 383)?

Reading the Signs

1. Write a rhetorical analysis of the effect of the graphic presentation that Gladstone uses to make her points.
2. Write a brief essay that presents the same message that Gladstone is conveying. Then compare your prose version with her graphic design. What different effects do they have on a reader? Share your essay with the class.
3. **CONNECTING TEXTS** In an essay, discuss the extent to which the echo chamber effect influenced the 2016 presidential election. To develop your ideas, you might consult John Herrman's "Inside Facebook's (Totally Insane, Unintentionally Gigantic, Hyperpartisan) Political-Media Machine" (p. 384).
4. Write an essay in response to Gladstone's question "How do we develop intellectually or morally if we can evade encounters with the unfamiliar, the unwelcome, and the unimagined?" (p. 383).

JOHN HERRMAN

Inside Facebook's (Totally Insane, Unintentionally Gigantic, Hyperpartisan) Political-Media Machine

John Herrman's in-depth analysis of the way in which Facebook has come to dominate not only the dissemination of the news in America, but exactly what news individual Facebook subscribers receive, is a case study in the "echo chamber" effect of contemporary news consumption. Revealing the ways in which Facebook employs the same data-mining techniques that it uses to construct consumer profiles for marketing purposes, Herrman shows how your Facebook news feed can become "bluer" or "redder," depending upon the kinds of comments that appear on your page. For with such third-party sources as the Liberty Alliance promoting ideological news content on Facebook in essentially the same way that consumer products merchandisers market their goods on social media, the inevitable outcome is the construction of a myriad of ideological closed circuits — with those within the circuit "sharing" the same ever-expanding messages. And there's no way out of the situation, Herrman concludes, for "Facebook's primacy is a foregone conclusion, and the question of Facebook's relationship to political discourse is absurd — they're one and the same." John Herrman covers technology and media for the *New York Times*.

Open your Facebook feed. What do you see? A photo of a close friend's child. An automatically generated slide show commemorating six years of friendship between two acquaintances. An eerily on-target ad for something you've been meaning to buy. A funny video. A sad video. A recently live video. Lots of video; more video than you remember from before. A somewhat less-on-target ad. Someone you saw yesterday feeling blessed. Someone you haven't seen in 10 years feeling worried.

And then: A family member who loves politics asking, "Is this really who we want to be president?" A coworker, whom you've never heard talk about politics, asking the same about a different candidate. A story about Donald Trump that "just can't be true" in a figurative sense. A story about Donald Trump that "just can't be true" in a literal sense. A video of Bernie Sanders speaking, overlaid with text, shared from a source you've never seen before, viewed 15 million times. An article questioning Hillary Clinton's honesty; a headline questioning Donald Trump's sanity. A few shares that go a bit too far: headlines you would never pass along yourself but that you might tap, read, and probably not forget.

Maybe you've noticed your feed becoming bluer; maybe you've felt it becoming redder. Either way, in the last year, it has almost certainly become more intense. You've seen a lot of media sources you don't recognize and a lot of posts bearing no memorable brand at all. You've seen politicians and celebrities and corporations weigh in directly; you've probably seen posts from the candidates themselves. You've seen people you're close to and people you're not, with increasing levels of urgency, declare it is now time to speak up, to take a stand, to set aside allegiances or hang-ups or political correctness or hate.

Facebook, in the years leading up to this election, hasn't just become nearly ubiquitous among American internet users; it has centralized online news consumption in an unprecedented way. According to the company, its site is used by more than 200 million people in the United States each month, out of a total population of 320 million. A 2016 Pew study found that 44 percent of Americans read or watch news on Facebook. These are approximate exterior dimensions and can tell us only so much. But we can know, based on these facts alone, that Facebook is hosting a huge portion of the political conversation in America.

The Facebook product, to users in 2016, is familiar yet subtly expansive. 5
Its algorithms have their pick of text, photos, and video produced and posted by established media organizations large and small, local and national, openly partisan or nominally unbiased. But there's also a new and distinctive sort of

operation that has become hard to miss: political news and advocacy pages made specifically for Facebook, uniquely positioned and cleverly engineered to reach audiences exclusively in the context of the news feed. These are news sources that essentially do not exist outside of Facebook, and you've probably never heard of them. They have names like Occupy Democrats; The Angry Patriot; US Chronicle; Addicting Info; RightAlerts; Being Liberal; Opposing Views; Fed-Up Americans; American News; and hundreds more. Some of these pages have millions of followers; many have hundreds of thousands.

Using a tool called CrowdTangle, which tracks engagement for Facebook pages across the network, you can see which pages are most shared, liked, and commented on, and which pages dominate the conversation around election topics. Using this data, I was able to speak to a wide array of the activists and entrepreneurs, advocates and opportunists, reporters and hobbyists who together make up 2016's most disruptive, and least understood, force in media.

Individually, these pages have meaningful audiences, but cumulatively, their audience is gigantic: tens of millions of people. On Facebook, they rival the reach of their better-funded counterparts in the political media, whether corporate giants like CNN or the *New York Times*, or openly ideological web operations like Breitbart or Mic. And unlike traditional media organizations, which have spent years trying to figure out how to lure readers out of the Facebook ecosystem and onto their sites, these new publishers are happy to live inside the world that Facebook has created. Their pages are accommodated but not actively courted by the company and are not a major part of its public messaging about media. But they are, perhaps, the purest expression of Facebook's design and of the incentives coded into its algorithm — a system that has already reshaped the web and has now inherited, for better or for worse, a great deal of America's political discourse.

In 2006, when Mark Zuckerberg dropped out of college to run his rapidly expanding start-up, Mark Provost was a student at Rogers State University in Claremore, Okla., and going through a rough patch. He had transferred restlessly between schools, and he was taking his time to graduate; a stock picking hobby that grew into a promising source of income had fallen apart. His outlook was further darkened by the financial crisis and by the years of personal unemployment that followed. When the Occupy movement began, he quickly got on board. It was only then, when Facebook was closing in on its billionth user, that he joined the network.

Now 36, Provost helps run US Uncut, a left-leaning Facebook page and website with more than 1.5 million followers, about as many as MSNBC has, from his apartment in Philadelphia. (Sample headlines: "Bernie Delegates Want You to See This DNC Scheme to Silence Them" and "This Sanders Delegate Unleashing on Hillary Clinton Is Going Absolutely Viral.") He frequently contributes to another popular page, The Other 98%, which has more than 2.7 million followers.

Occupy got him on Facebook, but it was the 2012 election that showed 10
him its potential. As he saw it, that election was defined by social media. He

mentioned a set of political memes that now feel generationally distant: Clint Eastwood's empty chair at the 2012 Republican National Convention and Mitt Romney's debate gaffe about "binders full of women." He thought it was a bit silly, but he saw in these viral moments a language in which activists like him could spread their message.

Provost's page now communicates frequently in memes, images with overlaid text. "May I suggest," began one, posted in May 2015, when opposition to the Trans-Pacific Partnership was gaining traction, "the first 535 jobs we ship overseas?" Behind the text was a photo of Congress. Many are more earnest. In an image posted shortly thereafter, a photo of Bernie Sanders was overlaid with a quote: "If Germany, Denmark, Sweden and many more provide tuition-free college," read the setup, before declaring in larger text, "we should be doing the same." It has been shared more than 84,000 times and liked 75,000 more. Not infrequently, this level of zeal can cross into wishful thinking. A post headlined "Did Hillary Clinton Just Admit on LIVE TV That Her Iraq War Vote Was a Bribe?" was shared widely enough to merit a response from Snopes, which called it "quite a stretch."

This year, political content has become more popular all across the platform: on homegrown Facebook pages, through media companies with a growing Facebook presence and through the sharing habits of users in general. But truly Facebook-native political pages have begun to create and refine a new approach to political news: cherry-picking and reconstituting the most effective tactics and tropes from activism, advocacy and journalism into a potent new mixture. This strange new class of media organization slots seamlessly into the news feed and is especially notable in what it asks, or doesn't ask, of its readers. The point is not to get them to click on more stories or to engage further with a brand. The point is to get them to share the post that's right in front of them. Everything else is secondary.

While web publishers have struggled to figure out how to take advantage of Facebook's audience, these pages have thrived. Unburdened of any allegiance to old forms of news media and the practice, or performance, of any sort of ideological balance, native Facebook page publishers have a freedom that more traditional publishers don't: to engage with Facebook purely on its terms. These are professional Facebook users straining to build media companies, in other words, not the other way around.

From a user's point of view, every share, like or comment is both an act of speech and an accretive piece of a public identity. Maybe some people want to be identified among their networks as news junkies, news curators, or as some sort of objective and well-informed reader. Many more people simply want to share specific beliefs, to tell people what they think or, just as important, what they don't. A newspaper-style story or a dry, matter-of-fact headline is adequate for this purpose. But even better is a headline, or meme, that skips straight to an ideological conclusion or rebuts an argument.

Rafael Rivero is an acquaintance of Provost's who, with his twin brother, 15
Omar, runs a page called Occupy Democrats, which passed three million

followers in June. This accelerating growth is attributed by Rivero, and by nearly every left-leaning page operator I spoke with, not just to interest in the election but especially to one campaign in particular: "Bernie Sanders is the Facebook candidate," Rivero says. The rise of Occupy Democrats essentially mirrored the rise of Sanders's primary run. On his page, Rivero started quoting text from Sanders's frequent email blasts, turning them into Facebook-ready memes with a consistent aesthetic: colors that pop, yellow on black. Rivero says that it's clear what his audience wants. "I've probably made 10,000 graphics, and it's like running 10,000 focus groups," he said. (Clinton was and is, of course, widely discussed by Facebook users: According to the company, in the last month 40.8 million people "generated interactions" around the candidate. But Rivero says that in the especially engaged, largely oppositional left-wing-page ecosystem, Clinton's message and cautious brand didn't carry.)

Because the Sanders campaign has come to an end, these sites have been left in a peculiar position, having lost their unifying figure as well as their largest source of engagement. Audiences grow quickly on Facebook but can disappear even more quickly; in the case of left-leaning pages, many had accumulated followings not just by speaking to Sanders supporters but also by being intensely critical, and often utterly dismissive, of Clinton.

Now that the nomination contest is over, Rivero has turned to making anti-Trump content. A post from earlier this month got straight to the point: "Donald Trump is unqualified, unstable and unfit to lead. Share if you agree!" More than 40,000 people did.

"It's like a meme war," Rivero says, "and politics is being won and lost on social media."

In retrospect, Facebook's takeover of online media looks rather like a slow-motion coup. Before social media, web publishers could draw an audience one of two ways: through a dedicated readership visiting its home page or through search engines. By 2009, this had started to change. Facebook had more than 300 million users, primarily accessing the service through desktop browsers, and publishers soon learned that a widely shared link could produce substantial traffic. In 2010, Facebook released widgets that publishers could embed on their sites, reminding readers to share, and these tools were widely deployed. By late 2012, when Facebook passed a billion users, referrals from the social network were sending visitors to publishers' websites at rates sometimes comparable to Google, the web's previous de facto distribution hub. Publishers took note of what worked on Facebook and adjusted accordingly.

This was, for most news organizations, a boon. The flood of visitors 20
aligned with two core goals of most media companies: to reach people and to make money. But as Facebook's growth continued, its influence was intensified by broader trends in internet use, primarily the use of smartphones, on which Facebook became more deeply enmeshed with users' daily routines. Soon, it became clear that Facebook wasn't just a source of readership; it was, increasingly, where readers lived.

Facebook, from a publisher's perspective, had seized the web's means of distribution by popular demand. A new reality set in, as a social-media network became an intermediary between publishers and their audiences. For media companies, the ability to reach an audience is fundamentally altered, made greater in some ways and in others more challenging. For a dedicated Facebook user, a vast array of sources, spanning multiple media and industries, is now processed through the same interface and sorting mechanism, alongside updates from friends, family, brands and celebrities.

From the start, some publishers cautiously regarded Facebook as a resource to be used only to the extent that it supported their existing businesses, wary of giving away more than they might get back. Others embraced it more fully, entering into formal partnerships for revenue sharing and video production, as the *New York Times* has done. Some new-media start-ups, most notably BuzzFeed, have pursued a comprehensively Facebook-centric production-and-distribution strategy. All have eventually run up against the same reality: A company that can claim nearly every internet-using adult as a user is less a partner than a context — a self-contained marketplace to which you have been granted access but which functions according to rules and incentives that you cannot control.

The news feed is designed, in Facebook's public messaging, to "show people the stories most relevant to them" and ranks stories "so that what's most important to each person shows up highest in their news feeds." It is a framework built around personal connections and sharing, where value is both expressed and conferred through the concept of engagement. Of course, engagement, in one form or another, is what media businesses have always sought, and provocation has always sold news. But now the incentives are literalized in buttons and written into software.

Any sufficiently complex system will generate a wide variety of results, some expected, some not; some desired, others less so. On July 31, a Facebook page called Make America Great posted its final story of the day. "No Media Is Telling You About the Muslim Who Attacked Donald Trump, So We Will . . .," read the headline, next to a small avatar of a pointing and yelling Trump. The story was accompanied by a photo of Khizr Khan, the father of a slain American soldier. Khan spoke a few days earlier at the Democratic National Convention, delivering a searing speech admonishing Trump for his comments about Muslims. Khan, pocket Constitution in hand, was juxtaposed with the logo of the Muslim Brotherhood in Egypt. "It is a sad day in America," the caption read, "where we the people must expose the TRUTH because the media is in the tank for 1 Presidential Candidate!"

Readers who clicked through to the story were led to an external website, 25
called Make America Great Today, where they were presented with a brief write-up blended almost seamlessly into a solid wall of fleshy ads. Khan, the story said — between ads for "(1) Odd Trick to 'Kill' Herpes Virus for Good" and "22 Tank Tops That Aren't Covering Anything" — is an agent of the Muslim Brotherhood and a "promoter of Islamic Shariah law." His late son,

the story suggests, could have been a "Muslim martyr" working as a double agent. A credit link beneath the story led to a similar-looking site called Conservative Post, from which the story's text was pulled verbatim. Conservative Post had apparently sourced its story from a longer post on a right-wing site called Shoebat.com.

Within 24 hours, the post was shared more than 3,500 times, collecting a further 3,000 reactions — thumbs-up likes, frowning emoji, angry emoji — as well as 850 comments, many lengthy and virtually all impassioned. A modest success. Each day, according to Facebook's analytics, posts from the Make America Great page are seen by 600,000 to 1.7 million people. In July, articles posted to the page, which has about 450,000 followers, were shared, commented on, or liked more than four million times, edging out, for example, the Facebook page of *USA Today*.

Make America Great, which inhabits the fuzzy margins of the political Facebook page ecosystem, is owned and operated by a 35-year-old online marketer named Adam Nicoloff. He started the page in August 2015 and runs it from his home outside St. Louis. Previously, Nicoloff provided web services and marketing help for local businesses; before that, he worked in restaurants. Today he has shifted his focus to Facebook pages and websites that he administers himself. Make America Great was his first foray into political pages, and it quickly became the most successful in a portfolio that includes men's lifestyle and parenting.

Nicoloff's business model is not dissimilar from the way most publishers use Facebook: build a big following, post links to articles on an outside website covered in ads and then hope the math works out in your favor. For many, it doesn't: Content is expensive, traffic is unpredictable and website ads are both cheap and alienating to readers. But as with most of these Facebook-native pages, Nicoloff's content costs comparatively little, and the sheer level of interest in Trump and in the type of inflammatory populist rhetoric he embraces has helped tip Nicoloff's system of advertising arbitrage into serious profitability. In July, visitors arriving to Nicoloff's website produced a little more than $30,000 in revenue. His costs, he said, total around $8,000, partly split between website hosting fees and advertising buys on Facebook itself.

Then, of course, there's the content, which, at a few dozen posts a day, Nicoloff is far too busy to produce himself. "I have two people in the Philippines who post for me," Nicoloff said, "a husband-and-wife combo." From 9 a.m. Eastern time to midnight, the contractors scour the internet for viral political stories, many explicitly pro-Trump. If something seems to be going viral elsewhere, it is copied to their site and promoted with an urgent headline. (The Khan story was posted at the end of the shift, near midnight Eastern time, or just before noon in Manila.) The resulting product is raw and frequently jarring, even by the standards of this campaign. "There's No Way I'll Send My Kids to Public School to Be Brainwashed by the LGBT Lobby," read one headline, linking to an essay ripped from Glenn Beck's The Blaze; "Alert: UN Backs Secret Obama Takeover of Police; Here's What We Know . . .," read another, copied from a site called The Federalist Papers Project. In the end, Nicoloff takes home what he jokingly described as a "doctor's salary" — in a good month, more than $20,000.

Terry Littlepage, an internet marketer based in Las Cruces, N.M., has taken 30
this model even further. He runs a collection of about 50 politically themed Facebook pages with names like The American Patriot and My Favorite Gun, which push visitors to a half-dozen external websites, stocked with content aggregated by a team of freelancers. He estimates that he spends about a thousand dollars a day advertising his pages on Facebook; as a result, they have more than 10 million followers. In a good month, Littlepage's properties bring in $60,000.

Nicoloff and Littlepage say that Trump has been good for business, but each admits to some discomfort. Nicoloff, a conservative, says that there were other candidates he preferred during the Republican primaries but that he had come around to the nominee. Littlepage is also a recent convert. During the primaries, he was a Cruz supporter, and he even tried making some left-wing pages on Facebook but discovered that they just didn't make him as much money.

In their angry, cascading comment threads, Make America Great's followers express no such ambivalence. Nearly every page operator I spoke to was astonished by the tone their commenters took, comparing them to things like torch-wielding mobs and sharks in a feeding frenzy. No doubt because of the page's name, some Trump supporters even mistake Nicoloff's page for an official organ of the campaign. Nicoloff says that he receives dozens of messages a day from Trump supporters, expecting or hoping to reach the man himself. Many, he says, are simply asking for money.

Many of these political news pages will likely find their cachet begin to evaporate after Nov. 8. But one company, the Liberty Alliance, may have found a way to create something sustainable and even potentially transformational, almost entirely within the ecosystem of Facebook. The Georgia-based firm was founded by Brandon Vallorani, formerly of Answers in Genesis, the organization that opened a museum in Kentucky promoting a literal biblical creation narrative. Today the Liberty Alliance has around 100 sites in its network, and about 150 Facebook pages, according to Onan Coca, the company's 36-year-old editor in chief. He estimates their cumulative follower count to be at least 50 million. Among the company's partners are the former congressman Allen West, the 2008 election personality Joe the Plumber, the conservative actor Kirk Cameron and the former "Saturday Night Live" cast member Victoria Jackson. Then there are Liberty's countless news-oriented pages, which together have become an almost ubiquitous presence on right-leaning political Facebook in the last few years. Their names are instructive and evocative: Eagle Rising; Fighting for Trump; Patriot Tribune; Revive America; US Herald; The Last Resistance.

A dozen or so of the sites are published in-house, but posts from the company's small team of writers are free to be shared among the entire network.

The deal for a would-be Liberty Alliance member is this: You bring the name and the audience, and the company will build you a prefab site, furnish it with ads, help you fill it with content and keep a cut of the revenue. Coca told me the company brought in $12 million in revenue last year. (The company declined to share documentation further corroborating his claims about followers and revenue.)

Because the pages are run independently, the editorial product is varied. 35
But it is almost universally tuned to the cadences and styles that seem to work best on partisan Facebook. It also tracks closely to conservative Facebook media's big narratives, which, in turn, track with the Trump campaign's messaging: Hillary Clinton is a crook and possibly mentally unfit; ISIS is winning; Black Lives Matter is the real racist movement; Donald Trump alone can save us; the system — all of it — is rigged. Whether the Liberty Alliance succeeds or fails will depend, at least in part, on Facebook's algorithm. Systemic changes to the ecosystem arrive through algorithmic adjustments, and the company recently adjusted the news feed to "further reduce clickbait headlines."

For now, the network hums along, mostly beneath the surface. A post from a Liberty Alliance page might find its way in front of a left-leaning user who might disagree with it or find it offensive, and who might choose to engage with the friend who posted it directly. But otherwise, such news exists primarily within the feeds of the already converted, its authorship obscured, its provenance unclear, its veracity questionable. It's an environment that's at best indifferent and at worst hostile to traditional media brands; but for this new breed of page operator, it's mostly upside. In front of largely hidden and utterly sympathetic audiences, incredible narratives can take shape, before emerging, mostly formed, into the national discourse.

Consider the trajectory of a post from August, from a Facebook page called Patriotic Folks, the headline of which read, "Spread This: Media Rigging the Polls, Hiding New Evidence Proving Trump Is Winning." The article cited a litany of social-media statistics highlighting Trump's superior engagement numbers, among them Trump's Facebook following, which is nearly twice as large as Clinton's. "Don't listen to the lying media — the only legitimate attack they have left is Trump's poll numbers," it said. "Social media proves the GOP nominee has strong foundation and a firm backing." The story spread across this right-wing Facebook ecosystem, eventually finding its way to Breitbart and finally to Sean Hannity's "Morning Minute," where he read through the statistics to his audience.

Before Hannity signed off, he posed a question: "So, does that mean anything?" It's a version of the question that everyone wants to answer about Facebook and politics, which is whether the site's churning political warfare is actually changing minds — or, for that matter, beginning to change the political discourse as a whole. How much of what happens on the platform is a reflection of a political mood and widely held beliefs, simply captured in a new medium, and how much of it might be created, or intensified, by the environment it provides? What is Facebook doing to our politics?

Appropriately, the answer to this question can be chosen and shared on Facebook in whichever way you prefer. You might share this story from the *New York Times Magazine*, wondering aloud to your friends whether our democracy has been fundamentally altered by this publishing-and-advertising platform of unprecedented scale. Or you might just relax and find some memes to share from one of countless pages that will let you air your political id. But for the page operators, the question is irrelevant to the task at hand. Facebook's primacy is a foregone conclusion, and the question of Facebook's relationship to political discourse is absurd — they're one and the same. As Rafael Rivero put it to me, "Facebook is where it's all happening."

Reading the Text

1. How do Facebook news feeds differ from traditional news sources, according to Herrman?
2. Explain in your own words how Facebook determines what will appear in your news feeds.
3. Summarize how, according to Herrman, Mark Provost uses Facebook to promote his political agenda.
4. What Facebook-related strategies did Adam Nicoloff and Terry Littlepage use to encourage the election of Donald Trump in 2016?
5. What significance does Herrman find in the growth of Liberty Alliance?

Reading the Signs

1. If you have a Facebook page, analyze a week's worth of news feeds that you receive. What do your results reveal about Facebook's profile of you? To what extent do you think that profile is accurate? Alternatively, study the news feeds of relatives or acquaintances, and prepare a political profile based on your Facebook information alone. What response do the profiles' subjects have to your results?
2. **CONNECTING TEXTS** Read Brooke Gladstone's "Influencing Machines: The Echo Chambers of the Internet" (p. 379). Adopting her perspective, write an essay in which you assess the applicability of the term *echo chamber* to describe Facebook's news feed practices.
3. **CONNECTING TEXTS** In class, brainstorm ways that an ordinary citizen can try to escape the echo chamber effects of digital media. Use the class's results to formulate an essay that evaluates the extent to which digital technology is threatening the free flow of information that has long been considered a cornerstone of a democratic society. To develop your ideas, consult Joseph Turow, "The Daily You: How the New Advertising Industry Is Defining Your Identity and Your Worth" (p. 265).
4. **CONNECTING TEXTS** Write an essay that argues your response to Herrman's question "What is Facebook doing to our politics?" (para. 38). To develop your ideas, consult the Introduction to Chapter 1, "American Paradox: Culture, Conflict, and Contradiction in the U.S.A." (p. 67).

Section 3

ENTERTAINMENT

Leonard Zhukovsky/Shutterstock

6

ON THE AIR

Television and Cultural Forms

From Mary Tyler Moore to *The Handmaid's Tale*

Once upon a time, women were housewives — at least that was the impression viewers were most likely to get in the early years of American TV from watching sitcom after sitcom featuring goofy housewives like Lucy Ricardo, elegant ones like Donna Stone, demure ones like Margaret Anderson, or slightly ditzy ones like Laura Petrie. And then, one day, Laura Petrie metamorphosed, like a caterpillar emerging from a cocoon, into Mary Richards, and suddenly women weren't all housewives any more.

The story we have just told — about the fictional housewives of *I Love Lucy*, *The Donna Reed Show*, *Father Knows Best*, and *The Dick Van Dyke Show*, followed by the unmarried news-producing protagonist of *The Mary Tyler Moore Show* — traces a semiotically significant arc from the patriarchal origins of American television to the emergence of the women's movement into mainstream popular culture. As the actress whose career most visibly exemplified this transformation, Mary Tyler Moore became a universally admired cultural symbol, her personal grace and charm contributing significantly to the acceptance of what was at the time a fairly radical change in prime-time TV.

But that was then. It has now been over forty years since Mary Richards got canned by new management at WJM, and a lot has happened in the interval. For one, we've seen a lot more non-housewives on the air — like factory workers Laverne and Shirley, cops Cagney and Lacey, and (in a clear nod to *MTM*) TV journalist Murphy Brown and *30 Rock*'s Liz Lemon. Such television programs, and many more like them, form a **system** of associated signs that point to the growing power of women in American society, but if we expand that system to include a number of much more recent women-centered series, a certain **difference** appears, marking a significant change in the tenor and tone of gender politics in America today. In short, things are getting darker.

This difference is most evident in Hulu's *The Handmaid's Tale*, a nightmarish dystopia based on Margaret Atwood's 1985 novel of the same title. The *1984* of feminist fiction, Atwood's story was uncompromising in its denunciation of the cultural backlash against women that she apprehended in the rise of such conservative movements as the Moral Majority. So as women donned handmaid attire in 2019 to protest threats against *Roe v. Wade*, the reappearance of Atwood's dark moral fable as a prime-time hit on streaming TV presented a striking signifier of the #MeToo era, reflecting a feeling that there was something intolerably Gileadish about America in the Age of Trump.

One sign that America was ready for such a politically charged program as *The Handmaid's Tale* in 2017 was the ongoing success of the Netflix offering *Orange Is the New Black*, a streaming series that also featured women imprisoned under essentially patriarchal conditions. But we can find a significant **difference** between the handmaid Offred and the busted drug courier Piper, for while Piper and her sister inmates have actually committed crimes, Offred's only "crime," in effect, lies in being a fertile woman. Thus, there is a certain qualification in the oppression endured by the women of *Orange Is the New Black* (a show that also has a comedic side) that is lacking

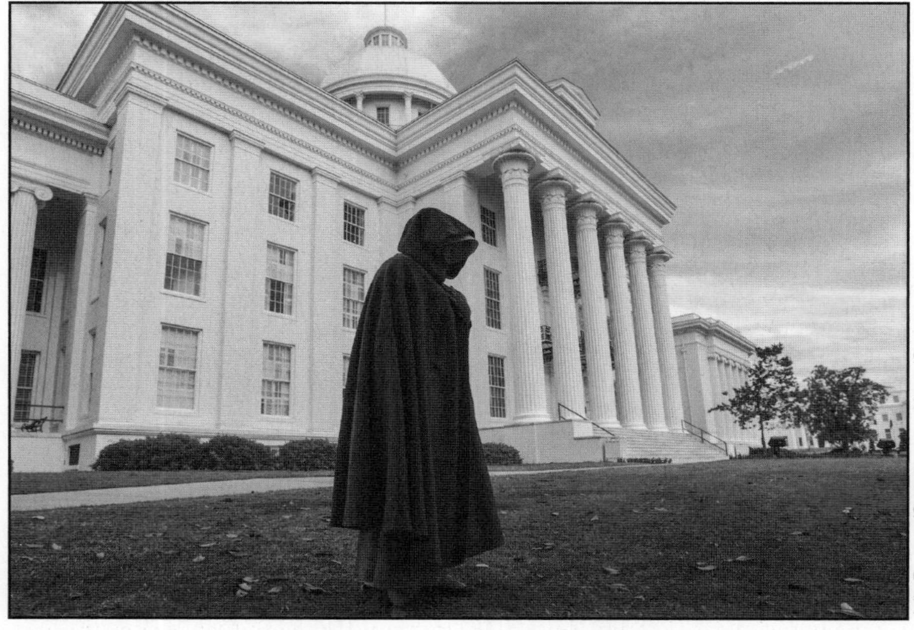

Julie Bennett/Getty Images News/Getty Images

A protestor dressed in handmaid attire, following a 2019 reproductive rights rally outside the Alabama State Capitol.

in *The Handmaid's Tale*, signifying a further darkening of mood between the release of the two programs. Toss in the extreme gender violence dramatized throughout the spectacular run of *Game of Thrones*, and the meaning of this trajectory becomes clear: it's as if the arc of the rainbow that sprouted from the skies of *MTM*'s Minneapolis finally came to earth in a prison yard.

Litchfield Is the New Mayberry

The preceding analysis demonstrates how you can interpret semiotically an entire system of television programs, illustrating how the associations among, and differences between, various series over a number of years can reveal broad movements within American social history. You have many more ways to take a semiotic approach to TV, of course, from interpreting a single episode of a television series to analyzing the cultural effects of the new media now available for television viewing—for while the days of "the box" are not over, digital TV platforms are revolutionizing the ways that audiences access their favorite content. For the purpose of this introduction, since we have already begun laying the groundwork for the analysis of a single TV episode by establishing a system of associations and differences in which the series to which it belongs can be situated, we will now study *Orange Is the New Black* more closely to show how understanding a television series as a whole is essential to interpreting a single episode, and how single episodes build up the larger picture that TV series create.

Let's begin by looking at the television genre that *Orange Is the New Black* belongs to, because the generic classification of a series has a great deal to do with its overall significance. There are a lot of genres to consider—including dramas, comedies, sitcoms, mysteries, crime shows, fantasies, Westerns, soap operas, game shows, documentaries, unscripted programs (reality TV), and so on and so forth. Along with the many sub-varieties within a given genre (for example, medical and law *dramas*, or *crime* procedurals and police shows), different categories of programming can be mixed together into any number of hybrid forms. For example, there are war dramas (like the 1960s series *Combat*) and war comedies (like *M*A*S*H*), family sitcoms (animated—*The Simpsons*—and nonanimated—*Leave It to Beaver*), and nonfamily sitcoms (*Seinfeld* and *Friends*), and shows that mix comedy and drama in such equal parts that a new classification has had to be created to account for them: the *dramedy*. *Orange Is the New Black*, with its dramatic as well as comic elements, belongs to this category, as well as to another, relatively rare, programming type focused on prison inmates as the main characters (examples include *Prison Break*, HBO's *Oz*, an Australian series called *Wentworth*, and a British series called *Bad Girls*).

As you can see, categorizing a TV program can take a lot of thought and research, and it's a good place to start your analysis of any TV series. After deciding what kind of program your topic is, you then want to look into its history to see how the series relates to that history. For example, say you are analyzing an animated family sitcom like *South Park* or *The Simpsons*. Your system would include such shows as *Father Knows Best*, *Leave It to Beaver*, *The Dick Van Dyke Show*, *The Flintstones*, and *Married with Children*. All of these shows can be associated with *South Park* and *The Simpsons*, but there are also some crucial differences. Like *Married with Children*, but unlike the other shows listed here, *South Park* and *The Simpsons* feature what are commonly called dysfunctional families, just like *Family Guy*, *Malcolm in the Middle*, and a host of dysfunctional family sitcoms that sprang up in the late 1980s and bourgeoned in the 1990s. The difference between the dysfunctional and the traditional family sitcoms points to a profound change in American attitudes toward family life itself. Reflecting an era of high divorce rates, and a growing, often feminist-inspired, audience resistance to the patriarchal propaganda promulgated in the golden age of family sitcoms during the 1950s and 1960s, the dysfunctional family sitcoms have proven to be an enduring sign of our times.

So, what about *Orange Is the New Black*? There aren't very many American prison-based dramedies to compare it to, but we can still find something of importance through a brief look at a classic sitcom, *The Andy Griffith Show*, that did involve a prison of sorts. Situated in Mayberry, an idealized southern village, that program focuses on a country sheriff who contends with local criminals and runs the local jail. But, of course, the whole small town scene never gets much naughtier than a spitball fight in an elementary school cafeteria, and that's precisely the point. It's a long stretch from the little-used and comedically sanitized jail in Mayberry to the women's prison at Litchfield, an evolution comparable to the cultural movement from *The Dick Van Dyke Show* to *The Mary Tyler Moore Show* to *The Handmaid's Tale*. Once again, things are getting a lot darker and grittier, and it is highly significant in this regard that *Orange Is the New Black* is largely a woman's show.

For this reason, the gender difference that marks *Orange Is the New Black* indicates that we would do well to look beyond the prison genre in our analysis to yet another television genre, one that includes such shows as *Sex and the City*, *The L Word*, and *Girls*, and that could be called *women's relationship* programs.

Orange Is the New Black's generic kinship with *The L Word* is explicitly indicated both in the ongoing saga of Piper and Alex's romance and in the opening scene of "The Chickening," the particular episode of *Orange Is the New Black* that we will analyze here. In the language of movie ratings, the scene is sexually explicit and involves nudity. Now, it may be difficult today to see how controversial it is to present such an explicit portrayal of a lesbian relationship on American television, but as late as 1997, when Ellen DeGeneres came out as a lesbian on her ABC series *Ellen*, consumer boycotts of the program's sponsors were threatened, advertising contracts were terminated, and the episode was not aired on all local stations. So, the fact that "The Chickening" could begin with the kind of scene that it does is itself a sign of just how far America has come in the treatment of human sexuality.

More evidence that *Orange Is the New Black* is more of a relationship or (perhaps more accurately) a sisterhood program — one that goes well beyond the more heterosexually oriented sisterhood series *Sex and the City* — than it is a prison series lies once again in a crucial difference. The traditional prison show focuses on either the innocence of its protagonist (*The Fugitive* is one instance) or the protagonist's attempts to escape (*The Prisoner* is a good example). In contrast, *Orange Is the New Black*'s protagonist is unquestionably guilty. In addition, escape is not posed as a desperate goal for the prisoners. At least in the show's first season, Litchfield is presented as a minimum-security prison with such "country club" amenities as yoga classes and verdant grounds into which Piper can take her morning cup of tea and read a book. In fact, the main plot point of "The Chickening" begins with Piper spotting a chicken wandering on the grounds while she sips her tea and enjoys the autumn foliage. Becoming an obvious symbol in the episode, that chicken also becomes a device around which the rather loosely structured story line can be organized.

And that story line raises another element in the system to which *Orange Is the New Black* belongs. Loosely plotted story lines, which continue from episode to episode without any attempt at closure, have become increasingly popular, forming a system of **postmodern** series from *Twin Peaks* to *The X-Files* to *Lost*. Like *Lost*, *Orange Is the New Black* is filled with flashbacks intended to reveal a little more of the backstories of the ensemble cast, but it never fills in all the blanks at once. To know fully what's going on, the audience must tune in to every episode, but with new twists developing every time around, the story line remains wide open (as it does in *Desperate Housewives*, which can, for its part, be called a postmodern soap opera).

So, to summarize where we are at this point, we might say that *Orange Is the New Black* is a sisterhood-themed postmodern soap opera, breaking old barriers to what can be represented on television and exploring new horizons of the human — especially women's — experience.

This takes us back to that chicken. Like Herman Melville's novel *Moby-Dick*, "The Chickening" draws explicit attention to the symbolism of an animal, in this case a chicken (one character named Red, who is especially obsessed with it, is even referred to as "Ahab" in the episode) without telling the viewer what that symbolism is. We *are* told the chicken's "story": the women believe that it is the sole survivor of a chicken massacre outside the fence that has come to haunt, as it were, the prison. But beyond this general significance, the inmates offer up a number of their own interpretations. To Red, for example, the chicken is a symbol of power, and she wants to cook and eat it to absorb that power. To the Latina prisoners, it is a symbol of forbidden fruits (they think it is filled with $1,000 worth of heroin). To the black prisoners, the chicken is a symbol of forbidden sweets (they think it is filled with candy). And to the prison warden (a man who, like most men in the show, is an exemplar of abusive patriarchal authority), the myth of the chicken is an annoyance that stirs up Litchfield's inmates and makes them more difficult to control.

The episode ends with Piper chasing the chicken through the yard, but just as she seems to have trapped it, it rather magically appears *outside* the prison fence, and the final shot shows Piper *inside* the fence gazing at something she cannot attain for herself. Does this mean that the chicken simply signifies "freedom"? That certainly seems to be one of its meanings, but the differences among the various inmates as to the chicken's significance suggest that the matter is more complicated than that. So, we need to dig a little further.

It *is* significant that the chicken is a hen and not a rooster (at least so the bird appears), for while the women of Litchfield interpret it differently, they share a sense that the hen represents something desired but out of reach (while the male warden would like to see the whole legend of the chicken suppressed). With its open-ended symbolism, the hen is thus expressly addressed to a female viewership, symbolizing whatever the viewer most desires but cannot quite attain.

We can now return to the overall significance of *Orange Is the New Black*. Belonging to a system of sisterhood television programs, the series establishes new boundaries of what it means to be a woman and how that can be represented on TV. Far edgier than *Sex and the City* and *Desperate Housewives*, the show transcends the conventional gender stereotypes that circumscribe these associated programs — in which heterosexual relationships, dieting, and fashion take up so much of the characters' time — to explore dimensions of women's experience that have hitherto been more or less taboo on American television. Ironically, this greater freedom of expression is set within the context of a prison story, which may be the most profound point of all: that only within the confines of a women's prison can a contemporary woman explore who she is.

Writing about Television

We began this chapter with a semiotic analysis of both a television series as a whole and a single episode of it to show how you can look at TV programs in the same way that you can look at any cultural phenomenon: as a series of signs, or signifiers, of the society that consumes them. But while you might find writing about television familiar from high school assignments in which you wrote about a favorite program — perhaps in a summary-writing exercise, a descriptive essay, or an opinion piece about what made a particular program your favorite — writing semiotic interpretations of TV shows is a different task. Although you still need to rely on your skills in description and summarization in writing semiotic analyses of TV, you should put aside your personal opinions of a show (that is, whether you like it or not) to construct interpretive arguments about its cultural significance.

Television offers an especially rich field of possible writing topics, ranging from a historical analysis of a whole category, or genre, of TV programming, or of a general trend, to an interpretation of a single TV show episode — or all of these topics combined. Whatever your approach to analyzing television,

Photofest

Enjoy it or not, *Game of Thrones* provides enormous potential for cultural analysis.

however, you will probably need to do some research. No one can be expected to know about all the TV programs (from both the past and the present) that can be associated with and differentiated from any particular show that you're analyzing, so you should plan to find reliable sources to help you contextualize whatever show you are interpreting.

From Symbols to Icons

When writing about TV, keep in mind that the ubiquity of televised (or digitized) images in our lives represents a shift from one kind of sign system to another. As Marshall McLuhan pointed out over fifty years ago in *The Gutenberg Galaxy* (1962), Western culture since the fifteenth century has defined itself around the printed word — the linear text that reads from left to right and top to bottom. The printed word, in the terminology of the American founder of semiotics, Charles Sanders Peirce, is a **symbolic sign**, one whose meaning is entirely arbitrary or conventional. A symbolic sign means what it does because those who use it have decided so. Words don't look like what they mean. Their significance is entirely abstract.

Not so with a visual **image**, which does resemble its object and is not entirely arbitrary. Although a photograph is not literally the thing it depicts and may reflect a good deal of staging and manipulation by the photographer, we often respond to it as if it were an innocent reflection of the world. Peirce

Discussing the Signs of Television

With your class, choose a current television program, and all watch the same episode (either individually as "homework" or together while you're in class). Interpret the episode semiotically. What values and cultural myths does the show project? What do the commercials broadcast during the show say about its presumed audience? Go beyond the episode's surface appeal or "message" to look at the particular images it uses to tell its story, always asking, "What is this program *really* saying?"

called such signs "icons," using this term to refer to any sign that visually resembles what it means. The way you interpret an **icon**, then, differs from the way you interpret a symbol or word. The interpretation of words involves your cognitive capabilities; the viewing of icons is far more sensuous, more a matter of vision than cognition. The shift from a civilization governed by the paradigm of the book to one dominated by the image accordingly involves a shift in the way we "read" our world, as the symbolic field of the printed page yields to the iconic field of the screen.

The change from a symbolic, or word-centered, world to an iconic universe filled with visual images carries profound cultural implications. For while we *can* read visual images actively and cognitively (which, of course, is the whole point of this book), the sheer visibility of icons tempts us to receive them uncritically and passively. Icons look so much like the realities they refer to that it's easy to forget that icons, too, are signs: images that people construct to carry **ideological** meanings.

Consider again the image of the American family as presented in the classic situation comedies of the 1950s and 1960s. White, suburban, and middle class, these families signified an American ideal that glorified patriarchal authority. Even *I Love Lucy*, a sitcom showcasing Lucille Ball, reinforced masculine privilege through such plotlines as Lucy's attempt to market her own line of "Vitameatavegamin" dietary supplements, an endeavor which, the show implied, was predestined to end in disaster due to female business incompetence. The advent of such "dysfunctional" family sitcoms as *Married with Children*, which undermined *male* authority and competence, thus signified a profound difference, a rejection of the old patriarchal values.

And Now a Word from Our Sponsors

Whatever show you choose to analyze, remember why it's on TV in the first place: to make money. In the early history of the medium in America, this was accomplished solely through commercial sponsorship. Viewers received free television content, but at the expense not only of having to watch the advertisements that accompanied the show but also in becoming subject to the restrictions that sponsors could influence over that content. Always on the alert for possible audience objection to controversial topics, TV's commercial sponsors have placed quite a number of limits on what can, and can't, be aired.

Network TV still has these limitations, but with first cable and now streaming television media that are paid for by consumer subscription, a lot of the barriers have come down. Leading the way into ever more daring programming with *The Sopranos*, HBO, for example, not only continues to push the boundaries of allowable sexual and violent content but has also stimulated such competitors as Showtime, whose racy series *The Affair* seems to be competing with HBO to see just where the limits may (or may not) lie. We've come a long way since Rob and Laura slept in separate beds, sheathed from neck to toe in conservative pajamas so no potential product consumers would be offended by the sight of a married couple in bed together.

Still, the majority of viewers watch commercially sponsored programs, and the advertising that accompanies such programs can provide a good deal of useful information as to who their intended audiences may be. Why is the nightly news often sponsored by over-the-counter painkillers, for example? Why is daytime TV, especially in the morning, typically accompanied by ads for vocational training schools? Why are youth-oriented prime-time shows filled with fast-food commercials, while family programs have a lot of car ads?

Your analysis of a single episode of a television program can also usefully include a survey of where the show fits in what cultural studies pioneer Raymond Williams called the "flow" of an evening's TV schedule. Flow refers to the sequence of TV programs and advertisements, from, say, the 5:00 p.m. news through the pre–prime time 7:00 to 8:00 slot, through prime time and

Exploring the Signs of Television: Viewing Habits

In your journal, explore your television-viewing habits and how the way you have watched TV has changed over time. When and why do you usually watch television? Have you transitioned from watching shows with your family or friends to watching them alone on a computer? Do you watch shows when they are broadcast, or do you watch them via Netflix or Hulu on your own time? Do you think of watching television as a social activity? If so, write about how the diverse technical options for watching television have complicated this notion. If not, what place does watching television occupy in your life? Consider as well whether your TV watching habits changed after stay-at-home orders brought on by COVID-19 and why.

on through to the 11:00 news and the late-night talk shows. What precedes your program? What follows? Can you determine the strategy behind your show's scheduling?

Reality Bites

With the full return of scripted television — a veritable renaissance of creativity that has seen TV eclipse film as a source of high-art popular culture — reality TV has lost some of its luster in recent years. It still generates a lot of programming, though, and its special stars over the years — from the Kardashian /Jenner clan to the Robertsons to *The Apprentice* host who went on to become president — continue to loom large over the cultural landscape. But RTV's significance has changed as America has changed, and it accordingly merits a brief analysis here, beginning with an overview of its history.

One might say that reality television began in 1948 with Allen Funt's *Candid Camera*, which featured the filming of real people (who didn't know they were on camera) as they reacted to out-of-the-ordinary situations concocted by the show's creators. The show's attraction lay in the humor that viewers could enjoy by watching other people get into minor jams. There is a name for this kind of humor that comes from psychoanalytic theory: *schadenfreude*, or taking pleasure in the misfortunes of others, as when we laugh at someone slipping on a banana peel. And we shall see that this appeal from the early days of reality TV is very much a part of the genre's popularity today.

After *Candid Camera* came the 1970s PBS series *An American Family*. In this program, a camera crew moved in with a suburban family named the Louds and filmed them in their day-to-day lives. The Louds were not contestants and there were no prizes to be won. The program was conceived as an experiment in cinema verité to see if it was possible for television to be authentically realistic. The experiment was a bit of a failure, however, as the Loud family members began to act out for the camera. The result was the eventual dissolution of the Loud's family structure and a general uneasiness about such experiments.

The next and probably most crucial step was when MTV launched *The Real World* in 1992. Like *An American Family*, *The Real World* (and similar programs like *Big Brother*) attempts to be realistic, with its constant camera recording a group of people living in the same house. Unlike *An American Family*, however, *The Real World* is a fantasy that caters to young-adult viewers, who can imagine themselves living in glamorous circumstances and vicariously enjoy the experience of becoming instant TV stars. That there is a certain tampering with reality in *The Real World*, a deliberate selection of participants based upon their appearance and how they can be cast into often-contrived romances as well as conflicts, constitutes a contradiction that differentiates *The Real World* from *An American Family* and leads us to the dawning of the reality revolution.

The astounding success of the inaugural versions of *Who Wants to Marry a Multi-Millionaire?* and *Survivor* established reality TV's full coming-of-age. In both programs, we can see strong traces of what made their pioneering predecessors popular. But through their introduction of a game show element, complete with contestants competing for huge cash prizes, a whole new dimension was added with complex layers of significance in an even more **overdetermined** fashion. Reality programs that include a game show dimension offer their viewers the vicarious chance to imagine themselves as being in the shoes of the contestants (after all, in principle, anyone can get on a game show) and winning lots of money. There's an element of schadenfreude here as well, if viewers take pleasure in watching the losers in game show competitions. But by adding the real-life element of marriage to the mix, *Who Wants to Marry a Multi-Millionaire?* (and such descendants as *The Bachelor*) brought an extra dimension of humiliation, not to mention voyeurism, to the genre. It's one thing to be caught on camera during the emotional upheaval of competing for large cash prizes, but it's quite another to be in an erotic competition, and lose, with millions watching you.

While game shows usually feature some sort of competition among the contestants, the *Survivor* series took such competition to a new level by compelling its contestants to engage in backstabbing conspiracies as they clawed their way to the top. (The 2006 season even added racial conflict to the mix by forming tribes according to race.) It isn't enough for tribe to compete against tribe; there has to be intratribal backbiting and betrayal as well. Such a subtext constitutes a kind of grotesque parody of American capitalism itself, in which the cutthroat competition of the workplace is moved to the wilderness.

A lot of RTV also is intended to evoke a kind of freak show appeal (consider the popularity of such shows as *Jersey Shore*, *Here Comes Honey Boo Boo*, and *My Super Sweet 16*), inviting its viewers to sneer at its central figures, but a good deal of reality programming expresses the values and desires of its highly segmented audiences, not its hostilities. From *Duck Dynasty*, which appealed to rural — and generally conservative — Americans, to *Dancing with the Stars* and various other talent show–themed programs, which, in the tradition of *American Idol*, address a host of **mass cultural** fantasies, RTV often presents its audiences with visions of their own lives and dreams. Some working-class Americans, for example, have found truck drivers (*Ice Road Truckers*) and commercial fishing crews (*Deadliest Catch*) to identify with, and homeowners and home buyers can choose from a plethora of do-it-yourself programs to help them purchase and maintain their houses.

In this respect, then, we can see how RTV has followed an evolutionary path that is quite similar to that of digital technology, because whether we get our content from a TV set or a computer, RTV enables us to customize our viewing down to the most granular details of our lifestyles and values. The medium that once pulled America together, if only by compelling everyone to watch the same limited programming on the same limited number of networks, is now, paradoxically enough, pulling things asunder as the

Reading about Television Online

The internet has given rise to a number of popular sites for TV criticism and community discussion, including tvworthwatching.com. Using a search engine, find a forum devoted to your favorite TV show and study how the community of fans interacts. What about the show you've chosen most interests fans? What topics are most popular or most contested? Does the conversation stick to television, or does it veer into discussions of users' personal lives or politics? Are you drawn to participate? Using the forum as a microcosm, reflect on how television might be considered a social adhesive. How do the fans of TV shows use the internet to bond over the show and with one another?

multitudinous choices of network, cable, and digital TV draw us ever further into our own self-mirroring echo chambers wherein we may find only our own chosen realities. And it is within such an environment that we may find yet another explanation for a country that appears to be coming apart at the seams — a darkly ironic revelation for a medium that, after all, involves a projection of light.

The Readings

We begin this chapter's readings with an essay by Neal Gabler suggesting that, having contributed to the atomization of American society, "TV has learned how to compensate for the increasing alienation it seems to induce" by filling its schedule with shows saturated with inauthentic "flocks" of friends and family relationships. Samantha Allen is next with a celebration of the way that HBO's *Euphoria* advances the evolution of television's presentation of trans characters. Claire Miye Stanford follows with an analysis of the feminist dimensions of ABC's *Nashville*, while Emily Nussbaum takes us back to Westeros for another look at a "sophisticated cable drama about a patriarchal subculture." Massimo Pigliucci then steps up to the lectern with a philosophical analysis of *The Big Bang Theory*'s critique of scientism, which is as accessible as the series he analyzes, and Brittany Levine Beckman concludes the readings with a rueful reflection on, um, "Why We Binge-Watch Stuff We Hate."

NEAL GABLER

The Social Networks

Do you like to binge-watch *Friends*, that sprightly comedy in which no one ever seems to be alone? Or *Sex and the City*, wherein busy Manhattan professional women always seem to have time to share a glass of water and some lettuce? Indeed, even today, wherever you look on television, Neal Gabler notes in this essay that originally appeared in the *Los Angeles Times*, you are certain to see "lots of folks spending the better part of their day surrounded by their friends and family in happy conviviality." Yet oddly enough, this sort of programming is appearing "at a time when it is increasingly difficult to find this kind of deep social interaction anyplace but on TV." Clearly, Gabler suggests, television is providing some sort of compensation for the social atomization that it itself has contributed to, and thus, all the simulated conviviality, while being a pleasant "dream," is "pure wish fulfillment," indeed, rather "phony," and, perhaps, sad. Neal Gabler is a well-known analyst and historian of American cinema and popular culture, and is the author of, among many books, *An Empire of Their Own: How the Jews Invented Hollywood* (1988).

With the new television season upon us, here are a few things you are virtually certain to see again and again and again: lots of folks spending the better part of their day surrounded by their friends and family in happy conviviality; folks wandering into the unlocked apartments and homes of friends, family, and neighbors at any time of the day or night as if this were the most natural thing in the world; friends and family sitting down and having lots of tearful heart-to-hearts; Little League games, school assemblies, and dance recitals, all attended by, you guessed it, scads of friends and family.

You're going to be seeing these scenes repeatedly because the basic unit of television is not the lone individual or the partnership or even the nuclear family. The basic unit of television is the flock — be it the extended family of brothers and sisters, grandfathers and grandmothers, nieces, nephews, and cousins, or the extended circle of friends, and, rest assured, it is always a circle. On television friends never come in pairs; they invariably congregate in groups of three or more.

That television has become quite possibly the primary purveyor in American life of friendship and of the extended family is no recent blip. Over the last twenty years, beginning with *Seinfeld* and moving on through *Friends*, *Sex and the City*, and more recently to *Desperate Housewives*, *Glee*, *The Big Bang Theory*, *How I Met Your Mother*, *Cougar Town*, and at least a half-dozen other shows, including this season's newbies *Raising Hope* and *Better with You*, television has become a kind of friendship machine, dispensing groups of people in constant and intimate contact with one another, sitting around in living rooms, restaurants, and coffee shops, sharing everything all the time. You might even say that friendship has become the basic theme of television, certainly of broadcast television, though cable has its own friendship orgies like *Men of a Certain Age*, *My Boys*, and *It's Always Sunny in Philadelphia*. Friendship is what television is about.

What makes this so remarkable is that it has been happening at a time when it is increasingly difficult to find this kind of deep social interaction anyplace but on TV. Nearly a decade ago, Harvard professor Robert Putnam observed in his classic *Bowling Alone* that Americans had become more and more disconnected from one another and from their society. As Putnam put it, "For the first two-thirds of the twentieth century a powerful tide bore Americans into ever deeper engagement in the life of their communities, but a few decades ago — silently, without warning — that tide reversed and we were overtaken by a treacherous current." It was a current that pulled Americans apart.

Moreover, the current that Putnam observed has, according to more recent 5
studies, only intensified in the last decade. One study found that Americans had one-third fewer nonfamily confidants than they had twenty years earlier, and 25 percent had no one in whom to confide whatsoever. Another study of 3,000 Americans found that on average they had only four close social contacts, but these included family members like one's own spouse. This decline in real friendships may account in part for the dramatic rise of virtual friendships like those on social-networking sites where being "friended" is less a sign of personal engagement than a quantitative measure of how many people your life has brushed and how many names you can collect, but this is friendship lite. Facebook, in fact, only underscores how much traditional friendship — friendship in which you meet, talk, and share — has become an anachronism and how much being "friended" is an ironic term.

Among the reasons Putnam cited for the increasing atomization in American life were economic pressures and anxieties; women entering the workplace in full-time employment by necessity and thus disengaging from their friends and neighbors; metropolitan sprawl, which meant more time spent commuting, greater social segregation, and the disruption of community boundaries; and last but by no means least, the rise of television itself, especially its splintering influence on later generations who have grown up addicted to the tube. It is no secret that watching television is not exactly a communal activity. Rather, we often use it to fill a communal void. But instead of bringing comfort, it seems only to remind us of our alienation. In Putnam's view, based on several studies, "TV is apparently especially attractive for people who feel unhappy, particularly when there is nothing else to do."

It's not that we prefer television to human contact. The laugh track attests that most people don't really want to be alone in front of their TV sets. They want to be part of a larger community. Yet another study indicates that TV provides a sort of simulacrum of community because the relationship between the TV viewer and the people he or she watches on the screen competes with and even substitutes for physical encounters with real people. It is Facebook with hundreds of "friends" but without any actual contact with any of them, only the virtual contact of watching.

But what none of these theories of television has noticed is that TV has learned how to compensate for the increasing alienation it seems to induce. And it compensates not by letting us kill time with "friends" on-screen but by providing us with those nonstop fantasies of friendship, which clearly give us a vicarious pleasure. Watch *Seinfeld* or *Friends* or *Sex and the City* or *Community* or *Men of a Certain Age* — the list is endless — and you'll see people who not only are never ever alone but people whose relationships are basically smooth, painless, uninhibited and deeply, deeply intimate — the kind of friendships we may have had in college but that most of us can only dream about now. How many adults do you know who manage to hang out with their friends every single day for hour after hour?

Or watch the incomparable *Modern Family* or *Brothers and Sisters* or *Parenthood* and you'll see big, happy family gatherings with lots of bonhomie and jokes and an outpouring of love. On the last there seems to be a huge extended family dinner every other night where most families would be lucky to have one such get-together each year at Thanksgiving. And don't forget those school assemblies, already mentioned, which everyone in the family takes off work to attend en masse or the weekend birthday parties where attendance is also compulsory.

One feels a little churlish pointing out how phony most of this intimacy 10
is. After all, these shows, even one as observant as *Modern Family*, aren't about realism. They aren't about the genuine emotional underpinnings of friendship or family, and they certainly aren't about the rough course that almost every relationship, be it with a friend or family member, takes — the inevitable squabbles, the sometimes long and even permanent ruptures, the obtuseness, the selfishness, the reprioritization, the expectations of reciprocity, the drifting apart, the agonizing sense of loneliness even within the flock. These shows are pure wish fulfillment. They offer us friends and family at one's beck and call but without any of the hassles. It is friendship as we want it to be.

For the fact is that we miss the friendships we no longer have, and we know that Facebook or emails cannot possibly compensate for the loss. So we sit in front of our television sets and enjoy the dream of friendship instead: a dream where we need never be alone, where there are a group of people who would do anything for us, and where everyone seems to understand us to our very core, just like Jerry and George, Chandler and Joey, Carrie and her girls, or the members of the McKinley High glee club. It is a powerful dream, and it is one that may now be the primary pleasure of television.

Reading the Text

1. Summarize in your own words what Gabler means by saying, "The basic unit of television is the flock" (para. 2).
2. How does Robert Putnam's research on friendship in America inform Gabler's argument?
3. Why does Gabler say that "being 'friended' is an ironic term" (para. 5)?
4. How does Gabler use concession to strengthen his argument?
5. In your own words, explain what Gabler means by "simulacrum of community" (para. 7)?

Reading the Signs

1. Write an argumentative essay in which you assess the validity of Gabler's claim that "instead of bringing comfort, [television] seems only to remind us of our alienation" (para. 6). To support your argument, you might interview friends or acquaintances about their reasons for watching television.
2. In an essay, analyze an episode of one of the friend-heavy TV programs that Gabler mentions, such as *The Big Bang Theory*, *Glee*, or *Modern Family*. To what extent does it confirm Gabler's assertion that "these shows are pure wish fulfillment" (para. 10)?
3. **CONNECTING TEXTS** Write an essay in which you support, oppose, or complicate Gabler's belief that Facebook offers "friendship lite" (para. 5). To develop your ideas, read Nancy Jo Sales's "From the Instamatic to Instagram: Social Media and the Secret Lives of Teenagers" (p. 360).
4. Adopting Gabler's perspective, analyze the friendships and interpersonal relations depicted in *How I Met Your Mother*, *The Good Place*, or *Modern Family*. To what extent do they replicate or deviate from the ones represented in the shows Gabler discusses? How do you think Gabler would explain any differences you see among these TV shows?

SAMANTHA ALLEN

How Euphoria *and Model Hunter Schafer Created the Most Interesting Trans Character on TV*

The inclusion of trans characters in a major television series has come a long way since the debut of *Transparent* in 2014, and HBO's *Euphoria* is a good example of the change. For while, as Samantha Allen explains in this review piece for the *Daily Beast*, Jules, the character played by Hunter Schafer, *is* a trans woman, she "is so many things besides transgender." Simply by treating Jules as a complex American teenager rather than as a one-dimensional poster child for all transgender people, *Euphoria* signals the beginning of a new era in which, in Allen's words, "we are *finally* entering a time when being transgender can be a footnote instead of the whole story." Samantha Allen is a GLAAD Award–winning journalist and the author of *Love & Estrogen* (2018).

The most interesting transgender character on television doesn't utter the words "I'm trans" until three episodes into her show.

The show is *Euphoria*, HBO's controversy-courting teen drama, and the character is Jules, a charismatic young transgender girl with Rapinoe-pink hair and a heart that looks for love in all the wrong places. Jules is brought to life by transgender model Hunter Schafer, acting the hell out of her debut role opposite Zendaya, who plays Jules's best friend Rue.

Euphoria is a series that clearly wants a reaction, regularly touching hot buttons like 9/11, the opioid crisis, and sexting — and a reaction *Euphoria* will get. But years from now, long after the hot takes have cooled and the show itself has been reduced to a blur of sex scenes in our collective cultural consciousness, we will still remember Jules. A character like her is hard to dream up, harder to portray, and harder still for a creator to handle with care.

The fact that Jules is transgender isn't exactly a secret in the episodes that HBO has aired thus far. The context clues are all there: a few oblique references in the dialogue, a handful of visual cues. Whereas the (still-groundbreaking) *Orange Is the New Black* seemed to go out of its way to announce that Laverne Cox's character Sophia was transgender in every single scene, *Euphoria* trusts its audience to pick up on the hints and follow along. "Yes, she's transgender," the show seems to say. "But that's not all there is to her."

Indeed, Jules — like transgender people more generally — is so many 5
things besides simply transgender. She is silly and has a strong sense of style. She likes to ride her bike through the orange groves, even at night. She spends way too much time on her phone. She melts under attention, even when it's coming from people who could prove dangerous.

It's not that *Euphoria* refuses to acknowledge Jules's gender identity or to use it as a plot point. The show does both. But it does so without reducing the rich complexity that is Jules to her transgender status and — so far — without trotting out the same tired transgender tropes that have plagued Hollywood since the days of *The Crying Game*.

Whereas that 1992 film revealed that a character was transgender as a plot twist, *Euphoria* is set in a high school where the Gen Z student body seems to already know, more or less, about Jules. Viewers who missed context clues might be surprised when Jules vocalizes that she's trans in the third episode — in a conversation with Rue, who cuts her off, because it's not new information — but *Euphoria* doesn't treat the revelation like a rug to be pulled out from under the audience. If you knew, fine. If you missed it, catch up. And although Jules's gender identity certainly plays a role in how the other characters treat her — be it sexual assault, verbal harassment, or erotic fetishization — Jules as a character is allowed to do so much more than endure violence and discrimination.

Narratively, she has spent much of *Euphoria* so far being courted via text message by an anonymous boy who found her profile on a gay dating app. The boy goes to her school. Drama predictably ensues. But Jules is most captivating to watch in her many richly-textured scenes with Rue, who develops a crush on Jules while struggling with drug addiction. *Euphoria* likes to take big swings, and it misses some of them, but the show always returns to this tender friendship between a cisgender young woman and her transgender BFF, who bond not just over shared histories of trauma but through bike rides and sleepovers and lunchroom banter.

Zendaya and Schafer capture the beauty of this cis-trans, platonic-romantic bond with a chemistry that arguably hasn't been seen on TV since the Emmy-nominated web series *Her Story*. (In an interview with *W Magazine*, Schafer said that she and Zendaya had formed "a really special bond" — and it shows.) "I hate everyone else in this world but you," Jules tells Rue, forehead to forehead, right before one of *Euphoria*'s most gut-wrenching moments to date.

It's clear that these characters love each other — or, at least, that they need 10
each other in ways deeper than teenagers possess the emotional maturity to express. But nothing about *Euphoria* suggests that this will be a fairy-tale romance in which Rue and Jules run away from their insular town and start a new life together. The show's prevailing atmosphere of doom will come for them, too. But for now, their bond is gorgeous and, quietly, a step forward for transgender representation writ large.

Euphoria, along with the very different show, *Pose*, is proving what many LGBT viewers have known all along: There are far more interesting things for transgender characters to do aside from get hurt. It should be obvious that transgender people are people first: people who have friends, people who love, people who yearn for lives bigger than the constraints of their current realities. Pain is unavoidable, so at least let us dream.

Yet showrunners and filmmakers still too often use transgender characters as empty rhetorical vehicles to make some broader point about injustice. While well-intentioned, this approach elides the humanity of these characters — and of the community they represent. They become mere cardboard cutouts to be knocked down, so that the show can then say, "See? That was wrong!" — when, in fact, the best way to humanize a marginalized group is to show them being, well, fully human. In that respect, much credit goes to writer-creator Sam Levinson, who directed Hari Nef in *Assassination Nation* last year — another piece of media that deftly acknowledges a character's gender identity without making it the central fact of her existence.

But it should be no surprise that Schafer herself reportedly helped Levinson "fill in little pieces" of Jules, as the actress told *W*, because the character feels authentic, lived-in, and, most important, complicated. The result isn't just the most interesting transgender character on television right now, but one of the most interesting, period.

Jules, much like Schafer herself, is a sign that we are *finally* entering a time when being transgender can be a footnote instead of the whole story.

Reading the Text

1. How does the depiction of the character of Jules in *Euphoria* differ from that of other transgender characters on TV, like Sophia on *Orange Is the New Black*, according to Allen?
2. What does *Euphoria*, along with televisions series like *Pose*, prove what "many LGBT viewers have known all along" (para. 11)?
3. What mistakes, in Allen's view, do traditional television and filmmakers usually make in their portrayal of transgender characters?
4. How does Allen characterize the relationship between Jules and Rue, and what attitude does she have toward that relationship?

Reading the Signs

1. Watch a variety of television programs that feature transgender characters — including *Euphoria* — and write an analytic essay describing how they portray their lives and personalities. To what extent do the programs that you are analyzing avoid showing "transgender characters as empty rhetorical vehicles to make some broader point about injustice" (para. 12)?
2. Research the history of TV series that feature LGBTQ+ characters and write an essay describing how their portrayal has evolved over the years. Alternately, write an essay comparing the historical treatment of LGBTQ+ characters on TV with their representation in advertising during the same period. How might the difference in media account for any differences you might find?
3. Write an essay comparing and contrasting the depiction of transgenderism in *Euphoria* and the groundbreaking TV series *Trans*.
4. **CONNECTING TEXTS** Adopting the perspective of David Denby ("High-School Confidential: Notes on Teen Movies," p. 510), write an essay in which you analyze whether *Euphoria* fits his category of a typical "teen" narrative.

CLAIRE MIYE STANFORD

You've Got the Wrong Song: Nashville *and Country Music Feminism*

Ever since Tammy Wynette counseled women to "Stand By Your Man" no matter what abuse he dishes out, country music has hardly been noteworthy for its feminist spirit. Such a background makes the country music–themed series *Nashville* all the more remarkable, Claire Miye Stanford argues in her review of the program, which she regards as "one of the most feminist television shows on television." In fact, for Stanford, *Nashville* resists simple political categorization and instead mixes femininity and feminism in the Dolly Parton tradition. Claire Miye Stanford is a freelance writer who has written for *The Millions, The Rumpus, Good,* and the *Los Angeles Review of Books,* in which this reading first appeared.

Both femininity and feminism have become harder and harder to define in 2013. In regard to the first, there are as many examples of femininity in the world as there are people (not just biological women) who embody them. As for the second, the term "feminism" is now so loaded with meaning, confusion, and incorrect associations that it has become all too common, especially among young women, to disavow the term entirely.

Into this complex terminology, enter Rayna James (Connie Britton) and Juliette Barnes (Hayden Panettiere), the lead characters of ABC's *Nashville*, created by former Nashville resident Callie Khouri. Khouri is a film veteran who wrote 1991's *Thelma & Louise*, a feminist classic that also won her the Academy Award for best original screenplay (typically a heavily male-dominated category). In its first season, the show has explored what it means to be both feminine and feminist in the world of country music and television.

Ultimately, any female-driven television show has to contend with these two concepts — whether that treatment is overt or more indirect, if only because every female-driven show will ultimately contend with the characters' love lives and how they interact with men (since their romantic interests are, almost always, male). But what stands out about *Nashville*, among all female-driven television shows, is that it places these omnipresent questions in unique contexts: professional, rather than personal, in the frame of a highly gendered genre, industry, city, and region.

But can a show that is so ostensibly interested in the "feminine" — in sexual and romantic relationships, in motherhood and daughterhood, in short skirts and spangly tops and big hair — also be feminist? That same question has been asked time and time again about country music itself, long considered a bastion of heteronormative, gendered songs about pick-up trucks. Historically, most feminist ire lands squarely on the shoulders of country music legend Tammy Wynette, and her biggest hit, 1968's "Stand By Your Man," in which Wynette advises the listener to forgive your man and, for that matter, to be "proud" of him, even when he's off having "good times / doing things that you don't understand." Whether these things that "you don't understand" are cheating, boozing, gambling, or other unsavory activities is not entirely clear, but still, Wynette counsels the listener to stand by him "'cause after all he's just a man"; in other words, he can't help it, it's in his Man Nature to mistreat you.

There are countless other songs, less famous than Wynette's, with the 5
same degrading message, but critics keep circling back to "Stand By Your Man" as a kind of shorthand for antifeminist doctrine in country music, and, to a greater extent, life in general. In 1992, Hillary Clinton referred to the song when responding to allegations of then-presidential-hopeful Bill's extramarital affairs. "I'm not sitting here — some little woman standing by my man like Tammy Wynette," she said in a *60 Minutes* interview. (In a whole other layer of feminist rhetoric, Clinton was pressured into apologizing to Wynette only days later by legions of country music fans who said it was an unfair comparison.)

Still, plenty of female country musicians have serious feminist chops, using their lyrics to take on political feminist issues from birth control and abortion to equal pay and spousal abuse. Loretta Lynn's 1975 song, "The Pill," is the first major song to mention oral contraceptives; more recently, Neko Case's 2002 song, "Pretty Girls," examines the judgment that comes with abortion. Other songs — about disappointment in marriage and motherhood, about not being slut-shamed for wearing a short skirt, about hitting your cheating husband upside the head with a cast-iron skillet — are not as overtly political, but still deal with realities of female experience head-on, without conforming to gender norms or social conventions.

Of all female country musicians, Dolly Parton presents the most interesting example of the tension that exists between femininity and feminism. Her 1980 classic hit, "9 to 5," is set to a catchy beat but makes a political point about being an ambitious woman in a discriminatory workplace. Lesser known, her 1968 song "Just Because I'm a Woman" took on sexual hypocrisy and double standards way before "slut-shaming" was even an established phrase. But these days, Parton is often discounted as an artist — and as a feminist — made into a punch line about breast implants and plastic surgery; even when she is held up as a feminist icon, the argument often comes with a tone of questioning surprise and an acknowledgment that her big hair, big breasts, and tiny waist make her a less-than-obvious feminist heroine.

In their music on the show, both Rayna and Juliette fall firmly in the Dolly Parton camp of female country music star; while their songs are not overtly political or feminist — no abortion or birth control talk here — they are very much about women standing on their own, standing up for themselves, and being respected. Juliette's hits include "Telescope," which warns a cheating lover that she knows full well what he's up to; "Boys and Buses," advising that chasing after boys is a waste of time; and "Undermine," a heartfelt ballad about how it's harder — but more worthwhile — to achieve something on your own than to undermine someone else. Rayna's songs, tinged with more experience, are more downcast, but they, too, advocate for standing one's ground: "Buried Under" tells the story of a woman grappling with finding out her lover's long-buried secrets; in "No One Will Ever Love You," the singer insists that her love is the best love the listener will ever find, and he should accept it.

Of all *Nashville*'s songs, the song that Juliette and Rayna fictionally "co-wrote" does the most to situate them within the world of women in country music. Titled "Wrong Song," the song is a fiery duet, addressed to a lying, cheating man, and in classic Rayna/Juliette fashion, it stands up for the woman, saying that she won't stand for that. But "Wrong Song" goes a step further than the usual woman-power advocacy, adding a meta-layer of commentary on country music (and music in general), turning the song into a defiant take on expectations for country music and female narratives in general. The song begins with a series of conditional ifs, setting up the typical country-song scenario — man drinks too much, does foolish thing, woman misses him and forgives him:

> If you think you're gonna hear
> how much I miss you
> If you're needing to feel better 'bout yourself
> If you're waiting to hear me
> say I forgive you
> 'Cause tequila turned you into someone else

The song then slows down, ever so slightly, as it winds up to the chorus, meanwhile deploying the Tammy Wynette shorthand for the disempowered woman, the country music stereotype who stands by her man no matter what he does:

> If you're looking for one more chance
> A little stand by your man

And then there comes the booming chorus, both women's voices coming together for the coup de grace, calling out all those songs before it for so easily forgiving wayward men, and also calling out the listener himself for expecting that they would forgive him, just because they are country music singers, just because they are ladies. If you think you're getting the stereotypical female narrative of passivity and forgiveness (à la "Stand By Your Man"), they tell the listener, then you've got the wrong song and the wrong girl:

> You've got the wrong song
> Coming through your speakers
> This one's about a liar and a cheater

Who didn't know what he had
'till it was gone
You've got the wrong girl
Cause I've got your number
I don't know what kind of spell
you think I'm under
This ain't a feel-good,
'Everything's fine' sing-along
You've got the wrong song

This song, this performance, is the epitome of *Nashville* womenhood: active, empowered, and take-charge. But this song is more than just a statement on behalf of the characters. In one catchy chorus, it takes on the music industry and its demands on female artists, and then goes a step further by putting that examination on television, a similar crucible of issues concerning money, sexuality, female image, and power.

10 As characters, Rayna and Juliette are strong women, still rare on television, but not impossible to find. As a show, though, *Nashville*— in its unapologetically pure focus on female characters, its self-aware examination of the struggles of female artists, and its critique of male-dominated industries— is one of the most feminist television shows on television.

Still, neither Rayna nor Juliette is a feminist, or, at least, we've never heard them say that they are. *Nashville* has never dropped the F-bomb, surely afraid of alienating part of its audience. As the show goes on, however, and as both Rayna and Juliette give more and more fictional interviews to television talk shows and magazines, the absence of the word "feminist" becomes a more glaring omission; after all, media love to ask women to define themselves in terms of feminism, especially strong, powerful women.

But that kind of definitive stance— feminist or not feminist— doesn't interest *Nashville*. The show is focused on individual characters rather than overarching labels, in showing how strong, powerful women live their strong, powerful lives. There are men on *Nashville*, too, but they are pretty much ineffectual; any success they have comes, directly or indirectly, as a result of their partnerships with the show's various women. Indeed, every woman on the show— not just Rayna and Juliette— is portrayed as a strong woman; they may have their faults, but all of them, from up-and-comer Scarlett O'Connor to Rayna's sister Tandy to more minor characters like the managers and political wives, have ambition, drive, and agency, as well as a self-possessed dignity that leaves no question about who is in control.

There is only one notable exception to this otherwise consistently empowered cast of female characters: the needy, conniving, and man-reliant Peggy Kenter, who has an affair with Rayna's husband and leaks Rayna's subsequent divorce to the tabloids. In both her demeanor and her actions, Peggy appears like a caricature of a helpless female, as if a reminder of all the ghosts of stereotypical soapy female characters past. Peggy is also notably the only character whose situation is presented without a trace of compassion; the show, it would seem, has no sympathy for a woman like Peggy — a woman who belongs in a different kind of world, on a different kind of show.

In fact, even though *Nashville* is billed as a primetime soap, it is much better described as a workplace drama, where the workplace is the country music mainstage. Along with reproductive rights, women's advancement and equal treatment in the workplace is one of the last — and most persistent — issues for feminism, a fact that makes *Nashville*'s portrait of this very particular workplace all the more interesting from a feminist point of view.

As in a workplace drama, we see the way the women express themselves 15
in front of others, but we also see what happens when the stage curtain is pulled back, and how that empowerment translates to both their personal lives and their behind-the-scenes business decisions. And it's in this offstage life that the show truly uses Rayna and Juliette to explore questions of feminism, especially when it looks at the challenges a woman faces when she insists on being in control of her own life.

These challenges are different for Rayna and Juliette, who are at distinct stages in both their careers and personal lives. For Rayna, married with two daughters, they manifest as a question of how to balance her career ambitions with being a good ("good") mother, daughter, and wife (and eventually ex-wife). Rayna never feels guilty about any of the decisions she makes related to her career; she misses her daughters when she is on the road, but she does not feel guilty or ashamed that she has left them with their (very loving) father. On the flip side, when her father has a heart attack, she flies back to Nashville immediately and says she might have to cancel that night's concert, but those decisions are made without agony, without any drama over where to put family and where to put career. This departure from female guilt over the intersection of professional and domestic priorities is refreshing.

Rayna also faces the challenge of how to stay relevant as a female artist and performer in her forties, an age our society deems over the hill. Again, the show defies the stereotypical storyline — one that might end in a middle-age crisis, substance abuse, or plastic surgery — and gives the character of Rayna the dignity of a real person, taking on a real professional challenge. Rayna has to work even harder to stay relevant; there is no such thing as resting on laurels, especially for a female celebrity over the age of thirty. And, as always, Rayna rises to the challenge, writing more songs, evolving her sound, taking more risks, going on tour. When faced with a challenge, Rayna does not break down; she steels herself and takes it on, and she succeeds — not by chance or wiles, but by hard work and force of will.

For Juliette — young, hot, and unattached — the challenges are different. More than anything, Juliette wants to be taken seriously: by her record label, by her employees, by her colleagues, by reviewers, by her fans. Her youth is a major part of her problem: her male-dominated world (her boss at the label, her manager, her roadies, her band, the predominately male reviewers) do not want to take her seriously. But, even more problematic for a young woman like Juliette is her attitude. She knows what she wants, and she does what she wants without thinking of the consequences.

Juliette's behavior is not always perfect, but her slips in judgment are exacerbated by her gender and her age, and these mistakes drive the show's examination of social and professional double standards. Were Juliette a man, she would be described as "driven" and "demanding" when she fires her manager or changes her set list at the last minute; instead, since she is a woman, she is seen as irrational. Were she a man, she would be called a "bad boy" for her brushes with the law and her late nights clubbing; since she is a woman, this behavior threatens to ruin her career and her image. When Juliette's ex-boyfriend blackmails her over a sex tape he secretly filmed, the show takes on one of the most gendered celebrity scandals: a sex tape for a male celebrity means almost nothing, but becomes part of a woman's permanent record.

Even when exploring the rivalry between Rayna and Juliette — one of 20
Nashville's central plotlines — the show treats the women with sophistication and dignity, making it clear from the start that it's a professional rivalry. It would be ideal if all women — or, for that matter, all people — could support each other even in competition, but in the world in which Rayna and Juliette operate, that isn't an option. This kind of competition is particularly endemic to women and particularly brutal, but professional competition transcends gender. Record labels only have so much promotional money to put behind artists; magazines only have so many pages to dedicate to female country music stars. In the plotline that will wrap up this season, Rayna and Juliette are both nominated for Female Country Music Artist of the Year. This turn of events is a brilliant move by the show in that it brings their competition to the forefront.

The show's recognition of this contest — and also the way the rivalry unfolds — again defies the typical portrayal of female envy. The very fact that competition is the major plot point of the show recognizes that women can compete in the first place — that women don't always "play nice," that a woman can want to be number one. Beyond that initial recognition, the rivalry itself is handled with sophistication and dignity. Other than a few snippy comments in the first few episodes when the show was finding its footing, both women are refreshingly direct (the gendered thing to say here would be that they aren't catty) about their relationship. Other than a few offhand statements, neither of them really talks about the other behind her back; when one of them is frustrated or angry at the other, she says so to her rival's face.

Most refreshingly, the competition stays entirely in the professional sphere. When Juliette is confronted with a giant billboard of Rayna's face as a celebrity endorsement, she does not react by commenting on Rayna's appearance or her age; she is pissed, but she is pissed because she wants an endorsement deal and a billboard of her own. When Rayna is forced to fly on Juliette's plane, she is also unhappy, but mostly about the fact that she doesn't have her own jet. Even when Juliette beds Rayna's long-ago love, the story focuses more on both women wanting him as a bandleader and songwriter — in a professional capacity — than a sexual or romantic rivalry.

In fact, in a brilliantly self-aware move, this season's closing plotline about Rayna and Juliette's award rivalry perfectly appropriates real-world media commentary about the show itself. When the show debuted in the fall, *Nashville*'s creator Khouri and stars Connie Britton and Hayden Panettiere both had to spend a lot of time (an inordinate amount of time) telling interviewers that the show was not about a "catfight" between the two women. In a recent episode, as Britton's Rayna and Panettiere's Juliette walked a red carpet together, reporters ask them how it feels to compete and Rayna, echoing Britton's real-life remarks, tells them, "If you're expecting a catfight, you're not going to get it."

Not only does this statement provide a new meta-commentary on female-driven narratives, but it also continues the themes established in "Wrong Song" of defying traditional expectations for women, both for the way women act and the way women are represented — and represent themselves. In other words, if viewers come to *Nashville* looking for the same old soapy female tropes — catfights, bitchiness, seduction, backstabbing — then they've got the wrong show.

Reading the Text

1. According to Stanford, how do the fictional *Nashville* characters Rayna James and Juliette Barnes compare with real-life country music stars Tammy Wynette and Dolly Parton?
2. Why does Stanford claim that the word "'feminism' is now so loaded with meaning, confusion, and incorrect associations that it has become all too common, especially among young women, to disavow the term entirely" (para. 1)?
3. Summarize in your own words the conventional motifs of mainstream country music. In what ways does *Nashville* depart from the genre's conventions?
4. What does Stanford mean by saying that "Wrong Song" adds "a meta-layer of commentary on country music (and music in general)" (para. 9)?

Reading the Signs

1. In class, list on the board the connotations class members attach to the word *feminism*. What do you think the sources of these connotations may be? Do you detect any differences between male and female students; if so, how do you account for them?
2. In an essay, argue for your own response to Stanford's question about *Nashville*: "Can a show that is so ostensibly interested in the 'feminine' . . . also be feminist?" (para. 4). As an alternative, focus your argument on a different program that features women characters, such as *Orange Is the New Black*.

3. Using Stanford's critique of femininity and feminism as a critical framework, analyze some songs popularized by current real-life country music artists such as Carrie Underwood, Kacey Musgraves, or Miranda Lambert. As an alternative, conduct a survey of country music lyrics by both male and female performers, and write an essay analyzing the gender politics implicit in these lyrics.
4. Write a semiotic analysis of a music superstar such as Lady Gaga, who is overtly political in her public persona and actions. In what ways might your subject of analysis reflect "the themes established in 'Wrong Song' of defying traditional expectations for women, both for the way women act and the way women are represented — and represent themselves" (para. 24)?
5. Adopting Stanford's perspective, analyze the gender dynamics you see in a different show that focuses on Southern female characters, *Here Comes Honey Boo Boo* or *Atlanta*. To what extent does the show replicate or defy "the same old soapy female tropes" (para. 24)? To develop your ideas, watch one or two episodes of the show.

EMILY NUSSBAUM

The Aristocrats: The Graphic Arts of Game of Thrones

In one sense, HBO's smash hit series *Game of Thrones*, like the novels it's based on, turns the past upside down. For unlike J. R. R. Tolkien's Middle Earth, with its clear-cut divisions between good and evil, George R. R. Martin's Westeros presents a world of almost total moral anarchy. But when it comes to television history, the show is very much in the tradition of such programs as *The Sopranos* and *Mad Men*, dramas set within patriarchal subcultures. The result, Emily Nussbaum observes in this review for the *New Yorker*, is a show that features "copious helpings of pay-cable nudity, much of it in scenes that don't strictly require a woman to display her impressive butt dimples as the backdrop for a monologue about kings." Emily Nussbaum is the television critic for the *New Yorker*.

For critics, sorting through television pilots is an act of triage. Last year, when *Game of Thrones* landed on my desk, I skimmed two episodes and made a quick call: we'd have to let this one go. The HBO series, based on the best-selling fantasy books by George R. R. Martin, looked as if it were another guts-and-corsets melodrama, like *The Borgias*, or that other one. In the première, a ten-year-old boy was shoved out of a tower window. The episode climaxed with what might be described as an Orientalist gang rape/wedding dance. I figured I might catch up later, if the buzz was good.

It was the right decision, even if I made it for the wrong reason. *Game of Thrones* is an ideal show to binge-watch on DVD: with its cliffhangers and Grand Guignol dazzle, it rewards a bloody, committed immersion in its foreign world — and by this I mean not only the medieval-ish landscape of Westeros (the show's mythical realm) but the genre from which it derives. Fantasy — like television itself, really — has long been burdened with audience condescension: the assumption that it's trash, or juvenile, something intrinsically icky and low. Several reviews of *Game of Thrones* have taken this stance, including two notable writeups in the *Times:* Ginia Bellafante sniffed that the show was "boy fiction" and Neil Genzlinger called it "vileness for voyeurism's sake," directed at "Dungeons & Dragons types."

It's true that *Game of Thrones* is unusually lurid, even within the arms race of pay cable: the show is so graphic that it was parodied on *Saturday Night Live*, with a "behind-the-scenes" skit in which a horny thirteen-year-old boy acted as a consultant. To watch it, you must steel yourself for baby-stabbing, as well as rat torture and murder by molten gold. But, once I began sliding in disks in a stupor, it became clear that, despite the show's Maltese vistas and asymmetrical midriff tops, this was not really an exotic property. To the contrary, *Game of Thrones* is the latest entry in television's most esteemed category: the sophisticated cable drama about a patriarchal subculture. This phenomenon launched with *The Sopranos*, but it now includes shows such as *Deadwood*, *Mad Men*, *Downton Abbey*, and *Big Love*. Each of these acclaimed series is a sprawling, multicharacter exploration of a closed, often violent hierarchical system. These worlds are picturesque, elegantly filmed, and ruled by rigid etiquette — lit up, for viewers, by the thrill of seeing brutality enforced (or, in the case of *Downton Abbey*, a really nice house kept in the family). And yet the undergirding strength of each series is its insight into what it means to be excluded from power: to be a woman, or a bastard, or a "half man."

The first season of *Game of Thrones* built up skillfully, sketching in ten episodes a conflict among the kingdoms of Westeros, each its own philosophical ecosystem. There were the Northern Starks, led by the gruffly ethical Ned Stark and his dignified wife, Catelyn, and their gruffly ethical and dignified children. There were the Southern Lannisters, a crowd of high-cheekboned beauties (and one lusty dwarf, played by the lust-worthy Peter Dinklage), who form a family constellation so twisted, charismatic, and cruel that it rivals *Flowers in the Attic* for blond dysfunction. Across the sea, there were the Dothraki, a Hun-like race of horseman warriors, whose brutal ruler, Drogo, took the delicate, unspellable Daenerys as a bride. A teen girl traded like currency by her brother, Daenerys was initiated into marriage through rape; in time, she began to embrace both that marriage and her desert queenhood. (Although the cast is mostly white, the dusky-race aesthetics of the Dothraki sequences are headclutchingly problematic.) By the finale, she was standing naked in the desert — widowed, traumatized, but triumphant, with three baby dragons crawling over her like vines. (This quick summary doesn't capture the complexity of the series' ensemble, which rivals a Bosch painting: there's also the whispery eunuch Spider; a scheming brothel owner named Littlefinger; and a ketchup-haired sorceress who gives birth to shadow babies.)

5 In the season's penultimate episode, the show made a radical move: it killed off the protagonist. On a public stage, Ned Stark was beheaded, on the orders of the teenage sadist King Joffrey, a sequence edited with unusual beauty and terror — birds fluttering in the air, a hushed soundtrack, and a truly poignant shot from Ned's point of view, as he looked out toward his two daughters. This primal act suggested the limits of ethical behavior in a brutalized universe, and also dramatized the show's vision of what aristocracy means: a succession of domestic traumas, as each new regent dispatches threats to his bloodline. (Or, as Joffrey's mother, Cersei, puts it, kinghood means "lying on a bed of weeds, ripping them out one by one, before they strangle you in your sleep.") It demonstrated, too, a willingness to risk alienating its audience.

This season, early episodes have suggested the outlines of a developing war, hopping among a confusing selection of Starks, semi-Starks, and members of the Baratheon clan. (There are so many musky twenty-something men with messy hair that a friend joked they should start an artisanal pickle factory in Red Hook.) Greater than the threat of war is the danger that, in time, the television adaptation may come to feel not so much epic as simply elephantine. Still, the most compelling plots remain those of the subalterns, who are forced to wield power from below. These characters range from heroic figures like the tomboy Arya Stark to villains like Littlefinger, but even the worst turn out to have psychic wounds that complicate their actions. If the show has a hero, it's Tyrion (Dinklage), who is capable of cruelty but also possesses insight and empathy, concealed beneath a carapace of Wildean wit. So far, his strategic gifts have proved more effective than the torture-with-rats approach. Power is "a trick, a shadow on the wall," the eunuch tells Tyrion. "And a very small man can cast a very large shadow."

Then, of course, there are the whores. From the start, the show has featured copious helpings of pay-cable nudity, much of it in scenes that don't strictly require a woman to display her impressive butt dimples as the backdrop for a monologue about kings. (The most common fan idiom for these sequences is "sexposition," but I've also seen them referred to as "data humps.") These scenes are at once a turn-on and a turn-off. At times, I found myself marveling at the way that HBO has solved the riddle of its own economic existence, merging *Hookers at the Point* with quasi-Shakespearean narrative. In the most egregious instance so far, Littlefinger tutored two prostitutes in how to moan in fake lesbianism for their customers, even as they moaned in fake lesbianism for us — a real Uroboros of titillation.

Viewed in another light, however, these sex scenes aren't always so gratuitous. Like *Mad Men*, *Game of Thrones* is elementally concerned with the way that meaningful consent dissolves when female bodies are treated as currency. War means raping the enemy's women; princesses go for a higher price, because their wombs are the coin of the realm, cementing strategic alliances. It helps that the narrative is equally fascinated by the ways in which women secure authority, and even pleasure, within these strictures, and that in the second season its bench of female characters has gotten even deeper — among them, a seafaring warrior princess, a butch knight, and Tyrion's prostitute girlfriend.

Game of Thrones is not coy about the way the engine of misogyny can grind the fingers of those who try to work it in their favor. An episode two weeks ago featured a sickening sequence in which King Joffrey ordered one prostitute — a character the audience had grown to care about — to rape another. The scenario might have been scripted by Andrea Dworkin; it seemed designed not to turn viewers on but to confront them with the logical endgame of this pornographic system. It echoed a very similar line-crossing moment in *The Sopranos*, when Ralphie beat a pregnant Bada Bing girl to death. But while the scene may have been righteous in theory, in practice it was jarring, and slightly incoherent, particularly since it included the creamy nudity we've come to expect as visual dessert.

As with *True Blood*, the show's most graphic elements — the cruel ones, 10
the fantasy ones, and the cruel-fantasy ones — speak to female as well as male viewers. (One of the nuttiest quotes I've ever read came from Alan Ball, *True Blood*'s showrunner, who said that a focus group had revealed that men watched his series for the sex and women for the romance. Please.) But there is something troubling about this sea of C.G.I.-perfect flesh, shaved and scentless and not especially medieval. It's unsettling to recall that these are not merely pretty women; they are unknown actresses who must strip, front and back, then mimic graphic sex and sexual torture, a skill increasingly key to attaining employment on cable dramas. During the filming of the second season, an Irish actress walked off the set when her scene shifted to what she termed "soft porn." Of course, not everyone strips: there are no truly explicit scenes of gay male sex, fewer lingering shots of male bodies, and the leading actresses stay mostly buttoned up. Artistically, *Game of Thrones* is in a different class from *House of Lies*, *Californication*, and *Entourage*. But it's still part of another colorful patriarchal subculture, the one called Los Angeles.

Reading the Text

1. Describe in your own words the genre to which Nussbaum categorizes *Game of Thrones*: "the sophisticated cable drama about a patriarchal subculture" (para. 3).
2. According to Nussbaum, how does *Game of Thrones* resemble shows like *Mad Men* and *The Sopranos*?
3. What does Nussbaum mean by saying "the most compelling plots remain those of the subalterns, who are forced to wield power from below" (para. 6)?
4. In your own words, describe Nussbaum's attitude toward the violence, nudity, and sex scenes in *Game of Thrones*.
5. Why does Nussbaum conclude that "there is something troubling about this sea of C.G.I-perfect flesh, shaved and scentless and not especially medieval" (para. 10)?

Reading the Signs

1. **CONNECTING TEXTS** Using Michael Parenti's "Class and Virtue" (p. 506), analyze how *Game of Thrones* reflects current American attitudes toward class and power.
2. In class, discuss how Nussbaum's review article, published in the *New Yorker*, differs from a scholarly analysis of a mass media product. For comparison, you might compare it to Massimo Pigliucci's essay, which is a scholarly article, in this chapter.
3. In class, brainstorm the system of "sword and sorcery" productions (*Lord of the Rings*, for example, or *Outlander*). In your own essay, locate *Game of Thrones* within this system and analyze how it both resembles and differs from the other entertainments in the system. What is the most crucial difference that you identify, and what does that difference signify?
4. Watch an episode of *Game of Thrones*. In an analytic essay, assess the extent to which the episode you choose demonstrates Nussbaum's assertion that "the undergirding strength of each series is its insight into what it means to be excluded from power: to be a woman, or a bastard, or a 'half man'" (para. 3).
5. When *Game of Thrones* concluded its run in 2019, it remained a top hit. Write an essay in which you interpret the reasons for the show's popularity. How can the show be seen as a sign of its time? To gather support for your position, you might interview a half dozen fans of the program about their attraction to it.

MASSIMO PIGLIUCCI

The One Paradigm to Rule Them All: Scientism and The Big Bang Theory

Mash up *Friends* with *Seinfeld*, toss in a dash of *Son of Flubber*, and what do you get? *The Big Bang Theory*, TV's long-playing Nielsen chart-topper. And one of the things that makes this hit series so popular, Massimo Pigliucci argues in this philosophical analysis of the show, is its persistent, and hilarious, takedowns of "scientism": that is, the belief that science has all the answers to life, the universe, and everything. For while the goofy geniuses of *The Big Bang Theory* do know an awful lot about, say, connecting every electrical device in their apartments to the internet, they don't always have a lot of simple common sense, which is where human capabilities beyond scientific acumen come in. And that's the point. Massimo Pigliucci is a former evolutionary biologist turned philosophy professor at the

City University of New York's Lehman College and Graduate Center, who is the author of *Nonsense on Stilts: How to Tell Science from Bunk* (2010).

Why is *The Big Bang Theory* so funny? Some fans think it's the writing; others, the acting; still others, the directing. Different aspects of the show no doubt work together on multiple levels. This essay explores one way in which the various facets — writing, acting, directing — come together to make us laugh. The characters of Sheldon Cooper, Leonard Hofstadter, Howard Wolowitz, and Rajesh "Raj" Koothrappali are so funny (in part) due to their extremely "scientistic" worldviews, entirely framed by their practice of science. The humor manifests as their scientific approach unfolds in everyday life. They, of course, invariably fail at various mundane tasks, in sharp contrast with their nonintellectual but much more pragmatic neighbor Penny. In this way, art teaches us something about life. Through the lens of *The Big Bang Theory*, we can see how attempts to develop a thoroughgoing scientistic worldview are bound to fail, calling for more balanced approaches to understanding the world around us.

The Data

In "The Hamburger Postulate," Leonard Hofstadter finally decides to ask his equally nerdy colleague, Leslie Winkle, to go out on a date:

> LEONARD: Leslie, I would like to propose an experiment. . . . I was thinking of a bi-social exploration with a neuro-chemical overlay.
>
> LESLIE: Wait, are you asking me out?
>
> LEONARD: I was going to characterize it as a modification of our colleagues slash friendship paradigm with the addition of a date-like component, but we don't need to quibble over terminology.

Leslie suggests they simplify things a bit, as in any good scientific experiment, by skipping the actual date and going straight to the kissing stage. This will determine empirically what sort of neuro-chemical arousal they get from the experience and hence determine whether they wish, in fact, to begin dating. Leslie reports that Leonard's kiss produces absolutely no arousal in her, ending their experiment and Leonard's inquiry. Having agreed with the parameters, he quietly leaves the lab, a bit wistful.

It's "Anything Can Happen Thursday Night" from "The Hofstadter Isotope," and the guys are — gasp — considering going out to a bar to pick up women. Leonard quickly comes back to Earth, muttering, "C'mon, Howard, the odds of us picking up girls in a bar are practically zero." Undaunted, Wolowitz replies, "Oh, really? Are you familiar with the Drake equation?" Sheldon unflinchingly recites the formula for the Drake equation, used to calculate the odds of finding an extraterrestrial civilization with whom to communicate.[1] "Yeah, that one!" Howard quickly injects and continues:

> You can modify it to calculate our chances of having sex by changing the formula to use the number of single women in Los Angeles, the number of those who might find us attractive, and what I call the Wolowitz coefficient: Neediness, times Stress, squared. In crunching the numbers I came up with a conservative 5,812 potential sex partners within a 40-mile radius.

Leonard muses that he must be joking. Stone-faced, Howard replies, "I'm a horny engineer, Leonard, I never joke about math or sex."

In "The Friendship Algorithm," Sheldon endeavors to develop a scientific approach to acquiring friends. He proceeds to demonstrate the power of the algorithm over the phone, trying to convince the irksome Barry Kripke to spend time with him. Sheldon, however, soon gets stuck in an infinite loop caused by the structure of his own algorithm. Howard notices this and promptly strolls over to Sheldon's whiteboard to modify the procedure, thereby helping Sheldon achieve his goal. Placing his hand over the phone, Sheldon muses, "A loop counter, and an escape to the least objectionable activity. Howard, that's brilliant. I'm surprised you saw that." Slowly making his way back to his chair, Howard rhetorically and sarcastically asks, "Gee, why can't Sheldon make friends?"

These examples illustrate the attempt to reduce complex social skills to 5
simple matters of logic, of the kind that might be implemented in a computer program. Once we are finished chuckling at Sheldon, Howard, Leonard, or Raj, the inevitable reaction is: dating or making friends simply isn't that cut and dried. This, in turn, leads us to ask: why even try to apply scientific methodologies to complex social interactions? Why think that science holds all of the answers?

The Background

Science is indisputably the most effective way human beings have developed to understand — and even control, to a point — the natural world. It used to be a branch of philosophy, until the scientific revolution of the seventeenth

[1]The actual equation looks like this: $N = R * fp * ne * fl * fi * fc * L$. Where N is the number of civilizations in our galaxy with whom communication is possible; R is the average galactic rate of star formation per year; fp is the fraction of stars with planets; ne is the average number of potentially life-sustaining planets per star; fl is the fraction of planets actually developing life; fi is the further fraction developing intelligent life; fc is the fraction of civilizations developing communication technology; and L is the length of time these civilizations produce detectable signals. You can play with the equation yourself here: www.activemind.com/Mysterious/Topics/SETI/drake_equation.html.

century. Galileo and Newton thought of themselves as "natural philosophers," and the very term *scientist* was coined by the philosopher William Whewell as recently as 1834, in analogy with the word *artist*. The root of the term, however, is the Latin *scientia,* which means knowledge broadly construed, not only in the sense of what we today consider scientific knowledge.

Scientism is the idea that science can and should be expanded to every domain of human knowledge or interest, including the social sciences and the humanities, or alternatively the idea that the only kind of knowledge really worth having is that provided by the natural sciences. The appeal of scientism may derive from another important idea that is fundamental to the practice of science: reductionism. Reductionism is a basic and very successful approach common to the physical and biological sciences, articulated by René Descartes (1596–1650) in his *Meditations on First Philosophy.* Descartes was interested in establishing firm epistemic foundations for mathematics, philosophy, and science. To this end, he proffered four principles that he discovered on which to build a successful science. The second and third principles summarized the practice of reductionism:

> The second, to divide each of the difficulties under examination into as many parts as possible, and as might be necessary for its adequate solution. The third, to conduct my thoughts in such order that, by commencing with objects the simplest and easiest to know, I might ascend by little and little, and, as it were, step by step, to the knowledge of the more complex; assigning in thought a certain order even to those objects which in their own nature do not stand in a relation of antecedence and sequence.[2]

The "divide and conquer" strategy (second principle), coupled with the "building from the bottom up" (third principle) approach, are exactly how physics has been able to subsume the entire domain of chemistry, and why molecular biology has been such a successful science since the discovery of the structure of DNA as recently as 1953. It is this triumph of the Cartesian method that has made reductionism a staple of the way science is done today.

Moreover, there is an intuitive appeal to reductionism and, by extension, to scientism, because of the common acknowledgment—among both

[2]In case you are really curious, here are the first and the fourth: "The first was never to accept anything for true which I did not clearly know to be such; that is to say, carefully to avoid precipitancy and prejudice, and to comprise nothing more in my judgment than what was presented to my mind so clearly and distinctly as to exclude all ground of doubt." And: "The last, in every case to make enumerations so complete, and reviews so general, that I might be assured that nothing was omitted."

scientists and philosophers — that the world is made of the same kind of basic stuff, be it quarks or superstrings. From this, it is tempting to conclude that a complete understanding of the world can be arrived at by simply studying the basic stuff of the universe carefully. Of course, science — particularly physics — is the discipline that studies the basic stuff of the universe. Perhaps this kind of thinking fuels the heated discussion between Leslie and Sheldon about string theory and loop quantum gravity in "The Codpiece Topology." If a complete understanding of everything depends on exploring the basic stuff of the universe, it is very important that you are studying the correct basic stuff.

The Ramifications

The term *scientism* is almost never used in a positive sense; rather, it is 10
ordinarily meant as an insult, usually hurled by (some) philosophers and humanists at scientists who seem to trespass on territory that does not belong to them. True, Howard's attempt to mathematically quantify the delicate art of human dating is amusing, as is Leslie and Leonard's experiment. And Sheldon's attempt at friendship is simply comical. Yet what accounts for the animosity associated with scientism?

Consider that staunchly valuing a scientific approach to things may hamper our ability to see the "bigger picture." These days, for instance, our society seems to be in the thrall of a quantification frenzy: we wish to measure (and compare) people's intelligence or learning or happiness by using simple, linear scales that afford us a feeling of precision and scientific accuracy. The risk, of course, is that we may miss the structure (and beauty?) of the forest because we are focused on counting the individual trees, discounting the importance of anything that is not amenable to a scientific-quantifying approach (think again of Sheldon's friendship algorithm) or straitjacketing complex phenomena (such as intelligence, learning, or happiness) into easily digestible numbers that make our decisions and our entire worldview much simpler than they would otherwise be.

Even Sheldon seems to get close to understanding this point during a conversation with his sister Missy in "The Pork Chop Indeterminacy." Introducing her to the rest of the gang, he says, "She is my twin sister, she thinks she is funny, but frankly I've never been able to see it." Missy knowingly replies, "That's because you have no measurable sense of humor, Shelly." Without skipping a beat, Sheldon rhetorically asks, "How exactly would one measure a sense of humor? A humor-mometer?" The delightful play on the term *measurable* shows that Missy, and not Sheldon, has a sense of humor exactly because humor resists quantifiable analysis.

Too much emphasis on science also risks becoming a sterile end, in and of itself, as in this exchange from "The Cooper-Hofstadter Polarization," where the boys proudly show Penny a new piece of software that Howard developed, which allows people from all over the world to take control of Leonard and Sheldon's apartment's fixtures:

> LEONARD: See?
> PENNY: No.
> SHELDON: [impatiently] Someone in Szechuan province, China, is using his computer to turn our lights on and off.
> PENNY: Oh, that's... handy. Ahem, here is a question: why?

When the four scientists answer, in unison, "Because we can," Penny shakes her head in exasperation. The exercise is fascinating to the boys because it shows that it can be done, even though there are much better (but less "scientific") ways of accomplishing the same goal. Penny would simply have them use the light switch (or, at most, buy a universal remote from Radio Shack.)

Philosophers who criticize scientistic approaches to human problems seek to highlight the ethical issues raised by a science-based view of everything. When we attempt to reduce, or reinterpret, the humanities and our everyday experience in scientific terms, we not only are bound to miss something important, we also risk dehumanizing our own and other people's existence, possibly even becoming callous about the dangers of doing certain types of science on the grounds that the latter represents in itself the highest conceivable goal. For instance, since the Large Hadron Collider (LHC), the world's highest energy particle accelerator, has gone into service near Geneva (Switzerland), there has been discussion of the possible dangers posed by some of the experiments planned for the facility. The controversy is briefly featured in "The Pork Chop Indeterminacy." Leonard informs Raj, "Some physicists are concerned that if the Supercollider actually works, it will create a black hole and swallow up the earth, ending life as we know it." Raj unsympathetically answers, "What a bunch of crybabies."

True, there doesn't seem to actually be any measurable (!) risk of a black 15
hole suddenly materializing inside the LHC and destroying the Earth, but science does have a long history of questionable effects on human life, from the tragedy of the eugenic movement (which from 1909 through the 1960s was responsible for the forced sterilization of sixty thousand individuals deemed to be genetically "unfit" in the United States) to the invention of nuclear weapons and the development of biological warfare. So an argument can be made that we shouldn't necessarily carry out certain types of scientific research just "because we can," as the boys explained to Penny. Science needs the guidance of external disciplines — such as ethics — as well as a serious engagement with public discourse to avoid eugenics-type Frankenstein scenarios. Yet this assumes the very thing that a scientistic approach denies: that meaningful rational discourse is possible or relevant outside of science itself.

Even if scientists know best, should science be used to improve the human condition without the explicit consent of the people whose lives are affected, in order to achieve the alleged improvement? And what constitutes an "improvement" in our existence, anyway? This question is implicitly posed in "The Gothowitz Deviation," when Leonard discovers that Sheldon is using positive reinforcement (a behavioral control technique devised by B. F. Skinner) with Penny — giving her chocolate every time she does something he likes:

LEONARD: You can't train my girlfriend like a lab rat.
SHELDON: Actually, it turns out I can.
LEONARD: Well, you shouldn't.
SHELDON: There is just no pleasing you, is there, Leonard? You weren't happy with my previous approach in dealing with her, so I decided to employ operant conditioning techniques. . . . I'm just tweaking her personality, sanding off the rough edges, if you will.
LEONARD: No, you are not sanding Penny!
SHELDON: Oh c'mon, you can't tell me that you are not intrigued by the possibility of building a better girlfriend.

The exchange is hilarious, but the underlying issue — the interplay between science at all costs and a consideration of extrascientific ethical values — has led to some horrifying outcomes, even in recent history. One of the most notorious cases is the Tuskegee syphilis experiment, conducted in Tuskegee, Alabama, between 1932 and 1972. Doctors working with the U.S. government began a study of 399 black men affected by syphilis, as well as an additional 201 used as controls, without telling the men in question that they had the disease. More crucially, once an effective cure became available — with the development of penicillin in the mid-1940s — the researchers knowingly withdrew treatment from the subjects. The study continued for decades and was terminated only because of a leak to the press, with the resulting controversy eventually leading to federal legislation to regulate scientific research that affected human subjects, as well as to the establishment of the Office for Human Research Protections.[3]

The Analysis

So, what exactly is the problem with scientism, and what solutions are available to us? The answers to these two questions are actually among the several comedic premises that make *The Big Bang Theory* work so well as a show:

[3]Disturbingly, however, some federal agencies can still engage in human research without consent, via a presidential executive order, presumably under the increasingly all-encompassing excuse of "national security."

respectively, the tendency of scientists to overreach, and the pushback we can generate by applying some common sense (along with, perhaps, good philosophical reflection). Again, there should be no question that science is by far the best toolbox that humanity has come up with to discover how the world works. Science also needs much defending, as it has been under increasing attack recently, with large portions of Americans denying the theory of evolution, rejecting the notion of anthropogenic climate change, or believing that somehow vaccines cause autism.[4] As Carl Sagan aptly put it in his *The Demon-Haunted World*, a classic collection of essays about pseudoscience and assorted nonsense, science is like a very precious candle in the dark, which deserves our respect and requires our protection.

Yet it should be equally clear that science has a proper domain of application (however large). This implies that there are areas where science doesn't belong or it is not particularly informative or has nothing to do with what we really want. One of the benefits of *The Big Bang Theory* is its effectiveness in demonstrating this point, especially through many of the lighthearted exchanges between Penny and Sheldon.

One such exchange is particularly relevant to the debate about 20
scientism. In "The Work Song Nanocluster," Sheldon volunteers to help Penny make her new "Penny Blossom" business enterprise become as profitable as possible. A bit surprised, Penny asks, "And you know about that stuff?" Sheldon, slightly scoffing, answers, "Penny, I'm a physicist. I have a working knowledge of the entire universe and everything it contains." Rather annoyed, Penny asks a question to test Sheldon's hypothesis: "Who's Radiohead?" This time skipping many beats, Sheldon musters, "I have a working knowledge of the *important* things in the universe." This is a near perfect example of the fallacy of scientism: physicists may one day be successful in arriving at a theory of everything, but "everything" has a very specific and limited meaning here, referring to the basic building blocks of the universe. It does not follow, either epistemologically or ontologically, that one can then simply apply the Cartesian method to work one's way up from superstrings to the cultural significance of Radiohead.[5] Moreover, Sheldon is offering a not-so-implicit value judgment here. Yet one could reasonably ask,

[4]For a fuller discussion of the relationship between science and pseudoscience, see my own *Nonsense on Stilts: How to Tell Science from Bunk* (Chicago: University of Chicago Press, 2010).

[5]Epistemology is the branch of philosophy that deals with what we can know, while ontology is the branch that attends to the existence of things. In this context, reductionism may be ontologically insufficient to explain reality, if it turns out that there are truly novel ("emergent") phenomena at higher levels of complexity that cannot be directly reduced to lower levels. Even if ontologically feasible, reductionism surely does not work epistemologically, because it would make for an unwieldy account of reality above the quantum level. For instance, while engineers certainly agree that a bridge is, ultimately, made of quarks (ontology), attempting to describe its macroscopic physical properties by developing a detailed quantum mechanical model of it (epistemology) would be sheer folly.

why is theoretical physics the only important mode of discourse? Or, more to the point, how could Sheldon prove or justify this position within science alone? Value judgments, again following David Hume, seem distinct from scientific discourse exactly because what is or can be done is no sure guide to what ought to be done.

Moreover, it is downright pernicious for science, as well as for society at large, when prominent scientists such as Stephen Hawking declare an entire field of inquiry (philosophy) dead. Hawking does so, while at the same time engaging in some (bad) philosophical reasoning throughout his book, particularly when he comments on the very nature of science — a classic domain of study for philosophy. Or consider again Sam Harris, who wrote an entire tome about how science can provide us with values, rejecting without argument one of the most fundamental distinctions made by philosophers, the one between empirical facts and values.[6] Harris does this while at the same time making a very particular (and entirely unacknowledged) set of philosophical choices right at the beginning of his book, such as taking on board a consequentialist ethical philosophy as the basis for his ideas about human happiness.

A much more reasonable view, I think, is that natural science, social science, philosophy, literature, and art each must have a respected place at the high table of societal discourse, because they are all necessary — and none sufficient — for human flourishing. Or, as it was so beautifully put in "The Panty Piñata Polarization,"

> SHELDON: Woman, you are playing with forces beyond your ken.
> PENNY: Yeah, well, your Ken can kiss my Barbie.

Philosophically, I can see no better way to articulate the message: sometimes, science is just not the point, and it certainly isn't the only point.

Reading the Text

1. Explain in your own words the meaning of "scientism."
2. In what ways does *The Big Bang Theory* satirize scientism?
3. What dangers does Pigliucci find in a belief in scientism?
4. Describe Pigliucci's attitude toward *The Big Bang Theory*. What evidence can you provide to support your description?
5. In offering his reading of *The Big Bang Theory*, Pigliucci refers to episodes in scientific history (such as the Tuskegee syphilis experiment) and to real-life scientists (such as Stephen Hawking). What effect do these sorts of references have on your response to his essay?

[6]To be fair, even some philosophers, such as W. V. O. Quine, have questioned the existence of a sharp distinction between facts and values, but they have done so within strict limits and based on careful arguments. Harris, instead, simply thinks that philosophical arguments are capable only of increasing the degree of boredom in the universe and accordingly dismisses them out of hand—an exceedingly anti-intellectual attitude exhibited by a self-styled public intellectual.

Reading the Signs

1. In class, brainstorm TV shows and films that feature scientists. Use the class's list as a starting point for your own essay, in which you analyze semiotically the popular image of scientists in modern entertainment. Do you find any differences in this image depending on genre (science fiction, comedy, or drama, for instance)? If so, what do they signify?
2. Write an essay in which you support, refute, or qualify Pigliucci's thesis that *The Big Bang Theory* is a critique of scientism.
3. In an essay, write your own response to Pigliucci's opening question: "Why is *The Big Bang Theory* so funny?" (para. 1).
4. Watch several episodes of *The Big Bang Theory*, with at least one from the show's early years and another that aired toward the series' conclusion. Write an essay in which you describe the evolution of the show. What changes do you identify, and what do they signify?
5. Write an essay in which you support, oppose, or complicate Pigliucci's contention that "When we attempt to reduce, or reinterpret, the humanities and our everyday experience in scientific terms, we not only are bound to miss something important, we also risk dehumanizing our own and other people's existence, possibly even becoming callous about the dangers of doing certain types of science on the grounds that the latter represents in itself the highest conceivable goal" (para. 14).

BRITTANY LEVINE BECKMAN

Why We Binge-Watch Stuff We Hate

In the nineteenth century, American readers of Charles Dickens's serialized novels had to wait for weeks for each new installment to cross the Atlantic. Today, thanks to streaming technology and content providers like Netflix, you can watch an entire season's worth of television episodes in a single sitting. This is called "binge-watching," and while a lot of people are very familiar with the phenomenon, Brittany Levine Beckman wants to know why she binge-watches not only programs she loves but those she hates as well. Seeking an answer, she interviewed communications studies scholars and psychologists, and what she discovered was that . . . well, maybe you should read her article to find out.

Two episodes into *Chilling Adventures of Sabrina*, I knew I hated it. Then I watched two more episodes — in the same sitting. Somehow, I finished all eight episodes of the Netflix show's first season in a matter of days. Why? I was under the spell of the hate-binge.

Being glued to the TV as I lose myself in a show I like makes sense; I'm enjoying myself. But this nonstop watching of something I dislike . . . does it make me a masochist? Nope, it just makes me human, according to psychology and communications experts.

Something you hate can suck you in just as much as a show that makes your heart sing—love and hate are both strong emotions, after all. The cardinal TV show sin if you're looking to attract binge-watchers is to be *boring*, says Paul Levinson, a communications professor at Fordham University and author of *New New Media*. "Once our emotions are unleashed, whether it's because we're very attracted to something or very repelled by something, if we feel strongly enough about it, we want to know more," Levinson says. He gives the example of President Trump to further his point: Even if you hate him, you can't seem to look away.

Yes, *Chilling Adventures* unleashed my emotions, so one point for Levinson. I was annoyed by Aunt Zelda's cigarette stick, the show's attempts at tackling social issues seemed shallow, Sabrina's choice between the mortal and witch worlds felt half-baked, and her family's coven was confusingly run by a man. I liked Sabrina's mysterious cousin Ambrose, though, so the series has some redeeming qualities. An episode or two beyond the halfway mark, I thought to myself: Maybe I should do something else? I quickly flicked that musing away. There's only a few more episodes left and everyone's talking about this show; there must be some redeeming quality I'm missing, I told myself. Besides, it'll take too long for me to settle on something new to watch, and I really don't want to go change the laundry.

These rationalizations can be tied to psychological research, says Alice 5
Atkin, a Ph.D. student at the University of Alberta's Neuroscience and Mental Health Institute who is studying video game players and their personality types. "When there are no good options about what to do, people tend to sort of default to the least objectionable decision," Atkin says. "Binge-watching a show you hate may not be particularly pleasant, but it's more pleasant than cleaning the bathroom or taking your dog for a walk when it's raining."

As for my completionist tendencies, Atkin says this has to do with a misconception about time and effort known as the sunk-cost fallacy. "When we invest time and resources and effort into something and we're not getting anything out of it, we feel like that time is wasted, and we don't want to waste our time, so we keep going, hoping eventually we'll get something out of it," she says. "Eventually what happens is you dislike it more and more, you waste more and more money, and things generally just get worse."

Greeaaattt.

In this age of Peak TV, you might think it'd be easy to toss one show aside and move onto something new. But it can seem overwhelming to start over. I've already spent 15 minutes scrolling through Netflix to decide what to watch in the first place. Why would I want to do that again?

This feeling can take hold just a few episodes in, Levinson says. "If you have given enough that you've watched an episode or two, it is preferable to keep watching than trying something new," he says. "Even an annoyance or dislike is more reliable than watching something new where we have no feeling associated."

If I don't like something by episode 2, that's when I start hoping for a 10
turnaround, a Hail Mary pass, something to bear fruit — especially if a show has social media buzz. And that keeps me watching more. When Netflix starts its 15-second countdown to the next episode, I let it passively lure me into the next one as I cross my fingers for the show to change course.

My hopeful desires have to do with social influence, Atkin says. In general, we tend to think other people know better. Others who are gushing about this show on Twitter can't be wrong, so less confident naysayers like myself keep watching to see what we're missing.

So how do I stop wasting my time on stuff I dislike? Atkin suggests turning autoplay off on streaming platforms and being more mindful when an episode ends. "If you've binge-watched before and you regretted it — maybe you didn't get enough sleep, or you didn't do your work — just remember that feeling. Remember that if you keep watching the show you'll regret it, and that should help you make a different decision."

I took Atkin's advice when I started watching *Sex Education*, a show I actually liked and would recommend for its relatable portrayal of awkward teen romance and skilled knit-work of diverse storylines. I eased myself in, watching two roughly one-hour episodes at kickoff. Before the third rolled onto my TV screen, I proudly shut off the TV. It was late and I had yoga in the morning. The same mindful decision-making continued the next day.

Reading the Text

1. What does it mean to "hate-binge" (para. 1), according to Beckman?
2. What is Paul Levinson's (para. 3) explanation for the phenomenon of binge-watching?
3. How does Alice Atkin use psychological research to explain the motivation behind binge-watching (paras. 5–6)?
4. How did Beckman train herself to stop hate-binging?

Reading the Signs

1. Write a journal entry describing your own experience with binge-watching. What motivates you to engage in this pastime? If you avoid binge-watching altogether, why does this activity not appeal to you?
2. **CONNECTING TEXTS** Binge-watching television programs — whether you love them or hate them — is largely made possible by digital technology. Referring

to David Courtwright's "How 'Limbic Capitalism' Preys on Our Addicted Brains" (p. 354), write an essay supporting, refuting, or complicating the argument that binge-watching television is a reflection of deliberate strategies on the part of streaming TV providers like Netflix.

3. In class, discuss the tone and style of this selection. How does its tone affect your response as a reader?
4. Survey members of the class to determine which TV programs they most often binge-watch and why. Analyze the results to determine any patterns that might exist in students' binge-watching behavior. Develop your analysis into an essay that proposes your own explanation for binge-watching.

Gavin Hellier/Alamy

7

THE HOLLYWOOD SIGN

The Culture of American Film

Global Warming with a Vengeance

Between May 2, 2008, and July 2, 2019, the Marvel Cinematic Universe released the first 23 installments in its ongoing *Avengers* series, grossing nearly $22 billion dollars worldwide — far surpassing the total box office for that other great American franchise, the *Star Wars* saga. Joining such other blockbusters as the *Harry Potter* movies and *The Lord of the Rings* — not to mention the Batman and Superman films — the never-ending cinematic adventures of the *Avengers* have effectively demonstrated the almost total dominance of fantasy story telling in America today, not only commercially but culturally as well. For fantasy has come to take the place of realism as the go-to genre for grappling with what most concerns us in contemporary American life, the space in which our society works through, and mythopoeically resolves, its deepest conflicts.

Consider, for example, the way that *Black Panther* dramatized conflicting visions of black power in a racially divided nation, paradoxically winning almost universal acclaim for its representation of the eventual triumph of a royal ruler over a revolutionary upstart. And consider as well the cataclysmic near-extinction event presented in *Avengers: Infinity War*, which metaphorically expressed the growing fear that global warming and climate change are threatening our very existence. That the great die-off was reversed in the immediate sequel, *Avengers: Endgame*, accentuates the fact that movies don't really solve our problems; they only make us feel better about them. Because, while time machines and other supernatural gadgets can bring the dead back to life in fantasy narratives, in the real world extinction is forever.

Pictorial Press Ltd/Alamy

Chadwick Boseman, Lupita Nyong'o, and Danai Gurira in a scene from *Black Panther*.

In more realistic apocalyptic storytelling, like *On the Beach* (1959), *Testament* (1983), and *The Day After* (1983), extinction isn't reversible. The dead stay dead in these bleak visions of a post-nuclear world, and — eventually, it is implied — everyone dies. The satirical representation of nuclear extinction in *Dr. Strangelove* (1964) adds dark comedy to the picture, but the essential message is the same, and it is hardly reassuring. Thus, the **difference** we encounter in movie sequences like *Avengers: Infinity War* and *Avengers: Endgame* becomes all the more significant, pointing to a cultural preference for reassurance over disturbing truths in our most popular entertainment artifacts.

For a further exploration in depth of this tendency in contemporary American film, let's look at another movie in the **system** of fantasy films that its creators presented *explicitly* as a metaphor for our fears of extinction, of nature striking back against humanity for the mess that we've made of the natural world. Here, too, we can find a signifier of the way that Hollywood mediates our worries by giving us what we want rather than the truth we need to hear.

For Godzilla's Sake!

It's a strange day in Hollywood when a gigantically destructive monster is cast as the *hero* of a movie. But that is exactly what happened when, in 2014, Gareth Edwards brought out the thirtieth installment in the never-ending Godzilla saga, reconstructing the iconic dragon/dinosaur as humanity's last hope against even more fearsome beasties. While not the first time that Godzilla had been so cast (in both Japanese and American versions of the story), Edwards's *Godzilla* offers a particularly instructive lesson in cinematic semiotics.

Analyzing *Godzilla* semiotically would appear to be a disarmingly easy task. After all, the marketers of the film went out of their way to state openly what the film "means." Even the description on the film's DVD package declares how "this spectacular adventure pits Godzilla, the world's most famous monster, against malevolent creatures that, bolstered by humanity's scientific arrogance, threaten our very existence." And just in case we miss the point, Edwards himself announced in a Comic-Con interview that "Godzilla is definitely a representation of the wrath of nature. We've taken it very seriously and the theme is man versus nature and Godzilla is certainly the nature side of it. You can't win that fight. Nature's always going to win and that's what the subtext of our movie is about. He's the punishment we deserve." And so, that would seem to wrap it all up — except that a careful semiotic reading of the movie reveals that this isn't what *Godzilla* is about at all. So let's look again.

Remember that a semiotic analysis takes us from the **denotation** of a sign to its **connotative significance** by situating it in a historically informed **system** of **associated** and **differentiated signs**. Using **abductive** reasoning, and keeping in mind the **overdetermined** nature of most cultural **signifiers**, the semiotic analysis arrives at an interpretation. We can do that here by beginning with a denotational plot summary of the movie: what it *shows*.

Although it takes some time to become clear to the viewer, the story concerns the discovery of a prehistoric species of subterranean monsters called MUTOs (for Massive Unidentified Terrestrial Organisms) who thrive on nuclear radiation. The dawning of the atomic age has drawn them to the surface to snack on all the nice nuclear goodies available in such facilities as atomic power plants and nuclear waste dumps, and the main action of the film begins (after setting up a backstory from fifteen years earlier) with a MUTO destroying a Japanese nuclear reactor, which just happens to be under surveillance by a shadowy international research organization called Monarch. This group has been monitoring a heretofore dormant Godzilla, who apparently has been sleeping under the reactor but awakes when the MUTO attacks. After trashing the power plant, the MUTO (a winged male) takes off to hook up with a wingless female MUTO on the U.S. mainland (after a catastrophic stopover in Hawaii), and a young U.S. Navy lieutenant, who happens to be the son of the head engineer of the now defunct Japanese reactor whose personal story opens the film, gets caught up in the mess and joins the attempt to stop the MUTOs. As the U.S. military helplessly attempts (and fails) to stop them, the MUTOs create a nest for hundreds of soon-to-hatch monsters (enough to destroy the solar system, it would seem) in San Francisco. But Godzilla — who is somehow able to hear and understand the MUTO's "language" as they communicate with each other (across the Pacific Ocean) — decides for reasons of his own (yes, Godzilla is a "he" this time around) that he should pursue the MUTOs and destroy them. In the end, he does and then swims off into the sunset as the survivors of a devastated San Francisco cheer him on, while the naval lieutenant is reunited with his beautiful wife and child, who have miraculously escaped the destruction thanks to Godzilla's intervention. While we have omitted some details very much worth pursuing in a longer treatment of the movie, this is its basic denotative setup.

The next step is to construct a system of associations and differences. As a giant reptilian monster, Godzilla can be associated with a larger **archetypal** phylum of monsters that includes medieval dragons, sea monsters, and other giant creatures that emerge from the natural world to threaten humanity. Such monsters, and their stories, have always signified a human apprehension that nature is hostile and must be conquered, and the monster characteristically is slain by a hero (or group of heroes) who thus restores human dominance over the natural world.

It is therefore significant that when the Japanese creators of the first Godzilla story used this ancient archetype, they introduced a certain *difference*. For while the original Godzilla was certainly a monster and a threat to humanity that had to be defeated, her existence as the result of nuclear bomb testing could nevertheless be traced to human, not natural, causes. This shifting of the blame, so to speak, from nature to culture, is of especial importance as we look further at the system to which *Godzilla* belongs. For in addition to its archetypal associations, *Godzilla* has cinematic ones. As a member of the monster movie subcategory of the larger action-thriller film genre, it can be associated with a long film history that usually casts the monster as a force to be destroyed. So the fact that, in this version of the film, the monster is the destroyer of much worse monsters and actually saves humanity introduces a second difference, one crucial to understanding the film's semiotic significance. And when we relate this latter difference to the one introduced in the 1954 origin story, we can see an emerging counter story to the usual man versus nature narrative, one in which man, not nature, is the problem.

Such a shift is a clear reflection of a growing historical apprehension that human activity, from the industrial revolution onward, is the real threat to

Photofest

A still of Godzilla from the 2014 movie.

human, and even planetary, survival. Guided by the comments made by the film's director, writers, and actors, we see that *Godzilla* can unquestionably be linked with a great many contemporary movies (like the *Avatar* films) wherein it is man's destructive threat to nature, rather than the other way around, that is at stake. Indeed, as a Monarch scientist in the movie tells an American admiral who is fighting the MUTOs, since human "arrogance" against nature is responsible for the MUTO mess, only nature (in the form of Godzilla) can restore the "balance." To a certain extent, then, *Godzilla* is a signifier of an ever-growing (especially in the era of climate change) apprehension that humanity is making a shambles of the Earth. That certainly is the view of the movie's creators and performers, and it is certainly what the movie says in its own dialogue. But, as is so often the case with commercial entertainment, there's a hitch, a contradiction, to consider, and we have to dig deeper to find it.

The key to the matter lies in looking not at what the movie *says* about itself but at what it *does*. And this is what *Godzilla* does: it depicts a symbolic creature of the nuclear age (Godzilla = Nature) destroying other creatures (the MUTOs), who are no less "natural" than he is. Thus, the film's final image of the joyful reunion of the naval lieutenant and his family, which Godzilla has made possible by defeating the MUTOs, is fundamentally reassuring. Because the real "message" of the movie is that no matter how much humans may damage the Earth, nature itself will fix everything. It's like saying "don't worry about global warming, because mother nature will clean up the mess before it gets completely out of hand."

If the movie was more honest, the MUTOs would have won. And Godzilla, as a cocreation of the nuclear age getting revenge on humanity (as Edwards claims), would have been on the MUTOs's side. But if the movie had done that, it wouldn't have grossed three quarters of a billion dollars, and that's the final signifier revealed by our analysis. For when performing a semiotic analysis of popular culture, you must never lose sight of the fact that popular culture exists to produce profits, and uplifting movies produce much higher profits than downers. An apocalyptic image of Godzilla and the MUTOs teaming up to trash the world would have been a downer indeed. So, *Godzilla* instead panders to its audience's desire to see the characters it most identifies with (the handsome naval lieutenant and his adorable family) live happily ever after, while at the same time reassuring everyone that although humanity may have messed up the planet, ultimately benign forces (somehow, somewhere) will take care of everything.

The Culture Industry

Filmmakers have been providing Americans with entertainments that have both reflected and shaped their hopes and desires for over a century now. Long before the advent of TV, movies offered viewers the glamour, romance, and sheer excitement that modern life seems to deny. So effective have movies been in molding audience desire that such early cultural critics as Theodor Adorno and Max Horkheimer[1] identified them as part of a vast, Hollywood-centered "culture industry" whose products successfully distracted their audiences from the inequities of modern life and, thus, effectively maintained the social status quo under capitalism by drawing everyone's attention away from it.

More recent analysts, however, are far less pessimistic. Indeed, for many cultural studies "populists," films, along with the rest of popular culture, can represent a kind of mass resistance to the political dominance — or what is often called the *hegemony* — of the social and economic powers-that-be. For such critics, films can provide utopian visions of a better world, stimulating their viewers to imagine how their society might be improved, and so, perhaps, inspiring them to go out and do something about it.

Whether you believe that films distract us from the real world or inspire us to imagine a better one, their central place in contemporary American culture demands interpretation, for their impact goes well beyond the movie theater or Prime rental. Far from being mere entertainments — as our reading of *Godzilla* demonstrates — movies constitute a profound part of our everyday lives, with every film festival and award becoming big news, and each major release becoming the talk of the country. Just think of the pressure you might feel to discuss the latest film sensation among your friends. Consider how, if you decide to save a few bucks, not watch the latest hit, and wait for the DVD release or to watch the film online, you can lose face and be seriously on the social outs. No, nothing is frivolous about the movies. You've been watching them all your life: now's the time to start thinking about them semiotically.

Interpreting the Signs of American Film

Interpreting a movie or a group of movies is not unlike interpreting a television program or group of programs. Again, you should suspend your personal feelings and aesthetic judgments about your subject. As with any semiotic analysis, your goal is to interpret the cultural significance of your topic, not to give it a thumbs-up or a thumbs-down. Thus, you may find it more rewarding to interpret films that promise to be culturally meaningful than to simply examine your favorite flick. Determining whether a film is culturally meaningful in the prewriting stage, of course, may be a hit-or-miss affair; you may find that your first choice does not present any particularly interesting grounds for interpretation. That's why it can be helpful to consider reasons a particular movie is special, such as enormous popularity or widespread critical attention. Of course, cult favorites, while often lacking in critical or popular

[1]**Theodor Adorno** (1903–1969) and **Max Horkheimer** (1895–1973) authored *Dialectic of Enlightenment* (1947), a book whose analyses included a scathing indictment of the culture industry. — EDS.

attention, can also be signs pointing toward their self-selected audiences and thus are strong candidates for analysis. Academy Award nominees and winners are also typically effective cultural signs.

Your interpretation of a movie or group of movies should begin with a construction of the **system** in which it belongs — that is, those movies, past and present, with which it can be **associated**. While tracing those associations, be on the lookout for striking **differences** from films that are otherwise like what you are analyzing, because those differences are what often reveal the significance of your subject.

Archetypes are useful features for film analysis as well. An archetype is anything that has been repeated in storytelling from ancient times to the present. There are character archetypes, such as the wise old man, represented by such figures as Yoda and Gandalf, and plot archetypes, such as the heroic quest, which forms the backbone of films like *The Lord of the Rings* trilogy. All those male buddy films — from *Butch Cassidy and the Sundance Kid* to *Lethal Weapon* to *Once Upon a Time in Hollywood* — hark back to archetypal male-bonding stories as old as *The Epic of Gilgamesh* (from the third millennium BCE) and the *Iliad*, while Cruella de Vil from *101 Dalmatians* is sister to the Wicked Witch of the West, Snow White's evil stepmother, and every other witch or crone dreamed up by the patriarchal imagination. All those sea monsters, from Jonah's "whale" to Moby-Dick to the great white shark in *Jaws*, are part of the same archetypal phylum, and every time a movie hero struggles to return home after a long journey — Dorothy to Kansas, Lassie to Timmy — a story as old as Exodus and the *Odyssey* is retold.

Hollywood is well aware of the enduring appeal of archetypes (see Linda Seger's selection in this chapter for a how-to description of archetypal scriptwriting), and director George Lucas's reliance on the work of anthropologist Joseph Campbell in his creation of the *Star Wars* saga is legendary. But it's not always the case that either creators or consumers are consciously aware of the archetypes before them. Part of a culture's collective unconscious, archetypal stories can send messages that their audiences only subliminally receive. A heavy dosage of male-bonding films in a given Hollywood season, for instance, can send the unspoken cultural message that a man can't really make friends with a woman and that women are simply the sexual reward

Discussing the Signs of Film

In any given year, one film may dominate the Hollywood box office, becoming a blockbuster that captures the public's cinematic imagination. In class, discuss which film would be your choice as this year's top hit. Then analyze the film semiotically. Why has *this* film so successfully appealed to so many moviegoers?

for manly men. Similarly, too many witches in a given Hollywood season can send the antifeminist message that women (especially older women) are bitches. Conversely, the modification of an archetype, as in the *female-*bonding film *Thelma and Louise*, or the introduction of Captain Marvel, can signify a feminist emergence.

Repetition with a Difference

Just as movies frequently repeat ancient archetypal character and plot types, they also may refer to other movies and modern cultural artifacts in what is called a **postmodern** manner. Postmodernism is, in effect, both a historical period and an attitude. As a historical period, postmodernism refers to the culture that emerged during the advent of twentieth-century mass media, one obsessed with electronic imagery and the products of mass culture. As an attitude, postmodernism rejects the values of the past, not to support new values but instead to ironize value systems as such. Thus, in the postmodern worldview, our traditional hierarchical distinctions valuing high culture over low culture, say, or creativity over imitation, tend to get flattened out. What was once viewed in terms of an oppositional hierarchy (origination is opposed to emulation and is superior to it) is reconceived and deconstructed. Postmodern artists, accordingly, tend to reproduce, with an ironic or parodic twist, already-existing cultural images in their work, especially if they can be drawn from mass culture and mass society. Roy Lichtenstein's cartoon canvases, for instance, parody popular comic strips, and Andy Warhol's *Campbell's Soup Cans* repeats the familiar labels of the Campbell Soup Company — thus mixing high culture and mass culture in a new, nonoppositional, relationship.

To put this another way, the postmodern worldview holds that it is no longer possible or desirable to create new images; rather, one surveys the vast range of available images that mass culture has to offer, and repeats them, but with a difference. Postmodern filmmakers accordingly allude to existing films in their work, as in the final scene of Tim Burton's *Batman*, which directly alludes to Alfred Hitchcock's *Vertigo*, or Oliver Stone and Quentin Tarantino's *Natural Born Killers*, which recalls *Bonnie and Clyde*. Such allusions to, and repetitions

Exploring the Signs of Film

In your journal, list your favorite movies. Then consider your list: What does it say about you? What **cultural mythologies** do the movies tend to reflect, and why do you think those myths appeal to you? What signs particularly appeal to your emotions? What sort of stories about human life do you most respond to?

of, existing cultural images in postmodern cinema are called *double-coding*, because of the way that the postmodern artifact simultaneously refers to existing cultural **codes** and recasts them in new contexts. The conclusion of *Batman*, for example, while echoing *Vertigo*'s climactic scene, differs dramatically in its significance, turning from Hitchcock's tragedy to Burton's quasi-farce.

Movies as Metaphors

As we have seen with the Godzilla movies, films often function as metaphors for larger cultural concerns. Consider, as further examples, the classic B-movies of the 1950s. Whenever some "blob" threatened to consume New York or some especially toxic slime escaped from a laboratory, the suggestion that science — especially nuclear science — was threatening to destroy the world filled the theater along with the popcorn fumes. And if it wasn't science that was the threat, Cold War filmmakers could scare us with communism, as in films such as *Invasion of the Body Snatchers,* with its metaphorical depiction of a town in which everyone looked the same but had really been taken over by aliens. "Beware of your neighbors," the movie seemed to warn. "They could be commies."

In such ways, an entire film can be a kind of metaphor, but you can find many smaller metaphors at work in the details of a movie as well. Early filmmakers, for example, put a tablecloth on the table in dining scenes to signify that the characters at the table were good, decent people (you can find such a metaphor in Charlie Chaplin's *The Kid*, where an impoverished tramp who can't afford socks or a bathrobe still has a nice tablecloth on the breakfast table). Sometimes a director's metaphors have a broad political significance, as at the end of the Rock Hudson/James Dean/Elizabeth Taylor classic *Giant*, where the parting shot presents a tableau of a white baby goat standing next to a black baby goat, which is juxtaposed with the image of a white baby

Reading Film Online

Most major films released in the United States have their own websites. You can find them listed online under the film's title or in print ads for the film. Select a current film, log on to its website, and analyze it semiotically. What images are used to attract your interest in the film? What interactive strategies, if any, are used to increase your commitment to the film? If you've seen the movie, how does the site's presentation of it compare with your experience of viewing it? Alternatively, analyze the posters designed to attract attention to a particular film; a useful resource is the Movie Poster Page (musicman.com/mp/mp.html).

standing in a crib side by side with a brown baby. Since the human babies are both the grandchildren of the film's protagonist (one of whose sons has married a Mexican woman, the other an Anglo), the goats are added to underscore (if rather heavy-handedly) the message of racial reconciliation that the director wanted to send.

Reading a film, then, is much like reading a novel. Both are texts filled with intentional and unintentional signs, metaphors, and archetypes, and both are cultural signifiers. The major difference is in their medium of expression. Literary texts are cast entirely in written words; films combine verbal language, visual imagery, and sound effects. Thus, we perceive literary and cinematic texts differently, for the written sign is perceived in a linear fashion that relies on one's cognitive and imaginative powers, while a film primarily targets the senses: one sees and hears (and sometimes even smells!) the story. That film is such a sensory experience often conceals its textuality. One is tempted to sit back and go with the flow, to say that it's only entertainment and doesn't have to "mean" anything at all. But even the most cartoonish cinematic entertainment can harbor a rather profound cultural significance. This chapter is intended to show you how to find it. Now it's your turn.

The Readings

Robert B. Ray's "The Thematic Paradigm" begins this chapter, revealing how American cinema has mediated some of this country's most profound cultural contradictions through its portrayals of "official" and "outlaw" heroes. Christine Folch follows with an analysis of the cultural differences that make sci-fi and fantasy movies all the rage in America but nothing special in India, while Linda Seger provides a how-to guide for creating the kind of archetypal characters that made *Star Wars* one of the most popular movie franchises of all time. Maya Phillips is next with an exploration of the narrative complexities involved in Disney's transformation of decades of comic book story lines into the Marvel Cinematic Universe. Abraham Riesman then takes on two of America's favorite superheroes and the cultural overtones of their ongoing conflict. The next three readings address the representation of race relations in film, with Matt Zoller Seitz presenting a critique of cinema's "'Magical Negro': a saintly African-American character who acts as a mentor to a questing white hero"; Mikhail Lyubansky deconstructing the racial signifiers implicit in *Black Panther*; and Jessica Hagedorn surveying a tradition of American filmmaking that stereotypes Asian women as either tragic or trivial. Taking a social-class-based approach to the codes of American cinema, Michael Parenti notes the caste biases inherent in a popular hit such as *Pretty Woman*, while David Denby explains why generations of teenagers flock to all those jocks-and-cheerleaders-versus-the-nerds movies. Wesley Morris concludes the chapter with an affectionate meditation on the rom-com: a venerable movie genre with an uncertain future.

ROBERT B. RAY

The Thematic Paradigm

Usually we consider movies to be merely entertainment, but as Robert B. Ray demonstrates in this selection from his book *A Certain Tendency of the Hollywood Cinema* (1985), American films have long reflected fundamental patterns and contradictions in our society's myths and values. Whether in real life or on the silver screen, Ray explains, Americans have always been ambivalent about the value of civilization, celebrating it through official heroes like George Washington and Jimmy Stewart, while at the same time questioning it through outlaw heroes like Davy Crockett and Huck Finn. Especially when presented together in the same film, these two hero types help mediate America's ambivalence, providing a mythic solution. Ray's analyses show how the movies are rich sources for cultural interpretation. Robert B. Ray is a professor of English at the University of Florida at Gainesville.

The dominant tradition of American cinema consistently found ways to overcome dichotomies. Often, the movies' reconciliatory pattern concentrated on a single character magically embodying diametrically opposite traits. A sensitive violinist was also a tough boxer (*Golden Boy*); a boxer was a gentle man who cared for pigeons (*On the Waterfront*). A gangster became a coward because he was brave (*Angels with Dirty Faces*); a soldier became brave because he was a coward (*Lives of a Bengal Lancer*). A war hero was a former pacifist (*Sergeant York*); a pacifist was a former war hero (*Billy Jack*). The ideal was a kind of inclusiveness that would permit all decisions to be undertaken with the knowledge that the alternative was equally available. The attractiveness of Destry's refusal to use guns (*Destry Rides Again*) depended on the tacit understanding that he could shoot with the best of them, Katharine Hepburn's and Claudette Colbert's revolts against conventionality (*Holiday*, *It Happened One Night*) on their status as aristocrats.

Such two-sided characters seemed particularly designed to appeal to a collective American imagination steeped in myths of inclusiveness. Indeed, in creating such characters, classic Hollywood had connected with what Erik Erikson has described as the fundamental American psychological pattern:

> The functioning American, as the heir of a history of extreme contrasts and abrupt changes, bases his final ego identity on some tentative combination of dynamic polarities such as migratory and sedentary, individualistic and standardized, competitive and co-operative, pious and free-thinking, responsible and cynical, etc. . . .

To leave his choices open, the American, on the whole, lives with two sets of "truths."[1]

The movies traded on one opposition in particular, American culture's traditional dichotomy of individual and community that had generated the most significant pair of competing myths: the outlaw hero and the official hero.[2] Embodied in the adventurer, explorer, gunfighter, wanderer, and loner, the outlaw hero stood for that part of the American imagination valuing self-determination and freedom from entanglements. By contrast, the official hero, normally portrayed as a teacher, lawyer, politician, farmer, or family man, represented the American belief in collective action, and the objective legal process that superseded private notions of right and wrong. While the outlaw hero found incarnations in the mythic figures of Davy Crockett, Jesse James, Huck Finn, and all of Leslie Fiedler's "Good Bad Boys" and Daniel Boorstin's "ring-tailed roarers," the official hero developed around legends associated with Washington, Jefferson, Lincoln, Lee, and other "Good Good Boys."

An extraordinary amount of the traditional American mythology adopted by Classic Hollywood derived from the variations worked by American ideology around this opposition of natural man versus civilized man. To the extent that these variations constituted the main tendency of American literature and legends, Hollywood, in relying on this mythology, committed itself to becoming what Robert Bresson has called "the Cinema."[3] A brief description of the competing values associated with this outlaw hero–official hero opposition will begin to suggest its pervasiveness in traditional American culture.

1. *Aging*: The attractiveness of the outlaw hero's childishness and pro- 5
pensity to whims, tantrums, and emotional decisions derived from America's cult of childhood. Fiedler observed that American literature celebrated "the notion that a mere falling short of adulthood is a guarantee of insight and even innocence." From Huck to Holden Caulfield, children in American literature were privileged, existing beyond society's confining rules. Often, they set the plot in motion (e.g., *Intruder in the Dust*, *To Kill a Mockingbird*), acting for the adults encumbered by daily affairs. As Fiedler also pointed out, this image of childhood "has impinged upon adult life itself, has become a 'career' like everything else in America,"[4] generating stories like *On the Road* or *Easy Rider* in which adults try desperately to postpone responsibilities by clinging to adolescent lifestyles.

[1]Erik H. Erikson, *Childhood and Society* (New York: Norton, 1963), p. 286.

[2]Leading discussions of the individual–community polarity in American culture can be found in *The Contrapuntal Civilization: Essays Toward a New Understanding of the American Experience*, ed. Michael Kammen (New York: Crowell, 1971). The most prominent analyses of American literature's use of this opposition remain Leslie A. Fiedler's *Love and Death in the American Novel* (New York: Stein and Day, 1966) and A. N. Kaul's *The American Vision* (New Haven: Yale University Press, 1963).

[3]Robert Bresson, *Notes on Cinematography*, trans. Jonathan Griffin (New York: Urizen Books, 1977), p. 12.

[4]Leslie A. Fiedler, *No! In Thunder* (New York: Stein and Day, 1972), pp. 253, 275.

While the outlaw heroes represented a flight from maturity, the official heroes embodied the best attributes of adulthood: sound reasoning and judgment, wisdom and sympathy based on experience. *Franklin's Autobiography* and *Poor Richard's Almanack* constituted this opposing tradition's basic texts, persuasive enough to appeal even to outsiders (*The Great Gatsby*). Despite the legends surrounding Franklin and the other Founding Fathers, however, the scarcity of mature heroes in American literature and mythology indicated American ideology's fundamental preference for youth, a quality that came to be associated with the country itself. Indeed, American stories often distorted the stock figure of the Wise Old Man, portraying him as mad (Ahab), useless (Rip Van Winkle), or evil (the Godfather).

2. *Society and Women*: The outlaw hero's distrust of civilization, typically represented by women and marriage, constituted a stock motif in American mythology. In his *Studies in Classic American Literature*, D. H. Lawrence detected the recurring pattern of flight, observing that the Founding Fathers had come to America "largely to get *away*. . . . Away from what? In the long run, away from themselves. Away from everything."[5] Sometimes, these heroes undertook this flight alone (Thoreau, *Catcher in the Rye*); more often, they joined ranks with other men: Huck with Jim, Ishmael with Queequeg, Jake Barnes with Bill Gorton. Women were avoided as representing the very entanglements this tradition sought to escape: society, the "settled life," confining responsibilities. The outlaw hero sought only uncompromising relationships, involving either a "bad" woman (whose morals deprived her of all rights to entangling domesticity) or other males (who themselves remained independent). Even the "bad" woman posed a threat, since marriage often uncovered the clinging "good" girl underneath. Typically, therefore, American stories avoided this problem by killing off the "bad" woman before the marriage could transpire (*Destry Rides Again*, *The Big Heat*, *The Far Country*). Subsequently, within the all-male group, women became taboo, except as the objects of lust.

The exceptional extent of American outlaw legends suggests an ideological anxiety about civilized life. Often, that anxiety took shape as a romanticizing of the dispossessed, as in the Beat Generation's cult of the bum, or the characters of Huck and "Thoreau," who worked to remain idle, unemployed, and unattached. A passage from Jerzy Kosinski's *Steps* demonstrated the extreme modern version of this romanticizing:

> I envied those [the poor and the criminals] who lived here and seemed so free, having nothing to regret and nothing to look forward to. In the world of birth certificates, medical examinations, punch cards, and computers, in the world of telephone books, passports, bank accounts,

[5]D. H. Lawrence, *Studies in Classic American Literature* (New York: Viking/Compass, 1961), p. 3. See also Fiedler's *Love and Death in the American Novel* and Sam Bluefarb's *The Escape Motif in the American Novel: Mark Twain to Richard Wright* (Columbus: Ohio State University Press, 1972).

insurance plans, wills, credit cards, pensions, mortgages and loans, they lived unattached.[6]

In contrast to the outlaw heroes, the official heroes were preeminently worldly, comfortable in society, and willing to undertake even those public duties demanding personal sacrifice. Political figures, particularly Washington and Lincoln, provided the principal examples of this tradition, but images of family also persisted in popular literature from *Little Women* to *Life with Father* and *Cheaper by the Dozen*. The most crucial figure in this tradition, however, was Horatio Alger, whose heroes' ambition provided the complement to Huck's disinterest. Alger's characters subscribed fully to the codes of civilization, devoting themselves to proper dress, manners, and behavior, and the attainment of the very things despised by the opposing tradition: the settled life and respectability.[7]

3. *Politics and the Law*: Writing about "The Philosophical Approach of the 10
Americans," Tocqueville noted "a general distaste for accepting any man's word as proof of anything." That distaste took shape as a traditional distrust of politics as collective activity, and of ideology as that activity's rationale. Such a disavowal of ideology was, of course, itself ideological, a tactic for discouraging systematic political intervention in a nineteenth-century America whose political and economic power remained in the hands of a privileged few. Tocqueville himself noted the results of this mythology of individualism which "disposes each citizen to isolate himself from the mass of his fellows and withdraw into the circle of family and friends; with this little society formed to his taste, he gladly leaves the greater society to look after itself."[8]

This hostility toward political solutions manifested itself further in an ambivalence about the law. The outlaw mythology portrayed the law, the sum of society's standards, as a collective, impersonal ideology imposed on the individual from without. Thus, the law represented the very thing this mythology sought to avoid. In its place, this tradition offered a natural law discovered intuitively by each man. As Tocqueville observed, Americans wanted "to escape from imposed systems ... to seek by themselves and in themselves for the only reason for things ... in most mental operations each American relies on individual effort and judgment" (p. 429). This sense of the law's inadequacy to needs detectable only by the heart generated a rich tradition of legends celebrating legal defiance in the name of some "natural" standard: Thoreau went to jail rather than pay taxes, Huck helped Jim (legally a slave) to escape, Billy the Kid murdered the sheriff's posse that had ambushed his boss,

[6]Jerzy Kosinski, *Steps* (New York: Random House, 1968), p. 133.

[7]See John G. Cawelti, *Apostles of the Self-Made Man: Changing Concepts of Success in America* (Chicago: University of Chicago Press, 1965), pp. 101–23.

[8]Alexis de Tocqueville, *Democracy in America*, ed. J. P. Mayer, trans. George Lawrence (Garden City, N.Y.: Anchor/Doubleday, 1969), pp. 430, 506. Irving Howe has confirmed Tocqueville's point, observing that Americans "make the suspicion of ideology into something approaching a national creed." *Politics and the Novel* (New York: Avon, 1970), p. 337.

Hester Prynne resisted the community's sexual mores. This mythology transformed all outlaws into Robin Hoods, who "correct" socially unjust laws (Jesse James, Bonnie and Clyde, John Wesley Harding). Furthermore, by customarily portraying the law as the tool of villains (who used it to revoke mining claims, foreclose on mortgages, and disallow election results — all on legal technicalities), this mythology betrayed a profound pessimism about the individual's access to the legal system.

If the outlaw hero's motto was "I don't know what the law says, but I do know what's right and wrong," the official hero's was "We are a nation of laws, not of men," or "No man can place himself above the law." To the outlaw hero's insistence on private standards of right and wrong, the official hero offered the admonition, "You cannot take the law into your own hands." Often, these official heroes were lawyers or politicians, at times (as with Washington and Lincoln), even the executors of the legal system itself. The values accompanying such heroes modified the assurance of Crockett's advice, "Be sure you're right, then go ahead."

In sum, the values associated with these two different sets of heroes contrasted markedly. Clearly, too, each tradition had its good and bad points. If the extreme individualism of the outlaw hero always verged on selfishness, the respectability of the official hero always threatened to involve either blandness or repression. If the outlaw tradition promised adventure and freedom, it also offered danger and loneliness. If the official tradition promised safety and comfort, it also offered entanglements and boredom.

The evident contradiction between these heroes provoked Daniel Boorstin's observation that "never did a more incongruous pair than Davy Crockett and George Washington live together in a national Valhalla." And yet, as Boorstin admits, "both Crockett and Washington were popular heroes, and both emerged into legendary fame during the first half of the nineteenth century."[9]

The parallel existence of these two contradictory traditions evinced 15
the general pattern of American mythology: the denial of the necessity for choice. In fact, this mythology often portrayed situations requiring decision as temporary aberrations from American life's normal course. By discouraging commitment to any single set of values, this mythology fostered an ideology of improvisation, individualism, and ad hoc solutions for problems depicted as crises. American writers have repeatedly attempted to justify this mythology in terms of material sources. Hence, Irving Howe's "explanation":

> It is when men no longer feel that they have adequate choices in their styles of life, when they conclude that there are no longer possibilities of honorable maneuver and compromise, when they decide that the time has come for "ultimate" social loyalties and political decisions — it is then that ideology begins to flourish. Ideology reflects a hardening of

[9]Daniel J. Boorstin, *The Americans: The National Experience* (New York: Random House, 1965), p. 337.

> commitment, the freezing of opinion into system.... The uniqueness of our history, the freshness of our land, the plenitude of our resources—all these have made possible, and rendered plausible, a style of political improvisation and intellectual free-wheeling.[10]

Despite such an account's pretext of objectivity, its language betrays an acceptance of the mythology it purports to describe: "honorable maneuver and compromise," "hardening," "freezing," "uniqueness," "freshness," and "plenitude" are all assumptive words from an ideology that denies its own status. Furthermore, even granting the legitimacy of the historians' authenticating causes, we are left with a persisting mythology increasingly discredited by historical developments. (In fact, such invalidation began in the early nineteenth century, and perhaps even before.)

The American mythology's refusal to choose between its two heroes went beyond the normal reconciliatory function attributed to myth by Lévi-Strauss. For the American tradition not only overcame binary oppositions; it systematically mythologized the certainty of being able to do so. Part of this process involved blurring the lines between the two sets of heroes. First, legends often brought the solemn official heroes back down to earth, providing the sober Washington with the cherry tree, the prudent Franklin with illegitimate children, and even the upright Jefferson with a slave mistress. On the other side, stories modified the outlaw hero's most potentially damaging quality, his tendency to selfish isolationism, by demonstrating that, however reluctantly, he would act for causes beyond himself. Thus, Huck grudgingly helped Jim escape, and Davy Crockett left the woods for three terms in Congress before dying in the Alamo for Texas independence. In this blurring process, Lincoln, a composite of opposing traits, emerged as the great American figure. His status as president made him an ex officio official hero. But his Western origins, melancholy solitude, and unaided decision-making all qualified him as a member of the other side. Finally, his ambivalent attitude toward the law played the most crucial role in his complex legend. As the chief executive, he inevitably stood for the principle that "we are a nation of laws and not men"; as the Great Emancipator, on the other hand, he provided the prime example of taking the law into one's own hands in the name of some higher standard.

Classic Hollywood's gallery of composite heroes (boxing musicians, rebellious aristocrats, pacifist soldiers) clearly derived from this mythology's rejection of final choices, a tendency whose traces Erikson detected in American psychology:

> The process of American identity formation seems to support an individual's ego identity as long as he can preserve a certain element of deliberate tentativeness of autonomous choice. The individual must be able to convince himself that the next step is up to him and that no

[10]*Politics and the Novel*, p. 164.

> matter where he is staying or going he always has the choice of leaving or turning in the opposite direction if he chooses to do so. In this country the migrant does not want to be told to move on, nor the sedentary man to stay where he is; for the life style (and the family history) of each contains the opposite element as a potential alternative which he wishes to consider his most private and individual decision.[11]

The reconciliatory pattern found its most typical incarnation, however, in one particular narrative: the story of the private man attempting to keep from being drawn into action on any but his own terms. In this story, the reluctant hero's ultimate willingness to help the community satisfied the official values. But by portraying this aid as demanding only a temporary involvement, the story preserved the values of individualism as well.

Like the contrasting heroes' epitomization of basic American dichotomies, the reluctant hero story provided a locus for displacement. Its most famous version, for example, *Adventures of Huckleberry Finn*, offered a typically individualistic solution to the nation's unresolved racial and sectional anxieties, thereby helping to forestall more systematic governmental measures. In adopting this story, Classic Hollywood retained its censoring power, using it, for example, in *Casablanca* to conceal the realistic threats to American self-determination posed by World War II.

Because the reluctant hero story was clearly the basis of the Western, American literature's repeated use of it prompted Leslie Fiedler to call the classic American novels "disguised westerns."[12] In the movies, too, this story appeared in every genre: in Westerns, of course (with *Shane* its most schematic articulation), but also in gangster movies (*Angels with Dirty Faces*, *Key Largo*), musicals (*Swing Time*), detective stories (*The Thin Man*), war films (*Air Force*), screwball comedy (*The Philadelphia Story*), "problem pictures" (*On the Waterfront*), and even science fiction (the Han Solo character in *Star Wars*). *Gone with the Wind*, in fact, had two selfish heroes who came around at the last moment, Scarlett (taking care of Melanie) and Rhett (running the Union blockade), incompatible only because they were so much alike. The natural culmination of this pattern, perfected by Hollywood in the 1930s and early 1940s, was *Casablanca*. Its version of the outlaw hero–official hero struggle (Rick versus Laszlo) proved stunningly effective, its resolution (their collaboration on the war effort) the prototypical Hollywood ending.

The reluctant hero story's tendency to minimize the official hero's role (by 20
making him dependent on the outsider's intervention) suggested an imbalance basic to the American mythology: Despite the existence of both heroes, the national ideology clearly preferred the outlaw. This ideology strove to make that figure's origins seem spontaneous, concealing the calculated, commercial efforts behind the mythologizing of typical examples like Billy the Kid and Davy Crockett. Its willingness, on the other hand, to allow the official

[11]*Childhood and Society*, p. 286.

[12]*Love and Death in the American Novel*, p. 355.

hero's traces to show enables Daniel Boorstin to observe of one such myth, "There were elements of spontaneity, of course, in the Washington legend, too, but it was, for the most part, a self-conscious product."[13]

The apparent spontaneity of the outlaw heroes assured their popularity. By contrast, the official values had to rely on a rational allegiance that often wavered. These heroes' different statuses accounted for a structure fundamental to American literature, and assumed by Classic Hollywood: a split between the moral center and the interest center of a story. Thus, while the typical Western contained warnings against violence as a solution, taking the law into one's own hands, and moral isolationism, it simultaneously glamorized the outlaw hero's intense self-possession and willingness to use force to settle what the law could not. In other circumstances, Ishmael's evenhanded philosophy paled beside Ahab's moral vehemence, consciously recognizable as destructive.

D. H. Lawrence called this split the profound "duplicity" at the heart of nineteenth-century American fiction, charging that the classic novels evinced "a tight mental allegiance to a morality which all [the author's] passion goes to destroy." Certainly, too, this "duplicity" involved the mythology's pattern of obscuring the necessity for choosing between contrasting values. Richard Chase has put the matter less pejoratively in an account that applies equally to the American cinema:

> The American novel tends to rest in contradictions and among extreme ranges of experience. When it attempts to resolve contradictions, it does so in oblique, morally equivocal ways. As a general rule it does so either in melodramatic actions or in pastoral idylls, although intermixed with both one may find the stirring instabilities of "American humor."[14]

Or, in other words, when faced with a difficult choice, American stories resolved it either simplistically (by refusing to acknowledge that a choice is necessary), sentimentally (by blurring the differences between the two sides), or by laughing the whole thing off.

Reading the Text

1. In your own words, describe the two basic hero types in American cinema that Ray describes.
2. How do these two hero types relate to America's "psychological pattern" (para. 2)?
3. Explain why, according to Ray, the outlaw hero typically mistrusts women.
4. Define what Ray means by the "reluctant hero" (para. 17).

[13]*The Americans: The National Experience*, p. 337.

[14]Richard Chase, *The American Novel and Its Tradition* (Garden City, N.Y.: Anchor/Doubleday, 1957), p. 1.

Reading the Signs

1. What sort of hero is Wonder Woman in *Wonder Woman 1984* (2020) or Natasha Romanov in *Black Widow* (2020)? Write an essay in which you apply Ray's categories of hero to your chosen character, supporting your argument with specific references to the film.
2. In class, brainstorm on the board official and outlaw heroes you've seen in movies. Then categorize these heroes according to characteristics they share (such as race, gender, profession, or social class). What patterns emerge in your categories, and what is the significance of those patterns?
3. Ray focuses on film, but his categories of hero can be used as a critical framework to analyze other media, including television. What kinds of heroes are the heroes in *Better Call Saul* or *Grey's Anatomy*? Alternately, select your own TV show and analyze its heroes.
4. Cartoon television series like *The Simpsons* and *Family Guy* feature characters that don't readily fit Ray's two main categories of hero. Invent a third type of hero to accommodate such characters.
5. In class, brainstorm a list of female heroes from film and television. Then try to categorize them according to Ray's article. Do the characters easily fit the categories Ray mentions, or do they seem to be mismatches? Do you feel a need to create an additional category? If so, what would it be?

CHRISTINE FOLCH

Why the West Loves Sci-Fi and Fantasy: A Cultural Explanation

Hollywood loves sci-fi and fantasy; Bollywood doesn't. Just why the Indian movie industry (which is the world's largest) is so uninterested in fantasy is an anthropological question that Christine Folch sets out to answer in this *Atlantic* analysis. The key, Folch believes, lies in history, a history that in the West has included a post-Enlightenment reign of scientific rationalism that has led to a general disenchantment with things-as-they-are, which fantasy strives to reverse by "re-enchant[ing] the world." Experiencing a different kind of history without this lens of disenchantment, Indians, Folch suggests, feel no need for cinematic fantasy, so Bollywood doesn't bother much with it. Christine Folch is an assistant professor of anthropology at Duke University.

Hollywood's had a long love affair with sci-fi and fantasy, but the romance has never been stronger than it is today. A quick glance into bookstores, television lineups, and upcoming films shows that the futuristic and fantastical is everywhere in American pop culture. In fact, of Hollywood's top earners since 1980, a mere eight have *not* featured wizardry, space or time travel, or apocalyptic destruction caused by aliens/zombies/Robert Downey Jr.'s acerbic wit. Now, with *Man of Steel*, it appears we will at last have an effective reboot of the most important superhero story of them all.

These tales of mystical worlds and improbable technological power appeal universally, right? Maybe not. Bollywood, not Hollywood, is the largest movie industry in the world. But only a handful of its top hits of the last four decades have dealt with science fiction themes, and even fewer are fantasy or horror. American films in those genres make much of their profits abroad, but they tend to underperform in front of Indian audiences.

This isn't to say that there aren't folk tales with magic and mythology in India. There are. That makes their absence in Bollywood and their overabundance in Hollywood all the more remarkable. Whereas Bollywood takes quotidian family dramas and imbues them with spectacular tales of love and wealth found-lost-regained amidst the pageantry of choreographed dance pieces, Hollywood goes to the supernatural and futurism. It's a sign that longing for mystery is universal, but the taste for science fiction and fantasy is cultural.

Cultural differences are fascinating because even as we learn about others, we learn about ourselves. As an anthropologist, I want to flip this conversation: Why are *we* so into science fiction and fantasy? Nineteenth-century German sociologist Max Weber had a useful theory about this: The answer may be that we in the West are "disenchanted." The world in which we live feels explainable, predictable, and boring. Weber posited that because of modern science, a rise in secularism, an impersonal market economy, and government administered through bureaucracies rather than bonds of loyalty, Western societies perceived the world as knowably rational and systematic, leading to a widespread loss of a sense of wonder and magic. Because reality is composed of processes that can be identified with a powerful-enough microscope or calculated with a fast-enough computer, so Weber's notion of disenchantment goes, there is no place for mystery. But this state of disenchantment is a difficult one because people seem to *like* wonder.

And so we turn to science fiction and fantasy in an attempt to re-enchant 5
the world. Children and childhood retain mystery, and so one tactic has been to take fairytales and rewrite them for adults and here we get the swords and sorcery of modern fantasy. Another strategy was to reinsert the speculative unknown into the very heart of scientific processes. But just because *we* have mined myth for magic — and, remember, even what we define as *myth* would have been called *religion* two millennia earlier (and the very fact that we think those two terms equivalent is also cultural) — does not mean that this fills the same need for wonder elsewhere.

India has developed many of the same features as America: a capitalist economy, an enormous bureaucratic government, and cutting-edge scientific expertise. But its intellectual history is different. Weber's argument is much more nuanced and substantive than the cursory description I have given here, but, in sum, disenchantment is rooted in the intellectual tradition of the 18th-century European Enlightenment with its struggles over the place of religion versus rationality. The aftermath of that contest in the West was to relegate the supernatural mysterious to a lower position than material-based reason. The key point is that this is a particular moment in cultural history, not some necessary and universal stage of human societal "development." Similarly, for that reason, I'd guess Japan's vibrant tradition of the supernatural in its anime, and China's recent taste for American FX spectacles, results from those countries' specific cultural contexts rather than from disenchantment. (And some of the ways the West looks to the non-West for re-enchantment are another, Orientalist can of worms best left for a different day.)

Anyone looking to debunk cultural explanations for the American/Indian sci-fi gap might point out that Hollywood has had the big-budget, dragons-and-droids market flooded for years. Perhaps Bollywood, for commercial reasons, doesn't want to jump in. Average production costs for American superhero blockbusters hover around $200 million these days, and audiences have come to expect the computer-generated spectacle that kind of money buys. But . . . *Star Wars* was made for $11 million in 1977 (less than $40 million now) and 25 percent of *Iron Man 3*'s $200 million budget was Robert Downey Jr.'s salary. Surely there's enough technical expertise and financial muscle in India to digitize a realistic Mars landing when the country's space program is on track to launch a real spacecraft (unmanned) to the red planet this upcoming November.

What about the fact that American blockbusters make tons of money worldwide? For films like *Avatar* and *The Hobbit*, foreign sales equal or exceed domestic U.S. sales. But India, the world's ninth-largest economy and second-most populous country, does not even rank in the top 12 foreign markets for the genre. The list of those markets reads like the attendees of a G-8 summit (plus some key trading partners): the United Kingdom, Japan, France, Germany, Italy, Mexico, Brazil, Spain, South Korea, Russia, Australia, and China. *Avatar* (2009) set the high-water mark for India, where South Asian audiences purchased $24 million worth of tickets—about 10 percent of foreign ticket sales worldwide. But for most science fiction, countries with smaller GDPs than India (Australia, Mexico, South Korea) are higher consumers. Of *Avengers*' (2012) $888 million worldwide, $12 million came from India; *Iron Man 3* is on track with similar numbers; and, to their credit, Indian audiences contributed a paltry $2.8 million to *Transformers 3*'s $434 million. Fantasy fares much worse. *The Hobbit* (2012) made $714 million worldwide; it took home $1.8 million in India. That is barely more than Croatia's $1.4 million.

The simplest conclusion to draw from this is that Bollywood doesn't produce science fiction and fantasy because Indian audiences aren't as keen on it. Local cultural production doesn't just result from economic wherewithal; desires and needs also matter. And desires and needs are cultural. This sometimes feels hard to accept because desires and needs feel so *natural*. Often we think that the way we live is normal and not cultural; this is what anthropologists call "tacit ethnocentrism," when we are not *trying* to be prejudiced, but we have unquestioned assumptions that somehow we are the normal human baseline and others somehow deviate from that.

10 Hollywood continues to make science fiction and fantasy movies because disenchantment creates a demand for these stories, but disenchantment predates Hollywood. We were journeying ten thousand leagues under the sea or scarcely surviving a war of the worlds before the film industry began. If the uptick of *Hunger Games*–inspired archery lessons and the CDC's humorous-but-practical Zombie Preparedness Guide are any indication, this is not going away any time soon. Re-enchantment delivers something more important than escapism or entertainment. Through its promise of a world of mystery and wonder, it offers the hope that we haven't seen all that there is.

Reading the Text

1. Explain in your own words Max Weber's notion of "disenchantment" (para. 4).
2. What is Folch's explanation for why Western film audiences find the supernatural and futurism appealing?
3. According to Folch, what are the cultural reasons Indian film audiences are not "keen on" (para. 9) science fiction and fantasy?
4. What was the Enlightenment, and how did it affect Western consciousness?
5. What does Folch mean by the anthropological term "tacit ethnocentrism" (para. 9)?

Reading the Signs

1. Research the last ten years of American movies, and determine how many of the most successful films were fantasies. Use your findings to write your own argument about why fantasy films appeal to American audiences, basing your claims on an analysis of particular movies.
2. Write an essay in which you support, refute, or modify the claim that the rise of fantasy films in America reflects market forces pandering to immature cinematic tastes.
3. Watch a classic Bollywood film such as *Sholay* (1975); *Dangal* (2016), the all-time most popular Indian film; or *Bala* (2019). In an essay, analyze the nature of its appeal to Indian audiences, using Folch's selection as a critical framework. What cultural needs and desires does the film seem to satisfy?
4. Folch claims that "Bollywood takes quotidian family dramas and imbues them with spectacular tales of love and wealth found-lost-regained amidst the pageantry of choreographed dance pieces" (para. 3). In an essay, compare an Indian film like *Shaandaar* (2015) with an American movie such as *My Big Fat Greek Wedding* (2002). How do the films you select depict family and interpersonal relations? What cultural explanations can you offer for your observations?

LINDA SEGER

Creating the Myth

To be a successful screenwriter, Linda Seger suggests in this selection from *Making a Good Script Great* (1987), you've got to know your archetypes. Seger reveals the secret behind the success of such characters as *Star Wars*'s Luke Skywalker and tells you how you can create such heroes yourself. In this how-to approach to the cinema, Seger echoes the more academic judgments of such semioticians of film as the late Umberto Eco — that the road to popular success in mass culture is paved with cultural myths and clichés. A script consultant and author, Seger has also given professional seminars on filmmaking around the world.

All of us have similar experiences. We share in the life journey of growth, development, and transformation. We live the same stories, whether they involve the search for a perfect mate, coming home, the search for fulfillment, going after an ideal, achieving the dream, or hunting for a precious treasure. Whatever our culture, there are universal stories that form the basis for all our particular stories. The trappings might be different, the twists and turns that create suspense might change from culture to culture, the particular characters may take different forms, but underneath it all, it's the same story, drawn from the same experiences.

Many of the most successful films are based on these universal stories. They deal with the basic journey we take in life. We identify with the heroes because we were once heroic (descriptive) or because we wish we could do what the hero does (prescriptive). When Joan Wilder finds the jewel and saves her sister, or James Bond saves the world, or Shane saves the family from the evil ranchers, we identify with the character, and subconsciously recognize the story as having some connection with our own lives. It's the same story as the fairy tales about getting the three golden hairs from the devil, or finding the treasure and winning the princess. And it's not all that different a story from the caveman killing the woolly beast or the Roman slave gaining his freedom through skill and courage. These are our stories — personally and collectively — and the most successful films contain these universal experiences.

Some of these stories are "search" stories. They address our desire to find some kind of rare and wonderful treasure. This might include the search for outer values such as job, relationship, or success; or for inner values such as respect, security, self-expression, love, or home. But it's all a similar search.

Some of these stories are "hero" stories. They come from our own experiences of overcoming adversity, as well as our desire to do great and special acts. We root for the hero and celebrate when he or she achieves the goal because we know that the hero's journey is in many ways similar to our own.

We call these stories *myths*. Myths are the common stories at the root of 5
our universal existence. They're found in all cultures and in all literature, ranging from the Greek myths to fairy tales, legends, and stories drawn from all of the world's religions.

A myth is a story that is "more than true." Many stories are true because one person, somewhere, at some time, lived it. It is based on fact. But a myth is more than true because it is lived by all of us, at some level. It's a story that connects and speaks to us all.

Some myths are true stories that attain mythic significance because the people involved seem larger than life, and seem to live their lives more intensely than common folk. Martin Luther King, Jr., Gandhi, Sir Edmund Hillary, and Lord Mountbatten personify the types of journeys we identify with, because we've taken similar journeys—even if only in a very small way.

Other myths revolve around make-believe characters who might capsulize for us the sum total of many of our journeys. Some of these make-believe characters might seem similar to the characters we meet in our dreams. Or they might be a composite of types of characters we've met.

In both cases, the myth is the "story beneath the story." It's the universal pattern that shows us that Gandhi's journey toward independence and Sir Edmund Hillary's journey to the top of Mount Everest contain many of the same dramatic beats. And these beats are the same beats that Rambo takes to set free the MIAs, that Indiana Jones takes to find the Lost Ark, and that Luke Skywalker takes to defeat the Evil Empire.

In *Hero with a Thousand Faces*, Joseph Campbell traces the elements that 10
form the hero myth. In their own work with myth, writer Chris Vogler and seminar leader Thomas Schlesinger have applied this criteria to *Star Wars*. The myth within the story helps explain why millions went to see this film again and again.

The hero myth has specific story beats that occur in all hero stories. They show who the hero is, what the hero needs, and how the story and character interact in order to create a transformation. The journey toward heroism is a process. This universal process forms the spine of all the particular stories, such as the *Star Wars* trilogy.

The Hero Myth

1. In most hero stories, the hero is introduced in ordinary surroundings, in a mundane world, doing mundane things. Generally, the hero begins as a non-hero; innocent, young, simple, or humble. In *Star Wars*, the first time we see Luke Skywalker, he's unhappy about having to do his chores, which consist of picking out some new droids for work. He wants to go out and have fun. He wants to leave his planet and go to the Academy, but he's stuck. This is

the setup of most myths. This is how we meet the hero before the call to adventure.

2. Then something new enters the hero's life. It's a catalyst that sets the story into motion. It might be a telephone call, as in *Romancing the Stone*, or the German attack in *The African Queen*, or the holograph of Princess Leia in *Star Wars*. Whatever form it takes, it's a new ingredient that pushes the hero into an extraordinary adventure. With this call, the stakes are established, and a problem is introduced that demands a solution.

3. Many times, however, the hero doesn't want to leave. He or she is a reluctant hero, afraid of the unknown, uncertain, perhaps, if he or she is up to the challenge. In *Star Wars*, Luke receives a double call to adventure. First, from Princess Leia in the holograph, and then through Obi-Wan Kenobi, who says he needs Luke's help. But Luke is not ready to go. He returns home, only to find that the Imperial Stormtroopers have burned his farmhouse and slaughtered his family. Now he is personally motivated, ready to enter into the adventure.

4. In any journey, the hero usually receives help, and the help often comes 15
from unusual sources. In many fairy tales, an old woman, a dwarf, a witch, or a wizard helps the hero. The hero achieves the goal because of this help, and because the hero is receptive to what this person has to give.

There are a number of fairy tales where the first and second sons are sent to complete a task, but they ignore the helpers, often scorning them. Many times they are severely punished for their lack of humility and unwillingness to accept help. Then the third son, the hero, comes along. He receives the help, accomplishes the task, and often wins the princess.

In *Star Wars*, Obi-Wan Kenobi is a perfect example of the "helper" character. He is a kind of mentor to Luke, one who teaches him the Way of the Force and whose teachings continue even after his death. This mentor character appears in most hero stories. He is the person who has special knowledge, special information, and special skills. This might be the prospector in *The Treasure of the Sierra Madre*, or the psychiatrist in *Ordinary People*, or Quint in *Jaws*, who knows all about sharks, or the Good Witch of the North who gives Dorothy the ruby slippers in *The Wizard of Oz*. In *Star Wars*, Obi-Wan gives Luke the light saber that was the special weapon of the Jedi Knight. With this, Luke is ready to move forward and do his training and meet adventure.

5. The hero is now ready to move into the special world where he or she will change from the ordinary into the extraordinary. This starts the hero's transformation, and sets up the obstacles that must be surmounted to reach the goal. Usually, this happens at the first Turning Point of the story, and leads into Act Two development. In *Star Wars*, Obi-Wan and Luke search for a pilot to take them to the planet of Alderaan, so that Obi-Wan can deliver the plans to Princess Leia's father. These plans are essential to the survival of the Rebel Forces. With this action, the adventure is ready to begin.

6. Now begin all the tests and obstacles necessary to overcome the enemy and accomplish the hero's goals. In fairy tales, this often means getting past

witches, outwitting the devil, avoiding robbers, or confronting evil. In Homer's *Odyssey*, it means blinding the Cyclops, escaping from the island of the Lotus-Eaters, resisting the temptation of the singing Sirens, and surviving a shipwreck. In *Star Wars*, innumerable adventures confront Luke. He and his cohorts must run to the *Millennium Falcon*, narrowly escaping the Storm-troopers before jumping into hyperspace. They must make it through the meteor shower after Alderaan has been destroyed. They must evade capture on the Death Star, rescue the Princess, and even survive a garbage crusher.

7. At some point in the story, the hero often hits rock bottom. He often has 20
a "death experience," leading to a type of rebirth. In *Star Wars*, Luke seems to have died when the serpent in the garbage-masher pulls him under, but he's saved just in time to ask R2D2 to stop the masher before they're crushed. This is often the "black moment" at the second turning point, the point when the worst is confronted, and the action now moves toward the exciting conclusion.

8. Now, the hero seizes the sword and takes possession of the treasure. He is now in charge, but he still has not completed the journey. Here Luke has the Princess and the plans, but the final confrontation is yet to begin. This starts the third-act escape scene, leading to the final climax.

9. The road back is often the chase scene. In many fairy tales, this is the point where the devil chases the hero and the hero has the last obstacles to overcome before really being free and safe. His challenge is to take what he has learned and integrate it into his daily life. He *must* return to renew the mundane world. In *Star Wars*, Darth Vader is in hot pursuit, planning to blow up the Rebel Planet.

10. Since every hero story is essentially a transformation story, we need to see the hero changed at the end, resurrected into a new type of life. He must face the final ordeal before being "reborn" as the hero, proving his courage and becoming transformed. This is the point, in many fairy tales, where the Miller's Son becomes the Prince or the King and marries the Princess. In *Star Wars*, Luke has survived, becoming quite a different person from the innocent young man he was in Act One.

At this point, the hero returns and is reintegrated into his society. In *Star Wars*, Luke has destroyed the Death Star, and he receives his great reward.

This is the classic "Hero Story." We might call this example a *mission* or *task* 25
myth, where the person has to complete a task, but the task itself is not the real treasure. The real reward for Luke is the love of the Princess and the safe, new world he had helped create.

A myth can have many variations. We see variations on this myth in James Bond films (although they lack much of the depth because the hero is not transformed), and in *The African Queen*, where Rose and Allnutt must blow up the *Louisa*, or in *Places in the Heart*, where Edna overcomes obstacles to achieve family stability.

The *treasure myth* is another variation on this theme, as seen in *Romancing the Stone*. In this story, Joan receives a map and a phone call which forces her into the adventure. She is helped by an American bird-catcher and a Mexican pickup-truck driver. She overcomes the obstacles of snakes, the jungle, waterfalls, shootouts, and finally receives the treasure, along with the "prince."

Whether the hero's journey is for a treasure or to complete a task, the elements remain the same. The humble, reluctant hero is called to an adventure. The hero is helped by a variety of unique characters. S/he must overcome a series of obstacles that transform him or her in the process, and then face the final challenge that draws on inner and outer resources.

The Healing Myth

Although the hero myth is the most popular story, many myths involve healing. In these stories, some character is "broken" and must leave home to become whole again.

The universal experience behind these healing stories is our psychological 30
need for rejuvenation, for balance. The journey of the hero into exile is not all that different from the weekend in Palm Springs, or the trip to Hawaii to get away from it all, or lying still in a hospital bed for some weeks to heal. In all cases, something is out of balance and the mythic journey moves toward wholeness.

Being broken can take several forms. It can be physical, emotional, or psychological. Usually, it's all three. In the process of being exiled or hiding out in the forest, the desert, or even the Amish farm in *Witness*, the person becomes whole, balanced, and receptive to love. Love in these stories is both a healing force and a reward.

Think of John Book in *Witness*. In Act One, we see a frenetic, insensitive man, afraid of commitment, critical and unreceptive to the feminine influences in his life. John is suffering from an "inner wound" which he doesn't know about. When he receives an "outer wound" from a gunshot, it forces him into exile, which begins his process of transformation.

At the beginning of Act Two, we see John delirious and close to death. This is a movement into the unconscious, a movement from the rational, active police life of Act One into a mysterious, feminine, more intuitive world. Since John's "inner problem" is the lack of balance with his feminine side, this delirium begins the process of transformation.

Later in Act Two, we see John beginning to change. He moves from his highly independent lifestyle toward the collective, communal life of his Amish hosts. John now gets up early to milk the cows and to assist with the chores. He uses his carpentry skills to help with the barn building and to complete the birdhouse. Gradually, he begins to develop relationships with Rachel and her son, Samuel. John's life slows down and he becomes more receptive, learning important lessons about love. In Act Three, John finally sees that the feminine is worth saving, and throws down his gun to save Rachel's life. A few beats later, when he has the opportunity to kill Paul, he chooses a nonviolent response instead. Although John doesn't "win" the Princess, he has nevertheless "won" love and wholeness. By the end of the film, we can see that the John Book of Act Three is a different kind of person from the John Book of Act One. He has a different kind of comradeship with his fellow police officers, he's more relaxed, and we can sense that somehow, this experience has formed a more integrated John Book.

Combination Myths

Many stories are combinations of several different myths. Think of *Ghost-* 35
busters, a simple and rather outrageous comedy about three men saving the city of New York from ghosts. Now think of the story of "Pandora's Box." It's about the woman who let loose all manner of evil upon the earth by opening a box she was told not to touch. In *Ghostbusters*, the EPA man is a Pandora figure. By shutting off the power to the containment center, he inadvertently unleashes all the ghosts upon New York City. Combine the story of "Pandora's Box" with a hero story, and notice that we have our three heroes battling the Marshmallow Man. One of them also "gets the Princess" when Dr. Peter Venkman finally receives the affections of Dana Barrett. By looking at these combinations, it is apparent that even *Ghostbusters* is more than "just a comedy."

Tootsie is a type of reworking of many Shakespearean stories where a woman has to dress as a man in order to accomplish a certain task. These Shakespearean stories are reminiscent of many fairy tales where the hero becomes invisible or takes on another persona, or wears a specific disguise to hide his or her real qualities. In the stories of "The Twelve Dancing Princesses" or "The Man in the Bearskin," disguise is necessary to achieve a goal. Combine these elements with the transformation themes of the hero myth where a hero (such as Michael) must overcome many obstacles to his success as an actor and a human being. It's not difficult to understand why the *Tootsie* story hooks us.

Archetypes

A myth includes certain characters that we see in many stories. These characters are called *archetypes*. They can be thought of as the original "pattern" or "character type" that will be found on the hero's journey. Archetypes take many forms, but they tend to fall within specific categories.

Earlier, we discussed some of the helpers who give advice to help the hero — such as the *wise old man* who possesses special knowledge and often serves as a mentor to the hero.

The female counterpart of the wise old man is the *good mother*. Whereas the wise old man has superior knowledge, the good mother is known for her nurturing qualities, and for her intuition. This figure often gives the hero particular objects to help on the journey. It might be a protective amulet, or the ruby slippers that Dorothy receives in *The Wizard of Oz* from the Good Witch of the North. Sometimes in fairy tales it's a cloak to make the person invisible, or ordinary objects that become extraordinary, as in "The Girl of Courage," an Afghan fairy tale about a maiden who receives a comb, a whetstone, and a mirror to help defeat the devil.

Many myths contain a *shadow figure*. This is a character who is the oppo- 40
site of the hero. Sometimes this figure helps the hero on the journey; other times this figure opposes the hero. The shadow figure can be the negative side of the hero, which could be the dark and hostile brother in "Cain and Abel," the stepsisters in "Cinderella," or the Robber Girl in "The Snow Queen." The shadow figure can also help the hero, as the whore with the heart of gold who saves the hero's life, or provides balance to his idealization of woman.

Many myths contain *animal archetypes* that can be positive or negative figures. In "St. George and the Dragon," the dragon is the negative force which is a violent and ravaging animal, not unlike the shark in *Jaws*. But in many stories, animals help the hero. Sometimes there are talking donkeys, or a dolphin which saves the hero, or magical horses or dogs.

The *trickster* is a mischievous archetypical figure who is always causing chaos, disturbing the peace, and generally being an anarchist. The trickster uses wit and cunning to achieve his or her ends. Sometimes the trickster is a harmless prankster or a "bad boy" who is funny and enjoyable. More often, the trickster is a con man, as in *The Sting*, or the devil, as in *The Exorcist*, who demanded all the skills of the priest to outwit him. The "Till Eulenspiegel" stories revolve around the trickster, as do the Spanish picaresque novels. Even the tales of Tom Sawyer have a trickster motif. In all countries, there are stories that revolve around this figure, whose job it is to outwit.

"Mythic" Problems and Solutions

We all grew up with myths. Most of us heard or read fairy tales when we were young. Some of us may have read Bible stories, or stories from other religions or other cultures. These stories are part of us. And the best way to work with them is to let them come out naturally as you write the script.

Of course, some filmmakers are better at this than others. George Lucas and Steven Spielberg have a strong sense of myth and incorporate it into their films. They both have spoken about their love of the stories from childhood, and of their desire to bring these types of stories to audiences. Their stories create some of the same sense of wonder and excitement as myths. Many of the necessary psychological beats are part of their stories, deepening the story beyond the ordinary action-adventure.

Myths bring depth to a hero story. If a filmmaker is thinking only about 45
the action and excitement of a story, audiences might fail to connect with

the hero's journey. But if the basic beats of the hero's journey are evident, a film will often inexplicably draw audiences, in spite of critics' responses to the film.

Take *Rambo*, for instance. Why was this violent, simple story so popular with audiences? I don't think it was because everyone agreed with its politics. I do think Sylvester Stallone is a master at incorporating the American myth into his filmmaking. That doesn't mean it's done consciously. Somehow he is naturally in sync with the myth, and the myth becomes integrated into his stories.

Clint Eastwood also does hero stories, and gives us the adventure of the myth and the transformation of the myth. . . . Eastwood's films have given more attention to the transformation of the hero, and have been receiving more serious critical attention as a result.

All of these filmmakers — Lucas, Spielberg, Stallone, and Eastwood — dramatize the hero myth in their own particular ways. And all of them prove that myths are marketable.

Application

It is an important part of the writer's or producer's work to continually find opportunities for deepening the themes within a script. Finding the myth beneath the modern story is part of that process. To find these myths, it's not a bad idea to reread some of Grimm's fairy tales or fairy tales from around the world to begin to get acquainted with various myths. You'll start to see patterns and elements that connect with our own human experience. Also, read Joseph Campbell and Greek mythology. If you're interested in Jungian psychology, you'll find many rich resources within a number of books on the subject. Since Jungian psychology deals with archetypes, you'll find many new characters to draw on for your own work.

With all of these resources to incorporate, it's important to remember that 50
the myth is not a story to force upon a script. It's more a pattern which you can bring out in your own stories when they seem to be heading in the direction of a myth.

As you work, ask yourself:

Do I have a myth working in my script? If so, what beats am I using of the hero's journey? Which ones seem to be missing?

Am I missing characters? Do I need a mentor type? A wise old man? A wizard? Would one of these characters help dimensionalize the hero's journey?

Could I create new emotional dimensions to the myth by starting my character as reluctant, naïve, simple, or decidedly "unheroic"?

Does my character get transformed in the process of the journey?

Have I used a strong three-act structure to support the myth, using the first turning point to move into the adventure and the second turning point to create a dark moment, or a reversal, or even a "near-death" experience?

Don't be afraid to create variations on the myth, but don't start with the myth itself. Let the myth grow naturally from your story. Developing myths is part of the rewriting process. If you begin with the myth, you'll find your writing becomes rigid, uncreative, and predictable. Working with the myth in the rewriting process will deepen your script, giving it new life as you find the story within the story.

Reading the Text

1. How does Seger define the "hero myth" (para. 11), and what are its typical stages?
2. In your own words, explain what Seger means by "the healing myth" (para. 29).
3. What is an "archetype" in film (para. 37)?

Reading the Signs

1. Seger is writing to aspiring screenwriters. How does her status as an industry insider affect her description of heroic archetypes?
2. **CONNECTING TEXTS** Focusing on gender issues, compare Seger's formulation of heroes with Robert B. Ray's in "The Thematic Paradigm" (p. 451). To what extent do Seger and Ray adequately explain the role of women — and men — in movies?
3. **CONNECTING TEXTS** Review Michael Parenti's "Class and Virtue" (p. 506), and write an essay identifying the myths behind the modern story *Pretty Woman* (1990).
4. Watch one of the *Harry Potter* films or a segment of the *Lord of the Rings* trilogy, and write an essay in which you explain the myths and archetypal characters the film includes. How might archetypal and mythic patterns explain the film's success? Alternately, select a dark film such as *Watchmen* (2009) or *Parasite* (2019).
5. Seger recommends that aspiring screenwriters read Grimm's fairy tales for inspiration. You can find them online. Read some of Grimm's tales, and then write an argument assessing the suitability of such tales as inspiration for films today.
6. **CONNECTING TEXTS** Read Mikhail Lyubansky's "The Racial Politics of *Black Panther*" (p. 492), then watch the film, paying particular attention to the character types. In an essay, analyze the film's use of archetypes. To what extent does it replicate, reinvent, or otherwise complicate archetypal characters?

MAYA PHILLIPS

The Narrative Experiment That Is the Marvel Cinematic Universe

As everyone knew at the time, the release of the mega-hit movie *Avengers: Endgame* in 2019 did not in the least signal the conclusion of the most profitable cinematic franchise in history. For like the real-world universe it inhabits, the Marvel Cinematic Universe promises to expand indefinitely, with no end in sight. But as Maya Phillips notes in this aesthetic approach to the M.C.U., such an expansive and interconnected story line presents special challenges to its creators, requiring the development of a nontraditional narrative format attuned to the complex interplay of old comics and new movies that underlies the whole enterprise. Will the whole thing collapse under its own weight eventually? Stay tuned. Maya Phillips is a member of *The New Yorker*'s editorial staff who writes for numerous print and online magazines.

Earlier this month, Marvel Studios announced that the prèmiere of *Avengers: Endgame* would be preceded by marathon screenings of all the movies in the Marvel Cinematic Universe, or M.C.U. Since the M.C.U. consists, to date, of twenty-two movies, the screenings were fifty-nine hours and seven minutes long. They topped the thirty-one-hour screenings held last year, before the prèmiere of *Avengers: Infinity War*, and the twenty-nine-hour screenings held in 2015, before the release of *Avengers: Age of Ultron*. An M.C.U. marathon is "equal parts dare, endurance test, and assertion of fan dominance," the reporter Alex Abad-Santos wrote, at Vox, after a pre-*Ultron* screening. Alex McLevy, a writer and editor at the A.V. Club, described the event he attended as "beyond anything I have ever experienced in a movie theater. . . . It's beautiful, and terrifying."

When *Iron Man* came out, in 2008, it was a standalone film. Moviegoers didn't know that it would kick off a titanic interconnected narrative that, during the next decade, would include aliens thrashing New York City (*The Avengers*); a space jailbreak (*Guardians of the Galaxy*); a *Terminator*-style robot insurrection (*Avengers: Age of Ultron*); a civil war (*Captain America: Civil War*); and an apocalypse (*Thor: Ragnarok*). Although the subtitle of the newest film, *Endgame*, suggests a conclusion, there are more movies on the horizon, including *Spider-Man: Far from Home*, sequels to *Black Panther* and *Doctor Strange*, and a third installment of *Guardians of the Galaxy*. Last month, Disney paid seventy-one billion dollars for 21st Century Fox's entertainment business, insuring that Marvel characters previously owned by Fox — including Deadpool, the X-Men, and the Fantastic Four — could appear in future additions to the M.C.U.

Though some fans complain about substandard movies and ever-lengthening runtimes, audiences remain invested in the M.C.U.: *Avengers: Infinity War* was the fourth-highest-grossing movie of all time, closely followed, in the top ten, by *The Avengers*, *Avengers: Age of Ultron*, and *Black Panther*. It seems likely, in other words, that the M.C.U. will continue to expand for the foreseeable future. This raises questions both superheroic and narratological. Will half of all the people on Earth, who were snuffed out at the end of *Infinity War*, ever be resurrected? And can the M.C.U. really keep expanding? How flexible is a story, ultimately? Can it be extended indefinitely without becoming meaningless, or will it reach some natural limit? How infinite can a fictional world be?

By most accounts, Aristotle laid out the ground rules of storytelling, in the fourth century B.C., in his *Poetics*. He argued that plot was at the core of narrative; a plot, he thought, needed to have a beginning, a middle, and an end, reflect an ordered structure of connected actions, and be self-contained. The most effective plots, he wrote, "should have a certain length, and this should be such as can readily be held in memory." *Poetics* has proved persuasive: many narrative theorists see an orderly, coherent, and contained plot as crucial to the act of storytelling.

5 The scholar Brian Richardson, in his essay "Beyond the Poetics of Plot: Alternative Forms of Narrative Progression and the Multiple Trajectories of Ulysses," offers his own definition of plot-based narrative — "a teleological sequence of events linked by some principle of causation; that is, the events are bound together in a trajectory that typically leads to some form of resolution or convergence" — before pointing out that "many narratives resist, elude, or reject" plot. Especially in the twentieth century, narratives began to "remain insistently fragmentary, open-ended, contradictory, or defiantly 'plotless.'" There are, it turns out, many kinds of plotlessness. Episodic storytelling, as in *Law & Order* or *The Simpsons*, utilizes smaller, loosely connected narratives to allow for the maintenance of a comforting, predictable stasis over all. Extended novels, such as Marcel Proust's *In Search of Lost Time*, allow a single narrative to emerge out of nonlinearity, in an effort to produce a more accurate representation of thought, memory, and experience.

In the book *A Theory of Narrative*, from 2008, Rick Altman, a professor emeritus of the cinematic arts at the University of Iowa, explores the peculiar narrative qualities of soap operas, which contain narrative twists and turns but get nowhere. "Unlike most novels and films, soaps are all middle," he writes. Despite their length, soaps tend to feel hemmed in. Science-fiction and fantasy narratives, by contrast, often seek to create a feeling of expansiveness: J. R. R. Tolkien created a world so detailed and all-encompassing that his narratives felt like pieces of something larger. Both soaps and fantasies may contain traditional plot-based narratives with moments of "resolution or convergence," but, in a sense, such moments aren't the point. It's the fictional world that's most alluring.

One might conclude that it's possible to break the Aristotelian mold — but narratives that deëmphasize or deconstruct plot must do so with good reason. The plotlessness of *The Simpsons* allows for the endless production of bite-size morsels of humor; the wandering narrative of *Ulysses* connects one character's internal landscape to a larger, interconnected view of life. Plotlessness works when it has a point.

Comic books, which are the direct ancestors of the M.C.U., may seem as if they belong to the tradition of expansive world-building that gave rise to *The Lord of the Rings*, *Dune*, *Game of Thrones*, and other epic fantasy worlds. In truth, comics have their own peculiar convention of nontraditional narrative, which has endowed them with a unique aesthetic. Its roots are in a dynamic of give and take that began, early on, between creators and audiences. Many superhero stories take place in similar environments — fictionalized versions of New York City, for example, which in different stories are portrayed in conflicting ways. As time went on, contradictions mounted. "At first, comic-book editors said, 'Who's paying attention to this?,' " Corey Creekmur, a colleague of Altman's, at the University of Iowa, who teaches classes on film and comic books and is the head of the film-studies program, told me. Then attentive readers began writing in. "Responding to fans, the editors started to say, 'Well, maybe we can think of all of these stories as linked, or connected.' " This led to the creation of teams such as the Justice League (which includes both Superman and Batman — residents of Metropolis and Gotham City, respectively) and the Avengers. Superheroes began living in shared worlds.

Marvel began adding more crossovers and teams to its roster; the Avengers first appeared in September, 1963. "It was canny cross-promotion," the writer Sean Howe notes in *Marvel Comics: The Untold Story*; by teaming fan-favorite characters with less popular heroes, Marvel hoped to increase interest across the board. But this also had "narrative effects that would become a Marvel Comics touchstone: the idea that these characters shared a world, that the actions of each had repercussions on the others, and that each comic was merely a thread of one Marvel-wide mega-story," he continues.

The proliferation of team-up narratives, of course, created its own set of 10
inconsistencies. Stan Lee, the creator of Spider-Man, the X-Men, and many other Marvel characters, "found it difficult to keep his stories straight when his lead characters were having adventures in their own books, but also teaming up with each other in The Avengers," the author Brian Robb writes in *A Brief History of Superheroes*. Even so, there was something brilliant about the method of addressing narrative inconsistencies by means of new narratives. It created a generative loop in which writers would produce stories, sometimes containing inconsistencies, and then write more stories to explain these discrepancies. Mistakes became opportunities. Fans grew even more engaged.

Eventually, team-ups and merged worlds changed the way comics were published. Mike O'Sullivan, the head writer and researcher of the *Official*

Handbook of the Marvel Universe, explains that, in the nineteen-sixties and seventies, readers would often encounter comic-book stories by means of single paper issues: "There was a finite start and finish to a self-contained story," he said. By the eighties, however, individual comic books were being republished, five or six at a time, in a trade-paperback format. Formerly independent stories were now merged; each multi-volume collection, in turn, pointed toward a larger, forever-expanding narrative. Today, that narrative includes not just M.C.U. movies but television shows: *Agent Carter*, *Agents of S.H.I.E.L.D.*, and Marvel's *Defenders* miniseries, on Netflix, contain references to big happenings in the M.C.U. O'Sullivan now heads a team responsible for combing through both the comics and films and recording every detail of every character arc and story line to preserve continuity. When his team spots an error, it confers with Marvel editors and Marvel Studios to decide how to then proceed in the Marvel canon going forward.

When filmmakers began working with the M.C.U., they may not have known what they were getting into. "At the time it was hard to understand the full scope of it," Jon Favreau, the director of *Iron Man* and *Iron Man 2*, said in a 2017 *Vanity Fair* piece on the beginnings of the M.C.U. "By the time I saw Avengers I understood how sophisticated the scope was. How difficult it is to juggle." (Favreau went on to executive-produce six more Marvel movies.) In theory, Favreau said, every M.C.U. movie should stand on its own. And yet anyone who's traced the journey of the Tesseract, the travels of Nick Fury, or the recurring character of Ronan the Accuser from one M.C.U. movie to the next knows that the films are as deeply invested in Easter eggs, teased plotlines, in-jokes, and interconnections as they are in traditional plot. "I know some people who've been frustrated when they'd go see a film and realize that it's not the whole story, or that it's just the first half," Creekmur said. "For some audiences, that's been fun. Other people just want to go see a movie, and now they're in for the long haul of a dozen more."

As the M.C.U. has expanded, the team-up movies in particular — *Avengers: Age of Ultron*, *Captain America: Civil War*, and *Avengers: Infinity War* — have grown unwieldy. Some films are so jam-packed that they feel airless, with meaningful character interaction confined to emotionally charged glances and insubstantial dialogue. Character development is put on hold until the heroes can retreat back to their individual properties, where they have more room to grow. In many accounts of M.C.U. marathoning, fans survive the onslaught of older movies only to find that they're indifferent to the newest installment. "Did the experience enhance my appreciation of the M.C.U.? Hard to say," the Indiewire critic David Ehrlich wrote, after attending a marathon last year.

One imagines that, with time, the intricate web linking the movies will get more frayed and insubstantial, and the new films will seem increasingly inessential. And yet, after a certain point, following a story for a long time becomes a story in itself. After watching nearly thirty hours of

Marvel adventures, Alex McLevy, the A.V. Club writer, concluded that "the experience overtakes the nature of the content." This is true of the M.C.U. more generally. When watching any individual movie, a kind of pattern recognition — an intellectual interest in how each new story evokes or departs from the others — replaces narrative pleasure. The narrative worth caring about becomes the story of one's own interaction with the M.C.U. Just as people ask, about historical events, "Where were you when it happened?," so fans ask where they were when *Iron Man* came out, when the Avengers first assembled, when heroes and villains battled in Wakanda. This is the story that's truly limitless.

Reading the Text

1. Summarize in your own words the historical development of the Marvel Cinematic Universe.
2. According to Phillips, how do Aristotle, Brian Richardson, and Rick Altman each define the basics of an effective plot?
3. What does Phillips mean by the "nontraditional narrative" (para. 8) of comics?
4. In Phillips' view, how has the Marvel Cinematic Universe become "unwieldy" (para. 13)?

Reading the Signs

1. Once upon a time, DC Comics, with its Superman/Batman lineup, ruled the superhero comic book roost. With the rise of the M.C.U., especially with its Avengers ensemble cast, it can be said that DC has taken a second place to Marvel in mass popularity. Write an essay proposing your own interpretation for why this happened. Conversely, write an essay challenging the contention that the M.C.U. is more popular than the DC world.
2. **CONNECTING TEXTS** Adopting Derek Thompson's perspective in "The Four-Letter Code to Selling Just About Anything" (p. 289), write an essay explaining why the M.C.U. movies remain so popular even though, as Phillips puts it, "character development is put on hold" (para. 13). Be sure to ground your analysis in a close reading of one or two M.C.U. films.
3. Until the appearance of *Iron Man* as a feature film in 2008, the character of Iron Man was not especially prominent among comic book superheroes. But it was *Iron Man* that, as Phillips remarks, really kicked off the colossal success of the M.C.U. universe. Write a semiotic analysis offering your own explanation for Iron Man's twenty-first century popularity.
4. **CONNECTING TEXTS** Using Jacob Silverman's explanation of Instagram's appeal (read "'Pics or It Didn't Happen': The Mantra of the Instagram Era," p. 368), as your critical framework, write an essay supporting, refuting, or modifying Phillips' claim that "the narrative worth caring about becomes the story of one's own interaction with the M.C.U." (para. 14).

ABRAHAM RIESMAN

What We Talk about When We Talk about Batman and Superman

Frenemies since 1940, Batman and Superman have coexisted in a complex relationship ever since DC Comics cloned the Caped Crusader from the superhero DNA of the Man of Steel. But, Abraham Riesman asks, why do we so often want to see them fighting each other? As Riesman argues in this historical interpretation of the men in spandex, they each stand for different ways of "how to do good," with Superman reflecting "an era of buoyant, blinkered consensus" and "operating on hope and inspiration" and Batman — only fully emerging from Superman's shadow in the troubled 1970s and 1980s — depending upon "fear and intimidation." So it really matters that every time the two have had a face-off in the past fifteen years or so, the Dark Knight has always gotten the upper hand: darkness over light. It could be a parable for our times. Abraham Riesman is a writer and editor at *New York Magazine*.

Are Batman and Superman allies or rivals, at their core? They're definitely not *enemies*, and that's only partly because they're both superheroes. For long stretches, particularly when the characters were new, they had a deeply chummy relationship, with Batman like a non-superpowered Superman — a lesser, but cheerful, do-gooder who also fought for truth, justice, and the American way. (It was kind of adorable, with Batman almost acting like a kid who smilingly looked up to his star-athlete older brother.)

And yet, for the past 30 years, the relationship has been punctuated by a series of spectacular fights — a gruesome tussle over ideology in 1986's graphic novel *Batman: The Dark Knight Returns*, a dramatic dust-up due to mind control in the 2003 comic-book story line "Hush," and, of course, an upcoming gladiator match in this weekend's big-screen tentpole *Batman v Superman: Dawn of Justice*. At this point, nobody really remembers that early, sunny friendship — when it comes to superheroes, pure friendship's boring. Batman and Superman are both, of course, good guys, but what we so often want to see is them fighting.

But why? Why are fans so desperate to see superheroes in conflict that they urge superhero writers to employ absurd narrative contrivances like mind control or alternate universes to make happen what would otherwise be vanishingly unlikely fights (a tactic used well over a dozen times in the history of Batman-Superman tales)? One big answer is no answer at all — who *wouldn't* want to see them fight? Every comics geek's inner adolescent is perpetually asking, *What's the point of having two heroes if you aren't also going to game out who'd win?* As comics critic Chris Sims put it in a column on the topic, "When you have characters and all you see them doing is winning, it's natural to wonder who would win harder if they ever had to compete. For that question, Superman and Batman make the perfect contenders."

But we also want to see them fight because, to an unusual degree even for comic books, the fights *mean* something. That is, they are about something — or some *things*. Namely: how to make a better world, with Superman operating through hope and inspiration, and Batman through fear and intimidation. As the villain Lex Luthor puts it in the new movie, it's "god versus man, day versus night."

5 Let's start with "god versus man." Superman is an alien — which is to say, celestial — creature, born on another planet but here completely alone, completely singular in his powers, which have at times included feats like reversing the spin of the Earth to turn back time. Batman is not just a man but a broken one, who inhabits a broken universe, his parents killed by a petty criminal and raised in an era of rapid urban decay — "an old-money billionaire, a human, an orphan who has seen the worst of the world and let it all but turn him to stone," in the words of critic Meg Downey. Superman, by contrast, "is a farm boy, an alien, raised with a stable adoptive family, who has seen the worst of the world and let it teach him a profound sense of empathy."

Which leads us to "day versus night." Superman has faith that humanity will tend toward goodness if you give it trust and hope; Batman lacks that faith and believes the world only gets in line if you grab it by the throat and never let go. The former spends his contemplative moments hoping for the best; the latter spends those moments vigilantly preparing for the worst. But this contrast isn't just characterological; it's also historical. The icons were created almost simultaneously, but Superman is unmistakably a figure of his early years — the 1940s and 1950s, an era of buoyant, blinkered wartime and postwar consensus (at least as it might have been felt by most white, boyish comic-book readers), when it seemed appropriate to deploy a godlike do-gooder to do things like help cats out of trees or return purses to de-pursed Metropolis women. (One of his early nicknames was the Man of Tomorrow, after all.) Batman came of age later, beginning in the 1970s, the era of American malaise and urban decay, using cynicism as a weapon for good and training his sights on a Gotham City so broken it often looked like a war zone (often fighting super-criminals who hoped not just to plunder the city but overturn any lingering faith its denizens had in the virtue of compassion and social order). Which of these two worldviews provides the better way to live a good and productive life? You can do both, of course — just as you can love both characters and write them in such a way where they get along with one another. But readers don't want just that — readers want to see the conflict.

And, in a real-world sense, most of them are on one side. Today, Batman is a far more popular character than Superman, and he typically wins whenever they go toe-to-toe in a story — which is, of course, ridiculous, considering he's just an earthling, but that only makes it all the more remarkable as a reflection of reader preferences and prejudices. Outside of comics and movies, too, his worldview predominates, in the form of a perennially apocalyptic vision of the near future. In all ways, Batman is winning in the battle of Batman vs. Superman, which is especially strange given how little New York today, say, looks like the Gotham of *The Dark Knight Returns*. But we've been living so long in Batman's universe that it can be hard to remember his worldview didn't always have the upper hand.

They began as friends — almost as doubles. Superman was created by Cleveland cartoonists Jerry Siegel and Joe Shuster and debuted in 1938 in the pages of *Action Comics* No. 1. At first, Superman only barely resembled the big blue Boy Scout we know today: He smirked while punching out slumlords, domestic abusers, and loan sharks and he seemed relatively unconcerned with preserving individual human life. He was, as Superman historian Glen Weldon puts it in his exhaustive and fascinating *Superman: The Unauthorized Biography*, a "bully for peace."

He was also an instant sensation. DC Comics knew it had a hit on its hands, but wanted a bigger one — which means they needed their star to be as family-friendly as possible. As comics historian Gerard Jones recounts in his chronicle of the era, *Men of Tomorrow: Geeks, Gangsters, and the Birth of the Comic Book*, DC exec Jack Liebowitz saw the nascent Man of Steel as "something that could be built and sustained here, a kind of entertainment that kids liked better than pulps and would continue to if given reason to keep coming back." Accordingly, in 1940, he and editor Whitney Ellsworth drew up a pristine code of conduct for superheroes that, among other tenets, forbade DC heroes from knowingly killing. It was not unlike the onset of the Hays Code in Hollywood, and by the time U.S. soldiers were being sent off to war in 1942, Superman had become cheery, lovable, and status quo–respecting.

Those were not adjectives you could use to describe the initial depictions 10
of Batman. He was first published in DC's 1939 comic *Detective Comics* No. 27, the creation of Bob Kane and Bill Finger. At first, he was a "weird figure of the dark" and an "avenger of evil," as one of the early stories put it. Unlike Superman, he had no special powers other than being exceedingly wealthy. He was more or less a rip-off of pulp hero The Shadow and spent his time in the darkness, attacking — and occasionally even murdering — evildoers. But, like Superman, he was also an instant smash — which meant the same image-buffering fate. In his new history of Batman, *The Caped Crusade: Batman and the Rise of Nerd Culture*, Weldon tells of newspaper editorials and church bulletins railing against dark, violent comic books.

As a result, the editorial leadership pushed Batman out of the shadows, making him brighter and poppier, and even turning the weird loner into a kind of doting father figure to a scrappy young ward named Robin (a relationship that could've really gotten dark and weird in different hands). "Adding Robin was no mere cosmetic tweak," writes Weldon, "it was a fundamental and permanent change that placed Batman in a new role of protector and provider." He stopped killing. He worked cheerfully with the Gotham police. He walked around in broad daylight. The Batman and Superman brands were more or less in sync.

Of course, Superman was a much more natural family-friendly sell than Batman, because comics writers couldn't quite eliminate all of the darkness from the character of the Dark Knight, as later they'd have trouble trying to turn Superman into something approaching an antihero: One of these characters was a benevolently powerful space-god, the other a weirdo orphan wearing bat ears. This probably, at least in part, explains Superman's bigger stature through the 1940s — his persona was a near-perfect vessel for imperious American confidence and social order. But Batman had his clean-cut pitch, too: He may not have had superpowers, but he was a kind of icon of self-improvement, since he had willed himself to reach the peak of human physical potential (well, willed and spent) and had fought a delightful gallery of enemies.

Oddly enough, it took DC a long time to figure out that these guys were two great tastes that could taste great together. Superman and Batman first appeared in an image together on the cover of a 1940 promotional tie-in comic for that year's World's Fair, but the interior pages showed no story where the two of them interacted. In 1941, there was a comic in which they stood side by side to help with a fund-raising drive for war orphans, but they had no dialogue with each other. That same year, they started appearing alongside one another on the covers of a new comics series called *World's Finest*, and on those covers, you saw them wordlessly playing baseball or going skiing — but once you opened the comic, you saw no stories where they actually hung out.

Superhero fiction has been a trans-media enterprise for longer than many give it credit for, and the genius notion of having Batman and Superman actually solve crimes together — as opposed to just convention-bid in tandem — apparently didn't materialize until a 1945 episode of Superman's spin-off radio show, *The Adventures of Superman*. Their first printed co-narrative came in *Superman* No. 76, published in 1952. There, Bruce Wayne and Clark Kent — who had no knowledge of each other's secret superhero-ing — found themselves in the same cabin on a cruise ship. When some criminals start a massive fire, Bruce turns out the cabin's light to change into his costume, and Clark takes the opportunity to do the same. But suddenly, they get caught in the act by light from the flames passing through the porthole. "Why — why, you're *Superman!*" Batman exclaims. "And you, Bruce Wayne . . . you're *Batman!*" Superman counters. "No time to talk this over now, *Superman!*" Batman says as they rush out of the cabin.

15 Their ensuing adventure set a template for the way they'd interact for the next 20-odd years: They complete each other and accentuate each other's different power-sets while having the same squeaky-clean tone and goals. Readers rarely saw a true ideological conflict between the two, and Batman subscribed to the Superman-ish notion that good can always triumph over evil, so long as we live clean lives and partner up with fellow do-gooders. The

only difference between them was their skill sets. "They had Batman be the master technician and Superman be the big jock," says Weldon. "Batman would be the ultimate brain and Superman would come over to Gotham for help on a case because *It's just too hard for me to figure!*" Occasionally, the two would have friendly contests (for example, No. 76 saw them performing feats of strength to win their respective cities the right to host an electronics convention), and they would occasionally challenge each other for the betterment of each (in No. 149, Batman and Superman each use an amnesia machine on themselves so they can try to re-discover each other's secret identities).

There were also real conflicts, though typically they unfolded under odd circumstances. "The logic of that time was heavily driven by covers," says comics historian and longtime DC executive Paul Levitz. You wanted to grab lucrative young eyeballs with insane vignettes on the front of a comic book and "two heroes fighting was a classically successful cover." The story on the inside was of secondary importance, largely built up to satisfy what was on the front. Irwin Donenfeld, the executive vice president of DC throughout much of the late '50s and early '60s, was particularly fond of this tactic, so you got nutso covers like that of *World's Finest* No. 109, in which a flying (!) Batman throws a massive cinderblock at Superman while a horrified Robin gazes at them and thinks to himself, *The sorcerer's spell that's been cast over* Batman *is forcing him to fight* Superman—*and now he has* super-powers *to do it with!* Such stories satisfied a fannish desire to see the two fight, but what made them even more exciting was how perverse they were—there's no way, after all, that these two would ever *really* have a problem with one another, right? And, whatever the fun of seeing them fight, you never had to worry too much about a permanent rupture: There was always some wacky explanation, like mind control, mistaken identity, or simply explaining that the tale was an "imaginary story," wholly removed from normal continuity. The chummy status quo would always return by the next issue. The gods were in their heaven, all was right with the world.

It was only in the '70s and '80s that Batman truly emerged from Superman's shadow, and it's hard to avoid the impression that the Dark Knight was a product of that time (just as Superman was a product of the mid-century). This was a period shadowed by the assassinations of two Superman-like symbols of hope—Robert F. Kennedy and Martin Luther King, Jr. Cities from coast to coast erupted into vicious race riots. A sitting president was tied to an insidious crime and resigned on live television. We lost a war for the first time and the economy skidded into an oil-slicked slowdown. At the cinema, audiences wanted heroes that were less like John Wayne and more like Dirty Harry.

In comics, they got one. For the first time since that brief window of grim violence in his earliest stories, the Dark Knight was dark again. That was a real reversal, given the deep, Technicolor imprint left by the '60s *Batman* TV show, which may be the clearest depiction of the soft-focus Batman of the Superman era (what could possibly have been at stake in that always-sunny playhouse Gotham?). The Batman comics, in a bid for brand synergy, got similarly goofy. But viewers grew tired of the show quickly, turning it from a brief hit into a canceled failure and cultural punch line and spawning a wave of angry fan letters asking DC's higher-ups to revise the character. One such letter, published in the pages of *Batman* No. 210: "Batman is a creature of the night. [He] prowls the streets of Gotham and retains an aura of mystery," it read. "Get the super-hero out, and the detective in!"

Batman comics were ailing in sales, so DC's leadership was willing to give it a shot. Under the guidance of editor Julius "Julie" Schwartz, upstart writer/artist team Denny O'Neil and Neal Adams were put in charge of *Batman*. As O'Neil recalls it, "I walked into Julie's office and he offered me *Batman* like this: 'We're going to keep publishing *Batman*, obviously, but we're not gonna do the camp thing anymore. Whaddaya got, my boy?' What I thought was this: we'll go back to 1939." O'Neil looked to Batsy's grim origin story for inspiration: "You've got this dark guy who's seen his parents killed and he spends his life symbolically avenging that death," he says. "That version of Batman seems to be the one that's right." O'Neil and Adams opted to have Batman scowl instead of smile, go out in the darkness and eschew the light, and meditate on how few people he could truly trust. "Superman has more faith in the system," says comics critic Ardo Omer. "Batman was created because the system failed him and continued to fail Gotham."

Batman was a much more natural icon of 1970s angst and anomie, 20
but the darker turn in comics also came to Metropolis, where Superman's virtues — once taken as self-evident — were being questioned in his own stories. O'Neil was brought on to write Superman tales, too, and felt it was no longer interesting to read about a perfect man who did only good. "The essence of fantasy melodrama is conflict," O'Neil says. "You've got a guy who, at his strongest and most powerful, could blow out a sun! How are you going to create conflict for that guy?" DC's leadership agreed. Through various in-story machinations, his powers were weakened for a while. But more important, doubting Superman became the order of the day. A 1972 tale penned by Elliot S. Maggin was boldly titled "Must There Be a Superman?" and saw the Man of Tomorrow realizing that he can't fix structural problems like poverty and oppression. "You stand so proud, *Superman*," read the opening narration, "in your *strength* and your *power* — with a pride that has found its way into the soul of every man who has stood above other men! But as with all men of *power*, you must eventually question yourself and your *use* of that *power*." Wait, were we talking about Kal-El of Krypton, or the United States of America?

As Americans began to distrust power, so too did Batman begin to distrust Superman. They still fought side by side in the pages of *World's Finest* and on the roster of DC's premier super-team, the Justice League, but there were cracks in the façade. In 1973's *World's Finest* No. 220, written by Bob Haney and drawn by Dick Dillin, the two are trying to crack a case, and the Kryptonian is turning up his nose at their villain's quest for "*illegal* revenge." "*I* can understand revenge," Batman says with a condescending scowl. "I took it myself against Joe Chill, my parents' killer! It's a human emotion — revenge!

Trouble with you, friend, is *you're* not human!" The ticked-off Superman punches a tree and asks, "*Who's* not human!?"

An ascendant Batman and Batman-ist worldview made concrete conflict almost inevitable, and matters came to a boiling point in 1983's *Batman and the Outsiders* No. 1, written by Mike W. Barr and drawn by Jim Aparo. During a meeting of the Justice League, Batman declares that he's had enough of the Superman-led squad's law-abiding approach to saving the world. He says he's going to break international regulations to rescue someone and when Superman tries to stop him, a furious Batman slaps his old friend's hand away and says he's resigning. Superman tries to appeal to the better angels of Batman's nature: "We've always served as an *example* to the others — " But the Dark Knight cuts him off. "I never asked for that, Superman!" he barks. "I never wanted men to *imitate* me — only *fear* me!"

Nowhere was their ideological conflict more pointed than in the most famous Batman story ever told, which is also the greatest Batman-Superman fight story ever told: writer/artist Frank Miller's 1986 masterwork *The Dark Knight Returns*. It's a dense tale set in a dystopian Gotham City tattooed with graffiti and beset by violent youths. Miller had been living in New York during its Koch-era nadir, getting mugged and seeing the tabloids scream about urban decay and the vigilantism of men like Bernhard Goetz. When Miller was commissioned to write a Batman tale, he decided to make Bruce Wayne what he called a "god of vengeance" — a pretty good description of Dirty Harry, actually, or other iconic antiheroes, like Travis Bickle and Rambo, who had already passed into American myth. "If he fights," Miller wrote in his notes for Batman, "it's in a way that leaves them too roughed up to talk." His ideal Batman "plays more on guilt and PRIMAL fears."

The result was, indeed, steeped in primal fear. In *The Dark Knight Returns*, an aging Bruce comes out of retirement and goes on a *Death Wish*esque crusade to clean up the streets by any means necessary. He has also come to hate the sunshiny outlook of Superman, a figure who — in Miller's depiction — has a naïve faith that it's morning in America. Miller's Superman has made a Faustian pact with the government, taking orders from President Reagan. (Well, he's not technically *called* Reagan, but any reader will recognize the fictional commander-in-chief's wrinkled smile and folksy chatter.) "I gave them my *obedience*," Clark thinks to himself while destroying some Soviet weaponry. "No, I *don't* like it. But I get to save lives — and the *media* stays quiet." When Batman leads an army of vigilantes during a night of chaos in Gotham, Superman is ordered to take down his erstwhile ally.

The fight that followed was the most perversely inventive one in the 25
canon. Superman arrives in Gotham and Batman completely beats the shit out of him. As it turns out, Superman may be strong, but Batman has two advantages: wealth and paranoia. His distrust of the Metropolis Marvel led him to come up with a cunning plan in preparation for the battle, and he can throw as many toys into it as he likes. He fires missiles at Superman; he wears a massive battle-suit that he plugs into the city's electrical grid, then

punches Superman *hard*; he has a pal hit the Man of Steel with some synthetic Kryptonite (Superman's historic weakness); and he ultimately wins, knocking Superman to a standstill. All the while, he takes pride in hurting Superman and meditates on their differing worldviews. "You sold us out, Clark," he thinks to himself. "Just like your *parents* taught you to. *My* parents taught me a *different* lesson — lying on this *street — shaking* in deep *shock — dying* for no reason at *all* — they showed me that the world only makes *sense* when you *force* it to."

A similar exchange punctuates writer/artist John Byrne's miniseries *The Man of Steel*, another influential recast of the Batman-Superman relationship, published the same year as *The Dark Knight Returns* (though less well known). Issue No. 3 chronicled a wholly rebooted version of the heroes' first meeting, devoid of the charming cruise-ship meet-up. Instead, the two of them, early in their careers, join together to catch a criminal — but they immediately question each other's approach to the task. Batman beats up a lowlife thug in an alleyway for information; Superman finds Batman right afterward and calls him an "outlaw" and an "inhuman monster." They decide to focus on taking down the villain, and, as they part ways, they reach a tense détente. "Well, I still won't say I fully approve of your methods, Batman," Superman says, flying away, "and I'm going to be keeping an eye on you, to make certain you don't *blow it* for the rest of us . . . but *good luck*."

But let's get back to *The Dark Knight Returns*. "In political terms, Superman would be a conservative and Batman would be a radical," Miller said when I interviewed him a few months ago. Miller himself identifies as a libertarian, so his protagonist's distrust of power makes all the sense in the world. But the political question of the book is, in my view, only a symptom of a larger philosophical matter. This Batman is utterly without faith in anything beyond his immediate control. Sure, he can trust his butler, his sidekick, and his weaponry — but that's about it. Everyone and everything else needs to be throttled and bent into shape, in order to wrestle with a world otherwise almost beyond repair. What's more, Batman hates Superman because Superman *does* have faith: faith in the government, faith in Reaganite prosperity, faith that Batman might be able to see reason and give up. In Batman's eyes, these are failings.

No one had ever before attempted to show these two being in such opposition, and so filled with bloodlust. But the crazy experiment was a massive success. For the first time, Batman comics started consistently outselling Superman ones, but the transformation went beyond mere sales. "It's difficult to overstate the influence *The Dark Knight Returns* has had on comics and the culture that has risen around them," Weldon writes. Thanks to Miller, the vision of Batman as a pitch-black bruiser and schemer was carved into the rock of superhero fandom. In 1989, Tim Burton's *Batman* hit theaters and, while it lacked the deep gothic mood of later screen hits like the influential *Batman: The Animated Series* and Christopher Nolan films that followed, it offered many of the dark, angry pleasures that *Dark Knight Returns* had surfaced — and it was a box-office smash unlike anything a DC character had ever seen.

Very few tales since then have dared to put the two heroes so viciously at odds as they were in *Dark Knight*, but every story of conflict since is shadowed by Miller's and Byrne's characterizations. In 1988's Batman story line "A Death in the Family" — written by Jim Starlin and drawn by Jim Aparo — Robin is brutally murdered by the Joker and a complicated diplomatic situation makes any Bat-revenge legally tricky. Clark flies in to tell Bruce to stay in line: "There's nothing you can do here," he says. Bruce fires off a massive punch to Clark's jaw, which of course doesn't even bruise the Man of Steel. "Feel better now?" Superman asks, frowning.

Even when they got along, after *Dark Knight*, there was often a steely sense that things *could* go awry between them. A 1990 Batman-Superman crossover story called "Dark Knight Over Metropolis" dealt with the theft of a ring made out of Kryptonite, and at the end, Supes opts to give the ring to Batsy for safekeeping, just in case someone evil ever takes over Superman's mind and he needs to be taken down. "I want the means to stop me," Clark says, "to be in the hands of a man I can trust with my life." It's a sweet moment, but also a grim one. Indeed, for all the talk of trust, Superman was dourly preparing for the worst and acting out of fear. In other words, much as Batman had acted like Superman in the middle of the century, we had somehow entered a world where Superman was acting like Batman.

Perhaps more important, the Batman mentality — paranoid, fatalistic, violent — was setting the pace for superhero fiction generally. Superman was killed by a rampaging monster in 1992. One year later, a brutal villain snapped Bruce Wayne's spine, and a younger, more vicious successor took over the Bat-mantle. Superman came back from the dead and the original Batman took back the cape and cowl, but they still fought increasingly apocalyptic threats that required harsh pragmatism to beat. The best-selling comics across the industry in the early-to mid-'90s were violent and oozing with themes as dark as the colors. America wasn't as decrepit and frightening as it had been in prior decades, especially in its cities, but in an age of increasing cynicism, Batman felt far more *au courant* than the Metropolis Marvel. As a new century dawned, conflicts between the two became more frequent in comics and, in nearly every one, Batman kept winning.

There was 2000's Justice League story line "Tower of Babel," written by Mark Waid and drawn by Howard Porter, in which we learned that Batman had detailed and brilliant plans to take down every member of the League, just in case — including Superman. There was the 2003 alternate-history tale *Superman: Red Son*, written by Mark Millar and drawn by Dave Johnson and Kilian Plunkett, which imagined a world where Kal-El of Krypton landed in the Soviet Union and became a Stalinist dictator — only to be challenged by an anarchist Russian Batman who uses his superior wit to knock the snot out of Soviet Supes before killing himself with a suicide bomb. There was that same year's *Batman* No. 612, written by Jeph Loeb and drawn by Jim Lee, where Batman uses that old Kryptonite ring to knock a mind-controlled Superman onto his butt. There were 2014's *Batman* Nos. 35 and 36, written by Scott

Snyder and drawn by Greg Capullo, wherein Superman gets mind-controlled yet again and Batsy spits a tiny pellet of Kryptonite-like material into Supes's eye to put him down. "Who wins in a fight?" Batman muses to himself in that last story. "The answer is always the same. Neither of us."

It's a nice rhetorical flourish, but in the real world, Batman *is* winning. Not only do creators nowadays think stories work better when he comes out on top, but he also outsells Superman on the comics stands and — much more important — at the box office. Way back in the earliest days of big-budget superhero filmmaking, 1978's *Superman: The Movie* was a sensation — but its sequels showed massively declining returns and that incarnation of the franchise was canned after 1987's loathed *Superman IV: The Quest for Peace*. Two years later, Batman struck big with the aforementioned Burton flick, which got two hit sequels: 1992's *Batman Returns* and 1995's *Batman Forever*. The failure of 1997's *Batman & Robin* put DC Comics-based movies in the wilderness for a while, but it was Batman who led them back to the Promised Land. Christopher Nolan's *Batman Begins* hit theaters in 2005 and was a surprise critical success, but the real action came with its two sequels. *The Dark Knight* and *The Dark Knight Rises* each made more than a billion dollars worldwide — numbers that were unthinkable for a superhero flick just a decade earlier. As many film critics noted, in the age of the War on Terror, this Batman seemed to be the hero we deserved.

Superman, on the other hand, couldn't get airborne. Bryan Singer's *Superman Returns* hit theaters in 2006 and it was as sunny, colorful, and hopeful as you'd want a Superman story to be. But Warner Bros. was disappointed in its performance and cancelled plans for a sequel. After years of failed proposals, a new Superman movie finally hit theaters in 2013: Zack Snyder's *Man of Steel*. It was a hit, raking in $668 million worldwide and giving Warner the confidence to use it as the starting point for its new DC Comics-based "shared universe" of interconnected films, the next of which is *Batman v Superman*. But at what price to his soul did Superman get this box-office victory? *Man of Steel* is a very dark movie. The visuals play out with gritty, color-drained filters. Superman spends much of the movie moping over a dead parent and wondering what the point of everything is. In the end, he has a horrifically violent battle with a fellow Kryptonian that levels Metropolis. He even grimly concludes that the only way to end that fight is to kill his rival (something the comics versions of Superman *and* Batman never do). The whole endeavor shows us a Superman who is brooding, angry, and pessimistic. In other words, it seems like the only way to do a successful Superman movie is to make it feel like a Batman movie. With *Batman v Superman,* they've just made another one.

The Batman perspective has some things going for it, of course: The world 35
can indeed look pretty dark, as our collective anxieties and casually apocalyptic political mood testify daily. But it is also not the 1970s or '80s anymore, and new threats like ISIS and climate change aside, the urban hellscapes which gave rise to the Dark Knight are distant memories at this point. Which does

make you wonder: How much is the cynicism of Batman a logical response to a terrifying future, and how much a self-perpetuating worldview with a locomotive logic of its own? And then there's the cost to comic-book *narrative*: If Batman and Superman are going to keep fighting, could we maybe let the Man of Steel win? Because if the political worldview of superhero fiction is going to hang in the balance with each battle, the least we could ask for is a little genuine suspense about which one of the do-gooders is going to come out on top.

Reading the Text

1. Summarize in your own words the history of the relationship between Batman and Superman, as Riesman presents it.
2. According to Riesman, how do Batman and Superman's fictional characters reflect cultural periods in real-life history?
3. Why does Riesman call *The Dark Knight Returns* (1986) "the greatest Batman-Superman fight story ever told" (para. 23)?
4. In the Batman-Superman fight, which character does Riesman believe is "winning" in recent years, and why?

Reading the Signs

1. **CONNECTING TEXTS** In class, form teams and debate Riesman's opening question: "Are Batman and Superman allies or rivals, at their core?" (para. 1). To develop your ideas, consult Robert B. Ray's "The Thematic Paradigm" (p. 451). Use the class debate as a brainstorming session for an essay in which you propose your own response to Riesman's question.
2. Write an essay in which you support, refute, or complicate Frank Miller's contention that "in political terms, Superman would be a conservative and Batman would be a radical" (para. 27).
3. Write an essay in which you analyze the rise of superheroes, like Deadpool, who are not squeaky-clean personalities. What does the popularity of such characters suggest about the mood of American society today?
4. In an essay, analyze a current female superhero such as Black Widow. To what extent is her mission "to do good," or is her heroism manifested in other ways? In what ways might her gender affect her creators' construction of her mission?

MATT ZOLLER SEITZ

The Offensive Movie Cliché That Won't Die

You've seen a satirical portrayal of him on *The Simpsons,* in the guise of Bleeding Gums Murphy, and he has appeared quite seriously in such movies as *The Legend of Bagger Vance, The Green Mile,* and *Legendary.* He's the "Magical Negro": "a saintly African American character who acts as a mentor to a questing white hero" in many recent movies. First identified as such by Spike Lee, as Matt Zoller Seitz observes in this critique of the character, the "Magical Negro" has his roots in such figures as Uncle Remus and Bill "Bojangles" Robinson, and his persistence in American popular culture can be read as a signifier of a larger cultural negotiation in which, Seitz argues, white America, finding itself no longer in complete control of the cultural and political agenda, is trying to strike a "deal." Matt Zoller Seitz is a television critic for *New York* and *Vulture* and is the founder of the online publication *The House Next Door.*

"You always know the right things to say," says Cal Chetley (Devon Graye), the high school wrestler hero of *Legendary*, in conversation with Harry "Red" Newman (Danny Glover), a local fisherman.

The hero seems bewildered and delighted as he says this. He's about to compete in an important match, reeling from melodramatic blows. When Harry shows up out of nowhere to give Cal a pep talk, the stage is set for a *Rocky*-style, go-the-distance ending. But if Cal had thought about Harry in terms of pop-culture stereotypes, he could have answered his own implied question: *How come you're always there when I need you, even though I barely know you?* Harry seems to stand apart from the rest of the community, even though he's a familiar and beloved part of it. The only character who speaks to Harry directly is Cal, and their conversations are always about Cal and his well-being. He's such the benevolent guardian angel figure that the cynical viewer half-expects him to be revealed as a figment of Cal's imagination.

He's not imaginary. He's a "Magical Negro": a saintly African American character who acts as a mentor to a questing white hero, who seems to be disconnected from the community that he adores so much, and who often seems to have an uncanny ability to say and do exactly what needs to be said or done in order to keep the story chugging along in the hero's favor.

We have Spike Lee to thank for popularizing this politically incorrect but very useful term. Lee used it in a 2001 appearance at college campuses. He was blasting a then-recent wave of such characters, played by the likes of Cuba Gooding Jr., in *What Dreams May Come* (a spirit guide helping Robin Williams rescue his wife from Hell), Will Smith in *The Legend of Bagger Vance* (a sherpa-on-the-green, mentoring Matt Damon's golfer), Laurence Fishburne in *The Matrix* (Obi-Wan to Keanu Reeves's Luke Skywalker), and Michael Clarke Duncan in *The Green Mile* (a gentle giant on death row whose touch heals white folks' illnesses).

5 The word choice is deliberately anachronistic — "negro" started to fall out of fashion about forty years ago. But that's why it's so devastating. The word "negro" was a transitional word that fell between the white-comforting "colored" and the more militantly self-determined and oppositional "black." It asked for dignity and autonomy without going that extra step asserting that it existed anyway, with or without white America's approval. "Negro" fits the sorts of characters that incensed Lee. Even though the movies take pains to insist that the African American character is as much a flesh-and-blood person as the white hero, the relationship is that of a master and servant. And not a *real* servant, either: one that really, truly lives to serve, has no life to speak of beyond his service to Da Man, and never seems to trouble himself with doubts about the cause to which he's devoting his time and energy. "How is it that black people have these powers but they use them for the benefit of white people?" Lee asked sarcastically.

The Magical Negro character (or as Lee called him, the "super-duper magical negro") wasn't invented in the 1990s. He's been around for at least a hundred years, accumulating enough examples (from Uncle Remus in *Song of the South* through the clock-keeper played by Bill Cobbs in *The Hudsucker Proxy*) to merit snarky lists, an entry in the urban dictionary, and a detailed Wikipedia page (turns out Stephen King's fiction has been a Magical Negro factory). The term gained an even wider audience when a candidate to chair the Republican National Committee mailed out a song titled "Barack the Magic Negro," with lyrics to the tune of the Peter, Paul and Mary hit. Outraged liberals focused on the surface racism encoded in the song title, ignoring the possibility that the song, however lead-footed in its humor, was rooted in something real.

What got lost in the flap over the song was the phrase's relevance to Obama's candidacy: There was (among Democrats, at least) a widespread sense that replacing George W. Bush with the Illinois senator would send a definitive signal that everything was different now, that it was time to rebuild, repair, rejuvenate, and move forward, not just toward a post-Bush society, but a post-racial one. It was an absurd hope, one that Obama himself seemed to resist endorsing at first, only to relent and begin publicly playing up his pioneer status as the first not-entirely-Caucasian man to pursue and then win the Democratic presidential nomination. Frequent *Salon* commenter David Ehrenstein tackled this subject in a memorable 2007 *Los Angeles Times* piece that called Obama a "magic negro" almost a year before that RNC ditty appeared. Likening Obama to a spiritual descendant of the noble, kind-hearted, often sexless black men portrayed by pioneering leading man Sidney Poitier, he wrote, "Like a comic-book superhero, Obama is there to help, out of the sheer goodness of a heart we need not know or understand. For as with all Magic Negroes, the less real he seems, the more desirable he becomes."

Suffice to say Obama's election triggered a paroxysm of paranoia, insecurity, and rage in roughly half the population (maybe more, if polls on immigration and the Park51 project are to be believed). These flare-ups of privilege (wherein an almost entirely white sector of the populace descended from once-despised immigrants embraces the idea that "we" have to protect or reclaim "our" country from "them") cast retrospective light on the Magical Negro resurgence, which flowered in earnest during the last Democratic administration and has been going full-steam ever since.

Between demographers' projections of a twenty-first-century majority-minority swap, Clinton's unprecedented (un-presidented?) comfort with African American culture (which he made official during the 1992 campaign, in an effective bit of pandering stagecraft, by playing sax on *The Arsenio Hall Show*), and hip-hop's supplanting rock as the country's unofficial national soundtrack, there was a sense, even in the pre-internet era, that the white man either wasn't in control anymore or soon wouldn't be. Whitey was just going to have to deal.

Things haven't played out quite so simply, of course. In every aspect of 10
quality of life that can be measured, nonwhite folks have always tended to be worse off than whites. That hasn't changed in the aughts, and the recession /depression has hit black men especially hard.

Looking back over the last twenty years' worth of cultural and demographic unrest, the M. N. phenomenon seems a form of psychological jujitsu — one that takes a subject that some white folks find unpleasant or even troubling to ponder (justifiably resentful black people's status in a country that, fifty years after the start of the modern civil rights struggle, is still run by, and mostly for, whites) and turns it into a source of gentle reassurance. Do "they" hate us? Oh, no! In fact, deep down they want "us" to succeed, and are happy to help "us" succeed, as long as we listen well and are polite. That's why Whoopi Goldberg put her life on hold to help Demi Moore get in touch with her dead boyfriend in *Ghost*, and Jennifer Hudson lived to serve Sarah Jessica Parker in the first *Sex and the City* movie. And it's why Danny Glover's character — one of but a few black men in an otherwise white town — takes such a keen interest in the life of a bantamweight high school wrestler who has apparently lived in the same town with Harry his entire life and recognizes him as a local eccentric, yet never bothered to get to know him before now.

People that enjoyed *Legendary* may say I'm being unfair to Harry, that there's more to him than Magical Negro-hood. And yes, it's true, at the end — spoiler alert! — we're told that he's not just a gravel-voiced sweetheart who likes to hang out by the local creek, catching fish and dispensing words of wisdom. He's actually quite influential — not *literally* magical, but nevertheless demi-godlike in his influence over the town and its history. But the specifics of Harry's character don't refute the label; quite the contrary. The revelation of Harry's influence is a nifty trick, one that's common in nearly all movies featuring nonwhite mentor/sidekick/deus ex machina characters. It seems appealing enough in the abstract. But it's weak soup when you look at such a character's role in the totality of the story.

Danny Glover, arguably one of cinema's most versatile and likable character actors, gets to play something close to God (he even narrates the story and turns out to have had a hand in three generations of local lives). But he doesn't get a good scene with anybody but the hero, doesn't get even the intimation of a private life, and barely speaks to anyone in the town that supposedly adores and respects him. Like the clock-tender in *The Hudsucker Proxy*, the HIV-stricken painter/saint from *In America*, and Ben Vereen's characters in *Pippin* and *All That Jazz*, Harry's aura of omnipotence is compensation for being shut out of the movie. It's a screenwriter's distraction that obscures the character's detachment from the heart of the narrative — and the character's essentially decorative nature. Like the hot-tempered black police captain who demands the maverick white detective's badge and the stern black woman judge who dresses down the kooky but irresponsible white heroine and warns her to get her life together, the Magical Negro is a glorified walk-on role, a narrative device with a pulse. The M. N. doesn't really drive the story, but is a glorified hood ornament attached to the end of a car that's being driven by white society, vigorously turning a little steering wheel that's not attached to anything.

Reading the Text

1. In your own words, define the term "Magical Negro" (para. 3). Why is it considered "anachronistic" (para. 5)?
2. What evidence does Seitz offer to suggest that the Danny Glover character in *Legendary* is a Magical Negro?
3. Why did some commentators dub Barack Obama, who was not a cinematic character, a Magical Negro during the 2008 presidential race?
4. Characterize Seitz's tone in this selection. In what ways does it affect your response to his argument?

Reading the Signs

1. **CONNECTING TEXTS** Write your own interpretation of the representation of African American characters in *Legendary*, *Ghost*, *Sex and the City*, *All That Jazz*, or another film that Seitz refers to. To develop your ideas, consult Michael Omi's "In Living Color: Race and American Culture" (p. 129). To what extent do the characters in the film you've selected display traits of "overt" or "inferential" racism, as Omi describes those concepts?
2. **CONNECTING TEXTS** Seitz attributes the recurrence of the Magical Negro stereotype, in part, to concern about changing demographics whereby whites would no longer be the dominant ethnic group in America. Considering today's political landscape, what signs do you see that support or complicate this explanation? Be sure to consider national voting patterns, particularly in the 2016 and 2020 presidential elections. To develop your ideas, read Mark Murphy's "The Uncivil War: How Cultural Sorting of America Divides Us" (p. 94).

3. Seitz comments parenthetically that "Stephen King's fiction has been a Magical Negro factory" (para. 6). Read at least one King novel that includes African American characters. Write an essay in which you support, refute, or modify this assertion.
4. Seitz is critical of the Magical Negro stereotype, but it has been argued that this representation of African Americans is a positive response to accusations that this demographic group too often is portrayed with overtly negative, violent stereotypes. Write an essay in which you evaluate this argument, taking care to base your claims on an analysis of specific films and characters.
5. Using Seitz's article as a critical framework, analyze the depiction of African American characters in a film such as *Suicide Squad* (2016) or *Birth of a Nation* (2016). To what extent does the film you select reinforce, redefine, or complicate mainstream depictions of African Americans?

MIKHAIL LYUBANSKY

The Racial Politics of Black Panther

The cultural impact of the blockbuster movie *Black Panther* can hardly be overestimated, with not the least of its effects being the complete revision of the old Hollywood maxim that Afrocentric films don't make for big box-office. But as Mikhail Lyubansky observes in this essay that originally appeared in *Psychology Today*, *Black Panther*'s significance goes beyond "the racial makeup of its talent and its box-office appeal" to offer a "racial commentary about our own world." Breaking the movie down into six racially analytic categories, Lyubansky offers a semiotic reading that notes both the explicit and sometimes "problematic" implicit racial signals that *Black Panther* sends. It all is, as they say, complicated. A teaching associate professor in the Department of Psychology at the University of Illinois, Urbana-Champaign, Lyubansky is co-editor of *Toward a Socially Responsible Psychology for a Global Era* and writes a blog for *Psychology Today* called Between the Lines.

Seen through a racial lens, *Black Panther* is an important film. Written and directed by black men, it tells a story about black characters in a fictional black land. Hollywood has essentially refused to make such Afrocentric films on the grounds that they wouldn't attract a sufficient audience. *Black Panther*'s box-office success may permanently disrupt this narrative, creating conditions for a more inclusive industry and a wider range of films.

But there is more to this film, racially speaking, than the racial makeup of its talent and its box-office appeal. *Black Panther* also offers racial commentary about our own world. To that end, below are six racial dynamics worth noting and unpacking. They are offered in the spirit of better appreciating a courageous film that not only tells an entertaining story but takes on important social issues and questions.

Warning: spoilers ahead.

1. The Black Panther is Black.

Well, duh! But as Kristen Page-Kirby pointed out, he "is not a superhero who happens to be black. His blackness . . . goes to the absolute center of his identity. . . ." There is really no white superhero equivalent. There cannot be, given this country's (and this world's!) racial politics. For T'Challa, his blackness and his Wakandan heritage are a source of pride. Other superheroes can exhibit national pride (hello, Captain America), but white pride is off-limits for heroes, just as it is off-limits for us mere mortals, at least those of us who value being part of the cultural mainstream. This is as it should be. For T'Challa, for other Africans, and for African Americans, racial pride is legitimately earned by overcoming or even just surviving an oppressive history and reality. White men (and women) can be proud too. Many have also overcome oppression and other obstacles, but their oppression was unrelated to their whiteness, and therefore, their pride cannot be related to whiteness either. T'Challa is aware of his blackness and is unapologetically proud of it.

2. The relationship between the Marvel Black Panther and prominent 1960s civil rights groups and leaders is . . . complicated.

Black Panther first appeared in Fantastic Four #52 (July 1966), three months 5
before the Black Panther Party was formally founded. Though the black panther logo was also used by the Lowndes County Freedom Organization, and the segregated World War II Black Panthers Tank Battalion, there seems to be no evidence that the comic was inspired by either. In fact, despite the similar names and proximate origin, cocreator Stan Lee said "the name was inspired by a pulp adventure hero who had a black panther sidekick." Indeed, sharing a name with an armed, revolutionary, socialist organization was sufficiently inconvenient that Marvel renamed the character to Black Leopard in Fantastic Four #119 (1972). T'Challa explains his reasoning to The Thing thus:

> "I contemplate a return to your country, Ben Grimm, where [the Black Panther name] has—political connotations. I neither condemn nor condone those who have taken up the name—but T'Challa is a law until himself. Hence, the new name—a minor point, at best, since the panther is a leopard."

The name change was short-lived, with the Panther returning less than a year later, but it seems that the creative team of the '60s and early '70s found the link to the Panther party more an annoyance and distraction than inspiration.

For their part, I'm certain that Black Panther Party leaders like Bobby Seale, Eldridge Cleaver, and Elaine Brown would have frowned at T'Challa cooperating with CIA operatives and the U.S. government more broadly. Yet, they would have certainly approved of the first mainstream superhero of African descent and likely found common ground over their mutual concern with the well-being and self-determination of black people. The Black Panther Party was more radical than the comic. How could it not be? Even with a black hero, Jack Kirby and Stan Lee were both white and Marvel was primarily targeting a white audience, while the Black Panther Party was black led and clearly focused on the black agenda. But as Jamil Smith aptly pointed out in his piece for *Time*, "the revolutionary thing about Black Panther is that it envisions a world not devoid of racism but one in which black people have the wealth, technology, and military might to level the playing field." With those resources in hand, the Black Panther Party might have adopted very different tactics.

Some writers have suggested that T'Challa's philosophy is similar to that of Martin Luther King Jr. For example, *N.Y. Post*'s Sara Stewart writes "T'Challa, though, is a pacifist, the Martin Luther King Jr. to Killmonger's Malcolm X." While I have previously made a comparison to MLK when discussing Professor Xavier, in this case I think the analogy, while well-intentioned, is not well informed.

First of all, while Malcolm X shared Killmonger's concerns about black inequality, by the time he was killed, he had come to realize that allies for the cause of liberation and equality exist across racial lines. Secondly, T'Challa is not a pacifist. To be sure, he does not enjoy violence and spares M'Baku's life in the first ritual battle. And when he lands what turns out to be the fatal blow against Killmonger, there seems to be more mourning and compassion than rejoicing. But he accepts both ritual battles and he is clearly willing to use violence when he puts on the Panther suit to do battle with Claw and other thugs. A reluctant warrior, perhaps, but T'Challa is clearly a warrior, not a pacifist. And while it's easy to imagine King saying "We are all one tribe," as T'Challa does in his speech to the United Nations, the film offers no examples of him engaging in nonviolent resistance, which distinguished King and his followers from the Black Panther Party, Malcolm X, and Stokely Carmichael, who agreed on the problems but not on the strategies.

10 None of this is intended as a criticism of either the film or its lead character. King, like the Black Panther Party, was also operating from a position of weakness, relative to the dominant power structure. As the head of a resource-rich, sovereign nation, T'Challa does not need to shame those who hold structural power to do the right thing. He can simply opt to do it, as he does near the end of the film when he decides that he and Wakanda have a moral duty to the world. Upon reaching this conclusion, he decides to focus his energy not on overpowering his enemies but on building an infrastructure that better supports the disenfranchised. This includes African American youth, but it also seems aimed at a much larger international community. Would King have supported such a global strategy? Had he had the resources to do

so, I think he would have, but so, I think, would have all the other prominent civil rights leaders of the 1960s. Besides the access to far greater resources, T'Challa has much in common with all of them.

3. Klaw is a representation of white supremacy.

The Black Panther film doesn't provide much of Ulysses Klaw's backstory, but he is the son of Nazi war criminal Colonel Fritz Klaue, a member of the Blitzkrieg Squad led by Baron Strucker, one of the leaders of Hydra. Klaue was sent to Wakanda by Adolf Hitler in order to learn the African nation's secrets. After the war ended, he "anglicized his name to Klaw and raised his son [Ulysses] with tales of Wakanda." After coming of age, Ulysses becomes an arms dealer in South Africa and travels to Wakanda where he forces (enslaves) Wakandans to mine Vibranium. Thus, Klaw (literally) represents the legacy of the Nazis and therefore also of white colonialism and white supremacy. As such, his primary motivation is greed. He has no interest in Wakandan culture or its people. He wants only to extract its valuable resource, Vibranium, and is willing to kill anyone in his way, including the Wakandan king, T'Chaka. Klaw seems to die in this film, but white supremacy has proven to be remarkably resilient. We will see Klaw again, probably soon.

4. CIA agent, Everett K. Ross, as a representation of the every(white)man.

If Klaw is the representation of white supremacy, then Ross is the comforting antithesis. He not only likes and respects T'Chaka's son, T'Challa (the Black Panther) but essentially earns his "pass" by stepping in front of a bullet to save one of T'Challa's guards. Though in many ways Ross essentially functions as a reverse "magic negro"[1] — a character whose sole purpose seems to be to promote the well-being of the lead (in this case, Black) characters — he is also an avatar, an audience surrogate who represents the way Panther is perceived by well-meaning white men (and women). In the words of Ross's creator, Christopher Priest, "Comics are traditionally created by white males for white males. I figured, and I believe rightly, that for *Black Panther* to succeed, it needed a white male at the center, and that white male had to give voice to the audience's misgivings or apprehensions or assumptions about this character."

[1]Spike Lee and others have appropriately criticized certain films for their use of "the magical negro," a black character (often with mystical powers or unusual wisdom) whose sole purpose seems to be to support the film's white protagonists. Though seemingly positively depicted, the one-dimensional nature of these characters strips them of their humanity. They exist only as a prop to support the growth or ambition of whiteness. There are no "magical negroes" in *Black Panther*, but Ross has many similar characteristics as the film's only nonvillainous white character in an Afrocentric story. He's moral, kind, courageous, and selfless — a good (white) man, if ever there was one, but either despite my whiteness or because of it, I found it difficult to relate to him. Perhaps this speaks to my discomfort with my own racial politics and reluctance to identify with the "white ally" ideal, or perhaps there is something just a bit off about a character whose only reason for being is to serve as a white conduit to a black story.

Importantly, the antiracist, while ideal, cannot remain skeptical toward blackness. To the contrary, he/she must (relatively soon) embrace the racial other and, at least in their own fantasies, become their allies and friends. Thus, despite having no special powers or even understanding of Wakandan culture and traditions, by shooting down the ships leaving Wakanda at Killmonger's orders, Ross winds up playing a vital role in not only assisting T'Challa but in preserving Wakandan traditions.

5. Erik Killmonger represents . . .

The racial symbolism of Killmonger is, for me, one of the more unsatisfying aspects of this film. It is tempting to think of Killmonger as a representation of his people, the African American counterpart to T'Challa's African identity. Indeed, the smart viewer will nod along when he challenges T'Challa's claim that he has no responsibility to help black Americans: "Not your own?" he asks, "Did life start on this continent? Aren't all people your people?"

Unfortunately, Killmonger is too filled with anger to respond affirmatively 15
to his own question. He is *justifiably* angry at his own people's oppression, but he has internalized the notion that one has to be either the conqueror or the conquered. He wants to free his people, but he seems willing to have other people (the oppressors) suffer in turn. It is not so much justice and freedom that Killmonger wants as the power to dominate others. This is not an uncommon phenomenon. There are studies (e.g., Nansel, Overpeck, Haynie, Ruam, & Scheidt, 2003) that show that those who are bullied are often more willing to carry weapons and perpetrate violence against others. Certainly, there are African Americans who hold such beliefs, but Killmonger is essentially the only representation of African Americans in the film. As such, the film could be read as an indictment not just of this particular point of view but of African American men more broadly. For those who already tend to blame racial inequality on so-called "black on black" violence, it is not much of a stretch to find that view vindicated in the film.

This is certainly not what the filmmakers intended and I hope not what most viewers come away with. The film is an indictment of Killmonger and his philosophy, but is sympathetic toward his (and his people's) suffering. We don't want Killmonger to unleash the power of Vibranium on an unsuspecting world, but we recognize the need to end oppression and racialized poverty. When Killmonger dies at the end of the film, there is, for many, little pleasure at his death. He needed to die because the philosophy of racialized vengeance has to die, but we nevertheless see him (rightfully) as a victim of unfortunate circumstances he could not control and we can understand and even relate to his anger, even as we reject his vision for how to make things better. As Nate Marshall so aptly pointed out, one of this film's many strengths is that it "fundamentally questions the nature of power, freedom, and responsibility." I agree. I have no objection to the Killmonger character. I just wish he wasn't the only significant African American character in the film. Here, as everywhere, there are the dangers of a single story.

6. **Wakanda has problems.**

There are lots of Wakanda fans out there and for good reason. With Wakanda, we all bear witness to an African country characterized not only by its natural beauty but by its natural resources and highly developed technologies. It is meaningful, as well, that Wakandan women seem to be valued for their strength and assertiveness, rather than repressed or punished. Certainly, T'Challa is a worthy leader surrounded by capable and talented warriors and advisors. There's much to like.

At the same time, the Wakanda we see in the first Black Panther film has its problems. For a supposed advanced nation, the Wakandans seem unusually highly invested in military technology and have opted to retain not only a family monarchy but a ritual fight that could (and does) result in an unpredictable and dangerous transfer of power.

It is problematic as well that Wakanda is so completely ethnically homogeneous that one must literally have a brand to gain entry. To be sure, deciding that Wakanda needs to become less insular is part of T'Challa's transformation, but the "old" Wakanda — the one we see throughout most of the film — seems rather invested in its own ethnic purity. Imagine a homogeneously white nation-state that brands its citizens and restricts entry only to its own people. It is an inaccurate and therefore unfair comparison,[2] but it still feels off, especially since one Wakandan tribe seems to live in relative isolation with little access to Wakanda's considerable resources and technology.

Moreover, it appears that the king's power is absolute. There is no (visible) 20
democratic process, no checks and balances, no protections for Wakandan citizens. With T'Challa on the throne, there is no need for concern, but strong societies are structured so that they can survive individual failings and difficult transitions. It is not at all clear that Wakanda can. Perhaps T'Challa will set all things right (there are benefits to absolute power). In the meantime, like the rest of the world, Wakanda has its share of domestic challenges too.

Reading the Text

1. In your own words, summarize Lyubansky's six categories of racial dynamics in *Black Panther*.
2. Synthesize Lyubansky's various comments about the role white characters play in *Black Panther* into an overall interpretation.
3. What negative stereotypes about African-American men does Lyubansky suggest *Black Panther* may perpetuate?
4. What "problems," as a fictional place, does Wakanda present in the movie, according to Lyubansky?

[2]This imaginary white country would presumably exist in a world in which most power and wealth is concentrated in white hands, which would make it part of the dominant group, while Wakanda is a small black oasis in a predominantly white world, which locates it in the margins of society.

Reading the Signs

1. Research Black Panther Party leaders such as Eldridge Cleaver and Bobby Seale, and write an essay supporting, challenging, or qualifying Lyubansky's position that they would have a mixed response to the movie.
2. Some critics have suggested that the T'Challa/Killmonger conflict is analogous to the historical difference between Martin Luther King, Jr. and Malcolm X. Basing your argument on a close reading of *Black Panther*, write an essay supporting, refuting, or qualifying this contention.
3. Even though Lyubansky says "there's much to like" about Wakanda, he goes on to claim that "it's also ethnically homogeneous," with a king whose "power is absolute" (para. 20). Write an essay supporting, refuting, or qualifying this contention.
4. **CONNECTING TEXTS** Lyubansky says "there are no 'magical Negroes' in *Black Panther*" (footnote 1). Read Matt Zoller Seitz's "The Offensive Movie Cliché That Won't Die (p. 488), and write an essay defending, refuting, or modifying this observation.

JESSICA HAGEDORN

Asian Women in Film: No Joy, No Luck

Why do movies always seem to portray Asian women as tragic victims of history and fate? Jessica Hagedorn asks this in this essay, which originally appeared in *Ms.* Even such movies as *The Joy Luck Club*, based on Amy Tan's breakthrough novel that elevated Asian American fiction to best-seller status, reinforce old stereotypes of the powerlessness of Asian and Asian American women. A screenwriter and novelist, Hagedorn calls for a different kind of storytelling that will show Asian women as powerful controllers of their own destinies. Jessica Hagedorn's publications include the novels *Dogeaters* (1990) and *Toxicology* (2011).

Pearl of the Orient. Whore. Geisha. Concubine. Whore. Hostess. Bar Girl. Mamasan. Whore. China Doll. Tokyo Rose. Whore. Butterfly. Whore. Miss Saigon. Whore. Dragon Lady. Lotus Blossom. Gook. Whore. Yellow Peril. Whore. Bangkok Bombshell. Whore. Hospitality Girl. Whore. Comfort Woman. Whore. Savage. Whore. Sultry. Whore. Faceless. Whore. Porcelain. Whore. Demure. Whore. Virgin. Whore. Mute. Whore. Model Minority. Whore. Victim. Whore. Woman Warrior. Whore. Mail-Order Bride. Whore. Mother. Wife. Lover. Daughter. Sister.

As I was growing up in the Philippines in the 1950s, my fertile imagination was colonized by thoroughly American fantasies. Yellowface variations on the exotic erotic loomed larger than life on the silver screen. I was mystified and enthralled by Hollywood's skewed representations of Asian women: sleek, evil goddesses with slanted eyes and cunning ways, or smiling, sarong-clad South Seas "maidens" with undulating hips, kinky black hair, and white skin darkened by makeup. Hardly any of the "Asian" characters were played by Asians. White actors like Sidney Toler and Warner Oland played "inscrutable Oriental detective" Charlie Chan with taped eyelids and a singsong, chop suey accent. Jennifer Jones was a Eurasian doctor swept up in a doomed "interracial romance" in *Love Is a Many Splendored Thing*. In my mother's youth, white actor Luise Rainer played the central role of the Patient Chinese Wife in the 1937 film adaptation of Pearl Buck's novel *The Good Earth*. Back then, not many thought to ask why; they were all too busy being grateful to see anyone in the movies remotely like themselves.

Cut to 1960: *The World of Suzie Wong*, another tragic East/West affair. I am now old enough to be impressed. Sexy, sassy Suzie (played by Nancy Kwan) works out of a bar patronized by white sailors, but doesn't seem bothered by any of it. For a hardworking girl turning nightly tricks to support her baby, she manages to parade an astonishing wardrobe in damn near every scene, down to matching handbags and shoes. The sailors are also strictly Hollywood, sanitized and not too menacing. Suzie and all the other prostitutes in this movie are cute, giggling, dancing sex machines with hearts of gold. William Holden plays an earnest, rather prim, Nice Guy painter seeking inspiration in The Other. Of course, Suzie falls madly in love with him. Typically, she tells him, "I not important," and "I'll be with you until you say — Suzie, go away." She also thinks being beaten by a man is a sign of true passion and is terribly disappointed when Mr. Nice Guy refuses to show his true feelings.

Next in Kwan's short-lived but memorable career was the kitschy 1961 musical *Flower Drum Song*, which, like *Suzie Wong*, is a thoroughly American commercial product. The female roles are typical of Hollywood musicals of the times: women are basically airheads, subservient to men. Kwan's counterpart is the Good Chinese Girl, played by Miyoshi Umeki, who was better playing the Loyal Japanese Girl in that other classic Hollywood tale of forbidden love, *Sayonara*. Remember? Umeki was so loyal, she committed double suicide with actor Red Buttons. I instinctively hated *Sayonara* when I first saw it as a child; now I understand why. Contrived tragic resolutions were the only way Hollywood got past the censors in those days. With one or two exceptions, somebody in these movies always had to die to pay for breaking racial and sexual taboos.

Until the recent onslaught of films by both Asian and Asian American film- 5
makers, Asian Pacific women have generally been perceived by Hollywood with a mixture of fascination, fear, and contempt. Most Hollywood movies either trivialize or exoticize us as people of color and as women. Our intelligence is underestimated, our humanity overlooked, and our diverse cultures treated

as interchangeable. If we are "good," we are childlike, submissive, silent, and eager for sex (see France Nuyen's glowing performance as Liat in the film version of *South Pacific*) or else we are tragic victim types (see *Casualties of War*, Brian De Palma's graphic 1989 drama set in Vietnam). And if we are not silent, suffering doormats, we are demonized dragon ladies — cunning, deceitful, sexual provocateurs. Give me the demonic any day — Anna May Wong as a villain slithering around in a slinky gown is at least gratifying to watch, neither servile nor passive. And she steals the show from Marlene Dietrich in Josef von Sternberg's *Shanghai Express*. From the 1920s through the 1930s, Wong was our only female "star." But even she was trapped in limited roles, in what filmmaker Renee Tajima has called the dragon lady / lotus blossom dichotomy.

Cut to 1985: There is a scene toward the end of the terribly dishonest but weirdly compelling Michael Cimino movie *Year of the Dragon* (cowritten by Oliver Stone) that is one of my favorite twisted movie moments of all time. If you ask a lot of my friends who've seen that movie (especially if they're Asian), it's one of their favorites too. The setting is a crowded Chinatown nightclub. There are two very young and very tough Jade Cobra gang girls in a shoot-out with Mickey Rourke, in the role of a demented Polish American cop who, in spite of being Mr. Ugly in the flesh — an arrogant, misogynistic bully devoid of any charm — wins the "good" Asian American anchorwoman in the film's absurd and implausible ending. This is a movie with an actual disclaimer as its lead-in, covering its ass in advance in response to anticipated complaints about "stereotypes."

My pleasure in the hard-edged power of the Chinatown gang girls in *Year of the Dragon* is my small revenge, the answer to all those Suzie Wong "I want to be your slave" female characters. The Jade Cobra girls are mere background to the white male foreground/focus of Cimino's movie. But long after the movie has faded into video-rental heaven, the Jade Cobra girls remain defiant, fabulous images in my memory, flaunting tight metallic dresses and spiky cock's-comb hairdos streaked electric red and blue.

Mickey Rourke looks down with world-weary pity at the unnamed Jade Cobra girl (Doreen Chan) he's just shot who lies sprawled and bleeding on the street: "You look like you're gonna die, beautiful."

JADE COBRA GIRL: "Oh yeah? [blood gushing from her mouth] I'm proud of it."

ROURKE: "You are? You got anything you wanna tell me before you go, sweetheart?"

JADE COBRA GIRL: "Yeah. [pause] Fuck you."

Cut to 1993: I've been told that like many New Yorkers, I watch movies with the right side of my brain on perpetual overdrive. I admit to being grouchy and overcritical, suspicious of sentiment, and cynical. When a critic like Richard Corliss of *Time* magazine gushes about *The Joy Luck Club* being "a fourfold *Terms of Endearment*," my gut instinct is to run the other way. I resent being told how to feel. I went to see the 1993 eight-handkerchief movie version of Amy Tan's bestseller with a group that included my ten-year-old daughter. I was caught between the sincere desire to be swept up by the turbulent mother-daughter sagas and my own stubborn resistance to being so obviously manipulated by the filmmakers. With every flashback came tragedy. The music soared; the voice-overs were solemn or wistful; tears, tears, and more tears flowed on-screen. Daughters were reverent; mothers carried dark secrets.

I was elated by the grandness and strength of the four mothers and the 10
luminous actors who portrayed them, but I was uneasy with the passivity of the Asian American daughters. They seemed to exist solely as receptors for their mothers' amazing life stories. It's almost as if by assimilating so easily into American society, they had lost all sense of self.

In spite of my resistance, my eyes watered as the desperate mother played by Kieu Chinh was forced to abandon her twin baby girls on a country road in war-torn China. (Kieu Chinh resembles my own mother and her twin sister, who suffered through the brutal Japanese occupation of the Philippines.) So far in this movie, an infant son had been deliberately drowned, a mother played by the gravely beautiful France Nuyen had gone catatonic with grief, a concubine had cut her flesh open to save her dying mother, an insecure daughter had been oppressed by her boorish Asian American husband, another insecure daughter had been left by her white husband, and so on. . . . The overall effect was numbing as far as I'm concerned, but a man sitting two rows in front of us broke down sobbing. A Chinese Filipino writer even more grouchy than me later complained, "Must ethnicity only be equated with suffering?"

Because change has been slow, *The Joy Luck Club* carries a lot of cultural baggage. It is a big-budget story about Chinese American women, directed by a Chinese American man, cowritten and coproduced by Chinese American women. That's a lot to be thankful for. And its box office success proves that an immigrant narrative told from female perspectives can have mass appeal. But my cynical side tells me that its success might mean only one thing in Hollywood: more weepy epics about Asian American mother-daughter relationships will be planned.

That the film finally got made was significant. By Hollywood standards (think white male; think money, money, money), a movie about Asian Americans even when adapted from a bestseller was a risky proposition. When I asked a producer I know about the film's rumored delays, he simply said, "It's still an *Asian* movie," surprised I had even asked. Equally interesting was director Wayne Wang's initial reluctance to be involved in the project; he told the *New York Times*, "I didn't want to do another Chinese movie."

Maybe he shouldn't have worried so much. After all, according to the media, the nineties are the decade of "Pacific Overtures" and East Asian chic. Madonna, the pop queen of shameless appropriation, cultivated Japanese high-tech style with her music video "Rain," while Janet Jackson faked kitschy orientalia in hers, titled "If." Critical attention was paid to movies from China, Japan, and Vietnam. But that didn't mean an honest appraisal of women's lives. Even on the art house circuit, filmmakers who should know better took the easy way out. Takehiro Nakajima's 1992 film *Okoge* presents one of the more original film roles for women in recent years. In Japanese, "okoge" means the crust of rice that sticks to the bottom of the rice pot; in pejorative slang, it means fag hag. The way "okoge" is used in the film seems a reappropriation of the term; the portrait Nakajima creates of Sayoko, the so-called fag hag, is clearly an affectionate one. Sayoko is a quirky, self-assured woman in contemporary Tokyo who does voice-overs for cartoons, has a thing for Frida Kahlo paintings, and is drawn to a gentle young gay man named Goh. But the other women's roles are disappointing, stereotypical "hysterical females" and the movie itself turns conventional halfway through. Sayoko sacrifices herself to a macho brute Goh desires, who rapes her as images of Frida Kahlo paintings and her beloved Goh rising from the ocean flash before her. She gives birth to a baby boy and endures a terrible life of poverty with the abusive rapist. This sudden change from spunky survivor to helpless, victimized woman is baffling. Whatever happened to her job? Or that arty little apartment of hers? Didn't her Frida Kahlo obsession teach her anything?

Then there was Tiana Thi Thanh Nga's *From Hollywood to Hanoi*, a 15
self-serving but fascinating documentary. Born in Vietnam to a privileged family that included an uncle who was defense minister in the Thieu government and an idolized father who served as press minister, Nga (a.k.a. Tiana) spent her adolescence in California. A former actor in martial arts movies and fitness teacher ("Karaticize with Tiana"), the vivacious Tiana decided to make a record of her journey back to Vietnam.

From Hollywood to Hanoi is at times unintentionally very funny. Tiana includes a quick scene of herself dancing with a white man at the Metropole hotel in Hanoi, and breathlessly announces: "That's me doing the tango with Oliver Stone!" Then she listens sympathetically to a horrifying account of the My Lai massacre by one of its few female survivors. In another scene, Tiana cheerfully addresses a food vendor on the streets of Hanoi: "Your hairdo is so pretty." The unimpressed, poker-faced woman gives a brusque, deadpan reply: "You want to eat, or what?" Sometimes it is hard to tell the difference between Tiana Thi Thanh Nga and her Hollywood persona: The real Tiana still seems to be playing one of her B-movie roles, which are mainly fun because they're fantasy. The time was certainly right to explore postwar Vietnam from a Vietnamese woman's perspective; it's too bad this film was done by a Valley Girl.

Nineteen ninety-three also brought Tran Anh Hung's *The Scent of Green Papaya*, a different kind of Vietnamese memento — this is a look back at the peaceful, lush country of the director's childhood memories. The film opens in Saigon, in 1951. A willowy ten-year-old girl named Mui comes to work for a troubled family headed by a melancholy musician and his kind, stoic wife. The men of this bourgeois household are idle, pampered types who take naps while the women do all the work. Mui is male fantasy: She is a devoted servant, enduring acts of cruel mischief with patience and dignity; as an adult, she barely speaks. She scrubs floors, shines shoes, and cooks with loving care and never a complaint. When she is sent off to work for another wealthy musician, she ends up being impregnated by him. The movie ends as the camera closes in on Mui's contented face. Languid and precious, *The Scent of Green Papaya* is visually haunting, but it suffers from the director's colonial fantasy of women as docile, domestic creatures. Steeped in highbrow nostalgia, it's the arty Vietnamese version of *My Fair Lady* with the wealthy musician as Professor Higgins, teaching Mui to read and write.

And then there is Ang Lee's tepid 1993 hit, *The Wedding Banquet*—a clever culture-clash farce in which traditional Chinese values collide with contemporary American sexual mores. The somewhat formulaic plot goes like this: Wai-Tung, a yuppie landlord, lives with his white lover, Simon, in a chic Manhattan brownstone. Wai-Tung is an only child and his aging parents in Taiwan long for a grandchild to continue the family legacy. Enter Wei-Wei, an artist who lives in a grungy loft owned by Wai-Tung. She slugs tequila straight from the bottle as she paints and flirts boldly with her young, uptight landlord, who brushes her off. "It's my fate. I am always attracted to handsome gay men," she mutters. After this setup, the movie goes downhill, all edges blurred in a cozy nest of happy endings. In a refrain of Sayoko's plight in *Okoge*, a pregnant, suddenly complacent Wei-Wei gives in to family pressures—and never gets her life back.

> "It takes a man to know what it is to be a real woman."
>
> —SONG LILING in *M. BUTTERFLY*

Ironically, two gender-bending films in which men play men playing women reveal more about the mythology of the prized Asian woman and the superficial trappings of gender than most movies that star real women. The slow-moving *M. Butterfly* presents the ultimate object of Western male desire as the spy/opera diva Song Liling, a Suzie Wong/Lotus Blossom played by actor John Lone with a five o'clock shadow and bobbing Adam's apple. The best and most profound of these forays into cross-dressing is the spectacular melodrama *Farewell My Concubine*, directed by Chen Kaige. Banned in China, *Farewell My Concubine* shared the prize for Best Film at the 1993 Cannes Film Festival with Jane Campion's *The Piano*. Sweeping through fifty years of tumultuous history in China, the story revolves around the lives of two male Beijing Opera stars and the woman who marries one of them. The three characters make an unforgettable triangle, struggling over love, art, friendship, and politics against the bloody backdrop of cultural upheaval. They are as capable of casually betraying each other as they are of selfless, heroic acts. The androgynous Dieyi, doomed to play the same female role of concubine over and over again, is portrayed with great vulnerability, wit, and grace by male Hong Kong pop star Leslie Cheung. Dieyi competes with the prostitute Juxian (Gong Li) for the love of his childhood protector and fellow opera star, Duan Xiaolou (Zhang Fengyi).

20 Cheung's highly stylized performance as the classic concubine-ready-to-die-for-love in the opera within the movie is all about female artifice. His sidelong glances, restrained passion, languid stance, small steps, and delicate, refined gestures say everything about what is considered desirable in Asian women — and are the antithesis of the feisty, outspoken woman played by Gong Li. The characters of Dieyi and Juxian both see suffering as part and parcel of love and life. Juxian matter-of-factly says to Duan Xiaolou before he agrees to marry her: "I'm used to hardship. If you take me in, I'll wait on you hand and foot. If you tire of me, I'll . . . kill myself. No big deal." It's an echo of Suzie Wong's servility, but the context is new. Even with her back to the wall, Juxian is not helpless or whiny. She attempts to manipulate a man while admitting to the harsh reality that is her life.

Dieyi and Juxian are the two sides of the truth of women's lives in most Asian countries. Juxian in particular — wife and ex-prostitute — could be seen as a thankless and stereotypical role. But like the characters Gong Li has played in Chinese director Zhang Yimou's films, *Red Sorghum*, *Raise the Red Lantern*, and especially *The Story of Qiu Ju*, Juxian is tough, obstinate, sensual, clever, oafish, beautiful, infuriating, cowardly, heroic, and banal. Above all, she is resilient. Gong Li is one of the few Asian Pacific actors whose roles have been drawn with intelligence, honesty, and depth. Nevertheless, the characters she plays are limited by the possibilities that exist for real women in China.

"Let's face it. Women still don't mean shit in China," my friend Meeling reminds me. What she says so bluntly about her culture rings painfully true, but in less obvious fashion for me. In the Philippines, infant girls aren't drowned, nor were their feet bound to make them more desirable. But sons were and are cherished. To this day, men of the bourgeois class are coddled and prized, much like the spoiled men of the elite household in *The Scent of Green Papaya*. We do not have a geisha tradition like Japan, but physical beauty is over-treasured. Our daughters are protected virgins or primed as potential beauty queens. And many of us have bought into the image of the white man as our handsome savior: G.I. Joe.

Buzz magazine recently featured an article entitled "Asian Women / L.A. Men," a report on a popular hangout that caters to white men's fantasies of nubile Thai women. The lines between movies and real life are blurred. Male screenwriters and cinematographers flock to this bar-restaurant, where the waitresses are eager to "audition" for roles. Many of these men have been to Bangkok while working on film crews for Vietnam War movies. They've come back to L.A., but for them, the movie never ends. In this particular fantasy the boys play G.I. Joe on a rescue mission in the urban jungle, saving the whore from herself. "A scene has developed here, a kind of R-rated *Cheers*," author Alan Rifkin writes. "The waitresses audition for sitcoms. The customers date the waitresses or just keep score."

Colonization of the imagination is a two-way street. And being enshrined on a pedestal as someone's Pearl of the Orient fantasy doesn't seem so demeaning, at first; who wouldn't want to be worshipped? Perhaps that's why

Asian women are the ultimate wet dream in most Hollywood movies; it's no secret how well we've been taught to play the role, to take care of our men. In Hollywood vehicles, we are objects of desire or derision; we exist to provide sex, color, and texture in what is essentially a white man's world. It is akin to what Toni Morrison calls "the Africanist presence" in literature. She writes: "Just as entertainers, through or by association with blackface, could render permissible topics that otherwise would have been taboo, so American writers were able to employ an imagined Africanist persona to articulate and imaginatively act out the forbidden in American culture." The same analogy could be made for the often titillating presence of Asian women in movies made by white men.

Movies are still the most seductive and powerful of artistic mediums, 25
manipulating us with ease by a powerful combination of sound and image. In many ways, as females and Asians, as audiences or performers, we have learned to settle for less — to accept the fact that we are either decorative, invisible, or one dimensional. When there are characters who look like us represented in a movie, we have also learned to view between the lines, or to add what is missing. For many of us, this way of watching has always been a necessity. We fill in the gaps. If a female character is presented as a mute, willowy beauty, we convince ourselves she is an ancestral ghost — so smart she doesn't have to speak at all. If she is a whore with a heart of gold, we claim her as a tough feminist icon. If she is a sexless, sanitized, boring nerd, we embrace her as a role model for our daughters, rather than the tragic whore. And if she is presented as an utterly devoted saint suffering nobly in silence, we lie and say she is just like our mothers. Larger than life. Magical and insidious. A movie is never just a movie, after all.

Reading the Text

1. Summarize in your own words Hagedorn's view of the traditional images of Asian women as presented in American film.
2. What is the chronology of Asian women in film that Hagedorn presents, and why do you think she gives us a historical overview?
3. Why does Hagedorn say that the film *The Joy Luck Club* "carries a lot of cultural baggage" (para. 11)?
4. What sort of images of Asian women does Hagedorn imply she would prefer to see?

Reading the Signs

1. Watch *The Joy Luck Club*, and write an essay in which you support, refute, or modify Hagedorn's interpretation of the film. Alternatively, view another film featuring Asian characters, such as *Better Luck Tomorrow* or *Crazy Rich Asians*, or a TV show with Asian characters, such as *Fresh off the Boat*, and use Hagedorn's article as a critical framework to evaluate your choice's representation of Asian characters.

2. **CONNECTING TEXTS** In class, form teams and debate the proposition that Hollywood writers and directors have a social responsibility to avoid stereotyping ethnic characters. To develop your team's arguments, brainstorm films that depict various ethnicities, and then discuss whether the portrayals are damaging or benign. You might also consult Michael Omi's "In Living Color: Race and American Culture" (p. 129).
3. Study a magazine that targets Asian American readers, such as *Tea*, *Hyphen*, or *Yolk*. Then write an essay in which you analyze whether Asian women in the magazine fit the stereotypes that Hagedorn describes, keeping in mind the magazine's intended readership (businessmen, twentysomethings of both sexes, and so forth).
4. **CONNECTING TEXTS** Watch one of the gender-bending films Hagedorn mentions (such as *M. Butterfly*), and write your own analysis of the gender roles portrayed in the film. To develop your ideas, consult Aaron Devor's "Gender Role Behaviors and Attitudes" (p. 150).
5. Few American films have featured Asian characters as protagonists. Watch an exception to this trend, *Harold & Kumar Go to White Castle* (2004), and write a semiotic analysis of the racial depictions in this film. To what extent does this film replicate or avoid the stereotypes Hagedorn discusses?

MICHAEL PARENTI

Class and Virtue

In 1993, a movie called *Indecent Proposal* presented a story in which a billionaire offers a newly poor middle-class woman a million dollars if she'll sleep with him for one night. In Michael Parenti's terms, what was really indecent about the movie was the way it showed the woman falling in love with the billionaire, thus making a romance out of a class outrage. But the movie could get away with it, partly because Hollywood has always conditioned audiences to root for the 1 percent and to ignore the inequities of class privilege. In this selection from *Make-Believe Media: The Politics of Entertainment* (1992), Parenti argues that Hollywood has long been in the business of representing the interests of the ruling classes. Whether it is forgiving the classist behavior in *Pretty Woman* or glamorizing the lives of the wealthy, Hollywood makes sure its audiences leave the theater thinking you can't be too rich. Michael Parenti is a writer who lectures widely at university campuses around the country. His most recent book, *Profit Pathology and Other Indecencies* (2015), continues to explore the impact of class power on social and political life.

The entertainment media present working people not only as unlettered and uncouth but also as less desirable and less moral than other people. Conversely, virtue is more likely to be ascribed to those characters whose speech and appearance are soundly middle- or upper-middle class.

Even a simple adventure story like *Treasure Island* (1934, 1950, 1972) manifests this implicit class perspective. There are two groups of acquisitive persons searching for a lost treasure. One, headed by a squire, has money enough to hire a ship and crew. The other, led by the rascal Long John Silver, has no money — so they sign up as part of the crew. The narrative implicitly assumes from the beginning that the squire has a moral claim to the treasure, while Long John Silver's gang does not. After all, it is the squire who puts up the venture capital for the ship. Having no investment in the undertaking other than their labor, Long John and his men, by definition, will be "stealing" the treasure, while the squire will be "discovering" it.

To be sure, there are other differences. Long John's men are cutthroats. The squire is not. Yet, one wonders if the difference between a bad pirate and a good squire is itself not preeminently a matter of having the right amount of disposable income. The squire is no less acquisitive than the conspirators. He just does with money what they must achieve with cutlasses. The squire and his associates dress in fine clothes, speak an educated diction, and drink brandy. Long John and his men dress slovenly, speak in guttural accents, and drink rum. From these indications alone, the viewer knows who are the good guys and who are the bad. Virtue is visually measured by one's approximation to proper class appearances.

Sometimes class contrasts are juxtaposed within one person, as in *The Three Faces of Eve* (1957), a movie about a woman who suffers from multiple personalities. When we first meet Eve (Joanne Woodward), she is a disturbed, strongly repressed, puritanically religious person, who speaks with a rural, poor-Southern accent. Her second personality is that of a wild, flirtatious woman who also speaks with a rural, poor-Southern accent. After much treatment by her psychiatrist, she is cured of these schizoid personalities and emerges with a healthy third one, the real Eve, a poised, self-possessed, pleasant woman. What is intriguing is that she now speaks with a cultivated, affluent, Smith College accent, free of any low-income regionalism or ruralism, much like Joanne Woodward herself. This transformation in class style and speech is used to indicate mental health without any awareness of the class bias thusly expressed.

Mental health is also the question in *A Woman under the Influence* (1974), 5
the story of a disturbed woman who is married to a hard-hat husband. He cannot handle — and inadvertently contributes to — her emotional deterioration. She is victimized by a spouse who is nothing more than an insensitive, working-class bull in a china shop. One comes away convinced that every unstable woman needs a kinder, gentler, and above all, more *middle-class* hubby if she wishes to avoid a mental crack-up.

Class prototypes abound in the 1980s television series *The A-Team*. In each episode, a Vietnam-era commando unit helps an underdog, be it a Latino immigrant or a disabled veteran, by vanquishing some menacing force such as organized crime, a business competitor, or corrupt government officials. As always with the make-believe media, the A-Team does good work on an individualized rather than collectively organized basis, helping particular victims by thwarting particular villains. The A-Team's leaders are two white males of privileged background. The lowest ranking members of the team, who do none of the thinking nor the leading, are working-class palookas. They show they are good with their hands, both by punching out the bad guys and by doing the maintenance work on the team's flying vehicles and cars. One of them, "B.A." (bad ass), played by the African American Mr. T., is visceral, tough, and purposely bad-mannered toward those he doesn't like. He projects an image of crudeness and ignorance and is associated with the physical side of things. In sum, the team has a brain (the intelligent white leaders) and a body with its simpler physical functions (the working-class characters), a hierarchy that corresponds to the social structure itself.[1]

Sometimes class bigotry is interwoven with gender bigotry, as in *Pretty Woman* (1990). A dreamboat millionaire corporate raider finds himself all alone for an extended stay in Hollywood (his girlfriend is unwilling to join him), so he quickly recruits a beautiful prostitute as his playmate of the month. She is paid three thousand dollars a week to wait around his super-posh hotel penthouse ready to perform the usual services and accompany him to business dinners at top restaurants. As prostitution goes, it is a dream gig. But there is one cloud on the horizon. She is low-class. She doesn't know which fork to use at those CEO power feasts, and she's bothersomely fidgety, wears tacky clothes, chews gum, and, y'know, doesn't talk so good. But with some tips from the hotel manager, she proves to be a veritable Eliza Doolittle in her class metamorphosis. She dresses in proper attire, sticks the gum away forever, and starts picking the right utensils at dinner. She also figures out how to speak a little more like Joanne Woodward without the benefit of a multiple personality syndrome, and she develops the capacity to sit in a poised, wordless, empty-headed fashion, every inch the expensive female ornament.

She is still a prostitute but a classy one. It is enough of a distinction for the handsome young corporate raider. Having liked her because she was charmingly cheap, he now loves her all the more because she has real polish and is a more suitable companion. So suitable that he decides to do the right thing by her: set her up in an apartment so he can make regular visits at regular prices. But now she wants the better things in life, like marriage, a nice house, and, above all, a different occupation, one that would allow her to use less of herself. She is furious at him for treating her like, well, a prostitute. She decides to give up her profession and get a high school diploma so that she might make

[1]Gina Marchetti, "Class, Ideology and Commercial Television: An Analysis of *The A-Team*," *Journal of Film and Video* 39, Spring 1987, pp. 19–28.

a better life for herself—perhaps as a filing clerk or receptionist or some other of the entry-level jobs awaiting young women with high school diplomas.[2]

After the usual girl-breaks-off-with-boy scenes, the millionaire prince returns. It seems he can't concentrate on making money without her. He even abandons his cutthroat schemes and enters into a less lucrative but supposedly more productive, caring business venture with a struggling old-time entrepreneur. The bad capitalist is transformed into a good capitalist. He then carries off his ex-prostitute for a lifetime of bliss. The moral is a familiar one, updated for post-Reagan yuppiedom: A woman can escape from economic and gender exploitation by winning the love and career advantages offered by a rich male. Sexual allure goes only so far unless it develops a material base and becomes a class act.[3]

Reading the Text

1. According to Parenti, what characteristics are typically attributed to working-class and upper-class film characters?
2. How does Parenti see the relationship between "class bigotry" and "gender bigotry" (para. 7).
3. What relationship does Parenti see between mental health and class values in films?

Reading the Signs

1. Watch *Hustlers*, *Wall Street*, *Unstoppable*, or *The Fighter*, and analyze the class issues that the movie raises. Alternatively, watch an episode of *Shark Tank*, and perform the same sort of analysis.
2. Do you agree with Parenti's interpretation of *Pretty Woman*? Write an argumentative essay in which you defend, challenge, or complicate his reading of the film.
3. **CONNECTING TEXTS** Read Aaron Devor's "Gender Role Behaviors and Attitudes" (p. 150). How would Devor explain the gender bigotry that Parenti finds in *Pretty Woman*?
4. Watch the 1954 film *On the Waterfront* with your class. How are labor unions and working-class characters portrayed in that film? Does the film display the class bigotry that Parenti describes?

[2]See the excellent review by Lydia Sargent, *Z Magazine*, April 1990, pp. 43–45.
[3]Ibid.

DAVID DENBY

High-School Confidential: Notes on Teen Movies

Face it: high school for most of us is one extended nightmare, a long-playing drama starring cheerleaders and football players who sneer at the mere mortals who must endure their haughty reign. So it's little wonder that, as David Denby argues in this *New Yorker* essay from 1999, teen movies so often feature loathsome cheerleaders and football stars who, one way or another, get theirs in this ever-popular movie genre. Indeed, Denby asks, "Who can doubt where Hollywood's twitchy, nearsighted writers and directors ranked — or feared they ranked — on the high-school totem pole?" Nerds at the bottom, where else, like the millions of suffering kids who flock to their films. Denby is a staff writer and film critic for the *New Yorker*.

The most hated young woman in America is a blonde — well, sometimes a redhead or a brunette, but usually a blonde. She has big hair flipped into a swirl of gold at one side of her face or arrayed in a sultry mane, like the magnificent pile of a forties movie star. She's tall and slender, with a waist as supple as a willow, but she's dressed in awful, spangled taste: her outfits could have been put together by warring catalogues. And she has a mouth on her, a low, slatternly tongue that devastates other kids with such insults as "You're vapor, you're Spam!" and "Do I look like Mother Teresa? If I did, I probably wouldn't mind talking to the geek squad." She has two or three friends exactly like her, and together they dominate their realm — the American high school as it appears in recent teen movies. They are like wicked princesses, who enjoy the misery of their subjects. Her coronation, of course, is the senior prom, when she expects to be voted "most popular" by her class. But, though she may be popular, she is certainly not liked, so her power is something of a mystery. She is beautiful and rich, yet in the end she is preëminent because . . . she is preëminent, a position she works to maintain with Joan Crawford–like tenacity. Everyone is afraid of her; that's why she's popular.

She has a male counterpart. He's usually a football player, muscular but dumb, with a face like a beer mug and only two ways of speaking — in a conspiratorial whisper, to a friend; or in a drill sergeant's sudden bellow. If her weapon is the snub, his is the lame but infuriating prank — the can of Sprite emptied into a knapsack, or something sticky, creamy, or adhesive deposited in a locker. Sprawling and dull in class, he comes alive in the halls and in the cafeteria. He hurls people against lockers; he spits, pours, and sprays; he has a projectile relationship with food. As the crown prince, he claims the best-looking girl for himself, though in a perverse display of power he may invite an outsider or an awkward girl — a "dog" — to the prom, setting her up for some special humiliation. When we first see him, he is riding high, and virtually the entire school colludes in his tyranny. No authority figure — no teacher or administrator — dares correct him.

Thus the villains of the recent high-school movies. Not every American teen movie has these two characters, and not every social queen or jock shares all the attributes I've mentioned. (Occasionally, a handsome, dark-haired athlete can be converted to sweetness and light.) But as genre figures these two types are hugely familiar; that is, they are a common memory, a collective trauma, or at least a social and erotic fantasy. Such movies of the past year [1999] as *Disturbing Behavior*, *She's All That*, *Ten Things I Hate about You*, and *Never Been Kissed* depend on them as stock figures. And they may have been figures in the minds of the Littleton shooters, Eric Harris and Dylan Klebold, who imagined they were living in a school like the one in so many of these movies — a poisonous system of status, snobbery, and exclusion.

Do genre films reflect reality? Or are they merely a set of conventions that refer to other films? Obviously, they wouldn't survive if they didn't provide emotional satisfaction to the people who make them and to the audiences who watch them. A half century ago, we didn't need to see ten Westerns a year in order to learn that the West got settled. We needed to see it settled ten times a year in order to provide ourselves with the emotional gratifications of righteous violence. By drawing his gun only when he was provoked, and in the service of the good, the classic Western hero transformed the gross tangibles of the expansionist drive (land, cattle, gold) into a principle of moral order. The gangster, by contrast, is a figure of chaos, a modern, urban person, and in the critic Robert Warshow's formulation he functions as a discordant element in an American society devoted to a compulsively "positive" outlook. When the gangster dies, he cleanses viewers of their own negative feelings.

High-school movies are also full of unease and odd, mixed-up emotions. 5
They may be flimsy in conception; they may be shot in lollipop colors, garlanded with mediocre pop scores, and cast with goofy young actors trying to make an impression. Yet this most commercial and frivolous of genres harbors a grievance against the world. It's a very specific grievance, quite different from the restless anger of such fifties adolescent-rebellion movies as *The Wild One*, in which someone asks Marlon Brando's biker "What are you rebelling against?" and the biker replies "What have you got?" The fifties teen outlaw was against anything that adults considered sacred. But no movie teenager now revolts against adult authority, for the simple reason that adults have no authority. Teachers are rarely more than a minimal, exasperated presence, administrators get turned into a joke, and parents are either absent or distantly benevolent. It's a teen world, bounded by school, mall, and car, with occasional moments set in the fast-food outlets where the kids work, or in the kids' upstairs bedrooms, with their pinups and rack stereo systems. The enemy is not authority; the enemy is other teens and the social system that they impose on one another.

The bad feeling in these movies may strike grownups as peculiar. After all, from a distance American kids appear to be having it easy these days. The teen audience is facing a healthy job market; at home, their parents are stuffing the den with computers and the garage with a bulky SUV. But most teens aren't thinking about the future job market. Lost in the eternal swoon of late adolescence, they're thinking about their identity, their friends, and their clothes. Adolescence is the present-tense moment in American life. Identity and status are fluid: abrupt, devastating reversals are always possible. (In a teen movie, a guy who swallows a bucket of cafeteria coleslaw can make himself a hero in an instant.) In these movies, accordingly, the senior prom is the equivalent of the shoot-out at the O.K. Corral; it's the moment when one's worth as a human being is settled at last. In the rather pedestrian new comedy *Never Been Kissed*, Drew Barrymore, as a twenty-five-year-old newspaper reporter, goes back to high school pretending to be a student, and immediately falls into her old, humiliating pattern of trying to impress the good-looking rich kids. Helplessly, she pushes for approval, and even gets herself chosen prom queen before finally coming to her senses. She finds it nearly impossible to let go.

Genre films dramatize not what happens but how things feel — the emotional coloring of memory. They fix subjectivity into fable. At actual schools, there is no unitary system of status; there are many groups to be a part of, many places to excel (or fail to excel), many avenues of escape and self-definition. And often the movies, too, revel in the arcana of high-school cliques. In last summer's *Disturbing Behavior*, a veteran student lays out the cafeteria ethnography for a newcomer: Motorheads, Blue Ribbons, Skaters, Micro-geeks ("drug of choice: Stephen Hawking's *A Brief History of Time* and a cup of jasmine tea on Saturday night"). Subjectively, though, the social system in *Disturbing Behavior* (a high-school version of *The Stepford Wives*) and in the other movies still feels coercive and claustrophobic: humiliation is the most vivid emotion of youth, so in memory it becomes the norm.

The movies try to turn the tables. The kids who cannot be the beautiful ones, or make out with them, or avoid being insulted by them — these are the heroes of the teen movies, the third in the trio of character types. The female outsider is usually an intellectual or an artist. (She scribbles in a diary, she draws or paints.) Physically awkward, she walks like a seal crossing a beach, and is prone to drop her books and dither in terror when she stands before a handsome boy. Her clothes, which ignore mall fashion, scandalize the social queens. Like them, she has a tongue, but she's tart and grammatical, tending toward feminist pungency and precise diction. She may mask her sense of vulnerability with sarcasm or with Plathian rue (she's stuck in the bell jar), but even when she lashes out she can't hide her craving for acceptance.

The male outsider, her friend, is usually a mass of stuttering or giggling sexual gloom: he wears shapeless clothes; he has an undeveloped body, either stringy or shrimpy; he's sometimes a Jew (in these movies, still the generic outsider). He's also brilliant, but in a morose, preoccupied way that suggests masturbatory absorption in some arcane system of knowledge. In a few special cases, the outsider is not a loser but a disengaged hipster, either saintly or satanic. (Christian Slater has played this role a couple of times.) This outsider wears black and keeps his hair long, and he knows how to please women. He sees through everything, so he's ironic by temperament and genuinely indifferent to the opinion of others — a natural aristocrat, who transcends the school's contemptible status system. There are whimsical variations on the outsider figure, too. In the recent *Rushmore*, an obnoxious teen hero, Max Fischer (Jason Schwartzman), runs the entire school: he can't pass his courses but he's a dynamo at extracurricular activities, with a knack for staging extraordinary events. He's a con man, a fundraiser, an entrepreneur — in other words, a contemporary artist.

10 In fact, the entire genre, which combines self-pity and ultimate vindication, might be called "Portrait of the Filmmaker as a Young Nerd." Who can doubt where Hollywood's twitchy, nearsighted writers and directors ranked — or feared they ranked — on the high-school totem pole? They are still angry, though occasionally the target of their resentment goes beyond the jocks and cheerleaders of their youth. Consider this anomaly: the young actors and models on the covers of half the magazines published in this country, the shirtless men with chests like burnished shields, the girls smiling, glowing, tweezed, full-lipped, full-breasted (but not too full), and with skin so honeyed that it seems lacquered — these are the physical ideals embodied by the villains of the teen movies. The social queens and jocks, using their looks to dominate others, represent an American barbarism of beauty. Isn't it possible that the detestation of them in teen movies is a veiled strike at the entire abs-hair advertising culture, with its unobtainable glories of perfection? A critic of consumerism might even see a spark of revolt in these movies. But only a spark.

My guess is that these films arise from remembered hurts which then get recast in symbolic form. For instance, a surprising number of the outsider heroes have no mother. Mom has died or run off with another man; her child, only half loved, is ill equipped for the emotional pressures of school. The motherless child, of course, is a shrewd commercial ploy that makes a direct appeal to the members of the audience, many of whom may feel like outsiders, too, and unloved, or not loved enough, or victims of some prejudice or exclusion. But the motherless child also has powers, and will someday be a success, an artist, a screenwriter. It's the wound and the bow all over again, in cargo pants.

As the female nerd attracts the attention of the handsomest boy in the senior class, the teen movie turns into a myth of social reversal — a Cinderella fantasy. Initially, his interest in her may be part of a stunt or a trick: he is leading her on, perhaps at the urging of his queenly girlfriend. But his gaze lights her up, and we see how attractive she really is. Will she fulfill the eternal American fantasy that you can vault up the class system by removing your specs? She wants her prince, and by degrees she wins him over, not just with her looks but with her superior nature, her essential goodness. In the male version of the Cinderella trip, a few years go by, and a pale little nerd (we see him at a reunion) has become rich. All that poking around with chemicals paid off. Max Fischer, of *Rushmore*, can't miss being richer than Warhol.

So the teen movie is wildly ambivalent. It may attack the consumerist ethos that produces winners and losers, but in the end it confirms what it is attacking. The girls need the seal of approval conferred by the converted jocks; the nerds need money and a girl. Perhaps it's no surprise that the outsiders can be validated only by the people who ostracized them. But let's not be too schematic: the outsider who joins the system also modifies it, opens it up to the creative power of social mobility, makes it bend and laugh, and perhaps this turn of events is not so different from the way things work in the real world, where merit and achievement stand a good chance of trumping appearance. The irony of the Littleton shootings is that Klebold and Harris, who were both proficient computer heads, seemed to have forgotten how the plot turns out. If they had held on for a few years they might have been working at a hip software company, or have started their own business, while the jocks who oppressed them would probably have wound up selling insurance or used cars. That's the one unquestionable social truth the teen movies reflect: geeks rule.

There is, of course, a menacing subgenre, in which the desire for revenge turns bloody. Thirty-one years ago, Lindsay Anderson's semi-surrealistic *If . . .* was set in an oppressive, class-ridden English boarding school, where a group of rebellious students drive the school population out into a courtyard and open fire on them with machine guns. In Brian De Palma's 1976 masterpiece *Carrie*, the pale, repressed heroine, played by Sissy Spacek, is courted at last by a handsome boy but gets violated — doused with pig's blood — just as she is named prom queen. Stunned but far from powerless, Carrie uses her telekinetic powers to set the room afire and burn down the school. *Carrie* is the primal school movie, so wildly lurid and funny that it exploded the clichés of the genre before the genre was quite set: The heroine may be a wrathful avenger, but the movie, based on a Stephen King book, was clearly a grinning-gargoyle fantasy. So, at first, was *Heathers*, in which Christian Slater's satanic outsider turns out to be a true devil. He and his girlfriend (played by a very young Winona Ryder) begin gleefully knocking off the rich, nasty girls and the jocks, in ways so patently absurd that their revenge seems a mere wicked dream. I think it's unlikely that these movies had a direct effect on the actions of the Littleton shooters, but the two boys would surely have recognized the emotional world of *Heathers* and *Disturbing Behavior* as their own. It's a place where feelings of victimization join fantasy, and you experience the social élites as so powerful that you must either become them or kill them.

15 But enough. It's possible to make teen movies that go beyond these fixed polarities — insider and outsider, blond-bitch queen and hunch-shouldered nerd. In Amy Heckerling's 1995 comedy *Clueless*, the big blonde played by Alicia Silverstone is a Rodeo Drive clotheshorse who is nonetheless possessed of extraordinary virtue. Freely dispensing advice and help, she's almost ironically good — a designing goddess with a cell phone. The movie offers a sunshiny satire of Beverly Hills affluence, which it sees as both absurdly swollen

and generous in spirit. The most original of the teen comedies, *Clueless* casts away self-pity. So does *Romy and Michele's High School Reunion* (1997), in which two gabby, lovable friends, played by Mira Sorvino and Lisa Kudrow, review the banalities of their high-school experience so knowingly that they might be criticizing the teen-movie genre itself. And easily the best American film of the year so far is Alexander Payne's *Election*, a high-school movie that inhabits a different aesthetic and moral world altogether from the rest of these pictures. *Election* shreds everyone's fantasies and illusions in a vision of high school that is bleak but supremely just. The movie's villain, an overachieving girl (Reese Witherspoon) who runs for class president, turns out to be its covert heroine, or, at least, its most poignant character. A cross between Pat and Dick Nixon, she's a lower-middle-class striver who works like crazy and never wins anyone's love. Even when she's on top, she feels excluded. Her loneliness is produced not by malicious cliques but by her own implacable will, a condition of the spirit that may be as comical and tragic as it is mysterious. *Election* escapes all the clichés; it graduates into art.

Reading the Text

1. Describe in your own words the stereotypical male and female villains common in teen movies.
2. What does Denby mean by the comment, "Adolescence is the present-tense moment in American life" (para. 6)?
3. What sort of characters are typically the heroes in teen films, in Denby's view?
4. In what ways does a Cinderella fantasy influence teen films?
5. What is the "menacing subgenre" (para. 14) of teen movies?

Reading the Signs

1. Using Denby's description of stock character types in teen movies as your critical framework, analyze the characters in a teen TV program, such as *Veronica Mars*, *Riverdale*, *Sex Education*, or *Pretty Little Liars*. Do you see the same conventions at work? How do you account for any differences you might see?
2. In class, brainstorm a list of current teen films. Then, using the list as evidence, write an essay in which you assess the validity of Denby's claim: "The enemy [in teen films] is not authority; the enemy is other teens and the social system that they impose on one another" (para. 5).
3. Watch *Love, Simon* (2018) or *Gretel & Hansel* (2020), and write an essay in which you argue whether it can be categorized as a teen film, at least as Denby defines the genre.
4. Denby asks, "Do genre films reflect reality? Or are they merely a set of conventions that refer to other films?" (para. 4). Write an essay in which you propose your own response to these questions, using as evidence your high school experience and specific teen films. In addition, you can consider as evidence teen-based TV programs such as *Glee* or a film such as *The Edge of Seventeen* (2016).

WESLEY MORRIS

Rom-Coms Were Corny and Retrograde. Why Do I Miss Them So Much?

Wesley Morris loves romantic comedies, and in this encyclopedic take on the theory and history of the genre he explains both what happened to them (they've gone the way of the Western) and why they still matter. In short, the "romantic comedy went into full decline during the same era in which feminist critics were rethinking all media directed at women . . . asking why women were continually offered roles in which their greatest achievement was a man," and Morris fully gets that. But he also believes that rom-coms "take our primal hunger to connect with one another and give it a story" — a story that Morris thinks is still worth telling. An article by a cinephile for cinephiles, this reading first appeared in *The New York Times*, where Wesley Morris is a staff writer and critic at large.

I have a confession to make: I miss Katherine Heigl. In the mid- to late- 2000s she spent five years doing romantic comedies, or what was left of them by the time she got there. She put up a decent fight. To watch her withstand the jeers of the boy-men in *Knocked Up*, the cave-manning of Gerard Butler in *The Ugly Truth*, or the bridesmaid-outfit montage in *27 Dresses* was to witness a genre's assault on one of its last dedicated practitioners. Heigl didn't get to show the luminance, flintiness, or idiosyncrasy of her romantic-comedy forebears; she was given too few moments of wit or insight. Instead, she was tough, stubborn, gainfully employed and — like most of the women in these movies, by that point — counterproductively heartless, tolerant of whatever partnership the plot backed her into. Her time as a romantic-comedy star was more a feat of survival than a cause for celebration. But as long as Heigl was around, so were romantic comedies, and that was something.

Now both are essentially gone, and we're making do with substitutions, decoys, and mirages: things that seem like romantic comedy but are actually fizzy soap operas (*Crazy Rich Asians*), teen movies (*To All the Boys I've Loved Before*), funny dramas (*You're the Worst*), TV Tinder (*Dating Around*), or sports (*The Bachelor*). Half the time, what gets labeled "romantic comedy" is just anything with ordinary women in it (*Book Club* is a deluxe ensemble comedy; *Mamma Mia! Here We Go Again* is the same, but with ABBA songs). Genuine romantic comedies have vanished entirely. In 2009, seven of the 50 highest-grossing films in North America were some kind of romantic comedy. Last year, virtually none were. So far *this* year, the thing that has come closest is a sendup that requires Rebel Wilson to imagine she's in a romantic comedy while she's actually in a coma. The conventions of romantic comedy are now considered absurd and foreign enough that a regular comedy can laugh about how ridiculous it would be to exist in a romantic one.

You could easily see the genre's demise as a form of justice. Don't women in movies have better things to do than wonder if they're going to meet some dude? Shouldn't they be running countries, curing diseases, shooting lasers out of their gloves, and spin-kicking anonymous goons over casino balconies? Also: How is it that a genre this old could rarely bring itself to include anyone other than wealthy straight white folks? At its worst, these movies could be painfully formulaic, corny, retrograde about gender and so unrealistic about love that they were often accused of poisoning real-life romance. (Back in 2008, a study in Scotland concluded that watching them can create unrealistic expectations of romantic partners.) *Good riddance,* you might cry. *Enjoy your spot in antiquity! Say hi to Westerns for me.*

I have no serious rebuttal to any of these objections. They're mostly true. I'm a single black gay man, and therefore an unlikely champion of the American romantic comedy: What's in these movies for me?

And yet here I am, in a state of panicked rumination: Who are we without 5
these movies? Romantic comedy is the only genre committed to letting relatively ordinary people — no capes, no spaceships, no infinite sequels — figure out how to deal meaningfully with another human being. These are the lowest-stakes movies we have that are also about our highest standards for ourselves, movies predicated on the improvement of communication, the deciphering of strangers, and the performance of more degrees of honesty than I ever knew existed — gentle, cruel, blunt, clarifying, T.M.I., strategic, tardy, medical, sexual, sartorial. They take our primal hunger to connect with one another and give it a story. And at their best, they do much more: They make you believe in the power of communion.

This was work determined, across the whole history of cinema, to find something funny about loneliness, curiosity, attraction, intimacy, conflict and rapprochement. So maybe it's the most featherweight of genres — but maybe it's also among the most important. This is moviemaking that explores a basic human wonder about how to connect with a person who's not you. And here we are dancing on its grave.

I've made it this far calling these movies what nobody does anymore. They're "rom-coms" now — old trade-publication lingo that replaced both the "romance" and the "comedy." But a pure Hollywood romantic comedy — according, at least, to me — needs both. It springs from a long literary tradition, from Shakespeare to Jane Austen: putting two people in proximity and conspiring, with wit and zing, for a match. Some of the pleasure lies in the way the two might begin as combatants and end up in each other's arms. Strangers become intimate. The estranged become reacquainted. The two people are, crucially, equal players in this narrative. The world of the movie orbits entirely around the both of them.

One ideal structure for this is the "drawbridge." The word applies more obviously to romantic melodramas, in which two lovers are kept apart by geography or time; I'm actually stealing this application from the *New Yorker* critic David Denby, who used it to describe the way Jude Law and Nicole Kidman find their way to each other across the brutal terrain of *Cold Mountain*. But the drawbridge is also perfect for the purer aims of romantic comedy. It represents two even halves lowering themselves toward each other — by making admissions, revealing vulnerabilities, giving in to magnetism — until both sides meet in the middle, ready to go somewhere deeper together, somewhere the audience won't see.

I was raised on two great eras of romantic comedies. First was the older, louder, wilder style, from the 1930s and 1940s, built on stars at the peak of their powers: Spencer Tracy shouting at Katharine Hepburn, Katharine Hepburn shouting at Cary Grant, Cary Grant shouting at Rosalind Russell, Rosalind Russell doing things with her posture that made shouting unnecessary. They imagined a certain parity of the sexes; their radical scheme, for the 1940s, was to balance the story between a man and a woman by making the woman formidable and remarkable and alive, in exactly the ways romantic-comedy heroines would later be criticized for not being. Many of them treated this quest for parity as a contest for supremacy, both in the relationship and in the plot. They were full of competition and gamesmanship and verbal battles between the sexes. Sometimes the men in them were a little like hapless, klutzy Henry Fonda in Preston Sturges's *The Lady Eve*: literally falling for women like Barbara Stanwyck.

10 Sex was rarely far from the surface, but in the '50s and '60s it really started to announce itself: The stars seemed either made of all the sex in the world (the Marilyn Monroes and Jane Russells) or none of it (Doris Day, the great movie virgin, defending herself against Rock Hudson's length and hair and teeth). And if right now looks bad for the romantic comedy, the frenetic 1970s were almost worse. Some of the movies may have been better — *What's Up, Doc?*, *Shampoo*, *Annie Hall*, *Starting Over* — but their approach to relationships was cockeyed. The people in them seem to have soured on love stories, and on one another. It was only as movies swelled into blockbusters that the conventional romantic comedy flourished again, repotted inside *Star Wars* and *Superman* and, a few years later, shoved into the Indiana Jones movies and *Ghostbusters*. And the old battle-of-the-sexes plot came back in two adventure fantasies Michael Douglas and Kathleen Turner made together in the first half of the '80s.

This was the other period I grew up on, a modern gloss on the classic style: Holly Hunter over- and outthinking William Hurt, Susan Sarandon tying Kevin Costner's tongue, Goldie Hawn squaring off against Burt Reynolds or Kurt Russell. Romance was giving in to 1980s corporate fever, and expanded to obsess over work and the workplace — in *Tootsie* and *Baby Boom*, *The Secret of My Success* and *Working Girl*. The stakes were bigger than companionship; the romance was, in part, with the office, and what it meant to be a woman working in one. In 1988, two of the five Best Picture nominees at the Oscars were romantic comedies: *Broadcast News* and *Moonstruck*. So, arguably, were two of 1989's: *Working Girl* and *The Accidental Tourist*.

Then, at the end of the decade, a movie came along that restored the genre to its easiest, smartest, most essential self, deploying the drawbridge structure as an act of discreet feminism and presenting two gainfully employed potential partners whose workplaces we never see. *When Harry Met Sally* opened in the summer of 1989, and it was a moon-landing sort of event, not because of the money it made but because, as written by Nora Ephron and directed by Rob Reiner, it formalized the genre with a thesis. On the last day of college, in 1977, Sally Albright (Meg Ryan) agrees to drive a friend's boyfriend, Harry Burns (Billy Crystal), from Chicago to New York. The drive alone — 15 very funny minutes — would have made the movie. He's crude, and a lech, and he hits on her, which she can't believe ("Amanda is my *friend!*"). They argue about the end of *Casablanca*. She insists they just be pals. He says, to her bafflement, that friendship's impossible: No man could coexist platonically with a woman, because he'd rather be having sex with her. Upon arrival in New York, she offers her hand to shake: "It was interesting." After that, the credits honestly could have rolled — but the movie skips ahead five years for a second encounter, then five more for a third. We watch two adversaries mature, warm to each other, then age into each other. Each is given a respective life and point of view; the molecular composition of the movie is different when they're together than when they're apart. They don't have to fall in love, but somebody has to win their argument, and it turns out to be both of them — she wouldn't have the sex without the friendship. So, drawbridge, and a draw.

To watch this movie now is to appreciate its traditionalism as a romantic comedy, one that would set the template for an explosion of them over the coming years. These movies know they're best left to stars — that the fun of them is in the chemistry of, say, Richard Gere and Julia Roberts or Drew Barrymore and Adam Sandler bringing out the best in each other — and the people who made *When Harry Met Sally* knew that Meg Ryan was a star, this buffet of bewilderment, surprise, wonder, self-assurance, and overreaction. Her faked deli orgasm is still up there with Sonny's getting whacked at the tollbooth and the baby carriage bumping down the staircase in *The Untouchables* — the famous passage that's always more perfect than you remember.

Dollar for dollar, she might trail Roberts as the biggest romantic-comedy star of that second boom. And yet nobody symbolizes the hazards of these movies better than Ryan does. She made about seven more of them, three with Tom Hanks, falling in more movie love than almost any of her peers. But the longer Ryan (and Roberts, and eventually Sandra Bullock and Barrymore) stayed in romantic comedies — and the longer romantic comedies kept rearranging the same tropes into new configurations — the more their personas seemed to smell a rat. A dozen years of these movies left the fictional Ryan sourly single enough to arrive at *Kate & Leopold* (2001) as a snappish wine guzzler who declares: "Maybe the whole love thing is just a grown-up version of Santa Claus, just a myth we've been fed since childhood. So we keep buying magazines, joining clubs and doing therapy and watching movies with hit pop songs played over love montages, all in a pathetic attempt to explain why our Love Santa keeps getting caught in the chimney." The queen of romantic comedies was now sneering at them.

15 But the movie had a plan. Ryan's ex has discovered some kind of wormhole (I know, I know) and accidentally imported an aristocrat from 1876. The aristocrat (a still-new Hugh Jackman) is living in the ex's apartment, trying to figure out how to work the toaster. Before he goes back to his own time, though, he's determined to restore Ryan's faith. She's looking for a big promotion at a New York market-research firm while also putting up with an oily pig of a boss. It's all too much. So there goes Meg Ryan climbing onto an altogether different bridge in order to take a leap — off the bridge, into a wormhole, *to go live in 1876!*

It made a kind of sense. The present didn't look great. Ryan seemed wiped out by the genre that made her a star, for about the same reasons real-life women were exasperated by modern romance. All the good men were either gay, taken, or from the nineteenth century.

It's a shame, though: On the evening of her leap, maybe a mile away, Carrie and Samantha and Miranda and Charlotte were probably out having cocktails. She could have commiserated with them. *Sex and the City*, which ran from 1998 to 2004, repurposed the vestigial glamour of the classical-Hollywood romantic comedy. The show proceeded from the belief that it was more fun and interesting to be out searching for somebody drawbridge-worthy than to actually lower your bridge. It was a show about dating that was highly conversant in correlated concerns — sex, love, work, hygiene, etiquette, decorum, things up the alley of the average Ryan character. But its priority was a friendship among women. And it was one of a few cultural products that marked a big shift in our depictions of men and women looking for love: they weren't looking *together* anymore.

The drawbridge had given way to separate locker rooms. On-screen, women were doing more on their own, often in what people wrote off as "chick flicks." Men did the same, in what we called "bromances." On a show like *Sex and the City*, straight men aren't really the women's social peers (their male friends are gay) or equal concerns of the plot — they're distant objects to be dissected and taxonomized, puzzled over and tested. (Other romances were really about the woman; the guy she fell for was just a placeholder for a desirable mate, an Easy-Bake man like the generic trophy girlfriends male protagonists have always won at the end of comedies.) Across the hall, in the men's room, were buddy movies like *Wedding Crashers*, *I Now Pronounce You Chuck & Larry*, *The Hangover*, and Judd Apatow's comedies, like *Knocked Up* or his glorious *The 40-Year-Old Virgin*. These movies feel a little like romantic comedies, but they exist almost entirely in a male world suspicious of women — they're tricky to deal with, likely to judge or nag, good for encouraging maturity but too mature for fun. Suddenly, homosocial relationships seemed preferable to heterosexual ones.

For women, evidently, all that drawbridge business was growing passé. Devotees like Nancy Meyers still believed in it, but movies like *Something's Gotta Give* and *It's Complicated* were about older women and men *re*-discovering romance. Younger stars weren't passing through romantic comedies at all; increasingly, they were making action movies. Around the time *Sex and the City* ceased TV operations, Angelina Jolie and Brad Pitt spent *Mr. & Mrs. Smith* as married hit people trying to assassinate each other. Jolie never made a proper romantic comedy at the height of her stardom. Being in one requires an acknowledgment that love is out of your hands, and the pleasure of the Angelina Jolie experience was that very little was out of her hands. She made more sense amid an uptick in women-fronted blockbusters, shooting at men, beating them up, killing them, avenging alongside them. This was another kind of equality, one certain romantic comedies predicted. In *Notting Hill*, Julia Roberts's movie-star character travels to London to promote some kind of sci-fi/action/superhero film called *Helix*. At the time I remember thinking: *I'd watch her in that!* Now it feels like there's a *Helix* every week.

20 We had to reckon with changing standards, too. The romantic comedy went into full decline during the same era in which feminist critics were rethinking all media directed at women — from fashion magazines to movies — asking why women were continually offered roles in which their greatest achievement was a man. In *Failure to Launch*, *You, Me and Dupree*, *Along Came Polly*, and *Knocked Up*, the men were practically rescue operations (forget the drawbridge; you needed FEMA), while the women around them were reduced to either saviors, bystanders, or obstacles. When they were more than that, they seemed borderline nuts (*How to Lose a Guy in 10 Days*) or borderline evil (*The Proposal*). The embrace of the Bechdel-Wallace Test, from Alison Bechdel's *Dykes to Watch Out For* comic strip — asking whether a movie has at least two women in it, who talk to each other, about something other than a man — codified that imbalance. The test reveals American movies' narrow interest in women, but once it came into frequent use a decade ago, it tended to deem the heterosexual romantic comedy as impolitic or subfeminist by default. Men are *all* Sally and her best friend, Marie, talk about. (And women are all Harry and *his* best friend, Jess, talk about.)

Eventually, it seemed reasonable to surmise that if you cared about a female character, it might be more satisfying to watch her solve a crime or fight for a promotion, to be an astronaut or Margaret Thatcher — anything besides trying to get to know a man. It became difficult, at some point, to even conceive of a romantic-comedy plot that could meet our moment; we're surrounded by films that come close but run into practical obstacles that force them to veer in some other direction. *The Big Sick* requires drawbridge work by the male lead, but not by the woman, who spends most of the movie in a coma; what makes him likable isn't courtship, but the more adult work of helping her parents care for her. (It's *them* he has to win over.) And the characters in *La La Land* meet cutely, but they so idealize work that their relationship becomes a job, too. Here, a romantic-comedy finale is possible only in the trick ending that precedes the actual, pragmatic one; it exists only as a what-if. Dreaming up a modern romantic-comedy plot that works — one that wouldn't send the wrong message or feel too unrealistic or too old-fashioned — seems risky. But I wonder if we're kidding ourselves; I wonder if we actually do want the risk.

Listen, there's a perfectly obvious industrial explanation for this, too. Major American studios have been releasing less, and middle-tier, middlebrow, midbudget adult movies are now virtually nonexistent as a priority. With the middle essentially vanished, gone, too, are trust in and patience for the kind of stardom that achieves nothing more than dinner and a movie.

Still, it's easy to feel as if we're in the midst of a major reconsideration, one in which the work of partnership has to wait. There's too much personal work to be done — corrections, upheavals, inclusions, reimaginings, representations. You know what they say: How you gonna love somebody else if you can't love yourself? This might be what's happening in the Netflix series *Russian Doll*, in which a loutish white software engineer (the Harry) learns that her fate is conjoined, via a kind of wormhole (I know!), with that of a fastidious, depressed young black yuppie (her Sally). In another version of this story, that connection would push them to fall in love. In this show, they're pushed toward something else — solving their own dark problems by finding a more basic recognition and care for one another as human beings. The show senses how disconnected we've become.

It's a disconnection I thought about last year, when — amid a tide of sexual-assault allegations in which men were accused of all sorts of heinous, psychopathic, *weird* stuff — along came news of an incident that people seemed to see as far more routine. It involved a couple of scenes between a young female photographer and a famous male comedian: a date during which, as the young woman described it to a reporter, he was sexually aggressive, she demurred and tried to communicate her discomfort, he pushed and pushed and basically turned into Pepé Le Pew and eventually she was on her way home, upset. The other Me Too horror stories could be harder to get our imaginations around (*How* many women? Why is the *Mossad* in this story?), but here was one that made immediate sense. People pored over the details she reported — about his choosing the wine, about his seeming eagerness to leave the oyster bar they went to, about his calling her a car. Women recognized a situation they'd been in more times than they cared to remember; men let the level of fury sink in and hoped they'd never been that guy.

25 I was most struck by the two cultural planets these people seemed to be coming from: not Venus and Mars, but romantic comedy and porn. There has been lots of research into what an endless supply of pornography, starting at a young age, has done to men — warping our judgment, patience, sympathy and imagination. But I've yet to find any comparable exploration of what we might get out of romantic comedy — an entire genre about people coming together, as opposed to one that prefers your coming alone. The stereotype was always that these movies were for women, but some of their value surely came from the fact that men and women *both* watched them, often together, everybody absorbing images of what it looked like to engage with each other.

The great thing about the drawbridge is that anybody can wind up on one. We might be readier to return to it than we know. In the past three years, we've made hits of downbeat love stories like *Moonlight* and *La La Land* and *A Star Is Born*. Maybe that's where we are right now: pragmatic, skeptical, in the mood for romantic tragedy, just like that previous ebb in the '70s. And yet I can't go a week without a website, magazine, or entertainment show shooting its confetti canon over some romantic comedy's anniversary or staging a reunion with its stars. But why are we going back to 1876 when the movies can just make more — funnier and crazier and browner and gayer ones? When they do, they should give Katherine Heigl a call. Maybe she wasn't done with them either.

Reading the Text

1. Summarize the trajectory of rom-com movies that Morris watched as he was growing up. How did they evolve over that period?
2. What were the causes of the decline of the rom-com, according to Morris?
3. In your own words, what does the narrative structure called "the drawbridge" mean?
4. Some critics say that the demise of the romantic comedy has been a positive change. How does Morris respond to that contention?

Reading the Signs

1. One of Morris's key defenses of the rom-com is that it "is the only genre committed to letting relatively ordinary people . . . figure out how to deal meaningfully with another human being" (para. 5). Currently, the movie industry is dominated by fantasy and superhero blockbusters like the *Avengers* and *Star Wars* films. Referring to at least one such film, write an essay supporting, refuting, or qualifying the contention that fantasy films cannot accomplish such an outcome.
2. In class, discuss the effect on Morris's argument of the personal, even autobiographical, approach in this essay.
3. In his conclusion Morris mentions three films — *Moonlight*, *La La Land*, and *A Star is Born* — that hint at being romantic comedies but fall short. Watch one of these films and write an essay analyzing whether it could be considered a rom-com after all or how it fails to be one.
4. *Marriage Story* was one of the most prominent films of 2019, the year in which Morris's essay was published. Described as a "comedy-drama," the movie could be described as a further evolution in the history of the rom-com. Basing your argument on a close reading of *Marriage Story*, write an essay supporting, refuting, or qualifying the thesis that *Marriage Story* is a romantic comedy that better expresses the emotional terrain of twenty-first-century life than do the traditional rom-coms that Morris misses.

YuryKo/Shutterstock

8

TANGLED ROOTS

The Cultural Politics of Popular Music

Get Back to Where You Once Belonged

A funny thing happened after the 2016 Grammy Awards. Paul McCartney (Sir Paul, if you prefer) was turned away from the door of a Hollywood club as he tried to join a post-Grammys party. While apparently he and his star-studded entourage had actually arrived at the wrong address (thus explaining why the club's security guard could not find his name on the invitation list), even McCartney seemed surprised when his name alone wasn't sufficient to be admitted. "How VIP do we gotta get?" he joked to his entourage, adding "we need another hit" to a group that included Beck and Taylor Hawkins, and then returned to his limo. TMZ even managed to get the whole thing on video.

In itself, the snafu was a rather amusing instance of a kind of real-world situation comedy, but we can find in it a deeper significance, an intimation that something had happened beyond the incredible fact that a bouncer either didn't know who Paul McCartney was or didn't care. For the party that McCartney was inadvertently trying to crash was hosted by an up-and-coming rapper named Tyga, and the worldwide reaction that followed indicated that this wasn't simply a generational changing of the guard. It went beyond that, signifying a cultural shift that, by the second decade of the twenty-first century, has rearranged the political geography of popular music.

This chapter is designed to show you how to decode the political significance of such events as what we will call "the McCartney affair" and of American popular music in general. We will not attempt to cover every genre, subgenre, or performer in that vast and ever-evolving world, nor will this introduction interpret any individual songs. We'll leave that job to you. Rather, this chapter is intended to open your eyes to the fact that musical entertainment today is, one way or another, politically significant, even when a given song or performer isn't regarded as being particularly political. For the politics of popular music extends well beyond the explicit messages of, say, the protest song tradition, the raps of Childish Gambino, or the LGBTQ+-affirming lyrics of Lady Gaga, ultimately involving entire genres of music and the audiences who embrace them. This is why we begin with the McCartney affair, because while on the surface it appears to denote nothing more than a security man's screw-up, having little (if anything) to do with politics, its cultural connotations, as seen through a semiotic lens, reveal an event whose significance goes to the very heart of American history.

It's Been a Long Time Coming

As with all semiotic analyses, the meaning of the McCartney affair becomes apparent within the **systems** of related signifiers with which it can be simultaneously **associated** and **differentiated**. As is useful with any semiotic analysis, the system that we begin with is a deeply historical one, tracing the American popular song tradition from its colonial-era origins in the spiritual and folk music traditions through such subsequent genres as minstrel, gospel, jazz, country, rhythm-and-blues, rock-and-roll, soul, Motown, and rap. Our review of this system is not intended to be exhaustive (indeed, a full examination of the history of American popular music would take volumes), but it will serve our purpose in illustrating the kind of research that you may want to conduct when writing analytic essays about popular music.

We can start with the American spiritual, which developed centuries ago in this country out of the religious hymnals of Protestant Christianity. But this fundamental taproot of the popular song tradition was divided from the start into two branching traditions that were racially demarcated as "white" spirituals and "black," shaped by the cultural traditions of Great Britain, on the one hand, and by the traditions that enslaved Africans brought to America with them, on the other. The result, in the latter case, was a hybrid musical form that creatively mixed African and European elements even as it was socially subordinated to the "white" music with which it was closely related. And this grounding pattern of cultural mixing and hierarchical ranking, as we shall see, would continue through most of the musical history to follow.

Now, given the way that both traditions of the spiritual were (and remain) an art form of the common folk, they can be seen as a current within the larger stream of the folk music tradition, wherein the dreams and desires, the hard times and heartbreaks, and the trials and tribulations of the poor are expressed. The spirituals of America's white colonists accordingly emphasized a religious salvation from worldly sin and suffering in a better place after death, while the spirituals of the slaves — though couched in the language of Christian salvation — expressed, in coded forms designed not to inflame their slave masters, a desire for freedom in *this* world, as exemplified in such songs as "Go Down, Moses."

By the nineteenth century, the spiritual had evolved a closely related genre that we know as gospel music, which too immediately divided along racial lines. This century also witnessed an especially ugly chapter in the history of American popular music involving insulting parodies of the lives and music of plantation slaves as performed by white performers in blackface. This was the minstrel tradition, and although it is now regarded with the same abhorrence as, say, D. W. Griffith's *Birth of a Nation*, minstrelsy led to the compositions of Stephen Foster, whose songs, like "My Old Kentucky Home," form one of the cornerstones of American popular music history.

It was nineteenth-century African Americans living in New Orleans who could be credited with inventing the next step in our historical survey, namely, jazz. Influenced by the march music of such white composers as John Philip Sousa, jazz, like so much of the music that preceded it, could be regarded as a racially hybridized musical genre. But, as had happened before, it quickly got the Jim Crow treatment, with a higher status "white" jazz tradition emerging that marginalized "black" jazz. Did this pattern end there? By no means. When rock-and-roll emerged in the 1950s, it did so from a complex blend of sources that included gospel (both white and black), country western, jazz, the blues,

Hogan Jazz Archives

Charles "Buddy" Bolden was popular with dance audiences in New Orleans and was known for his crowd-pleasing musical style. He formed his group, Buddy Bolden's Band, in 1895. They are pictured here in 1905.

rhythm-and-blues, and rockabilly, but this essential hybridity was quickly stratified, thus repeating the familiar refrain. It was as if Rosetta Tharpe — regarded as one of the earliest pioneers of rock-and-roll — was ordered along with Rosa Parks to the back of the bus, as southern radio stations refused to broadcast such black rock pioneers as Chuck Berry, Bo Diddley, and Little Richard. It was in this environment that record producer Sam Phillips famously quipped, "If I could find a white boy who could sing like a black man I'd make a million dollars." Phillips never did make his million, but he did discover Elvis Presley, who, though not the inventor of rock-and-roll as some believe, was its first superstar, enjoying its greatest rewards to that point.

By the early 1960s, a concerted campaign to suppress black contributions to rock-and-roll had essentially white-washed the genre. The likes of Frankie Avalon, Annette Funicello, Pat Boone, and Ricky Nelson had become rock-and-roll stars, while the Beach Boys were using Chuck Berry's riffs even as Berry remained in jail, imprisoned under the Mann Act for allegedly transporting a minor across state lines for "immoral purposes." The old pattern was being repeated yet again as the tangled roots of America's most popular mid-twentieth-century music genre were teased apart on behalf of white racial supremacy.

And then came the British Invasion.

In what is arguably the most ironic development in the history of American popular music, it was a wave of mostly working-class English performers, nurtured on rhythm-and-blues, who brought the African roots of rock-and-roll back to prominence in America. Led by the Beatles (who covered such 1950s black stars as Chuck Berry and Little Richard) and the Rolling Stones (who began as a blues cover band), the Brits revived the original spirit of rock. But, whether they intended to or not, their colossal success in the States resulted in yet another repetition of the now-familiar story of racial subordination that had blemished the preceding history of American popular music. For while the white superstars of rock honored and acknowledged the black musicians who had inspired them (this is particularly true for Keith Richards and Eric Clapton), and black icons like Jimi Hendrix and the Chambers Brothers were very much a part of rock's golden age, the greatest successes were enjoyed largely by the white rockers who reaped the harvest that their black predecessors planted — when they weren't simply stealing from them.

Exploring the Signs of Popular Music

Musical taste usually involves both a rejection and an embrace of individual songs, not to mention entire genres or sub-genres. In your journal, discuss those songs and genres that you *don't* like, carefully analyzing the reasons for your opinions. Can you find any significant patterns in your tastes?

The Turning Point

But even as rock-and-roll came to dominate America's musical horizon, soul music and its pop offshoot, the Motown sound, were rising as well. Indeed, with Berry Gordy's founding of Motown Records in 1959, a crucial turning point was reached in the long history that we have sketched here, introducing a critical **difference** that would eventually turn upside down the pattern of white supremacy. Because for the first time in this history, the commercial production as well as the composition and performance of African American music was in the hands of black entrepreneurs. Extremely popular with white audiences, producing crossover artists like The Supremes and the Jackson Five, Motown nevertheless was able to maintain its distinct racial identity and was never fully appropriated by white artists (the success of such "blue-eyed soul" performers as The Righteous Brothers notwithstanding), nor was it subordinated to a more successful "white" version. This time, things really had changed, and the stage was set for our final chapter in the contextualizing history within which the McCartney affair signifies. This was the rap revolution.

Blending African and Afro-Caribbean musical traditions with modern technology, rap/hip-hop has endured for almost half a century as an uncompromising popular music genre that has crossed over to white audiences without losing its racial and cultural identity. Creating its own corporate labels (like Death Row Records), producers (e.g., the post–NWA Dr. Dre), and entrepreneurs (like Jay-Z), rap/hip-hop has emerged as America's most popular music form while sustaining its status as the voice of black America. The crashing and burning of Vanilla Ice was a striking signifier of how things had changed, how rap, no matter how popular with white teens, was not going to be appropriated, and that even with the eventual success of white rappers such as Eminem and Macklemore, the black origins of rap were not going to be erased. White performers might be admitted to the party, but there would be no questions as to the identity of the party's hosts.

It is in the light of this reversal of American musical history, then, that we can most fully understand the significance of the moment when Paul McCartney was turned away at the door of a party hosted by a rapper. For,

Discussing the Signs of Popular Music

As the introduction to this chapter and a number of its readings indicate, race, and racial politics, have been a part of the history of popular music in America since its original European colonization. In class, conduct a conversation about this history, including a discussion of the reversals that have occurred in recent years. What do you think the future of American popular music holds?

trivial as it was in itself and caused by a case of mistaken identity rather than by any deliberate politically motivated snub, it signified the end of an era. American music was never going to be the same.

Country Road

In the midst of this fundamental shift in American popular music, country music, for its part, became politically self-conscious. A descendent of the folk traditions of the British Isles, country developed a set repertoire of themes cherished by America's rural white working class (parodied in Steve Goodman's and John Prine's Nashville spoof, "You Never Even Called Me by My Name"), which include, in country singer David Allan Coe's words, "mama, or trains, or trucks, or prison, or getting drunk." But in the 1960s it developed an ideological stance as well, defiantly facing off against the proponents of that era's cultural revolution with such "traditional values" ballads as Merle Haggard's "Okie from Muskogie." And though "outlaw" performer Johnny Cash formed musical alliances with the likes of Bob Dylan, and country rock emerged in the 1970s as a major segment of the pop music market, country purists continued to nurture a conservative political ethos consciously at odds with the predominant trends within popular music as a whole.

By the 1980s, as rap moved from the street to the Top Ten, country had unofficially acquired a racial connotation, with country fandom coming to signify not only traditional American values but white identity politics as well. This became particularly evident in the fan backlash against Beyoncé's appearance alongside the Dixie Chicks at the 2016 Country Music Awards, as well as when Lil Nas X's country/rap hybrid "Old Town Road" was dropped from *Billboard*'s Hot Country Songs list in 2019. And when, in 2017, most country stars refrained from commenting on the Unite the Right white supremacist rally in Charlottesville, their silence was widely attributed to the fear that their careers would be ruined if they did — in the way that the Dixie Chicks were ostracized by country fans when they criticized President George W. Bush in the run-up to the Iraq War. But perhaps the most striking signifier of the racial connotations of country music appeared in 2013 when Brad Paisley and LL Cool J joined to address the tensions between rap and country in "Accidental Racist" — a "country-hop" duet that in its defense of the Confederate battle flag and downplaying of the legacy of slavery backfired spectacularly.

The Ties That Don't Bind

The analysis that we have pursued so far focuses on the racial dimensions of American popular music history, but, as with most semiotic interpretations, the topic is **overdetermined**. You might want, of course, to take any of a number of other approaches. One of those approaches, which we have mentioned

Reading Popular Music Online

Choose a popular song and write a semiotic analysis of its lyrics, which you can find online, taking care to examine not only the song's lyrics and music but its historical context and relations to other songs both like and unlike it. Be careful to write an objective analysis, not a fan appreciation.

but not yet pursued, involves the typical American attitude toward social class, which, as was noted in Chapter 2, tends to underplay the role of class in America, preferring a mythology of social mobility within which class status can always be changed. So it is significant that even though both the black and white traditions of popular music share class characteristics, race, as we have seen, has divided what could have been a common heritage.

Given the social origins of most of the pioneers of the blues, bebop, soul, Motown, and hip-hop, the cross-over successes of these musical genres might appear to signify an expression of class consciousness and solidarity among black and white fans of American popular music. But such a conclusion is qualified, if not outright contradicted, by the middle-class status of a large proportion of the white fans who have embraced black music as an expression not of class struggle but of their rebellion against adult authority. Finding in African American music a parallel to their own sense of oppression by "the Establishment," or "the Man," white youth have adopted black cultural forms since the middle of the twentieth century, prompting Norman Mailer to refer to Beat hipsters in 1957 as "White Negroes," while suburban fans of gangsta' rap in the 1980s and 1990s were commonly referred to as "wannabes." Thus, the widespread adoption of black music by white American youth would appear to point less to genuine class solidarity than to something more like cultural appropriation.

Thus, as so many Americans of all races today are falling further and further behind an economic upper class that is appropriating a disproportionate share of America's wealth, a truly class-conscious popular music has yet to appear in any noticeable way. Rather than uniting in opposition to this apparent betrayal of the American dream, economically struggling Americans continue to divide racially — a division that became painfully evident in the most divisive political event of this century.

Rebels with a Cause: The Rebirth of the Protest Song

We refer here to the 2016 presidential election, when millions of working-class white voters helped elect a billionaire real estate developer to the presidency of the United States. If you will excuse the pun, race once again trumped class in American consciousness. It is significant, then, that in the return of the protest song in response to the election — with high-profile recordings from the likes of YG & Nipsey Hussle, Childish Gambino, and Janelle Monáe — there has been virtually nothing to be heard from the world of country music. It isn't as if the core audience for country, which continues to face stagnant wages, unemployment, declining communities, and an endless opioid epidemic, doesn't have plenty to protest. But with a few exceptions (such as Kacey Musgraves's Grammy-winning album *Same Trailer Different Park*), the stars of the genre, with their eyes to what happened to the Dixie Chicks, seem suddenly to have little to say.

But country artists aren't the only ones lingering on the sidelines. While rock and folk led the way in the protest-filled sixties, neither has made much of an impact in the revival of the protest song today. Despite a tradition that stretches from the union organizing songs of Joe Hill through the protest songs of such performers as Woody Guthrie, the Weavers, Bob Dylan, Phil Ochs, and Joan Baez, folk music has been in commercial decline for many years, while rock has lost much of its political edge (Neil Young notwithstanding) along with its commercial predominance. So this lack of political presence in the music world today isn't very surprising. But it is another sign of a changing of the guard in American popular music, the torch having passed to rap and rhythm-and-blues.

Coda: The Diva

Even as rock-and-roll yielded to rap, a multiracial eruption of women performers — led by Madonna in the 1980s, whose dance steps blazed a pathway followed by the likes of Britney Spears, Christina Aguilera, Jennifer Lopez, Beyoncé, Rihanna, Katy Perry, Taylor Swift, Ariana Grande, and Lady Gaga — achieved a gender-based revolution in the history of American popular music, overturning a tradition of male dominance. Arguably more popular — or at least more profitable — than rap, the choreographed spectacles of what could be called diva pop have eclipsed the male-dominated world of rock to create a woman-centered music empire that has made the latest tweets of its leading performers front page news. A full semiotic treatment of this revolution would entail the creation of a historicized system of associations and differences not unlike the one that we have presented in this introduction on the racial politics of popular music. We will leave that analysis up to you.

The Readings

Nolan Gasser opens the chapter with an uneasy reflection on the ways in which the digital revolution has paradoxically fragmented musical audiences in what is already an increasingly divided America. Clara McNulty-Finn follows with a historical survey of the evolution of rap/hip-hop, while Nadra Nittle shows how the "country-hop" fusion in Lil Nas X's "Old Time Road" is simply a continuation of a long history of African American contributions to the evolution of country music. Jon Meacham and Tim McGraw are next with a meditation on the political conflict between rap/hip-hop and country, and how popular music has always reflected America's cultural and ideological divisions. Christina Newland's "A Cultural History of the Diva" takes an admiring look at the spoiled princesses of pop, while DJ Louie XIV contemplates the possible extinction of pop stars as we have known them. Daniel Person's search for an explanation as to why there are so few references to the natural world in contemporary popular music and Dani Deahl's analysis of the YouTube-encouraged rise of K-pop to global stature conclude the readings.

NOLAN GASSER

Music Is Supposed to Unify Us. Is the Streaming Revolution Fragmenting Us Instead?

As the architect of Pandora's Music Genome Project, Nolan Gasser had a vision: this was "to democratize music, to free it from the hegemony of record executives and DJs, and to better enable artists to connect directly with fans." But along the way, something unexpected happened, for with the ability to choose from a large variety of digital music platforms, offering custom-curated playlists, the music audience has become fragmented — like so much else in the world of niche-marketed popular culture. But this tendency not only runs contrary to the inherent capacity of music to unify human beings, it threatens to further divide an already deeply divided America, Gasser believes. So "Let's take out the earbuds and turn up the speakers again," he exhorts, and get back to the garden, shall we? Gasser is a composer, pianist, and musicologist.

When the digital music revolution began in the early 21st century, I had a front-row seat. As the architect of Pandora Radio's Music Genome Project, it was my job to devise a system to analyze and categorize all styles of music so that a machine-learning algorithm could more successfully lead listeners to new music they would enjoy. The goals of this project — which became the core of Pandora's streaming service — were lofty. Pandora's founders, and the music analysts who worked with me, wanted nothing less than to democratize music, to free it from the hegemony of record executives and DJs, and to better enable artists to connect directly with fans.

Yet, as with every revolution, there were unforeseen consequences.

Today Pandora, Spotify, Tidal, Apple Music, YouTube and other digital services give us instant access to virtually any song. But that has also invited fragmentation that affects the recording industry and how we experience music. As fewer people use the same platform, it's hard for under-the-radar artists to find their fans or earn a living. In turn, fans will never find — or share — a potential new favorite song if it's not available on their platform of choice. The collective listening of days-gone-by has been replaced by earbuds and a personal playlist.

This no doubt reflects our larger zeitgeist of cultural fragmentation. No longer do we have — as Roger Waters sang on Pink Floyd's "The Wall" — "13 channels" of garbage "on the TV to choose from"; today we seemingly have 13,000 options. There are musical moments that still unite us: the "Hamilton" cast album, maybe a Super Bowl halftime performance, or when we stop to mourn a musician such as Prince, collectively swaying to "Purple Rain." But these now seem few and far between.

5 Is our musical isolation playing a contributing role in the broader fragmentation of our society? That would be terribly ironic — because music, as much as any other human invention, is an inherent unifier. Starting in our youth, music helps us find and define our immediate social cliques and communities, becoming the soundtrack of our emerging identity: Are we mods or rockers, East Coasters or West Coasters, Swifties or KatyCats? On a deeper level, the music of our respective cultures binds us together via their underlying rhythms, harmonies, and scales: the major/minor scales of the West, the pentatonic scales of China, the microtonal inflections of the Middle East, etc. We also share specific songs in our collective national memory: "Amazing Grace" at a church service or "Happy Birthday" at a dinner party.

But our connection to music goes even deeper, to our very core as human beings. The physical properties of sound and our neurocognitive ability to process it mean we humans share many universal musical perceptions: the strength of octaves, fifths, and fourths; a distinction of consonance from dissonance (with general preference for the former); a recognition of "happy" and "sad" songs across cultures; a love for major and minor triads, etc. Octaves, for example, are as structural in Beethoven and the Beatles as they are in Indian ragas or Balinese gamelan — and generally heard whenever men and women sing the same melody.

We also have a uniquely human ability to *entrain*, which means to physically lock into a steady beat. We take it for granted that we can entrain when we all clap or stomp or dance to the beat of the music — at a baseball game, a rally, a concert or a dance club. But no other animal can do this. Rhythm provides music with its emotional charge, its vitality and flow, and its unifying force. Entrainment gives rise to collaboration and cooperation. Indeed, this innate quality may have enabled our very capacity for culture in the first place.

Music, by its very nature, invites us to unify — with our fellow humans, our fellow Americans, and our fellow travelers in any circles we occupy. We should let it. More than that, we should empower it. Let's take out the earbuds and turn up the speakers again — at least from time to time. Sing in a choir. Jam. Launch a fan club for your favorite band. Start a singalong at your next dinner party.

Certainly, the digital music revolution offers many blessings to us as individuals. It enhances our taste and lets us discover things that bring us joy. But as we lament our too fragmented society, let us turn to music to bond with one another. It may not heal all the divisions we face, but it's hard to feel disconnected when you're sharing a song.

Reading the Text

1. According to Gasser, what were the original goals of Pandora Radio's Music Genome Project?
2. What unintended consequences have resulted from the music streaming revolution, in Gasser's view?
3. Describe in your own words how music helps us form our sense of identity.
4. Explain what Gasser means when he says that "Music, by its very nature, invites us to unify" (para. 8).

Reading the Signs

1. **CONNECTING TEXTS** Write an essay responding to Gasser's contention that the disunifying effects of streaming music services "[reflect] our larger zeitgeist of cultural fragmentation" (para. 4). To develop your ideas, read Mark Murphy's "The Uncivil War: How Cultural Sorting of America Divides Us" (p. 94).
2. In your journal, describe how your own music preferences developed. To what extent did "music [help you] find and define [your] immediate social cliques and communities, becoming the soundtrack of [your] emerging identity" (para. 5)? Compare your list of preferences with your classmates' lists.
3. Hold a class discussion identifying as many categories of contemporary popular music as you can, then in groups interpret the significance of those categories. Share your group's conclusions with the class. To what extent do your results demonstrate the sort of "cultural fragmentation" (para. 4) that Gasser discusses?
4. Gasser enjoins his readers to listen to music collectively, to "Sing in a choir. Jam. Launch a fan club for your favorite band" (para. 8). In class, form small groups, with each investigating a different part of campus student life (for instance, the dorms, fraternal organizations, clubs, and organizations based on ethnicity) to determine if they already engage in enjoying music collectively. Use your results to prepare a set of recommendations addressed to student leaders on how to make music a productive and prominent part of campus life.

CLARA McNULTY-FINN

The Evolution of Rap

Rap has come a long way since DJs Kool Herc and Hollywood began experimenting with funk and disco in the 1970s. Arguably the most popular of popular musical genres today, rap/hip-hop continues to evolve, and in this survey of its evolution from the 1990s into the new millennium, Clara McNulty-Finn looks at the changes that have taken place in the era of social networking. The "gangsta rap" era has become the anything-goes age, in which "successful hip-hop artists rap about everything from thrift shopping to the sheer excess of their lifestyles." Clara McNulty-Finn is a writer and editor for the *Harvard Political Review*.

Even those unfamiliar with the genre can recognize that rap and hip-hop are not what they used to be. A pre-2005 hip-hop or rap hit can be easily distinguished from a track released in the past decade, and artists who have gotten into the game within the last ten years bear little similarity to what was the norm for '90s-era rappers.

Earlier hip-hop music has a distinct tone with a relatively consistent theme of "hood politics," a term referenced by Nas in his 2002 hit "One Mic." Meanwhile, the artists themselves maintained strict "gangster" personas: most of the genre's biggest names, such as The Notorious B.I.G. and Jay-Z, were known drug dealers and many were convicted criminals.

Just a decade later, some of the most successful rap hits relay messages formerly unheard of in the genre while the artists themselves come from a variety of backgrounds. Rappers such as Macklemore have hits about formerly taboo subjects like homosexuality, and artists such as Drake, a former Canadian child actor, prove that being a "thug" is no longer a prerequisite to success. In fact, in an interview with ABC, Drake confessed that he was once described as "the furthest thing from hood."

Indeed, everything from the definition of mainstream hip-hop to the function of record labels to the personas of the artists themselves has evolved over the past decade. While some aspects of this evolution are obvious, it is in the subtleties of these changes that the inextricable link between social and musical development is revealed. The hip-hop/rap genre, despite having garnered a reputation of violence and misogyny, is a uniquely genuine voice amidst the development of our culture.

Lyrics and Society

5 Perhaps the most striking difference between 1990s hip-hop and more modern tracks is the lyrics. In general, hip-hop in the previous decade had a relatively narrow focus. Songs were less about an artist's success and more about his or her rise to it; even the most financially successful rappers wrote about violence, crime, and living in poverty. According to Rauly Ramirez, manager of Billboard's Hip-Hop chart, '90s rappers "would create this persona," portraying themselves as thugs and gangsters because that was "the character [they] had to be to succeed." The necessity for an artist to create and maintain this character led to a common theme among rap songs in the '90s. Rap was the story of the ghetto life and the anthem of gangsters, which prevented hip-hop from joining pop and rock in the mainstream.

Those who did listen to hip-hop, however, found that even as artists were carefully constructing their persona, there was honesty in their lyrics. Poppa Sims, a lyricist associated with the major record label Bad Boy Records, emphasized that in writing openly about violence and drugs, '90s hip-hop artists forced listeners to consider the "underlying reasons behind these things . . . it was survival." Indeed, the early era of rap publicized the notion that poverty begets crime. On his 2002 debut album "Gangster and a Gentleman," artist Styles P claimed that after a childhood of abuse and poverty, "the best thing that happened" to him was breaking into the crack industry because he was finally "gettin' everything that [he] was askin' about."

While, a decade later, rap lyrics still tell an artist's story, each rapper has a different one; artists no longer need to write about the "ghetto life" to be signed by a major record label. The definition of who a rapper can be, and what stories hip-hop can tell, has broadened indefinitely since the mid-2000s. Ramirez pinpoints the origins of this transition to the release of Kanye West's 2004 debut album, "The College Dropout." Rather than focusing on drug dealing or violence or living on the streets, the album addressed religion, West's pursuit of music, and as he says on the track "Breathe In Breathe Out," his desire to "say something significant."

In the years following the release of Kanye's first album, more and more rappers moved away from "gangsta rap" and towards developing their individuality as artists. Today's most successful hip-hop artists rap about everything from thrift shopping to the sheer excess of their lifestyles. Even as sexuality increasingly perpetuates mainstream hip-hop, artists are less afraid to present a softer side to relationships as well. In J Cole's 2013 hit "Power Trip," the sole reference to drug usage was the line "love is a drug, like the strongest stuff ever" and Drake, whose album "Take Care" topped the Hip-Hop/Rap Charts in 2012, confessed in "Shot for Me" that he "never cheated, for the record." Indeed, contrary to the themes of aggression and illegality that perpetuated earlier hip-hop, many of today's biggest artists have taken a gentler approach towards romance even amidst the genre's misogynistic reputation.

Social Media and the Internet

The internet, and in particular the role of social media, has become an irrefutable reflection of societal development. Websites like Tumblr and Facebook, where users can express themselves by publishing photos or writing blog posts, seem to emphasize a fresh pursuit of individuality and self-expression. Meanwhile, a person's ability to share these updates with "followers" or "friends" suggests a simultaneous desire to achieve a sense of community. According to WAJZ-FM program director J Will, it is this rising relevance of social media sites that bears responsibility for many of the stylistic developments within the hip-hop genre.

Prior to the rise of social media, an artist's sole means of establishing a fan base was to capture the attention of a record label. With only a few major labels in the business, this reliance on agents contributed to the streamlined message seen in '90s rap lyrics. But as emerging rap artist Miles From Nothing puts it, "we're in an era where artists don't need agents. If they know how to use sites like SoundCloud and YouTube, they can get themselves out there." Ramirez agrees, admitting that in many respects social media outlets have replaced the function of A&R scouts, who ordinarily are responsible for recruiting artists to different record labels.

Not having to uphold the expectations of a record label allows artists to craft their own message while still finding success. Immortal Technique is one rapper whose albums underscore the effects of this artistic freedom. Immortal Technique, who has released five albums since 2002, has not signed with a record label, giving him the freedom to rap about controversial political and social issues. In his 2008 album *The 3rd World*, for example, he raps that the United States government "[calls] us terrorists after they ruined our countries . . . and that's not socialist mythology, this is urban warfare." While not all unsigned artists choose to pursue such controversial themes, they are able to create a loyal fan base through social media and music sharing sites while maintaining complete control over the music they're producing.

Even as sites like YouTube allow rappers more freedom in constructing their messages, social media outlets like Twitter and Instagram give listeners an entirely new level of access to their favorite artist's daily life. Will suggests that, because we live in an internet-infused world "where people want to connect with one another," we crave a sincerity-driven connection with rap artists. As the barriers between these artists and their fans break away, honesty has become an integral part of a record's success and an artist's longevity. It used to be "very much about painting a picture," Ramirez notes. "Now it's about being yourself."

Underground versus the Mainstream, Then and Now

The rise of the internet age affected one other crucial aspect of the hip-hop genre. With social media providing increased visibility for artists, what constitutes a mainstream rapper, and the relationship between artists and radio stations, has changed completely. Underground '90s rap, according to Ramirez, stuck to politically and socially conscious messages as opposed to "the [gangster] theme that perpetuated a lot of mainstream hip-hop." While '90s mainstream artists signed with major labels and maintained a "thug" persona, underground groups such as Public Enemy spat lyrics like "how the hell can a color be no good for a neighborhood," a line from their 2000 track "Who Stole the Soul."

Fast-forward a decade and, with the aid of social media, there is no longer a single theme for mainstream hip-hop artists. As Will puts it, mainstream music has become about "how well [a track's] message resonates with the typical person." The more universal a song, the larger an audience it will reach; now that hip-hop has become more accepted by the masses, the potential for rap artists to make it big is even greater.

15 That being said, even artists who avoid the mainstream by remaining independent of any major record label can still find financial success. Of the 75 rap albums that topped the Billboard Rap charts since 2010, nearly 15 percent were produced by artists considered outside of the mainstream. However, despite the fact that underground rappers now have the potential to succeed financially, because they rap about themes that appeal only to a loyal niche of listeners, Will admits that "the chance of their music actually making it onto radio is unlikely."

The hip-hop that does play on the radio is different from '90s rap not only in message but in sound. Ally Reid, station manager at FLY 92.3, says that she has seen an increase in collaboration between hip-hop artists and vocalists from other genres. "There are genres that used to exist," she observes, listing rap and pop as examples, but "a lot of those boundaries have really . . . broken away." Ramirez agrees, adding that "the songs that fly up to the top of the rap charts . . . are a blending of the genres. They're the most digestible." Hip-hop artists who do choose to sign with major labels such as Columbia or Republic Records are encouraged to find pop artists to sing catchy hooks, or add more of a dance beat to their record, in order to achieve success on a mainstream scale.

What Hasn't Changed

Of course, some aspects of the genre haven't changed. As Poppa Sims puts it, in addition to a commitment to honest communication, an artist's "longevity comes from the fact that [he or she] put in real, hard work." Most of today's biggest rappers, such as Eminem, Jay-Z, and Lil Wayne, debuted in the '90s era of rap, and have since worked to establish their own record labels and production companies while continuing to record in order to secure their footholds in the music industry.

But this type of decades-long success is also dependent on an artist's commitment to telling their story and maintaining a consistent message, even if it requires doing more of the production legwork to avoid the inherent limitations of signing with a label. If a rapper can't get people to "familiarize themselves with who they are, then they're easily forgotten," Sims attests. An artist's success, therefore, is contingent upon his or her sincerity across albums. Ramirez cites artist 50 Cent as an example of how damaging a lack of honesty can be. "He defined a very strong persona early on," Ramirez says, but people just "wanted to see him as a person." Because 50 never adapted to the demand for sincerity in hip-hop music, he remains removed from the comparative success of fellow "mainstream" artists.

There seems to be a general agreement that these basic strategies for success won't be changing anytime soon. Ramirez predicts that as long as social media remains relevant, "doors will continue to open . . . for different characters and different styles," and it will become even easier for new artists to break into the game and for rappers to find success independently. More and more hip-hop artists are finding their way into the mainstream as well. Will attributes this to more listeners "opening up their ears to the genre, and understanding that this is just another way people are communicating." As it continues to evolve alongside the development of social media and the internet, rap will only strengthen its foothold in the music world. In the words of Will, "hip-hop is here to stay."

Reading the Text

1. Summarize in your own words how the lyrics of hip-hop/rap have changed since the early 1990s.
2. According to McNulty-Finn, how has the rise of social media affected the evolution of hip-hop/rap?
3. What, in McNulty-Finn's view, distinguishes mainstream hip-hop that receives radio play from "underground," often self-produced music?
4. What evidence does McNulty-Finn provide to support her contention that "the hip-hop/rap genre, despite having garnered a reputation of violence and misogyny, is a uniquely genuine voice amidst the development of our culture" (para. 4)?

Reading the Signs

1. Write a journal entry in which you brainstorm your favorite musical artists, whether their music is rap or another genre. Then discuss why you are attracted to these artists. What do your musical choices say about your identity?
2. In class, conduct a debate on whether hip-hop/rap is, as McNulty-Finn contends, "a uniquely genuine voice amidst the development of our culture" (para. 4). To support your team's position, be sure to garner evidence drawn from both the early days of hip-hop/rap and current incarnations of the genre.
3. Write an essay in which you support, oppose, or modify Rauly Ramirez's belief that Kanye West was pivotal in defining what a rapper could be. To support your thesis, ground your analysis in readings of both West's songs and their accompanying videos.

4. **CONNECTING TEXTS** Rap has long been embraced by nonblack performers and audiences. Write an essay on the effect that rap's acceptance "by the masses" (para. 14), as McNulty-Finn puts it, has had on the genre. Is it simply an evolution of a musical form that has had many changes in its short life already, or do you view it as an unfortunate appropriation of a particular ethnicity's culture? To develop your ideas, read Zahir Janmohamed's "Your Cultural Attire" (p. 144).

NADRA NITTLE

Lil Nas X Isn't an Anomaly

When Charley Pride was in his prime, a lot of his fans didn't realize that he was black, which pretty much sums up the history of country music as Nadra Nittle surveys it in this reading, which details the often-suppressed contributions of African American musicians to the evolution of a musical genre that is commonly coded as being for white people. This coding became explicit in the controversy surrounding Lil Nas X's country-hop single "Old Town Road," which climbed into Billboard's Top Twenty in its Hot Country Chart before being removed for not really being "country" music. But the tangled roots of country aren't so easily unravelled, and the whole genre might well be renamed "black-and-country" music, Nittle suggests. Nittle is a reporter for The Goods by Vox.

When the writer and activist James Baldwin took part in a Cambridge University debate about America's race problem in 1965, he invoked the trope of the Western film to argue that the American dream had indeed come at black people's expense. For all of their contributions to the United States, African Americans existed on society's margins. "It comes as a great shock around the age of 5 or 6 or 7 to discover that the flag to which you have pledged allegiance . . . has not pledged allegiance to you," he said. "It comes as a great shock to discover that Gary Cooper killing off the Indians, when you were rooting for Gary Cooper, that the Indians were *you*."

The nearly all-white Cambridge audience chuckled at Baldwin's recollection of this epiphany. They may have been English, but they viewed the "cowboy" to be white because American pop culture had made that idea global. More than 50 years later, that perception still holds. Most things country-and-western, including cowboys, music, and fashion, are widely linked to white men, from John Wayne to Johnny Cash.

No moment in recent memory demonstrates this quite like the debates sparked by the wildly successful single "Old Town Road," recorded by African American rapper Lil Nas X, who describes the song as "country-trap." In March, Billboard removed the track from the Hot Country chart (where it had broken the Top 20), explaining that it had been a mistake to categorize it as country.

This led Lil Nas X supporters to argue that Billboard's move stemmed from either racial bias or bias against rap music. Country-pop songs have been staples on country charts for decades, but "country-trap," "hick-hop," and "hip-haw," as rap-country blends have been nicknamed, have yet to become standard in the genre. Since some fans blame this on anti-blackness, Billboard's decision to pull "Old Town Road" from the country charts has raised questions about the purpose of musical genres and the historic exclusion of African Americans from country music. "When one understands that 'country' music is a marketing genre and that black country people are a culture, one begins to peel away the layers of perception and the definitions of who should be playing a certain type of music and why," Dom Flemons, the neo-traditional country musician known as the American Songster, told me.

In late May, the debates about "Old Town Road" stretched beyond the 5
music when Wrangler announced it was launching a Lil Nas X collection. The news prompted some consumers to accuse the jeans company of "taking the cowboy outta country" and threaten a boycott.

The fans who were angry that the company would team up with a rapper essentially characterized the pairing as "cultural appropriation," a charge that has generated outcry from African Americans who balk at the idea that cowboys or country music should be considered the sole provenance of white people. "The idea that Lil Nas X is perpetuating some form of cultural appropriation by recording and having success in the country genre is simply absurd," pop culture commentator Jawn Murray told me. "How can you appropriate something you played a significant part in shaping?"

Josh Garrett-Davis, the Autry Museum of the West's Gamble associate curator of Western history, popular culture, and firearms, said the efforts to whitewash the country-and-western tradition go back years. "There's a lot of media, whether the classic cowboy paintings or the Wild West shows, that were all sort of reinforcing this idea that the cowboy hero is white," he told me.

The racial segregation of musical genres would also perpetuate the idea that African Americans played no role in country-and-western customs. Still, the black influence on these practices lives on through the black rodeo, the black musicians recording country music today, and the millions of African Americans who remain connected to their country roots.

Fifty-four percent of African Americans live in the South; that figure includes Lil Nas X, who hails from Atlanta. But many of the black people located elsewhere have close ties to the region too. I was born in Chicago to an African American mother from Jackson, Tennessee, the destination of my first plane flight. By elementary school, I spent summers there with my aunts, uncles, and grandmother, who enjoyed canning and baking but could also handle a rifle, if need be. In fact, my grandmother took me on a wild quail hunt when I couldn't have been older than a second-grader. Inevitably, I'd leave Tennessee with words like "yonder" and "reckon" in my vocabulary, much to the amusement of my Midwestern relatives when I returned to Illinois.

As an adult, I live in Los Angeles, but the influence of the South on my 10
early years hasn't vanished. It's why I gravitate to Southern gothic films like *Eve's Bayou*, why the last book I finished was *A Secret History of Memphis Hoodoo*, and why I'll randomly call my mother to verify whether I went to Dollywood, Opryland, or both one childhood summer. While I don't own Wranglers, I have cowboy boots from Tony Lama, Frye, and Tecovas — symbols of the four years I spent living in New Mexico and Texas during the aughts.

The high concentration of African Americans in the South, largely the legacy of slavery, means the disputes that have surfaced in the wake of "Old Town Road's" success are about much more than cowboys and country music. The narrow framing of the African American identity as urban and the erasure of black people from the American mythos lie at the core of these controversies. By rejecting the notion that country-and-western culture is wholly white, black people aren't just pushing for historical accuracy but demanding — as Baldwin did decades ago — to be acknowledged as authentically American.

The Dialogue about Black People in Country Music Isn't New

Charles L. Hughes, author of *Country Soul: Making Music and Making Race in the American South*, said that country music has long struggled with its relationships to blackness and black musicians. Also director of the Lynne and Henry Turley Memphis Center at Rhodes College in Memphis, Hughes said that black music history has shaped country music nonetheless. "But the space for black artists has been very limited," he told me. "Black musicians have been very marginalized. I think the reason this ['Old Town Road' debate] has become such a massive cultural moment is that our understanding of rural comes from country music, even though African American folks have long been a central part of the story."

Even a superstar like Beyoncé faced barriers when she tried to go country. In 2016, the Grammys rejected her song "Daddy Lessons," featuring the Dixie Chicks, for consideration in the country category although it included guitars, a banjo, and horns — for a Zydeco twist. And when she performed the song at the 2016 Country Music Awards, some country music fans lashed out. Wrote one CMA viewer of Beyoncé, "SHE DOES NOT BELONG!!!! When have they ever invited ANY country singer to their BET awards . . . NEVER!!!! STOP IT." Another viewer demanded a boycott of the CMAs, lest Beyoncé "ruin our music," to which another responded, " 'your music'? you mad and don't even know the history of country music."

That history includes the banjo, a country music staple that likely evolved from a three-stringed West African instrument known as the akonting. Prohibited from playing the drums, which they could use to send messages to each other, enslaved Africans in the US perfected their banjo skills and also thrived as fiddle and harmonica players. In the 1920s, these black musicians played blues songs for African American audiences and folk songs for white listeners. Their tweaks to the blues ultimately gave rise to bluegrass and western swing, which became country-and-western.

Racial segregation in the music business has muted this history. The tunes black people recorded were classified as "race music" and separated from country-and-western. "It's really a result of the way the recording industry in the early 20th century developed this idea of musical genres," Hughes said. "The categories would be defined by race or ethnicity. They [record executives] wanted to be able to sell records to a particular market, so the string band traditions were moved to the category of hillbilly music, which later became country, and sold to white audiences. The gospel and the blues were sold to black audiences."

Although these genre divides were arbitrary, they changed the once flexible nature of Southern music, according to Grammy-winning musician Flemons. Artists began to record music in ways that easily lent themselves to classification, and after World War II, "race" music and "hillbilly" became "rhythm and blues" and "country and western," respectively. "This is the main reason most people would never associate black music and country music as having the same root," Flemons explained. "This does not mean that black audiences do not know or like country music."

A 2018 CBS News poll of 1,009 people found that 7 percent of African Americans consider country to be their favorite genre, roughly the same percentage who listed rock, rap, or classical as their preferred form of music. R&B was the most popular among black survey respondents, with 39 percent identifying it as their top musical style. By comparison, 26 percent of white respondents listed country as their favorite, edging out all other categories.

My mother is a black country music fan. While reporting this story, I phoned her to confirm her favorite country artists — Dolly Parton, Linda Ronstadt, Kris Kristofferson, Kenny Rogers, Crystal Gayle, Glenn Campbell. The conversation took a turn when she recalled asking my grandmother, her mother, if she was familiar with Carl Perkins's music. He was the rockabilly pioneer who influenced the Beatles, Jimi Hendrix, Eric Clapton, and Elvis Presley, who famously covered his "Blue Suede Shoes." My grandmother quipped that of course she knew Perkins's music; she'd grown up with the man.

Although Perkins was white and my grandmother was black, they were both the children of struggling Tennessee sharecroppers, a population among which the racial divides of the Jim Crow South weren't as fixed. After his rise to stardom, Perkins discussed how an elderly black field worker named John Westbrook taught him guitar. His story isn't an anomaly. "There's a laundry list of black background vocalists and musicians who have recorded and toured with white country superstars," Murray, the pop culture commentator, told me, "giving them that authentic bluesy-soul that has helped translate their country records into megahits."

The marketing of country as "the music of white America" may have 20 cemented the idea in the public Imagination that African Americans had little to do with the art form, but it didn't stop African American artists such as Ray Charles, Charley Pride, Big Bill Broonzy, the Pointer Sisters, and Linda Martell from performing country. Today, African American artists continue to leave their mark on the music, especially Darius Rucker, one of three black men, along with DeFord Bailey and Charley Pride, to be named a Grand Ole Opry member. An eclectic mix of black artists, including Jimmie Allen, Kane Brown, the Carolina Chocolate Drops, Mickey Guyton, Cowboy Troy, and Flemons are also thriving in the country and folk music scene. Cowboy Troy is a country rapper, but he certainly hasn't made the splash that Lil Nas X has.

Flemons, who last year released the album *Black Cowboys*, said he's always used his music to blur the lines between genres. "As a 21st-century musician, I have not found a need to limit my interests or my music to arbitrary lines set 100 years ago," he said.

African Americans Played Crucial Roles in the Old West

Just as country music has never been an exclusively white art form, the Old West itself was never solely white. Scores of indigenous peoples lived on the land before anyone of European descent set foot in the region. Moreover, people of color played important roles in Lewis and Clark's two-year expedition to explore the West in the early 1800s. Without the help of Sacagawea, the enslaved Shoshone woman who translated for Lewis and Clark and knew which foods to eat and the layout of some of the land to be explored, the expedition may have ended in failure. York, the black man William Clark enslaved, also helped the expedition succeed. As with many African Americans who ventured West, however, York's contributions were often omitted from history books. "One of the missions of the Autry Museum is to expand that often narrow or mythic perception people have of the American West," Carolyn Brucken, the Autry's chief curator and director of research, told me. "You can't talk about the beginning of the American West without talking about African Americans and Native Americans."

In Texas, many black men became skilled cowhands when white ranchers left their land and cattle behind to fight in the Civil War. When enslaved black people won their freedom, the ranchers hired them to be ranch hands and cowhands, or "cowboys." Brucken estimates that at least one out of four cowboys was a black man. Photographs of 19th-century cowboys reveal pride on their faces and self-expression in their choice of clothing, Brucken said. They mostly wore functional apparel that allowed them to tend to cattle. "At the same time, you can see rodeo performers modifying them into an early version of the street style look," she said. "They decorated their chaps, and by the early 20th century, they were influencing one of the first subcultures, railroad workers, who started imitating how they dressed."

Since African Americans made up a significant percentage of cowboys, Brucken says they have just as much right to country-and-western culture, including the clothes and music, as anyone. But while black filmmakers such as Oscar Micheaux, Fred Williamson, and Mario Van Peebles depicted the experiences of African Americans in the West in films like *The Homesteader*, *Adios Amigo*, and *Posse*, most major Western films left out the experiences of African Americans. "Is it white centrality or white supremacy?" Garrett-Davis, also of the Autry Museum, asked about the role of whiteness in the Western. He's unsure whether Westerns alone are responsible for the racial myths about the cowboy. "I don't know that they're only to blame, but they are to blame to a degree. If they weren't challenging American race relations, they were complicit."

The Black Rodeo Tradition Continues to Thrive

Black rodeos across the country work to dispel the notion that there were 25
no black cowboys. For 35 years, the traveling Bill Pickett Invitational Rodeo (BPIR) has paid tribute to the "forgotten cowboys of color." Started in Denver in 1984 by music promoter Lu Vason, the rodeo is named after Bill Pickett. Born in Texas in 1870, Pickett was a Wild West show performer and actor who invented the rodeo event known as bulldogging, or steer wrestling. Bulldogging is still practiced today, but the name BM Pickett often elicits blank stares from the public, according to BPIR president Valeria Howard-Cunningham. "I'm not sure before we started the rodeo how many people knew about Bill Pickett," she told me. "You know, being a person in the Wild West, he was the first black actor in a Western show. Some people — they don't know anything about rodeo or black rodeo. It's just not something they're interested in."

The Arizona Black Rodeo in Phoenix, which began about 15 years ago, also educates the public about the black presence on the frontier. It includes events such as bronco busting, steer and calf roping, bull riding, and women's barrel races. Black women such as Mary Ellen Pleasant, Biddy Mason, and Stagecoach Mary Fields were not cowgirls, per se, but they are Western legends just like cowboys Bill Pickett and Nat Love are. "We can incorporate how important the black cowboy was to American history," Cloves Campbell, Arizona Black Rodeo's coordinator, told me. "You'll see cowboys dressed up in certain outfits to show the history of the cowboy, the Buffalo soldiers, and their contributions to the West."

Today, some African Americans still identify as cowboys. Rodeo competitor and horseman Ramontay McConnell is one of them. The 23-year-old leads trainings and clinics on roping and reining horses, agility exercises, and cow pinning. When he steps out in Portland with muddy boots, a cowboy hat, and a horse, he definitely turns heads, he told me.

For the most part, people respond positively to the sight of a black cowboy. While McConnell often dresses the part, other times he mounts his horse in athletic wear. "Wearing boots and jeans doesn't make a cowboy a cowboy," he said. "People think a cowboy is the Marlboro Man chewing tobacco or smoking cigarettes on a horse." This is also why McConnell, a country music fan, said he considers the backlash Wrangler has faced for collaborating with Lil Nas X to be "nonsense." He believes the time has come to expand the cowboy's image.

Flemons said the Lil Nas X debate extends beyond cowboys to all the African Americans who headed West to achieve the American dream. Since black people are typically associated with urban environments — although most do not live in inner cities — their legitimacy as country people isn't universally accepted.

That "Old Town Road" has broken streaming records and won support 30
from none other than country giant Billy Ray Cyrus, featured on the remix, signals that there's more interest in the black-and-country perspective than entertainment industry executives likely realized. "This is what makes the controversy over 'Old Town Road' so interesting to me as a historian," Flemons said. "[Lil Nas X] has decided to reference black rural culture and black cowboys in the form of popular music, and it is not only being celebrated by the audience; it is being demanded."

Reading the Text

1. Summarize the history of the black contribution to country-and-western music as Nittle presents it.
2. What was the original response to Lil Nas X's "country-trap" (para. 3) hit "Old Town Road" on the part of Billboard? What sparked that reaction?
3. What were the contributions of black cowboys to the development of cowboy and country music, according to Nittle?
4. How does Nittle's essay respond to the claim that Lil Nas X is engaging in "cultural appropriation" (para. 6) in "Old Town Road"?
5. How did the record industry's creation of musical genres contribute to the racializing of different categories of music, as Nittle describes it?

Reading the Signs

1. **CONNECTING TEXTS** Nittle notes that the Wrangler Jeans company was accused of "cultural appropriation" for bringing out a Lil Nas X collection in the wake of "Old Town Road." Read Zahir Janmohamed's "Your Cultural Attire" (p. 144), and write an essay supporting, refuting, or qualifying the thesis that the essential hybridity in popular musical history prevents any one culture from "appropriating" the musical forms of another.
2. Write an essay discussing how Nadra Nittle's relation of her family's history of country-western fandom affects the presentation of her argument.
3. Research the history of rock-and-roll music and write an essay supporting, refuting, or modifying the thesis that the history of rock parallels that of country-western. Develop your argument by analyzing the work of specific artists of each musical genre.

4. Survey Western-themed movies produced by both black and white filmmakers, and focus on analyzing one produced by a director of each race. Compare the depiction of cowboys and other Western characters in each film. To what extent do they depict a monocultural or a multicultural mythic "West"? How do you account for any differences that you might see?

JON MEACHAM AND TIM MCGRAW

How Country Music Explains America's Divided History

A divided America today expresses itself in its music, and this division is nowhere so evident as in the opposition between the fans of country music and those of rap/hip-hop. But as journalist Jon Meacham and country music star Tim McGraw remind us in this essay, America has been here before, from the Civil War's competing anthems "Dixie" and "The Battle Hymn of the Republic," to the sixties' "Ballad of the Green Berets" and "Give Peace a Chance." Focusing on Johnny Cash's and Merle Haggard's sometimes ambivalent responses to the culture wars of their time, Meacham and McGraw point to the past to help illuminate a present in which it is often difficult for musicians to enter the political fray without "alienating nearly half of the folks a performer is trying to reach." But that, they believe, is exactly what they must do to keep the chain of American history, and music, unbroken. Meacham is a Pulitzer Prize–winning journalist and historian and a contributing writer to the *New York Times Book Review*, and McGraw is an American singer, actor, and record producer. Meacham and McGraw cowrote *Songs of America: Patriotism, Protest, and the Music That Made a Nation* (2019).

On Jan. 30, 1966, Ed Sullivan went on the air with a typical program. Dinah Shore was there, as were the Four Tops. There were three comedy acts, including one featuring the Italian puppet Topo Gigio. But the most resonant performance of the evening came when Staff Sgt. Barry Sadler, a member of the Army Special Forces, sang "The Ballad of the Green Berets." Standing ramrod straight, in uniform, before an image of the Green Beret insignia bearing the Latin motto "De oppresso liber" ("To free the oppressed"), Sergeant Sadler painted a portrait of valor and strength. Later that year, the song hit No. 1.

From Woodstock to the marches for peace in Washington, it's easy to think that the soundtrack of the antiwar counterculture defined the age: John Lennon's call to "Give Peace a Chance" has a more dominant place in the popular memory than John Mitchum's prose poem to the nation of Richard Nixon, "America: Why I Love Her," which was popularized by John Wayne.

Yet for every hippie, there was a hawk — and therein lies a useful history lesson. We tend to caricature and oversimplify the past, thus making the tensions and tumult of our own time seem uniquely difficult. But we do ourselves, and the past, a disservice by falling prey to the narcissism of the present. By failing to appreciate the complexities of history, we risk losing a sense of proportion about the relative gravity of contemporary problems and our odds of success in overcoming them. If we can more intimately and accurately grasp the nature of previous eras, we are more likely to see that debate, dissension, and disagreement are far more often the rule than the exception.

We're always arguing, always fighting, always restless — and our music is a mirror and a maker of that once and future truth. "Battle Hymn of the Republic" versus "Dixie"; "The Ballad of the Green Berets" versus "Fortunate Son"; "Born in the U.S.A." versus "God Bless the U.S.A.": The whole panoply of America can be detected in the songs that echo through our public squares. And country music — the ancestral lifeblood of our mutual home, Nashville — offers a divided America a revealing case study. Liberals may think that country music is hopelessly red, and conservatives may believe it is inexorably nationalistic, but the genre, like the Republic itself, has been more subtle and challenging.

In 1969, the country musician Merle Haggard gave Middle America — what 5
Nixon called "the great silent majority" — an anthem with "Okie From Muskogee": "We don't smoke marijuana in Muskogee / We don't take no trips on LSD / We don't burn no draft cards down on Main Street / We like living right, and being free." But was it the red-meat conservative song many fans made it out to be? Haggard could be ambivalent about it. In a 1970 interview in *Rolling Stone*, he was blunt about the counterculture protesters: "I don't like their views on life, their filth, their visible self-disrespect." But he also said he wrote the song as a satire, and in later years he said that he'd been "dumb as a rock" when he wrote it.

Haggard's ambivalence was emblematic of how many people felt at the time: sometimes hawkish, sometimes dovish. And the best music of the era struck notes not only of strident patriotism but of lamentation about the human cost of war. There was Loretta Lynn's "Dear Uncle Sam"; Jimmy Webb's "Galveston," popularized by Glen Campbell; and "Green, Green Grass of Home," a haunting, fatalistic ballad told, it's revealed in the final verse, by an inmate facing execution. For soldiers who themselves felt under a kind of death sentence, the song spoke volumes.

Or take Johnny Cash, whose complicated views on the war were fairly representative of his fellow country stars. Neither a ferocious hawk nor a reflexive dove, Cash toured East Asia for the U.S.O. But he harbored doubts about the war, and in "Singin' in Viet Nam Talkin' Blues," he sang "about that little trip into living hell / And if I ever go back over there anymore / Hope there's none of our boys there for me to sing for."

In 1974, the year Nixon was forced from office, Cash wrote a more traditionally patriotic song, "Ragged Old Flag." Seemingly sentimental, it's in fact a complex piece — a defense of the flag at a time when it's "been abused / She's been burned, dishonored, denied, refused," while also calling Nixon's lies to account: "And the government for which she stands / Is scandalized throughout the land." The song captures Cash's ambivalence about American glory and American sin: "But she's in pretty good shape for the shape she's in." The same could well be said for the nation for which it stood, and stands.

As ever, Elvis Presley tells us much about the age. In concert in the 1970s, Presley popularized "American Trilogy," which opened with a bit of "Dixie," shifted to a section of "Battle Hymn of the Republic," moved on to a verse of "All My Trials," and then climaxed with a return to "Glory, glory hallelujah." The turn to "All My Trials," about the deathbed words of a parent to a child, is perhaps the composition's most intriguing element: "Hush, little baby / Don't you cry," then concluding, "All my trials will soon be over." The point of the trilogy, it seems, is that the clash of visions of "Dixie" and "Battle Hymn of the Republic" — of, really, the clash between the blackface lyrics of Daniel Emmett's "Dixie" and the ennobling "Battle Hymn" verses of Julia Ward Howe — may only end in the coming of the Lord.

10 In our own divided time, polarization can make it difficult for artists to enter the arena in the same way Haggard and Cash did. To sing explicitly about politics risks alienating nearly half of the folks a performer is trying to reach. But history tells us that the great songs (and great books, plays, and other artistic vehicles) that speak to the current public moment have an enduring and vital role — all the more so when they are emotionally reflective rather than ideologically reflexive.

In the meantime — and that's where so much of life is lived, in the meantime — the trials endure, the story unfolds, and music plays on.

Reading the Text

1. Summarize in your own words the history of politically divided popular music in America, as Meacham and McGraw describe it.
2. What was the significance of Barry Sadler's appearance on *The Ed Sullivan Show* in 1966?
3. How, according to Meacham and McGraw, does the current state of polarization in America discourage performers from getting involved in political controversy?

Reading the Signs

1. Brainstorm in class a list of popular songs that express a current political controversy in America and write an essay detailing and analyzing your findings. What positions do the artists take, and how do they convey their message through their music?

2. By referring to history, Meacham and McGraw want to reassure their readers that America has been politically polarized in the past and has survived. Write an essay in which you assess the degree to which their attempt at reassurance is persuasive.
3. Meacham and McGraw refer to country artists like Johnny Cash and Merle Haggard, who eventually made overtures to the musicians on the left and thus ameliorated some of the hostility between country and rock in the 1960s and 1970s. Referring to contemporary artists on different sides of America's political divide, identify whether any such crossovers are appearing now. If you cannot think of any, write an analysis of why no musical meeting of the minds has occurred, even in the midst of the COVID-19 outbreak.
4. **CONNECTING TEXTS** Meacham and McGraw, and Nolan Gasser in "Music Is Supposed to Unify Us. Is the Streaming Revolution Fragmenting Us Instead?" (p. 533), suggest that music has "an enduring and vital role" (para. 10) in a polarized America. Write an essay in which you define in your own terms how that role might be performed today. If you think music can play no such role, write an essay in which you argue that their position is overly optimistic.

CHRISTINA NEWLAND

A Cultural History of the Diva

"If the original meaning of diva was 'goddess,' there's a ring of truth therein," Christina Newland observes in this historical survey of the pop divas of the past half century, for these "women are not like the rest of us mere mortals." From Barbara Streisand and Dolly Parton to Beyoncé and Rihanna, divas are distinguished by their extravagance, and in spite of their "temper tantrums, tackiness, and solid gold bathtubs," we love them anyway "because they invent their own rules," Newland believes, and "nobody gets to tell them no." Christina Newland is a journalist who writes on film and culture for *The Guardian*, VICE, *Sight and Sound*, and Canvas, among others.

"I'm a working girl. I don't make people bend over backwards, and I don't like that in people. I'm definitely no diva," Dolly Parton once told a reporter.

The word "diva" immediately conjures a particular kind of woman, and it's almost always used pejoratively. Dolly, often referred to as a country music diva par excellence, resists the label for all the reasons one might expect: a negative rep. To be a diva is to be a spoiled bitch; to have one's talent come second to one's egotism and flair for drama.

Originally, to be a diva meant to be a female opera singer, and its etymology comes from a Latin word literally meaning "goddess." The first woman to be known as a "diva" was Italian silent actress Lyda Borelli, a gorgeous waif whose looks and figure were madly copycatted by Italian teenagers of the 1910s. The label has long come to mean a woman celebrity of stage or screen; sometimes actresses, but usually singers, of a certain temperament. Being a diva connotes a particular kind of womanly arrogance. Tellingly, much like the word "slut", it has no equally powerful corresponding masculine term.

Parton may not see her behaviour as diva-ish — and it rarely is — but that hardly matters when it comes to how the world regards her. It doesn't matter that she grew up dirt-poor in rural Tennessee or that she's been part of pop culture for five decades, but simply that she's a cartoonishly buxom peroxide blonde with a series of smart-mouthed quips.

Hard work and a salt of the earth upbringing don't preclude women from 5
being called divas. Like Parton, you can build your empire from nowhere and end up with a theme park named after you, or like Barbra Streisand, be a working-class Jewish girl from the Bronx and become one of the best-selling recording artists of all time. But if you're a diva, those humble origins are quickly forgotten. Rihanna — a Barbadian immigrant whose father was a drug addict — is not often seen through the prism of the male rags-to-riches story.

Beyoncé attempted to reclaim the term when she sang the words "diva is a female version of a hustler" on the 2008 album *I Am . . . Sasha Fierce*. *FACT* magazine editor-in-chief Al Horner sees this as a turning point in the perception of the diva. "It's not a moment of self-criticism, but self-celebration," he says. "It sums up the sea change nicely."

It's often more about perception than reality, and so when we consider the profiles of women like Streisand or Rihanna, it's less about how they really do behave so much as the persona attached to them. Did Babs really clone her pet dog twice? Does Rih request her own private dancefloor wherever she goes? Did Mariah Carey play "Fantasy" while she delivered her children, so they could be born listening to the sound of her voice? I mean, probably. We lap up reports of mural-sized self portraits, peach-colored toilet paper, and riders demanding ten white kittens. It's fun to watch women who've worked for their power and money get to behave in silly, petulant ways with it.

"For fans of someone like Mariah Carey, being a diva is a massive part of her mythology — something to be celebrated," Horner points out. "In an entertainment world dominated by men, you have a mixed race woman of Afro-Venezuelan and Irish descent who made insane demands because her talent was so great that she could. I think to a lot of fans, this was a manifestation of strength; of a refusal to shut up and know her place, or to just smile and be pretty."

There are scores of famous women who've been tagged with the "diva" label over the years, including powerhouse singers like Aretha Franklin and Patti Lupone. The '70s divas were dispersed across musical genres — Donna Summer, Cher, Grace Jones, and Parton herself. Streisand is often seen as one of the ultra-divas of the second half of the 20th century, with her big crooning style and tendency to demand she always be photographed from her "good side." Madonna, too, was never afraid of showing a big personality and the wardrobe to match. She famously remarked, "I always thought I should be treated like a star." It only takes a cursory viewing of backstage tour doc *Madonna: Truth or Dare* to see that she takes the idea seriously.

In contemporary parlance, maybe the word "extra" would go some way 10
in describing the aesthetic of the diva. Fluttery oversized false lashes, baby pink fur stoles, turbans with matching tangerine caftans, rhinestone-encrusted crop tops; you'd be inclined to think that I'd just listed a set of outfits from *Drag Race*. But these are all existing accouterments of women like Streisand, Madonna, Beyoncé, and Parton.

"It's a good thing I was born a girl, or I'd have been a drag queen," Parton once said. She has a point: the diva is often so ultra-feminine that she inspires parody or drag. Streisand was famous for her matchy-matchy leopard-print gear and ultra-long fingernails; Parton for her bedazzled clothes and variety of blonde wigs. Zsa Zsa Gabor, the part-time star and full-time glamourpuss of mid-century Hollywood, exaggerated her frame by allowing her billowing fabrics to take up plenty of space, and dripped with a vulgar excess of diamonds. As *Telegraph* writer Bethan Holt wrote of her, Zsa Zsa would have been "a gift to the age of Instagram."

The IDGAF spirit of Rihanna's fully transparent, Swarovski-encrusted Adam Selman gown from 2014, complete with retro skullcap, personifies the spirit of the diva. But her hilariously chic tendency to leave functions and abscond with wine glasses is perhaps ultimate proof of her diva credentials — especially since she can clearly afford to replace restaurant glassware.

Reclaiming the word "diva" might prove tricky, given that so many take it as shorthand for a bratty form of bitchiness. The public seems to hate a celebrity who's not gracious, especially when that celebrity is a powerful woman. But isn't there something radical in the diva's refusal to be gracious, or tasteful, or one of countless other polite adjectives?

If the original meaning of diva was "goddess," there's a ring of truth therein: These women are not like the rest of us mere mortals. "I think at some point, pop culture stopped recognizing the term as a slight on women and began recognizing it as a politicized term," Horner points out. Temper tantrums, tackiness, and solid gold bathtubs aside, we love divas because they invent their own rules. Nobody gets to tell them no.

Reading the Text

1. According to Newland, what is the history of the word *diva*?
2. What are the negative connotations associated with the word *diva*, as Newland explains them?
3. What are the specific characteristics that define diva-hood, in Newland's survey of the type?
4. Why does Newland appear to like divas in spite of their extravagant behavior?

Reading the Signs

1. Before reading Newland's essay, brainstorm in your journal the connotations that the term *diva* has for you. Compare your brainstorm with that of other class members. Then read Newland's selection. To what extent does it confirm, redefine, or complicate the class's brainstormed notions? How do you account for any differences between her explanation and the class's?
2. **CONNECTING TEXTS** Using Newland's article as a critical framework, write an essay that critiques DJ Louie XIV's claims that pop music, and pop stars in particular, are "dead" (read "Has the Pop Star Been Killed?," p. 554).
3. **CONNECTING TEXTS** With the relative eclipse of the popularity of rock-and-roll, divas and rappers have emerged as America's most popular music performers. After reading the introduction to this chapter, write an essay presenting your own argument for why this has happened, keeping in mind that the "diva" is not a racially connotative musical identity.
4. In an essay, argue whether you would classify Billie Eilish as a "diva." If so, why does she fit that category; if not, why not? And how would you categorize her style?

DJ LOUIE XIV

Has the Pop Star Been Killed?

DJ Louie XIV thinks that the age of the pop star — that "brand of musical supernova usually associated with '80s titans like Michael Jackson and Madonna" — is coming to an end, especially in the wake of "an utter litany of flops" from the likes of Katy Perry, Kesha, Lorde, Fergie, Miley Cyrus, Timberlake, and Swift. With the exception of Drake and Bruno Mars, the next generation of pop stars just doesn't seem to be hitting the top of the charts, DJ Louie observes, and the future is hard to predict. But no worries, "There are only so many times something can be compared to Michael Jackson," he observes, and a change in pop history is long overdue. DJ Louis IV writes for *Vanity Fair* and is the host of the podcast *Tuning*.

For most of the last century, "pop music" has been a durable single phrase with two distinct meanings: a statement of fact about the most listened to music of the moment as well as a genre with specific traits. And for a majority of that time, the two definitions have neatly intersected. Pop songs from "I Want to Hold Your Hand" to "Umbrella" have also been the most popular songs of their day.

And especially since the 1980s, pop has been the domain of a particular type of entertainer: a virtuoso performer, visual artist, cultural maven, pop arbiter, and chart baron known as a pop star.

But thanks in part to the pluralizing forces of the internet, pop — like so many other things — has splintered. In the last two years, the popular-music ecosystem has proven more hospitable to SoundCloud rappers, novelty E.D.M./country hybrids, and a freestyle from Cardi B than it's been to once-indomitable pop stars like Taylor Swift. Meanwhile, former and would-be pop stars like Kesha, Troye Sivan, and Carly Rae Jepsen have grown into artists with devoted cult followings as opposed to global superstars. While there are exceptions — Bruno Mars in particular mimics the established pop-star formula to massive success — something novel is clearly afoot: pop music is no longer the most popular music in 2018.

Pop as a genre is squishy. Since "popular" is in the name, it's somewhat beholden to trends. There have, however, been some constants: big, broad emotions, a light touch driven by melody, and music and lyrics that are uncomplicated and familiar. Pop nicks elements from other genres — a guitar lick, a rap — but funnels everything through a tried-and-true structure, two verses and a bridge punctuated with an inescapable hook.

5 More pertinently, pop music is inextricably linked to the pop star, a brand of musical supernova usually associated with '80s titans like Michael Jackson and Madonna. These larger-than-life entertainers defined a well-worn — and perhaps now rundown — version of musical superstardom, trading in a mastery of visual mediums, untouchable virtuosity, and uber-polished live performance, usually incorporating dance. Mostly, though, their all-in take on pure pop music dominated the charts. In their decades-long careers, Jackson accumulated thirteen No. 1 singles, Madonna, twelve. Their contemporaries — Whitney Houston, Mariah Carey, and Janet Jackson among them — followed that path to similar success.

And for the next four decades, a flood of descendants followed in their tracks. Britney, Beyoncé, Justin Timberlake, Chris Brown, Jennifer Lopez, Rihanna, and Lady Gaga all built on the model set forth by Jackson and Madonna. While the elements were touched up to suit the moment, every successive generation took the same approach and filled the same general groove — and the chart positions — of their predecessors with scientific precision. As such, direct comparisons, for better or worse, were inescapable.

The last few years, however, have seen a huge disruption in this lineage. The idea of "the Flop" has traveled from movie blockbusters to pop albums, particularly those released by pop stars with woefully little impact. Both 2017 and 2018 played host to an utter litany of flops. Katy Perry, Kesha, Lorde, Fergie, Miley Cyrus, Timberlake, and Swift, all of whom recently owned the zeitgeist, have released notably underperforming albums; half of those albums failed to achieve a single top 10 hit. Even Beyoncé, a chronic cultural arbiter and megastar, has not reached the top 5 as a lead artist on the Hot 100 since 2013's "Drunk in Love." Her latest, *Everything Is Love* — a collaboration with her husband, Jay-Z — will be the latest test of her unique stature as a pop-cultural agenda-setter who endures without multiformat hit singles.

Meanwhile, the battalion of starlets who should be next in line — Selena Gomez, Demi Lovato, Camila Cabello, Dua Lipa, Charlie Puth, Charli XCX, and Shawn Mendes — have struggled to convert a smattering of hits into sustained runs at the top of the charts, even several albums into their careers. Ariana Grande, one of the most successful New Gen pop starlets, now in her fourth album cycle, has yet to score a No. 1 single. Most others have been pushed to the fringe, sustained by rabid core fan bases consisting largely of gay men and hipsters, but not cultural sovereignty.

Meanwhile, a quick scan of the top Hot 100 over the last twelve months reveals a disparate smorgasbord, much of it once inconceivable as chart hits. SoundCloud rap oddities like Lil Pump's "Gucci Gang" and XXXTentacion's "Sad!," as well as Migos's Dadaist take on trap music, are top 10 staples. Toothless nu-rock acts like Imagine Dragons have launched numerous hits. So have E.D.M./country collaborations like Florida Georgia Line's and Bebe Rexha's "Meant to Be" and Zedd, Grey, and Maren Morris's "The Middle," artists most people couldn't pick out of a lineup.

10 There have been no fewer than six top 10 singles featuring Cardi B, an unpolished stripper-turned-Instagram-star-turned-rapper-turned-breakout sensation of the year whose fame is predicated on the opposite of virtuosity. Cardi exploded with her completely unguarded social-media persona and "Bodak Yellow," a tough, loose rap song which is only "pop" in that it's massively popular, not because it shares much DNA with "Don't Stop 'Til You Get Enough." She says it herself, "I don't dance now, I make money moves."

And then of course there's Drake, the paragon for a new brand of pop stardom that shifts markedly, but not fully, away from the Jacksonian model. Drake often sings but is primarily a rapper, emblematic of hip-hop's firm grip on pop culture. He doesn't dance either, at least not in a polished way, and much of his music — confessional, insular, idiosyncratic — is wildly hooky, but owes very little to the dance pop of Jackson, or the pop ballads of Whitney and Mariah (although one could argue he draws on Janet's later, more intimate style of R&B).

Drake has, however, sustained a stranglehold on the charts once reserved for those artists, either redefining pop in his image or successfully nudging it from the center of the landscape. The success of his progeny like Post Malone proves this approach isn't singular to him, either. Fittingly, this past week, Drake passed Jackson as the solo male artist with the most weeks at No. 1 on the singles charts.

There are many factors at work here. The kind of huge album sales which once served as the benchmark for pop stardom have been steadily disintegrating since the explosion of MP3s in the early 2000s. Additionally the public, as opposed to record labels, now has an unprecedented ability to choose hits by simply streaming them or creating a viral meme. And radio play, while still a huge factor in chart position, is just a piece of a bigger pie that includes downloads, social-media buzz, and, increasingly, streaming numbers. This egalitarian environment allows a longer trail of artists to sustain careers, but it's also a reactive one where it's hard for any single act not named Drake to maintain the omnipresence critical to stars like Jackson.

Bruno Mars is the most obvious, and singular, exception to this trend. Pop stars have always drawn on what came before them, but rarely have they pantomimed the past as cravenly as Mars has, expertly cribbing old styles from Jackson, the Police, the Time, and Boyz II Men without updating the formula. As with the ninth *Jurassic Park* movie, people may buy tickets to access an old feeling. But whether Mars is an exception to this trend as opposed to the desperate last gasp of a dying breed is an open question.

So is pop music still popular? It hasn't completely receded. And it will be 15
interesting to see what the next couple of years bring. In 2015, Justin Bieber was able to synthesize then-fashionable E.D.M. and trop-house sounds into three No. 1 singles. What will new Bieber music sound like in 2018 or '19? It's not so hard to envision a world where Bieber's new stuff sounds a lot like, well, Drake. Either way, something is shifting and perhaps we were overdue. There are only so many times something can be compared to Michael Jackson. And indeed, 40 years is a long trend for something as perennially mutable, and undefinable, as pop music.

Reading the Text

1. How has the way we consume music via the internet and social media affected the status of popular music and pop stars, according to DJ Louie XIV?
2. What is the musical essence of popular music, as DJ Louie XIV describes it?
3. Why does DJ Louie XIV call Drake "the paragon for a new brand of pop stardom" (para. 11)?
4. What are DJ Louie XIV's predictions for the future of pop music?

Reading the Signs

1. Have each member of your class note the music that they regularly hear in public places (their place of work, the dentist's office, a grocery store, the gym, wherever they go). In class, list on the board all the kinds of music the class collectively heard. Use these results as evidence in an essay in which you propose your own definition of what counts as "popular music." To what extent do the class results echo DJ Louis XIV's notions of what is popular?
2. Write an essay in which you demonstrate, challenge, or qualify DJ Louie XIV's claim that "pop music is inextricably linked to the pop star" (para. 5). Is it really individual artists and not bands that produce successful pop songs? How do you explain any patterns that you might see in who or what gains the status of "pop" success?
3. DJ Louie XIV attributes the fact that some pop stars such as Miley Cyrus and Beyoncé have recently had "flops" to the overall demise of pop music. Focus on one or two such artists, and write an essay in which you propose your own

explanation for their flops. Are they indeed victims of the fate of a musical genre, or is DJ Louie XIV jumping to conclusions on the basis of inadequate data? Write an essay arguing your position on this question.

4. Michael Jackson and Madonna have often been credited (or blamed) for introducing dance as an integral part of pop music to the extent that it sometimes takes precedence over the music itself. Write an essay expressing your own opinion on the way that choreography often upstages musicality in contemporary pop.

DANIEL PERSON

When Did Pop Culture and Nature Part Ways?

When Joni Mitchell wrote the anthem for the Woodstock generation, her refrain was that "we've got to get ourselves / Back to the garden." But that was then, and now, as Daniel Person observes in this article from Outsideonline.com, "references to nature are disturbingly sparse in current pop culture, be it books, music, or movies." Searching for answers as to why this should be the case, Person cites the obvious explanation that America has become an increasingly urbanized nation in recent decades, out of touch with its natural environment, but also finds a more surprising hypothesis offered by some research psychologists who think that television is the culprit. So if we're going to nurture that connection with nature which we'll need to save what's left, it's time to turn off the screen and, as John Muir put it, "Climb the mountains and get their good tidings." Person is a writer who focuses on culture, history, and the environment.

These days, when Pelin and Selin Kesebir hear a song on the radio, they can't help but listen for references to nature: a flower, a sunset, or "the birds up above" (Paul McCartney, "Till There Was You," 1963). But nature-related words, Pelin observes, "really are hard to come by in current song lyrics."

This is no off-hand gripe from the 37-year-old identical twins, who both hold PhD's in psychology. According to a paper they published in March in the journal *Perspectives on Psychological Science,* references to nature are disturbingly sparse in current pop culture, be it books, music, or movies — and they've more or less been in steady decline since 1950. This, the researchers suggest, likely corresponds with a general decline in the public's engagement with nature. After all, artists tend to write about what they know or try to create things they think the audience can relate to.

To be clear: the Kesebirs are not critiquing pop culture itself. That's a debate that extends well beyond the parameters of their study. What they do argue is that music on the radio and books on the bestseller list provide a tidy capsule about what society is experiencing at any given time. That the experience involves less and less nature, they argue, is bad for both our minds and nature itself.

The sisters' interest in nature references in art was piqued in 2015 when a number of high-profile writers protested the decision by the editors at the Oxford Junior Dictionary to jettison words like "clover" and "blackberry" in favor of words like "blog" and, um, "BlackBerry." (How quickly tech lingo becomes dated.) They realized that while it seems almost self-evident that society is less connected to nature than it used to be, actually showing that with data is difficult. Some studies have looked at how much time people spend doing "nature-based activities," like hiking, but the Kesebirs found this approach lacking, since it doesn't account for more ephemeral moments like spending a lunch break beneath a blooming cherry tree. Songs and books, they argue, have a way of capturing the zeitgeist of culture, making it a good proxy for measuring trends in society.

One of the strengths of the Kesebirs' research is that they analyzed 5
thousands of works — they looked at some 6,000 songs released since 1950 alone — which allowed them to see clear trends in the din of millions of songs and books. To arrive at their results, the sisters compiled lists of common flowers, birds, trees, and general nature words (like "rainbow") and then, using various online databases, tracked how often they appeared in lyrics, movie plot summaries, and books since 1900. With slight variations, the trends followed a typical line, increasing between the turn of the 20th century and 1950, then plunging in the second half of the 20th century and beginning of the 21st. To make sure these declines were specific to nature-related words, the Kesebirs also compiled a random assortment of human-related words — like "bowl" and "brick" — and looked at their trends as well. Those words became more and more common in art over the course of the 20th century.

One may reasonably wonder whether these trends are the product of pop culture's whims. Woody Guthrie, preeminent folk singer of the mid-20th century, wrote reams of music about green Douglas firs (see "Roll on Columbia") and redwood forests (see "This Land Is Your Land"). That was fitting for a man who grew up in rural Oklahoma and traveled the country on freight trains. The modern British rock band Radiohead, held in equally high regard for its songwriting but with a less nomadic pedigree, seems mostly interested in nature as metaphor for paranoia and alienation (see 1995's "Fake Plastic Trees"). The 1960s happened to be the height of the Beach Boys' fame (just look at the cover of *Surfin' Safari*), and John Wayne was popular in the 1950s, so lots of movies had sweeping panoramas of the Mojave Desert. Does that mean the people watching the Duke were better connected to nature? The Kesebirs say yes. "Culture products are agents of socialization that can evoke curiosity, respect, and concern for the natural world," they write. In nonpsychology speak, this means that movies about New York City make people want to go to the city. Movies about the desert (unless they're horrifying survival stories) make people want to go to the desert. It's a chicken and an egg situation: authors, musicians, and screenwriters write about what people are interested in, and in turn people become interested in what the artists are writing about.

What's causing the decline? With people moving off farms and into cities over the course of the 20th century, it would seem inevitable that nature demanded less of their attention. But the researchers note that urbanization was a fairly steady fact of life in the English-speaking world over the entire century, meaning it doesn't tell the full story of the rise in nature words before the 1950s drop-off. A more plausible culprit, they write, is television, which first appeared in living rooms in the 1950s.

Beyond the psychological problems that this growing disconnect from nature presents, it's bad for the environment. "Emotional affinity for nature is associated with environmentally protective behavior," the Kesebirs write. "In one experiment, participants who viewed a brief video of natural spaces engaged in more sustainable behavior than did participants who viewed a video of human-based spaces."

Looking at the Kesebirs' research, one data set stands from the norm: between 2000 and 2010, nature references in popular music actually rose slightly. Selin says the rise is statistically significant and that she and her sister can't definitively say what caused it. Looking over the songs included in the study, one wonders if it was tied to the mainstream success country music enjoyed that decade, which often evokes pastoral scenes of fireflies and sunsets, the way Jason Aldean does in his 2009 hit "Big Green Tractor." Or it could just be a fluke. Selin says that the trend could be a momentary blip in the downward trend. (A sampling of Nikki Minaj's latest offerings suggests she's right.)

10 Regardless, the Kesebirs say "cultural leadership" is needed on the issue, given both the psychological and environmental benefits of appreciating the outdoors. "Public figures such as celebrities could . . . help spread a sense of the joys of nature," Pelin says. Take a page, in other words, from Paul McCartney, who sang on the *White Album*, in 1968:

Find me in my field of grass Mother
Nature's son.
Swaying daisies sing a lazy song beneath the sun.

Reading the Text

1. Summarize the results of Pelin and Selin Kesebir's research into whether popular music in America expresses an interest in and concern for the natural world.
2. What explanation do the Kesebirs offer for the decline of references to nature in modern popular music?
3. What do Pelin and Selin Kesebir mean by saying that the cause of nature's decline in pop music is "a chicken and egg situation" (para. 6)?

READING THE SIGNS

1. In the 1960s, young people often yearned for a more natural life outside the cities and suburbs in which they grew up. This was nowhere so well expressed as in Joni Mitchell's lyric from "Woodstock" that "we have to get back to the garden." Surveying contemporary popular music lyrics, can you find any equivalent longings? What do your results reveal about millennials and Gen Z?
2. Person notes the conventional explanation for the decline of nature awareness in American consciousness, which focuses on the shift from a rural/agricultural to an urban/suburban society during the twentieth century. In contrast, the Kesebirs correlate the drop in references to nature in popular music that they find starting in the 1950s with the rise of television in the same decade. Write an essay in which you present your assessment of this interpretation's persuasiveness. Or might the Kesebirs' hypothesis confuse correlation with causation?
3. With sustainability and worry about global climate change emerging as major concerns among Generation Z in 2019, a revival of interest in nature could be expected to emerge. Conduct a survey of the popular music current at the time you read this essay and write an essay analyzing your findings. Has nature re-emerged as a topic in popular songs? If not, offer your own explanation for why it hasn't.

DANI DEAHL

Monsta X and Steve Aoki: How K-pop Took Over YouTube

It's been a long time since Brian Epstein repackaged a group of young English rockers who sported black leather jackets and pompadour haircuts and whose American debut on *The Ed Sullivan Show* in 1964 launched the worldwide craze known as "Beatlemania." Since then, heavily choreographed performances by musical ensembles of singer-dancers (think NSYNC and Spice Girls) have been one of pop music's most enduring, and popular, genres, a genre that has now gone global with the explosion of K-pop onto the American scene. And as this overview by *The Verge*'s Dani Deahl explains, the international rise of K-pop is more than a musical phenomenon: it is a reflection of the way in which popular music is consumed in the digital era. Tailor made for YouTube, K-pop not only has created its own popular music cosmos but is also, in *The Verge*'s view, a part of "the future of music." Deahl is a music producer, DJ, journalist, and blogger.

The middle of Texas should be an unlikely place for a sold-out K-pop show. But at the Smart Financial Center outside Houston in late July, thousands of fans gathered with homemade banners, tribute costumes, and armfuls of merchandise as they waited in line to see Monsta X, a K-pop group on their third world tour. These fans didn't get here because of radio play or by combing through bins at a music store. Instead, everyone I ask says they've shown up thanks to one specific site: YouTube.

Online, K-pop's addictive tunes and big-budget videos are raking in billions of streams, making new fans across the globe, and continually breaking YouTube records. Stateside, acts like BTS and Blackpink are becoming red carpet regulars and selling out stadiums, as Monsta X has for the show I'm at in Texas. So how did this genre go beyond South Korea's borders to the world's biggest stages? The rapid growth of YouTube is a crucial component, but it's also the way K-pop is so perfectly packaged to spread on YouTube itself.

"They're the Olympian athletes of the pop world," says Steve Aoki, who recently collaborated with Monsta X on the single "Play It Cool." "They're trained athletes at what they do. Whether it's in media training, to their dancing, to their singing. Koreans have mastered that, so everyone else has to catch up, or at least take note and learn."

The first modern K-pop group, Seo Taiji and Boys, debuted in 1992. But most Americans wouldn't be familiar with the genre until two decades later when Psy's "Gangnam Style" became the first video on YouTube to reach 1 billion views in 2012.

Top Photo Corporation/Alamy

Monsta X in concert

5 "The history of K-pop outside of Korea is really closely tied to the spread of the technology that people use to discover it and to listen to it," says Kevin Allocca, head of culture and trends at YouTube.

"K-pop Is More Than Just Music"

YouTube started seeing rapid jumps in views of K-pop videos as early as 2011 when views jumped three-fold in a single year to 2.3 billion. Those views were mostly coming from international fans, and that's still the case today. "If you look at the top 25 most-watched K-pop groups over the past year, 90 percent of the views are coming from outside of South Korea," Allocca says.

K-pop had its audio-visual formula in place long before YouTube was a popular destination for discovering music, giving the genre an early advantage as YouTube matured. In the '90s, Lee Soo-man, founder of South Korean company SM Entertainment, developed a branding strategy called "cultural technology" that was meant to create massive hits and "set global trends, from not only music but also costume, choreography, and music video."

SM Entertainment literally wrote a manual for its employees on how to popularize K-pop artists outside South Korea using these elements. According to *The New Yorker*, it details things like "the precise color of eyeshadow a performer should wear in a particular country; the exact hand gestures he or she should make; and the camera angles to be used in the videos (a three-hundred-and-sixty-degree group shot to open the video, followed by a montage of individual closeups)."

Those techniques have been honed over time, resulting in modern K-pop videos that are designed to hook people in the first few seconds, even if the person watching doesn't understand the lyrics. They use things like quick cuts, fast zooms, tons of locations, flashy sets, and, of course, impeccable performances.

10 Super-sharp choreography has become a hallmark for K-pop, and acts like Monsta X develop new routines for every single music video. This isn't your normal choreography, either. Seeing a group perform complex moves with razor-like precision is mesmerizing to watch. Because it's so important, songs are often written with this in mind. "As I'm working on the drop, I want to imagine these guys dancing to the song," Aoki says of his collaboration with Monsta X. "Because 50 percent of the song is the visual part of it."

"They're the Olympian Athletes of the Pop World."

Monsta X member I.M says the videos also make each song easier for "the audience to "understand," which helps them connect with a broader set of viewers. "K-pop is more than just music because we always prepare choreography with the stage song," I.M says. "That's why we are preparing music video[s] every single time."

The formula is working, and it's allowed K-pop to spread faster on YouTube than any other style of music. "Half of the biggest 24-hour debuts on YouTube are all K-pop groups," Allocca says. Additionally, he says the top K-pop songs also get almost twice as many likes and five times as many comments as the top songs from other genres.

Once fans are on board, there's more to draw them in. K-pop acts publish additional content around the music videos for fans to watch, like behind the scenes looks, videos that highlight different members of the group, "dance practice" videos that teach fans the choreography to a song, and videos to learn the chants that you're supposed to use when you're at the show. As Simon from Eat Your Kimchi previously told *The Verge*, "The record labels will actually release a song to the official fan groups before it hits the actual airwaves. The fan groups can memorize a fan chant of a song, so at the actual debut performance of the song they can sing along with it. It's a crucial part of the marketing."

The fans also create tons of content on their own for YouTube. They make reaction videos, dance cover videos, guides that give new fans crash courses on groups, and provide lyric translations in other languages. It all helps people access and participate in the K-pop fandom, regardless of language or where they are in the world. "Being a fan at sort of a deeper level with these artists means connecting with them in ways that go beyond just listening to the music," Allocca says.

"They're not passive listeners," Aoki says of K-pop fans. "They know every 15
single song. They watch every single video. Each one of those people are a view on every single video that reached 500 million views on YouTube."

The official videos that are produced by the biggest K-pop acts can be incredibly reference-dense, creating a rich mythology for fans to unpack. Some symbols are less concrete than others, so it's up to the fans to figure out what they all mean, and that's often done online. "One of the places that these communities can gather is in the comments," says Allocca, "and they will both be debating things, but they'll also be sort of pointing out things in the video to each other or giving you a sort of a pathway into something that they've noticed to help you appreciate this thing as the work of art that they see it as."

There are tons of Easter eggs in the English-language video for Monsta X and Steve Aoki's "Play It Cool," for example, including the words "Airplane Mode" appearing in Korean, a reference to lyrics in the Korean-language version of the same song. But many of Monsta X's other videos go even further. They've had videos tease out stories dealing with time travel, societal reform, and the seven deadly sins, which have led to tons of fan theories being hashed out in YouTube comments.

Before streaming and social media, music was largely curated by a select few in the record industry — entities like radio DJs, labels, and critics. Now, it's curated by the masses, by fans who can pick and choose exactly what they want to see and listen to. "It's a very big platform," says Monsta X's Minhyuk. "And, K-pop isn't just the music." I.M nods in agreement. "It's really easy to get inside of that channel and watch whatever you want," he says.

"You can see some video what is related with that video, too. So I think it's really important to us." "Everything is available," chimes in bandmate Kihyun. "There's no limit."

People discover music differently now, and K-pop makes the most of this on YouTube. Online platforms allow people from all over the world to dictate what is popular and to connect — not just with the artists but with each other — in new and often meaningful ways. "I'm surrounded by non-Koreans singing Korean," Aoki says. "I love that a nondominant language is becoming a force. I'm glad I'm part of this day and age where I can be part of that process and help push that out there to the world. Because the world's much bigger than just English."

I.M smiles as he talks about the future. "We hope the world gets ready 20
for us."

Reading the Text

1. In your own words, what does Steve Aoki mean by saying that K-pop artists are "the Olympian athletes of the pop world" (para. 3)?
2. Summarize the audio and visual features that characterize K-pop, according to this article.
3. How has YouTube contributed to the popularity of K-pop, in the author's view?
4. In what ways are K-pop fans not "passive listeners," according to Deahl?

Reading the Signs

1. Deahl claims that K-pop videos broadcast on YouTube create "a rich mythology for fans to unpack" (para. 16). Watch a Monsta X and Steve Aoki video on YouTube and write a semiotic analysis of its cultural references. In your analysis, consider whether the desire to "get" these references may be part of the genre's appeal.
2. **CONNECTING TEXTS** In an argumentative essay, support, dispute, or complicate the proposition that K-pop is, in part, an "appropriation" of American musical styles and popular culture. To develop your ideas, read Zahir Janmohamed's "Your Cultural Attire" (p. 144).
3. **CONNECTING TEXTS** Write an essay in which you present your own explanation for the popularity of K-pop in America. To develop your ideas, consider the extent to which K-pop resembles or deviates from American pop music norms. To develop your ideas, read Derek Thompson's "The Four-Letter Code to Selling Just About Anything" (p. 289).
4. What role does K-pop's encouragement of fan participation play in the spread of this genre's popularity? To develop evidence for your argument, interview several K-pop fans about the audience-created content broadcast on YouTube. To what extent does it shape their experience of K-pop music?

GLOSSARY

abduction (n.) A form of logical inference, first proposed by Charles Sanders Peirce, by which one seeks the most likely explanatory hypothesis or cause for a phenomenon. For example, the most likely explanation for the fact that in teen horror movies the first victims of the murderous monster are the cheerleader and the football player is that the majority of the teen audience enjoys the imaginative revenge of seeing snooty high school types done in.

archetype (n.) A recurring character type or plot pattern found in literature, mythology, and popular culture. Sea monsters like Jonah's whale and Moby-Dick are archetypes, as are stories that involve long sea journeys or descents into the underworld.

associate (v.), **association** (n.) One of the relationships, along with difference, that establish the significance of a sign within a sign system or code. In the system of edgy cartoon comedies, for instance, *South Park* and *The Simpsons* are associated and project a similar meaning. See also **difference** and **system**.

canon (n.) Books or works that are considered essential to a literary tradition, as the plays of Shakespeare are part of the canon of English literature.

class (n.) A group of related objects or people. Those who share the same economic status in a society are said to be of the same social class: for example, working class, middle class, upper class. Members of a social class tend to share similar interests and political viewpoints.

code (n.) A system of **signs** or values that assigns meanings to the elements that belong to it. Thus, a traffic code defines a red light as a "stop" signal and a green light as a "go," while a fashion code determines whether an article of clothing is stylish. To *decode* a system is to figure out its meanings, as in interpreting the tattooing and body-piercing fads.

commodification (n.) The transforming of an abstraction or behavior into a product for sale. For example, selling mass-produced hamburgers as an expression of rule-breaking defiance and individualism.

connotation (n.) The meaning suggested by a word, as opposed to its objective reference, or **denotation**. Thus, the word *flag* might connote (or suggest) feelings of patriotism, while it literally denotes (or refers to) a pennant-like object.

consumption (n.) The use of products and services, as opposed to their production. A *consumer culture* is one that consumes more than it produces. As a consumer culture, for example, America uses more goods than it manufactures, which results in a trade deficit with those *producer cultures* (such as China) with which America trades.

context (n.) The environment in which a **sign** can be interpreted. In the context of a college classroom, for example, T-shirts, jeans, and sneakers are interpreted as ordinary casual dress. Wearing the same outfit in the context of a job interview at an investment bank would be interpreted as meaning that you're not serious about wanting the job.

cultural studies (n.) The academic study of ordinary, everyday culture rather than **high culture**. See also **culture**; **culture industry**; **mass culture**; **popular culture**.

culture (n.) The overall system of values and traditions shared by a group of people. Not exactly synonymous with *society*, which can include numerous cultures within its boundaries, a culture encompasses the worldviews of those who belong to it. Thus, the United States, which is a multicultural society, includes the differing worldviews of people of African, Asian, Latin American, Native American, and European descent. See also **cultural studies**; **culture industry**; **high culture**; **mass culture**; **popular culture**.

culture industry (n.) The commercial forces behind the production of **mass culture** or entertainment. See also **cultural studies**; **culture**; **high culture**; **mass culture**; **popular culture**.

denotation (n.) The particular object or class of objects to which a word refers. Contrast with **connotation**.

difference (n.), **differentiate** (v.) One of the relationships, along with association, that establishes the significance of a sign within a sign system or code. In the traffic system, a red light, for instance, is distinct from a green light and thus bears a different meaning ("stop" instead of "go"). See also **association** and **system**.

discourse (n.) The words, concepts, and presuppositions that constitute the knowledge and understanding of a particular community, often academic or professional.

dominant culture (n.) The group within a **multicultural** society whose traditions, values, and beliefs are held to be normative, as the European tradition is the dominant culture in the United States.

Eurocentric (adj.) Related to a worldview founded on the traditions and history of European culture, usually at the expense of non-European cultures.

function (n.) The utility of an object, as opposed to its cultural meaning. Spandex or Lycra shorts, for example, have a functional value for cyclists because they're lightweight and aerodynamic. On the other hand, such shorts are a general fashion item for both men and women because of their cultural meaning, not their function. Many noncyclists wear spandex to project an image of hard-bodied fitness, sexiness, or just plain trendiness, for instance.

gender (n.) One's sexual identity and the roles that follow from it, as determined by the norms of one's culture rather than by biology or genetics. The assumption that women should be foremost in the nurturing of children is a gender norm; the fact that only women can give birth is a biological phenomenon.

high culture (n.) The products of the elite arts, including classical music, literature, drama, opera, painting, and sculpture. See also **cultural studies**; **culture**; **culture industry**; **mass culture**; **popular culture**.

icon (n.), **iconic** (adj.) In **semiotics**, a **sign** that visibly resembles its referent, as a photograph looks like the thing it represents. More broadly, an icon is someone (often a celebrity) who enjoys a commanding or representative place in popular culture. Beyoncé is a music video icon. Contrast with **symbol**.

ideology (n.) The beliefs, interests, and values that determine one's interpretations or judgments and that are often associated with one's social class. For example, in the ideology of modern business, a business is designed to produce profits, not social benefits.

image (n.) Literally, a pictorial representation; more generally, the identity that one projects to others through such things as clothing, grooming, speech, and behavior.

mass culture (n.) A subset of **popular culture** that includes the popular entertainments that are commercially produced for widespread consumption. See also **cultural studies**; **culture**; **culture industry**; **high culture**.

mass media (n. pl.) The means of communication, often controlled by the **culture industry**, that include newspapers, popular magazines, radio, television, film, and the internet.

multiculturalism (n.), **multicultural** (adj.) In American education, the movement to incorporate the traditions, history, and beliefs of the United States' non-European cultures into a traditionally *monocultural* (or single-culture) curriculum dominated by European thought and history.

mythology (n.) The overall framework of values and beliefs incorporated in a given cultural system or worldview. Any given belief within such a structure — like the belief that "a woman's place is in the home" — is called a *myth*.

overdetermination (n.) Originally a term from Freudian psychoanalytic theory to describe the multiple causes of a psychological effect, overdetermination more generally describes the many possible causes for any social phenomenon. Combined with abductive reasoning, overdetermination is a key element in **semiotic** interpretation. See also **abduction**.

politics (n.) Essentially, the practice of promoting one's interests in a competitive social environment. Not restricted to electioneering; there may be office politics, classroom politics, academic politics, and sexual politics.

popular culture (n.) That segment of a **culture** that incorporates the activities of everyday life, including the consumption of consumer goods and the production and enjoyment of mass-produced entertainments. See also **cultural studies**; **culture industry**; **high culture**; **mass culture**.

postmodernism (n.), **postmodern** (adj.) The worldview behind some contemporary literature, art, music, architecture, and philosophy that rejects traditional attempts to make meaning out of human history and experience. For the *postmodern* artist, art does not attempt to create new explanatory myths or **symbols** but rather recycles or repeats existing images, as does the art of Andy Warhol.

proxemics (n.) The study of human uses of space in interactions with other humans, including body language, facial expression, distance between subjects, gestures, and so on.

semiotics (n.) In short, the study of **signs**. Synonymous with *semiology*, semiotics is concerned with both the theory and the practice of interpreting linguistic, cultural, and behavioral sign systems. One who practices *semiotic analysis* is called a *semiotician* or *semiologist*.

sign (n.) Anything that bears a meaning. Words, objects, images, and forms of behavior are all signs whose meanings are determined by the particular **codes**, or **systems**, in which they appear.

signify (v.) To mean or to represent something, sometimes explicitly—as a red traffic signal means STOP—and often implicitly—as when one moves from the denotation of a sign to its cultural connotation. See also **denotation** and **connotation**.

symbol (n.), **symbolic** (adj.) A **sign**, according to semiotician Charles Sanders Peirce, whose significance is arbitrary. The meaning of the word *bear*, for example, is arbitrarily determined by those who use it. Contrast with **icon**.

system (n.) The **code**, or network, within which a **sign** functions and so achieves its meaning through its associational and differential relations with other signs. The English language is a sign system, as is a fashion code.

text (n.) A complex of **signs**, which may be linguistic, imagistic, behavioral, and/or musical, that can be read or interpreted.

ACKNOWLEDGMENTS

Samantha Allen, "How 'Euphoria' and Model Hunter Schafer Created the Most Interesting Trans Character on TV," *The Daily Beast*, July 7, 2019. Copyright © 2019, The Daily Beast. 2128245:1219MB. Reprinted by permission.

Kwame Anthony Appiah, "What Does It Mean to 'Look Like Me'?" *The New York Times*, September 2019. Copyright © 2019 by The New York Times. All rights reserved. Used under license.

Chris Arning, "What Can Semiotics Contribute to Packaging Design?" Copyright © Creative Semiotics. Used with permission.

Brittany Levine Beckman, "Why We Binge-Watch Stuff We Hate," *Mashable*, January 24, 2019. Copyright © 2019 Mashable, Inc. Reprinted by permission of Ziff Davis.

Deborah Blum, "The Gender Blur: Where Does Biology End and Society Take Over?" from *UTNE Reader*, Sept.–Oct. 1998. Copyright © 1998 by Deborah Blum. Reprinted by permission of ICM Partners.

Patti Schifter Caravello, "Judging Quality on the Web" by Patti Schifter Caravello, UCLA Research Library. Reprinted with permission of the Estate of Patrice S. Caravello.

Julia B. Corbett, "A Faint Green Sell: Advertising and the Natural World," from *Enviropop: Studies in Environmental Rhetoric and Popular Cultures*, eds. Mark Meister & Phyllis M. Japp, pp. 81–94. Copyright © 2002 by Mark Meister and Phyllis M. Japp. Reproduced with permission of ABC-CLIO, LLC; permission conveyed through Copyright Clearance Center, Inc.

David Courtwright, "How 'Limbic Capitalism' Preys on Our Addicted Brains," *Quillette*, May 31, 2019. Copyright © 2019 by Quillette Pty Ltd. All rights reserved. Used under license.

Steve Craig, "Men's Men and Women's Women: How TV Commercials Portray Gender to Different Audiences," from *Issues and Effects of Mass Communication: Other Voices*. Reprinted by permission of the author.

Dani Deahl, "Monsta X and Steve Aoki: How K-pop Took Over," from *The Future of Music*, season 2, episode 4, *The Verge*, September 11, 2019. Copyright © 2019 by Vox Media, Inc. Used with permission.

David Denby, "High School Confidential: Notes on Teen Movies," *The New Yorker*, May 31, 1999. Copyright © 1999 David Denby. Reprinted by permission of the author.

Aaron Devor, "Gender Role Behaviors and Attitudes," from *Gender Blending: Confronting the Limits of Duality* by Aaron Devor. Copyright © 1989 by Indiana University Press. Reprinted with permission of Indiana University Press.

Barbara Ehrenreich, excerpt from the "Introduction," from *Bright-Sided: How the Relentless Promotion of Positive Thinking Has Undermined America*. Copyright © 2009 by Barbara Ehrenreich. Reprinted by permission of the ICM Partners.

Alicia Eler, "There's a Lot More to a Selfie Than Meets the Eye," *Salon*, August 18, 2019, excerpted with permission from *The Selfie Generation: Exploring Our Notions of Privacy, Sex Consent, and Culture*. Copyright © 2019 by Skyhorse Publishing, Inc. Used with permission.

Judy Estrin, "I Helped Create the Internet, and I'm Worried about What It's Doing to Young People," *Pacific Standard*, April 29, 2019. Copyright © 2019 The Social Justice Foundation. Reprinted by permission.

Christine Folch, "Why the West Loves Sci-Fi and Fantasy: A Cultural Explanation," *The Atlantic*, June 13, 2013. © 2013 by Christine Folch. Used with permission of the author.

Thomas Frank and Matt Weiland, "Commodify Your Dissent," published as "Why Johnny Can't Dissent" in *The Baffler*, 1997. Copyright © 1997 The Baffler Literary Magazine, Inc. Reprinted by permission of Thomas Frank.

Neal Gabler, "The Social Networks," *The Los Angeles Times*, October 17, 2010. Used with permission from the author.

Trip Gabriel, "For Students in Internet Age, No Shame in Copy and Paste," *The New York Times*, August 2, 2010. Copyright © 2010 by The New York Times. All rights reserved. Used under license.

Nolan Gasser, "Music Is Supposed to Unify Us. Is the Streaming Revolution Fragmenting Us Instead?" *Los Angeles Times*, June 16, 2019. Reprinted by permission of the author.

Sophie Gilbert, "Millennial Burnout Is Being Televised," *The Atlantic*, January 22, 2019. Copyright © 2019 The Atlantic Media Co., as first published in *The Atlantic Magazine*. All rights reserved. Distributed by Tribune Content Agency, LLC.

Brooke Gladstone, "Influencing Machines: The Echo Chambers of the Internet," from *The Influencing Machine: Brooke Gladstone on the Media*, Illustrated by Josh Neufeld. Copyright © 2011 by Brooke Gladstone and Josh Neufeld. Used by permission of W. W. Norton & Company, Inc.

Malcolm Gladwell, "The Science of Shopping," from *The New Yorker*, November 4, 1996. Reprinted with permission from the author.

Wade Graham, "Are We Greening Our Cities, or Just Greenwashing Them?" *Los Angeles Times*, March 6, 2016. Used with permission from the author.

Jessica Hagedorn, "Asian Women in Film: No Joy, No Luck." First published in *Ms Magazine*, Jan.–Feb. 1994. Copyright © 1994 by Jessica Hagedorn. Reprinted by permission of Jessica Hagedorn, c/o Harold Schmidt Literary Agency.

Rachelle Hampton, "Which People?" *Slate*, Feb 13, 2019. Copyright © 2019 by The Slate Group. All rights reserved. Used under license.

John Herman, "Inside Facebook's (Totally Insane, Unintentionally Gigantic, Hyperpartisan) Political-Media Machine," *The New York Times*, August 24, 2016. Copyright © 2016 The New York Times. All rights reserved. Used under license.

Jordyn Holman, "Millennials Tried to Kill the American Mall, But Gen Z Might Save It," *Bloomberg*, April 25, 2019. Copyright © 2019 by Bloomberg L.P. All rights reserved. Used with permission.

Michael Hulshof-Schmidt and Robert Hulshof-Schmidt, "What's In an Acronym? Parsing the LGBTQQIP2SAA Community." Used with permission from the authors.

Zahir Janmohamed, "Your Cultural Attire," *Oregon Humanities*, August 22, 2017. Reprinted by permission of the author.

Scott Jaschik, "A Stand against Wikipedia," *Inside Higher Education*, January 26, 2007. Copyright © 2007. Reprinted by permission of the author and publisher.

DJ Louie XIV, "Has the Pop Star Been Killed?" *Vanity Fair*, June 22, 2018. Copyright © 2018 by Conde Nast. Reprinted by permission.

Rachel Lowry, "Straddling Online and Offline Profiles, Millennials Search for Identity," *Deseret News*, June 2, 2013. Copyright © 2013 by Deseret News. Reused with permission.

Alfred Lubrano, "The Shock of Education: How College Corrupts" in *Limbo: Blue-Collar Roots, White Collar Dreams*. Copyright © 2004 by Alfred Lubrano. Reprinted with permission of John Wiley & Sons, Inc.

Mikhail Lyubansky, "The Racial Politics of Black Panther," *Psychology Today*, February 20, 2018. Reprinted by permission of the author.

Mark Manson, "The Disease of More," from *Everything Is F*cked: A Book About Hope*, by Mark Manson. Copyright © 2019 by Mark Manson. Reprinted by permission of the author.

Clara McNulty-Finn, "The Evolution of Rap," *The Harvard Political Review*, April 10, 2014. Copyright © 2014 by Clara McNulty-Finn. Used with permission.

Jon Meacham and Tim McGraw, "The Music of American Politics; NYT 6/15/19" from *Songs of America: Patriotism, Protest, and the Music That Made a Nation*, copyright © 2019 by Project #268866, Inc. and Merewether LLC. Used by permission of Random House, an imprint and division of Penguin Random House LLC. All rights reserved.

Wesley Morris, "Rom-Coms Were Corny and Retrograde. Why Do I Miss Them So Much?" *The New York Times*, April 24, 2019. Copyright © 2019 by The New York Times. All rights reserved. Used under license.

Mark Murphy, "The Uncivil War: How Cultural Sorting of America Divides Us," *Savannah Morning News*, July 28, 2018. Reprinted by permission of the author.

Mariah Burton Nelson, "I Won. I'm Sorry." Originally published in *Self Magazine*, 1998 Reprinted with permission of the author.

Christina Newland, "The Cultural History of the Diva," *Vice*, March 5, 2018. Reprinted by permission of the author.

Nadra Nittle, "Lil Nas X Isn't an Anomaly," *Vox.com*, June 5, 2019. https://www.vox.com/the-goods/2019/6/5/18653880/lil-nas-x-country-music-billboard-wrangler-old-town-road. Copyright © 2019 by Vox Media, Inc. Used with permission.

Emily Nussbaum, "The Aristocrats: The Graphic Arts of *Game of Thrones*," *The New Yorker*, May 7, 2012. Copyright © 2012 by Conde Nast. Reprinted by permission.

Michael Omi, "In Living Color: Race and American Culture," from *Cultural Politics in Contemporary America*, ed. by Ian Angus and Sut Jhally. Copyright © 1989 by Michael Omi. Used with permission.

George Packer, "Celebrating Inequality" by George Packer, Copyright © 2013 by George Packer, originally appeared in *The New York Times*, used by permission of The Wylie Agency, LLC.

Michael Parenti, "Class and Virtue," from *Make-Believe Media*, 1e, by Michael Parenti. Copyright © 1992 South-Western, a part of Cengage, Inc. Reproduced by permission. www.cengage.com/permissions.

Dave Patterson, "Shame by a Thousand Looks," originally appeared in *Salon*, April 6, 2019. Copyright © 2019 by Dave Patterson. Used with permission.

Troy Patterson, "The Politics of the Hoodie," *The New York Times*, March 2, 2016. Copyright © 2016 The New York Times. All rights reserved. Used under license.

Daniel Person, "When Did Pop Culture and Nature Part Ways?" originally appeared in *Outside*, May 17, 2017. Copyright © 2017 by Daniel Person. Used with permission.

Maya Phillips, "The Narrative Experiment That Is the Marvel Cinematic Universe," *The New Yorker*, April 26, 2019. Copyright © 2019 Conde Nast. Reprinted by permission.

Massimo Pigliucci, "The One Paradigm to Rule Them All: Scientism and *The Big Bang Theory*" Republished with permission of John Wiley & Sons, from *The Big Bang Theory and Philosophy Rock, Paper, Scissors, Aristotle, Locke*. Copyright © 2012 by John Wiley & Sons; permission conveyed through Copyright Clearance Center, Inc.

Michael Pollan, "Supermarket Pastoral," from *The Omnivore's Dilemma: A Natural History of Four Meals*, copyright © 2006 by Michael Pollan. Used by permission of Penguin Press, an imprint of Penguin Publishing Group, a division of Penguin Random House LLC. All rights reserved.

Robert B. Ray, "The Thematic Paradigm." Reproduced with permission of Princeton University Press from *A Certain Tendency of the Hollywood Cinema, 1930–1980*, Princeton University Press, 1985; permission conveyed through Copyright Clearance Center, Inc.

Abraham Riesman, "What We Talk about When We Talk about Batman and Superman," *Vulture*, March 22, 2016. Copyright © New York Magazine. Used with permission.

James A. Roberts, "The Treadmill of Consumption," from *Shiny Objects* by James A. Roberts, pp. 95–101. Copyright © 2011 by James A. Roberts. Used by permission of HarperCollins Publishers.

Nancy Jo Sales, "From the Instamatic to Instagram: Social Media and the Secret Lives of Teenagers," excerpt from *American Girls: Social Media and the Secret Lives of Teenagers* by Nancy Jo Sales, copyright © 2016 by Nancy Jo Sales. Used by permission of Alfred A. Knopf, an imprint of the Knopf Doubleday Publishing Group, a division of Penguin Random House LLC. All rights reserved.

Juliet Schor, "Selling to Children," from *Born to Buy: The Commercialized Child and the New Consumer Culture*, by Juliet Schor. Copyright © 2004 by Juliet Schor. Reprinted with the permission of Scribner, a division of Simon & Schuster, Inc. All rights reserved.

Linda Seger, "Creating the Myth," excerpt from *Making a Good Script Great*. Copyright ©1987 by Linda Seger. Reprinted by permission of the author.

Matt Zoller Seitz, "The Offensive Movie Cliché That Won't Die," *Salon.com*. 9/14/2010. Copyright © 2010 by Salon. This article first appeared in *Salon.com*, at http://www.Salon.com. An online version remains in the Salon archives. Reprinted with permission.

Jesse Sell, "Gamer Identity," *MIT Game Lab/Massachusetts Institute of Technology*, November 18, 2014. Reprinted by permission of the author.

Laurence Shames, "The More Factor," from *The Hunger for More: Searching for Values in an Age of Greed*. Copyright © 1989 by Laurence Shames. Published by Times Books, a division of Random House, Inc. Reprinted with permission of the Stuart Krichevsky Literary Agency, Inc.

Judith Shulevitz, excerpt from "Alexa, How Will You Change Us?" *The Atlantic*, November 2018. Copyright © 2018 The Atlantic Media Co., as first published in *The Atlantic Magazine*. All rights reserved. Distributed by Tribune Content Agency, LLC.

Jacob Silverman, "'Pics or It Didn't Happen': —The Mantra of the Instagram Era," *The Guardian*, February 26, 2015. Copyright Guardian News & Media Ltd, 2015. Reprinted by permission.

Jack Solomon, "Masters of Desire: The Culture of American Advertising," excerpt(s) from *The Signs of Our Time: Semiotics, the Hidden Message of Environments, Objects, and Cultural Images* by Jack Solomon, copyright © 1988 by Jack Solomon. Used by permission of Tarcher, an imprint of Penguin Publishing Group, a division of Penguin Random House LLC. All rights reserved.

Claire Miye Stanford, "You've Got the Wrong Song: *Nashville* and Country Music Feminism." This article was originally published in the *Los Angeles Review of Books* (www.lareviewofbooks.org). Copyright © 2013 Los Angeles Review of Books. Used with permission.

Derek Thompson, "The Four-Letter Code to Selling Just About Anything," *The Atlantic*, January/February 2017. Copyright © 2017 The Atlantic Media Co., as first published in *The Atlantic Magazine*. All rights reserved. Distributed by Tribune Content Agency, LLC.

Jia Tolentino, "How 'Empowerment' Became Something for Women to Buy," *The New York Times*, April 12, 2016. Copyright © 2016 The New York Times. All rights reserved. Used under license.

Joseph Turow, "Introduction," from *The Daily You: How the New Advertising Industry Is Defining Your Identity and Your Worth* by Joseph Turow. Copyright © 2012 by Joseph Turow. Reprinted by permission of Yale University Press.

James B. Twitchell, "What We Are to Advertisers," from *Lead Us Into Temptation: The Triumph of American Materialism* by James B. Twitchell. Copyright © 1999 by James B. Twitchell. Reprinted by permission of the author.

INDEX OF AUTHORS AND TITLES

"Alexa, How Will You Change Us?" (Shulevitz), 346

Allen, Samantha. *How* Euphoria *and Model Hunter Schafer Created the Most Interesting Trans Character on TV*, 412

Anglerfish in the Machine: Horror and Re-enchantment in Stranger Things, *The* (Creek), 31

Appiah, Kwame Anthony. *What Does It Mean to "Look Like Me"?*, 178

Are We Greening Our Cities, or Just Greenwashing Them? (Graham), 114

Aristocrats: The Graphic Arts of Game of Thrones, *The* (Nussbaum), 423

Arning, Chris. *What Can Semiotics Contribute to Packaging Design?*, 217

Asian Women in Film: No Joy, No Luck (Hagedorn), 498

Banks: Progressive or Conventional? (Bodea), 45

Barbie: Queen of Dolls and Consumerism (Lin), 38

Beckman, Brittany Levine. *Why We Binge-Watch Stuff We Hate*, 436

Blum, Deborah. *The Gender Blur: Where Does Biology End and Society Take Over?*, 156

Bodea, Irina. *Banks: Progressive or Conventional?*, 45

Bright-Sided (Ehrenreich), 77

Caravello, Patti S. *Judging Quality on the Web*, 53

Celebrating Inequality (Packer), 86

Class and Virtue (Parenti), 506

Commodify Your Dissent (Frank), 228

Corbett, Julia B. *A Faint Green Sell: Advertising and the Natural World*, 305

Courtwright, David. *How "Limbic Capitalism" Preys on Our Addicted Brains*, 354

Craig, Steve. *Men's Men and Women's Women*, 273

Creating the Myth (Seger), 463

Creek, Jeremy. *The Anglerfish in the Machine: Horror and Re-enchantment in* Stranger Things, 31

Cultural History of the Diva, A (Newland), 551

Daily You: How the New Advertising Industry Is Defining Your Identity and Your Worth, The (Turow), 265
Deahl, Dani. *Monsta X and Steve Aoki: How K-Pop Took Over YouTube*, 561
Denby, David. *High-School Confidential: Notes on Teen Movies*, 510
Devor, Aaron. *Gender Role Behaviors and Attitudes*, 150
Disease of More, The (Manson), 89

Ehrenreich, Barbara. *Bright-Sided*, 77
Eler, Alicia. *There's a Lot More to a Selfie Than Meets the Eye*, 340
Estrin, Judy. *I Helped Create the Internet, and I'm Worried about What It's Doing to Young People*, 337
Evolution of Rap, The (McNulty-Finn), 536

Faint Green Sell: Advertising and the Natural World, A (Corbett), 305
Folch, Christine. *Why the West Loves Sci-Fi and Fantasy: A Cultural Explanation*, 459
For Students in Internet Age, No Shame in Copy and Paste (Gabriel), 55
Four-Letter Code to Selling Just About Anything: What Makes Things Cool?, The (Thompson), 289
Frank, Thomas. *Commodify Your Dissent*, 228
From the Instamatic to Instagram: Social Media and the Secret Lives of Teenagers (Sales), 360

Gabler, Neal. *The Social Networks*, 409
Gabriel, Trip. *For Students in Internet Age, No Shame in Copy and Paste*, 55
Gamer Identity (Sell), 350
Gasser, Nolan. *Music Is Supposed to Unify Us. Is the Streaming Revolution Fragmenting Us Instead?*, 533
Gender Blur: Where Does Biology End and Society Take Over?, The (Blum), 156
Gender Role Behaviors and Attitudes (Devor), 150
Gilbert, Sophie. *Millennial Burnout Is Being Televised*, 170
Gladstone, Brooke. *Influencing Machines: The Echo Chambers of the Internet*, 379
Gladwell, Malcolm. *The Science of Shopping*, 200
Graham, Wade. *Are We Greening Our Cities, or Just Greenwashing Them?*, 114

Hagedorn, Jessica. *Asian Women in Film: No Joy, No Luck*, 498
Hampton, Rachelle. *Which People?*, 141
Has the Pop Star Been Killed? (XIV), 554
Herrman, John. *Inside Facebook's (Totally Insane, Unintentionally Gigantic, Hyperpartisan) Political-Media Machine*, 384
High-School Confidential: Notes on Teen Movies (Denby), 510
Holman, Jordyn. *Millennials Tried to Kill the American Mall, But Gen Z Might Save It*, 207
How Country Music Explains America's Divided History (Meacham and McGraw), 548
How "Empowerment" Became Something for Women to Buy (Tolentino), 285
How Euphoria *and Model Hunter Schafer Created the Most Interesting Trans Character on TV* (Allen), 412
How "Limbic Capitalism" Preys on Our Addicted Brains (Courtwright), 354
Hulshof-Schmidt, Michael. *What's in an Acronym? Parsing the LGBTQQIP2SAA Community*, 163

I Helped Create the Internet, and I'm Worried about What It's Doing to Young People (Estrin), 337
I Won. I'm Sorry. (Nelson), 107
In Living Color: Race and American Culture (Omi), 129
Influencing Machines: The Echo Chambers of the Internet (Gladstone), 379
Inside Facebook's (Totally Insane, Unintentionally Gigantic, Hyperpartisan) Political-Media Machine (Herrman), 384

Janmohamed, Zahir. *Your Cultural Attire*, 144
Jaschik, Scott. *A Stand against Wikipedia*, 51
Judging Quality on the Web (Caravello), 53

Lil Nas X Isn't an Anomaly (Nittle), 541
Lin, Amy. *Barbie: Queen of Dolls and Consumerism*, 38
Lowry, Rachel. *Straddling Online and Offline Profiles, Millennials Search for Identity*, 166
Lubrano, Alfred. *The Shock of Education: How College Corrupts*, 100
Lyubansky, Mikhail. *The Racial Politics of* Black Panther, 492

Manson, Mark. *The Disease of More*, 89
Masters of Desire: The Culture of American Advertising (Solomon), 250
McNulty-Finn, Clara. *The Evolution of Rap*, 536
Meacham, Jon and Tim McGraw. *How Country Music Explains America's Divided History*, 548
Men's Men and Women's Women (Craig), 273
Millennial Burnout Is Being Televised (Gilbert), 170
Millennials Tried to Kill the American Mall, But Gen Z Might Save It (Holman), 207
Monsta X and Steve Aoki: How K-Pop Took Over YouTube (Deahl), 561
More Factor, The (Shames), 193
Morris, Wesley. *Rom-Coms Were Corny and Retrograde. Why Do I Miss Them So Much?*, 516
Murphy, Mark. *The Uncivil War: How Cultural Sorting of America Divides Us*, 94
Music Is Supposed to Unify Us. Is the Streaming Revolution Fragmenting Us Instead? (Gasser), 533

Narrative Experiment That Is the Marvel Cinematic Universe, The (Phillips), 472
Nelson, Mariah Burton. *I Won. I'm Sorry.*, 107
Newland, Christina. *A Cultural History of the Diva*, 551
Nittle, Nadra. *Lil Nas X Isn't an Anomaly*, 541
Nussbaum, Emily. *The Aristocrats: The Graphic Arts of* Game of Thrones, 423

Offensive Movie Cliché That Won't Die, The (Seitz), 488
Omi, Michael. *In Living Color: Race and American Culture*, 129
One Paradigm to Rule Them All: Scientism and The Big Bang Theory, *The* (Pigliucci), 427

Packer, George. *Celebrating Inequality*, 86
Parenti, Michael. *Class and Virtue*, 506
Patterson, Dave. *Shame by a Thousand Looks*, 175
Patterson, Troy. *The Politics of the Hoodie*, 224
Person, Daniel. *When Did Pop Culture and Nature Part Ways?*, 558
Phillips, Maya. *The Narrative Experiment That Is the Marvel Cinematic Universe*, 472
"Pics or It Didn't Happen": The Mantra of the Instagram Era (Silverman), 368
Pigliucci, Massimo. *The One Paradigm to Rule Them All: Scientism and* The Big Bang Theory, 427
Politics of the Hoodie, The (Patterson), 224
Pollan, Michael. *Supermarket Pastoral*, 211

Racial Politics of Black Panther, *The* (Lyubansky), 492
Ray, Robert B. *The Thematic Paradigm*, 451
Riesman, Abraham. *What We Talk about When We Talk about Batman and Superman*, 477
Roberts, James A. *The Treadmill of Consumption*, 233

Rom-Coms Were Corny and Retrograde. Why Do I Miss Them So Much? (Morris), 516

Sales, Nancy Jo. *From the Instamatic to Instagram: Social Media and the Secret Lives of Teenagers*, 360
Schor, Juliet B. *Selling to Children: The Marketing of Cool*, 296
Science of Shopping, The (Gladwell), 200
Seger, Linda. *Creating the Myth*, 463
Seitz, Matt Zoller. *The Offensive Movie Cliché That Won't Die*, 488
Sell, Jesse. *Gamer Identity*, 350
Selling to Children: The Marketing of Cool (Schor), 296
Shame by a Thousand Looks (Patterson), 175
Shames, Laurence. *The More Factor*, 193
Shock of Education: How College Corrupts, The (Lubrano), 100
Shulevitz, Judith. *"Alexa, How Will You Change Us?"*, 346
Silverman, Jacob. *"Pics or It Didn't Happen": The Mantra of the Instagram Era*, 368
Social Networks, The (Gabler), 409
Solomon, Jack. *Masters of Desire: The Culture of American Advertising*, 250
Stand against Wikipedia, A (Jaschik), 51
Stanford, Claire Miye. *You've Got the Wrong Song:* Nashville *and Country Music Feminism*, 416
Straddling Online and Offline Profiles, Millennials Search for Identity (Lowry), 166
Supermarket Pastoral (Pollan), 211

Thematic Paradigm, The (Ray), 451
There's a Lot More to a Selfie Than Meets the Eye (Eler), 340
Thompson, Derek. *The Four-Letter Code to Selling Just About Anything: What Makes Things Cool?*, 289
Tolentino, Jia. *How "Empowerment" Became Something for Women to Buy*, 285
Treadmill of Consumption, The (Roberts), 233
Turow, Joseph. *The Daily You: How the New Advertising Industry Is Defining Your Identity and Your Worth*, 265
Twitchell, James B. *What We Are to Advertisers*, 261

Uncivil War: How Cultural Sorting of America Divides Us, The (Murphy), 94

What Can Semiotics Contribute to Packaging Design? (Arning), 217
What Does It Mean to "Look Like Me"? (Appiah), 178
What We Are to Advertisers (Twitchell), 261
What We Talk about When We Talk about Batman and Superman (Riesman), 477
What's in an Acronym? Parsing the LGBTQQIP2SAA Community (Hulshof-Schmidt), 163
When Did Pop Culture and Nature Part Ways? (Person), 558
Which People? (Hampton), 141
Why the West Loves Sci-Fi and Fantasy: A Cultural Explanation (Folch), 459
Why We Binge-Watch Stuff We Hate (Beckman), 436

XIV, DJ Louie. *Has the Pop Star Been Killed?*, 554

Your Cultural Attire (Janmohamed), 144
You've Got the Wrong Song: Nashville *and Country Music Feminism* (Stanford), 416